Isaac Kashdan,
American Chess Grandmaster

Isaac Kashdan, American Chess Grandmaster

A Career Summary with 757 Games

Peter P. Lahde

McFarland & Company, Inc., Publishers

Jefferson, North Carolina

ALSO OF INTEREST AND FROM MCFARLAND

Albert Beauregard Hodges: The Man Chess Made
(John S. Hilbert and Peter P. Lahde, 2013 [2008])

The present work is a reprint of the library bound edition of Isaac
Kashdan, American Chess Grandmaster: A Career Summary
with 757 Games, *first published in 2009 by McFarland.*

LIBRARY OF CONGRESS CATALOGUING-IN-PUBLICATION DATA

Lahde, Peter P.
Isaac Kashdan, American chess Grandmaster : a career
summary with 757 games / Peter P. Lahde.
p.   cm.
Includes bibliographical references and indexes.

ISBN 978-1-4766-9295-1
softcover : acid free paper ∞

1. Kashdan, Isaac, 1905–1985.   2. Chess players—United States—Biography.
3. Chess—Collection of games.   I. Title.
GV1439.K373L34 2023   794.1092—dc22 [B]   2009017982

British Library cataloguing data are available

Edited and designed by Robert Franklin

Front cover image: © ktsdesign/Shutterstock

Printed in the United States of America

*McFarland & Company, Inc., Publishers
Box 611, Jefferson, North Carolina 28640
www.mcfarlandpub.com*

In memory of my wife,
Susanna Katherine Lahde
(1934–2008)

Acknowledgments

This book has been my most rewarding project, thanks to many people who have helped make it possible. It began with trips to the Cleveland Public Library when Alice Lorenth was the person in charge of the Fine Arts and Special Collections Department, which included the vast collection of books on chess. Later, Jeffrey Martin was most helpful in getting the material I requested. The Library of Congress in Washington, D.C., has been an excellent source, particularly in obtaining microfilm through Inter-Library Loan. I made several visits to Cleveland and two to Washington.

One of the first persons who gave me assistance was Larry Parr, a former president of the United States Chess Federation, who sent me many games I did not have at the time. He had access to the games with Albert Pinkus, a player with whom Kashdan had many encounters. He also told me about how to get chess columns from newspapers.

Another valuable source beyond the chess columns I was already familiar with, was a German language newspaper, the *New Yorker Staats-Zeitung*. It was through Jack O'Keefe that I learned about this.

Also of valuable assistance was John Donaldson, who sent me many games and also pages of publications such as the *California Chess Reporter*.

Andy Ansel was helpful with games Kashdan played with Fred Reinfeld. Early in this project I had contacted Calle Erlandson of Sweden who was able to supply me with Kashdan games that he played with players from Sweden. Then around 2006 I was able to find out about Peter Holmgren of Sweden, who supplied me with the missing games from the Stockholm Olympiad of 1937. (A book that will include all the games of that event is planned but has not yet been published.) Dale Brandreth supplied me with many games, but in particular all the games I was missing from the Chicago International of 1926. A book about this event has not yet been published either, but Dale is in possession of all the games.

There are others that I should also recognize as having assisted me in this project. They include Neil Brennen, Arthur Dake, Vlastimil Fiala, Tony Gillam, John S. Hilbert, Dave Lonerean, Russell Miller, Bruce Nelson, and Aidan Woodger. I am sure there are others whom I have failed to mention.

My greatest addition to the games came in 2005 when, through the internet, I was able to contact Richard Kashdan, the son of Isaac. After several exchanges with Richard he told me about his cousin, Teddy Seidenfeld, who was in possession of many of the original score sheets of the games of Isaac Kashdan. Teddy sent me copies of more than 200 of these games. Of these more than 30 were new to me. Neither Richard nor Teddy asked for any compensation for the big effort that went in to this. Many thanks also go to Richard for providing me with many personal insights that I would not have been able to include otherwise.

I must not forget to give special recognition to Mark Ishee, who helped me immensely with computer related problems, particularly in putting games in Chess Base in the correct order when they were received at a later date and in making it possible to convert to a file so the publisher could read the diagrams. Without him this whole project would not have been possible.

Table of Contents

Part Two: The Games of Isaac Kashdan

Part Three: Appendices and Indexes

Introduction

When I started more than twenty years ago to collect the games of Isaac Kashdan I had no idea where it would lead. It took that time to make the contacts to obtain all the games and to find his many involvements with chess. You could say that chess was his life.

The book is divided into three parts. Part One is "The Career of Isaac Kashdan" and Part Two is "The Games of Isaac Kashdan." In this latter, the 661 tournament and match games are presented first. A good number of them are with Kashdan's own annotations. These are followed by the 56 games he played in simultaneous exhibitions. This primarily concentrates on the period from 1931 to 1934 when he made nationwide tours. Then follow the 16 games he played in the national speed tournaments in 1941 to 1945 and a few other speed tourneys. Finally, the last grouping has 24 exhibition, consultation, and practice games and one postal game. All of these games are numbered from 1 through 758.

Part One begins with the early years in some detail and then discusses the fantastic record Kashdan set in the team tournaments from 1928 to 1937. His record in the biannual U.S. Championships from 1936 through 1948 is a highlight. Part One moves all the way through the later career and on to the final years.

Part Three gives tournament crosstables, a bibliography of tournament, biographical and games collections books, an appendix listing some of his best games, and three indexes. An index of players, and an index of ECO openings are both keyed to Part Two game numbers; a General Index refers to page numbers.

Kashdan first learned the moves of chess at about age 17 while attending Stuyvesant High School, in New York City, in 1923. He became interested in solving chess problems and took part in several competitions. In fact he won several honors because he was able to solve problems faster then any other player including masters. He found, when he played more chess, that problem solving had improved his game considerably.

His first international success came in the Team Tournament at The Hague in 1928, where he achieved the best score of any player by winning 12 games, drawing 2 and losing only 1 for a record 86.7 percent. This allowed the United States to take second place behind Hungary. In 1930 he took part in four international tournaments in Europe, scoring three first places and one second. In these four events he scored 27 wins, 6 draws and only 2 losses, for a record of 84.4 percent. He continued to compete successfully in international events for the next two years.

Kashdan's greatest achievements in international competition were the five Olympic team tournaments starting with The Hague 1928, followed by Hamburg 1930, Prague 1931, Folkestone 1933, and finally Stockholm 1937. For these five events he scored 52 wins, five losses, and 22 draws. This gave him a record of 79.8 percent. He won five individual medals, two gold (1928, 1937), one silver (1933) and two bronze (1930, 1931).

To supplement his income he went on tour giving exhibitions of simultaneous play between 1931 and 1934 with excellent results. In most of these displays he scored better than 80 percent.

Kashdan also competed in all the United States Championships from 1936 through 1948, with the exception of 1944. This resulted in a tie for first in 1942, in which Reshevsky won the play-off, and two second places, in 1946 and 1948. For these six events he scored 71.2 percent, putting him in third place in the history of the U.S. championship, behind Bobby Fischer at 83.3 percent, and Reuben Fine at 78.0.

Kashdan also competed in what is now known as the U.S. Open: Milwaukee 1935, Philadelphia 1936, and Boston 1938. Later he played at Corpus Christi (Texas) 1947, Baltimore 1948, and Fort Worth 1951. His best results among these events were a tie for first with Horowitz in 1938, and the championship in 1947.

Kashdan was recognized for his accomplishments in international competition in 1954 when he was awarded the grandmaster title. In 1955 he competed for the last time in an international competition, the match between the USSR and the USA. Also that year he became chess editor for the *Los Angeles Times*. He remained in this capacity for 27 years. His last competitive game was played in 1961.

Kashdan did not rest on his laurels, but contributed to the furtherance of chess by directing many tournaments. Especially notable were the Piatigorsky Cup tournaments in 1963 and 1966; and between 1971 and 1981 he directed all 11 of the Lone Pine tournaments. He was also involved in the administration of the U.S. Chess Federation.

Missing Games

The main purpose of this book has been the presentation of all the games by Kashdan that I could find, particularly his tournament and match games but also those he played in simultaneous exhibitions, in speed tournaments, and on other occasions. Without a doubt most chess players would be interested in his tournament and match games. While I along with other researchers have been able to find some 661 such games, certainly more can still be found. Among the most important games that are still missing from tournaments and matches are listed here:

Hallgarten 1925-26 Pinkus (2), H. Steiner (2) Samuels (2) Smirka, Bornholz
Manhattan 1925-6 Kupchik, H. Steiner, Beihoff, Cohen, Samuels, Berman, Field, Halper
Rice Progressive 1926 H. Steiner, Berman, Feuer, Mishook, Simchow, Zatulove, Bartha
Manhattan 1926-7 Marózcy, Horowitz, Bornholz, Cohen, Willman, Bartha, Field, deVries
New York Junior 1927 Pinkus (2), Santasiere (2), Bornholz (2), Tholfsen, Smirka
Manhattan 1927-8 Kupchik (2), H. Steiner
Manhattan Junior 1927-8 Horowitz (2), Pinkus
The Hague Olympics 1928 Marin

Stockholm 1930 Ståhlberg (incomplete)
Match: Stoltz Stoltz (4)
Hastings 1931-2 Sultan Khan, Stoltz
Manhattan 1932-3 Pinkus, Cohen
Folkestone 1933 Grünfeld, Ståhlberg
Chicago (Prelims) 1934 Engholm, Elo, Waggoner
Chicago (Finals) 1934 Reshevsky
Syracuse 1934 Dake, Kupchik, H. Steiner, Santasiere, Martin, Reinfeld (incomplete)
Manhattan 1934 MacMurray, Schwartz, Jackson
Milwaukee (Prelims) 1935 Belson, Santasiere, Woods, Rathman
Milwaukee (Finals) 1935 Morton
Philadelphia (Prelims) 1936 Kupchik, Reinfeld, Grossman, Elo, Isenberg, Holland, Glover, Jackson
Philadelphia (Finals) 1936 Dake, Santasiere, Hanauer, Morton
Poughkeepsie 1936 Martinson, Battell, Broughton, Evans, Wood
San Juan 1936 Benitez, Cancio, Prieto
Manhattan 1936-7 Willman, MacMurray, Jackson
Match: Simonson Simonson (2)
Manhattan 1937-8 Willman, Platz, Soudakoff, Newman, Tenner
Boston 1938 Horowitz, Blumin, Polland, Rosenzweig, Dahlstrom
Hamilton 1939 Pinkus, Shainswit, Willman, Chernev, Garfinkel
Havana 1940 Blanco, Meylan
Hamilton 1941 Evans
New York 1942 Pinkus, Levin, Lessing, Hahlbohm
Manhattan 1944 Pinkus, Denker, Kevitz, Willman, Pavey, Rothman, Kramer, R. Byrne
Corpus Christi 1947 Gibson, Sandrin, Kramer, H. Steiner, Santasiere, Hartleb
Manhattan Masters 1948 Kramer, Bisguier, D. Byrne, Vasconcellos, Williams
Hollywood Invitational 1953 Levin, Rivise, Keckhut, Geller
Santa Barbara 1954 Reissman, Russell, Martin

The United States deserved to win [at the 1931 Prague Olympics]. It was a great advantage having a player at Board 1 who could hold his own with anyone. Kashdan will henceforth be reckoned among the world's greatest masters (*British Chess Magazine*, September 1931).

It has never been a disgrace to lose to Kashdan (*If You Must Play Chess*, 1947, by Arnold Denker).

Alekhine stated around in the early thirties that Kashdan might become the next world champion (*The Oxford Companion to Chess*, 1992, by Hooper and Whyld).

There was no question in anybody's mind that had he played a match with Marshall in 1931 or 1932 Kash would have won the title of U.S. Champion; but those were depression years and it could not be arranged. Kashdan's superiority, however, was recognized in that he was placed on first board in the team tournaments (*The World's Great Chess Games*, 1951, by Reuben Fine).

Kashdan was always considered a cautious player and he was considered the leading American expert of the endgame (*A Passion for Chess*, 1958, by Reuben Fine).

Kashdan was a gifted positional player who had a notorious fondness for gaining the two bishops. Kashdan's ability to extract victories from seemingly even positions earned him, the nickname *der kleine Capablanca* (the little Capablanca) (*A Picture History of Chess*, 1981, by Fred Wilson).

Kashdan once appeared on Groucho Marx's television show "You Bet Your Life" and Groucho called him "Mr. Ash Can" throughout the show.... In the 1930's the Mexican government offered all foreign chess masters appointments as chess instructors in the Army. Both Kashdan and Fine were made lieutenants (Bill Wall; source lost).

Kashdan was a giant of the chess world, a man with important accomplishments in every phase of the game. He was a kind and considerate man, always well mannered, who commanded respect (*Los Angeles Times*, 1985, by Jack Peters).

PART ONE

The Career
of Isaac Kashdan

1

The Early Years

The Years 1923–1929

Isaac Kashdan was born in New York City on November 19, 1905. He learned chess at Stuyvesant High School in 1921. By his own admission he was not one of the top players of his school. Later, he attended City College of New York and played on their team. The first games that we have a record of were played in 1923. The *American Chess Bulletin* (ACB November 1923) reports of a match he played representing the International Chess Club against a team from the Manhattan Chess Club. He played on board three and lost to Frink. (The veteran Albert Hodges, former U.S. Champion, also played for the Internationals on board one.) This match took place on September 29 in 1923. Later that year (ACB December 1), Morris Schapiro gave a simultaneous exhibition against 25 players. Kashdan won his game along with seven others. The master also gave up 4 draws, while winning 14. The next year on April 27, 1924 (ACB May-June 1924), Alexander Alekhine, who was to become world champion in 1927, gave an exhibition on 26 boards against some of the strongest players in New York. He scored 16 wins, while drawing five and losing five. Only five of the wins by Alekhine have survived; Kashdan was one of the players who defeated him. All we know about the game is that the opening was a Ruy Lopez. The results of all the players who played Alekhine are given on page 127 of the *American Chess Bulletin*. Kashdan played in several tournaments that year, such as the Stuyvesant Championship and the Rice Progressive Championship. While some of his games have survived, how he fared in those two events overall is not known. He also won the championship of the Hungarian Chess Club.

What he was best known for at this time was his prowess in solving chess problems. Already, at age 18 he captured the Problem Solving Contest of 1924. For this he received a gold medal. His winning time was 1 hour and 5 minutes (ACB April 1924).

Then in 1925 he outscored such veterans as Kupchik, Chajes and Jaffe to win another problem-solving contest. He himself was the composer of many chess problems. In 1933, when he was editor of *The Chess Review* in its first year, he published two of them. One might assume that these problems were composed in earlier years. But he continued to compete in problem-solving contests for many more years, many times winning first prize.

Early in 1925 he played in the Hallgarten Tournament. He won his preliminary section by scoring 5½ points. In the final, a double round affair, he placed third out of seven players behind Albert Pinkus and Herman Steiner. Later that year he competed in his first Manhattan Chess Club Championship, which concluded in early 1926. He placed second behind the veteran Kupchik. He was only half a point behind the winner, scoring 9 wins, 5 draws and no losses. This event included such strong masters such as Maróczy, Horowitz, H. Steiner and Pinkus. Another event that year was the Rice Progressive Championship, which he won, going through the tournament undefeated: 6 wins and 3 draws.

Chicago International 1926

Because of his successes in the tournaments cited above, he was invited to his first international tournament in Chicago during August and early September of 1926. The United States Champion, Frank Marshall, was the eventual winner. For the first time Kashdan faced the current champion in a losing effort. His final score was not impressive, as in later rounds he suffered some setbacks. But he still ended up with a plus score with 5 wins, 4 draws, and 3 losses, placing him sixth out of 13 players. He was deprived of a share of the prize money by losing to N.W. Banks of Detroit, the checker champion. (All the games by Kashdan are included in the present volume, thanks to Dale Brandreth, who has the scores of the yet unpublished tournament.)

The following year he was involved in several tournaments, again with quite impressive

A young Isaac Kashdan (courtesy Cleveland Public Library).

results. First came the Manhattan Chess Club Championship where he tied for second and third. Out of 14 games, he won 10, drew 1, and lost 3. Next, came the Manhattan Junior Masters Tournament, which he won with a score of 5 wins, 1 draw and no losses. Last, came the Manhattan Championship that started late in 1927 and ended early the next year. Here he had a very poor result, winning only 1 game out of 8, drawing 3 and losing the rest.

The Hague Olympiad 1928

Kashdan was invited to play in his first team tournament, at The Hague Olympiad in the Netherlands. This was the first time he traveled to Europe. The event took place from July 23 to August 3, 1928. The United States team consisted of Kashdan, H. Steiner, Factor, Tholfsen, and Hanauer. Seventeen teams competed in this, only the second such team event. (The first one took place in London in 1927, but the United States did not take part.) The *Brooklyn Daily*

Eagle (August 28, 1928) reported on the event upon the arrival of Kashdan back in the states.

> Isaac Kashdan was one of the five members of the quintet who landed the United States in second place in the Olympic team tournament at the recent meeting of the international Chess Federation at The Hague. He was the scoring ace for the Americans and returned here yesterday as a passenger on board the steamship Veendam of the Holland-American Line.

Kashdan, a member of the Manhattan Chess Club, returned with two medals, one of which was awarded to him as a member of the runner-up team in the competition. The other, a special award, was presented to him by Dr. A. Rueb, president of the International Chess Federation, for making the best individual score of any of the players representing the 17 countries involved.

The youthful New Yorker, at age 22, played 15 games, winning 12. He drew 2 against Reca of Argentina and Pokorný of Czechoslovakia, and lost only 1, to Makarczyk of Poland. This gave him a total score of 13–2, whereas A. Muffang of France, who made the next highest individual score, was credited with 12½–3½. Kashdan received a warm reception from the members of the Manhattan Chess Club and many visitors when he arrived back at the club.

Then later that year going into 1929 he competed in the Manhattan Chess Club Championship, coming in third behind Kevitz (8 points) and Kupchik (6½ points). Kashdan scored 6 points, winning 4, drawing 2, and losing to Kevitz and Willman. He then competed in the Metropolitan Chess League, winning from Lajos Steiner, of Hungary but losing again to Frank Marshall. He also played against the world champion, Alexander Alekhine. Alekhine played three games against consultation partners; one of these was with Kashdan and Herman Steiner on March 24, 1929. It was a disappointing loss by the partners in only 21 moves.

Kashdan played again in the 1929-30 Manhattan Championship. This time he had one of his best results. Of the ten games he played, he won 8, drew 1 and lost only 1. This was good enough for first place. He suffered a surprising loss to Samuels. But he defeated the previous year's champion Kevitz in their individual encounter. Kevitz, on the other hand, had the dismal score of 2 out of 10 games, placing him next to last. Kupchik came in second with 7, which was 1½ points behind the winner. Horowitz and Samuels tied for third. Another low score was obtained by Herman Steiner with four points, placing him eighth in this 11 player round robin.

2

The Early Thirties

Lajos Steiner Match 1930

In April 1930 a match took place between the Hungarian player Lajos Steiner and Isaac Kashdan. Many observers were interested to see how Kashdan would fare against a strong international master. Up to this point, he had never been tested in match play. The match, set for 12 games, started out with a draw in the first game. In the second, with the Black pieces, Kashdan succumbed in 57 moves in a Petroff Defense. In the third game Kashdan came back to even the match. It was a Queen's Pawn Opening in which Steiner defended with the Cambridge Springs Defense. It was one of the games that Kashdan himself later annotated. Steiner moved ahead again by winning the fourth game but again Kashdan evened the match in the fifth. But then, with the sixth game, Kashdan won for the first time with the black pieces to move ahead and he did not relinquish his lead. He also won the next game, the seventh, again a Ruy Lopez, but this time Kashdan had White. The eighth game ended in a draw. By winning the ninth game, Steiner came within one point—but, clinching the victory, Kashdan then won the final game. While the match was originally planned for 12 games, Kashdan's play was so decisive that the match was concluded after 10. The match started on April 19 and finished on May 3. The *American Chess Bulletin* (May-June 1930) offered these remarks: "This splendid victory, coupled with his unsurpassed play for the United States team at The Hague in 1928, and the fact that he is the Manhattan C.C. Champion, marks Kashdan as in the foremost ranks of American experts."

Another match against the veteran Charles Jaffe (born in Russia around 1879) took place in June 1930. This match lasted only three games as Kashdan won all three. Even so, it was not easy: every game went over 50 moves.

Hamburg Olympiad 1930

The next team competition took place in Hamburg, Germany. It was on the occasion of the 100th birthday of the Hamburg Chess Club. Eighteen teams competed in this July 1930 Hamburg Chess Olympiad. For the first time the United States Champion played in this competition. The U.S. team consisted of Marshall, Kashdan, H. Steiner, Anderson and

Phillips. While Marshall was a welcome addition to the team, the players Anderson and Phillips had a minus score. Marshall scored 10 wins, 5 draws, and 2 losses for 73.5 percent. Kashdan scored 12 wins, 4 draws and only 1 loss, giving him 82.4 percent. Two players had a better percentage than Kashdan. They were Rubinstein of Poland with 88.2, by scoring 13 wins, 4 draws and no losses. Next came Flohr of Czechoslovakia who had 85.3 percent with 14 wins, 1 draw, but 2 losses. Herman Steiner for the United States also had a plus score, winning 7, drawing 2, and losing 6. This was the lowest ranking of an American team in the pre-war era. The teams placed as follows:

1.	Poland	48½	10.	Latvia	35
2.	Hungary	47	11.	Denmark	31
3.	Germany	44½	12.	France	28½
4.	Austria	43½	13.	Rumania	28½
5.	Czechoslovakia	42½	14.	Lithuania	22½
6.	U.S.A.	41½	15.	Iceland	22
7.	Holland	41	16.	Spain	21½
8.	England	40½	17.	Finland	18
9.	Sweden	40	18.	Norway	16

Berlin Quadrangular 1930

The year 1930 was to be Kashdan's busiest, so far as playing in European events. Besides the team competition at Hamburg he played in four other tournaments. After the Hamburg Olympiad he traveled to Berlin in August to take part in the Quadrangular tournament. It was a double round affair consisting of two American players, Kashdan and H. Steiner, and two Germans, Sämisch and Helling. Kashdan was victorious, winning 4 games and drawing 2. Herman Steiner scored the two draws with Kashdan.

Frankfurt International 1930

Next was the tournament at Frankfurt where he faced much stiffer competition than at Berlin. This 12 player round robin took place from September 6 to 18, 1930. While Kashdan did not lose a game, scoring 7 wins and 4 draws, he was relegated to second by Nimzovitch even though the latter lost one game. Nimzovitch came out the victor with 9 wins, 1 draw and 1 loss. Their individual encounter was a draw.

Gyor 1930

This event in Hungary was a round robin tourney with ten players. It took place from October 2 to 12, 1930. Kashdan made the excellent score of 8 wins, 1 draw and no losses. The opposition were all local players from Hungary with the exception of Herman Steiner of the United States. On this occasion Kashdan was successful in defeating Steiner. Steiner had held Kashdan to two draws at Berlin. While playing in Gyor, Kashdan met Bogoljubow, who did not play in the event but was watching. He mentioned to Kashdan that they were planning a tournament in Stockholm later that year and he invited him to play in it. He accepted the invitation.

Stockholm 1930

While still winning the tournament at Stockholm, Kashdan had his first taste of defeat at the hands of Spielmann from Austria. In these four tournaments he played in 1930 in Europe his overall score was 23 wins, 8 draws, and 1 loss. At Stockholm he scored 4 wins, 1 draw, and 1 loss. This tournament ran from October 20 to 27, 1930. The Swedish players in the event were Ståhlberg, Stoltz and Lundin. Germany was represented by Bogoljubow and Rellstab. And Spielmann came from Austria. Kashdan won from Bogoljubow, Stoltz, Rellstab and Lundin. He had a draw with Ståhlberg and lost to Spielmann. That gave him 4½ points and victory. Bogoljubow tied for second with Stoltz, scoring 4 points each. While still in Sweden a match was arranged between Stoltz and Kashdan from October 30 to November 5. It was only the third match he had ever played and, surprisingly, he lost by a score of 3½ to 2½. Stoltz won the first game, which was given in many newspapers at the time. What was probably the second game is the only other game that apparently has survived. (Thanks to Calle Erlandson for finding the game in a Swedish newspaper.) This game ended in a draw. Kashdan then won the third game. The final game Stoltz won with the Black pieces.

New York International 1931

An international tournament was held in New York which included the former world champion, Capablanca. The competition began on April 18 and concluded on May 2, 1931. The following players also competed in the event: Frank J. Marshall (U.S. title holder), Isaac Kashdan, Edward Lasker, Abraham Kupchik, Israel Horowitz, Alexander Kevitz, Herman Steiner, Anthony Santasiere, all of New York: and Arthur Dake of Portland, Oregon, and I.S. Turover of Washington, D.C. Kashdan performed as might have been expected, placing second behind Capablanca and not losing a game. Capablanca was also undefeated but he had fewer draws than Kashdan and captured first prize with a score of 9 wins and 2 draws, for a score of 10 points. Kashdan had 6 wins and 5 draws for a score of 8½. Marshall had the dismal score of 4 points, with 3 wins, 2 draws, and 6 defeats. This was also the first time in tournament play that Kashdan defeated Marshall. The complete crosstable appears in Part Three along with other tournament results.

Prague Olympiad 1931

The next team competition took place at Prague, Czechoslovakia, from August 11 to 26, 1931. For the first time Marshall, the United States Champion, ceded the number one board to Kashdan for the U.S. team. The lineup then was as follows: Kashdan, Marshall,

Horowitz, H. Steiner, and Dake. This is how the *American Chess Bulletin* (July-August 1931) described it:

> Second at The Hague in 1928; sixth at Hamburg in 1930, and first at Prague in 1931! That's the record of our players in the three team tournaments of the International Chess Federation, affiliation with which for Americans was made possible through the National Chess Federation of U.S.A. After Paul Morphy came Harry Pillsbury; then Frank J. Marshall, and now Isaac Kashdan. A galaxy of names of which this country will always be proud. Each in his turn forced Europe to a full recognition of the chess ability as developed in this country.

The U.S. team won 12 of the 18 matches outright, made 3 even scores, and lost 3. But the final standings were awarded according to games scores and not match points. The American team came in ahead of the Poles with a score of 48 points against 47 points. Here are the individual scores for the U.S. team:

	Won	Lost	Drawn	Score
Kashdan	8	1	8	12–5
Marshall	7	3	6	10–6
Dake	5	2	7	8½–5½
Horowitz	6	1	6	9–4
H. Steiner	7	2	3	8½–3½

Bled International 1931

Without a doubt this international tournament at Bled, Slovenia (then part of Yugoslavia), was by far the strongest event in which Kashdan ever competed. The tournament began on August 23 and lasted to September 26, 1931. This 26 round event was a double round affair with 14 players. The world champion, Alexander Alekhine, did not disappoint. He won the event without losing a game. His score was 15 wins, 11 draws, and no losses. Kashdan came close in one of his two games with Alekhine, when he could have won at a critical point in the game, but he missed his opportunity and had to settle for a draw. The other game between these players was also a hard fought draw. At the half way point Kashdan was in second place. For most of the tournament Kashdan had an excellent chance to be in contention but then faltered in the last seven rounds. Here he could only score four draws and suffered three defeats. This ruined his chances for a high place in the final standings. He ended up in a tie for fourth place with Flohr, Stoltz and Vidmar. To get an idea how strong the tournament was; even the tailender was undefeated in 15 of his games.
Here are the final standings of the players:

	Won	Lost	Drawn	Score
1. Alekhine	15	0	11	20½–5½
2. Bogoljubow	12	8	6	15–11
3. Nimzovitch	8	6	12	14–12
4–7. Flohr	8	7	11	13½–12½
4–7. Kashdan	7	6	13	13½–12½
4–7. Stoltz	8	7	11	13½–12½
4–7. Vidmar	5	4	17	13½–12½

	Won	Lost	Drawn	Score
8. Tartakower	6	6	14	13–13
9. Spielmann	5	6	15	12½–13½
10. Kostić	6	8	12	12–14
11. Maróczy	6	8	12	12–14
12–13. Asztalos	3	8	15	10½–15½
12–13. Colle	8	13	5	10½–15½
14. Pirc	2	11	13	8½–17½

While still playing in the tournament in Yugoslavia, Kashdan reported that he would be returning to the States on October 16. He also indicated he was planning to go on a second tour of the country. Kashdan gave two exhibitions in simultaneous play in December. The first one took place on December 10 at the Montclair (New Jersey) Chess Club, where, opposed by 36 players, he achieved a score of 31 wins, 4 draws, and 1 loss. Then on December 12, he encountered 24 players at the Manhattan Chess Club, where he won 16, drew 6, and lost 2.

Hastings Christmas Tournament 1931-32

Kashdan, because of his growing reputation, received another invitation to compete in a tournament in Europe. It was the annual tournament at Hastings, England, which takes place right after Christmas. The tournament was scheduled to start on December 28 and conclude on January 6, 1932. The foreign masters in the event besides Kashdan were Flohr from Czechoslovakia, Euwe from the Netherlands, Stoltz from Sweden, and Sultan Khan from India. The English participants were Jackson, Menchik, Yates, Michell, and Sir George Thomas.

Salo Flohr captured first place, shaking off Kashdan only in the last round. Both players were undefeated. For three days they were neck and neck and then the exciting race came to an end when Stoltz drew with Kashdan in the final round, while Flohr won from Yates. So Flohr took top honors with 7 wins and 2 draws. Besides his draw with Kashdan, Flohr also drew with Euwe. Kashdan had one more draw than Flohr. His draws besides that to Flohr were to Sultan Khan, the Indian representative, and Stoltz.

London International 1932

Another tournament was planned under the auspices of the *Sunday Referee* of London only a few weeks after the Hastings tournament ended. Again, Kashdan was invited to compete. The 11-round tournament—with "a select company of masters" said the *British Chess Magazine* (March 1932)—was to commence on February 1 and conclude on February 12, 1932. (This gave Kashdan time to give some exhibitions while in England; a more detailed account of these exhibitions is given in Chapter 3, dealing with the simultaneous exhibitions.)

The London contest was again won by Alekhine, just as in Bled. The world champion scored 9 points without losing a game. He gave up draws to Flohr, Kashdan, Maróczy, and

George Thomas. Second place went to Flohr, who scored 8 points, winning 6 games, drawing 4, but losing 1 to Tartakower. Kashdan tied with Sultan Khan for third with 7½ points. Kashdan won 5 games, had 5 draws, and lost to Maróczy. Sultan Khan had 6 wins, 3 draws, and 2 losses. Maróczy placed fifth, winning 2 games, drawing 8, and losing but 1; this gave him 6 points. That score was equaled by Tartakower, winning 5 games, drawing 2, and losing 4.

Rounding out the field were Koltanowski, scoring 5 points for seventh place; Vera Menchik with 4½ points for eighth place, an excellent result for the lady in such strong company; Milner-Barry and Sir George scoring 3½ points to tie for ninth place; and Winter, 12th, with 2½ points.

Pasadena International 1932

The tournament called the California Chess Congress took place at Pasadena from August 15 to August 28, 1932. World Champion Alexander Alekhine was the main attraction to the event. In the recent tournaments at Bled in 1931 and later in London 1932 he was undefeated. But here he was handed his first defeat by Arthur Dake. Also, for the first time Kashdan faced the cream of the crop of the American players, which included Sammy Reshevsky and Reuben Fine. But Kashdan was still the leading American player, and he placed second to Alekhine. This was also the only time that Alekhine defeated Kashdan. All other games between them had ended in draws. Here are the final standings:

	Won	Drawn	Lost	Score
1. Alekhine	7	3	1	8½–2½
2. Kashdan	5	5	1	7½–3½
3. Dake	3	6	2	6–5
4. Reshevsky	5	2	4	6–5
5. H. Steiner	4	4	3	6–5
6. Borochow	4	3	4	5½–5½
7. J. Bernstein	2	6	3	5–6
8. Factor	3	4	4	5–6
9. Fine	2	6	3	5–6
10. Reinfeld	3	4	4	5–6
11. Araiza	2	3	6	3½–7½
12. Fink	2	2	7	3–8

Mexico City International 1932

The next tournament that Kashdan competed in was in Mexico City in 1932. He was joined here by World Champion Alekhine. They played eight of the strongest players from Mexico, making it a total of ten competitors. The tournament began on October 6 and lasted until October 16. The Mexican players were out-matched by Alekhine and Kashdan, despite strong resistance (in fact, the game between Kashdan and Medina went 101 moves; Kashdan had to play the endgame very carefully to squeeze out a win). The game between Alekhine and Kashdan ended in a draw. It is noteworthy that this was the sixth time the two masters had met and the fifth time they had drawn. Only in Pasadena was Alekhine able to take a game from Kashdan. The leaders were separated by 2½ points from the Mexican contingent.

A Visit to Dallas 1932

After the tournament in Mexico, Kashdan was invited to give exhibitions in Dallas, Texas. From October 25 to October 29, 1932, he gave two simultaneous exhibitions, two lectures, and a simultaneous consultation exhibition there. He took part in a rapid transit (speed) tournament, which was held in order to give local fans a chance to try their individual skill against the master. In the first simultaneous exhibition he won 23 games, drew 1 and lost 1. There was great interest in the rapid-transit tournament. Kashdan won all 58 of his games. The scores of the other players were as follows: second, Thompson 6½; third, Anderson 6; fourth, Hartsfield 5½; fifth, Barrington 4; sixth, Hart 2; seventh, Brantley 1½; eighth, Kempster ½; and ninth, Payne 0. The simultaneous consultation exhibition was a more difficult task for the master, as there were two players at every board against him. He played not just the white pieces but also black on some boards. He scored 7 wins and 1 loss. Before returning to New York, he also gave exhibitions in Chicago and Cleveland.

On November 22, Kashdan made his first visit to Boston. He gave a simultaneous exhibition there against 40 opponents at the Boston City Club. He won 35 of his games, lost 3 and drew 2.

Early 1933

After his stops at Dallas, Chicago and Cleveland late in 1932, Kashdan returned to New York uncertain about his future plans. He had an invitation to compete again at Hastings and he was tempted to go. But his friends discouraged this. Then the thought occurred to him of editing a chess magazine. He received the needed support, primarily from Israel Horowitz. The result was that he became chief editor of *The Chess Review*, with Horowitz as the associate editor. It started with the January issue for 1933.

He started to play in the Manhattan Chess Club Championship but after five games he dropped out with a score of 2 wins, 1 draw, and 2 losses. His wins were over Pinkus and Cohen. His reason for withdrawing was the pressure of business.

He did compete in some of the games in the Metropolitan Chess League. Noteworthy was his victory over Reuben Fine on April 21 in the match between the top teams in the league, namely the Manhattan and Marshall chess clubs. But Kashdan's win was the only one for the Manhattans and so they lost the match by a score of 2½ to 5½. Then on April 30 he competed also on first board in the intercity match against Philadelphia. The Manhattan team triumphed with a score of 9–4. But Kashdan was held to a draw by Levin.

He considered writing two books, one on the Bled tournament in 1931, selecting 50 of the best games. This he was going to co-edit with Fred Reinfeld, but it never materialized.

He also had planned to write a book of his own games both in America and abroad titled *Chess Holidays*. This was never published, but in 1936 he did annotate a good number of his games in *Chess Review*. He published a book on the Folkestone Olympiad later in 1933.

Before the team tournament at Folkestone, England, early in June 1933 he married Helen Cohen. This was a happy union that would last a lifetime. She also would accompany her husband to the team tournament in England.

Folkestone Olympiad 1933

The biggest event of 1933 was the Folkestone Olympiad to be held in England during the month of June. The American team was already fixed as far as boards one and two were concerned. As happened with the Prague Olympiad 1931, Frank Marshall, the United States Champion, relinquished the number one spot to Kashdan. But a tournament was held to determine the other three places. In this, Reuben Fine was the winner, with Dake coming in second and Simonson placing third.

Helen Kashdan accompanied her husband on the voyage to Folkestone. The book of the tournament which Isaac Kashdan later published has a picture of the American team players with his wife.*

The tournament started on June 12 and concluded on June 23. The tournament consisted of 15 teams. A team from Estonia was registered but never arrived.

The battle went neck-and-neck but the United States finally edged out their nearest rival, Czechoslovakia, for first place. The Czech team started the 15th round morning play with a magnificent win by Flohr against Kashdan, while Opočenský proved altogether too good for Simonson. So the U.S. team succumbed by a score of 1½ to 2½. Earlier they had lost the match with Sweden, who placed third and won their match against the United States by the same score, 2½ to 1½. Against Salo Flohr, Kashdan suffered his only loss. Flohr, playing White, had built up a winning position but faltered when he made an inferior move that would have allowed Kashdan to escape with a draw. Flohr could have played two different moves delivering check but instead chose a third move, which would have given Kashdan the exchange. But Kashdan overlooked it and resigned two moves later.

Here are the individual scores of the American team:

	Played	Won	Drawn	Lost	Total	Percent
Kashdan	14	7	6	1	10	71.4
Marshall	10	4	6	0	7	70
Fine	13	6	6	1	9	69.2
Dake	13	9	2	2	10	76.9
Simonson	6	2	2	2	3	50

The results of the teams were as follows (not match results but individual game score totals determined the placings):

*Arnold Denker recalled two incidents in his 1995 book The Bobby Fischer I Knew. (Denker was the first alternate should any of the regular team members not be able to go.) On the voyage to Folkestone, Al "Buddy" Simonson had a few drinks too many and passed out in "Kash" and Helen's room. It did not seem to upset Kashdan too much; he said, "We all know that Buddy can't hold more than one drink. Let him sleep it off." The other incident Denker places at the Hastings tournament of 1931-1932. But this is unlikely as the Kashdans were not married yet. More likely it also occurred at Folkestone: The Indian player Sultan Khan took a liking to Mrs. Kashdan. He offered Isaac 150 English pounds for her to join his harem. He said to Kash: "It will be much easier for you to replace her, than for me to find another Helen at my age." Rather than Kash being upset about this, he found it rather amusing.

The team representing the United States at Folkstone in 1933. The players are, from left to right, Arthur Dake, Helen Kashdan, Isaac Kashdan, Albert Simonson, Frank Marshall, and Reuben Fine (courtesy *Chess Review*).

1.	United States	39	9.	Latvia	27½
2.	Czechoslovakia	37½	10.	England	27
3.	Sweden	34	11.	Italy	24½
4.	Poland	34	12.	Denmark	22½
5.	Hungary	34	13.	Iceland	17
6.	Austria	33½	14.	Belgium	17
7.	Lithuania	30½	15.	Scotland	14
8.	France	28	[16.	Estonia	0]

A Challenge to Marshall 1933

Negotiations for a match between Frank J. Marshall and Isaac Kashdan for the chess championship of the United States were underway. The basic terms had been agreed upon; to make it official Kashdan started the ball rolling by issuing a formal challenge with the following letter:

October 11, 1933

Dear Mr. Marshall:

There has been frequent discussion in the last two years regarding a match for the American Chess Championship, which you held so long and so honorably. I have been generally mentioned as the logical contender.

I wish now to lay my challenge before you, and request that you state under what conditions you would play me for the title. You will realize that times have changed considerably since the last Championship Match, and that the terms set at that time are no real precedent for a present encounter.

I suggest that we hold an amicable meeting in the presence of our respective friends. If this is satisfactory to you, I shall ask Messrs. Harold M. Phillips, Leonard B. Meyer, and Fritz Brieger to be present. Will you name a time and a place that will be convenient to you? We can then discuss the various matters that may come up in arranging the match, and I trust bring it to an early fruition.

Very truly yours,
Isaac Kashdan

This open letter was published in the October 1933 *Chess Review*. A few days later, on October 15, Marshall replied and a meeting was arranged on October 21. The conditions laid down included a purse of $5,000 to be raised by the challenger. Unfortunately that amount could not be raised in the end because of the Great Depression. The match never took place. Instead Marshall agreed to a round robin tournament to be held to determine the next champion of the United States, which was held in 1936.

Resigns as Chief Editor of Chess Review

In the November-December, 1933, issue Kashdan officially gave his resignation as head of *Chess Review*. He felt that some of the difficulties that were encountered during the year were pretty much resolved. He also stated that he believed he could do more for the game by resuming his active playing career, which precluded giving the necessary time and care as editor to the magazine.

Plays Against 26 Teams

Opposed by 26 teams, for the most part composed of four players each, Isaac Kashdan gave a simultaneous exhibition late in November or early December of 1933. The event took place at the Labor Temple in Woodside. That meant that about 100 players were involved. His score was 22 wins, 2 losses and 2 draws. Only the teams from Columbia and the Marshall Chess Club forced the resignation of the international master; the teams that drew against him were James Monroe High School and the Hawthorne Chess Club.

Metropolitan League Play

The final match between the leading adversaries for the Metropolitan League championship—the Manhattan and the Marshall chess clubs—took place on April 21, 1934. This time Kashdan played again Reuben Fine, not on board one but on board four. Their individual encounter ended in a draw. This was sufficient for the Manhattan team to win the match, 4½ to 3½. They had lost the matches to the Marshall club the previous three years. Later, Kashdan played board one for Manhattan against a team from Philadelphia. His opponent was again Levin but this time Kashdan lost. The match was nevertheless won by the Manhattans with a score of 10–6.

35th Western Chess Congress, Chicago 1934

Folkestone was the only tournament Kashdan played in 1933. Not having further obligations as the editor of Chess Review allowed him to become more active again in tournament play. He took part in the 35th Western Chess Congress in Chicago in July. He faced again, as at Pasadena 1932, the cream of American masters. First he needed to play in the preliminaries before he could advance to the finals. This he easily accomplished although he suffered a loss to Reshevsky. His score was 6 points, half a point behind Reshevsky. In the final, Kashdan's poor showing was unexpected. The leading scorers were Reshevsky and Fine, with 7½ points each. Third was Arthur Dake with 6½, fourth was Denker with 5½, and in fifth place was Kashdan with an even score of 2 wins, 5 draws, and 2 losses for 4½ points.

Syracuse International 1934

By winning the Syracuse Masters Tournament in August 1934, following closely upon his triumph in the Western Chess Association Meeting in Chicago, Sammy Reshevsky passed another milestone on the way to American chess supremacy. If American players had been ranked at that time, Sammy would have been entitled to the No. 1 position.

Kashdan staged a comeback after his poor showing in the Western and after a slow start made a "garrison" finish to achieve second place. Third and fourth prizes were shared by Arthur Dake and Reuben Fine. Abraham Kupchik, after a gallant struggle which kept him at Reshevsky's pace during the major portion of the tourney, was disheartened by his only loss, to Horowitz—and weakened. He finished fifth (information from Chess Review, October 1934).

The final standings:

	Won	Lost		Won	Lost
1. Reshevsky	12	2	9. Reinfeld	6	8
2. Kashdan	10½	3½	10. Santasiere	6	8
3. Dake	10	4	11. Denker	5	9
4. Fine	10	4	12. Seitz	5	9
5. Kupchik	9½	4½	13. Araiza	4½	9½
6. Horowitz	8½	5½	14. Tholfsen	3	11
7. H. Steiner	8	6	15. Martin	½	13½
8. Monticelli	6½	7½			

Manhattan Chess Club Championship 1934

Kashdan had competed in the Manhattan Chess Club Championship in 1932, but did not complete the schedule. In the 1934 tournament he made a very strong showing. He tied with Kupchik for the lead, scoring 11 wins, 2 losses and no draws. The two losses he suffered were to Cohen and MacMurray. Kupchik achieved his total with 10 wins, 2 draws, and 1 loss—to Kashdan. It was one of the strongest Manhattan championships and also included Horowitz, Denker, and Simonson. The playoff game to determine the winner went to Kupchik.

Later in April 1935 Kashdan took part in the annual final Metropolitan League Match. His opponent on board two was Fred Reinfeld. The game was won by Kashdan. The match was won by his Manhattan club by the lopsided margin of 7–1. Only Reshevsky on board three was able to win his game against Horowitz for the Marshall club. Kupchik won for Manhattan from Santasiere on board one.

3

The Simultaneous Exhibitions

Kashdan returned on December 5, 1930, from his European trip to New York on the steamship *George Washington*, and received a warm welcome at the Manhattan Chess Club. He gave his first simultaneous exhibition there on the evening of December 20. There were 23 opponents, the result being that club champion Kashdan won 20, lost 2, and drew 1. His next performance was at the Rice Progressive Chess Club, where he played 20 games. He won every game but one, which was a draw. Then on New Year's Day, Kashdan partnered with Lubowski, and played an exciting consultation game. The opponents were Jaffe and Mishook. The game ended in a draw.

For four consecutive years Kashdan made nationwide tours giving simultaneous exhibitions. In some years he also went into Canada. The first of these tours took place in 1931. Kashdan hardly published any of his wins although in most of these displays he would score 90 percent or better. A researcher will find more of his losses than wins, as the local newspapers would proudly show off one of their own who had defeated the master.

Kashdan, the Manhattan Chess Club Champion, embarked on his first tour on February 3, 1931. He visited ten cities, ending with a visit to the Newark Rice Chess Club on March 28. Here are the results of these engagements:

	Played	*Won*	*Lost*	*Drawn*
Binghamton	12	12	0	0
Scranton	19	16	2	1
Philadelphia	16	9	2	5
Cincinnati	32	27	1	4
Cincinnati	17	16	0	1
St. Louis	34	31	0	3
Iowa City	21	20	0	1
Chicago	10	9	1	0
Peoria	11	11	0	0
Allentown	27	25	1	1
Newark	40	33	2	5
Totals	239	209	9	21

Early in 1932, after the conclusion of the Hastings tournament in England, he had three weeks before the tournament in London started. He took advantage of that interval to give exhibitions in that country. He was the guest of the Liverpool Chess Club for three days. He also visited Bournemouth, Tunbridge Wells, and London. Here is what the *British Chess Magazine* for March 1932 reported:

> Kashdan has found time to give a few simultaneous displays despite the strenuous efforts in the *Sunday Referee* Festival. On January 27 he played 29 games at the Kingston and Thames Valley Club, winning 24, drawing 4, and losing 1. The following day he traveled to Bournemouth and the result of his display there was 28 won, 1 drawn, and 1 lost. On the Saturday following he played at Tunbridge Wells, winning 19, losing 1, and drawing 1. On February 7 a strong entry of 29 took the field against him at Montefiore Hall, by arrangement of the Maccabeans; here his figures reverted to 24 won, 4 drawn, and 1 lost. His final engagement was at Liverpool where he lost only 4 in two displays of 20 each and three consultation games against strong couples, and giving a short lecture before each display.

After an absence of three months, Kashdan returned home on board the steamship *Deutschland* of the Hamburg-America Line. The champion of the Manhattan Chess Club was warmly welcomed home by a host of admirers on March 3, 1932.

In recognition of the achievements of Isaac I. Kashdan, a testimonial exhibition was arranged for him at Empire City Chess Club on April 24. Kashdan opposed 108 opponents on 27 games, with four consulting on each table. The result was quite surprising with Kashdan winning only 6 games, drawing 8, and losing 13. This definitely was not one of his better days.

During the months of May to July he went on one of his longest exhibition tours. The displays started on May 8 in Reading, Pennsylvania, and ended on June 18 in Portland, Oregon. The largest group he encountered on May 13, was in the town of Allentown, Pennsylvania. Of the 60 players who opposed him, he won 57, drawing 2, and losing only 1. It is interesting to note that Kashdan did not publish any of his games as many other masters did. Naturally the local papers would feature games won by or drawn by local players. On this tour he achieved the fantastic record for the 505 games played, winning 467, drawing 20, and losing 18. This gave him a phenomenal total of nearly 94.5 percent. Here are the results:

		Played	Won	Lost	Drawn
May 9	Reading, Pa.	37	37	0	0
May 10	Wilkes-Barre	20	19	1	0
May 11	Scranton, Pa.	21	20	0	1
May 12	Binghamton, N.Y.	21	20	0	1
May 13	Allentown, Pa.	60	57	1	2
May 14	Philadelphia	24	18	4	2
May 16	Harrisburg, Pa.	17	16	0	1
May 20	Cincinnati	29	26	0	3
June 4	Chicago	17	13	2	2
June 11	Chicago	19	17	1	1
June 15	Minneapolis	27	23	3	1
June 20	Omaha	40	38	1	1
June 22	St. Louis	40	36	2	2
June 25	St. Louis	18	18	0	0

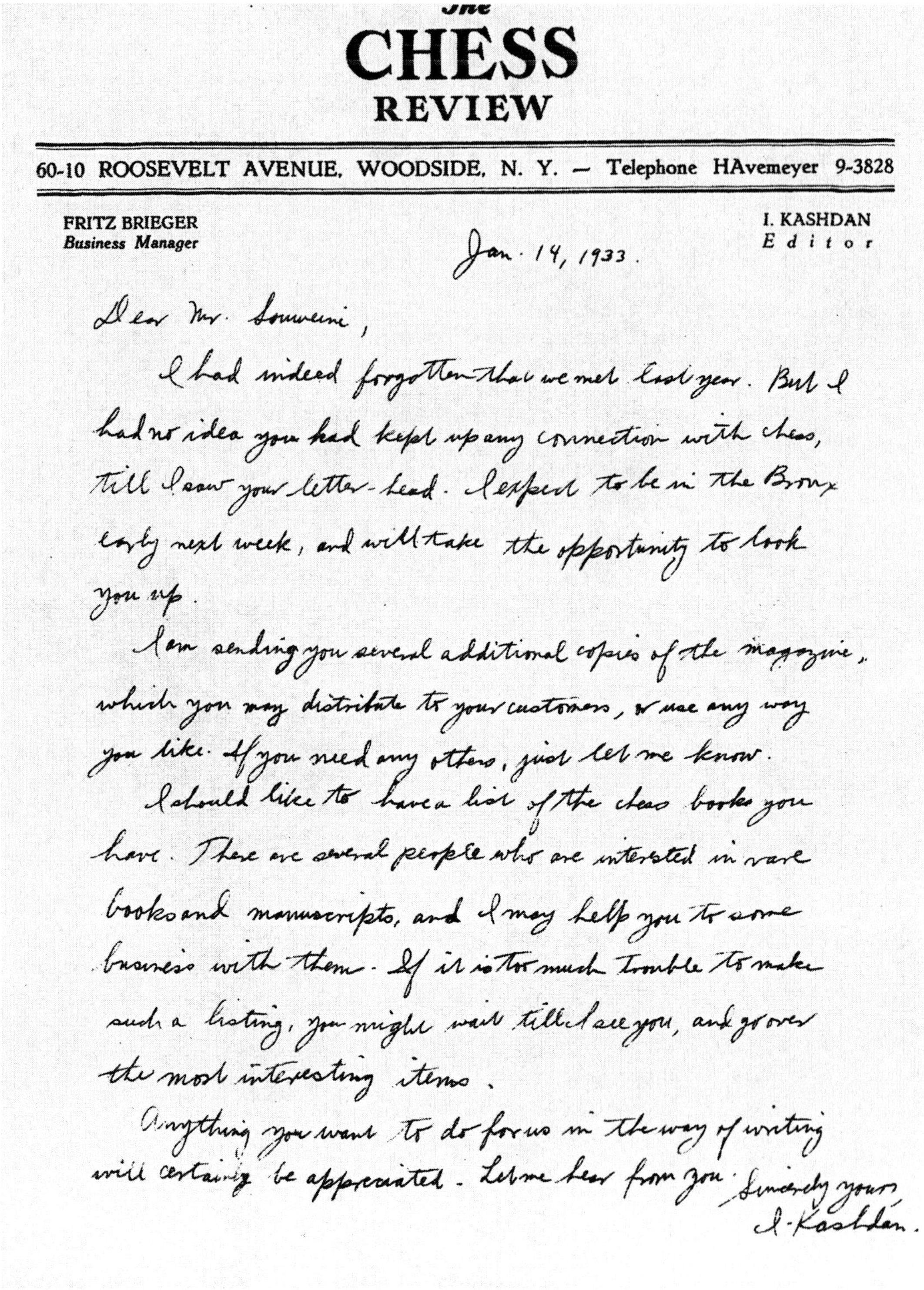

CHESS
REVIEW

60-10 ROOSEVELT AVENUE, WOODSIDE, N. Y. — Telephone HAvemeyer 9-3828

FRITZ BRIEGER
Business Manager

Jan. 14, 1933.

I. KASHDAN
Editor

Dear Mr. Souweine,

I had indeed forgotten that we met last year. But I had no idea you had kept up any connection with chess, till I saw your letter-head. I expect to be in the Bronx early next week, and will take the opportunity to look you up.

I am sending you several additional copies of the magazine, which you may distribute to your customers, or use any way you like. If you need any others, just let me know.

I should like to have a list of the chess books you have. There are several people who are interested in rare books and manuscripts, and I may help you to some business with them. If it is too much trouble to make such a listing, you might wait till I see you, and go over the most interesting items.

Anything you want to do for us in the way of writing will certainly be appreciated. Let me hear from you. Sincerely yours,

I. Kashdan.

As can be seen by the letterhead Kashdan had just assumed the editorship to *Chess Review*. In the letter he asked Mr. Souweine if he would distribute copies of the magazine (contributed by Richard Kashdan).

		Played	Won	Lost	Drawn
June 28	Denver	26	24	1	1
June 30	Billings, Montana	15	15	0	0
July 2	Yellowstone Park, Wyo.	16	15	0	1
July 15	Seattle	34	31	2	1
July 18	Portland, Ore.	24	24	0	0
Totals		505	467	18	20

Kashdan wrote a letter to a Mr. MacMahon on July 23, indicating that he would be interested in giving an exhibition in San Francisco or Oakland. Whether these events ever materialized in those cities is not clear. He did mention in the letter his latest exhibition in Portland, Oregon. (A copy of the letter is shown herewith.)

Later that year he also gave more exhibitions, such as in Dallas on October 25 and Tulsa on October 30. He also gave several exhibitions while he was playing in a tournament in Mexico. He gave his first ever exhibition in Boston on November 22, where he won 35, lost 3, and drew 2.

He gave a simultaneous exhibition on January 16, 1933, at Reading, Pennsylvania. He encountered 40 players, winning 39 and losing only 1. (The previous year he started his nation-wide tour at Reading against 37 players, beating them all.)

He also embarked on a tour of the Eastern and Midwestern states in the month of May, but for a much shorter time than he had spent the previous year. He visited 11 cities and compiled a record of 225 wins, 33 draws, and 21 losses out of 279 games played.

		Played	Won	Lost	Drawn
May 1	Binghamton	21	19	0	2
May 6	Detroit	34	28	3	3
May 15	Minneapolis	15	14	0	1
May 17	Springfield, Mo.	19	17	0	2
May 18	St. Louis	20	18	1	1
May 25	Cleveland	36	32	1	3
May 26	Buffalo, N.Y.	18	15	1	2
May 27	Toronto	28	21	2	5
May 29	Montreal	48	32	6	10
May 30	Collinsville, Conn.	28	25	3	0
May 31	Philadelphia	12	4	4	4
Totals		279	225	21	33

Kashdan's fourth and final nationwide tour was not as completely reported. But we have the results from what was given in the *Brooklyn Daily Eagle,* for April 4, 1934 ("Isaac Kashdan, who is expected shortly to meet United States Champion Frank J. Marshall in a title match, recently concluded a tour in which he encountered 616 opponents in simultaneous play"). Here are the results for 1934:

		Played	Won	Lost	Drawn
February 9	Binghamton, N.Y.	14	13	0	1
February 14	Washington, D.C.	23	20	0	3
February 17	Montreal	72	58	5	9

TELEPHONE PROSPECT 3940

HOTEL WORTH
641 POST STREET
SAN FRANCISCO
CALIFORNIA

July 23, 1932.

Dear Mr. MacMahon,

Thank you for your kind letter.
I appreciate that your suggestions
have been helpful. It will be a
pleasure to meet you soon, and I shall
be glad to co-operate in anything you
plan at L. A.

The situation re Minneapolis is this.
I know Mr. Barnes, who is running the
tournament, and there is no chance of a
repetition of the Tulsa episode. When
he invited me there, I asked for my
fare and a hundred dollar retainer,
which is only fair in view of the effort.
They have till Wednesday to notify
me definitely. I think the chance of
their meeting those terms rather slim

. but am not anxious about it. I shall let you know the final outcome in a few days.

While in Portland, I played 24, winning them all. There is a possibility of an exhibition either in San Francisco or Oakland before I go South, but nothing sure yet.

Give Dake my best regards. Can you send me the result of his big display?

Cordially yours,

I. Kashdan.

A letter by Kashdan to a Mr. MacMahon. The tournament in Minneapolis referred to was the 33rd Western Chess Association meeting that Kashdan did not attend (although Reshevsky and Fine competed). Instead he was considering giving exhibitions in California (contributed by Richard Kashdan).

		Played	Won	Lost	Drawn
February 18	Montreal	73	50	7	16
February 21	Toronto	39	34	1	4
March 3	Chicago	?			
March 4	Irving Park, Ill.	?			
March 6	Milwaukee	?			
March 9–11	Winnipeg	?			
March 13	Omaha	?			
March 15–22	Denver	32	29	0	3
March 24–26	Dallas	?			

The *Washington Post* for February 17, 1934, gave details of the simul in that city—the results of all the opponents that faced the master. Only three players were able to achieve a draw (the fact was mentioned that many of the strong players of the Capital City did not compete).

His overall performance was 532 wins, 28 losses, and 56 draws from the 616 games. This gave him a total of nearly 91 percent. Considering the large number of players he encountered in Canada, this was quite an impressive accomplishment.

He continued to give exhibitions in 1935 but not on the scale of the previous four years. He gave a display in August at the Mt. Vernon Chess Club where he was opposed by 16 players. He won all the games except for a loss to expert M. Krieger. Later, probably in October, he faced 21 adversaries at the Empire Chess Club in New York City. He won 16, drew 4, and lost to Dr. Gassen. One of the draws was achieved by Adele Rivero, who later held the American woman's title.

In 1936 while in San Juan, where he won a tournament in November, he also gave two exhibitions. He started off against 31 players at Ponce. Here he won all but one; the lone player to draw him was Sugranes. The next day he made it a clean sweep over 26 at the Casino Yauco.

Early in 1937 at the newly organized Kings Chess Club in Brooklyn, N.Y., Kashdan gave an exhibition, winning 21 while giving up 1 draw and 1 loss. Later that year in Washington, D.C., he encountered 16 players, winning 15 and losing 1 game, to Martin Stark. Later, he encountered 20 players in Richmond, winning them all. Playing against 17 at the Scarsdale Golf Club, Kashdan made it a clean sweep on all boards. Among his opponents was N. Marache, grandson of Napoleon Marache, a contemporary of Paul Morphy.

On February 13, 1938, Kashdan gave an exhibition of simultaneous play at the Manhattan Old Fellows Temple. Of the 22 games he won 18, drew 3, and lost 1. He also played a consultation game against two players of the club, Myron Granger and Sol Raunheim. In this game he took the black pieces and lost the game.

While he continued to give exhibitions every year, nothing was reported until 1947, when he gave an exhibition in Baltimore. One of the games that he lost was given in *Chess Review*. All that is known is that he played against 38 players. How he scored was not reported. Another game was given in 1949 when he was opposed by, among others, the strong expert Irving Rivise. That game he lost; no further information on this event was given. While playing in the United States Open at Fort Worth in August 1951, he also gave some exhibitions. One of those games we have with his own score sheet and a partial game of another. How he fared in this exhibition, however, is also not known.

Kashdan reported, as chess editor of the *Los Angeles Times*, an exhibition he gave at the Covina Country Club on April 7, 1956. Here, he encountered 28 players, winning all but 1. The remaining game was a draw with William Rogers.

Chess Life in the July 5, 1960, edition, reported of a simul he gave in Coronado, California. He played 30, won 28, drew with Rubalcaba, and lost to James Miller.

4

The Late Thirties

36th Western Championship, Milwaukee 1935

The 36th Annual Western Congress took place in July and the beginning of August in Milwaukee, Wisconsin. In the preliminaries Kashdan won section B with a score of 6 wins and 3 draws. Reuben Fine won Section A, also scoring 6 wins and 3 draws. Arthur Dake won Section C with 8 wins and 1 draw.

In the finals Fine was the winner with 6 wins and 4 draws. Dake was second with a score of 5 wins and 5 draws. Kashdan was also undefeated and placed third with a score of only 3 wins and 7 draws. Kashdan would edit a book, his second, dealing with this tournament. (The first one dealt with the Folkestone Olympiad of 1933.)

New York State Championship 1935

Kashdan was expected to play in the Warsaw Olympiad, but for some reason he chose not to go. Instead he played for the first time in the New York State Championship. The tournament took place from August 19 to 24, 1935. The competition was not especially strong and he won it handily. He did give up one draw to Lessing and his game with Reinfeld lasted over 80 moves. He scored 6 wins with 1 draw.

First United States Championship, New York 1936

The year 1936 was one of the busiest of Kashdan's career. It started out with his annotating several of his earlier games and contributing them to *Chess Review* starting in January. They included those that he played in the Olympiads at The Hague 1928, Hamburg 1930, and Prague 1931. In addition there were games he played in tournaments in Europe, especially Bled 1931. And, finally, he offered annotated games of his in the October 1936 *Chess Review* of the just completed U.S. Championship. He also contributed articles to *Chess Review* starting in February dealing with the endgame.

He advertised in February and later that he would be available to give exhibitions, lectures and private lessons at the Manhattan Chess Club. But, interestingly, for a short time he switched from the Manhattan Club to the Empire City Club. That is the reason he did not compete in the match between the Manhattan and the Marshall club. Instead, he played at least two games for the Empire club. One of those games was against Frank J. Marshall and ended in a draw. The other game was against Jaffe who represented the Rice Progressive club; it was also a draw.

This was the year when the first tournament for the United States championship was held—a 16 player round robin. Previously, the title had been decided in match play. The title holder, Marshall, agreed late in 1935 that a championship should be held that would include the best players in the country. Marshall did not compete in the championship tournament, although he remained active playing in other tournaments. Eight players were seeded into the tournament. They were, in addition to Kashdan, Reshevsky, Fine, Dake, Horowitz, Kupchik, Kevitz and H. Steiner. There were no clear favorites as to who was most likely to win. It was felt that Reshevsky, Fine, and Kashdan had the best chances. That left eight places open. These were decided by four preliminary sections of eight players each. Two of these players from each section would then advance to the finals. The following players advanced from these sections: A—Factor and Simonson; B—Denker and Adams; C—Treysman and Bernstein; and D—Morton and Hanauer. The preliminaries started in March and concluded early in April.

The first game of the finals was played on April 25. Kashdan first defeated Albert C. Simonson, a young player who qualified only by going through the preliminaries but who actually took clear second in the finals. Kashdan then proceeded to win his next three games against Bernstein, Horowitz, and Denker, in that order. This gave Kashdan the lead after four rounds with a perfect score. Treysman was close behind with 3½, followed by Dake, Fine, and Horowitz with 3 points.

In round five Kashdan was upset by Hanauer, but this still left him in the lead. Five players trailed him a half point behind: Dake, Fine, Horowitz, Steiner, and Treysman. In the sixth round Kashdan defeated Factor, giving him 5 points. Now only Dake and Horowitz were trailing him by half a point. It is interesting to note that the eventual winner, Reshevsky, was not among the leaders. He started out poorly, posting only 1½ points in the first four rounds. But then he won the next two games to be at 3½ points and was tied for seventh after 6 rounds. In round seven Kashdan faced one of the favorites, Reuben Fine. It was a hard fought game and only after 73 moves was Kashdan forced to resign. This gave Arthur Dake a chance to take the lead with 5½ points. Tied for second with 5 points were then Kashdan, Fine, and Horowitz.

In round eight Kashdan faced the other favorite, Reshevsky. He lost this game rather quickly, a Scotch Gambit in 29 moves. Kashdan played for material gain, but this gave Reshevsky too much of a lead in development, and Kashdan already had a lost game after 19 moves. The situation after eight rounds looked like this: Dake was leading with 6½ points, Fine was second with 6, Reshevsky and Treysman were tied for third at 5½, and then came Kashdan tied at 5 points with Horowitz, Kupchik and Simonson. In round nine, Kashdan played to a draw with Dake. This put Kashdan in a tie for sixth with 5½ points, and Dake holding the lead with 7. In round 10 Kashdan faced Herman Steiner and went on to win that game. His 6 points put him in a tie for fifth with Fine. The leader now was Treysman with 7½ points, as Dake lost to Reshevsky. In round 11 Kashdan suffered an upset in a long game with Treysman that went 81 moves, allowing Treysman to remain in first place with 8½ points. Reshevsky moved up to second with 8 points, tied with Simonson, Dake was third, Fine and Kupchik tied for fourth, and only then, in sixth place with 6½ points, came Kashdan. In round 12 Kashdan won from Adams, which put him in a tie for fifth place with 7½ points, and in round 13 he drew with Kevitz to tie for sixth with 8 points. The lead was still shared by Reshevsky and Simonson with 10 points as both won their games. This certainly looked like a close finish with only two rounds to go, and was a big surprise so far as Simonson was concerned.

Kashdan made up some lost ground as he won his game in round 14 over Kupchik; his 9 points put him fifth. Reshevsky and Simonson both won, standing at 11 points, followed by Treysman at 10½ and then Fine with 9½.

Kashdan also won his last round game from Morton. That gave him a final standing of clear fifth with 10 points (9 wins, 2 draws, 4 losses). The games by the leaders, Reshevsky and Simonson, took an exciting turn. Reshevsky agreed to draw with Kupchik in his game. So by winning his last game Simonson could have won the tournament but instead he lost his game with Factor, who was not a strong contender. This allowed Reshevsky to win the first United States Championship by half a point. The final standings were:

1. Reshevsky	11½	9. Horowitz	7
2. Simonson	11	10. Factor	6½
3.–4. Fine	10½	11.–12. Denker	6
3.–4. Treysman	10½	11.–12. Steiner, H	6
5. Kashdan	10	13. Bernstein, S	5½
6.–7. Dake	9	14. Hanauer	4½
6.–7. Kupchik	9	15.–16. Adams	3
8. Kevitz	7½	15.–16. Morton	3

37th Western Championship, Philadelphia 1936

A few months after the U.S. championship Kashdan competed in the 37th annual meeting of the American Chess Federation. It began on August 15 in Philadelphia. It continued for two weeks and it proved to be one of the most grueling in the long history of this event. The contest was divided into four sections. The top three players in each section would then advance to the finals. Kashdan played in section I and made an excellent score, winning 8 and drawing 3 of his games to take the top spot by half a point. His draws came against Kupchik, Reinfeld and Grossman. He did have one close call against Glover, who, however, blundered so badly later in the game that Kashdan won. Since the tournament lasted only two weeks, two games had to be played on each day. In the finals Kashdan did not do so well and had to be content with fourth place, scoring 7 points. He won 6 games and drew 4, but lost to Horowitz and Polland. Horowitz was the winner with 8 points. Half a point behind were Dake and Denker.

New York State Championship 1936

Kashdan again competed in the New York State Championship, the event he had won the year before. This year was no different. It took place in Poughkeepsie from August 30 to September 5, 1936. The Western Championship tournament in Philadelphia was to have ended on August 30 and it is not clear how Kashdan could have played two games on the same day in two different locations. Perhaps he was allowed to start the first game a day late; he was after all the champion. This tournament was not nearly as strong as the two previous ones, and he had an easy time, giving up only one draw to the runner-up Helms. He scored 10 wins and the 1 draw.

Puerto Rico International 1936

Not much later Kashdan again took part in a tournament at San Juan. He was invited by the Puerto Rico Chess Federation along with Marshall and Jakob Seitz of Germany to play in this international event, held from November 16 to 22. Five players from the home country made up the rest of the field. It started out with Marshall going into an early lead. Then Seitz overtook him, but Kashdan remained in the background as he had several games that were unfinished. In the end Kashdan triumphed by defeating Marshall, all the Puerto Rican players, and giving up only one draw to Seitz.

At the conclusion of the tournament, Kashdan gave two simultaneous exhibitions. He started out by playing against 31. He won 30 and gave up only one draw. The next day he made a clean sweep against all 26 opponents.

Manhattan Chess Club Championship 1936-37

As if that was not enough chess in one year, Kashdan again competed in the Manhattan Chess Club Championship, which started late in 1936 and lasted until early 1937. In this event he was also successful despite strong opposition. Besides Kashdan there were Abraham Kupchik, Robert Willman, and Arnold Denker among the 12 competitors. Kashdan had to share the top spot with Simonson. They both scored 9 wins and 2 draws. But then in the playoff Kashdan was victorious as he won the first game and then drew the next two. With the conclusion of this match Kashdan had competed in three tournaments and this match without losing a game. His record stood at 30 wins, 6 draws, and no losses.

Then Kashdan proceeded to give some simultaneous displays. He opened up the new Manhattan club's activities with an exhibition, winning 21 games, losing 2, and drawing 1. Later in 1937 he went to Washington, D.C., where he played against 17, winning 15, losing 1 and drawing 1. Shortly thereafter he made a clean sweep of 20 games at Richmond, Virginia. Playing against 17 in Scarsdale, New York, Kashdan succeeded in making another clean sweep. Among the opponents was N. Marache, a grandson of Napoleon Marache, contemporary of Paul Morphy.

Stockholm Olympiad 1937

The biggest event of the year for the United States was the team tournament at Stockholm. Samuel Reshevsky and Reuben Fine had moved ahead of Kashdan in the rankings, Reshevsky mainly for having won the United States Championship the year before, and Fine

Kashdan (left) and Marshall engaged in a friendly game around 1935. The onlookers are not identified (courtesy *Chess Review*).

because of his international successes in Europe. That put Kashdan in the third position playing for the United States. Frank Marshall took the fourth spot, and Israel Horowitz was the reserve player. As in all the prior team competitions, Marshall was the team captain.

The team tournament started on July 31 and lasted until August 13, 1937. That meant that for some rounds two games had to be played on one day. Nineteen teams competed, all from Europe except for Argentina and the United States. The United States won by the fantastic margin of 6 points, scoring 56½. Hungary came in second, scoring 48½ points; Poland and Argentina tied for third with 47. Here is how *Chess Review* (September 1937) described it:

> The U.S.A. was clearly the class of the field: no lost matches and only three draws allowed (against Hungary, Holland, and Latvia). But Hungary was the only other undefeated team, but too many drawn matches made a big difference in the point score. Strangely enough Poland, which won three more matches than Hungary, only came third. Argentina, on the other hand, won three less matches than Poland, and lost two more matches than the Polish team—and yet was fourth by only half a point. The explanation is that the Argentine players won their matches by large scores and lost by narrower scores. Three of the American masters particularly distinguished themselves by making the best scores of all players in their respective categories: Fine at second board, Kashdan at third, and Horowitz among the reserves; to which should be added that Frank J. Marshall, the veteran of the team and its captain, completed his schedule, without loss of a game. Marshall, incidentally, celebrated his sixtieth birthday during the tourney. Sammy Reshevsky had a difficult time on first board, having his hands full with some of the world's strongest masters included in the opposition.

Following are the individual results for the American team:

	Played	Won	Drawn	Lost	Total	Percentage
1. Reshevsky	16	6	7	3	9½	59.4
2. Fine	15	9	5	1	11½	76.7
3. Kashdan	16	13	2	1	14	87.5
4. Marshall	10	3	7	–	6½	65
5. Horowitz	15	11	4	–	13	86.7

That gave Kashdan the best score of any of the other players in the team competition. He was closely followed by Horowitz. In third position with 84.6 percent came Regedzinski of Poland.

The team results were as follows:

1. United States	54½	11. Latvia	37½
2. Hungary	48½	12. Finland	34
3. Poland	47	13. England	34
4. Argentina	47	14. Italy	26½
5. Czechoslovakia	45	15. Denmark	25½
6. Holland	44	16. Iceland	23
7. Estonia	41½	17. Belgium	22½
8. Lithuania	41½	18. Norway	19½
9. Yugoslavia	40	19. Scotland	14
10. Sweden	38½		

The record for Kashdan for all five Olympiads:

	Played	Won	Drawn	Lost	Total	Percentage
1928 The Hague	15	12	2	1	13	86.7
1930 Hamburg	17	12	4	1	14	82.4
1931 Prague	17	8	8	1	12	70.6
1933 Folkestone	14	7	6	1	10	71.4
1937 Stockholm	16	13	2	1	14	87.5
Totals	79	52	22	5	63	79.5

Kashdan won four team medals: three gold (1931, 1933, 1937), one silver (1928), and five individual medals: two gold (1928, 1937), one silver (1933), two bronze (1930, 1931). No wonder Kashdan was called the hero of the Olympics.

Manhattan Chess Club Championship 1937

The Manhattan Championship consisted of only eight players this year. Kashdan defended his title successfully as he went through undefeated, winning four games and drawing three for 5½–1½ points. Robert Willman, a former champion, came in second scoring 5–2. Except for Denker the event was not as strong as in previous years.

Metropolitan League Matches 1938

Since Kashdan could no longer make his living by playing chess in tournaments and exhibitions, he advertised in January 1938 in *Chess Review* that he would be a special agent for Prudential Insurance Company. He invited anyone interested to consult him for life insurance and investments.

Kashdan gave an exhibition of simultaneous play on February 12 at the Manhattan Odd Fellows Temple. He conducted 22 games, winning 18, drawing 3, and losing 1. A consulting pair, Sol Raunheim and Myran Granger, were the only players to defeat the Manhattan champion.

Kashdan also took part in two matches played between the Manhattan and the Marshall Chess Club. The first one took place on March 12 and ended in a tie, with a score of 8–8. But Kashdan ended up on the losing end on board three against Fine. The return match took place after the United States Championship on May 21. Kashdan played to a draw here against former U.S. champion Frank Marshall on board two. The Marshall club won this match by the narrow score of 8½ to 7½.

Simonson Match 1938

Just prior to the championship Kashdan played a match against A. C. Simonson. The match did not get much publicity because of the upcoming United States Championship. But it turned into a surprisingly lopsided win for Kashdan, 4–0. That came as quite a surprise as Simonson scored better than Kashdan in the first United States Championship and did so again in 1938.

Helen Kashdan in the United States Women's Championship 1938

Mrs. Kashdan took quite an interest in chess herself. She even formed a chess club that would consist of seven men and eight women. They met twice a month to improve their skill. Then in February there was even a tournament underway. The next month she took part in the Marshall Chess Club Women's tournament. The preliminaries were divided into two section. She scored 5–2 in her section, to tie for second. This qualified her to compete in the first United States Championship tournament for women that then took place in April. May Karff was the eventual winner of the event, giving up only one draw to runner-up Mary Bain. Eleven women took part. Helen Kashdan had three wins to place ninth in the event. Her husband was glad to see her play in the tournament. He reports that she now understands why he worries about his clock. The article in *Chess Review*, May issue, then goes on to say: "Mrs. Kashdan is a sweet person. When she captured the queen of one of her opponents and gave check with the knight at the same time, she actually apologized."

Second United States Championship, New York 1938

This time again as in the first United States Championship there were preliminary tournaments held to qualify for the finals. But several players were seeded, including Kashdan,

Reshevsky, Fine, Horowitz, Dake, Simonson, Polland, Kupchik, Treysman and Morton. The tournament started on April 2 and ended on April 24.

Kashdan started the first round with a win over Santasiere. The second round resulted in a draw with Horowitz. In round three he suffered his first upset by losing to Cohen, giving him only an even score up to this point. Then began a remarkable winning streak for him. In the fourth round he won over the veteran Kupchik; round five was a win over Morton and round six resulted in a win over Reinfeld. Round seven brought a win over Bernstein and in round eight he beat Polland in only 18 moves. Round 9 saw a win over Treysman. That gave Kashdan a score of 7½ points after nine rounds. This put him close to Reshevsky, who held the lead with 8 points, followed by Simonson with 6½. Fine and Dake were tied for fourth with 6 points.

In round 10 Kashdan had to be content with a draw against Hanauer. But Reshevsky drew with Cohen. Again round 11 brought a draw against Simonson. Even with those two draws Kashdan was temporarily thrust into the lead since Reshevsky had a bye in round 11. Kashdan went on to win his next game against Shainswit in round 12. Then came round 13 where he faced one the favorites, Reuben Fine, and lost. It was a great game and Fine considered it worthy of inclusion in his collection of his best games. Even here Kashdan was trailing by only half a point. Both Reshevsky and Fine were leading with 10 points. This included a bye for both of them. Kashdan did not have his bye until round 17. But then things went downhill as Kashdan lost the next three games in succession, beginning with the upset loss to Suesman, the tailender in round 14. He went on to lose to Reshevsky in round 15, which was not surprising, and then suffered another defeat, by Arthur Dake, in round 16. He had the bye in the last round. Reshevsky was leading the tournament after 16 rounds, with Fine only half a point behind. As it happened, the two were paired against each other in the last round. If Fine won he would win the tournament. But he could only draw, so Reshevsky won the second United States Championship as well. The scores of the leaders were as follows: first, Reshevsky 13; second, Fine 12½; third, Simonson 11; fourth, Horowitz 10; and fifth, Kashdan with 9½ points (scoring 8 wins, 3 draws, and 5 losses).

39th American Chess Federation Tournament, Boston 1938

The American Chess Federation tournament took place from July 11 to 23 in Boston. Because of the large number of players it was divided into six sections of seven players each. The top two players from each section then would advance to the Masters' Tournament. Then the lower scorers played in the Consolation Master's Tournament, and the Class A tournament. Also this year, there was a Women's Championship. Kashdan easily won his section, scoring 4 wins and 2 draws. Runner-up was Collins, half a point behind. Horowitz also qualified from his section with 5 wins and a draw and Jaffe was able to equal this score as his only draw was with Horowitz. Horowitz and Kashdan were the favorites in the finals. They both tied for top honors, winning 8, drawing 2 and losing 1. Their individual game was a draw. Again Mrs. Kashdan competed in the women's tournament.

The very first game in the finals pitted Kashdan against Santasiere. It was a long drawn out affair lasting 127 moves. No fewer than four times the game was adjourned. In those days during adjournment a player could be assisted by others for the best continuation of the game. It was later reported by Horowitz that Kashdan himself talked himself out of first prize. Here is what Horowitz reported in the book *The Best of Chess* in an article entitled "Legislating Morals":

> More than once has the result of an important event depended upon extracurricular third-party analysis. In the U.S. Open, Boston, 1938 the Santasiere–Kashdan imbroglio had extended to more than 120 moves. About the fourth adjournment Santasiere was a pawn to the good in a tricky ending. Nearly all the contestants submitted analysis to best Kashdan, who was a threat to premier honors. After some 20-odd hours of this wide-open *sub rosa* analysis, S. was positive that he had discovered the winning line; K. was equally certain that the position was a draw. Before play was resumed, however, Santasiere magnanimously exhibited the win. "Kash," said he, "this is how I am going to beat you." Kashdan was unimpressed. "And this," He replied, "is how I am going to draw you," showing a variation which Santasiere had not taken into account. Kashdan was right. He was going to draw. But he would have been "righter" had he not spoken out of turn. For no sooner had word got around that Kashdan had found the draw than the analysts came up with a new idea, this time a clear-cut win. As matters turned out, this was the first time in chess history where a player talked himself out of first prize.

As it turned out Kashdan shared first prize with Horowitz and also the playoff did not produce a clear winner. So if the Santasiere game had been a draw, Kashdan alone would have been first.

Horowitz Playoff Match 1938

It was decided to determine the American Chess Federation champion with a ten game match as Horowitz and Kashdan were co-winners of the tournament (see above). The first game was played on October 15, nearly three months after the tournament had ended. Kashdan obtained a winning position only to let Horowitz escape with a draw later in the game. The second game also ended in a draw. Kashdan, playing White, lost the third game. The fourth was a draw again, as was the fifth, but Horowitz could have won by sacrificing his queen and after several exchanges he would have regained the queen and in the end be a piece up. This game was played on November 19, which was Kashdan's 33rd birthday. Several days passed until the sixth game was played on December 4. Kashdan had chances to win, but weak moves near the end allowed Horowitz to escape with a draw. Finally, Kashdan was able to win, in game seven. The rest of the games all ended in draws. The tenth game was completed on the last day of the year. That meant that each player was able to win two games of the ten played. It was decided not to break the tie with further play, and both players would therefore share the title of Champion of the American Chess Federation for 1938.

New York State Championship, Hamilton 1939

In January Kashdan gave a simultaneous exhibition at the Franklin Chess Club of Philadelphia. There are no details available about the results. Then, starting in February, Kashdan took part in at least three Metropolitan League matches. First came the match with the Rice Progressive Chess Club. Kashdan was paired on board five against Lessing. The game ended in a draw. The match was won by the Manhattan club by the narrow margin of 5½ to 4½. The annual match with the Marshall Chess club took place on March 25. In this contest he played White against Sid Bernstein on board three. Again a draw was the outcome. But the Marshall Chess Club scored their fifth consecutive win over the Manhattan club by a score of 11–6 with one game unfinished. The Manhattan club also played a match with Philadelphia on April 30. Here Kashdan, playing on board one, scored a win over Levin. The match ended in a victory for the Manhattan team by a score of 10½ to 5½.

Kashdan then took part in the New York State Championship at Hamilton from August 21 to 26. Denker won the championship section, winning 5 and drawing 4 games. Kashdan was also undefeated but had one more draw than Denker to place second with 4 wins and 5 draws. This event was much stronger than the previous year and resulted in many more draws.

In November he took part in another match that was not part of the Metro League. This match was between the Manhattan and the Westside Y.M.C.A. Kashdan drew his game against Forster on board two. The Manhattans won the match by a score of 9½ to 3½.

5

The Forties

Havana International 1940

Kashdan and Koltanowski were invited from the United States to compete in a tournament in Havana against the best players that Cuba had to offer. The contest took place at the end of January. The Americans came through without losing a single game. Kashdan scored 6 wins and 3 draws. Kolty gave up two more draws to come in second with 4 wins and 5 draws. The rest of the Cuban field scored as follows: third, Planas 6; fourth, Aleman 5½; fifth, Blanco 4; sixth, Gonzalez 4; seventh-eighth, Meylan and Paz 3½; ninth, Mora 2; and tenth, Florido 1½.

Third United States Championship, New York 1940

At the same time the men played for the United States Championship, a championship for the women took place. Kashdan's wife, Helen, competed in the preliminary section, scoring a respectable 5 points out of 9. This was good enough to qualify for the finals. But Mrs. Kashdan declined because of business reasons.

The men's competition took place in New York from April 27 to May 19, 1940. *Chess Review* called the third U.S. Championship one of the most bitterly fought competitions in all of chess history. Reshevsky was leading by only half a point ahead of Fine going into the last round. As it happened, they were paired against each other for the last round. It soon became clear that Reshevsky's game was hopeless. It was even reported there were tears in his eyes. It must have been the most miserable moment of his life! When most other players would have resigned he fought on—and, then, an inexact move by Fine allowed Reshevsky to draw this fateful game.

Chess Review gave this analysis of the play by Kashdan:

Kashdan showed a welcome return to his grand form of about ten years ago, and actually led the tournament until the thirteenth round, when he lost the WAR OF NERVES to Reshevsky. Kashdan committed a serious blunder on his 54th move. Had he played the correct move the game would have ended in a draw. In the following round, a loss to Adams (who produced a magnificent game) pulled him down still further. But it speaks well for Kashdan that he was the only player who was able to remain in the vicinity of Reshevsky and Fine!

The final results were as follows: First place, Reshevsky, undefeated, winning 10 and drawing 6 games, for 13 out of 16 points; half a point behind in second place was Fine with 10 wins, 5 draws, and 1 loss to Kupchik. Kashdan came in third at 10½, two points behind Fine, winning 7, drawing 7 and losing 2 games. Pinkus and Simonson tied for fourth-fifth with 10 points. Kupchik and Denker tied for sixth-seventh at 9½. There was a four-way tie for eighth place at 7½ among Bernstein, Polland, Reinfeld and Shainswit. Adams and Seidman had 7 points and Green and Hanauer each had 6. Bringing up the rear were Wolliston at 3 points and Littman with 2.

Kashdan made a brief return as an editor along with Horowitz of *Chess Review* during the months of November and December. Earlier in the year the assistant to Horowitz, Harold Morton, was killed in a car accident. Horowitz was also injured but he recovered quickly.

Lasker Memorial

Emanuel Lasker, the German former world champion, died on January 11, 1941, in Manhattan. In his honor a memorial was given on the evening of March 3, 1941, at the Capitol Hotel in New York. More than 500 chess players were present for the occasion.

The main event was a multiple simultaneous display, with five of the leading American grandmasters plying their skills on the chess board. More then 100 players took part in this mass exhibition. The following are the individual scores of the masters:

	Won	Lost	Drawn
Samuel Reshevsky	16	1	2
Reuben Fine	24	0	0
Isaac Kashdan	16	1	4
Frank Marshall/Olaf Ulvestad	16	3	4
Albert Pinkus	19	0	3

Marshall tired after about an hour of play. His games were taken over by Ulvestad. Pinkus took the place of Capablanca, who could not leave from Cuba in time to participate.

New York State Tournament, Hamilton 1941

This was without a doubt the strongest state tournament in American history. All the best players in the country took part in this event. The 1941 Congress of New York State took place in the town of Hamilton, at Colgate University, from August 16 to 23. It broke all records for attendance, and quality and number of players. Among the entrants were Samuel Reshevsky, the current U.S. Champion, and Reuben Fine, runner-up in the (1940) U.S. Championship. Kashdan, Denker, Willman and Santasiere were the other strong contenders.

The tournament was won by Reuben Fine. He scored 8 points, winning 6 and drawing 4 games. Reshevsky played below form by drawing a won game with Fine, and then in his last game with the tailender H. Evans, only achieving a draw (he unsoundly sacrificed his queen, and was forced to give perpetual check to obtain the draw). Kashdan and Reshevsky both had 4 wins and 6 draws to enter a three-way tie for second-third-fourth at 7 points. A score of 7 points was also achieved by Denker but he won 5 games, drew 4, and lost 1. The remaining scores were Willman fifth with 6½; Santasiere sixth with 4½; Seidman and Cruz tied for seventh with 4 points; Shainswit with 3, Hewlett with 2½, and in eleventh and last place H. Evans, with 1½ points.

Manhattan Chess Club Formal Opening 1941

On October 8, 1941, was the official opening of the new quarters of the Manhattan Chess Club. Some 200 people came on this occasion, including the widow of former champion Dr. Emanuel Lasker. Edward Lasker was also present. The highlight of the evening was a rapid transit tournament with ten of the top players.

The result was the somewhat surprising win for Jack Moscowitz, with a score of 7–2. Reuben Fine was just a half point behind. Fine had outplayed the eventual tournament winner in the first game, but then lost to Horowitz and then also to Pinkus. In a three way-tie for third were Kashdan, Pinkus and Denker with 5½ points each.

Fourth United States Championship, New York 1942

Santasiere, a strong master, observed that Kashdan had not played any serious chess for seven months until he started playing in the Metropolitan League matches in March 1942. In one of those matches he faced Pilnick of City College, in a game that he won. Then on April 4 he played in the annual match between the Marshall Chess and the Manhattan Chess Club. Although Kashdan won his match for Manhattan from Hanauer on board 3, the Marshall club won by one point.

Only six days later on April 10 the United States Championship began. This was the fourth championship to have been held every two years since 1936. Again all the best players of the country were present with the exception of Fine. Reshevsky and Kashdan were favored as possible winners and they did not disappoint.

Kashdan gave a round by round account of the action. This appeared in *Chess Review*, in the May, 1942, issue:

> On Friday night, April 10, promptly at 7 P.M., the race was on, in the same old room at the Hotel Astor. On the following pages you will find some extracts from my "round by round diary" of the contest.
>
> **Round 1:** Reshevsky starts out with a brilliant win over Seidman. This looks bad for us. We are accustomed to shaky, uncertain play by the champion in the early rounds, and a grand recovery in the later chapters. If he starts out in excellent form, and improves as he goes, who can stop him? But it is rather early to lose heart, so let's go. I beat Pilnick in this round; Denker, Steiner and Altman are the other winners.
>
> **Round 2:** Reshevsky beats Levin after a fair fight. I am paired with Horowitz. The advance dope had established us as the logical contenders, though the champion was a prohibitive favorite to repeat. This is the first "crucial" game then. It is a hard middle game and still tougher ending. With a pawn plus, I can just squeeze out a win in a knight and

pawn ending. Reshevsky and I have already shaken off the field, being the only ones with two victories.

Round 3: After 21 moves Reshevsky offers Green a draw, which is accepted. The rules state that a minimum of 30 moves must be played before a draw can be agreed upon. The audience is dissatisfied, as the position is quite complicated. But the players and the referee are in accord, which ends the matter. I take first place for the time being by a win over Seidman, two bishops being the deciding factor. I have the impression that Reshevsky, for the first time since I have known him, has shown lack of fighting spirit. It may not mean anything, but I am encouraged.

Round 4: Reshevsky comes back with a win over Altman, while I draw with Levin. I seem to have the better of my game at all times, but cannot find the crusher. There is now a triple tie for first at 3½ points. Denker being the party of the third part. He drew with Steiner in the second round, and beat Pinkus, Lessing and Baker. We will have to watch him.

Round 5: I am lucky against Green. He outplays me in the opening, gets a beautiful position, then misses an important tempo which would win a pawn and maintain the better position. The adjourned position is still complicated. It is a draw with best play, but Green weakens and I win. Whew! Reshevsky beats Levy, not without his own share of worries, and Denker wins against Hahlbohm. Still three against the field.

Round 6: Here is the first big break of the tournament. Reshevsky beats Denker in a drawn position when Denker oversteps the time limit. This causes a commotion and a near-riot. The spectators and officials all get a look at the clock, which is carried about and handled by all and sundry. There is a wide divergence of opinion, but the referee has ruled, and is later upheld by the tournament committee. [It should be pointed out here that Denker felt that it was not he, but Reshevsky who lost on time, as the clock had been turned around when it was picked up!—PPL.] I beat Altman and leave early, only learning of the excitement the next day. From now on Reshevsky and I are the only ones in the running for premier honors.

Round 7, 8, 9: It is getting monotonous. Reshevsky and I keep winning and now have 8½ points out of 9. We have had some close calls. Pinkus had the better game against Reshevsky, got short of time, and on the fifteenth move overlooked a pretty rook sacrifice which would have forced the game. Against me Pinkus had a draw at adjournment, overreached himself trying to win, wound up on the losing end of a rook endgame. My most difficult game of the tournament came against Denker. Two bishops did it again. Other leading scores at the end of round 9 are: Horowitz 6½ (he has scored 6 out of 7 since losing to me), Denker 6; Steiner 5½.

Round 10: I lose to Steiner while Reshevsky wins in short order against Baker. For the first time there is a gap of a full point between us with only six rounds to go. Is this the end? In the last three championship tournaments I have led up to about this stage, then collapsed. Everyone I meet reminds me of this, and draws the normal conclusion. But the "slum" is only one game long so far, so don't lose your nerve, son. Steiner thoroughly deserves the win. He plays a dashing gambit, he wins the exchange as the only way for me to avoid mate. He allows me considerable counter play thereafter and it gets close again, but in time pressure I overlook Steiner's queen sacrifice which wins at once. He can win against any defense, as it turns out, so I cannot spare any regrets.

Round 11: Hahlbohm plays the King's Gambit against Reshevsky, an unsound variation analyzed by Keres. We smile indulgently. The Chicago expert will soon be punished for his audacity. But Reshevsky is worried, plays very carefully, and the upshot is the exchange of major pieces, and complete equality. The game is finally drawn by repetition of moves, breaking the winning streak which had reached seven straight for the champion. Here is my chance to regain some ground. I win a pawn against Lessing, and adjourn in a position with reasonable winning prospects. I do not make the best try, and also draw. I am still a point behind, and five to go. Oh, well, I am pretty safe for second, which is not too bad.

Round 12: I beat Baker in 17 moves, my shortest game of the tournament, join the spectators for a time, then go home. It is Saturday, I can spend part of the afternoon and all evening with the family, which does not happen often during chess tournaments. Reshevsky is playing [Carl] Pilnick, and keeps on playing Pilnick for three sessions and a total of 93 moves. Pilnick gets a fine opening, weakens a bit, finally loses a pawn. It develops into a queen ending, but Reshevsky seems sure of his win. The result is not known until Monday night. By that time Reshevsky is three pawns up, has his king in safety against any threat of perpetual check, and what else can go wrong? You guessed it, or did you know? Stalemate? An odd chance, and noble reward for Pilnick's stubborn resistance. So there is only half a point for me to make up, and still have to play Reshevsky. We're in the ballgame.

Round 13: Reshevsky and I both win, against Chernev and Hahlbohm respectively. We are to meet in the next round, presumably for the decisive encounter. I am to have the White pieces, can play my opening. I look over a number of games Reshevsky has played recently, try to spot his weakness. If he has any, I should appreciate the information. But I do not decide on the first move until five minutes before the session begins.

Round 14: I get to the hotel two minutes late, my first tardiness in the tournament. I have just closed a business deal and feeling properly keyed up. Next day I learn that in the newspaper that I have failed to play my "favorite" Ruy Lopez. Actually I had a wide variety of openings, essaying the Ruy only twice. Reshevsky defends irregularly, getting better control of the center, though my development is superior. I play to break up his formation, too early as it turns out, and he develops a formidable position, timing his moves perfectly. At one point he can win a pawn, at a cost in time which would permit me to advance in the center and the king side. Here is a hard decision. If he plays to win and succeeds, the championship is his. Should he lose, I would be half a point ahead, with every prospect of retaining the lead in the last round. He decides to play safe, forcing the exchange of the remaining minor pieces. We are left with queen, two rooks each, the pawns sufficiently blocked so that little headway can be made. After a few moves we agree to a draw. Rather dull all told, and the decision is yet to be handed down.

Round 15: Reshevsky vs. Horowitz, and I am paired with Chernev. Horowitz, after building up a good score, has done poorly. Successive losses to Pinkus and Steiner, after having better games against both, were mainly responsible, and Horowitz has no chance for a prize. Success against Reshevsky is a sufficient end in itself, however, and both are ready for a real battle. I am somewhat interested in their table, but my task is to beat Chernev, enough to occupy me fully. I succeed in a pretty finish, an unusual mating position with just the rooks. Now I can watch what is happening, with no further control over proceedings. Horowitz outplays Reshevsky, winning a pawn in the midgame complications and another ending just before adjournment. It looks all over for the spectators, but opposite color bishops and Reshevsky's better placed king offer drawing chances. I refuse congratulations, wonder what it will feel like to be champion, decide to postpone such thoughts for one more day.

The game is played off Thursday afternoon, April 20, at the Manhattan Chess Club. It has been a long three weeks. I am thinking back to 1934, when I challenged Frank Marshall to a match for the American championship, and the number of times I have tried for the title since. This is my best chance. Just a few good moves, friend Horowitz. Things go along very nicely. Horowitz now has a passed pawn on d6, he advances it to d7. It is all over. No, wait. That white pawn on b4 threatens to sneak in. Reshevsky has worked out a devilish resource from nowhere. Horowitz is worried about it, finally exchanges pawns. In the resulting position Reshevsky can just draw, and does. There was a win, we discover on analysis, and very easy, too, once we see it. It was not so simple in the pressure of actual play, with the clock ticking remorselessly. So it ends in a tie for first; Reshevsky and I are co-champions pro tem. We have a match to play, which is perhaps the best ending.

The results for the top six:

	Won	Lost	Drawn	Scores
1–2. Kashdan	11	1	3	12½–2½
1–2. Reshevsky	10	0	5	12½–2½
3–4. Denker	9	3	3	10½–4½
3–4. Pinkus	10	4	1	10½–4½
5. Steiner, H.	8	3	4	10–5
6. Horowitz	6	3	6	9–6

Prizes were awarded as follows: Kashdan and Reshevsky received $226.81 each; Denker and Pinkus $90.72 each; Steiner $45.36; others $4.30 per point scored.

First United States Lightning Championship 1942

Just prior to the Lightning Championship (the first U.S. speed championship), Kashdan took part in such a tournament at the Manhattan Chess Club. This may have been a tune-up for the national event. This tournament was won by Moscowitz with 10 wins and only 1 draw. Kashdan and Horowitz tied for second with 9 wins and 2 losses.

The next event in which Kashdan took part was the first United States Lightning Championship, or the Rapid Transit Championship as it was known then. It was held in the Grand Oak Ball Room at the Hotel Capital, Eighth Avenue and 51st Street, New York City, on July 5, 1942. It was called a novel lightning tournament. The way the game is played, a move must be made by each player every 10 seconds. Forty-eight players competed in four groups of 12 each for the national title. The three top scoring players of each group would advance to the finals of the Championship division.

In Group A Reshevsky advanced to the finals with a perfect score of 11 wins. The other two players to advance were Green and Seidman. Fine, in Group B, did nearly as well, losing only 1 game to score 10–1. Yanofsky, the Canadian champion, and Nadell also advanced in Group B. Kashdan was the leading player in Group C, with 9 wins, 1 draw and 1 loss; he, Pinkus and Shainswit advanced to the finals. In Group D, Horowitz was the leading player with 10 wins and 1 draw; he advanced to the finals, with Helms and Denker.

In the finals it was a close contest between Reshevsky and Fine. They were paired in the next to the last round. It was a long and close game that Fine finally won after 74 moves. In the next round Fine lost to Seidman for his only loss in the finals. This gave him first place with 10 points and a cash prize of $75. As Reshevsky gave up 2 draws in addition to his loss to Fine, he took clear second with 9 points and the $50 prize. Shainswit was the surprising third place finisher with 7½ points and $25 in prize money. Fourth place was taken by Horowitz with a score of 7–5 and $15 prize money. Kashdan placed fifth, winning 6 games and losing 5, to take home $10 in prize money. Here are the results in the finals:

	Won	Lost	Drawn	Totals			Won	Lost	Drawn	Totals
1. Fine	10	1	0	10–1	7. Seidman	5	5	1	5½
2. Reshevsky	8	1	2	9–2	8. Pinkus	4	5	2	5
3. Shainswit	7	3	1	7½–3½	9. Denker	2	6	3	3½
4. Horowitz	7	4	0	7–4	10. Yanofsky	2	6	3	3½
5. Kashdan	6	5	0	6–5	11. Nadell	1	8	2	2
6. Green	5	5	1	5½–5½	12. Helms	1	9	1	1½

Reshevsky Playoff for the National Title 1942

There were no provisions to break the tie for the United States Championship. But Kashdan felt strongly that there should be a playoff. When he made the request to the U.S. Chess Federation, arrangements were made and the match was set to start on October 7. (He could easily not have made such a request and he would have been listed in the record book as co-champion.) It was also reported that Kashdan would be preparing for the match by playing some training games with Milton Hanauer. Whether he actually played such preparatory games is not known.

Reshevsky and Kashdan agreed to a match of 14 games to determine the better player and the right to the title of United States Champion. The first four games were scheduled at various Army bases in New York State: October 7, Fort Jay, on Governors Island; October 10, Camp Upton, at Yaphank; October 13, Pine Camp, at Great Bend; and October 15, Plattsburg Barracks, at Plattsburg.

The fifth game was to take place November 15 and match would then continue at the rate of three games a week. These games were not yet arranged at the beginning of the contest. But they would be held in clubs in New York and within a radius of 200 miles of New York City.

Chess fans were looking forward to a close, exciting contest. Reshevsky was a fighting champion with a remarkable record. Since losing to Horowitz in the fourth round of the 1936 tourney, in which he gained the title, he had played a total of 74 U.S. championship games without losing a single encounter! Kashdan has aspired to the title for many years. This was the chance he has been waiting for and he could be expected to do the utmost. His recent record showed that he was in top form.

The first game of the match started as scheduled on October 7, 1942, at Fort Jay. The match committee consisted of Maurice Wertheim, chairman; Fritz Brieger, treasurer; and Samuel Gradstein, secretary. Reshevsky had the white pieces. Near the beginning Kashdan was forced to give up two pawns. But then he did his best to enliven the play for the entertainment of those present. In the end he had to pay the price.

Reshevsky, thrown early on the defense, fought practically with his back to the wall. He did not castle until the 22nd move. From then on he took the initiative and in a series of master strokes, under pressure of time for both, soon caused Kashdan's hopes to fade. The latter's position was hopeless when, after 35 moves, his clock indicated he had consumed two hours and 16 minutes. Thereupon the referee, Kenneth Harkness, announced a forfeiture under the time limit rule, which called for 45 moves in the first two hours and 15 minutes. The greatest discrepancy occurred after ten moves, at which stage Reshevsky had taken an hour and 15 minutes as against 33 minutes for Kashdan.

Two days later, at Camp Upton, the second game was contested at the library of the Recreation Center. Lieutenant Harte, as special service officer, was host of the evening. It was Kashdan's turn to taste a bit of triumph. With the kings castled on opposite sides of the board, in a Ruy Lopez opening by Kashdan, there was again plenty of tension and time pressure. Reshevsky's loss of a pawn on the 22nd move led to a lost position after 47 moves. Although the game was adjourned, Reshevsky resigned the following day without resuming play.

Next, this epoch-making chess junket took the principals to Plattsburg, New York, on Lake Champlain, where, in the calm stillness of the post headquarters library, the third game was contested on the evening of October 15. Captain Clarence McFarland was the special service officer in charge.

Reshevsky varied early in the course of the game, by dint of protracted study, and set Kashdan a hard problem which the latter, good problemist though he was, failed to solve. Reshevsky won in 40 moves and recovered his lead.

The game showed the old story of overly lengthy study in the opening and the middle game and then the making of moves at lightning speed to finish in the set time limit. Reshevsky consumed 2 hours and 11 minutes while Kashdan took 2 hours and 14 minutes. With the position extremely critical, each had six minutes left for 11 moves. That Reshevsky succeeded in working out a mating combination under these conditions, once again brought out his strength—coolness under pressure.

Kashdan played the fourth game with courage and skill, crushing his opponent with sledgehammer blows in the final stages. From the very beginning, Reshevsky's position was tight, cramped. The opening was a Ruy Lopez and Reshevsky again chose the Steinitz Defense Deferred, as in the second game. Kashdan varied the routine on his fifth move when he branched into the Duras Variation. It was with maneuvers like this that Kashdan showed great virtuosity in avoiding prepared defenses.

> Reshevsky pondered for half an hour over his 16th move, eventually played 16. ... Kh8, a passive continuation which Fine regards as a mistake. On his 29th turn, Reshevsky's clock registered one hour and 58 minutes. Two minutes and 15 moves to go. Again Reshevsky displayed his amazing ability to play the final moves in lightning speed. He made all 15 moves within the time limit—but lost the game.
>
> Losing is still a new experience for Reshevsky and he has not yet learned how to resign gracefully. At the adjournment he was in an obviously lost position but did not resign directly to Kashdan. The resignation was tendered to his opponent during the adjournment through your reporter.
>
> The outcome of the match is anybody's guess. The co-champions are still playing aggressive, wide open chess. It is becoming obvious that this is no ordinary match with one dull draw after another. As we commented last month, the co-champions are definitely out for blood [Chess Review].

The fifth game was again a win by White (the first five games were all won by the player having the white pieces). Here it was Reshevsky with White and he opened 1. d4 as he had in the first and third games. Kashdan answered 1. ... Nf6 as he had before. After 2. c4, however, Kashdan varied by playing 2. ... e6 (in the earlier two games he played 2. ... g6; those two games turned into the Grünfeld Defense). Game five went 3. Nc3 Bb4, which made it a Nimzo-Indian—quite a surprise since it usually means Black exchanges bishop for knight and Kashdan was known to prefer the bishop over the knight. (Reshevsky, analyzing this game in his book *Reshevsky on Chess*, said, "It may well be that Kashdan's faith in the two bishops handicaps him in this variation.") The game was still even after Kashdan played Nd6 on his 24th move. With correct play the game should have ended in a draw. But Kashdan made weak moves on his 26th and 27th turns, which allowed Reshevsky to take the whole point after 38 moves.

Kashdan could again have equalized the contest by winning the sixth game with the white pieces. Since he had been successful in the other two games with the Ruy Lopez, it made sense to use it again, and this he did. But Reshevsky put up a stout resistance and did not make any inferior moves. Though Kashdan kept up the pressure throughout the game, Reshevsky did not waver. So the result was a draw.

Reshevsky opened game seven again with 1. d4 and Kashdan replied 1. ... Nf6, again resorting for the second (and last) time in the match to the Nimzo-Indian (with 2. c4 e6, 3. Nc3 Bb4). Reshevsky varied from game five on the 4th move with Qc2, thinking perhaps that Kashdan was better prepared this time for 4. a3. Kashdan played on even terms until move 19, an inferior one that allowed Reshevsky to get the initiative. But then with 43. b4 he allowed Kashdan to equalize. Then on move 50 Kashdan mistakenly played h4, when e4 might have drawn.

For the eighth game Kashdan again used the Ruy Lopez (with which he had won games two and four and drawn game six), and Reshevsky had to summon all his defensive resources to reach a draw.

Reshevsky opened the ninth with d4 and Kashdan chose the Grünfeld Defense as he had in games one and three. This time, Kashdan defended correctly and Reshevsky had to be content with a draw. This was the only game Kashdan did not lose with the Black pieces.

In the tenth game Kashdan for the first time opened 1. d4. Perhaps he should have continued with the Ruy Lopez as he had success with it. Reshevsky as Black also chose the Grünfeld Defense. Kashdan played 4. Bf4 as he had done in game one. Reshevsky varied from that game when he played 5. ... c6 instead of castling as in game 1. But this time Kashdan made inferior moves at his 23rd and 24th turns and was forced to resign on the 39th move. This was the only game in the whole match won by Black (White won seven of the games and only three games were draws). The score now stood at 6½ to 3½.

In the eleventh match game Reshevsky again resorted to 1. d4 as he had in all other games with White. This was the only Queen's Gambit of the match. The game was level until Kashdan made an inferior move with 36. ... Rc2, when Rc6 would have ended the game in a draw (both Reshevsky and Alekhine came to that same conclusion after the game). Kashdan lasted until the 57th move but then he shook hands with Reshevsky, ending the game and the match. Kashdan's opportunity to become United States Champion was not to be. The last game was played on December 27, 1942; final score Reshevsky 7½–3½.

The match for the United States Championship in 1942 caused tremendous interest in the chess world. No fewer than three champions analyzed all of the games. World Champion Alexander Alekhine annotated all of the games, with other games, in the book *107 Great Chess Battles*, translated, rendered into algebraic, and edited by E.G. Winter in 1980. Reuben Fine, at the time ranked second behind Reshevsky in the U.S. but not competing in the fourth Championship tournament, then wrote a booklet, *Reshevsky–Kashdan 1942-1943 United States Championship Chess Match*, with annotations to all the games. And then, Anthony Santasiere, a former champion of the Marshall Chess Club in 1936, annotated all the games for the *American Chess Bulletin*.

For the *Chess Review* magazine, there were several annotators. Game One was annotated by Reuben Fine. Kashdan only annotated Game Two. Game Three was annotated by Reshevsky, and the fourth game, which Kashdan won, was annotated by Reuben Fine. Reshevsky annotated Game Five. Israel Horowitz annotated Game Six and Fine Game Seven. Games 8, 9, 10, and 11 were also annotated by Horowitz. Reshevsky published his first book of his best games in 1948 under the title *Reshevsky on Chess*. It had analyses of all the six games he won in the match.

Second United States Speed Championship 1943

The second United States Speed Championship was again held in New York City, on July 4, 1943, and again at the Capital Hotel. This time there were 47 contestants, in view of about 200 spectators. Again four preliminary sections were played, with the top three players of each section qualifying for the finals. In the preliminaries, Reshevsky in Group B lost only 1½ points. Fine, playing in Group A, gave up only 1 point by drawing two of his games. Kashdan scored 10–1 in Group C to win his section. Horowitz also won his section, with 9½ points.

In the finals it was again the rivalry of Fine and Reshevsky that would decide the winners. And again it was Fine who prevailed in the end, concluding with their individual encounter. Fine did not lose or draw a single game. He won all 11 of his games. Reshevsky, besides losing to Fine, also gave up one other point, to score 9. This time the surprise was the veteran Kupchik, at age 51, who placed third with 7 points. Kashdan came in fourth again with six points, but this included 5 wins, 4 losses, and 2 draws. One of his losses was to Feldman who did not win another game. The previous year he had no draws. Also he moved up a notch by placing fourth. Horowitz, who placed ahead of Kashdan in 1942, scored only 5 points, a minus score. Denker, usually also a strong contender did not even qualify for the finals. The results for the finals were:

	Won	Lost	Drawn	Total			Won	Lost	Drawn	Total
1. Fine	11	0	0	11–0	7. Horowitz	4	5	2	5
2. Reshevsky	8	1	2	9–2	8. Seidman	3	5	3	4½
3. Kupchik	7	4	0	7–4	9. Sussman	3	5	3	4½
4. Kashdan	5	4	2	6–5	10. Adams	3	7	1	3½
5. Green	5	5	1	5½–5½	11. Feldman	1	7	3	2½
6. Heitner	3	4	4	5–6	12. Schwartz	2	8	1	2½

Then on September 1, Kashdan took part in the Metropolitan Speed Championship held in New York. It was a double round affair among ten players. Fine did not compete, and Reshevsky took top honors, winning 15 games and drawing 3. Among his victims was Kashdan (but in their other game Kashdan held Reshevsky to a draw). The other two draws were obtained by Adams and Horowitz. Kashdan came in second, winning 12, drawing 3, and losing 3.

Metropolitan Chess League 1944

Playing for the Manhattan Chess Club, Kashdan competed in the annual match against the Marshall Chess Club, coming out the winner on board four over the veteran Edward

Lasker. This was an important victory as it enabled the Manhattans to win the match by the narrow margin of 6½ to 5½. This also gave the Manhattan club the league victory over all the other teams as it went through the competition winning all five matches.

Kashdan planned to compete in the fifth United States Championship that started on April 15 in New York but was advised by his doctor not to play. His place was taken by DiCamillo. Denker and Fine fought it out in the 1944 championship. Denker was the winner mainly because he beat Fine. This was also the year when Helen and Isaac Kashdan had their second child, naming him Richard.

Third United States Speed Championship 1944

Next came the annual United States Rapid Transit Championship or what later became known as the United States Speed Championship. It took place on June 25, 1944, with 60 competitors. There were five preliminary sections with Kashdan and Willman taking the lead in section C with 9 wins against 2 losses. Fine won his section with 11 zip.

Reuben Fine had won the U.S. speed title the previous two times it took place, in 1942 and 1943. This year was no different as again he showed his superiority. His score was 10 wins against 1 loss (to Partos). In second place, surprisingly, came Horowitz with 8 wins, 2 losses, and a draw. Third was taken by Kevitz with 8 wins and 3 losses. And only then came Reshevsky in fourth place, winning 7, losing 3, and drawing 1. Kashdan again could do no better than fifth and his score—6 wins, 4 losses, 1 draw—was only half a point better than the year before. Next came Partos with an even score, winning 5, losing 5, and drawing 1. He was the giant killer as he defeated Fine, Kevitz and Denker, drawing with Kashdan. Denker was seventh with 4½ points; Green and Willman tied for eighth with 4; Seidman had 3 for tenth, Pavey 2½ for eleventh, and Rivise with 2 points was in last place. The players that did not qualify for the finals competed in lesser sections.

The results for the finals were as follows:

	Won	Lost	Drawn	Total			Won	Lost	Drawn	Total
1. Fine	10	1	0	11	7. Denker	4	6	1	4½
2. Horowitz	8	2	1	8½	8. Green	3	6	2	4
3. Kevitz	8	3	0	8	9. Willman	4	7	0	4
4. Reshevsky	7	3	1	7½	10. Seidman	3	8	0	3
5. Kashdan	6	4	1	6½	11. Pavey	2	8	1	2½
6. Partos	5	5	1	5½	12. Rivise	2	9	0	2

Manhattan Championship 1944-45

The winner in this Manhattan Championship for 1944-45 was Albert Pinkus, winning 9, losing 1, and drawing 2 of his games. Kashdan, with 6 wins, 1 loss, and 5 draws, tied for second with Arnold Denker at 8½ points. Kashdan's loss was to Jackson as he overstepped the time limit, but his opponent with correct play should have won anyway. Denker arrived at his score with 7 wins, 2 losses, and 3 draws.

Fourth United States Speed Championship 1945

Reuben Fine yet again proved that he was the number one player when it came to speed chess in the United States. For the fourth time in a row he captured the Speed Championship Tournament held at the Hotel Astor in New York on June 24, 1945. This year, as before, the 48 players were divided into four groups in the preliminaries, the top three from each group advancing to the finals. Fine qualified in Group A with a score of 8½–2½; the same score was also achieved by Pinkus. In Group B, Moscowitz and Pavey tied for the lead. Kashdan, playing in his final speed championship, led Group C with a score of 9–2. Group D was Shainswit's, with 8½. Fine did not lose a game in the finals, but he gave up two draws to go with his 9 wins. Shainswit was also undefeated to come in second, he gave up 4 draws to go with his 7 wins. Kashdan and Pavey tied for third, both scoring 6 wins, 3 draws, and 2 losses. This improved Kashdan's score from the previous year by one point. Reshevsky did not compete this year.

The final standings:

	Won	Lost	Drawn	Total			Won	Lost	Drawn	Total
1. Fine	9	0	2	10	7. Moscowitz	3	3	5	5½
2. Shainswit	7	0	4	9	8. Mugridge	3	7	2	4
3. Kashdan	6	2	3	7½	9. Pinkus	2	6	3	3½
4. Pavey	6	2	3	7½	10. D. Byrne	2	8	1	2½
5. Horowitz	5	4	2	6	11. Saltzberg	2	8	1	2½
6. Tenner	4	3	4	6	12. Helms	1	8	2	2

Pan-American Chess Congress, Hollywood 1945

A major international tournament was held in Hollywood from July 28 to August 12, 1945. Many of the top U.S. players competed: Samuel Reshevsky, Reuben Fine, Israel Horowitz, Herman Steiner, and Isaac Kashdan. Players from South America included Rossetto, Araiza, Dr. Cruz, and Camarena. In all there were 13 players. Among the spectators were movie stars such as Humphrey Bogart, Julie London, and Carmen Miranda, to name only three.

Reshevsky took first place with 9 wins and 3 draws for 10½ points. Fine was also undefeated but won only 6, while drawing also 6 games, for 9 points. Pilnik captured third place with a score of 8½ points. Fourth was Horowitz with 8. Kashdan placed fifth, winning 5, losing 3, and drawing 4 of his games, for 7 points. Rounding out the field were Rossetto scoring 6½ for sixth; followed by Adams and Steiner both scoring 5½ points to tie for seventh; Araiza and Dr. Cruz scored 5 points to tie for ninth place; Broderman was eleventh with 3½ and Seidman scored 3 points for twelfth place—but the latter had to forfeit two games as he was called back to active duty. The two players profiting from this were Kashdan and Steiner. Camerana came in last with only 1 point.

United States vs. USSR Radio Match 1945

The first of the team matches between the USSR and the United States took place September 1–3, 1945. It was contested on 10 boards played in two rounds. Denker, because of his winning the 1944 U.S. championship, took first board. Reshevsky played on board 2, Reuben Fine board 3, Horowitz board 4, Kashdan board 5, Steiner 6, Pinkus 7, Seidman 8, Kupchik 9, and Santasiere, board 10. Botvinnik defeated Denker in both games, as did Smyslow over Reshevsky on board 2. Fine salvaged one draw against Keres on board 3, Horowitz was able to win one of his games over Flohr, while losing the other one. Kashdan lost both of his games to Kotov. Steiner was the only player with a plus score for the U.S., winning one and drawing the other to Bondarevsky. Pinkus scored two draws with Lilienthal on board 7. Ragozin won both games from Seidman; Kupchik drew one game with Makagonov, while losing the other one. And Santasiere lost both of his games to Bronstein. The disastrous score for the United States was 2 wins, 5 draws, 13 losses.

Manhattan Speed Tournament 1945

Shortly after the team match with the USSR, on September 11, 1945, Kashdan played in a speed tournament at the Marshall Chess Club. He won the event in a strong field with a score of 11½ points. Second was Kupchik with 10 points. Third and fourth went to Horowitz and Rossetto with 9½ points; Green placed fifth with 8½ points; Pilnik and Pinkus tied for sixth with 7½ points. Others competing were Denker, Shainswit, and Seidman.

Metropolitan Championship 1946

Despite a loss to Santasiere, Kashdan was able to win the New York Metropolitan Championship early in 1946. It was contested by 10 strong players during August and September. This was intended as a valuable training for the team members for the upcoming match with the Soviet Union. Play took place at both the Manhattan and Marshall chess clubs.

The results were: first, Kashdan 7–2 (5 wins, 2 draws, 1 loss); second, Pinkus 6½–2½; third, Bernstein 5½; followed by Santasiere and Seidman with 5 points each; Shainswit 4; Willman and Moscowitz 3½ each; and Rothman and Shipman 2½ points each.

Swedish Speed Tournament 1946

Several of the American players who were going to take part in the match with the Soviet Union stopped in Sweden to play in a speed tournament, European style, on September 2, 1946 (see *Chess Review* for October 1946). The speed tournaments in Europe were contested with a certain time limit for the game, 5 or 10 minutes, instead of 10 seconds per move. Since the Americans were not used to this, they were at a disadvantage. After the preliminaries, 10 players advanced to the finals. The Americans were Reshevsky (the tournament winner with 7½ points in nine games), Dake, Pinkus, Kashdan, Ulvestad and Horowitz. The Swedish players were: Ekstrom, Danielsson, Sundberg and Holm.

The results follow:

	Won	Lost	Drawn	Score
1. Samuel Reshevsky (USA)	7	1	1	7½–1½
2.–3. Arthur Dake (USA)	5	2	2	6–3
2.–3. Folke Ekstrom (Sweden)	5	2	2	6–3
4. Albert Pinkus (USA)	4	2	3	5½–3½
5. Gosta Danielson (Sweden)	4	3	2	5–4
6.–7. Isaac Kashdan (USA)	4	5	0	4–5
6.–7. Olaf Ulvestad (USA)	4	5	0	4–5
8. Israel Horowitz (USA)	2	4	3	3½–5½
9. Bertil Sundberg (Sweden)	2	5	2	3–6
10. Gosta Holm (Sweden)	0	8	1	½–8½

United States vs. USSR, Moscow 1946

The match between the Soviet Union and the United States was not a radio match as the year before, but instead the American team traveled to Moscow, via Leningrad. Several of the wives accompanied their husbands on this trip, including Mrs. Dake and Mrs. Horowitz. Helen Kashdan could not come as they had two small children now, Howard, 5 years old, and Richard, 2.

The official opening ceremonies for the match took place on September 12, with the actual games starting the following day. It was an ominous start for the Americans as they mustered only 3 points to the Russians' 7. The American could not win a single game, and had to be content with six draws. A much better result was achieved two days later when they lost by only one game; winning 3, drawing 3 and losing 4. The winners in the second round for the Americans were Kashdan, Kevitz, and Ulvestad. Kashdan and Kevitz were the heroes as they achieved plus scores to go along with their draws in the first round. This also avenged the loss Kashdan sustained in the match with Kotov the year before. Kevitz's win was over Bondarevsky. Ulvestad ended up even with Bronstein. Also Horowitz against Bolelavsky, and Dake over Lilienthal had even scores, each with both games drawn. Reshevsky on board 1 against Botvinnik, and Fine on board 2 against Keres could only get one draw each in the two games they played.

Sixth United States Championship 1946

The sixth biennial United States Championship took place from October 26 to November 13, 1946. Reshevsky regained the title he had won in 1942 when he defeated Kashdan in the playoff. Neither Reshevsky nor Kashdan competed in 1944. This allowed Denker to score an upset victory over Fine in 1944. Fine did not compete this year; in fact, 1944 was the last time he competed in a U.S. championship. This year a playoff was not needed, as Reshevsky came through undefeated with a score of 14 wins, 4 draws and no losses, for 16 points. Kashdan came in second; in addition to losing to Reshevsky in the last round he also lost one other game, this to Horowitz in round 3. He ended up with 11 wins, 5 draws, and 2 losses, for a score of 13½ points (or 2½ points behind the winner). In third place was

Santasiere, scoring 13 points, winning 9, drawing 8, and losing only 1. Levin came in fourth, scoring 12½ points, winning 9, drawing 7, and losing 2. Denker and Horowitz tied for fifth with 12 points each. Steiner was seventh with 11, Pinkus eighth with 10½, Kramer ninth with 9½. The rest of the field consisted of Sandrin 8 points, Ulvestad 7½, Rubinov 7, a four-way tie among Adams, DiCamillo, Rothman, and Suesman for 6½; Drexel 5, Fink 4, and Kowalski 3½. Isaacs withdrew after 8 rounds, so his result was cancelled.

Metropolitan Chess League 1946-47

Kashdan played in at least four games in the Metropolitan Chess League for the 1946-1947 season, winning 2 and drawing 2. He scored wins over Collins and Weinstock, both games appearing in the *American Chess Bulletin*. In the third game, Goodman was proud to score a draw with the international master, so he annotated it in the *Chess Correspondent*. The fourth game came against Hanauer in the annual match between the Marshall and the Manhattan clubs played on May 10, 1947. Hanauer defended well to achieve a draw. Kashdan, representing the Manhattan Chess Club, played on board 3. The Manhattan club scored a convincing victory, allowing the Marshall only 5 draws, while the other 11 games were won by Manhattan.

A Reception for Former Champion Euwe

A reception was held in honor of Max Euwe, the former world champion (1935–1937), in Brooklyn on June 12, 1947. Among those in attendance were Isaac Kashdan, Arnold Denker, and Israel Horowitz. Dr. Euwe concluded the festivities with a simultaneous exhibition on 40 boards, winning 23, drawing 10 and losing 7. (Kashdan, Denker and Horowitz did not compete.)

48th United States Open, Corpus Christi 1947

The United States Open took place at Corpus Christi in Texas in the month of August. It was one of the best results ever achieved by Kashdan, who won 10 of his 13 games, while drawing the other 3. Here is how *Chess Review* described his triumph:

> When the expansive Texans put on a show, you can expect it to be the biggest and the best of its kind. The U.S. Chess Federation Open Championship didn't fall short of these superlatives. The largest entry in the forty-eight year history of the event made it seem more like a rodeo than a chess tournament. KASHDAN CLINCHES LAURELS AT CHESS, is the way the *New York Times* headlined the article on the next to the last day of the tournament. And then went on to say: Isaac I. Kashdan of New York gained the title of Open champion of the United States Chess Federation and the first prize of $1000 tonight, when he drew his game in the twelfth and semi-final round with Miguel Cuellar of Colombia in a Ruy Lopez after 36 moves. The half point gave the New Yorker a total score of 10½–1½, which cannot be reached by anyone of his rivals. Kashdan, who will play his last opponent tomorrow, came to the end of his successful campaign with a record of not having been defeated. He was held to a draw in three matches.
> Earlier in the day, Kashdan required 70 moves to win his eleventh round game from Norman

T. Whitaker of Shady Side, Md., after he had finished his adjourned game from the tenth round with Bob Steinmeyer of St. Louis, who was forced to resign after eighty-three moves. It was Kashdan's superior endgame strategy that counted. In his game with Whitaker, Kashdan, with the black pieces in a Ruy Lopez, worked out of a difficult position and outplayed his opponent in a neat endgame.

The next day (August 22) the *New York Times* gave this account

> Isaac Kashdan of New York, who became the new open champion of the United States Chess Federation yesterday, finished his schedule today be defeating R. G. Wade, the New Zealand title holder, in a Slav Defense lasting thirty-four moves.
>
> Undefeated in thirteen games, Kashdan's score at the close was 11½–1½. His three drawn games were with George Kramer, Anthony Santasiere, and Miguel Cuellar. Second and third prizes were shared by Santasiere and Abe Yanofsky of Winnipeg, Canada, who triumphed in adjourned matches.

He had beaten, among others, Yanofsky, Steiner, and Ulvestad. Coupled with his second place in the previous year's U.S. championship, it made Kashdan's position as one of the top American players more solid than ever.

Runners-up were Canada's champion, youthful Dan Abe Yanofsky, and Anthony Santasiere, winner of the Ventnor tournament. Each had 10–3. Fourth place went to Miguel Cuellar of Colombia. He tallied 9½ points.

An interesting sidelight worth reporting, is about what was probably the first game ever played on television. It was reported in *Chess Digest*, November 1970 (Ken Smith was the editor):

> In 1947 there was a young player who had been playing chess only five months and was playing in the U.S. Open at Corpus Christi. He was chosen to play Grandmaster Isaac Kashdan in a rapid transit game on television which was probably the first complete game ever shown on national television. It just so happened that the Grandmaster played a variation of the Ruy Lopez that the boy knew thoroughly and the result was a draw.

This boy was Ken Smith, 16 years old at the time. But he lost the game to Kashdan in the tournament. A few months before in 1947, Ken Smith had played in the U.S. Junior Open at Oak Ridge and scored credibly because of his good opening knowledge.

Since winning the United States Open in 1947, Herman Helms in his chess column in the *Brooklyn Daily Eagle* reported on who would represent the United States in the upcoming world championships the next year. Here is what he wrote in the *Eagle* on August 28, 1947:

Chess Unit Vindicated by Kashdan's Victory

> The policy of the United States Chess Federation, adopted sometime ago in the matter of American representation abroad and specifically with regard to the world championship which led the governing body to name Samuel Reshevsky of Boston and Isaac Kashdan of Brooklyn as our representatives in the proposed tournament at Noordwijk, has been vindicated by the outcome of the annual open tournament at Corpus Christi, Texas.
>
> Kashdan, by finishing first without the loss of a game, substantially supported the claim made by many in his behalf that he is entitled to be recognized as a fit candidate for the position which formerly was generally conceded to Reuben Fine. Unfortunately for the chances of the Brooklyn master, however, the delegates at the recent meeting of the International Chess Federation (FIDE) at The Hague thought and voted differently, as a result of which Reshevsky and Fine will represent this country in a tournament for the world title, to be held next year in Holland and Russia.*

*Unfortunately Fine did not compete and the United States was represented only by Reshevsky.

Meanwhile Kashdan, former co-champion with Reshevsky and runner-up to him in the 1946 title tournament, can afford to rest on his laurels. Interviewed last night, Kashdan stated that while he was disappointed in not sharing with Reshevsky and Fine the honor of representing this country in the 1948 world title tournament, he had been assured at Corpus Christi of being seeded in to the zonal preliminaries to be held the next year. Asked concerning his opinion of the Swiss system of pairings, which was used at Corpus Christi, he said it had worked out fairly well. Since then he has treated the subject mathematically and ascertained that the best results could be obtained from a schedule of rounds equivalent to 25 percent of the total number of entries.

Argentina–United States Radio Match 1947

Prior to the radio match with Argentina, Kashdan gave a simultaneous exhibition in Baltimore. He encountered 38 players, winning 31, drawing 6, and losing only 1 game (to LaPoint). The event was sponsored by the Maryland Chess Club.

Then on November 2, 1947, a radio match took place between the Jockey Club of Argentina and the Manhattan Chess Club of New York. The United States suffered a surprising defeat. Only Reshevsky on board 1 was able to win, against Ståhlberg. Kashdan on board 2 lost to Najdorf. Two more wins were scored by the team from Argentina. The United States was able to score only five draws in addition to the win by Reshevsky; giving Argentina the victory with 6½ to 3½.

Manhattan Masters Tournament 1948

Just prior to the United States Open, a tournament was held among the top players of the Manhattan Chess Club. Eight players took part. Eighteen-year-old George Kramer emerged as the winner, half a point ahead of Kashdan. Both players went through the event undefeated. But Kramer had 5 wins and 2 draws, while Kashdan, now 42 years of age, scored 4 wins and 3 draws. Another youngster, Arthur Bisguier, and Albert Pinkus tied for third with four points. Donald Byrne had an even score to place fifth. In sixth place was Boris Siff with 2½ points, ahead of Vasconcellos with 2; in last place was Joseph Williams with 1 draw and 6 losses. Only two games by Kashdan have been found, one of them against Siff, one of the best efforts of Kashdan's career. The event was arranged by the Manhattan Chess Club as a tune-up for the U.S. Open.

49th United States Open, Baltimore 1948

The 49th United States Open took place in Baltimore from July 5 to July 17. Among the 74 entrants were the defending champion Isaac Kashdan (1947), and former champions Herman Steiner (1946), Anthony Santasiere (1945), and Norman Whitaker (1930). With a brilliant recovery after a poor start, Weaver Adams won the event with a score of 9½ to 2½. Losing 1½ points in the first four rounds, Adams then settled down and in championship form lost only one more point in the remaining eight rounds. These were draws to Kashdan and Ulvestad. In coming from behind, he passed Kashdan, to whom he had given

a 1½ point advantage after the first four rounds. After winning his first four games, Kashdan lost to Kramer in round 5. In addition to Adams he also drew with Ulvestad, Evans,
and Pinkus. This gave Kashdan a tie for second place with a score of 9–3, shared with
Kramer and Ulvestad.

Seventh United States Championship, South Fallsburg 1948

The seventh United States Championship, for the first time, did not take place in New
York City, but in South Fallsburg, but still in the state of New York. The tournament started
on August 11 and ended on August 30, 1948. It was the last time Kashdan would play in the
U.S. championships.

For the second time in a row, Kashdan captured second place in the championship.
But this time Reshevsky did not play, and instead Herman Steiner was the winner. Half a
point was the winning margin. Steiner scored 12 wins, 6 draws, and 1 loss, while Kashdan
won also 12 wins, but with 5 draws, and 2 losses. Kashdan was leading the tournament after
8 rounds, with a score of 7–1, having won 6 and drawn 2. Steiner at the time stood at 6–2.
Going into the last round, Kashdan and Steiner were tied at 14–4. In the last round Kashdan faced Kramer and should have won. He definitely had the better game. But by resourceful play Kramer was able to draw. Steiner faced Howard in his last game, and he ran into
trouble and should have lost, but Howard made inferior moves in the end allowing Steiner
to win the game and the tournament. Kashdan came very close to ending up either in a tie
or an outright win for the tournament. In third place, 1½ points behind were Kramer and
Ulvestad, both scoring 13 points.

The results for Kashdan in the various United States championships were quite impressive, and deserve to be recorded. Here are the results for the six tournaments he played in
starting in 1936 to 1948 (he did not participate in 1944) according to Andy Soltis: "Out of
a total of 98 games, he won 58. Only four players scored more wins than that: Samuel
Reshevsky 127, Larry Evans 79, Walter Browne 67, and Bobby Fischer 61. Kashdan had 25
draws, and only 15 losses. That gave him a 71.2 percentage. Only two players ever did better than that—Bobby Fischer with 83.3, and Reuben Fine with 78 percent."

New York International 1948-49

Kashdan was expected to represent the United States at Saltsjöbaden, Sweden, during
July 1948, in the zonal competition leading eventually to the determination of a challenger
to play against the new world champion. He had earned this selection because of his winning the United States Open in 1947. However, he felt that the $1,000 he would receive in
expense money would not be sufficient and turned down the opportunity, leaving the United
States without representation at Saltsjöbaden (Reshevsky, however, was already seeded into
the tournament that would follow the event in Sweden).

Just prior to the New York tournament, Kashdan was one of the Americans who took
part in a cable match against France. The match ended in a tie, 3½ to 3½. Kashdan played

on board 4; his game over Raizman was adjudicated a win. Horowitz, playing on board 3, lost to Rossolimo, also by adjudication. The other five games were drawn.

The New York International started on December 23, 1948, and ended January 2, 1949. The event was won by Reuben Fine with 8 points, winning 7 and drawing 2. In second place came Miguel Najdorf with 6½ points. Former world champion Max Euwe tied for third with Pilnik, winning 5 points. Next came Horowitz and Kramer with even score of 4½ points each. Kashdan and Bisguier tied for seventh with 4 points. Denker was ninth with 2, ahead of Steiner who had only 1½ points. Kashdan started out well, winning 2, drawing 1, and losing 1 after four rounds. But he ended up in the minus column, winning 3, drawing 2, but losing 4.

6

The Fifties

Kashdan and Family Move to California

Kashdan and his wife, Helen, and their sons Howard and Richard, were busy relocating during 1949 and 1950 from New York to Los Angeles. A letter written by Kashdan to Mrs. Marshall of the Marshall Chess Club mentions that an unexpected trip to Los Angeles on May 20, 1949, made it necessary to postpone an event that was planned. He also expected to be back by June 15. This was perhaps for the purpose of locating living quarters. All this was made necessary because their son Howard was ill. The doctors had advised them that it would be better suited for their son to live in California because of the climate. Their son Howard was about 9 years old at the time, born in 1941. He died in 1955. The official cause of death was "idiopathic pulmonary fibrosis," which is probably "cystic fibrosis." Their younger son, Richard, born in 1944, is a lawyer with offices in San Francisco. Howard's health is one reason Kashdan did not compete in any events in 1949 and 1950.

There may also have been another reason. Early in 1950, to be exact from February 11 to 14, a radio match was held between Yugoslavia and the United States. Kashdan was to be one of the team members but a week before he had to undergo surgery for a perforated ulcer that prevented him from taking part.

52nd United States Open, Fort Worth 1951

Just prior to the United States Open in 1951, Kashdan played in his first match between North and South California. He played on first board and scored a win over Fink.

Later that year he competed in the United States Open, which took place in Fort Worth from July 9 to July 21. The winner of this event was the then 19 year old Larry Evans. He had previously won the title of the Marshall Chess Club three times, besides winning a national title and the United States Lightning (or Speed) tournament this year. Evans scored 10 points, winning 8 of his games and drawing 4 with no defeats. Second place went to Al Sandrin, who also scored 8 wins, but with 3 draws and 1 loss. Kashdan was in a tie with Eliot Hearst for third place with 9 points. Kashdan achieved his score by winning 8 games, drawing 2 and losing 2. His losses came to Dr. Gonzalez of Cuba and Norman Whitaker from Maryland. Hearst won 8 of his games, drew 4 and lost only 1.

JACQUES COE & CO.

MEMBERS

NEW YORK STOCK EXCHANGE COMMODITY EXCHANGE, INC.
NEW YORK CURB EXCHANGE CHICAGO BOARD OF TRADE
(ASSOCIATE) NEW YORK PRODUCE EXCHANGE
NEW YORK COFFEE AND SUGAR EXCHANGE, INC.

39 BROADWAY
NEW YORK 6, N.Y.

May 3, 1949

Mrs. Caroline D. Marshall,
23 West 10th St.,
New York City.

Dear Mrs. Marshall:

Something unexpected has just come up which has forced
me to postpone my trip two weeks. I expect to leave
for Los Angeles on May 20, and be back about June 15.

I could give the exhibition anytime from May 16 to 19,
if you wanted to arrange it for one of those nights.
I would talk on endgames, which I think should be interesting, and play as many as you wish in the simultaneous.

Would you let me know on this, and I shall confirm whatever date you select. I shall be looking forward to an
interesting event at the Marshall Chess Club.

Sincerely yours,

Isaac Kashdan

Isaac Kashdan

This letter was written to Mrs. Caroline Marshall, the widow of Frank Marshall, who died in 1944. Mrs. Marshall was at the time the secretary of the Marshall Chess Club. She had invited Mr. Kashdan to give an exhibition at the club. Probably because of this urgent trip to California, he had to reschedule the event. The trip to California was probably due to his doctor advising him and his family to relocate there because of the illness of his older son, Howard (contributed by Richard Kashdan).

Kashdan started out winning his first three games, but then in round 4 had a draw with Larry Evans, the eventual winner. Then came a surprising defeat against Gonzalez in round 5. He got back on the winning track by winning over Westbrock in round 6 and Liepnieks in round 7. In round 8 he drew with Hearst, with whom he tied for third. He then won over Brieger in round 9. In round 10 he suffered his loss to Norman Whitaker. He finished by winning over two youngsters—Mednis and Sherwin—who made their mark in later events in the two final rounds.

Later that year Kashdan took part in a match with a team from Hollywood against a team from Havana. He played second board and won the first game with White over Ortega and the return encounter ended in a draw. Herman Steiner played first board and also scored 1½ points over Gonzalez. The match was won by California with a score of 11½ to 7½. The visiting team from Cuba won the second round by a score of 5½ to 4½.

Hollywood International 1952

The Hollywood International was so called because of the participation of Gligorić from Yugoslavia and Pomar of Spain. The event took place from April 26 to May 7, 1952. It was not surprising that Gligorić ended up the winner of the tournament. Kashdan started out well enough, winning over Mrs. Graf in round 1, and winning his second game over Pafnutieff. Then in round 3 he faced Herman Steiner to whom he lost. In the fourth round he was on the losing end with Gligorić. But then his third loss in a row was a surprise when he lost to Joyner, a player he should have beaten. He won over Martin in round 6. After a draw with Dake in the seventh round, in the eighth he lost to Pomar. In the last round he could only draw with another local player, Jim Cross. That gave him a minus score of 3 wins, 2 draws, and 4 losses. His poor showing may be partially explained as he was also working and for that reason was forced to delay some of his games with the local players to the next weekend.

Hollywood Invitational 1953

Kashdan was the winner of the Hollywood Invitational Tournament. Herman Steiner's chess column in the Sunday *Los Angeles Times*, April 12, 1953, had this to say:

> Isaac Kashdan, last week won the first prize of $150 in the 1953 Hollywood Invitational Tournament with the fine score of 18½ to ½. He did not lose a single game and his only draw was with the Editor, Herman Steiner.
> Second prize of $100 went to Eugene Levin with a final score of 16–3. Third place with $75 prize was won by your editor, who finished his games before his departure to a tournament in Argentina. His final score was 15½ to 3½.
> Sven Almgren with 15–4 was fourth, winning $50, and James Cross won $25 as fifth place winner with 14–5. Irving Rivise was sixth, 13–6, and M. Altschiller has a chance to tie him if he wins his final game this week.

This was a fantastic achievement for Kashdan, winning 18 of the 19 games outright and only drawing one game, without a loss. Several of the games in Part II were obtained from his own score sheets.

North vs. South California Match 1954

Prior to the California Open, Kashdan took part in the annual North-South California Match in June of 1954. He played on board one for the South team, in a loss against Imre Koenig. He would also play him in 1955, 1956, 1957, and 1960. The overall result was in his favor, with 2 wins, 2 draws, and 1 loss.

Kashdan playing with his children probably around 1950. Howard was the older, and Richard is the younger (courtesy *Atlantic Chess News*).

California Open 1954

Then Kashdan took part in the California Open. He placed in a tie for third with a score of 5½ points out of 7 games. He scored wins in round 1 over Reissman; in round 2 over Russell; in round 3 over Martin; in round 4 over Burger; in round 5 over Rivise. After five straight wins he drew with Zemitis. In the final round he lost to Herman Steiner.

The event had a large turnout, 81 players. It was run on the Swiss system. The winner was Herman Steiner who won 6 games and drew with Zemitis. Second was Schmitt with 6 points. Kashdan was tied for third, at 5½ points, with three other players, Zemitis, Almgren, and Pafnutieff.

Pan-American Chess Congress, Hollywood 1954

The Pan-American Chess Congress took place from June 10 to June 24, in Hollywood, California, with 74 players in a Swiss system event. It brought together the cream of the top American players. The winner was Arthur Bisguier who scored 11½ points, winning 10 of his games, drawing 3 and losing only 1. Larry Evans came in second with 11 points, also with 10 wins, but with 2 draws and 2 losses. Herman Steiner, and Nicholas Rossolimo tied for third with 10½. In fifth place were Pomar of Spain and Sherwin, both scoring 10 points.

Kashdan (left) playing Taimanov in the match between the United States and the Soviet Union in 1955 (courtesy *Chess Review*).

Isaac Kashdan, now reckoned among the veterans, suffered 3 losses, which relegated him to seventh place. He had 8 wins, and 3 draws for 9½ points.

North vs. South California Match 1955

The annual match between North and South California took place on May 20 at San Luis Obispo, with 59 players on each side. Kashdan, South, played board 1 and drew with Imre Koenig. Herman Steiner won his game over Zemitis on board 2. But the North was the winner by a score of 35 to 24.

USSR–United States Match 1955

A match between Russia and the United States was played from June 29 to July 5, 1955, in Moscow. This was a return match; the year before, the Soviet team had come to New York and that year Kashdan did not compete. Unlike the matches played between these two countries in the forties, these were played in four rounds instead of two, with 8 players to a side. Each team was also allowed two reserves. The line-up for the American team was as follows: Board 1. Reshevsky; 2. Bisguier; 3. Evans; 4. D. Byrne; 5. R. Byrne; 6. Horowitz; 7. Kashdan; and 8. Steiner. Pavey and Kevitz were the reserves. Four players, Reshevsky, Bisguier, Evans, and Horowitz departed from New York on June 22. The other four team members, and 16 others, including officials and wives of the players, departed from New York the next day.

On the afternoon of June 24, a radiogram from Helsinki reached the office of the *American Chess Bulletin*. "Safe Helsinki" was the laconic message, which straightway was telephoned to Mrs. Kashdan in Brooklyn, for whom it was intended. Mrs. Kashdan, and their two boys are remaining in the East with relatives until his return, before going home to California [*American Chess Bulletin*, May-June, 1955].

The Kashdan's older son, Howard, would die later that year on December 23, 1955.

The match was won by the Soviet Union by a score of 25 to 7—the worst showing of the American team in the four matches that were played. In 1945 the score was 15½–4½ in favor of the Soviets. In 1946 the U.S. team scored 3 wins (Kashdan, Kevitz, Ulvestad) and 9 draws (Reshevsky, Fine, Kashdan, Steiner, Kevitz, and both Horowitz and Dake twice). The result in 1954 was 20–12 in favor of the Soviets; the American team scored 6 wins, 12 draws, and 14 losses. In the 1955 team match the only win was scored by Reshevsky. The results per round were (with the Soviet team given first), round 1: 5½–2½; round 2: 7–1; round 3: 5½–2½; round 4: 7–1. The only player for the Americans to achieve a plus score was Reshevsky on board 1 over Botvinnik: winning 1 and drawing 3. Otherwise the best American showing was that of Kashdan and Evans. They both scored 3 draws and 1 loss. Kashdan's USCF rating after this event was 2525, which placed him seventh in the United States.

Also that year Kashdan was awarded the Grandmaster title by FIDE, the world chess federation. He had deserved the honor much sooner, especially because of the fantastic results he achieved in the international team competitions in the thirties. But at that time the title was not yet conferred. This also coincided with his last international competition.

7

The Later Years

Chess Editor of the Los Angeles Times 1956

One of the most noteworthy posts Isaac Kashdan would take on was that of editor of the chess column of the *Los Angeles Times*. His predecessor Herman Steiner died prematurely, in 1955, and Kashdan then held the position for 27 years, until 1982. Here is the letter he wrote in the newspaper on January 8, 1956, when he officially was made the editor of the chess column:

> I have just been notified by the Times I am to edit the chess column, as successor to the late Herman Steiner. Mr. Steiner was my friend for over 30 years. I knew him better than most for the love he had for chess and the zeal with which he played and taught the game. The column reflected the dignity of the man, his knowledge of the game and its personalities, his desire to promote and develop interest in chess. I have submitted the material for the column for the last four weeks. There have been some changes in format, and there may be others. In the main I shall endeavor to continue the column in the good spirit with which it was conducted for 20 odd years.

In 1957, Kashdan proposed a significant change in the time control of games as a result of the time scrambles that occurred in the match between Samuel Reshevsky and Donald Byrne. It was well known at the time that Reshevsky would spend excessive time on the opening and middle game and then would face a shortage of time in the endgame. In several of his games this could have resulted in a loss. But more often than not he could make the best moves even when short of time. In this particular match Reshevsky did not lose a game, but it still could have meant the difference between a win and a draw. As reported in the English magazine *Chess*, October 5, 1957, Kashdan made a suggestion to improve the time-control system. His suggestion was a time delay, which allows a player in the last five minutes of the game on his clock an extra 30 seconds for each move (so if he makes the move within 30 seconds there is no forfeit). This was actually adopted many years later. He was ahead of his time with this improvement of the time-control system.

In 1959 Kashdan was appointed to the FIDE editorial post (FIDE is the French acronym for the Fédération Internationale des Échecs). The *FIDE Review* was a magazine published quarterly. That year in June he gave a simultaneous exhibition in Howthorne at the Northrop Aircraft Corporation. He met 35 opponents, winning 31 of those games, while drawing 1 and losing 3.

North vs. South California Matches 1956–1961

The matches between North and South California was the only competitive activity Kashdan took part in during the years 1956 to 1961. In every one of these matches Kashdan would represent the South and play on board one.

The first of them took place on May 27, 1956, and here again as in 1955, he was opposed by Imre Koenig. This time Kashdan was the winner, in 46 moves.

On June 2, 1957, his adversary was again Imre Koenig and the result was a peaceful draw. At that time Kashdan was already the editor of the chess column of the *Los Angeles Times*. Here are some excerpts from his report on the match that appeared on June 9.

> In a record breaking match with 73 players to each side, the Southern California forces held fast against a determined onslaught by the Northern delegation, and left the field winning by the closest possible margin, 37–36. The North proved stronger on the upper boards winning 4½ points of the first seven. This contrasted with last year, when the South did not lose a single game on the first ten boards. This was the second successive victory for the South. The totals for the series are now 14 for the North, 7 for the South, and 3 tie matches.

Then Kashdan gave the complete results for all 73 boards. It is interesting to note that his son, Richard, then 13 years old, played on one of the lower boards.

He then skipped the next two years only to take on Imre Koenig once again in 1960. The outcome this time was a win for Kashdan in just 25 moves.

The following year Kashdan, again and for the last time, would play in the annual North vs. South California Matches in 1961. But, this time his opponent Boris Siff was an old adversary he had played a few times earlier when they both lived in the eastern United States. In fact, an earlier game against Siff that Kashdan won was a brilliant effort that ranks among the best games he ever played. But this time Kashdan was outplayed, so this can be considered the revenge for Siff. He won in rather short order. This was the last game Kashdan would play competitively. He was one of the most active participants in these California matches, playing in seven from 1951 on.

The Olympiad, Leipzig 1960

Later that year in October he was selected as the non-playing captain for the American team in the 1960 Olympiad held in Leipzig, East Germany. The team was headed by Fischer, followed by Lombardy, Robert Byrne, Bisguier, Rossolimo, and Weinstein. The team finished second behind the Soviet Union. As team captain, Kashdan brought the knowledge and experience that he had gained since the 1930s and that is needed in international team competition.

Remains Active

He continued to give exhibitions in California. One such event took place in Coronado in May of 1960. He was opposed by 30 players. Only one player was able to win and another achieved a draw. Kashdan won the rest of the games.

In July and August 1961 a match between Bobby Fischer and Samuel Reshevsky took place. The match was to be for 16 games. But after 11 games Fischer refused to continue. The sponsors, Gregor and Jacqueline Piatigorsky, wanted to change the schedule for the 12th game so that they could attend a concert and also see the game later. Fischer refused to reschedule it. The match ended with each player winning two games and the rest were drawn. Kashdan, as the referee to the match, felt that Fischer should have continued to play. He expressed his disappointment in a letter to *Chess Life*, December 1961. Fischer in his book, *My 60 Memorable Games*, annotates the fifth game of the match. In it he gives Kashdan credit for showing a quicker win for Fischer. After the game Kashdan demonstrated a win in five moves on the 49th move which would have resulted in mate. Instead it took Fischer nine more moves before Reshevsky resigned.

First Piatigorsky Cup Tournament 1963

In 1963 Kashdan was the director of the Piatigorsky Cup tournament. This tournament was so named because Jacqueline Piatigorsky donated the cup and the prizes for the event. It took place in Santa Monica, California, from July 2 to July 28. It was a double round affair with two Soviet players, two U.S. players and four top ranked players from other countries. The two Russians, Paul Keres and Petrosian, tied for the title. The other participants were Najdorf and Panno of Argentina, Olafsson of Iceland, Gligorić of Yugoslavia, and the two American representatives, Reshevsky and Benko. Unfortunately Fischer was not one of the American players. Kashdan was the editor of a book on the tournament to which he wrote quite an extensive introduction. Following is only a small part of it to show how he viewed his involvement now as a non-player.

> The writer of these lines was chosen to direct the tournament. It was a rewarding experience. Some thirty years ago, when I was considered the leading American player, I would have much preferred to sit across the board and match wits with these redoubtable antagonists. However, there is also a role for the umpire and director of an event, and I was happy to take an active part in the Piatigorsky Cup Tournament.

Delegate to FIDE 1964

In 1964 Kashdan became a delegate to the FIDE Congress, representing the United States. He wrote in *Chess Life*, January 1965 issue, of his experience in that capacity.

> Although I have frequently been in the team tournaments, both as player and captain, this was my first experience as delegate to the FIDE meetings. I found the proceedings interesting and worthwhile. I made every effort to be present at the sessions and to make whatever impact I could in the matters that were important to us. The one handicap was that I was also team captain, and had to divide my time as equitably as I could between the two responsibilities.
>
> One big advantage was that Jerry Spann has been at a number of meetings, and developed considerable respect for himself and for the United States. The friendships he made were valuable, and the advise he gave me before I left also proved immediately helpful.

He then went on to discuss specifics.

The April 1964 issue of *Chess Life* reported that Kashdan would conduct a Trans World

Airline Tour that would have a heavy accent on chess. The dates will be from November 16 to December 7.

> The main feature of the tour will be nine days spent in Tel Aviv, Israel in conjunction with the finals of the Chess Olympiad. The tour will leave New York on November 16, will take in Tel Aviv from November 17 through November 25. From Israel, the tour will wend its way to Italy, Switzerland, France, and Great Britain under Mr. Kashdan's direction. In each of the countries visited, there will be chess lectures, simultaneous play and casual meetings with the leading chess figures.

Second Piatigorsky Cup Tournament 1966

The second Piatigorsky Cup tournament took place from July 17 to August 15, 1966, in Santa Monica, California. The number of players was increased to ten from eight. Also the prize fund was increased to $20,000. This time the event also included the United States Champion, Bobby Fischer. He was the youngest of the competitors at age 23. The event included Reshevsky, again, for the U.S., two players from the Soviet Union, Spassky and Petrosian, and Larsen from Denmark, Portisch from Hungary, Unzicker from Germany, Najdorf from Argentina, Ivkov from Yugoslavia, and Donner from Holland. Fischer started poorly in the first half, getting only 3½ points out of 9 in this double round tourney. But then he made a big spurt in the last half gaining 7½ points out of 9 to almost catch the winner. Spassky won the event with 11½ points, with Fischer only half a point behind to place second. Kashdan stated that Petrosian had told him before his game with Fischer that he would offer him a draw, because he wanted to see Fischer take second place because of his great comeback in the second half. Later he did offer Fischer a draw in his game, even though he claimed that he had a demonstrable win. But this was not too convincing.

The event, just like the first Piatigorsky Cup in 1963, was directed by Kashdan. An interesting sidelight was Fischer's insistence that he play on a smaller board then the one that was provided. Kashdan's wife, Helen, was instructed to locate a smaller set that Fischer could use. She found a set that was acceptable to Fischer. Now the question was if the other players would agree to this special favor given to Fischer. Only Najdorf did not find this acceptable, although he later relented. It also should be noted that Kashdan was again the editor of the tournament book that appeared two years later. All the games were annotated by the players themselves. It was regarded as one of the best tournament books ever written.

California Chess Hall of Fame

In 1968, Herman Steiner was inducted into the California Chess Hall of Fame; the honor was bestowed posthumously, as he died in 1955. The following year, Isaac Kashdan, also very deserving, followed Steiner into the Hall of Fame.

Kashdan was impressed with the successes that Fischer had in tournament play in 1970. Fischer's record stood at 50 wins, 23 draws, and only 3 losses. Kashdan called this "the most successful year for any chess player of our time."

Kashdan was also involved in the qualifying match that would eventually make Fischer a candidate for the world championship. The event took place in Denver in 1971 and it was against Grandmaster Bent Larsen. As he had in the preceding match against Taimanov, Fischer won the match 6 zip, without even a draw. Kashdan was the reporter for the AP and UPI and several newspapers. An amazingly versatile writer, he reported for AP with games in descriptive notation, for UPI in algebraic, and to the *New York Times* plus a Yugoslav and a Swedish magazine as well, and all the articles had to be different! After the match, "Kash" would dash off the articles, his wife would go to AP and he to UPI, to get the results on the morning wire services.

Lone Pine Tournaments

The Louis D. Statham International tournaments at Lone Pine in California began in 1971. These would be held every year for eleven years until 1981. Kashdan was the tournament director in every one. In 1972 it was held in March just prior to the Fischer–Spassky match. Kashdan reported on it in the June issue of *Chess Life*. He stated that this would prove to be one of the great happenings of American chess, at least once a year. These events were made possible by the Texas born inventor Louis D. Statham, who now made his living in the small town of Lone Pine. Kashdan mentioned in *Chess Life* that Statham wanted the strongest players he could attract so he raised the prize fund from the $2500 of the previous year to $5500. There were 33 players in the field in 1971 and in 1972 that number increased only to 35 but it was a much stronger event. By 1979 the number had increased to 73 players. While the Piatigorsky Cup events in 1963 and 1966 were organized and financially supported by Mr. and Mrs. Piatigorsky, this time another benefactor from California would make it possible to have chess tournaments there of international significance. These events were conducted on the Swiss system in which only masters, and experts under 21, could compete.

Fischer–Spassky Match 1972

This event, often called the match of the century, started in June 1972. It was for the World Chess Championship, between the title holder, Boris Spassky of the Soviet Union, and Bobby Fischer of the United States. It had been called the match of the century because for the first time since 1948 the challenger came from a country that was not the Soviet Union. Kashdan called it "the single most important chess event in the history of the game."

Kashdan again played an important role in this event. He reported from Iceland, where the match was held, for the Associated Press (AP) and the *Los Angeles Times*. He would also report on the event in his chess column for the newspaper.

Several of the top American grandmasters made predictions as to the outcome of the match. Robert Byrne and Herbert Seidman predicted right on the money with 12½ to 8½. Kashdan said it would be 12½–8½ or 13–8 for Fischer. Five grandmasters predicted a win for Spassky, while 12 thought that Fischer would win. The East German chess periodical *Schach Echo* even went so far as to say it would take a "miracle" to prevent Fischer from becoming the new champion. Fischer won by the score of 12½–8½ over Spassky.

Kashdan (right) as the tournament director of the Los Angeles International presents the trophy to Svetozar Gligorić, the winner of the event in 1974 (courtesy *Chess Life*).

Final Years

In 1982 Kashdan suffered a stroke that forced him to discontinue his activity with chess. In 1983 at the United States Open in Pasadena the U.S. Chess Federation recognized his many achievements by making him Honorary Chairman of the event. (Just a little over 50 years before, at the International Tournament in Pasadena in 1932, Kashdan scored one of his greatest triumphs, coming in ahead of his American rivals by placing second behind World Champion Alexander Alekhine.)

His eyesight went bad and he was confined for several years to a wheelchair. He died at the age of 79 at his home in West Los Angeles on February 20, 1985, survived by his wife Helen and son Richard. The U.S. Chess Federation recognized his many achievements in chess by inducting him into the United States Chess Hall of Fame the following year.

Arnold Denker, who knew him well, wrote a wonderful article in *Chess Life* on his death, that shows the kind of person he was and how he was regarded by his peers; an excerpt:

> For me, Kash was a flesh-and-blood whom I knew well and deeply respected. And, yes, I was fond of Kash. In the most important sense Kash was unlike other grandmasters whom I have known. I never detected a trace of anger or violence in the man. I remember occasions when he became annoyed at some unkind or nasty remark. He would never react meanly, but he did have a quiet humor leavened, when necessary, with sarcasm. Kash was then, different from the rest of us. And so was his chess. As a player, he resembled a scientist. Kashdan was a great

player indeed. During his heyday from 1930–1934, he and Salo Flohr were regarded as the two key challengers for Alekhine's crown. Kash's strength was in the endgame and he was often called *der kleine Capablanca* because of this. In the middle game, there was a slightest touch of rigidity; he loved the two bishops too much.

The Kashdan Legacy

BY ARNOLD DENKER

Grandmaster Isaac Kashdan, honorary chairman of the 1983 U.S. Open, came to the awards banquet in a wheelchair, accompanied by Helen, his wife of fifty years. He had been felled by a stroke some months ago, but was now counterattacking and making good progress. One of the stories he might tell, if he were not so modest, would be that he was largely responsible for our present U.S. championship tournament. It came about this way: For years, Frank Marshall had a hammerlock on the title, steadfastly refusing to meet his chief rival, "Kash," in a match. From 1925 until 1935, Kashdan was kept waiting, even though it was a foregone conclusion who the winner of such a great match would be. Finally, after lengthy negotiations, some of Kashdan's friends were able to work out a deal. Marshall would relinquish his title to the winner of a round-robin tournament. Another of Isaac's friends, Fritz Brieger, and others then arranged the first official U.S. Championship in 1936, which was held at the famous Astor Hotel in New York City. Unfortunately for Kash, it came too late. For Samuel Reshevsky and Reuben Fine, it was just in time.

Kashdan and his wife, Helen, at the U.S. Open in 1983 (courtesy *Chess Life*).

71

PART TWO

The Games
of Isaac Kashdan

The Outstanding Games

*Bishop vs. knight games.   †High quality endgames.   ‡ The "immortal" game.

Tournament and Match Games (1–661)

1 Kupchik–Kashdan [A13]
Rice Progressive Championship, 1924 *[Fall]*

1. Nf3 Nf6 2. c4 e6 3. b3 d5 4. Bb2 Nbd7 5. g3 c6 6. Bg2 Bd6 7. 0–0 0–0 8. d3 Re8 9. Nbd2 e5 10. cxd5 Nxd5 11. Rc1 f6 12. e4 Ne7 13. Nc4 Bc7 14. d4 exd4 15. Nxd4 Ne5 16. Qc2 N7g6 17. Rcd1 Qe7 18. Nf5 Bxf5 19. exf5 Nf8 20. Ba3 Qf7 21. Nd6 Bxd6 22. Bxd6 Rad8 23. h3 Ned7 24. Rd4 Nb6 25. Rfd1 Rd7 26. a4 Red8 27. a5 Nc8 28. Bc5 Rxd4 29. Rxd4 Rxd4 30. Bxd4 a6 31. Bf1 Qc7 32. Bc5 Qd8 33. Qc4+ Kh8 34. Qb4 Nd7 35. Be3 Qc7 36. Bf4 c5 37. Qe4 Ne5 38. Bg2 b6 39. Qa8 g6 40. Bxe5 fxe5 41. fxg6 1–0 (*American Chess Bulletin*, January 1925, p. 12)

2 Chajes–Kashdan [D45]
Rice Progressive Championship, 1924 *[Fall]*

1. d4 Nf6 2. Nf3 c6 3. c4 d5 4. e3 e6 5. Nc3 Nbd7 6. Qc2 Be7 7. a3 dxc4 The move which usually equalizes the game. 8. Bxc4 c5 9. 0–0 0–0 10. Rd1 a6 11. dxc5 Bxc5 12. b4 Be7 A move later, with a similar choice, White plays Ba7. But that would be inferior here. 13. Bb2 13. b5 is refuted here by Qc7 14. Bd3 (if Be2 axb5 15. Bxb5 Nd5 and Black wins), Nc5, with a fine game. 13. ... b5 14. Ba2 Bb7 15. Rac1 Rc8 16. Bb1 Bad, because after the exchange of bishops, a serious weakness is left at c4. 16. Qe2 was best. 16. ... Be4 17. Qd2 Bxb1 18. Rxb1 Nb6 19. Qe2 Qc7 20. Ba1 Nbd5 Stronger than the more plausible Nc4, which would be answered by 21. a4, giving White the advantage. 21. Rbc1 Qb7 22. Nd4 Rfd8 23. Qf3 Rc7 24. Ne4 Nxe4 25. Qxe4 Rxc1 26. Rxc1 Rc8 27. Rd1 Exchanging would leave Black with a definite advantage on the queenside. 27. ... Bf6 28. h4 Rc4 29. Qf3 Bxh4 This

leads to difficulties, but is probably the best.
30. Nf5

After
30. Nf5

30. ... f6? An oversight in time pressure.
Correct was 30. ... exf5 Qe7. The game might
then proceed: 32. Bd4 g6 33. Re5 Re1+ 34. Kh2
Qf8 (threatening Bf6 and Qh6+, with a win-
ning endgame); 35. Rc5 Rf1 36. g3 Be7 37. Kg2
Rb1 and Black continues with Qh6 and wins. If
38. Rxf5 then Qh6 still follows. **31. Nd6 Qc7
32. Nxc4 Qxc4 33. e4 Ne7 34. Qh5 Ng6
35. Qc5 Qa2 36. Rd8+ Kf7 37. Rd7+
Kg8 38. Bd4 Qd2 39. Qc8+ Nf8 40. Rd8**
Here I had hoped for 40. Bc5? Bxf2+! 41. Bxf2
Qxd7, but the master is much too wily. **1—0**
Annotated by Kashdan (*American Chess Bulletin*,
1925, p. 32)

3 Kashdan–Soos [D30]
Stuyvasant Championship, 1924 *[Fall]*

**1. Nf3 d5 2. c4 e6 3. d4 Nc6 4. Nc3
Nf6 5. Bg5 Be7 6. e3 Na5 7. Qa4+ Nc6
8. Bxf6 gxf6 9. cxd5 exd5 10. Bb5 Qd6
11. Rc1 Bd7 12. Qb3 a6 13. a3 Rc8
14. Bd3 Na5 15. Qxd5 Qxd5 16. Nxd5
Bd8 17. Nh4 c6 18. Bf5 Nb3 19. Rc3
Bxf5 20. Nxf5 Ba5 21. Nb4 Rd8
22. Rxb3 Rd5 23. e4 Rd7 24. Ke2 Kd8
25. Nxc6+ Kc8 26. Nxa5 Kb8 27. Rc1
Ka8 28. Rb6 Rg8 29. Nd6 Rgd8
30. Ndxb7 Ka7 31. Rb4 Re8 32. Nc6+
Ka8 33. Nc5 Rc7 34. Rb6 1—0** (*New
Yorker Staats-Zeitung*, November 2, 1924)

4 Kashdan–Newberger [B21]
Stuyvesant Championship, 1924 *[Fall]*

1. e4 c5 2. d4 cxd4 3. Nf3 e5 4. Bc4

Nc6 5. c3 dxc3 6. Nxc3 Bb4 7. 0–0
Bxc3 8. bxc3 h6 9. Ba3 Nge7 10. Qd6
Ng6 11. Rad1 Qe7 12. Qxg6 fxg6 13. Bxe7
Kxe7 14. Nh4 d5 15. Nxg6+ Kf6
16. Nxh8 dxc4 17. f4 Bg4 18. fxe5+ Ke6
19. Rd6+ Kxe5 20. Nf7+ Kxe4 21. h3
Bh5 22. g4 Bxf7 23. Rxf7 Rd8 24. Rxd8
Nxd8 25. Rxg7 Kd3 26. Rd7+ Kxc3
27. Rxd8 Kc2 28. g5 1—0 (*New Yorker Staats-
Zeitung*, December 7, 1924)

5 Kashdan–Treystman [C13]
Stuyvesant Championship, 1925 *[Winter]*

**1. e4 e6 2. d4 d5 3. Nc3 Nf6 4. Bg5
Be7 5. e5 Nfd7 6. h4 a6 7. Qg4 f6
8. Bf4 g6 9. h5 f5 10. Qh3 g5 11. Bd2
h6 12. g4 f4 13. Bd3 c5 14. Nf3 cxd4
15. Ne2 Nc6 16. Nexd4 Nxd4 17. Nxd4
Nxe5 18. 0–0 0–0 19. Rfe1 Bd6 20. Bc3
Qc7 21. Re2 f3 22. Re3 Rf4 23. Nxf3
Nxg4 24. Re2 e5 25. Bg6 Nxf2 26. Qg2
Rg4 27. Kxf2 Rxg2+ 28. Kxg2 Bg4 0–1**
(*New Yorker Staats-Zeitung*, January 25, 1925)

6 Kashdan (Stuyvesant)–
Schleifer (Brooklyn) [C66]
Met League Match, New York, 1925 *[Winter]*

**1. e4 e5 2. Nf3 Nc6 3. Bb5 Nf6 4. 0–0
d6 5. d4 exd4 6. Nxd4 Bd7 7. Bxc6
bxc6 8. Qf3 Be7 9. e5 dxe5 10. Nxc6
Bxc6 11. Qxc6+ Nd7 12. Nc3 Rb8
13. Be3 Rxb2 14. Nb5 Bd6 15. Rad1
Rxb5 16. Qxb5 0–0 17. c4 Qe7 18. Bxa7
e4 19. Rfe1 f5 20. c5 Nxc5 21. Bxc5
Bxc5 22. Rd7 Qe5 23. Qc4+ Kh8
24. Rd5**

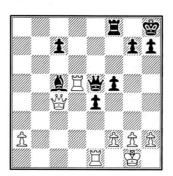

After
24. Rd5

24. ... Bxf2+ 25. Kxf2 Qxh2 26. Qb4 Kg8 27. Qb3 Qh4+ 28. Qg3 Qe7 29. Red1 c6 30. Re5 Qa7+ 31. Qe3 Qxa2+ 32. Qd2 Qb3 33. Re7 f4 34. Rxe4 Qg3+ 35. Kg1 f3 36. Qa2+ Kh8 37. Qf2 Qb8 38. gxf3 Rf6 39. Red4 Rf8 40. Qh4 Qb6 41. Kg2 Qb3 42. Qg3 Qg8 43. Qd6 Rc8 44. Qd8 1–0 (*New Yorker Staats-Zeitung*, March 22, 1925)

7 Santasiere (Marshall)– Kashdan (Stuyvesant) [A45]

Met League Match, New York, 1925 *[Spring]*

1. d4 Nf6 2. e3 e6 3. Bd3 c5 4. c3 b6 5. f4 Bb7 6. Nf3 Be7 7. Nbd2 0–0 8. e4 Nc6 9. 0–0 Rc8 10. a3 Qc7 11. e5 Ng4 12. Ne4 f5 13. Ng3 cxd4 14. cxd4 Na5 15. h3 Nh6 16. Bd2 Bd5 17. Bxa5 bxa5 18. Qd2 Qb6 19. Ne2 Rb8 20. Rfb1 Rfc8 21. Ne1 a4 22. Nc2 Qb7 23. Ne3 Be4 24. Nc3 Bxd3 25. Qxd3 Qb3 26. Kh2 g5 27. g3 Kh8 28. d5 gxf4 29. gxf4 Rg8 30. Nc4 Rbc8 31. Nd2 Qb6

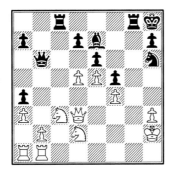

After 31. ... Qb6

32. Nd1? Qg1 mate 0–1 (*New Yorker Staats-Zeitung*, March 29, 1925)

8 Frink (Columbia)–Kashdan (Stuyvesant) [D46]

Met League Match, New York, 1925 *[Spring]*

1. d4 Nf6 2. Nf3 c6 3. c4 e6 4. Nc3 d5 5. e3 Nbd7 6. Bd3 Be7 7. 0–0 0–0 8. e4 dxe4 9. Nxe4 c5 10. b3 b6 11. dxc5 Nxc5 12. Nxc5 Bxc5 13. Bb2 Bb7 14. Qe2 Qe7 15. Rad1 Rad8 16. Ne5 Rfe8 17. Ng4 Nxg4 18. Qxg4 e5 19. Rfe1 f6 20. Bf5 e4 21. Qh4 h6 22. Qg4 e3

23. fxe3 Rxd1 24. Qxd1 Bxe3+ 25. Kh1 Qd8 26. Bg6 Qa8 27. Qg4 Re7 28. Bd4 h5 29. Qh3 Bxd4 30. Rxe7 Black won in three moves. 1–0 (*New Yorker Staats-Zeitung*, March 29, 1925)

9 Kashdan–Bornholz [D66]

Albert Hallgarten (Prelims), 1925 *[Fall]*

1. d4 Nf6 2. c4 e6 3. Nc3 d5 4. Nf3 c6 5. Bg5 Be7 6. e3 Nbd7 7. Rc1 0–0 8. Bd3 dxc4 9. Bxc4 b5 10. Bd3 a6 11. e4 c5 12. e5 Nd5 13. Bxe7 Qxe7 14. Ne4 c4 15. Bb1 Qb4+ 16. Qd2 Qxd2+ 17. Kxd2 f6 18. exf6 N7xf6 19. Nc5 Ng4 20. Rhf1 Nf4 21. h3 Nf6 22. g3 N4h5 23. Ng5 Rd8 24. Ngxe6 Bxe6 25. Nxe6 Rd6 26. Rfe1 Re8 27. Nc5 Rxd4+ 28. Kc3 Rxe1 29. Rxe1 Rd6 30. Bf5 Nd5+ 31. Kc2 Nb4+ 32. Kb1 Nf6 33. a3 Nbd5 34. Re6 Rxe6 35. Bxe6+ Kf8 36. Nxa6 Ke7 37. Bxd5 Nxd5 38. Kc2 Kd6 39. Kd2 Ke5 40. Nc5 g6 41. f4+ Kf5 42. a4 b4 43. a5 h5 44. a6 h4 45. a7 Nb6 46. gxh4 Kxf4 47. Nd7 Na8 48. Nf8 Kf5 49. Ke3 Nc7 50. Nd7 Na8 51. Kd4 c3 52. bxc3 b3 53. Kd3 b2 54. Kc2 Ke6 55. Nf8+ Kf7 56. Nxg6 0–1 (*En Passant*, January–March 1955)

10 Winter–Kashdan [C80]

Albert Hallgarten (Prelims), 1925 *[Fall]*

1. e4 e5 2. Nf3 Nc6 3. Bb5 a6 4. Ba4 Nf6 5. 0–0 Nxe4 6. d4 b5 7. Bb3 d5 8. dxe5 Be6 9. a4 Na5 10. Nc3 Nxc3 11. bxc3 c5 12. axb5 axb5 13. Bg5 Be7 14. Bxe7 Kxe7 15. Qe2 Qd7 16. Qe3 Rhc8 17. Rae1 Kf8 18. Ng5 Kg8 19. f4 c4 20. Ba2 Nc6 21. Bb1 Qa7 22. f5 Bd7 23. e6 fxe6 24. fxe6 Be8 25. Kh1 Qxe3 26. Rxe3 Bg6 27. Kg1 h6 28. Nf3 Re8 29. Nd4 Nxd4 30. cxd4 b4 31. Re5 Ra5 32. g4 c3 33. h4 Be4 34. Re1 Ra1 35. Kf2 b3 36. R5xe4 dxe4 37. d5 Ra5 38. Rd1 bxc2 39. Bxc2 Ra2 40. Rc1 Kf8 41. Ke3 Ke7 42. Bxe4 Rc8 43. Kf4 Kd6 44. Kf5 Rf8+! 0–1 (*New Yorker Staats-Zeitung*, November 1, 1925)

11 Berman–Kashdan [D66]
Albert Hallgarten (Prelims), 1925 *[Fall]*

1. d4 Nf6 2. Nf3 e6 3. c4 d5 4. Nc3
c6 5. Bg5 Nbd7 6. e3 Be7 7. Rc1 0–0
8. Bd3 h6 9. Bh4 dxc4 10. Bxc4 a6
11. a3 c5 12. 0–0 b5 13. Ba2 Bb7
14. Qe2 c4 15. Bb1 Re8 16. Ne5 Nf8
17. f4 Nd5 18. Be1 Nxc3 19. Bxc3 Rc8
20. Qh5 f5 21. Qf7+ Kh7 22. d5 Bc5
23. Qxb7 Bxe3+ 24. Kh1 Rc7 25. Qxa6
Bxc1 26. Rxc1 Qxd5 27. Qc6 Rd8 28. h3
Qc5 29. Ba5 Rdc8 30. Qxc5 Rxc5
31. Rd1 g5 32. Bb6 gxf4 33. Bxc5 Rxc5
34. Nd7 Nxd7 35. Rxd7+ Kg6 36. Kg1
c3 37. bxc3 Rxc3 38. Bd3 Rxa3
39. Bxb5 f3 40. g3 Ra2 41. Bf1 e5
42. Rd6+ Kg7 43. Rd5 Kf6 44. Rd6+
Kg7 ½–½ (*New Yorker Staats-Zeitung*, November 15, 1925)

12 Kashdan–Norwood [D24]
Albert Hallgarten (Prelims), 1925 *[Fall]*

1. d4 d5 2. c4 e6 3. Nf3 Nf6 4. Nc3
dxc4 5. a4 c6 6. e3 Be7 7. Bxc4 0–0
8. 0–0 Nbd7 9. b3 Qb6 10. Bb2 Rd8
11. Qe2 Nd5 12. Ne4 N7f6 13. a5 Qc7
14. Nc5 Rb8 15. Nh4 b6 16. axb6 axb6
17. Na6 Bxa6 18. Bxa6 b5 19. Rfc1 Rb6
20. e4 Nf4 21. Qe3 Ng6 22. d5 exd5
23. Bd4 c5 24. Nxg6 hxg6 25. Bxc5
Bxc5 26. Rxc5 Qe5 27. Rcc1 d4 28. Qd3
Nxe4 29. Re1 Nc5 30. Rxe5 Nxd3
31. Rxb5 Rxb5 32. Bxb5 Nc5 33. b4
Ne4 34. Bd3 Nc3 35. Kf1 Kf8 36. b5
Rb8 37. Ra3 Rb7 38. Rb3 Ke7 39. Rb4
Kf6 40. f4 g5 41. Rxd4 gxf4 42. Rxf4+
Ke5 43. Rc4 Nd5 44. Kf2 f5 45. Rc8 g6
46. Rc6 Nb4 47. Rc5+ Kd6 48. Rc3
Rb6 49. h4 Nd5 50. Rb3 Kc5 51. Kf3
Re6 52. Be2 Re4 53. g3 Re6 54. Ra3
Rd6 55. Ra6 Nb6 56. Ra7 Nd5 57. Ra8
Nc7 58. Rc8 Kb6 59. Rb8+ Kc5 60. Kf4
Re6 61. Rc8 Kb6 62. Kf3 Rd6 63. Rh8
Ne6 64. Bc4 Nc7 65. h5 gxh5 66. Rxh5
Rd4 67. Rh4 Rd6 68. Rf4 Kc5 69. Be2
Rd5 70. Rc4+ Kb6 71. Rc6+ Kb7
72. Kf4 Kb8 73. b6 Ne8 74. Bf3 Rd3
75. Rg6 Nd6 76. Rg8+ Nc8 77. b7

Rxf3+ 78. Kxf3 Kxb7 79. Rxc8 Kxc8
80. Kf4 Kd7 81. Kxf5 Ke7 82. Kg6 Kf8
83. g4 Kg8 84. g5 Kh8 85. Kf7 1–0
(*New Yorker Staats-Zeitung*, November 8, 1925)

13 Field–Kashdan [C77]
Albert Hallgarten (Prelims), 1925 *[Fall]*

1. e4 e5 2. Nf3 Nc6 3. Bb5 a6 4. Ba4
Nf6 5. c3 Nxe4 6. Qe2 Nc5 7. Nxe5
Be7 But not Nxa4 as then 8. Nxc6+ wins the
Queen. 8. Bxc6 dxc6 9. d4 Ne6 10. 0–0
0–0 11. f4 f6 12. Nd3 Re8 13. Be3 Nf8
14. Nd2 Bf5 15. b4 Qd5 16. g4 Bg6 17. f5
Bf7 18. Nf4 Qb5 19. Qf3 Qb6 20. Ne4
a5 21. Nc5 Qb5 22. Nce6 Bxe6 23. Nxe6
Nxe6 24. fxe6 axb4 25. cxb4 Bxb4
26. Rab1 Rxa2 27. g5 Rxe6 28. gxf6 Rxf6
29. Qh3 Rg6+ 30. Kh1 Qd5+ 31. Qf3
Bd6 0–1 (*Brooklyn Daily Eagle*, October 29,
1925)

14 Pinkus–Kashdan [C97]
Albert Hallgarten (Prelims), 1925 *[Fall]*

1. e4 e5 2. Nf3 Nc6 3. Bb5 a6 4. Ba4
Nf6 5. 0–0 Be7 6. Re1 b5 7. Bb3 d6
8. c3 0–0 9. h3 Na5 10. Bc2 c5 11. d4
Qc7 12. Nbd2 Bd7 13. Nf1 Rac8 14. d5
Ne8 15. g4 g6 16. Bh6 Ng7 17. Ng3 Nb7
18. Kh2 c4 19. Rg1 f6 20. Qd2 Rf7
21. Rg2 a5 22. Rag1 b4 23. Nh4 bxc3
24. bxc3 Kh8 25. Ne2 Nc5 26. Be3
Kg8 27. Nf3 Rb8 28. Rb1 Rff8 29. Rgg1
a4 30. Rb4 Na6 31. Rbb1 a3 32. Rgd1
Qa5 33. Ba7 Rb2 34. Rxb2 axb2
35. Bb1 Nc5 36. Bxc5 Qxc5 37. Ng3
Qa3 38. Kg2 Bd8 39. Rf1 Ba5 40. Ne2
f5 41. gxf5 gxf5 42. Qh6 Bd8 43. Ng5
Bxg5 44. Qxg5 fxe4 45. Ng3 Qxc3
46. Bxe4 Qd4 47. Qh6 Bf5 48. f3 Bxe4
49. Nxe4 Qxe4! For if 50. fxe4 Rxf1+ followed
by b1(Q). 0–1 (*Brooklyn Daily Eagle*, November
12, 1925)

15 Kashdan–Bertha [C66]
Albert Hallgarten (Prelims), 1925 *[Fall]*

1. e4 e5 2. Nf3 Nc6 3. Bb5 Nf6 4. 0–0
d6 5. d4 Bd7 6. Nc3 Be7 7. Bg5 exd4
8. Nxd4 0–0 9. Bxc6 bxc6 10. Qd3 Re8

11. Rae1 h6 12. Bc1 Bf8 13. f4 c5 14. Nf3 Bc6 15. Nd5 Bxd5 16. exd5 Qd7 17. b3 c6 18. dxc6 Qxc6 19. c4 a5 20. Bb2 Nd7 21. Nh4 a4 22. Nf3 axb3 23. Qxb3 g6 24. Qc3 f6 25. Qc2 Kf7 26. Nh4 Rxe1 27. Qxg6+ Ke7 28. Rxe1+ Kd8 29. Bxf6+ Kc7 1–0 (*Brooklyn Daily Eagle,* November 12, 1925)

16 Kashdan–Bornholz [D66]
Albert Hallgarten (Finals), 1925 *[Fall]*

1. d4 Nf6 2. c4 e6 3. Nc3 d5 4. Nf3 c6 5. Bg5 Be7 6. e3 Nbd7 7. Rc1 0–0 8. Bd3 dxc4 9. Bxc4 b5 10. Bd3 a6 11. e4 c5 12. e5 Nd5 13. Bxe7 Qxe7 14. Ne4 c4 15. Bb1 Qb4+ 16. Qd2 Qxd2+ 17. Kxd2 f6 18. exf6 N7xf6 19. Nc5 Ng4 20. Rhf1 Nf4 21. h3 Nf6 22. g3 N4h5 23. Ng5 Rd8 24. Ngxe6 Bxe6 25. Nxe6 Rd6 26. Rfe1 Re8 27. Nc5 Rxd4+ 28. Kc3 Rxe1 29. Rxe1 Rd6 30. Bf5 Nd5+ 31. Kc2 Nb4+ 32. Kb1 Nf6 33. a3 Nbd5 34. Re6 Rxe6 35. Bxe6+ Kf8 36. Nxa6 Ke7 37. Bxd5 Nxd5 38. Kc2 Kd6 39. Kd2 Ke5 40. Nc5 g6 41. f4+ Kf5 42. a4 b4 43. a5 h5 44. a6 h4 45. a7 Nb6 46. gxh4 Kxf4 47. Nd7 Na8 48. Nf8 Kf5 49. Ke3 Nc7 50. Nd7 Na8 51. Kd4 c3 52. bxc3 b3 53. Kd3 b2 54. Kc2 Ke6 55. Nf8+ Kf7 56. Nxg6 1–0 (*Brooklyn Daily Eagle,* November 25, 1925)

17 Kashdan–Smirka [A35]
Albert Hallgarten (Finals), 1925 *[Fall]*

1. Nf3 c5 2. c4 Nc6 3. Nc3 e6 4. d4 cxd4 5. Nxd4 Bb4 6. Ndb5 Nf6 7. a3 Bxc3+ 8. Nxc3 0–0 9. g3 d5 10. Bg2 dxc4 11. Qa4 Nd4 12. 0–0 b5 13. Qd1 Rb8 14. Bf4 Rb6 15. Be5 Nc6 16. Qxd8 Nxd8 17. Bc7 Ra6 18. Rad1 Nb7 19. Nxb5 Nd5 20. Be5 f6 21. Bd4 Bd7 22. Nc7 Rd6 23. Nxd5 exd5 24. Bxa7 Bc6 25. Rd2 Rfd8 26. Bb6 R8d7 27. Bd4 f5 28. Bc3 Rd8 29. Bb4 R6d7 30. Rd4 Kf7 31. Rfd1 Ke6 32. R1d2 g5 33. f3 h5 34. Kf2 Rf7 35. Ke1 Rfd7 36. h3 Ra8 37. e4 dxe4 38. fxe4 Rxd4

39. Rxd4 fxe4 40. Bxe4 Bxe4 41. Rxe4+ Kd5 42. Rc7 Nc5 43. Bxc5 Kxc5 44. Kd2 Rd8+ 45. Kc2 Rd5 46. Rh7 Rd3 47. Rxh5 Rxg3 48. h4 Rg2+ 49. Kb1 Kd4 50. Rxg5 Rh2 51. Rg4+ Kc5 52. a4 Kb4 53. Ka2 Kc5 54. Rg3 Rxh4 55. Ka3 Rh1 56. Rg5+ Kd4 57. Rb5 Rb1 58. Ka2 Rh1 59. a5 Rh6 60. Ka3 Rh1 61. Rg5 Ra1+ 62. Kb4 Rb1 63. Rg2 c3 64. b3 Rc1 65. Ra2 Rh1 66. a6 Rh7 67. Ra5 Ra7 68. Kb5 c2 69. Ra1 Kc3 70. b4 Rd7 71. Rc1 Rd4 72. Rxc2+ Kxc2 73. a7 Rd8 74. Ka6 Kb3 75. b5 Kc4 76. b6 Kc5 77. b7 Rd6+ 78. Ka5 Rd1 79. Ka4 Kc4 80. Ka3 Kc3 Even with two pawns about to queen, Kashdan could not win. ½–½ (*New Yorker Staats-Zeitung,* November 22, 1925)

18 Kashdan–Tenner [B45]
Manhattan Club Championship, 1925 *[Winter]*

1. Nf3 c5 2. e4 Nc6 3. d4 cxd4 4. Nxd4 Nf6 5. Nc3 e6 6. g3 Bb4 7. Bg2 Qa5 8. 0–0 Bxc3 9. bxc3 Qxc3 10. Nxc6 dxc6 11. Rb1 0–0 12. Qe2 b6 13. e5 Nd5 14. Rb3 Qa5 15. c4 Ne7 16. Rd1 Qa6 17. Ba3 Qb7 18. Qd2 f6 19. Qd6 Kf7 20. Bxc6 Nxc6 21. Qxf8+ Kg6 22. Qe8+ 1–0 (*Brooklyn Daily Eagle,* January 26, 1926)

19 Pinkus–Kashdan [D52]
Manhattan Club Championship, 1925 *[Winter]*

1. d4 Nf6 2. c4 e6 3. Nc3 d5 4. Bg5 Nbd7 5. Nf3 c6 6. e3 Qa5 7. Bxf6 Nxf6 8. Nd2 Bb4 9. Qc2 Ne4 10. Ndxe4 dxe4 11. Be2 0–0 12. 0–0 f5 13. a3 Be7 14. Rad1 Bd7 15. f3 exf3 16. Bxf3 e5 17. dxe5 Be6 18. Nd5?! cxd5 19. cxd5 Bd7 20. d6 Bg5 21. Bd5+ Kh8 22. e6 Bc6 23. e7 Bxd5 24. exf8Q+ Rxf8 25. Rxf5 Bxe3+ 26. Kh1 Rxf5 27. d7 Rf8 28. Qc8 Kg8 29. Qe8 Bf2 30. b4 Qc7 31. Qe7 Bxg2+ 32. Kxg2 Qc6+ 33. Kf1 Qc4+ 0–1 (*Brooklyn Daily Eagle,* January 26, 1926)

20 Kashdan–Maróczy [D67]
Manhattan Club Championship, 1925
[Winter]

1. d4 Nf6 2. c4 e6 3. Nf3 d5 4. Nc3
Nbd7 5. Bg5 Be7 6. e3 0–0 7. Rc1 c6
8. Bd3 dxc4 9. Bxc4 Nd5 10. Bxe7
Qxe7 11. e4 Nxc3 12. Rxc3 e5 13. 0–0
exd4 14. Qxd4 Nb6 15. Bb3 Be6 16. Re1
Bxb3 17. axb3 Rad8 18. Qe3 Rfe8
19. g3 Qd6 20. Qf4 Qxf4 21. gxf4 Re6
22. f5 Red6 23. Kg2 f6 24. Rce3 Nd7
25. Kg3 Re8 26. R1e2 Rd1 27. Rd2
Rxd2 28. Nxd2 Nc5 29. f4 Rd8 30. Nc4
Rd3 31. Rxd3 Nxd3 32. Kf3 b5 33. Na5
c5 34. Nb7 c4 35. bxc4 bxc4 36. Ke3
Nxb2 37. Kd4 Kf8 38. Nd6 Nd3
39. Ke3 ½–½ (*Brooklyn Daily Eagle*, January
21, 1926)

21 Norwood–Kashdan [B02]
Manhattan Club Championship, 1925
[Winter]

1. e4 Nf6 2. e5 Nd5 3. Nc3 More usual
is 3. c4 but the text is also good. 3. ... Nxc3
4. dxc3 d5 5. Bd3 c5 6. Bf4 Nc6 7. Qd2
c4 In view of this it would have been better for
White to have played 5. Be2 instead of the text.
8. Be2 Bf5 9. Nf3 e6 10. 0–0–0 b5
11. Qe3 Qa5 12. Kb1 After 12. a3 the attack
by Black would still be strong. 12. ... b4
13. Nh4 bxc3 14. Nxf5 Rb8 The point of
Black's 13th move. 15. Nxg7+ Bxg7 16. b3
0–0 17. Qg3 cxb3 18. axb3

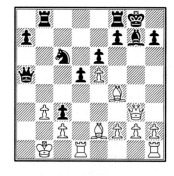

After
18. axb3

White has no time for 18. Bh6 as Qxa2 19. Kc1
Qa1 would be mate! 18. ... Nb4 19. Qxc3
Qa2+ 20. Kc1 Rfc8! Wins a piece by force!

21. Bc4 dxc4 22. Qb2 Qa5 23. Kb1 cxb3
24. c3 Rxc3 25. Qxc3 Qa2+ 26. Kc1 b2+
27. Qxb2 Nd3+ 28. Rxd3 Rxb2 29. Rd8+
Bf8 30. Kd1 Qb1+ 31. Bc1 Qc2+ And mate
next move! 0–1 (*New York Post*, March 3, 1926)

22 Kashdan–Bornholtz [D44]
Manhattan Club Championship, 1925
[Winter]

1. d4 Nf6 2. c4 c6 3. Nc3 d5 4. Nf3
e6 5. Bg5 dxc4 6. a4 Bb4 7. Rc1 Nbd7
8. e3 b5 9. Be2 0–0 10. 0–0 Qa5
11. Ne5 Nxe5 12. dxe5 Bxc3 13. exf6
Bxf6 14. Bxf6 gxf6 15. Qd6 Bb7
16. Qe7 Rab8 17. Qxf6 Qd8 18. Qh6
Qe7 19. axb5 cxb5 20. b3 cxb3 21. Rc7!
Forcing the draw! 21. ... Qd8 22. Rd1 b2
23. Rcd7! ½–½ Contributed by Brennen.
(*En Passant*, January–March 1955)

23 Horowitz–Kashdan [B03]
Manhattan Club Championship, 1926
[Winter]

1. e4 Nf6 2. e5 Nd5 3. c4 Nb6 4. d4
d6 5. exd6 exd6 6. d5 Be7 7. Nc3 0–0
8. Bd3 Re8 9. Nge2 N8d7 10. b3 Nc5
11. Bc2 Bg4 12. 0–0 Bf6 13. f3 Bh5
14. Nd4 a5 15. Qd2 Bg6 16. Bxg6 hxg6
17. Bb2 a4 18. Ncb5 Qd7 19. Qc2 Re3
20. Rad1 axb3 21. axb3 Nxb3 22. Nxb3
Bxb2 23. Nd2 Bf6 24. Ne4 Ra4
25. Nxf6+ gxf6 26. Rd4 Qe7 27. Rh4 f5
28. g3 c6 29. Qb2 Qe5 30. Nd4 Nxc4
31. Qxb7 cxd5 32. Nxf5 gxf5 33. Qc8+
Qe8 34. Qxf5 Re6 35. Qh5 Kg7
36. Qxd5 Ne3 0–1 (*New Yorker Staats-Zeitung*,
March 14, 1926)

24 Kashdan–Sharp [C43]
Manhattan vs. Franklin Match, 1926
[February 22, 1926]

1. e4 e5 2. Nf3 Nf6 3. d4 Nxe4
4. dxe5 d5 5. exd6 Bxd6 6. Bc4 0–0
7. 0–0 Nc6 8. Re1 Bg4! 9. h3 Nxf2
10. Qe2 Nxh3+ 11. gxh3 Nd4 12. hxg4
Nxe2+ 13. Rxe2 Qd7 14. Rg2 Bc5+
15. Kh2 Qd1 16. Nbd2 Rad8 17. Bd3

Rfe8 18. Ne4 Qxf3 19. Nxc5 Re1 20. Nb3
c5 21. Bg5 Rxa1 22. Nxa1 Re8 23. Nb3
Qd5 24. Bf5 g6 25. Bh6 Re1 26. c4 Qd8
27. Kg3 gxf5 28. gxf5 Kh8 29. Rd2 Qf6
30. Bf4 h5 31. Rd5 Qg7+ 0–1 (*The Gambit* 1926)

25 Kashdan–Kupchik [C99]

Rice Progressive Championship, 1926 *[Spring]*

1. e4 e5 2. Nf3 Nc6 3. Bb5 a6 4. Ba4
Nf6 5. 0–0 Be7 6. Re1 b5 7. Bb3 d6
8. c3 Na5 9. Bc2 c5 10. d4 Qc7 11. h3
0–0 12. Nbd2 cxd4 13. cxd4 Nc6 14. d5
Na5 15. Nf1 Bd7 16. a4 Rfc8 17. Ne3
Rab8 18. axb5 axb5 19. Bd2 Ra8
20. Bd3 g6 21. Bb4 Bf8 22. Nd2 Nb7
23. Nb3 Qb6 24. Qd2 Nc5 25. Nxc5
dxc5 26. Bc3 Bd6 27. b3 Nh5 28. Ng4
f6 29. g3 Bf8 30. Kh2 Qd6 31. Rf1 Bg7
32. f4 Rxa1 33. Bxa1 Ra8 34. fxe5 fxe5
35. Nh6+ Bxh6 36. Qxh6 Ra2+ 37. Kg1
Ra8 Here Black had a simple win with 37. ...
Bxa3 38. Bxe5 Rg2+ 39. Kh1 Nxg3+ 40. Bxg3
Rxg3 winning. 38. Qg5 c4 39. Be2 Bxh3
40. Bxh5 Qc5+ 41. Kh1 Bxf1 42. Bxg6
Qf2 43. Bf5+ Kf7 44. Qh5+ Kf8
45. Qh6+ Ke8 46. Qe6+ 1–0 (*Brooklyn
Daily Eagle*, April 22, 1926)

26 Kashdan–Chajes [B72]

Rice Progressive Championship, 1926 *[Spring]*

1. e4 c5 2. Nf3 Nc6 3. d4 cxd4
4. Nxd4 Nf6 5. Nc3 d6 6. Be2 g6 7. Be3
Bg7 8. h3 0–0 9. Qd2 Re8 10. 0–0 Bd7
11. f4 Rc8 12. Rad1 Na5 13. e5 Nh5
14. Bxh5 Nc4 15. Qe2 Nxb2 16. Ne4
Nxd1 17. Qxd1 gxh5 18. Qxh5 Rf8
19. Rf3 Qa5 20. Rg3 f6 21. Rxg7+! Kxg7
22. exf6+ 1–0 (*Brooklyn Daily Eagle*, March
11, 1926)

27 Kashdan–Kupchik [C86]

Chicago International (1), 1926
[August 21, 1926]

1. e4 e5 2. Nf3 Nc6 3. Bb5 a6 4. Ba4
Nf6 5. 0–0 Be7 6. Qe2 b5 7. Bb3 d6
8. a4 Bg4 9. c3 0–0 10. axb5 axb5

11. Rxa8 Qxa8 12. Qxb5 Rb8 13. Qa4
Qh7 14. Bc2 Nd8 15. Qc4 Ne6 16. Qe2
Nf4 17. Qe3 Qc8 18. Nh4 Ne2+ 19. Kh1
Nxc1 20. Rxc1 Rxb2 21. Nf5 Bxf5
22. exf5 Qa6 23. Bd3 Qb7 24. f3 Nd5
25. Qe1 Nf4 26. Bf1 Bg5 27. Rd1 h6
28. Na3 Qc8 29. Nc4 Rb8 30. Rb1 Ra8
31. g3 Nd5 32. Bd3 Ra2 33. Qe4 Nf6
34. Qc6 Qd7 35. Qxd7 Nxd7 36. Rb7
Nc5 37. Bb1 Ra1 38. Rb8+ Kh7 39. h4
Bf6 40. Ne3 Nd7 41. Rb2 Nb6 42. Kg2
d5 43. Bd3 Na4 44. Rc2 c6 45. Ng4
Kg8 46. c4 Nc5 47. Bf1 d4 48. Nf2 Be7
49. Ne4 Nxe4 50. fxe4 Bb4 51. Rb2 c5
52. Be2 Kf8 53. Kf2 Ke7 54. Bd3 Kd6
55. Be2 Ke7 56. Bf1 Kf6 57. Bh3 g6
58. fxg6 fxg6 59. Bg4 Ra3 60. Be2 Ke6
61. Bf1 Kd6 62. Kg2 Ra1 63. d3 Ke7
64. Rf2 h5 65. Be2 Re1 66. Bf1 Ra1
67. Be2 Bd2 68. Bf1 Be1 69. Rf3 Ra2+
70. Kg1 Bd2 71. Be2 Be3+ 72. Kf1 Ra1+
73. Kg2 Rg1+ 74. Kh3 Re1 75. Bf1 Rd1
76. g4 Ke6 77. gxh5 gxh5 78. Rf5 Bf4
79. Be2 Rd2 80. Rf8 (The move order
seems to be incorrect) 80. ... Be3 81. Bf1
Bf4 82. Be2 Bh6 83. Rf2 Bf4 84. Rg2
Kd7 85. Bf1 Rd1 86. Rf2 Rb1 87. Kg2
Rb8 88. Kf3 Kc7 89. Ra2 Rf8 90. Bh3
Kb6 91. Rb2+ Kc7 92. Rb5 Kd6
93. Rb6+ Kc7 94. Rb5 Be3+ 95. Bf5
Kc6 96. Ra5 ½–½ (Contributed by Dale
Brandreth)

28 Torre–Kashdan [A46]

Chicago International (2), 1926 *[August]*

1. d4 Nf6 2. Nf3 c6 3. Bf4 d6 4. h3
Bf5 5. Nbd2 Nbd7 6. e3 h6 7. Bc4 e6
8. Rc1 Be7 9. Qe2 d5 10. Bd3 Ne4
11. Ne5 0–0 12. 0–0 Nxe5 13. Bxe5
Nxd2 14. Qxd2 Bxd3 15. Qxd3 f5 16. f4
Bf6 17. Qe2 Bxe5 18. dxe5 Qe7 19. Kh2
Kh7 20. g4 g6 21. Rg1 Rg8 22. Rg3 Rg7
23. c4 Rf8 24. cxd5 exd5 25. gxf5 gxf5
26. Rxg7+ Qxg7 27. Rg1 Qf7 28. Qe1
Re8 29. Qb4 Qe7 30. Qd4 b6 31. a4
Rd8 32. a5 c5 33. Qd3 Qe6 34. axb6
axb6 35. Qa6 Rg8 36. Qb7+ Kh8
37. Rxg8+ Kxg8 ½–½ (*New York Sun*, September 1, 1926)

29 Kashdan–Maróczy [C00]

Chicago International (3), 1926 *[August]*

1. e4 e6 2. Nc3 d5 3. g3 dxe4 4. Nxe4 Bd7 5. Nf3 Bc6 6. Qe2 Nf6 7. d3 Nbd7 8. Bg2 Be7 9. Bd2 0–0 10. 0–0 Nc5 11. Ne5 Bd5 12. Rae1 Ncxe4 13. dxe4 Bxe4 14. Bxe4 Nxe4 15. Qxe4 Qxd2 16. Qxb7 Bd6 17. Qe4 Bxe5 18. Qxe5 Qxc2 19. Rc1 Qa4 20. a3 c6 21. Rc5 Rfd8 22. Qc3 Rd6 23. b4 Qa6 24. Rc1 Rad8 25. Qb3 Qe2 26. Qc4 Qf3 27. Re1 Rd5 28. Qa6 Rd2 29. Rf1 Ra2 30. Ra5 h5 31. Qxa7 h4 32. Qe7 Rd4 33. Ra8+ Kh7 0–1 (Contributed by Dale Brandreth)

30 Showalter–Kashdan [B05]

Chicago International (4), 1926
[August–September 1926]

1. e4 Nf6 2. e5 Nd5 3. d4 d6 4. Nf3 Bg4 5. Bc4 e6 6. h3 Bh5 7. Qe2 c6 8. 0–0 Nd7 9. exd6 Interesting complications would result after 9. Re1, with which White would sacrifice a pawn. 9. ... Bxd6 10. Bb3 0–0 11. c4 Nf4 12. Bxf4 Bxf4 13. Qe4 Qf6 14. Nc3 Rad8 Black has the better position. The White d pawn is weak and black's bishops are powerful. 15. g3 Bb8 16. Nh4 Nb6 17. d5 The pawn is about to be lost. 17. ... exd5 18. cxd5 Rfe8 19. Qd3 cxd5 20. Rae1 If 20. Nxd5, then ...Nxd5 21. Bxd5 Re5, etc. 20. ... Be5! 21. f4 Bd4+ 22. Kh2 Rxe1 23. Rxe1

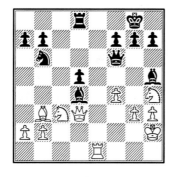

After
23. Rxe1

23. ... g5! Powerfully played! Black wants to keep his bishop and in this he succeeds. 24. Ng2 It would be wrong to capture the pawn, then would follow 24. fxg5 Qf2+ 25. Ng2

Bf3 etc. 24. ... Bg6 25. fxg5 Bxd3 26. gxf6 Bxf6 27. Nf4 Bc4 28. Bc2 Exchanging bishops would not help either. 28. ... d4 29. Ne4 Be7 30. Nd3 Nd5 31. b3 Bb5 32. Nef2 Ne3 Here the knight is in a dominating position and can only be eliminated at the cost of worsening his position. 33. Bb1 Re8 34. Ng4 Nxg4+ 35. hxg4 Bd6 36. Rxe8+ Bxe8 37. Kg2 Bc6+ 38. Kf2 Be4 39. Bc2 Kg7 40. Ne1 White has to do something as the king would simply march to g4. 40. ... Bxc2 41. Nxc2 d3 42. Ne3 Bc5 43. Kf3 Bxe3 44. Kxe3 Kg6 What now follows is simply counting the moves. White could calmly resign here. 45. Kxd3 Kg5 46. Ke3 Kxg4 47. Kf2 f5 48. Kg2 h5 49. Kh2 h4 50. gxh4 Kxh4 51. Kg2 Kg4 0–1 (*Kagans Neueste Schachnachrichten*, 1926)

31 Kashdan–Marshall [D52]

Chicago International (5), 1926 *[August]*

1. d4 d5 2. c4 e6 3. Nc3 Nf6 4. Nf3 Nbd7 5. Bg5 c6 6. e3 Qa5 7. cxd5 Nxd5 8. Qb3 Bb4 9. Rc1 e5 10. Nxe5 Nxe5 11. dxe5 Be6 12. a3 Nxc3 13. Qb4 Qxb4 14. axb4 Na2 15. Rc5 Nxb4 16. e4 a5 17. Be2 h6 18. Be3 b6 19. Rc3 c5 20. f4 g6 21. 0–0 0–0–0 22. Bxc5 bxc5 23. Rxc5+ Kd7 24. f5 gxf5 25. exf5 Bd5 26. Bb5+ Bc6 27. Bxc6+ Nxc6 28. Rd1+ Ke7! The saving move. But not 28. ... Kc7 as after 29. Rfe1 Black would lose the knight. 29. Rxd8 Nxd8 30. Rxa5 Nc6 31. Rb5 Re8 32. Rb7+ Kf8 33. Rb6 Rc8 34. b4 Nxe5 35. h3 Kg7 36. g4 Rc2 37. Rb8 Rb2 0–1 (*New York Sun*, September 4, 1926)

32 Isaacs–Kashdan [C55]

Chicago International (6), 1926 *[August]*

1. e4 e5 2. Nf3 Nc6 3. Bc4 Nf6 4. d4 exd4 5. 0–0 Be7 6. Re1 Nxe4 7. Rxe4 d5 8. Rxe7+ Nxe7 9. Bd3 c5 10. b4 cxb4 11. Nxd4 0–0 12. Bb2 f5 13. Nd2 Nc6 14. N2f3 Bd7 15. Qd2 Qf6 16. Rb1 Qd6 17. Qg5 Qg6 18. Qxg6 hxg6 19. Nxc6 bxc6 20. Ne5 Be8 21. Bd4 a5 22. f4 Rf6 23. h3 Re6 24. g4 fxg4

25. hxg4 Rc8 26. Bc5 Bf7 27. Kf2 g5 28. Bf5 gxf4 29. Nxf7 Kxf7 30. Bxe6+ Kxe6 31. Re1+ Kf6 32. Kf3 Rh8 33. Kxf4 Rh2 34. g5+ Kg6 35. Rc1 Rh4+ 36. Ke5 Rc4 37. Bd4 Kxg5 38. Rg1+ Kh4 39. Rg2 g5 40. Bb6 a4 41. Bd8 Kh3 42. Rd2 g4 43. Bb6 g3 44. Bd4 c5 45. Bg1 d4 46. Kd5 Rc3 47. Re2 Kg4 48. Rd2 Kf3 49. Kd6 Ke4 50. Kc6 a3 51. Kb5 Kd5 52. Re2 d3 53. cxd3 b3 54. axb3 Rxb3+ 55. Ka4 Rb2 56. Re1 a2 57. Ra1 Rb1 58. Rxa2 Rxg1 59. Kb5 Rd1 60. Rc2 Kd4 61. Rxc5 g2 0–1 (Contributed by Dale Brandreth)

33 Kashdan–Edward Lasker [D49]
Chicago International (7), 1926 *[August]*

1. d4 d5 2. c4 e6 3. Nc3 c6 4. e3 Nd7 5. Nf3 Ngf6 6. Bd3 dxc4 7. Bxc4 b5 8. Bd3 a6 9. e4 c5 10. e5 cxd4 11. Nxb5 Nxe5 12. Nxe5 axb5 13. Bxb5+ Bd7 14. Bxd7+ Nxd7 15. Nxd7 Qxd7 16. 0–0 Be7 17. Qg4 0–0 18. Rd1 Rfd8 19. Bf4 Ra5 20. Qg3 f6 21. a3 21. Bc7? would fail to 21. ... Rg5 22. Qf4 e5. 21. ... e5 22. Bd2 Rd5 23. b4 e4 24. Qb3 Kf8 25. Re1 f5 26. a4 Re8 27. Rac1 Bd6 28. b5 Rc5 29. Bb4 Rxc1 30. Rxc1 Qe7 31. Bxd6 Qxd6 32. b6 e3 33. fxe3 dxe3 34. Rc7 Qf6 35. Qa3+ Kg8 36. Qb3+ Kf8 37. Qb4+ Kg8 38. Qc4+ Kf8 39. Qc5+ Kg8 40. Rc8 Qa1+ 41. Qc1 Qxa4 42. b7 e2 43. Rxe8+ Qxe8 44. Kf2 Qe5 45. Qc4+ Kf8 46. Qb4+ Kf7 47. Ke1 Qd5 48. Qb1 Qa5+ 49. Kxe2 Qe5+ 50. Kf1 Qb8 51. Qxf5+ Ke7 52. Qg5+ Kf7 53. Qd5+ Ke7 54. g3 g6 55. Qd4 h5 56. Qg7+ Kd8 57. Qf8+ Kc7 58. Qxb8+ Kxb8 59. Kf2 Kxb7 60. Kf3 h4 61. Kg4 hxg3 62. hxg3 1–0 (Contributed by Dale Brandreth)

34 Jaffe–Kashdan [C83]
Chicago International (8), 1926 *[August]*

1. e4 e5 2. Nf3 Nc6 3. Bb5 a6 4. Ba4 Nf6 5. 0–0 Nxe4 6. d4 b5 7. Bb3 d5 8. dxe5 Be6 9. c3 Be7 10. Qe2 Nc5 11. Bc2 d4 12. Rd1 Bc4 13. Qe1 d3

14. Na3 Qc8 15. Bb1 Qg4 16. h3 Qg6 17. Nxc4 bxc4 18. b4 Ne4 19. a4 a5 20. b5 Bc5 21. Ra2 Ne7 22. Nd4 Nd5 23. Bd2 0–0 24. f3 Nxd2 25. Qxd2 Qb6 26. Kh1 Bxd4 27. cxd4 Qxd4 28. Re1 c3 29. Qxd3 Qxd3 30. Bxd3 Nb4 31. Bc4 Nxa2 32. Bxa2 Rfd8 33. e6 fxe6 34. Rxe6 Kf8 35. Rc6 Rd1+ 36. Kh2 Ra1 37. Bb3 Ra3 38. Bc2 Rd8 39. Rxc7 Rd2 40. Be4 Raa2 41. Kg3 Rxg2+ 42. Kf4 Rxa4 43. b6 Rb4 44. b7 Rgb2 45. Rxc3 Rxb7 46. Bxb7 Rxb7 47. Rc8+ Kf7 48. Ra8 Rb4+ 49. Kg3 Rb5 50. Ra7+ Kg6 51. h4 h6 52. Ra8 Kh5 53. Ra7 g5 54. hxg5 Kxg5 55. Rg7+ Kf6 56. Ra7 h5 57. Kh4 Rf5 58. Kg3 Ke6 59. Ra6+ Kd7 60. f4 Kc7 61. Kf3 Kb7 62. Rh6 Rc5 63. Ke4 Kc7 ½–½ (Contributed by Dale Brandreth)

35 Kashdan–Factor [C73]
Chicago International (10), 1926 *[August]*

1. e4 e5 2. Nf3 Nc6 3. Bb5 a6 4. Ba4 Nf6 5. 0–0 d6 6. Bxc6+ bxc6 7. d4 exd4 8. Nxd4 Bd7 9. Qf3 c5 10. Nf5 Bxf5 11. Qxf5 Qd7 12. Qf3 Qg4 13. Qd3 Be7 14. Nc3 0–0 15. Bd2 Rfe8 16. Rae1 Nd7 17. f4 Nb6 18. e5 dxe5 19. Rxe5 Rad8?? 20. Rxe7 1–0 (Contributed by Dale Brandreth)

36 Fink–Kashdan [B18]
Chicago International (11), 1926 *[August]*

1. e4 c6 2. d4 d5 3. Nc3 dxe4 4. Nxe4 Bf5 5. Ng3 Bg6 6. Nf3 Nf6 7. Be2 e6 8. 0–0 Nbd7 9. c3 Bd6 10. Nd2 Qc7 11. Nc4 Bf4 12. Bxf4 Qxf4 13. Qb3 0–0–0 14. a4 h5 15. Rfe1 h4 16. Nf1 Ne4 17. f3 Ng3 18. Na5 Nxe2+ 19. Rxe2 Qc7 20. Nc4 Rh5 21. Nfe3 e5 22. a5 e4 23. fxe4 Bxe4 24. Qb4 c5 25. dxc5 Nxc5 26. Na3 Bd3 27. Qg4+ Ne6 28. Qxh5 Nf4 29. Qxh4 Bxe2 30. Nac2 Qe5 31. Qf2 Rh8 32. Ra4 Nd3 33. Qg3 Qxg3 34. hxg3 Nxb2 35. Rf4 f6 36. Nd4 Bd3 37. Ndf5 Bxf5 38. Nxf5 Rd8 39. Nxg7 Rd3 40. Nh5 Rxc3 41. Rxf6 Rc5 42. g4 Rxa5 43. Rf8+ Kd7 44. Rf7+

Kc6 45. Rg7 Nc4 46. g5 Ne5 47. Nf4 b5
48. g6 b4 49. Re7 Nxg6 50. Re6+ Kc7
51. Rxg6 b3 52. Nd3 Ra2 53. Rf6 Rd2
54. Rf7+ Kc8 55. Rxa7 Rxd3 56. Ra1
b2 57. Rb1 Rd2 58. Kh2 Kd7 59. Kg3
Kd6 60. Kf3 Kc5 61. g4 Kd4 62. g5
½–½ (Contributed by Dale Brandreth)

37 Kashdan–Chajes [A54]
Chicago International (12), 1926
[September 1, 1926]

1. Nf3 Nf6 2. c4 d6 3. Nc3 e5 4. d4 e4
5. Nd2 Qe7 6. Qc2 Bf5 7. f3 Nc6 8. fxe4
Bg6 9. e3 0–0–0 10. a3 d5 11. cxd5
Nxd5 12. Nxd5 Rxd5 13. Bd3 Rh5
14. Nf3 Qd8 15. Bd2 Bd6 16. 0–0–0
Re8 17. Bc3 Be7 18. g4 Rh3 19. Qg2
Rxf3 20. Qxf3 f6 21. h4 h6 22. g5 fxg5
23. d5 Nb8 24. h5 Bh7 25. Bxg7 Nd7
26. e5 Bxd3 27. Rxd3 Nc5 28. Rc3 Kb8
29. Rd1 Na4 30. Rc2 Qd7 31. d6 cxd6
32. Qf7 Rc8 33. exd6 Rxc2+ 34. Kxc2
Qc6+ 35. Kb1 Bd8 36. Rc1 Nc5 37. Qf5
b6 38. b4 Qb5 39. Ka2 Qd7 40. Rxc5
1–0 (Contributed by Dale Brandreth)

38 Banks–Kashdan [A46]
Chicago International (13), 1926
[September 2, 1926]

1. d4 Nf6 2. Nf3 c6 3. Bg5 e6 In con-
sideration came 3. ... Ne4 followed by Qb6.
4. Nbd2 d5 5. e3 Nbd7 6. Bd3 Qb6 The
Black queen attacks very little and White defends the attacked pawn with the rook. Best was
here 6. ... c5 or castling. 7. Rb1 Be7 8. 0–0
0–0 9. Ne5 Re8 10. Ndf3 More aggressive
would have been 10. f4. 10. ... Nf8 11. c3
N6d7 12. Bxe7 Rxe7 13. Nxd7 Bxd7
14. Qc2 f6 15. Nh4 c5 16. f4 Be8
17. Qf2 Ng6 18. g4 Nxh4 19. Qxh4 Bg6
20. Bxg6 hxg6 21. Rf3 Ree8 22. Rh3
Kf7 23. f5! Energetically played. 23. ... Rh8
24. fxg6+ Kxg6 25. Qg3 To capture the
rook would have been bad, as the Black queen
with so many pawns on the board could have
been better used against the mobile rooks.
25. ... cxd4 26. exd4 e5?

After
26. ... e5

Simple and safer would have been 26. ... Rxh3
27. Qxh3 Kf7, etc. The text gives White chances
to give the game a neat if not quite correct winning combination. The onlookers really enjoy
these kind of games as opposed to positionally
attractive games. 27. Rxh8 Rxh8 28. g5
Rh5 29. gxf6+ Rg5 30. Qxg5+!? This
sacrifice was not considered by his opponent.
Therefore it is no wonder that he did not find
the best continuation. 30. ... Kxg5 31. f7
Qd8? This loses! Correct was 31. ... Qg6! 32. Rf1
(a little better is 32. f8(Q) Qxb1+ 33. Kg2+
34. Kg1, etc. with drawing chances. Kh4+ 33. Kh1
Qe4+ 34. Kg1 Kh3! 35. Kf2 exd 36. cxd Qd4+
etc. and Black also wins either the b or h pawn
and has enough time, the queen to get to f8.
The Black passed pawns would then decide. An
instructive position. 32. Rf1 Qf8 33. dxe5
a5 34. e6 Kg6 35. Rf2 b5 36. a3 b4
37. axb4 axb4 38. e7 Short and decisive!
38. ... Qxf7 39. Rxf7 Kxf7 40. cxb4
Kxe7 41. Kf2 Kd6 42. Ke3 Kc6 43. Kd4
g5 44. h3 Kb5 45. Kxd5 Kxb4 46. Ke5
1–0 (*Kagans Neueste Schachnachrichten*, 1926)

39 Kashdan–Kupchik [D93]
Rice Progressive Memorial, 1926 *[Winter]*

1. d4 Nf6 2. c4 g6 3. Nc3 Bg7 4. Nf3
d5 5. Bf4 c6 6. e3 0–0 7. h3 Nbd7
8. cxd5 Nxd5 9. Nxd5 cxd5 10. Bd3
Qa5+ 11. Qd2 Qxd2+ 12. Kxd2 f5
13. Bc7 Nb8 14. Rac1 Nc6 15. Rc5 e6
16. a3 Bd7 17. Rhc1 Rfc8 18. Bd6 Bf8
19. Bxf8 Kxf8 20. Bb5 Ke7 21. Ne1 Kd6
22. Nd3 a6 23. Ba4 b6 24. R5c3 Na5
25. Rxc8 Bxc8 26. f4 Bd7 27. Bd1
Nc4+ 28. Ke2 a5 ½–½ (*New York Sun*, December 24, 1926)

40 Chajes–Kashdan [C83]
Rice Progressive Memorial, 1926 *[Winter]*

1. e4 e5 2. Nf3 Nc6 3. Bb5 a6 4. Ba4
Nf6 5. 0-0 Nxe4 6. d4 b5 7. Bb3 d5
8. dxe5 Be7 9. c3 Be6 10. Nbd2 0-0
11. Bc2 Nc5 12. Nb3 Nxb3 13. axb3 f5
14. Nd4 Nxd4 15. Qxd4 c5 16. Qd3 Qc7
17. Qg3 Kh8 18. Rd1 d4 19. Bf4 a5
20. Racl dxc3 21. bxc3 Rfd8 22. h4
Rxd1+ 23. Rxd1 Rd8 24. Ra1 b4 25. h5
bxc3 26. Qxc3 Rd4 27. Be3 Rb4 28. h6
g6 29. g3 Kg8 30. Rc1 c4 31. Bd3 Bc5
32. Bxc4 Bxc4 33. bxc4 Bxe3 34. Qxe3
a4 35. e6 Rb3 36. Qg5 Rb2 37. Rd1 Rb8
38. Rd7 Qa5 39. Qf6 1-0 (*Brooklyn Daily
Eagle*, December 30, 1926)

41 Kashdan–Jaffe [C24]
Rice Progressive Memorial, 1926 *[Winter]*

1. e4 e5 2. Bc4 Nf6 3. d4 exd4 4. Nf3
Nxe4 5. Qxd4 Nf6 6. Nc3 Nc6 7. Qh4
Be7 8. Bg5 d5 9. 0-0-0 Be6 10. Nxd5
Bxd5 11. Bxd5 Nxd5 12. c4 Bxg5+
13. Nxg5 h6 14. Rhe1+ Kf8 15. Rxd5
Qf6 16. Re3 Ne7 17. Rf3 Nxd5 18. Rxf6
Nxf6 19. Ne4 Ne8 20. Nc5 b6 21. Nd7+
Kg8 22. Qe7 Nd6 23. Ne5 Rc8 24. f3
a5 25. h4 Kh7 26. Nxf7 Rhe8 27. Qd7
Nxf7 28. Qxf7 c6 29. a4 Re1+ 30. Kc2
Rd8 31. g4 Re2+ 32. Kb1 Rdd2 33. Qf5+
Kg8 34. Qc8+ Kh7 35. Qf5+ ½-½ (*Brooklyn Daily Eagle*, December 30, 1926)

42 Jaffe–Kashdan [A46]
Rice Progressive Memorial, 1926 *[Winter]*

1. d4 Nf6 2. Nf3 c6 3. e3 d5 4. Bd3
Bg4 5. h3 Bh5 6. c4 e6 7. Nbd2 Nbd7
8. Qb3 Qc7 9. 0-0 Bd6 10. c5 Be7
11. Qc3 a5 12. b3 b6 13. cxb6 Qxb6
14. Bb2 0-0 15. Rfc1 Rfc8 16. g4 Bg6
17. Bxg6 hxg6 18. Qd3 c5 19. Rc2 cxd4
20. exd4 Rc7 21. Rxc7 Qxc7 22. Rc1 Qf4
23. Ne5 Nxe5 24. dxe5 Nd7 25. Qd4
Qh6 26. Rc7 Bc5 27. Qd3 Qf4 28. Nf3
Qg3+ 29. Kh1 Qxh3+ 30. Kg1 Qg3+
31. Kh1 Bxf2 32. Qe2 Nc5 33. Rxc5
Bxc5 34. Nd4 Rc8 35. Qd1 Qxe5

36. Kg2 Qe4+ 37. Kh3 Bxd4 38. Bxd4
Rc2 39. Be5 Qe3+ 40. Bg3 Qh6+
41. Bh4 Rc3+ 0-1 (*Brooklyn Daily Eagle*, December 23, 1926)

43 Kashdan–Chajes [C43]
Rice Progressive Memorial, 1926 *[Winter]*

1. e4 e5 2. Nf3 Nf6 3. d4 Nxe4 4. Bd3
d5 5. Nxe5 Nd7 6. 0-0 Nxe5 7. dxe5
Nc5 8. Nc3 c6 9. f4 g6 10. Ne2 Nxd3
11. Qxd3 Bf5 12. Qc3 Qb6+ 13. Be3 Qb4
14. Qxb4 Bxb4 15. Rac1 Be7 16. Rfd1 b5
17. c3 Bd7 18. a4 a6 19. a5 0-0 20. b4
Rfe8 21. Kf2 Rac8 22. Bc5 Bxc5+
23. bxc5 Bg4 24. Rd2 Bxe2 25. Rxe2
Rb8 26. Rb1 h5 27. Ke3 f6 28. Kd4 Kf7
29. g3 Rb7 30. h3 Rbe7 ½-½ (*Brooklyn
Daily Eagle*, January 6, 1927)

44 Kupchik–Kashdan [B03]
Rice Progressive Memorial, 1926 *[Winter]*

1. e4 Nf6 2. e5 Nd5 3. d4 d6 4. exd6
cxd6 Here is 4. ... exd6 or 4. ... Qxd6 more
common. **5. Bd3** As Black has served notice
that he plans to fianchetto the king's bishop,
this does not promise much. **5. ... Nc6 6. c3
g6 7. Nf3 Bg7 8. 0-0 0-0 9. Re1 Kh8**
Here 9. ... Bg4 would have come to naught, as
h3 forces Black to exchange or retreat. **10. Bc4
Nb6 11. Bb3 Bf5 12. Bg5 h6 13. Bh4 d5
14. Nbd2 Qd7 15. Nf1 Rfe8 16. Ne3 Be4
17. Nd2 Bd3 18. Nf3 Be4 19. Nd2 Bd3
20. Ndf1 Ba6 21. Qf3 e6** Creating a hole at
f6, but it was difficult to find a good continuation. **22. Ng4 Qc7 23. Qh3 h5** White
threatened 24. Nxh6, followed by Bg5. **24. Nf6
Rf8 25. Ne3 Qf4 26. g3 Qh6 27. f4**
White threatens 28. Bg5 winning the queen.
**27. ... Bxf6 28. Bxf6+ Kg8 29. Rad1 Na5
30. Ng4!** (*see diagram*)
The knight that White could have exchanged
at move 20, now becomes most annoying, while
Black's queen's bishop, for which it might have
been exchanged, is now hopelessly out of play.
**30. ... Qh7 31. Ne5 Nxb3 32. axb3 Bb5
33. g4 Nd7 34. Nxd7 Bxd7 35. Re5 Rfc8**
Black wriggles, but cannot escape. If 35. ... hxg4
then 36. Qxg4 followed by Rd3 and Rh3.

After
30. Ng4

36. gxh5 Kf8 37. Rd2 Bb5 38. Rg2 gxh5 39. Kh1! Neatly destroying Black's last hope. If 30. Rxh4? Qb1+ would draw by perpetual check. Now the rook can interpose. 39. ... Ke8 40. Rxe6+! fxe6 41. Qxe6+ Kf8 42. Rg8+ Qxg8 43. Qe7 mate 1–0 (*The Chess Amateur*, April 1928)

45 Smirka–Kashdan [D43]
Manhattan Junior Masters, 1927 *[Winter]*

1. d4 Nf6 2. Nf3 c6 3. c4 d5 4. Nc3 e6 5. Bg5 h6 6. Bxf6 Qxf6 7. e3 Nd7 8. Bd3 Bd6 9. 0–0 Qe7 10. cxd5 cxd5 11. e4 dxe4 12. Nxe4 0–0 13. Rc1 Bf4 14. Rc3 b6 15. g3 Bb8 16. Bb1 Bb7 17. Qc2 f5 18. Ned2 Bd6 19. Nh4 Qf6 20. Qa4 Rfd8 21. Bd3 a6 22. Bc4 g5 23. Re1 Nf8 24. Rce3 Re8 25. Rxe6 Rxe6 26. Rxe6 Nxe6 27. Qd7 gxh4 28. Bxe6+ Kh8 29. Qxb7 Re8 30. d5 hxg3 31. hxg3 Bxg3 32. fxg3 Qd4+ 33. Kf1 Qxd2 34. Qf7 Qc1+ 35. Kg2 Qxb2+ 36. Kh3 Ra8 37. Qxf5 Qg7 38. d6 Rf8 39. Qd5 Qf6 40. d7 Kg7 41. Kg4 b5 42. Kh3 a5 43. Bf5! Rb8 44. Bd3 b4 45. Qxa5 Rb6 46. Qd5 Rd6 47. Qe4 Rd4 48. Qh7+ Kf8 49. Bc4! Rxc4! 50. Qh8+! Qxh8 51. d8Q+ Kg7 52. Qe7+ Kg6 53. Qe6+ Qf6 54. Qxc4 An especially fine endgame where Kashdan had to call on all his defensive resources. ½–½ (*Brooklyn Daily Eagle*, January 20, 1927)

46 Tholfsen–Kashdan [D48]
Manhattan Junior Masters, 1927 *[Winter]*

1. d4 Nf6 2. Nf3 d5 3. c4 c6 4. Nc3 e6 5. e3 Nbd7 6. Bd3 dxc4 7. Bxc4 b5

8. Bd3 a6 9. Qe2 c5 10. 0–0 Bb7 11. Rd1 Qb6 12. a4 c4 13. Bb1 b4 14. Na2 Rc8 15. e4 Be7 16. Bg5 0–0 17. d5 exd5 18. e5 Qe6 19. Bf4 Nh5 20. Bg5 Bc5 21. Nd4 Bxd4 22. Bxh7+ Kxh7 23. Qxh5+ Kg8 24. Rxd4 f6 25. exf6 Nxf6 26. Qg6 Rce8 27. f3 a5 28. Rad1 Nd7 29. Qh5 Qf7 30. Qh4 Re2 31. Nc1 Rxb2 32. Rg4 Ne5 33. Rg3 d4 34. Qxd4 Rxg2+ 35. Kxg2 Nxf3 36. Qe3 Ne1+ White resigns, for if 37. Kh3 Qh5+ 38. Bh4 Bc8+ etc. Or if 37. Kg1 then Qf1 mate! 0–1 (*Brooklyn Daily Eagle*, February 17, 1927)

47 Bornholz–Kashdan [C49]
Manhattan Club Championship, 1927

1. e4 e5 2. Nf3 Nc6 3. Nc3 Nf6 4. Bb5 Bb4 5. 0–0 0–0 6. d3 d6 7. Bg5 Bxc3 8. bxc3 Qe7 9. Re1 Nd8 10. d4 Ne6 11. Bc1 c6 12. Bf1 Qc7 13. g3 Re8 14. Bg2 Nf8 15. Qd3 c5 16. d5 Bd7 17. Nh4 Ng6 18. Nxg6 fxg6 19. c4 h6 20. Bd2 b5 21. h3 b4 22. f4 exf4 23. gxf4 Nh5 24. e5 Bf5 25. Be4 Bxe4 26. Rxe4 dxe5 27. d6 Qc6 28. Rxe5 Red8 29. Be3 Rxd6 30. Rd5 Rxd5 31. cxd5 Qd6 32. Qc4 Rc8 33. Rd1 Qe7 34. Bf2 Qf6 35. Bxc5 Nxf4 36. Qxb4 Qg5+ 37. Kf2 Qg2+ 38. Ke3 Re8+ 39. Kxf4 g5+ 40. Kf5 Qf3+ 0–1 (*Brooklyn Daily Eagle*, January 27, 1927)

48 Kashdan–Tenner [C99]
Manhattan Club Championship, 1927

1. e4 e5 2. Nf3 Nc6 3. Bb5 a6 4. Ba4 Nf6 5. 0–0 Be7 6. Re1 b5 7. Bb3 d6 8. c3 Na5 9. Bc2 c5 10. d4 Qc7 11. Nbd2 0–0 12. h3 cxd4 13. cxd4 Nc6 14. d5 Nb4 15. Bb1 a5 16. a4 bxa4 17. Rxa4 Ba6 18. Ra3 Rfc8 19. Nf1 Nd7 20. Ne3 Nc5 21. Nf5 Bf8 22. Nh2 Bb5 23. Ng4 f6 24. Rg3 Kh8 25. Bh6 Be8 26. Nxf6 Bg6 27. Bg5 gxf6 28. Bxf6+ Kg8 29. Nh4 Kf7 30. Qe2 Ke8 31. Nxg6 hxg6 32. Rxg6 Qf7 33. Qg4 Ncd3 34. Bh4 Rc7 35. Rf6 Qh7 36. Bxd3 Nxd3 37. Re3 Nf4 38. g3 Rg7 39. Qf5 Qxf5 40. Rxf5 Ng6 41. Bg5 Rh7 42. Kg2 Rb8 43. Rf6

Nh8 44. Re6+ Kf7 45. Ra3 Rb5 46. b3 Kg8 47. Re8 Ra7 48. Be3 Ra6 49. Bh6 Ng6 50. Bxf8 Nxf8 51. b4 Kf7 52. Rc8 Nd7 53. Rc6 Ra7 54. Rxd6 Rxb4 55. Re6 Nc5 56. Rf3+ Kg7 57. Rxe5 Nxe4 58. Re3 Nd6 59. Re6 Rd7 60. Re7+ Rxe7 61. Rxe7+ Kf8 62. Rd7 Nb7 63. Rc7 a4 64. Rc8+ Ke7 65. Ra8 Nc5 66. h4 Rb6 67. Ra5 Kd6 68. h5 Kxd5 69. g4 Kc4 70. g5 Kb4 71. Ra8 Ne6 72. g6 Nf4+ 73. Kg3 Nxh5+ 74. Kh4 Ng7 75. Kg5 Rb5+ 76. Kh6 Nf5+ 77. Kh7 Rb7+ 78. Kh8 a3 0–1 (*Brooklyn Daily Eagle*, March 17, 1927)

49 Kupchik–Kashdan [D13]
Manhattan Club Championship, 1927

1. Nf3 Nf6 2. d4 d5 3. c4 c6 4. cxd5 cxd5 5. Nc3 Nc6 6. g3 e6 7. Bg2 Bd6 8. 0–0 0–0 9. a3 a6 10. Qc2 Na5 11. Nd2 Qc7 12. e4 dxe4 13. Ndxe4 Nxe4 14. Bxe4 h6 15. b4 Nc6 16. Rd1 Bd7 17. Bb2 Rac8 18. Rac1 Ne7 19. Qe2 Bc6 20. d5 exd5 21. Nxd5 Nxd5 22. Bxd5 Rfe8 23. Qg4! Be5 24. Bxc6 bxc6 25. Rd7 Qb8 26. Bxe5 Qxe5 27. Qf3 Re7 28. Rxe7 Qxe7 29. Rxc6 Rxc6 30. Qxc6 Qe2 31. Kg2 g6 32. a4 h5 33. b5 axb5 34. axb5 h4 35. b6 Kg7 36. b7 hxg3 37. hxg3 Qe5 38. g4 Qf4 39. Kf1 Qe5 40. Qc8 On 40. ... Qb5+ 41. Kg1 Qb1+ 42. Kh2 White wins. 1–0 (*Brooklyn Daily Eagle*, April 7, 1927)

50 Kashdan–Pinkus [D45]
Manhattan Club Championship, 1927

1. d4 d5 2. c4 e6 3. Nf3 c6 4. Nc3 Nd7 5. e3 Ngf6 6. Qc2 Be7 7. cxd5 exd5 8. Bd3 0–0 9. 0–0 Bd6 10. Bd2 Re8 11. Rae1 Nf8 12. e4 dxe4 13. Nxe4 Nxe4 14. Bxe4 Be6 15. Ng5 h6 16. Bh7+ Kh8 17. Rxe6 hxg5 18. Rxe8 Qxe8 19. Bf5 Qd8 20. Qb3 Qf6 21. Qh3+ Kg8 22. Qg4 Bf4 23. Bc3 Re8 24. g3 Bc7 25. d5 Be5 26. dxc6 Bxc3 27. c7 Ne6 28. Bxe6 fxe6 29. Rc1 Bd4 30. c8Q Qxf2+ 31. Kh1 Rxc8 32. Rxc8+ Kf7 33. Qh5+ Ke7 34. Qe8+ Kd6 35. Qd8+ Ke5 36. Qxg5+ Ke4

37. Qf4+ Qxf4 38. gxf4 Bxb2 39. Rc4+ Kf5 40. Kg2 1–0 (*Brooklyn Daily Eagle*, April 7, 1927)

51 H. Steiner–Kashdan [A48]
Manhattan Club Championship, 1927

1. d4 Nf6 2. Nf3 g6 3. Bf4 Bg7 4. h3 0–0 5. Nbd2 c5 6. dxc5 Na6 7. Be3 Nd5 8. Bd4 Bxd4 9. Nxd4 Nxc5 10. e4 Nf6 11. Bd3 e5 12. N4f3 Qc7 13. 0–0 d5 14. Qe2 Bd7 15. Rfe1 Rae8 16. Rad1 Bc6 17. exd5 Nxd5 18. Bb5 Nf4 19. Qf1 Bxb5 20. Qxb5 e4 21. Nh2 Re5 22. Ng4 Rg5 23. Qc4 Nxh3+ 24. gxh3 h5 25. Nxe4 Qf4 26. Qd4 Nxe4 27. Rxe4 Qf3 28. Re3 Qc6 29. f4 1–0 (Contributed by Larry Parr)

52 Kevitz–Kashdan [D85]
Manhattan Club Championship, 1927

1. c4 Nf6 2. Nc3 d5 3. cxd5 Nxd5 4. d4 g6 5. e4 Nxc3 6. bxc3 c5 7. dxc5 Qxd1+ 8. Kxd1 Bd7 9. Bc4 Bc6 10. f3 Nd7 11. Be3 e6 12. Nh3 Bxc5 13. Ke2 Rc8 14. Rab1 Bxe3 15. Kxe3 Bxe4 16. fxe4 Rxc4 17. Rxb7 Rxc3+ 18. Ke2 Rc2+ 19. Ke3 Nb6 20. Kd3 Rc6 21. Rxa7 0–0 22. Rf1 Rd8+ 23. Ke3 Nc4+ 24. Kf4 h6 25. Rc1 Rd3 26. Nf2 g5+ 27. Kg4 Ne5+ 28. Kh5 Rxc1 29. Nxd3 Nxd3 30. Kxh6 Rc8 31. Kxg5 Kg7 32. h4 Rc2 33. g3 Nc5 34. h5 Nxe4+ 35. Kf4 Rc4 36. Ra5 Ng5+! If now 37. Kxg5 then f6 is mate. 37. Ke3 Rc3+ 38. Kf4 Kf6 39. Ra6 Rc4+ 40. Ke3 Rg4 41. Kf2 Kf5 42. Ra7 Ne4+ 43. Ke1 f6 44. h6 Rxg3 0–1 (*New Yorker Staats-Zeitung*, September 4, 1930)

53 Berman–Kashdan [A32]
Manhattan Club Championship, 1927

1. d4 Nf6 2. Nf3 c5 3. c4 e6 4. g3 cxd4 5. Nxd4 Bb4+ 6. Bd2 Qb6 7. Bxb4 Qxb4+ 8. Nc3 Qxb2 9. Ncb5 Na6 10. Bg2 0–0 11. Nd6 Nc5 12. 0–0 Qb6 13. Nb3 Ne8 14. Nxc8 Rxc8 15. Nxc5 Qxc5 16. Qxd7 Rc7 17. Qa4 b6 18. Rfd1 Qxc4 19. Qxc4 Rxc4 20. Rd7 Ra4 21. f4 g6 22. h3 Nf6 23. Rc7 Rd8 24. Kf2 Rd2 25. a3 h5 26. Ke3 Rb2 27. Rc3 b5

28. Bc6 Nd5+ 29. Bxd5 exd5 30. Rd1
Rc4 31. Rcd3 Re4+ 32. Kf3 Rbxe2 0–1
(*New Yorker Staats-Zeitung*, September 4, 1927)

54 Kashdan (Manhattan)– Santasiere (Progressive) [A12]
Metropolitan Chess League, 1927

1. Nf3 Nf6 2. c4 c6 3. g3 d5 4. b3 Bf5
5. Bg2 h6 6. 0–0 e6 7. Bb2 Nbd7 8. d4
Bd6 9. Nbd2 Qc7 10. Nh4 Bh7 11. cxd5
exd5 12. Bh3 0–0 13. Nf5 Rfe8 14. Nxd6
Qxd6 15. Nf3 Nf8 16. Ne5 Ne6 17. Rc1
Ng5 18. Bg2 Bf5 19. h3 Re7 20. Qd2
Rae8 21. Qa5 b6 22. Qa3 Qxa3 23. Bxa3
c5 24. f4 Nxh3+ 25. Kh1 Ne4 26. Bf3 f6
27. Nd3 Nd2 28. Bxd5+ Kh7 29. Bg2
Nxf1 30. Bxf1 Rxe2 31. Bxh3 Bxh3 0–1
(*Brooklyn Daily Eagle*, April 7, 1927)

55 Kashdan–Berman [C49]
Junior Masters Tournament, 1927 *[August]*

1. e4 e5 2. Nf3 Nc6 3. Nc3 Nf6 4. Bb5
Bb4 5. 0–0 0–0 6. d3 d6 7. Bg5 Bxc3
8. bxc3 Qe7 9. Re1 Nd8 10. d4 Ne6?
11. Bc1 Rd8 12. Bf1 c5 13. Nh4 Qc7 14. d5
Nf4 15. g3 Nh3+ 16. Kg2 h6 17. Nf5 Ng5
18. f3 Bxf5 19. exf5 e4? 20. fxe4 Ngxe4
21. c4 Re8 22. Bb2 Qa5 23. Bd3 Qb4
24. Rb1 Nc3 25. Bxc3 Qxc3 26. Rxe8+
Rxe8 27. Rxb7 Re1 28. Qf3 h5 29. Qf4
Re5 30. Rb8+ Kh7 31. Qg5 Qe1 32. Kh3
Re3 33. Kh4 Qf2 34. Qg6+! A pretty conclusion. If 34. ... fxg6 then 35. fxg6 + Kh6
36. Rh8 mate! **1–0** (*Brooklyn Daily Eagle*, August 18, 1927)

56 Kashdan–Pinkus [C47]
Junior Masters Tournament, round 4, 1927
[August]

1. e4 e5 2. Nf3 Nc6 3. d4 exd4
4. Nxd4 Nf6 5. Nc3 Bb4 6. Nxc6 bxc6
7. Bd3 d5 8. exd5 cxd5 9. 0–0 0–0
10. Bg5 c6 11. Qf3 Be7 12. Rae1 h6
13. Bc1 Bd6 14. h3 Rb8 15. Ne2 c5 16. c3
Bb7 17. Ng3 d4 18. Ne4 Nxe4 19. Bxe4
Ba6 20. Bd3 c4 21. Be4 Qa5 22. cxd4
c3 23. bxc3 Bxf1 24. Kxf1 f5 25. Bd5+

Kh7 26. Bb3 Rbc8 27. c4 Rce8 28. Rd1
Bb8 29. c5 Qc7 30. g3 Qe7 31. Kg2 f4
32. g4 Qh4 33. d5 Qf6 34. d6 a5 35. c6
Ba7 36. c7 Re2! A neat idea, so if 37. Qxe2
then f6+ wins the queen for the rook. 37. c8Q
Rxc8 38. Qxe2 Rc3 39. Qe4+ This is how
the game is described in BDE: Kashdan at the
critical juncture sacrificed the exchange. This
enabled him to establish strong pawns in the
center, which forced their way through to victory. **1–0** (*Brooklyn Daily Eagle*, August 25, 1927)

57 Berman–Kashdan [B04]
Junior Masters Tournament, 1927 *[August]*

1. e4 Nf6 2. e5 Nd5 3. d4 d6 4. Nf3
Nc6 5. Bb5 a6 6. Bxc6+ bxc6 7. c4 Nb6
8. Qe2 Bf5 9. Nc3 e6 10. 0–0 Be7
11. Rd1 0–0 12. Nd2? This move loses a
pawn. Better was either Be3 or b3. 12. ... dxe5
13. Nb3 If 13. Qxe5 then Bf6 wins the d pawn.
13. ... exd4 14. Nxd4 Qe8 15. Bf4 Rc8
16. b3 Bg6 17. Ne4 c5 18. Nf3 f6 19. Nc3
e5 20. Be3 Bd6 21. a4? e4 If 21. Nh4 Qe5
wins the knight at c3, because of the mate
threat. And if Nd2 also loses to Qe5 because of
the mate threat and the unprotected knight at
c3. Hence White resigns. **0–1** (*New York Post*,
September 7, 1927)

58 Winter–Kashdan [D51]
Cable Match, London vs. New York, 1927
[November 5]

1. d4 Nf6 2. c4 e6 3. Nc3 d5 4. Bg5
Nbd7 5. e3 c6 6. Bd3 Qa5 7. Bh4 Bb4
8. Nge2 dxc4 9. Bxc4 Qh5 10. Bg3 Ne4
11. Qb3 Nxg3 12. Nxg3 Qa5 13. 0–0 0–0–0
14. f4 Nb6 15. Be2 Nd5 16. Nce4 f5
17. Ng5 Bd2 18. Rf3 c5 19. Bc4 cxd4
20. Bxd5 exd5 21. exd4 h6 22. Nh3 b6
23. Nf1 Bb4 24. Nf2 Be6 Creditably played
by both sides, Black remains with two bishops,
but after Nd3 and Ne4, White obtains some
compensation in position. **½–½** (*American Chess
Bulletin*, November 1927)

59 Kashdan–Horowitz [C41]
Manhattan Club Championship, 1928
[January]

1. e4 e5 2. Nf3 d6 3. d4 Nf6 4. Nc3 Nbd7 5. Bc4 Be7 6. 0–0 c6 7. a4 0–0 8. Qe2 Qc7 9. h3 h6 10. Ba2 exd4 11. Nxd4 Re8 12. Qf3 Ne5 13. Qg3 Nh5 14. Qh2 d5! 15. Be3 Bd6 16. f4 Ng6 17. e5 Nxe5!! 18. Ncb5 cxb5 19. Nxb5 Qe7 20. Nxd6 Nd7! 21. Nf5 Qe4 22. Rae1 Qxf5 23. g4 Qg6 24. f5 Qc6 25. gxh5 Nf6 26. Qg2 Kh7 27. Bb3 b6 28. Kh2 Bb7 29. Qf3 Nxh5! 30. Qxh5 d4 31. Qg4 dxe3 32. f6 g6 33. Rf4 Rad8 34. Bxf7 Rd2+ 35. Re2 Rxe2+ 36. Qxe2 Qh1+ One of Horowitz's earliest brilliancies. 0–1 (*Brooklyn Daily Eagle*, January 12, 1928)

60 H. Steiner–Kashdan [E11]
Manhattan Club Championship, 1928
[January]

1. d4 Nf6 2. Nf3 e6 3. c4 Bb4+ 4. Bd2 Qe7 5. a3 Bxd2+ 6. Nbxd2 d6 7. e4 e5 8. d5 0–0 9. Be2 Nh5 10. g3 Bh3 11. Nf1 Nf6 12. Qc2 Nbd7 13. Ne3 Nc5 14. b4 Ncxe4 15. Ng1 Qd7 16. Nxh3 Qxh3 17. Bf1 Qh5 18. Be2 Qh6 19. 0–0 g6 20. Kg2 c6 21. Bd3 cxd5 22. Nxd5 Nxd5 23. Bxe4 Ne7 24. Bxb7 Rab8 25. Bf3 Nf5 26. Bd5 Nd4 27. Qd3 Kh8 28. Rae1 Qg7 29. f4 f5 30. Rd1 a5 31. b5 a4 32. fxe5 dxe5 33. Rfe1 Nb3 34. Qc3 e4 35. Qxg7+ Kxg7 36. Bc6 Rfd8 37. Rxd8 Rxd8 38. Bd5 Rd6 39. Kf2 Kf6 40. Ke3 Ke5 41. h4 h6 42. Rh1 Nd4 43. Rb1 Rb6 44. Kf2 g5 45. Rb4 e3+ 46. Kxe3 Nc2+ 47. Kd2 Nxb4 48. axb4 gxh4 49. gxh4 Rxb5! 0–1 (*Brooklyn Daily Eagle*, February 2, 1928)

61 Kashdan–Pinkus [D65]
Manhattan Club Championship, 1928
[February]

1. d4 d5 2. Nf3 Nf6 3. c4 e6 4. Nc3 Nbd7 5. Bg5 c6 6. e3 Be7 7. Rc1 0–0 8. Qc2 a6 9. cxd5 exd5 10. Bd3 Re8 11. 0–0 Nf8 12. a3 Ng6 13. Ne5 Ng4 14. Bxe7 Qxe7 15. Nxg6 hxg6 16. h3 Nf6 17. Na4 Ne4 18. Bxe4 dxe4 19. Qc5 Qf6 20. Qb6 g5 21. Qc7 Qd8 22. Qxd8 Rxd8 23. Rc5 f6 24. Rfc1 Be6 25. Nc3 f5

26. Na4 Rd5 27. Rxd5 Bxd5 28. Nc5 Rb8 29. Kf1 Kf7 30. Ke2 Re8 31. f3 If 31. Nxb7 Rb8 32. Nd6+ Kf6 regains the pawn. 31. ... Re7 32. fxe4 Bxe4 33. Nxe4 Rxe4 34. Kf3 Kf6 35. Rc5 Re6 36. b4 g6 37. a4 Rd6 38. b5 axb5 39. axb5 Rd5 40. Rxd5 cxd5 41. Kg3 Kg7 42. Kf3 Kh6 43. g3 ½–½ (*Brooklyn Daily Eagle*, February 9, 1928)

62 Horowitz–Kashdan [C01]
Manhattan Club Championship, 1928
[February]

1. e4 e6 2. d4 d5 3. exd5 exd5 4. Bd3 Nf6 5. Nf3 Bd6 6. 0–0 0–0 7. Bg5 Bg4 8. Nc3 c6 9. Qd2 Bxf3 10. gxf3 Nbd7 11. Kh1 Qc7 12. Rg1 Kh8 13. Bxf6 Nxf6 14. Qg5 Rg8 15. Qh4 Be7 16. Rg5 Rae8 17. Re5 Bd6 18. Rf5 Qd8? 19. Rxf6 g6 Of course not 19. ... Qxf6? 20. Qxh7 mate. 20. Rf4 Bxf4 21. Qxf4 Re6 22. Qxf7 Rf6 23. Qxb7 Rg7 24. Qa6 Qb8 25. Re1 Qxb2 26. Nxd5 Rxf3 27. Qxc6 Rxf2 28. Nf6 Rg8 29. Qe6 Rf8 30. Ng4 1–0 (*Brooklyn Daily Eagle*, February 16, 1928)

63 Pinkus–Kashdan [A50]
Manhattan Club Championship, 1928
[March]

1. d4 Nf6 2. c4 e6 3. Nc3 b6? 4. e4 Bb7 5. f3 Bb4 6. Bd3 Nc6 7. a3 Bxc3+ 8. bxc3 e5 9. Be3 Qe7 10. Ne2 0–0 11. 0–0 d6 12. Ng3 Bc8 13. Qe2 Na5 14. Rad1 c5 15. f4 Ng4 16. fxe5 Qh4 17. h3 Qxg3 18. Bf4 Qh4 19. hxg4 dxe5 20. Bxe5 cxd4 21. cxd4 Bxg4 22. Qe3 Rac8 23. Bd6 Rfd8 24. c5 bxc5 25. Bxc5 Rc6 26. Qf4 Qh5 27. Rb1 Rh6 28. Rb8 Nc6 29. Rxd8+ Nxd8 30. Be7 Nc6 31. Bg5 Re6 32. d5 Re8 33. dxc6 h6 34. Bc4 Be6 35. Bxe6 fxe6 36. Be7! If 36. ... Rxe7? then 37. Qf8+. 1–0 (*Brooklyn Daily Eagle*, April 12, 1928)

64 Kashdan (Manhattan)– Schmid (Empire) [A85]
Metropolitan Chess League, 1928

1. d4 e6 2. c4 f5 3. Nc3 Nf6 4. Nf3

Bb4 5. Qb3 c5 6. Bd2 Nc6 7. a3 Bxc3
8. Bxc3 cxd4 9. Nxd4 0−0 10. g3 Ne4
11. Bg2 Nxd4 12. Bxd4 Qa5+ 13. Qb4
Qc7 14. 0−0 b6 15. a4 Bb7 16. a5 bxa5
17. Rxa5 Bc6 18. Rfa1 Rfb8 19. Qa3 a6
20. Rxa6 Bb7 21. Ra4 e5 22. Ba7 Rf8
23. Qd3 d6 24. Be3 Qc6 25. Ra7 From
this point on the score is incorrect. White won
on the 31st move. **1−0** (*New Yorker Staats-Zeitung*, April 1, 1928)

65 Kashdan (Manhattan)−
Tholfsen (Marshall) [C86]

Metropolitan Chess League, 1928 *[Board 4]*

1. e4 e5 2. Nf3 Nc6 3. Bb5 a6 4. Ba4
Nf6 5. 0−0 Be7 6. Qe2 d6 7. c3 b5
8. Bb3 Bg4 9. h3 Bxf3 10. Qxf3 0−0
11. d3 Na5 12. Bc2 c5 13. Nd2 Nc6
14. Re1 Qc7 15. Nf1 Nd8 16. Ne3 g6
17. Ng4 Ne8 18. Bh6 Ng7 19. Nf6+ Bxf6
20. Qxf6 Nde6 21. a4 Qd8 22. Qxd8
Rfxd8 23. axb5 axb5 24. Bb3 Nc7 25. f4
exf4 26. Bg5 Rxa1 27. Rxa1 Ra8
28. Rxa8+ Nxa8 29. Bxf4 Ne8 30. e5
dxe5 31. Bxe5 Kf8 32. Kf2 Ke7 33. Ke3
f6 34. Bh2 Nb6 35. g4 Nd6 36. Bg8 h5
37. gxh5 gxh5 38. b3 Nf5+ 39. Ke4 Ng7
40. Bc7 Nd7 41. Kd5 Ne8 42. Bf4 f5
43. Kc6 Ndf6 44. Bd5 **1−0** (*New Yorker
Staats-Zeitung*, April 8, 1928)

66 Klein (Rice)−Kashdan
(Manhattan) [D48]

Metropolitan Chess League, 1928 *[Board 1]*

1. d4 c6 2. c4 d5 3. Nc3 Nf6 4. e3 e6
5. Nf3 Nbd7 6. Bd3 dxc4 7. Bxc4 b5
8. Bd3 a6 9. 0−0 c5 10. b3 Bb7 11. Bb2
Be7 12. Rc1 0−0 13. Qe2 Qb6 14. Rfd1
cxd4 15. exd4 Rfd8 16. Ne5 Nf8 17. Ne4
Ng6 18. Nxg6 hxg6 19. Nc5 Bd5 20. Bb1
Rac8 21. b4 Bc4 22. Bd3 Bxd3 23. Rxd3
Nd5 24. Qd2 Nxb4 25. Qxb4 Bxc5
26. dxc5 Rxd3 27. h3 Qd8 28. Qe1 Qd5
29. Qb4 Rd1+ 30. Rxd1 Qxd1+ 31. Kh2
Qd5 32. Qc3 f6 33. Ba3 Qe5+ 34. Qxe5
fxe5 35. Bb4 a5 36. Bxa5 Rxc5 And
White won. **1−0** (*New Yorker Staats-Zeitung*,
April 15, 1928)

67 Honlinger (Austria)−
Kashdan [D52]

Hague Olympiad, round 1, 1928 *[July 23]*

1. d4 Nf6 2. c4 e6 3. Nc3 d5 4. Bg5
Nbd7 5. e3 c6 6. Nf3 Qa5 7. Nd2 Bb4
8. Qc2 e5 9. dxe5 Ne4 10. Ndxe4 dxe4
11. e6 fxe6 12. Bh4 Nc5 13. 0−0−0 0−0
14. Nxe4 Qxa2 15. Nxc5 Qa1+ 16. Qb1
Qxb1+ 17. Kxb1 Bxc5 18. Be2 e5 19. h3
Bf5+ 20. Ka1 a5 21. Bg4 a4 22. Bxf5
Rxf5 23. Rd7 Rf7 24. Rhd1 Raf8 25. Kb1
h6 26. Kc2 Rxd7 27. Rxd7 Rf7 28. Rd8+
Rf8 29. Kd3 Rxd8+ 30. Bxd8 Kf7
31. Bc7 Ke6 32. Ke4 Bd6 33. Bb6 Bb4
34. f4 Bc3! 35. f5+ Kf7 36. Kd3 Bxb2
37. Kc2 Ba3 38. e4 h5 39. g4 hxg4
40. hxg4 Be7 41. Be3 b5 42. c5 Bh4
43. Kb2 Be1 44. Ka3 Bc3 45. Bc1 Kf6
46. g5+ Kf7 47. Ka2 b4 48. g6+ Kf6
49. Kb1 Bd4 50. Bd2 Bxc5 51. Be1 Ke7
White was threatening Bh4 mate! 52. Bh4+
Ke8 53. Be1 b3 54. Kb2 Bd4+ 55. Ka3
c5 **0−1** (*Cleveland Sunday News*,1928)

68 Kashdan−E. Steiner
(Hungary) [B29]

Hague Olympiad, round 2, 1928 *[July 23]*

1. e4 c5 2. Nf3 Nf6 3. Nc3 d5 4. exd5
Nxd5 5. d4 Nxc3 6. bxc3 e6 7. Bd3 Nd7
8. 0−0 Be7 9. Qe2 Nf6 10. Bb5+ Bd7
11. Ne5 0−0 12. dxc5 Bxb5 13. Qxb5 Qc7
14. Nd3 Ne4 15. Rb1 Nxc3 16. Qxb7
Rfc8 17. Qxc7 Rxc7 18. Rb2 Bxc5
19. Nxc5 Rxc5 20. Be3 Rc7 21. g3 a5
22. a3 Na4 23. Ra2 Nc3 24. Rb2 Na4
25. Ra2 f6 26. Kg2 Rb8 27. Bd2 Rb5
28. Re1 Kf7 29. Re3 e5 30. Rd3 Ke6
31. Kf1 Nc5 32. Rc3 Rd7 33. Be3 Ne4
34. Rb3 Rbd5 35. c4 Rd1+ 36. Kg2 a4
37. Rb4 Nc3 38. Rc2 R1d3 39. Rb6+
Kf7 40. Ra6 Nd1 41. Bb6 Rxa3 42. c5
Rc3 43. Rxc3 Nxc3 44. c6 Re7 45. Bd8
Nb5 46. Bxe7 Kxe7 47. Rxa4 Kd6
48. Rc4 Kc7 49. Kf3 f5 50. Ke3 Nd6
51. Rc5 Nf7 52. f4 exf4+ 53. Kxf4 g6
54. Rc2 h6 55. h4 h5 56. Re2 Nd8
57. Kg5 Nxc6 58. Kxg6 Nd4 59. Rd2
Nf3 60. Rf2 **1−0** (*The Hague* 1928)

69 Kashdan–Naegeli (Switzerland) [B83]

Hague Olympiad, round 3, 1928 *[July 24]*

1. e4 c5 2. Nf3 Nc6 3. d4 cxd4
4. Nxd4 Nf6 5. Nc3 d6 6. Be2 e6 7. 0-0
Be7 8. Be3 a6 9. f3 Qc7 10. a4 0-0
11. Nb3 b6 12. Qe1 Bb7 13. Qg3 Kh8
14. Rad1 Ne5 15. f4 Nc4 16. Bxc4 Qxc4
17. e5 dxe5 18. fxe5 Nd5 19. Rd4 Qc7
20. Nxd5 Bxd5 21. Rc1 b5 22. axb5 axb5
23. Rg4 Rg8 24. Nd4 b4 25. Nb5 Qb7
26. Nd6 Bxd6 27. exd6 f6 28. Bc5 b3
29. cxb3 Qxb3 30. Qxb3 Bxb3 31. Bb6
e5 32. Rg3 Be6 33. Rd3 Ra6 34. Bc7
Bd7 35. b4 Rga8 36. Ba5 Kg8 37. Rc7
Rd8 38. Rb7 Bc6 39. Bxd8 Bxb7
40. Ba5 Bc6 41. d7 In round four Kashdan
did not play. **1–0** (*The Hague*, 1928)

70 Kashdan–Blumich (Germany) [B09]

Hague Olympiad, round 5, 1928 *[July 25]*

1. e4 d6 2. d4 Nf6 3. Nc3 g6 4. f4 Bg7
5. Nf3 0-0 6. Bc4 c5 7. dxc5 Qa5
8. Qe2 Nxe4 9. Qxe4 Bxc3+ 10. Kf2
Bg7 11. cxd6 exd6 12. Ng5 Bd7 13. Qd5
Qxd5 14. Bxd5 Nc6 15. c3 h6 16. Ne4
Be6 17. Rd1 Bd4+ 18. cxd4 For if now
...Bxd5 then 19. Nf6+ regains the piece and
White is a piece up. The United States had the
bye in round 6. **1–0** (*The Hague*, 1928)

71 Kashdan–Taube (Latvia) [B18]

Hague Olympiad, round 7, 1928 *[July 27]*

1. e4 c6 2. d4 d5 3. Nc3 dxe4 4. Nxe4
Bf5 The advantage of the Caro Kann over the
French Defense or other chess openings is that
this bishop can easily be developed. On the
other hand, Black has no good way to challenge
the center with either ...e5 or ...c5, and White
maintains the freer game. Instead of the text
...Nf6 is playable, and leads to interesting games.
5. Ng3 Bg6 6. Nf3 Nd7 To prevent Ne5.
7. Bd3 e6 8. 0-0 Bd6 9. Qe2 Re1 might
have been more accurate to avoid the loss of a
move on the exchange of bishops. But I was play-

ing for the eventual f4, when the rook would
be needed on f1. 9. ... Ne7 9. ... Nf6 10. Nf5
forces the exchange of bishop for knight. But
9. ... Bxd3 10. Qxd3 Nf6 was preferable, and
then Black might continue with ...Qc7 and
...0-0-0. 10. Ng5! Making it difficult for Black
to castle, for if now 10. ... 0-0 11. Nxe6! fxe6
12. Qxe6+ wins. 10. ... Nf6 11. N3e4 Ned5
12. f4 0-0 The threat was 13. Nxd6 Qxd6
14. f5. But 12. ... Be7 should have been played
as a defensive measure. 13. Nxd6 Qxd6
14. Bxg6 hxg6 15. Bd2 Now the White
knight is splendidly placed, and White is ready
to prepare for a direct attack on the kingside.
15. ... Rad8 16. Rad1 The center must be
securely held before any advance. 16. ...
Qc7 17. c4 Ne7 17. ... Nb6 18. Bc3 Nfd7,
would have offered more security against the
coming threat on h7 by defending the other
knight. 18. Bc3 Rd7 19. Qe3 Qb6 20. Qh3
Nf5

After
20. ... Nf5

Believing he would force White to retreat to
defend the d pawn. But White's reply comes as
a forceful surprise. 21. c5 Qb5 22. d5! Now
there is no good answer to the threat of Bxf6.
22. ... Qxc5+ 23. Kh1 Nh5 Losing a piece,
but 23. ... Nh6 24. Bxf6 gxf6 25. Ne4! wins. Or
23. ... Rfd8 24. Bxf6 gxf6 25. Qh7+ 26. Kf8
dxe6! and Black is lost. 24. g4 Rxd5 25. gxh5
gxh5 26. Qxh5 Nh6 27. Bxg7! By far the
strongest continuation, as it at once disrupts
the whole king position. 27. ... Kxg7 If 27. ...
Rxd1 28. Rxd1 Kxg7 29. Nxe6+ wins the queen.
28. Rg1 There is no defense to all the threats of
discovered check. **1–0** Annotations by Kashdan. (*Chess Review*, April 1936)

72 Makarczyk (Poland)–Kashdan [D36]

Hague Olympiad, round 8, 1928 *[July 27]*

1. d4 Nf6 2. c4 e6 3. Nc3 d5 4. Bg5 Nbd7 5. e3 c6 6. cxd5 exd5 7. Bd3 Be7 8. Qc2 0–0 9. Nge2 Re8 10. Ng3 Nf8 11. Nf5 Bxf5 12. Bxf5 Ne4 13. Bxe7 Qxe7 14. 0–0 Ng6 15. Nxe4 dxe4 16. g3 Rad8 17. Qa4 Nh4 18. gxh4 Qxh4 19. f4 Rd5 20. Qxa7 Rxf5 21. Qxb7 Rf6 22. Rae1 g5 23. fxg5 Qxg5+ 24. Kh1 Kh8 25. Qc7 Rg6 26. Rg1 Qf5 27. Rxg6 hxg6 28. Qg3 Kg7 29. Qg2 Rh8 30. Rf1 Qe6 31. b3 Rh3 32. Qe2 g5 33. Rg1 Qf5 34. Qg4 Qxg4 35. Rxg4 Rxe3 36. Rxg5+ Kf6 37. Rc5 Re2 38. a4 Rd2 39. a5 e3 40. Re5 Rd3 41. Kg2 Rxb3 42. Kf3 Ra3 43. h4 Kg7 44. Rg5+ Kh7 45. Rc5 Rd3 46. a6 Rxd4 47. Ra5 Rd8 48. a7 Ra8 49. Kxe3 c5 50. Ke4 Kg6 51. Kd5 Kh5 52. Kxc5 Kxh4 53. Kb6 Kg4 54. Kb7 Rxa7+ 55. Rxa7 f5 56. Kc6 1–0 (*Brooklyn Daily Eagle*, August 16, 1928)

73 Kashdan–Dunkelblum (Belgium) [C28]

Hague Olympiad, round 9, 1928 *[July 29]*

1. e4 e5 2. Nc3 Nf6 3. Bc4 Nc6 4. d3 Na5 5. f4 Nxc4 6. dxc4 Bb4 7. fxe5 Nxe4 8. Qd4 Nxc3 9. bxc3 Be7 10. Ne2 0–0 11. 0–0 d6 12. Bf4 dxe5 13. Bxe5 f6 14. Bg3 c6 15. c5 Qd5 16. Bf2 Rd8 17. Nf4 Qf7 18. Qe4 Re8 19. Rfe1 Bd7 20. Qa4 b5 21. Qb3 Bf8 22. Rxe8 Rxe8 23. Rd1 Bg4 24. Rd2 Re4 25. Rd4 Re5 26. Qxf7+ Kxf7 27. Nd3 Rg5 28. Be3 Rg6 29. Rd8 Bf5 30. Ra8 Rg4 31. Rxa7+ Kg8 32. Ra8 Ra4 33. Rxa4 bxa4 34. Kf2 Kf7 35. Ke2 g5 36. Kd2 Be4 37. g3 Be7 38. Nb2 a3 39. Nc4 Ke6 40. Nxa3 Kd5 41. c4+ Ke6 42. Nb1 Kd7 43. Nc3 Bf3 44. Kd3 f5 45. Bd4 Bh5 46. Na4 Be8 47. Be5 Kc8 48. Kd4 Kb7 49. Nb2 Bh5 50. Nd3 Bd8 51. Nb4 Bd1 52. Bg7 Ba5 53. c3 Bxb4 54. cxb4 f4 55. gxf4 gxf4 56. Bh6 f3 57. Be3 Bc2 58. Kc3 Ba4 59. b5 Bd1 60. Kb4 Bc2 61. a4 Bd1 62. a5 1–0 (*Cleveland News*, 1928)

74 Stoltz (Sweden)–Kashdan [C47]

Hague Olympiad, round 10, 1928 *[July 30]*

1. e4 e5 2. Nf3 Nc6 3. d4 exd4 4. Nxd4 Nf6 5. Nc3 Bb4 6. Nxc6 bxc6 7. Bd3 d5 8. exd5 cxd5 9. 0–0 0–0 10. Bg5 c6 11. Qf3 Be7 12. Rae1 Rb8 13. Ne2 Ne4 14. Bxe7 Qxe7 15. Nd4 Rxb2 16. Nxc6 Qc5 17. Bxe4 dxe4 18. Qxe4 Ba6 19. Re3 Qxc2 20. Qxc2 Rxc2 21. Nb4 Bxf1 22. Nxc2 Bc4 23. Ra3 Rb8 24. h3 Rb7 25. Rc3 Be6 26. Nd4 Bd7 27. Rb3 Rxb3 28. axb3 From here on this is a famous endgame Kf8 29. Kf1 Ke7 30. Ke2 Kd6 31. Kd3 Kd5 32. h4 To avoid losing a pawn Bc8! 33. Nf3 Ba6+ 34. Kc3 h6 35. Nd4 g6 36. Nc2 Ke4 37. Ne3 f5 38. Kd2 f4 39. Ng4 h5 40. Nf6+ Kf5 41. Nd7 Bc8 42. Nf8 g5 43. g3 43. hxg5, Kxg5 loses the knight gxh4 44. gxh4 Kg4 45. Ng6 Bf5 46. Ne7 Be6 47. b4 Kxh4 48. Kd3 Kg4 49. Ke4 h4 50. Nc6 Bf5+ 51. Kd5 f3! Otherwise Ne5+ followed by Nf3, now the pawn queens by force 52. b5 h3 53. Nxa7 h2 54. b6 h1Q 55. Nc6 Qb1 56. Kc5 Be4 0–1 (Kashdan's scoresheet)

75 Pokorný (Czechoslovakia)– Kashdan [E16]

Hague Olympiad, round 11, 1928 *[July 30]*

1. d4 Nf6 2. Nf3 e6 3. c4 b6 4. g3 Bb7 5. Bg2 Bb4+ 6. Bd2 Qe7 7. 0–0 Bxd2 8. Qxd2 0–0 9. Nc3 d6 10. Rfe1 Ne4 11. Qc2 Nxc3 12. Ng5 Qxg5 13. Bxb7 Nd7 14. Bxa8 Nxe2+ 15. Rxe2 Rxa8 16. Qe4 Rf8 17. f4 Qd8 18. b4 Nf6 19. Qd3 c6 20. a4 Qd7 21. b5 a5 22. bxa6 Qa7 23. a5 Qxa6 24. Rea2 Rb8 25. axb6 Qxb6 26. Ra8 g6 27. Rb1 Qxb1+ 28. Qxb1 Rxa8 29. Qb7 Ra1+ 30. Kg2 Ng4 31. Qb8+ Kg7 32. Qb2 Ra6 33. Kf3 Nf6 34. d5 cxd5 35. cxd5 e5 36. fxe5 dxe5 37. Qxe5 Ra5 38. g4 Rxd5 39. Qc3 g5 40. h3 h6 41. Qb2 ½–½ (Kashdan's scoresheet)

76 Reca (Argentina)–Kashdan [B18]

Hague Olympiad, round 12, 1928 *[July 31]*

1. e4 c6 2. d4 d5 3. Nc3 dxe4 4. Nxe4 Bf5 5. Ng3 Bg6 6. f4 e6 7. Nf3 Nd7 8. Bd3 Bd6 9. 0–0 Qc7 10. Ne5 Ne7 11. c3 0–0 12. Kh1 Rad8 13. Nxg6 hxg6 14. Qf3 Nf6 15. Ne4 Nxe4 16. Bxe4 b6 17. Be3 Nd5 18. Bg1 Rc8 19. g3 Nf6 20. Bd3 c5 21. Ba6 Rcd8 22. a4 cxd4 23. Bxd4 e5 24. fxe5 Bxe5 25. Bxe5 Qxe5 26. Rfe1 Qg5 27. Rad1 Rxd1 28. Rxd1 Re8 29. Bf1 Qg4 30. Qxg4 Nxg4 31. Kg1 Re4 32. Bb5 Ne5 33. Kf2 a6 34. Bxa6 Rxa4 35. Be2 Ra8 36. Rd5 f6 37. Rb5 Rb8 38. c4 Rc8 39. Rxb6 Nxc4 40. Rb7 Ne5 41. b4 Rc3 42. b5 Rb3 43. b6 Kh7 44. h4 g5 45. hxg5 Kg6 46. gxf6 Kxf6 47. Ba6 Nc6 48. Be2 Na5 49. Ra7 Nc6 50. Rf7+ Kg6 51. Rd7 Rxb6 52. Rd6+ Kg5 53. g4 g6 54. Re6 Kh6 55. Bd3 Kg7 56. Rxg6+ Kf7 57. Rd6 Rb2+ 58. Kg3 Ne5 59. Bf5 Rb7 60. g5 Re7 61. Kh4 Kg7 62. Kh5 Re8 63. g6 Re7 64. Kg5 Nc4 65. Rd4 Ne5 66. Be4 Nd7 67. Kf5 Nf8 68. Rd6 Rc7 69. Kg5 ½–½ (Kashdan's scoresheet)

77 Kashdan–Nardo (Italy) [C42]

Hague Olympiad, round 13, 1928 *[July 31]*

1. e4 e5 2. Nf3 Nf6 3. Nxe5 d6 4. Nf3 Nxe4 5. d4 d5 6. Bd3 Bg4 7. 0–0 Bd6 8. c4 f5 9. c5 Be7 10. Qb3 Bxf3 11. gxf3 Bg5 12. f4 Bh4 13. Qxb7 Bxf2+ 14. Rxf2 Nxf2 15. Kxf2 Qh4+ 16. Ke2 Qxh2+ 17. Kd1 Qh1+ 18. Kc2 Qg2+ 19. Bd2 0–0 20. Qxa8 h5 21. Nc3 c6 22. Ne2 1–0 (*The Hague*, 1928)

78 Weenink (Holland)–Kashdan [C47]

Hague Olympiad, round 14, 1928 *[August 1]*

1. e4 e5 2. Nf3 Nc6 3. Nc3 Nf6 4. d4 exd4 5. Nxd4 Bb4 6. Nxc6 bxc6 7. Bd3 d5 8. exd5 Qe7+ 9. Qe2 Qxe2+ 10. Bxe2 Ne4 11. Bd2 Nxd2 12. Kxd2 cxd5 13. a3 Bxc3+ 14. Kxc3 Ke7 15. Bf3 Be6 16. Rad1

Kd6 17. Kd2 c6 18. Kc1 Kc7 19. Rd2 a5 20. Re1 Rab8 21. Re5 Kd6 22. Re3 Rb6 23. c3 Rhb8 24. Re1 Ke7 25. Re3 Kf6 26. Ree2 g5 27. g3 Rb3 28. g4 Rd8 29. Re1 c5 30. Bd1 Rb6 31. Rh1 d4 32. h4 h6 33. hxg5+ hxg5 34. Bc2 Rbd6 35. cxd4 cxd4 36. Rh6+ Ke7 37. Bd1 Rc8+ 38. Rc2 Rxc2+ 39. Bxc2 d3 40. Bd1 d2+ 41. Kc2 Bb3+ 42. Kxb3 Rxh6 0–1 (*The Hague*, 1928)

79 Kashdan–Brody (Rumania) [B15]

Hague Olympiad, round 15, 1928 *[August 3]*

1. e4 c6 2. d4 d5 3. Nc3 dxe4 4. Nxe4 Nf6 5. Ng3 e5 6. Nf3 exd4 7. Nxd4 c5 8. Qe2+ Qe7 9. Qxe7+ Bxe7 10. Ndf5 Bxf5 11. Nxf5 g6 12. Nxe7 Kxe7 13. Bc4 Nbd7 14. 0–0 h6 15. Bf4 Kf8 16. Rfe1 Kg7 17. Re7 Rhf8 18. Be6 Rae8 19. Rxd7 Rxe6 20. Rxb7 Re2 21. Rc1 Nd5 22. Bd6 Rfe8 23. g3 Nb4 24. Bxc5 Nxc2 25. Bxa7 g5 26. h3 h5 27. Rc7 Ne1 28. g4 hxg4 29. hxg4 Kg6 30. Rb7 R2e4 31. Kf1 Nf3 32. Kg2 Ne5 33. f3 Re2+ 34. Kg3 Rh8 35. Bg1 Rd8 36. Rf1 Nd3 37. Bf2 Rh8 38. Rb6+ f6 39. f4! Nxf4 40. Rxf6+ Kg7 41. Rxf4 gxf4+ 42. Kf3 Rd2 43. Be1 Rh3+ 44. Kxf4 Rd5 45. Bc3+ Kg6 46. Re1 Rd6 47. Re7 Rhd3 48. Rg7+ Kh6 49. g5+ Kh5 50. Rh7+ 1–0 (*Revista de Sah*, 1928) In round 17 Kashdan played Marín of Spain and won in 35 moves. It was a Queen's Pawn Opening. That game is not available.

80 Norman-Hansen (Denmark)– Kashdan [C77]

Hague Olympiad, round 16, 1928 *[August 3]*

1. e4 e5 2. Nf3 Nc6 3. Bb5 a6 4. Ba4 Nf6 5. Nc3 d6 6. d4 Bd7 7. d5 Ne7 8. Bxd7+ Qxd7 9. 0–0 h6 10. Qd3 g5 11. Ne2 Nh5 12. c4 Nf4 13. Bxf4 gxf4 14. Nh4 Rg8 15. Kh1 Qg4 16. g3 Bg7 17. Rg1 0–0–0 18. Rab1 fxg3 19. fxg3 f5 20. Nxf5 Nxf5 21. exf5 Rdf8 22. Rgf1 e4 23. Qe3 Rxf5 24. Nf4 Be5 25. Qxe4 h5 26. Rf3 h4 27. Rbf1 Rff8 28. Qe1

Bxb2 29. h3 Qd7 30. g4 Be5 31. Ne6
Rxf3 32. Rxf3 Qa4 33. Qe2 Kb8 34. Rb3
Qa5 35. g5 Bg3 36. Rf3 Qb6 37. Kg2
Qb1 38. Rf7 Be5 39. Rf1 Qh7 40. Kh1
Qg6 41. a4 c6 42. Rd1 cxd5 43. cxd5
Qf5 44. Qd3 Qf2 45. Rd2 Qe1+ 46. Kg2
Rc8 47. Re2 Qc1 48. Qf5 a5 49. Qf1 Qa3
50. Qf3 Rc3 51. Qf8+ Ka7 52. Qf2+ Ka6
53. Rc2 Rxc2 54. Qxc2 Qg3+ 55. Kf1
Qxh3+ 56. Qg2 Qd3+ 57. Qe2 Qxe2+
58. Kxe2 b5 59. Nc7+ Kb6 60. Nxb5
Kc5 61. Kf3 h3 62. g6 Kxd5 63. Nc7+
Kc4 64. Ne6 d5 65. g7 Bxg7 66. Nxg7
d4 67. Nf5 d3 68. Kg3 Kb3 69. Kxh3
Kxa4 70. Kg3 d2 71. Ne3 Kb3 72. Kf3
Kb2 73. Ke2 Kc1 74. Nd1 a4 75. Nc3
Kc2 0–1 (Kashdan's scoresheet)

81 Kashdan–Tenner [C97]
Manhattan Club Championship, 1929

1. e4 e5 2. Nf3 Nc6 3. Bb5 a6 4. Ba4
Nf6 5. 0–0 Be7 6. Re1 b5 7. Bb3 d6
8. c3 Na5 9. Bc2 c5 10. d4 Qc7 11. h3
0–0 12. d5 Nb7 13. Nbd2 Nd8 14. a4
b4 15. Nc4 Ne8 16. a5 bxc3 17. bxc3 f6
18. Nfd2 g6 19. Nb6 Rb8 20. Ndc4 Nf7
21. Nxc8 Rxc8 22. Nb6 Rd8 23. Qe2
Qa7 24. Rb1 Nc7 25. Ba4 Rb8 26. Bc6
Nd8 27. Bh6 Rf7 28. Bd7 Nb7 29. Bg4
Nxa5 30. Nc8 Rxc8 31. Bxc8 Bf8
32. Bxf8 Rxf8 33. Qa2 Rxc8 34. Qxa5
Rb8 35. c4 Kf7 36. Qa4 Ke7 37. Rb3 f5
38. f4? Rb4 39. Rxb4 cxb4+ 40. Kf1 Qc5
41. Qc2 fxe4 42. Qxe4 Kd8 43. fxe5
dxe5 44. Qxe5 Qxc4+ 45. Kg1 Qc5+
46. Kh1 Kc8 47. Rd1 Kb7 48. Qe4 Qd6
49. Rc1 Nb5 50. Rc6 Nc3 51. Qc4 Qd7
52. Qxa6+ Kb8 53. Rb6+ 1–0 (*New York
Sun*, December 21, 1928)

82 Kline–Kashdan [C77]
Manhattan Club Championship, 1929

1. e4 e5 2. Nf3 Nc6 3. Bb5 a6 4. Ba4
Nf6 5. Nc3 d6 6. Bxc6+ bxc6 7. d4 exd4
8. Nxd4 Bd7 9. 0–0 Be7 10. Bf4 0–0
11. Qd3 Qb8 12. b3 Qb4 13. Rad1 Rfe8
14. Nde2 Bf8 15. f3 a5 16. Bd2 Qb6+
17. Kh1 Bc8 18. Na4 Qa6 19. Bg5 Nd7

20. c4 Nb6 21. Nxb6 Qxb6 22. Nc3 Qc5
23. Be3 Qh5 24. Ne2 f5 25. Ng3 fxe4
26. fxe4 Qg6 27. Nf5 d5 28. exd5 cxd5
29. cxd5 Ba6 30. Qc3 Bxf1 31. Rxf1 Bd6
32. Bd4 Re4 33. g3 Rf8 34. Nxd6 Rxf1+
35. Kg2 Rff4 36. Nxe4 Qxe4+ 0–1
(*Brooklyn Daily Eagle*, December 27, 1929)

83 Kashdan–Fishman [B01]
Manhattan Club Championship, 1929

1. e4 d5 2. exd5 Qxd5 3. Nc3 Qd8
4. d4 Nf6 5. Bc4 g6 6. Nf3 Bg7 7. Bg5
a6 8. Qe2 0–0 9. 0–0–0 b5 10. Bb3
Bb7 11. Rhe1 Re8 12. Ne5 e6 13. d5 Qe7
14. dxe6 fxe6 15. Ng4 Kf7 16. Rd4 c5
17. Rf4 Nbd7 18. Rd1 c4 19. Rxd7 Qxd7
20. Ne5+ Kg8 21. Nxd7 Nxd7 22. Bxc4
bxc4 23. Rxc4 Nf8 24. Ne4 Bxe4
25. Qxe4 h6 26. Be7 Rab8 27. Bxf8
Bxb2+ 28. Kd1 1–0 (*New York Sun*, January
4, 1929)

84 Kupchik–Kashdan [D43]
Manhattan Club Championship, 1929

1. d4 Nf6 2. Nf3 e6 3. c4 d5 4. Bg5
h6 5. Bxf6 Qxf6 6. Nc3 c6 7. e3 Nd7
8. Bd3 Bb4 9. Qb3 Bxc3+ 10. Qxc3
dxc4 11. Bxc4 c5 12. Rd1 0–0 13. 0–0
cxd4 14. Rxd4 Nb6 15. Rfd1 Nxc4
16. Rxc4 b6 17. Qxf6 gxf6 18. Rc7 e5
19. Kf1 Be6 20. a3 Rfc8 21. Rdc1 Rxc7
22. Rxc7 Rc8 23. Rxc8+ Bxc8 24. Ke2
Kf8 25. e4 Ke7 26. Nh4 Kd6 27. Kd2
Kc5 28. Kc3 a5 29. b3 h5 30. f3 Bd7
31. h3 Bc8 32. g4 hxg4 33. fxg4 Bb7
34. Kd3 Ba6+ 35. Kc3 Bf1 36. Nf5 Bxh3
37. Ne3 Kb5 38. Kd3 Kc5 39. Kc3 Kb5
40. Kc2 Kc5 41. Kd3 b5 42. Kc3 b4+
43. axb4+ axb4+ 44. Kd3 Kb5 45. Ke2
Kc5 ½–½ (*New York Sun*, January 4, 1929)

85 Kevitz–Kashdan [D52]
Manhattan Club Championship, 1929

1. c4 Nf6 2. d4 e6 3. Nf3 d5 4. Nc3
c6 5. Bg5 Nbd7 6. e3 Qa5 7. Qb3 Ne4
8. cxd5 Nxg5 9. Nxg5 exd5 10. Bd3 Be7
11. Nf3 0–0 12. 0–0 Re8 13. Qc2 Nf6
14. Ne5 Bd6 15. f4 c5 16. Rad1 c4 17. Be2

b5 18. Bf3 b4 An oversight excusable perhaps in the light of White's pretty rejoinder. Bb7 should have been played. **19. Nxd5 Bxe5 20. dxe5 Nxd5 21. Bxd5 Rb8 22. Bxc4 Bb7 23. Rd7 Rf8 24. Qb3** White wins a third pawn, after which he would soon force the issue. **1–0** (*American Chess Bulletin*, January 1929, p. 9)

86 Kashdan–L. Steiner [C90]
Metropolitan Chess League, 1929

1. e4 e5 2. Nf3 Nc6 3. Bb5 a6 4. Ba4 Nf6 5. 0–0 Be7 6. Re1 b5 7. Bb3 d6 8. c3 Na5 9. Bc2 c5 10. d4 Qc7 11. h3 Nc6 12. Nbd2 g5 13. d5 Nd8 14. Nf1 g4 15. hxg4 Bxg4 16. Ne3 h5 17. a4 Rb8 18. axb5 axb5 19. Ra6 Bc8 20. Ra3 h4 21. Nh2 Nh5 22. Qf3 Bg5 23. Nf5 Bxc1 24. Rxc1 Nf4 25. Ng4 Bxf5 26. exf5 Qe7 27. f6 Qb7 28. c4 bxc4 29. Re1 Kf8 30. Rae3 Ng6 31. Bxg6 fxg6 32. Nxe5! This fine sacrifice breaks up the position completely and prepares for the entry of the major pieces. **32. ... dxe5 33. Rxe5 Nf7 34. Re7 Qxb2 35. Qf4 Rd8 36. Rxf7+! Kxf7 37. Qc7+ Kxf6 38. Qf4+** Checkmate is forced in two moves, hence Black resigns **1–0** (*American Chess Bulletin*, 1929, p. 70)

87 Marshall (Marshall)–Kashdan (Manhattan) [E11]
Metropolitan Chess League, 1929

1. d4 Nf6 2. Nf3 e6 3. c4 Bb4+ 4. Bd2 Qe7 5. Nc3 b6 6. e3 Bb7 7. Bd3 Bxc3 8. Bxc3 Ne4 9. Bxe4 Bxe4 10. 0–0 0–0 11. Nd2 Bb7 12. e4 d6 13. Qe2 Nd7 14. Rae1 e5 15. f4 exd4 16. Bxd4 f5 17. Qd3 Rae8 18. Qg3 Nf6 19. exf5 Qf7 20. Qg5 h6 21. Qh4 Ne4 22. Nxe4 Rxe4 23. Rxe4 Bxe4 24. Re1 d5 25. cxd5 Qxd5 26. Bxg7! White true to form, seizes the opportunity for a brilliancy. **26. ... Rxf5** If 26. ... Kxg7, then 27. Qe7+ recovers the piece with a pawn to boot. **27. Be5 Kh7 28. Rxe4!** Another fine conception which wins the game by force. **28. ... Qxe4 29. Qe7+ Kg6 30. Qe8+ Kh7 31. Qd7+** 31. Qh8+ at once leads to a direct checkmate, but the time limit had to be taken into account. **31. ... Kg6**

32. Qe6+ Kh7 33. Qe7+ Kg6 34. Qe8+ Kh7 35. Qh8+ Kg6 36. Qg8+ Kh5 37. Qe8+ Kg4 38. Qg6+ Kh4 39. Bf6+ Rxf6 40. g3+ Kh3 41. Qh5 mate 1–0 (*American Chess Bulletin*, 1929, p. 91)

88 Lier (Scandinavia)–Kashdan [C83]
Metropolitan Chess League, 1929

1. e4 e5 2. Nf3 Nc6 3. Bb5 a6 4. Ba4 Nf6 5. 0–0 Nxe4 6. d4 b5 7. Bb3 d5 8. dxe5 Be6 9. c3 Be7 10. Nbd2 0–0 11. Bc2 f5 12. exf6 Rxf6 13. Nd4 Nxd4 14. cxd4 Bd6 15. Re1 Bxh2+! 16. Kxh2 Rh6+ 17. Kg1 Qh4 18. f3 Qh2+ Overlooking 18. ... Qf2 mate! **19. Kf1 Qh1+ 20. Ke2 Qxg2+ 0–1** (*Brooklyn Daily Eagle*, February 27, 1929)

89 Kashdan (Manhattan)– Santasiere (Marshall) [B84]
Metropolitan Chess League, 1929
[April 5, 1930]

1. e4 c5 2. Nf3 d6 3. d4 cxd4 4. Nxd4 Nf6 If 4. ... Nc6 5. c4! Nf6 6. Nc3 with a much stronger game for White, due to the complete control of the center. Black must try to avoid this formation by the timely attack on the e pawn. **5. Nc3** The simplest reply. If 5. Bd3 Nbd7 6. c4? Nc5, exchanging the important king's bishop. **5. ... a6** Black avoids the normal Nc6, planning to bring the knight via d7 to c5. The whole maneuver involves considerable loss of time, and White is enabled to build up a strong attacking game. **6. Be2 e6** An alternative development for the king's bishop is ...g6 and ...Bg7 with a chance for play on the long diagonal. **7. 0–0 Qc7**

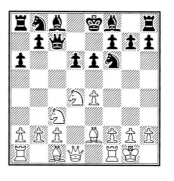

After
7. ... Qc7

The tempting ...b5 would be premature because of 8. Bf3! Bb7 (or 8. ... Ra7 9. Be3 and Black is in difficulties); 9. e5! Nd5 (if 9. ... Bxf3 10. Qxf3 wins at least a pawn, or 9. dxe5 10. Bxb7 Ra7 11. Nc6! Qxd1 12. Rxd1 Rxb7?? 13. Rd8 mate) 10. Nxd5 exd5 11. exd6 Bxd6 12. Re1+ with a decisive advantage. **8. a4** Now preventing b5, and forcing Black to assume a weaker formation on the queenside. **8. ... b6 9. f4** It is important to play this before Bf3, so that the bishop will not impede the coming attack. **9. ... Bb7 10. Bf3 Nbd7 11. Qe2 Be7 12. Be3 Rc8 13. Rad1 0-0** A bit better was first ...Nc5, forcing the bishop at e3 to move, in order to defend the e pawn. After the next move, White obtains a stronger grouping for his pieces. **14. g4!** The proper plan. White is secure in the center, and fully justified in attempting to open new lines of attack on the king's wing. **14. ... Nc5 15. Qg2** Protecting the pawn, and placing the queen on the right file for future activity. **15. ... Rfd8 16. g5 Ne8?** On this square, the knight is immobile and prevents the rooks from ever defending the kingside. Better was 16. Nfd7. If then 17. f5 (but not 17. b4 Nb3! threatening Qxc3) Ne5 18. f6 Bf8, with fair chances. With 17. h4, however, White would still have all the advantage. **17. f5** Leaving a hole at e4, but Black will have no time to establish himself there. **17. ... exf5** If ...e5 18. Nb3, and Black is no better off, in view of his weak queenside pawns. **18. Nxf5** Playing for the open f file. 18. exf5 is also strong, as a knight could be established at d5, and both f6 and g6 would soon be threatened. **18. ... Bf8 19. Bg4** If 19. Nh6+ gxh6 20. gxh6 Kh8 21. Bd4+ f6 22. Bg4 or Bh5, Bxh6! and Black can escape. The text is a useful preparation for this idea. **19. ... Nd7** Not ...g6 20. Nh6+ Bxh6 21. Bxc8 wins the exchange. Black hardly has a useful move left. **20. Qf2** *(see diagram)*

But here 20. Nxh6+! could have been played, with the continuation ...gxh6 21. Bxd7 Rxd7 22. gxh6+ Kh8 (or ...Bg7 23. hxg7 with a winning position.) 23. Bd4+ f6 24. Rxf6! Nxf6 25. Bxf6+ Bg7 26. Bxg7+ Kg8 (if 26. ... Rxg7, White will easily win the ending) 27. Bd4+ Kf8 28. Rf1+ Rf7 29. Qg7+! Ke8 30. Qg8+ wins the rook. The text is also effective and demonstrates clearly the weakness of the Black game. **20. ...**

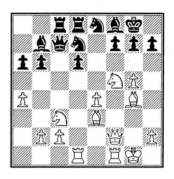

After
20. Qf2

Ne5 The threat was Ne7+! Bxe7 22. Qxf7+ etc. If 20. ... Nc5 21. b4! Nxe4 22. Nxe4 Bxe4 23. Bxb6 wins the exchange. and on 21. ... Nd7 22. Ne7+! again wins. **21. Be2** Preventing Nc4, when 22. Bxc4 Qxc4 23. Bxb6 suffices. Now there is no good way to protect the b pawn. Black's reply allows the combination previously planned. **21. ... Nd7 22. Ne7+! Bxe7 23. Qxf7+ Kh8 24. Qxe7 h6** There was nothing better than ...Nef6, giving up a piece, when the game was hopeless, of course. The text allows a forced mate in six moves. It is remarkable how completely shut out the Black pieces are from the action on the kingside. **25. Rf8+ Kh7** If ...Nxf8 26. Qxf8+ Kh7 27. g6+ Kxg6 28. Qf5 mate! **26. g6+ Kxg6 27. Qf7+ Kh7 28. Qf5+ g6 29. Qf7+ Ng7 30. Qg8 mate** An odd problem-like finish. **1-0** Annotated by Kashdan from *Chess Review*, August 1936. (*Brooklyn Daily Eagle*, April 10, 1929)

90 Mlotkowski-Kashdan [C58]
Metropolitan Chess League, 1930

1. e4 e5 2. Nf3 Nc6 3. Bc4 Nf6 4. Ng5 d5 5. exd5 Na5 6. b3 Nxc4 7. bxc4 Bc5 8. 0-0 0-0 9. d3 h6 10. Nf3 Re8 11. Be3 Bxe3 12. fxe3 e4 13. Nd4 Ng4 14. Qd2 exd3 15. Rf3 c5 16. Nb3 dxc2 17. Na3 Qd6 18. g3 Ne5 19. Rf4 Bg4 20. Raf1 Bh3 21. Re1 g5 22. Rf2 g4 23. Nb5 Qb6 24. d6 Rad8 25. e4 a6 26. Qxh6 axb5 27. Qg5+ Ng6 28. Rf6 Rxd6 **0-1** (*Chess*, May 1949, p. 191)

91 Fischman (NY City College)– Kashdan (Manhattan) [D03]
Metropolitan Chess League, 1930

1. d4 Nf6 2. Nf3 e6 3. Bg5 d5 4. e3
Nbd7 5. Bd3 c5 6. c3 Qb6 7. Qc2 c4
8. Be2 Ne4 9. Bf4 Be7 10. Nbd2 Ndf6
11. 0–0 0–0 12. Ne5 Nxd2 13. Qxd2 g5!
So if 14. Bxg5 then Ne4 wins a piece. 14. Bg3
Ne4 15. Qc2 f5 16. f3 Nxg3 17. hxg3
Bd6 18. f4 Qc7 19. b3 b5 20. a4 cxb3
21. Qxb3 bxa4 22. Rxa4 a5 23. c4 Bxe5
24. fxe5 Bd7 25. Ra3 Rfb8 26. Qa2 Bc6
27. Bf3 Rd8 28. Ra1 Qb7 29. Rxa5 Rxa5
30. Qxa5 Rd7 31. Qa6 g4 32. cxd5 Bxd5
33. Bxd5 Qxd5 34. Ra5 Qb7? 35. Qxe6+
Rf7 36. Qe8+ Kg7 37. Qd8 Re7 38. Ra8
1–0 (*American Chess Bulletin*, March 1929, p. 52)

92 Kashdan–Kline [C26]
Metropolitan Chess League, 1930

1. e4 e5 2. Nc3 Nf6 3. Bc4 Bc5 4. f4
d6 5. f5 c6 6. Qf3 b5 7. Bb3 a5 8. a4 b4
9. Nce2 d5 10. d3 Ra7 11. Bg5 d4 12. g4
Be7 13. h4 Ba6 14. Bd2 h5 15. g5 Ng4
16. Ng3 Nd7 17. Nxh5 Rxh5 18. Qxg4
Rh8 19. f6 Nxf6 20. gxf6 Bxf6 21. Nf3
Bc8 22. Qg3 Qd6 23. Bg5 Bxg5
24. Qxg5 f6 25. Qg6+ Kd8 26. Ng5 Qf8
27. Nf7+ Rxf7 28. Qxf7 1–0 (*Brooklyn Daily
Eagle*, March 27, 1930)

93 Kashdan–Kevitz [A55]
Manhattan Club Championship, 1930
[February 14]

1. d4 Nf6 2. c4 d6 3. Nc3 Nbd7 4. e4
e5 5. Nf3 Be7 6. Be2 0–0 7. 0–0 Re8
8. d5 Nc5 9. Qc2 a5 10. Be3 b6 11. h3
Rf8 12. a3 Ne8 13. b4 axb4 14. axb4
Rxa1 15. Rxa1 Na6 16. Qb3 Nb8 17. Ra8
Ba6 18. Qa4 Bb7 19. Ra7 Bc8 20. Nb5
Bd7 21. Rb7 Bxb5 22. Qxb5 Qc8
23. Ra7 Qd7 24. Bxb6 Qxb5 25. cxb5
cxb6 26. Rxe7 Nf6 27. Rb7 Nbd7
28. Nd2 Rb8 29. Rc7 Kf8 30. Bg4 Ke7
31. Bxd7 Nxd7 32. Nc4 g6 33. g4 h6
34. Kg2 Kd8 35. Rc6 Ke7 36. Nxd6 Ra8
37. Nc8+ Ke8 38. Nxb6 Nxb6 39. Rxb6
Ra4 40. Rb8+ Ke7 41. b6 Rxb4 42. Kf3
Kd7 43. Ke3 Rb3+ 44. Kd2 Rxh3
45. Kc2 Rf3 46. Rf8! 1–0 (*Brooklyn Daily
Eagle*, February 20, 1930)

94 Samuels–Kashdan [C15]
Manhattan Club Championship, 1930

1. e4 e6 2. d4 d5 3. Nc3 Bb4 4. Nge2
Nf6 5. Bg5 dxe4 6. a3 Be7 7. Bxf6 gxf6
8. Nxe4 b6 9. Qd3 Ba6 10. Qf3 c6
11. 0–0–0 f5 12. N4g3 Qd5 13. Qc3 Nd7
14. Kb1 Bb7 15. Nc1 Nf6 16. Be2 0–0
17. Bf3 Qd6 18. Nd3 Kh8 19. Ne5 Rac8
20. Bh5 f4 21. Nxf7+ Rxf7 22. Bxf7
fxg3 23. hxg3 Kg7 24. Bh5 c5 25. d5
exd5 26. Qe3 Ne4 27. Bf3 Qf6 28. c4
Qg5 29. Bxe4 Qxe3 30. fxe3 dxe4
31. Rd7 1–0 (*Brooklyn Daily Eagle*, April 17,
1930)

95 Horowitz–Kashdan [A12]
Manhattan Club Championship, 1930

1. Nf3 Nf6 2. c4 c6 A sounder system of
defense than ...c5, when 3. Nc3 Nc6 4. d4! is
in White's favor. 3. g3 d5 4. Bg2 Bf5 This
is an effective diagonal, and it balances the pressure of the fianchettoed bishop. 5. b3 e6
6. 0–0 Be7 7. d3 If 7. Nh4 to exchange the
bishop, ...Be4 8. f3 Bxh3 9. Rxb3 g5 wins. 7. ...
h6 A useful precaution, to provide a retreat for
the bishop. 8. Bb2 0–0 9. Nbd2 Nbd7
10. Qc2 Qc7 11. e4 The e pawn remains
pinned, and for a time a source of weakness.
White might have better continued his development with Rfd1 and Rac1, as Black will find it
harder to undertake anything. 11. ... dxe4
12. dxe4 Bh7 13. Ne1 A loss of time, as the
knight is no better at d3 than its former square.
The idea is to play f4, but this proves to have
its drawbacks. A good alternative was 13. Qc3
with e5 to come at the proper moment. 13. ...
Bb4 Attacking the e pawn by the threat of
...Bxd2, which requires attention. 14. Rd1 Rfd8
15. a3 Eventually necessary, as the bishop is
annoyingly placed, but it somewhat weakens the
queenside. 15. ... Bd6 16. h3 An aimless
move, which gives Black further time. 16. f4
would not do because of ...Bc5+ 17. Kh1 Ng4
winning the exchange. But 13. Nd3 was more
consistent than the text. 16. ... Be5 Exchanging the bishops gives Black more opportunities
for exploiting the weakness in White's center and
queenside. 17. Nd3 Bxb2 18. Qxb2 Qd6!

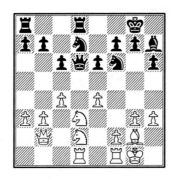

After
18. ... Qd6

A strong move, as it is difficult to protect the knight, and it has no good square. **19. Rfe1** If 19. e5 Qxd3 20. Ne4 Qxd1+! 21. Rxd1 Rxd1+ 22. Nxe4, with three pieces for the queen, which is more than equivalent. Or 20. exf6 Qc2 21. Qxc2 Bxc2 22. Rc1 Bd3 23. Rfe1 Nxe5 with an easy game. The text is played to win the queen, but he must still give up both rooks, and in addition Black retains command of the open file. **19. ... Qxd3** Accepting the offer, and relying on the text move to save the day. **20. Nf1 Nc5!** The point. White must take the queen at once, and cannot avoid the loss of the second rook. **21. Rxd3 Nxd3 22. Qe2 Nxe1 23. Qxe1 e5** Avoiding e4, which would give White more chances. Now the minor pieces will have little to do, on either side. **24. g4 Rd3 25. Qb4 b6 26. Ng3 c5 27. Qb5 Rad8 28. b4** This loses a pawn, but it is difficult for White to proceed and in the long run as the pressure of the two rooks is bound to succeed. **28. ... Rxa3 29. bxc5 Ra5! 30. Qc6 Rxc5 31. Qb7 Rxc4 32. Qxa7 Rc6** With a passed pawn ahead, the issue is now a matter of time. **33. Nf5 Bxf5 34. exf5 Rc1+** Starting a process of readjustment, which puts the rooks in the best position for both attack and defense. If ...Rcd6 35. Qe7 would be annoying. **35. Kh2 Rb1 36. Qa2** If now 36. Qe7 Re8, followed by e4 is strong. **36. ... Rb4 37. Qa3 Rbd4 38. Qb3 R8d6 39. Qb5 e4** Keeping the bishop out of play, and threatening Rd2, etc. **40. Bf1 Rd2 41. Kg3 Rc2 42. Qe5 Rdc6** If 42. ... Rdd2 43. Qb8+ Kh2 44. Qxb6 Rxf2 45. Qxf2! would lead to a draw. But the rooks must soon enter the king's field, with a dangerous attack. **43. Bb5** The only chance for some counter play, but it falls short, and enables a rather quick finish. **43. ... R6c3+ 44. Kh4** If

44. Kg2 e3 will win without much trouble. **44. ... Rf3 45. Be8 Rcc3** Black can easily avoid the checks. If 46. Bxf7+ Kxf7 47. e6+ Kf8 48. Qd6+ Kg8 49. Qd8+ Kh7. A curious point is that if White did not have his g pawn, he could force a stalemate by 50. Qh8+!. **0–1** Analysis by Kashdan in *Chess Review*, August 1936, p. 184. (*New York Sun*, January 24, 1930)

96 Pinkus–Kashdan [C42]
Manhattan Club Championship, 1930
[December 25, 1929]

1. e4 e5 2. Nf3 Nf6 3. Nxe5 d6 4. Nf3 Nxe4 5. Qe2 Qe7 6. d3 Nf6 7. Bg5 Be6 8. Nc3 h6 9. Bxf6 Qxf6 10. d4 Qe7 11. 0-0-0 d5 12. Ne5 c6 13. f4 Nd7 14. Qf3 0-0-0 15. Bd3 Nxe5 16. dxe5 d4 17. Ne2 Qc5 18. a3 Be7 19. Ng3 g6 20. Rhe1 Rhe8 21. f5 Bd5 22. Qg4 Bg5+ 23. Kb1 gxf5 24. Nxf5 Be6 25. Qg3 Qd5 26. b3 Bxf5 27. Bxf5+ Kb8 28. e6+ Ka8 29. Re5 Qd6 30. Re4 fxe6 31. Qxd6 Rxd6 32. Bg6 Rf8 33. c3 d3 34. Rd4 Rxd4 35. cxd4 d2 36. Kc2 Rf2 37. Be4 Kb8 38. Bf3 Kc7 39. h4 Bf4 40. Kd3 h5 41. Ke4 Bh6 42. g3 Bf8 43. Bxh5 Bxa3 44. Bf3 Bd6 45. g4 Be7 46. h5 Bg5 47. Rh1 Kd6 48. Bd1 Rf6 49. Kd3 a5 50. Rh3 b5 51. Kc2 b4 52. Rf3 Rxf3 53. Bxf3 c5 54. dxc5+ Kxc5 55. Kd3 Bh6 56. Bd1 Kd5 57. Bf3+ Ke5 58. Bd1 Bf4 59. Be2 Kf6 60. Ke4 e5 61. Bd1 Kg5 62. Be2 Kh4 63. Bd1 Kg3 64. Kf5 Kf2 65. g5 Ke1 66. Bc2 Be3 67. g6 Bh6 68. Kf6 e4 69. g7 Bxg7+ 70. Kxg7 e3 71. h6 e2 **0–1** (*New York Sun*, January 3, 1930)

97 Kashdan–Willman [E20]
Manhattan Club Championship, 1930
[January 19, 1930]

1. d4 Nf6 2. c4 e6 3. Nc3 Bb4 4. Bd2 0-0 5. Qc2 c5 6. dxc5 Nc6 7. Nf3 Bxc5 8. e3 d5 9. cxd5 exd5 10. Be2 Qe7 11. 0-0 Bg4 12. Rac1 Bb6 13. Qb3 Rac8 14. Rfd1 Rfd8 15. Nb5 Ne4 16. Re1 Be6 17. Nbd4 Nxd4 18. Nxd4 Qg5 19. Nxe6 fxe6 20. a4 Rxc1 21. Rxc1 Rf8 22. Rc2 h5 23. a5 Bc5 24. Bd3 Qe5 25. Bxe4

dxe4 26. Bc3 Qf5 27. Qxb7 Qg4
28. Qxg7+ Qxg7 29. Bxg7 Rd8 30. Kf1
Bb4 31. Bc3 Rc8 32. Rd2 Bxc3 33. bxc3
Rxc3 34. g3 Rc7 35. a6 Kf7 36. Rb2 Kf6
37. Rb7 Rc1+ 38. Kg2 Ra1 39. Rxa7 Kf5
40. Ra8 Kg6 41. a7 Kg7 42. g4 hxg4
43. Kg3 Ra2 44. Kxg4 Kf7 45. Kg5 Kg7
46. h4 Kh7 47. Kf6 Rxf2+ 48. Kxe6 Ra2
49. Rd8 Ra6+ 50. Rd6 Ra4 51. Rd7+
Kg6 52. Kd5 Kh5 53. Kc6 Kxh4
54. Kb7 Kg4 55. Rf7 1–0 (*New York Sun*,
February 14, 1930)

98 Berman–Kashdan [D90]

Manhattan Club Championship, 1930
[December 15, 1929]

1. Nf3 Nf6 2. c4 g6 3. d4 Bg7 4. Nc3
d5 The Grünfeld Defense. It allows White to
establish a center, with the plan of later attacking it by ...c5 or even ...e5. The opening has not
worked out too well in master practice, as Black
has difficulty in finding good squares for his
queenside pieces. 5. cxd5 An interesting alternative is 5. Bg5 Ne4! 6. exd5, etc. But not
6. Nxd5? Nxg5 7. Nxg5 e6! wins a piece. 5. Qb3
was played several times in the Alekhine–Euwe
championship match, and 5. Bf4 is another
good choice. 5. ... Nxd5 6. Qb3 6. e4 Nxc3
7. bxc3 c5 gives Black better chances, with a target in the center. 6. ... Nxc3 7. bxc3 c5 8. e3
0–0 9. Ba3 Nd7 Inferior would be 9. cxd4
10. cxd4 when White pieces are much freer, and
the center is entirely in his possession. The outcome of the entire game hinges on whether
White can force Black to make this exchange,
Black on the other hand will attempt to defend
his c pawn, and play for ...e5. 10. Bc4 If 10. dxc5
Qc7 will soon regain the pawn with advantage.
The text loses time, as the bishop cannot be
maintained on c4. 10. Be2 was in order. 10. ...
Rb8 Preparing the following advance which
gains ground for Black on the queenside.
11. 0–0 b5 12. Be2 Qc7 13. Rfd1 Re8 Intending ...e5 which as yet would not do because
of 14. dxc5 Nxc5 15. Qd5, winning at least the
exchange. 14. dxc5 Losing patience. White
finally makes the break. It leads to some difficult,
trappy play, from which Black can emerge quite
satisfactorily; however, 14. Rac1, and if e5

15. dxc5, etc. would give White more lasting
pressure. 14. ... Nxc5 15. Qd5 Na4 This
seems to win at least a pawn, and it would appear as if White's last move was a blunder. But
he had looked some distance ahead, and finds
the resource which avoids any loss of material.
16. Bxb5 Nxc3 17. Qc6 The only move, but
it just proves insufficient. 17. ... Qxc6 18. Bxc6
Nxd1 19. Rxd1 But not 19. Bxe8? Bxd1 wins.
But now if 19. ... Rf8 20. Bxe7, so that Black
must return the exchange. 19. ... Be6
20. Bxe8 Rxe8 21. Bc5 a5 22. a3 Bb3
The idea of this and the next move, is to induce
the rook to move away from the first rank. Then
the Black rook can enter with gain of tempo,
in view of the mating threat. 23. Rb1 Ba2
24. Rb5 Attacking the pawn looks tempting,
but it falls in with Black's plan. 24. Rd1 was
safer. 24. ... Bc3 25. Bd4 If 25. Nd4 Rc8!
threatening ...Bc4 and if the bishop moves,
Bxd4 wins a piece. Relatively best was 25. h3.
25. ... Rc8! Threatening ...Bxd4, and if
26. Bxc3 Rxc3, the a pawn falls because of the
threat of mate. 26. h3 a4 Now the threat of
...Bxc3 and ...Rc3 practically forces White's
reply. 27. Rc5 Rxc5 28. Bxc5

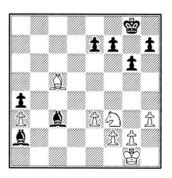

After
28. Bxc5

28. ... e5! Starting the final phase of the
game. The knight is shut out of play, and the
White king will also be seriously hampered by
the bishops. Black's plan is to march his king to
b3 which in the long run cannot be stopped.
29. Nh2 The knight must move to a weaker
square, in order to allow the king to advance to
check the march of the Black monarch. 29. ...
f6 30. f3 Kf7 31. Kf2 Ke6 32. e4 f5
33. Ke3 Bc4 Limiting the king's moves and
at the same time stalemating the knight. 34. g3
Hoping to get some play by f4. If at present

34. f4? exf4+ 35. Kxf4 Be5+ wins the unhappy knight. The text does not help matters, however. **34. ... Be1!** Threatening to win a piece by ...Bxg3 and if 35. g4 f4 mate!! A surprising outcome which amply demonstrates the power of the bishops. **35. exf5+ gxf5 36. g4** The last effort to free the knight, but Black's reply again threatens mate, and finally captures a piece. **36. ... Kd5** This game did not appear in the final tournament table. The reason for this is that Berman withdrew from the event before he played half of his games. In that case the games do not count. 0–1 Annotated by Kashdan in *Chess Review*, August 1936. (*New Yorker Staats-Zeitung*, December 22, 1929)

99 Jackson–Kashdan [A46]
Manhattan Club Championship, 1930
[December 7, 1929]

1. Nf3 Nf6 2. d4 e6 3. e3 c5 4. Bd3 Nc6 5. 0–0 Be7 6. Nbd2 0–0 7. c3 d5 8. Qe2 Bd7 9. dxc5 Bxc5 10. e4 Qc7 11. e5 Ng4 12. Bxh7+ Kxh7 13. Ng5+ Kg8 14. Qxg4 Qxe5 15. Nb3 Bb6 16. Bf4 Qf6 17. Bd6 Rfe8 18. Qh5 Qf5 19. Rad1 Ne7 20. Rd3 Qg6 21. Qxg6 Nxg6 22. Re1 f6 23. Nf3 Rac8 24. h4 Kf7 25. h5 Ne7 26. Nh4 g5 27. hxg6+ Nxg6 28. Nxg6 Kxg6 29. Rg3+ Kf7 30. Rh3 Rh8 31. Rxh8 Rxh8 32. Nc5 Bc8 33. Nd3 e5 34. Bc5 Bc7 35. Bxa7? b6 36. a4 Bf5 37. Nb4 Ra8 38. Bxb6 Bxb6 39. Nxd5 Bd8 40. Ra1 Bc2 41. Nb4 Bxa4 42. b3 Bc6 43. Rd1 Be8 44. c4 Bb6 45. Nd5 Bd4 46. Kf1 Ra2 47. f4 Bd7 48. fxe5 fxe5 49. Ne3 Bc6 50. Nd5 Ke6 51. Nf4+ exf4 52. Rxd4 Bxg2+ 53. Kg1 Ke5 54. Rd8 Ke4 55. c5 Ke3 56. b4 Bf3 57. Re8+ Be4 0–1 (*New York Sun*, December 20, 1929) Contributed by Jack O'Keefe.

100 Kashdan–Arons [B01]
Manhattan Club Championship, 1930
[December 8, 1929]

1. e4 d5 2. exd5 Qxd5 3. Nc3 Qa5 4. Nf3 Nf6 5. d4 c6 6. Ne5 Nbd7 7. Nc4 Qd8 8. Bg5 e6 9. Ne4 Be7 10. Ned6+ Kf8 11. Qf3 Nb6 12. Nxc8 Rxc8 13. Nxb6

axb6 14. 0–0–0 b5 15. Kb1 Ra8 16. Be2 Qd5 17. Qxd5 Nxd5 18. Bd2 Bf6 19. c3 Ke7 20. f4 Kd7 21. Bd3 g6 22. g4 h5 23. f5 exf5 24. gxf5 g5 25. Rdg1 Rag8 26. h3 Be7 27. Be4 Nf4 28. Rf1 Bd6 29. Bf3 Nxh3 30. Rxh3 g4 31. Rhh1 gxf3 32. Rxf3 Rg2 33. Kc2 h4 34. Kd3 Bg3 35. Rh3 Re8 36. Bg5 Be1 37. Bc1 Ree2 38. a3 Bg3 39. b3 Rh2 40. Rxh2 Rxh2 41. Bf4 Bxf4 42. Rxf4 Ke7 43. d5 cxd5 44. Rb4 Kd6 45. Rxb5 Kc6 46. Rb4 h3 47. Rh4 Rh1 48. Kc2 h2 49. Kb2 Kd6 50. a4 Ke5 51. a5 Kxf5 52. b4 Kg5 53. Rh8 d4 54. cxd4 Rd1 55. Rxh2 Rxd4 56. Kc3 Rd7 57. b5 f5 58. b6 f4 59. Rb2 Rd8 60. Rg2+ Kf5 61. Rg7 Rb8 62. Kd4 Rd8+ 63. Kc5 Rb8 64. Rxb7 Rxb7 65. a6 Rb8 66. a7 Ra8 67. b7 Rxa7 68. b8Q Rf7 69. Qe8 Kf6 70. Kd6 f3 71. Qg8 Rg7 72. Qf8+ Rf7 73. Qh6+ Kf5 74. Qe6+ Kf4 75. Qxf7+ 1–0 (Kashdan's scoresheet)

101 Kashdan–H. Steiner [C83]
Manhattan Club Championship, 1930
[December 20, 1929]

1. e4 e5 2. Nf3 Nc6 3. Bb5 a6 4. Ba4 Nf6 5. 0–0 Nxe4 6. d4 b5 7. Bb3 d5 8. dxe5 Be6 9. c3 Be7 10. Nbd2 0–0 11. Bc2 f5 12. exf6 Nxf6 13. Nb3 Bg4 14. Qd3 Bxf3 15. Qxf3 Ne5 16. Qh3 Ng6 17. Nd4 Rf7 18. Bf5 Nf8 19. Ne6 Nxe6 20. Bxe6 Bd6 21. Bg5 c6 22. Bxf7+ Kxf7 23. Bxf6 Qxf6 24. Qxh7 Re8 25. Rae1 Re5 26. Re3 Rf5 27. Qh8 Bf8 28. f4 d4 29. cxd4 Qxd4 30. Qh3 Rf6 31. Kh1 Qc4 32. Qf3 Qxa2 33. b3 a5 34. f5 a4 35. bxa4 bxa4 36. Re6 Qc4 37. Rfe1 Qh4 38. g3 Qg5 39. Qxc6 Qxf5 40. Rxf6+ gxf6 41. Qc4+ Kg7 42. Rf1 Qd7 43. Rf4 f5 44. Kg2 a3 45. Rd4 Qf7 46. Qxf7+ Kxf7 47. Kf3 Ke6 48. h4 Bh6 49. Ra4 Bc1 50. Ra5 Kf6 51. Ra6+ 1–0 (Kashdan's scoresheet)

102 Kashdan–Kussman [C83]
Manhattan Club Championship, 1930

1. e4 e5 2. Nf3 Nc6 3. Bb5 a6 4. Ba4

Nf6 5. 0–0 Nxe4 6. d4 b5 7. Bb3 d5
8. dxe5 Be6 9. c3 Be7 10. Nbd2 0–0
11. Bc2 f5 12. exf6 Nxf6 13. Nb3 Bg4
14. Qd3 Ne4 15. Nbd4 Nxd4 16. Nxd4
Bd6 17. h3 Qh4 18. f4 Ng3 19. hxg4 g5
20. Nf5 Qh1+ 21. Kf2 Qxf1+ 22. Qxf1
Nxf1 23. Kxf1 Bxf4 24. Bxf4 gxf4
25. Re1 Rfe8 26. Rxe8+ Rxe8 27. Bb3
c6 28. Nd4 1–0 (Kashdan's scoresheet)

103 Kashdan–L. Steiner [C66]
Match, Game 1, 1930 *[April]*

1. e4 e5 2. Nf3 Nc6 3. Nc3 Nf6 4. Bb5
d6 5. d4 Bd7 6. 0–0 Be7 7. Re1 exd4
8. Nxd4 0–0 9. Bf1 Re8 10. h3 Bf8
11. Bg5 h6 12. Bh4 g5 13. Bg3 Nxd4
14. Qxd4 Nh5 15. Bh2 Bg7 16. Qd1 Nf4
17. Bxf4 gxf4 18. Qf3 Bxc3 19. Qxc3 Re5
20. Rad1 Bc6 21. b4 Qe7 22. f3 Kh7
23. b5 Bxb5 24. Bxb5 Rxb5 25. Rd5
Rc5 26. Rxc5 dxc5 27. e5 Rd8 28. e6
fxe6 29. Qe5 Qd6 30. Qxe6 Qxe6
31. Rxe6 Rd2 32. Re7+ Kg6 33. Rxc7
Rxc2 34. Rxb7 Rxa2 35. Re7 Ra5
36. Kf2 Kg5 37. Rg7+ Kf6 38. Rh7 Ra2+
A more promising winning attempt is 38. Kg6
39. c7 a6. **39. Ke1 Rxg2 40. Rxa7 Rh2
41. Rc7 Rxh3 42. Rxc5 Rxf3 43. Ke2
Ra3** A famous endgame position which is considered drawn in most cases. **44. Kf2 Kg6
45. Rc8 h5 46. Rg8+ Kf5 47. Rf8+ Kg4
48. Rg8+ Kh3 49. Rf8 Ra4 50. Kf3 h4
51. Rh8 Ra1 52. Kxf4 Rf1+ 53. Ke3 Kg3
54. Rg8+ Kh2 55. Ke2 Rf5 56. Rg7 h3
57. Rg8 Ra5 58. Kf2 Ra2+ 59. Kf1 Rg2
60. Rh8 Rg4 61. Kf2 Rf4+ 62. Ke3 Rf5
63. Ke2 Rg5 64. Kf2 Rg3 65. Rh7 Ra3
66. Rg7 Ra2+ 67. Kf1 Ra1+ 68. Kf2 Kh1
69. Rg8 h2 70. Rg7 Ra2+ 71. Kf1 Ra1+
72. Kf2 Rg1 73. Rf7** ½–½ (*American Chess
Bulletin*, May-June 1930)

104 L. Steiner–Kashdan [C42]
Match, Game 2, 1930 *[April]*

1. e4 e5 2. Nf3 Nf6 3. Nxe5 d6 4. Nf3
Nxe4 5. Qe2 Qe7 6. d3 Nf6 7. Bg5 Be6
8. Nc3 h6 9. Bxf6 Qxf6 10. d4 Qe7
11. 0–0–0 d5 12. Ne5 c6 13. f4 Nd7

14. Qf2 0–0–0 15. Bd3 Nxe5 16. fxe5
c5 17. Rhf1 g6 18. Kb1 c4 19. Be2 b5
20. Nxb5 Qb7 21. Nc3 Ba3 22. Na4
Bxb2 23. Nxb2 c3 24. Ba6! Qxa6
25. Nd3 Kb8 26. Ka1 Ka8 27. Rb1 Rb8
28. Nc5 Qa3 29. Rb3 Rxb3 30. cxb3
Bf5 31. Na4 c2 32. Qd2 Rb8 33. Nc5
Rb4 34. Qxh6 a5 35. g4 Rxd4? The capture 35. ... Bxg4 seems to win. The rook is ready
to block at b8, while the bishop is ready to return to f5. **36. Qf8+ Ka7 37. Qe7+ Kb6
38. Nd7+ Bxd7 39. Qxa3 Rd1+ 40. Qc1
Bxg4 41. Kb2 Rxc1 42. Kxc1 Bf5 43. h4
Be6 44. Kxc2 Kc5 45. Rf4 d4 46. Kd3
a4 47. Rxd4 axb3 48. axb3 Bxb3
49. Ke3 Bd5 50. Rd2 Be6 51. Kf4 Bb3
52. Kg5 Be6 53. Kf6 Kc4 54. Rd6 Bd5
55. Rxd5 Kxd5 56. Kxf7 Kxe5 57. Kxg6**
1–0 (*American Chess Bulletin*, May-June 1930)

105 Kashdan–L. Steiner [D52]
Match, Game 3, 1930 *[April]*

1. d4 d5 2. c4 c6 3. Nf3 Nf6 4. Nc3 e6
5. Bg5 Nbd7 6. e3 Qa5 The Cambridge
Springs Defense, which usually leads to very interesting play, and is one of the strongest counters to the Queen's Pawn Openings. **7. Qb3**
7. Nd2 is the usual reply, and 7. cxd5 has also
been played with good results. The text avoids
the more complicated attacks, but it allows Black
the gain of a bishop for a knight with an easy development. **7. ... Ne4 8. cxd5** If 8. Bf4 g5!
9. Bg3 (not 9. Nxg5 10. Bxg5 dxc4 and 11. ...
Qxg5 wins), h5 with advantage. **8. ... exd5
9. Bd3 Bb4?!** This attack is easily parried.
Black can gain time by Nxg5 10. Nxg5 Be7 (this
is where the bishop belongs) 11. Nf3 0–0, etc.
**10. Rc1 Nxg5 11. Nxg5 h6 12. Nf3 0–0
13. 0–0 Re8 14. a3 Bxc3** After this exchange
White gets the advantage, because of his better
development, and also because of the mobility
of his queenside pawns, which threaten to advance and create weaknesses in Black's game. It
was better to retreat, 14. ... Be7, though White
would have some attack by 15. e4 dxe4 16. Nxe4.
**15. Qxc3 Qxc3 16. Rxc3 Nf6 17. b4 Be6
18. Rfc1 Ne4 19. Bxe4** Playing this position
today, I would prefer 19. R3c2. The bishop is
useful to enforce b5, and the Black knight can

always be disposed of. **19. ... dxe4 20. Nd2 Bd5 21. Rc5?!** More accurate is 21. a4. I played the text to induce the following advance, which I judged would be weak for Black. **21. ... b6** Sounder was 21. ... Rad8 22. a4 a6 and it is questionable whether White can break through to any advantage. **22. R5c3 a5 23. Nc4!** Now Black's pawns are seriously weakened, and subject to attack, whether the knight is exchanged or not. **23. ... axb4 24. axb4 Ra6** Believing he can set up a sufficient defense, as indicated in the next note. If 24. ... Bxc4 25. Rxc4 Ra4 26. Rxc6 Rxb4 27. g4! White would have the better ending, with a strongly supported passed pawn, against the isolated b pawn and kingside pawns of Black. **25. Ne5 Re6** Defending the pawn, which cannot yet be taken because of the mating threat, and intending b5, after which everything would be secure. If White has any winning plan, it must therefore be tried at once. **26. b5!** Although only a pawn sacrifice, it is very dangerous and had to be calculated, as the pawn will go right on to queen should White's attack miscarry. **26. ... cxb5 27. Rc8+ Kh7 28. Rd8!**

After 28. Rd8

An important tempo, and essential part of the idea. Wrong would be 28. Nxf7 b4 29. Rh8+ Kg6 30. Ne5+ Rxe5! 31. dxe5 b3 wins. Or 28. Nd7 Rd6 29. Rd8 Rc6! and Black will escape. **28. ... Bc4** Black's last chance to offer some resistance was 28. ... f6 29. Rxd5 fxe5; on the other hand, if 28. ... Bb3, White wins brilliantly with 29. h4! f6 30. h5!! fxe5 31. Rcc8. **29. Nd7!** Threatening to win the exchange, which strangely enough cannot be avoided, despite the rook's mobility. If 29. ... Re7 30. Nf8+ Kg8 31. Ng6+, or 29. ... Rc6 30. Nb8! wins. Black decides to get his king nearer the center.

29. ... Kg6 30. d5 Gaining time, as the rook still cannot escape. Of course if 30. ... Bxd5 31. Nf8+ wins a piece. **30. ... Re7 31. d6** If 31. ... Re6 32. Nf8+ Kf6 33. d7! and Black is worse off. **31. ... Rxd7 32. Rxd7 Bd3 33. Rb7 Kf6 34. f3** If 34. ... Ke6 35. d7 and Rc8 wins. Or 34. ... exf3 35. gxf3 Bc4 36. Rd1 is decisive. **1–0** Annotated by Kashdan in *Chess Review*, January 1936. (*Brooklyn Daily Eagle*, May 22, 1930)

106 L. Steiner–Kashdan [C17]
Match, Game 4, 1930 *[April-May]*

1. e4 e6 2. d4 d5 3. Nc3 Bb4 4. e5 c5 5. Bd2 cxd4 6. Nb5 Bf8 7. Qg4 Nc6 8. Nf3 a6 9. Nbxd4 Nge7 10. Bd3 Qc7 11. Qg3 Nxd4 12. Nxd4 Ng6 The correct way to attack is with 12. ... Nc6. **13. Nf3 Bd7 14. h4 Bb5 15. Bxb5+ axb5 16. h5 Ne7 17. Nd4 Qc4 18. Qd3 Nc6 19. Nxb5 Rxa2 20. Qxc4 Rxa1+ 21. Ke2 Rxh1 22. Qa4 Be7 23. Qa8+ Nd8 24. Nd6+ Bxd6 25. exd6 Rh4 26. Ba5 Kd7 27. b3 e5 28. Qb8 Nc6 29. Qxb7+!** This decides the game more quickly than winning the exchange. **29. ... Kxd6 30. Qc7+ Kc5 31. b4+** Black will win the knight. **1–0** (*Lajos Steiner*, Game 25, p. 26, book by Woodger)

107 Kashdan–L. Steiner [A15]
Match, Game 5, 1930 *[April-May]*

1. Nf3 Nf6 2. c4 d5 3. cxd5 Nxd5 4. e4 Nf6 5. Nc3 g6 6. Bc4 Bg7 7. e5 Ng4 8. e6 fxe6 9. Qe2 0–0 10. Bxe6+ Kh8 11. 0–0 Nc6 12. Ng5 Nge5 13. Qe4 Nd4 14. Bxc8 Rxc8 15. d3 h6

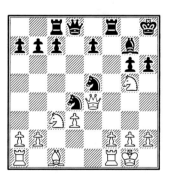

After 15. ... h6

16. f4 Ng4 17. Nf3 Nxf3+ 18. Qxf3 Ne5 19. Qxb7 Nxd3 20. Be3 Rb8 21. Qc6 Rxb2 22. Qxg6 Qd6 23. Qxd6 exd6 24. Rad1 Nb4 25. Bd4 Nxa2 26. Nd5 Bxd4+ 27. Rxd4 c6 28. Ne7 Re8 29. Re4 Kh7 30. f5 Nc3 31. Re3 Ne2+ 32. Kh1 c5 33. f6 c4 34. g4 c3 35. g5 Nf4 But not 35. ... hxg5 as then 36. Rh3 is mate! 36. Rxf4 Rb1+ 37. Kg2 c2 38. g6+ Kh8 39. Rc3 c1Q 40. Rxc1 Rxc1 41. g7+ Kh7 42. f7 Rc2+ 43. Rf2 1–0 (*American Chess Bulletin*, May-June 1930)

108 L. Steiner–Kashdan [C97]
Match, Game 6, 1930 *[April-May]*

1. e4 e5 2. Nf3 Nc6 3. Bb5 a6 4. Ba4 Nf6 5. 0–0 Be7 6. Re1 b5 7. Bb3 d6 8. c3 Na5 9. Bc2 c5 10. d4 Qc7 This system of defense is probably the strongest against the Ruy Lopez. The object is to maintain the center, force White to either exchange pawns or play d5, and then get some activity on the queenside by opening a file. White will attempt a direct kingside attack, and will maneuver his pieces in that direction. 11. h3 0–0 12. Nbd2 Bd7 Nc6 is customary, but Black's intention is to occupy the c file as soon as possible. Bb7 was perhaps better for that purpose, but he does not want to relinquish his hold on f5. 13. Nf1 Rac8 Threatening ...cxd4, and compelling White to declare himself in the center. 14. d5 Blocking the lines, and announcing that he is basing his plans on the coming kingside advance. 14. ... Ne8 Preparing to take up a solid defensive formation. White's main threat is to plant a knight on f5, which must not be allowed. 15. g4 g6 16. Ng3 Ng7 17. Bh6 f6 Now there is no immediate danger, and Black can look to the other side of the board for a counter demonstration. 18. Nd2 Preparing for f4, but as will be seen, Black gains as much ground as White by the exchange. Another plan is Kh2, followed by Rg1, and after due preparation h4. However, Black has enough resources to meet any such advance. 18. ... Rb8 19. b3 Nb7 20. f4 Opening the f file, but in return giving Black a strong square for the knight, which he hastens to occupy. 20. ... exf4 21. Bxf4 Nd8 22. Qe2 Nf7 23. Rf1 Qc8 With the

idea of ...h5 in some positions, breaking up the White formation, and also anticipating a possible sacrifice on g5, such as actually occurred later. 24. Rf2 Ne5 25. Raf1 c4! Now that the White pieces are definitely fixed on the kingside, Black is ready for forceful measures on the other wing. 26. b4 a5 Finally gaining his objective, for if 27. bxa5 Ra8. 27. a3 axb4 28. axb4 Ra8 29. Nf3 Ra3 This and the next moves show the marked effect the rook is to have on the game. 30. Bd2 Ra2 31. Bb1 Ra1 An excellent move and an integral part of the coming combination. 32. Bh6?

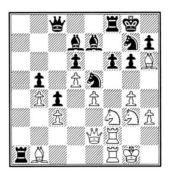

After
32. Bh6

Wiser would have been 32. Bc2, to exchange rooks, or if ...Ra2 33. Bb1, etc. White wished to prevent ...h5, which accounts for the text. 32. ... Bxg4!! The stage is completely set, and everything just works out. It is remarkable that every White piece has some effect upon the soundness of the sacrifice. 33. hxg4 Qxg4 34. Nd4 The piece cannot be saved. If 34. Kh2 Nxf3+ 35. Qxf3 Qh4+, and Qxh6. Or 34. Kg2 Nh5! 35. Bxf8?? Nf4+. Finally, if 34. Rg2 Nxf3+ 35. Qxf3 Qxf3 36. Rxf3 Rxb1+ wins easily. The text offers most chances. 34. ... Qxg3+ 35. Rg2 Qxc3 36. Nf5! From this point White struggles manfully, though in a seemingly hopeless cause, and makes a battle of it right to the end. 36. ... Nxf5 37. exf5 g5 Giving up the exchange, but securing the position and relying on the extra pawn to win. 38. Bxf8 Bxf8 39. Qh5 Qxb4 This grab provides a sufficient defense. 40. Rxg5+ Gambling for a possible perpetual check, rather than waiting and suffering a lingering death. The Black king can escape, but he is led on a merry chase. 40. ... fxg5 41. Qxg5+ Kf7 42. Qh5+ Ke7 43. Qxh7+ Kd8 44. f6 If Qg8, or Qb7, Nd7

is a simple defense. The text protects the bishop.
44. ... c3 45. Qb7 Qc5+ White was threatening mate in two. If 45. ... Nd7 46. Bf5 with some chances. Or 45. ... Rxb1? 46. Qb8+ Kd7 47. Qb7+ Ke8 48. f7+ Kd8 49. Qb8+, and a draw is forced. **46. Kg2 Qc7 47. Qxb5 c2** This would seem to finish it, but White has a last try, and creates another interesting diversion before finally yielding. **48. f7 Nxf7 49. Rxf7** Once more threatening mate, by 50. Rxf8+ Ke7 51. Qe8, should Black be tempted to make another queen at this point. **49. ... Qxf7 50. Qb8+ Ke7 51. Qc7+ Kf6 52. Qc3+ Kg5** After 53. Qg3+ Kh6 54. Qe6+ Kg7 55. Qc3+ Qf6 and the king finally escapes, and Black is left with a rook ahead. **0–1** Annotated by Kashdan in *Chess Life*, January 1936. (*American Chess Bulletin*, May-June 1930)

109 Kashdan–L. Steiner [C79]
Match, Game 7, 1930 *[May]*

1. e4 e5 2. Nf3 Nc6 3. Bb5 a6 4. Ba4 Nf6 5. 0–0 d6 6. d4 b5 7. dxe5 bxa4 8. exf6 Qxf6 9. Nc3 Bd7 10. Nxa4 h6 11. Nc3 g5 12. Nd5 Qd8 13. Nd4 Bg7 14. Nxc6 Bxc6 15. c4 a5 16. Rb1 a4 17. Be3 0–0 18. Bd4 f6 19. f4 Bd7 20. fxg5 hxg5 21. Qh5 Be8 22. Qf3 Bg6 23. Rbe1 Rb8 24. Qc3 c6 25. Nxf6+ Bxf6 26. Bxf6 Qb6+ 27. Kh1 Qb4 28. Qg3 Qxc4 29. Qxg5 Qf7 30. h4 Kh7 31. Bc3 Qxf1+ 32. Rxf1 Rxf1+ 33. Kh2 Rf7 34. Bd2 Rg7 35. Qh6+ Kg8 36. Bc3 Rbb7 37. Bxg7 Rxg7 38. Qf4 Kh7 39. g4 Rf7 40. Qxd6 Bxe4 41. h5 Bd5 42. g5 Kg8 **1–0** (*American Chess Bulletin*, July-August 1930)

110 L. Steiner–Kashdan [C42]
Match, Game 8, 1930 *[May]*

1. e4 e5 2. Nf3 Nf6 3. Nxe5 d6 4. Nf3 Nxe4 5. Qe2 Qe7 6. d3 Nf6 7. Bg5 Qxe2+ 8. Bxe2 Be7 9. Nc3 h6 10. Bh4 Nc6 11. Nb5 Kd8 12. 0–0–0 Nd5 13. Bg3 a6 14. Nbd4 Nxd4 15. Nxd4 Bf6 16. Nb3 Be6 17. Bf3 Nb4 18. Kb1 a5 19. Nc1 a4 20. c3 Nc6 21. d4 Re8 22. Be2 Bf5+ 23. Bd3 Bxd3+ 24. Nxd3 Kd7 25. Nf4 Ra5 26. Rhe1 Rxe1 27. Rxe1

Rf5 28. Nd3 h5 29. Bf4 Ne7 30. Bc1 Nd5 31. Kc2 b5 32. Be3 Be7 33. b3 axb3+ 34. axb3 Nxe3+ 35. fxe3 d5 36. Kd2 Bd6 37. Rh1 Rg5 38. Ne1 c5 39. Ke2 b4 40. dxc5 Bxc5 41. cxb4 Bxb4 42. Nd3 Bd6 43. Kf3 Rg6 44. g3 Rf6+ 45. Ke2 h4 46. gxh4 Rh6 47. Rg1 g6 48. Rg4 Bxh2 49. Rd4 Ke6 50. Nc5+ Kd6 51. Ne4+ Kc6 52. Ng5 f5 53. Ra4 Bc7 54. Nf3 Rh8 55. Ra1 Bb6 56. Ne5+ Kc7 57. Rc1+ Kb7 58. Rd1 Rxh4 59. Rxd5 Rh2+ 60. Kd3 Rh3 61. Nc4 Bxe3 **½–½** (*Brooklyn Daily Eagle*, May 9, 1930)

111 Kashdan–L. Steiner [C87]
Match, Game 9, 1930 *[May]*

1. e4 e5 2. Nf3 Nc6 3. Bb5 a6 4. Ba4 Nf6 5. 0–0 Be7 6. Re1 d6 7. Bxc6+ bxc6 8. d4 Nd7 9. dxe5 dxe5 10. Nbd2 f6 11. Nb3 a5 12. Bd2 a4 13. Na5 Ra6 14. Qe2 Nc5 15. Rad1 Be6 16. Nb7 Qc8 17. Nxc5 Bxc5

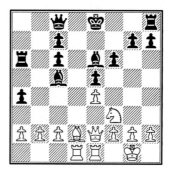

After
17. ... Bxc5

18. Nxe5 fxe5 19. Qh5+ Kf8 20. Qxe5 Bd6 21. Qg5 h6 22. Qh4 Kg8 23. f4 Kh7 24. f5 Bf7 25. g4 Be5 26. Kh1 Re8 27. g5 c5 28. g6+ Bxg6 29. fxg6+ Rxg6 30. b3 axb3 31. axb3 Bd4 32. c3 Bf6 33. Qf2 Qb7 34. Qf5 Re5 35. Qf3 Bh4 36. Bf4 Re7 37. Re2 Rf6 38. Qe3 Qxb3 39. Rg1 Qc4 40. Rg4 g5 41. Bg3 h5 42. Rxh4 gxh4 43. Bxh4 Rf1+ 44. Kg2 Ref7 45. Bf2 Rd1 46. Re1 Rg7+ **0–1** (*Brooklyn Daily Eagle*, May 9, 1930)

112 L. Steiner–Kashdan [C99]
Match, Game 10, 1930 *[May]*

1. e4 e5 2. Nf3 Nc6 3. Bb5 a6 4. Ba4

Nf6 5. 0–0 Be7 6. Re1 b5 7. Bb3 d6
8. c3 Na5 9. Bc2 c5 10. d4 Qc7 11. h3
0–0 12. Nbd2 cxd4 13. cxd4 Nc6 14. d5
Nb4 15. Bb1 a5 16. a3 Na6 17. b3 Nc5
18. Nf1 Bd7 19. Ra2 Rac8 20. Ng3 Qb7
21. Kh2 Ne8 22. Ng1 Bh4 23. Nf5 Bxf5
24. exf5 Nc7 25. Nf3 Bf6 26. Bg5 Nxd5
27. Bxf6 Nxf6 28. g4 Nce4 29. Re3 Nc3
30. Qg1 Nfd5 31. Re1 Nxa2 32. f6 Nxf6
33. Nh4 Nc3 34. g5 Nfe4 35. Bd3 Qd5
36. Re3 g6 37. Rf3 Nd2 0–1 (*Brooklyn Daily Eagle*, May 22, 1930)

113 Kashdan–Jaffe [C49]
Match, Game 1, 1930 *[June]*

1. e4 e5 2. Nf3 Nc6 3. Nc3 Nf6 4. Bb5
Bb4 5. Nd5 Nxd5 6. exd5 e4 7. dxc6
bxc6 8. Ba4 exf3 9. Qxf3 Qe7+ 10. Qe2
Ba6 11. Qxe7+ Bxe7 12. d3 Bf6 13. Rb1
0–0 14. Bf4 Rfe8+ 15. Kd2 Be5 16. Bxe5
Rxe5 17. Rhe1 Rae8 18. f4 Rxe1 19. Rxe1
Rxe1 20. Kxe1 Kf8 21. Kd2 Ke7 22. b4
Bb7 23. g3 d5 24. Ke3 Kd6 25. Kd4 Bc8
26. c4 dxc4 27. dxc4 Bd7 28. Bc2 g6
29. Be4 f6 30. a3 Be6 31. h4 Bg4
32. Bd3 Bf5 33. Be2 h5 34. Bf3 Be6
35. a4 c5+ 36. bxc5+ Kd7 37. Be4 Bf5
38. c6+ Kd6 39. c5+ Ke6 40. Bxf5+ Kxf5
41. Kc4 Kg4 42. Kb5 Kxg3 43. Ka6 Kxf4
44. Kb7 g5 45. hxg5 fxg5 46. Kxc7 h4
47. Kb8 h3 48. c7 h2 49. c8Q h1Q 50. c6
Qh6 51. c7 Qd6 52. Ka8 g4 53. Qb7
1–0 (*Brooklyn Daily Eagle*, June 5, 1930)

114 Jaffe–Kashdan [C77]
Match, Game 2, 1930 *[June]*

1. e4 e5 2. Nf3 Nc6 3. Bb5 a6 4. Ba4
Nf6 5. Qe2 Be7 6. c3 b5 7. Bb3 0–0
8. d4 exd4 9. cxd4 d5 10. e5 Ne4 11. 0–0
Bg4 12. Rd1 Bh4 13. Be3 Na5 14. h3
Nxb3 15. axb3 Bh5 16. g4 Bg6 17. Nc3 f5
18. exf6 Qxf6 19. Nxh4 Nxc3 20. bxc3
Qxh4 21. Kh2 Qe7 22. Re1 Be4 23. f4
Qd6 24. Rf1 Rf6 25. g5 Re6 26. Qg4 a5
27. Qg3 Bf5 28. Rfe1 Bc2 29. b4 a4
30. Bc1 Rae8 31. Re5 Qc6 32. Ra2 Be4
33. Rf2 g6 34. Qg4 R6e7 35. Bb2 Rf7
36. Qe2 Ref8 37. Qd2 Qc4 38. Kg3 Ra8
39. Qe2 Qxe2 40. Rxe2 a3 41. Ba1 c6

42. Re6 Ra6 43. Re8+ Rf8 44. Rxf8+
Kxf8 45. Ra2 Bd3 46. Rd2 Bc4 47. Rd1
Ra7 48. Re1 a2 49. Bb2 Bd3 50. Kf2 Bb1
51. Ba1 Ra3 52. Ke3 Bf5 53. h4 Kg7
54. Re2 h6 55. Kd2 hxg5 56. hxg5 Kf7
57. Kc1 Bd3 58. Re1 Rb3 59. Bb2 Be4
60. Ba1 Rb1+ 61. Kd2 Ke6 62. Ke2 Kf5
63. Kf2 Kxf4 64. Rf1 Kxg5 0–1 (*Brooklyn Daily Eagle*, June 12, 1930)

115 Kashdan–Jaffe [D52]
Match, Game 3, 1930 *[June]*

1. d4 Nf6 2. c4 e6 3. Nc3 d5 4. Bg5
Nbd7 5. e3 c6 6. Nf3 Qa5 7. Qb3 Ne4
8. cxd5 exd5 9. Bd3 Nxg5 10. Nxg5 h6
11. Nf3 Be7 12. 0–0 0–0 13. Rae1 Qc7
14. Bb1 Rd8 15. Qc2 Nf8 16. Ne5 Bd6
17. f4 f5 18. Qe2 g6 19. g4 fxg4 20. Nxg4
Qg7 21. Kh1 Be6 22. f5 gxf5 23. Bxf5
Bxf5 24. Rxf5 Nh7 25. Rg1 Kh8 26. Ne5
Bxe5 27. Rxg7 Bxg7 28. Qg4 Rg8
29. Ne2 Bf6 30. Qh5 Bg5 31. Nf4 Bxf4

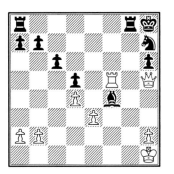

After
31. ... Bxf4

32. exf4 Rg7 33. Rf7 Rxf7 34. Qxf7
Rf8 35. Qxb7 Rxf4 36. Qxc6 Nf6
37. Qc8+ Ng8 38. Qc7 Rf5 39. Qxa7
Nf6 40. b4 Rf1+ 41. Kg2 Rb1 42. Qb8+
Kg7 43. b5 Rb2+ 44. Kf3 Rxa2
45. Qc7+ Kg6 46. b6 Ra3+ 47. Kf4
Nh5+ 48. Ke5 Nf6 49. Qc6 Re3+
50. Kd6 Kf7 51. Qc7+ Kf8 52. Qc8+ Re8
53. b7 Kf7 54. b8Q 1–0 (*Brooklyn Daily Eagle*, June 12, 1930)

116 Gromer (France)–Kashdan [C77]
Hamburg Olympiad, round 1, 1930 *[July 13]*

1. e4 e5 2. Nf3 Nc6 3. Bb5 a6 4. Ba4

Nf6 5. d3 d6 6. Bxc6+ bxc6 7. Nc3 c5
8. Ne2 Nh5 9. Ng3 Nxg3 10. hxg3 Be7
11. Nh4 g6 12. Bh6 Be6 13. Qd2 Bf6
14. Nf3 Qd7 15. Bg5 Bg7 16. Bh6 f6
17. Bxg7 Qxg7 18. Qh6 Qxh6 19. Rxh6
Kf7 20. Kd2 Kg7 21. Rah1 a5 22. b3 a4
23. Ng1 c6 24. f4 Bg4 25. R6h4 h5
26. Nf3 Rhf8 27. R4h2 d5 28. Kc3 Rfe8
29. Re1 axb3 30. axb3 exf4 31. gxf4 Re7
32. Rhh1 Rae8 33. Nd2 Bf5 34. Re2 Re6
35. Rhe1 Kh6 36. b4 cxb4+ 37. Kxb4
dxe4 38. dxe4 g5 39. fxg5+ fxg5
40. Kc3 h4 41. e5 g4 42. Nb3 Kg5
43. Nd4 Rh6 44. e6 c5 45. Nxf5 Kxf5
46. Rf1+ Kg6 47. Re4 Kg5 48. Rff4 g3
49. Rg4+ Kf5 50. Rgf4+ Kg5 51. Rg4+
½–½ (*The Gambit*, August 1930, p. 215)

117 Kashdan–Asgeirsson (Iceland) [C26]

Hamburg Olympiad, round 2, 1930 *[July 14]*

1. e4 e5 2. Nc3 Nf6 3. Bc4 Bb4
4. Nge2 d6 5. 0–0 Be6 6. Nd5 c6
7. Nxf6+ Qxf6 8. Bxe6 fxe6 9. c3 Ba5
10. d4 0–0 11. Qb3 Bb6 12. a4 Rf7 13. a5
Bd8 14. Bd2 d5 15. Rae1 Bxa5 16. dxe5
Qxe5 17. Nf4 dxe4 18. Qc4 Nd7 19. Rxe4
Qb5 20. Qxb5 cxb5 21. Nxe6 Nf6
22. Re5 a6 23. Ra1 Re8 24. Rxa5 Rfe7
25. Nxg7 Rxe5 26. Nxe8 Rxe8 27. Kf1
Kf7 28. Ra1 Re4 29. f3 Ra4 30. Rxa4
bxa4 31. Ke2 Ke6 32. Kd3 Kd5 33. c4+
Kc5 34. Bg5 Ne8 35. Be7+ Kc6 36. g4
b5 37. h4 Ng7 38. h5 Ne6 39. cxb5+
axb5 40. Ke4 Nc5+ 41. Kd4 Ne6+
42. Ke5 Nc5 43. g5 b4 44. g6 hxg6
45. hxg6 a3 46. bxa3 bxa3 47. Kf5 1–0
(*The Gambit*, August 1930, p. 216)

118 Krogius (Finland)–Kashdan [C55]

Hamburg Olympiad, round 3, 1930 *[July 15]*

1. e4 e5 2. Nf3 Nc6 3. Nc3 Nf6
4. Bc4? Nxe4! 5. Nxe4 d5 6. Qe2 dxc4
7. Qxc4 Be6 8. Qa4 a6 9. Nxe5? b5
10. Nxc6 Qd5 11. Nc3 Qxg2 12. Qe4
Qxe4+ 13. Nxe4 Bd5 14. 0–0 Bxc6
15. Re1 0–0–0 16. d3 h6 17. Bd2 f5

18. Ng3 g6 19. a3 Bg7 20. Re6 Rd6
21. Rxd6 cxd6 22. c3 Re8 23. Kf1 Kd7
24. f4? Bf6 25. Re1 Rxe1+ 26. Kxe1 After
the exchange of rooks the advantage goes to
Black as the bishop is better posted than the
knight. 26. ... Ke6 27. Be3 g5 28. Ne2
Bd7! 29. Nd4+ Kf7 30. Kf2 Kg6 31. Nc2
Bc6 32. Nd4 Bd7 33. Nc2 Bc8 34. Nd4
Kh5 35. Kg3 g4 36. Kg2 Kg6 37. c4!
bxc4 38. dxc4 Bb7+ 39. Kf2 Be4
40. Ke2 h5 41. b4 h4 42. Bf2 g3
43. hxg3 hxg3 44. Bg1 Kh5 45. Ne6
Kg4 46. b5 a5 47. a4 Bb2 48. Be3 g2!
49. Kf2 Kh3 50. Kg1 Kg3 51. b6 Bc3
52. Nc7 Be1 53. Nd5 Kh3 54. b7 Bg3
55. b8Q Bh2+ 56. Kf2 g1Q+ 57. Ke2
Qg2+ 58. Bf2 Qf3+ 59. Ke1 Bxd5
60. Qh8+ Kg2 61. Qg7+ Bg3 0–1 (*Hamburg 1930*)

119 Rubinstein (Poland)–Kashdan [E44]

Hamburg Olympiad, round 4, 1930 *[July 15]*

1. d4 Nf6 2. c4 e6 3. Nc3 Bb4 4. e3
b6 5. Nge2 Ne4 6. f3 Bxc3+ 7. bxc3
Nd6 8. Ng3 Nc6 9. Qa4 h5 10. Bd3 h4
11. Ne4 Nxe4 12. Bxe4 Bb7 13. 0–0 Qf6
14. f4 Na5 15. Bxb7 Nxb7 16. e4 h3
17. g3 Nd6 18. e5 Qg6 19. exd6 Qe4
20. Rf2 Qe1+ 21. Rf1 Qe4 22. Rf2 Qe1+
The game in round 5 was forfeited by Macht
who had not yet arrived. ½–½ (*The Gambit*,
August 1930, p. 217)

120 Apscheneck [i.e., Apšenieks] (Latvia)–Kashdan [A46]

Hamburg Olympiad, round 6, 1930 *[July 17]*

1. d4 Nf6 2. Nf3 e6 3. Bg5 c5 4. e4
Turning the opening into a position akin to
that of the Sicilian Defense. 4. ... cxd4 5. e5
Inviting complications, but this pawn will pres-
ently be a bone of contention. 5. ... h6 6. Bh4
g5 7. Bg3 Ne4 8. Qxd4 Nxg3 9. hxg3
Nc6 10. Qe4 Qb6 11. Nbd2 Preferring to
give up the b pawn rather than retard the development to b3. 11. ... Qxb2 12. Rb1 Qc3
13. Rb3 Qa5 14. Bd3 g4 15. Rb5 Ng5 instead would have relieved the pressure upon the

pawn menaced in the center. **15. ... Qa3 16. Ng1** Necessary in order to avoid loss of the rook on h1. **16. ... a6 17. Rb3** Retreat all the way to b1 was in order here. **17. ... Qc1+ 18. Ke2 Qa1 19. c3 Na5 20. Rb1 Qxc3 21. Qxg4 Nc6 22. Ne4** Unsuspectingly White walks into the trap set for him. He loses a piece and the game. **22. ... Qxd3+! 0–1** (*The World*, August 24, 1930)

121 Kashdan–Dr. Balogh (Rumania) [C90]

Hamburg Olympiad, round 8, 1930 *[July 18]*

1. e4 e5 2. Nf3 Nc6 3. Bb5 a6 4. Ba4 Nf6 5. 0–0 Be7 6. Re1 b5 7. Bb3 d6 8. c3 Na5 9. Bc2 c5 10. d4 Qc7 11. h3 Nc6 12. d5 Nd8 13. Nbd2 0–0 14. a4 Ra7 15. Nf1 Ne8 16. Be3 f6 17. Bd3 Bd7 18. axb5 axb5 19. Qe2 Rxa1 20. Rxa1 Qb7 21. b4 Nf7 22. Qa2 Nc7 23. Qa7 Qxa7 24. Rxa7 Rc8 25. N3d2 Kf8 26. bxc5 dxc5 27. c4 Ke8 28. cxb5 Nxb5 29. Rxd7 Kxd7 30. Bxb5+ Kc7 31. Bd3 Rb8 32. f3 Rb4 33. Kf2 Rb2 34. Ke2 Nd8 35. f4 Nf7 36. Kf3 Nd6 37. Nc4 Nxc4 38. Bxc4 Rb4 39. Nd2 Kd6 40. fxe5+ fxe5 41. Bd3 Kd7 42. Nc4 Bd6 43. Bf2 Rb3 44. Ke2 Rb8 45. Bg3 Re8 46. Bc2 Kc7 47. Ba4 Rb8 48. Bxe5 Bxe5 49. Nxe5 Rb4 50. Bc2 Kd6 51. Nf7+ Ke7 52. Ng5 h6 53. Ne6 Kf7 54. Kd3 1–0 (*The Gambit*, August 1930, p. 219)

122 Ståhlberg (Sweden)– Kashdan [E23]

Hamburg Olympiad, round 9, 1930 *[July 19]*

1. d4 Nf6 2. c4 e6 3. Nc3 Bb4 One of Nimzovitch's favorites. The idea is either to double White's pawns, or gain a stronghold with the knight at e4, which can be supported by f5, and the fianchetto of the bishop at c8. **4. Qb3** Perhaps the strongest reply, as it gains time, and prepares, is ...Bxc3+, to play Qxc3. Other moves which have been tried here are Qc2, d5!, or 4. e3 b6 5 Nge2, followed by a3, or the simple Bd2. **4. ... c5 5. dxc5 Nc6 6. Nf3 Ne4** More consistent with Black's original plan than 6. ... Bxc5, but the latter would be just as effec-

tive. Black's gain of time with the text is more apparent than real. **7. Bd2 Nxc5** Or 7. ... Nxd2 8. Nxd2 f5 9. e3 Bxc5 with a good game. **8. Qc2 0–0** I did not know this at the time, but this proved to be a new move. The usual play was 8. ... f5, in order, after ...Bxc3, to play ...Ne4 very soon. **9. e4** Ståhlberg realized that I had avoided the "book" line, and thought this would take advantage of it. However, the e pawn proved to be a weakness. Correct was 9. a3 Bxc3 10. Bxc3 f5 11. b4! Ne4 12. Bb2. The scope of the queen's bishop, and Black's backward d pawn would give White the advantage. **9. ... Qf6!** An unusual looking move, as the queen is generally developed on the other wing, or at e7. But here there is a threat, by ...Bxc3, followed by Qg6, which will require careful defense by White. **10. 0–0–0 b6** Black cannot yet win the pawn. If 10. ... Bxc3 11. Bxc3 Qf4+ 12. Nd2! Qxf2? 13. b4 Na6 14. b5 wins. The text, besides developing the queen's bishop, prepares for the retreat ...Nb7 in this variation, thus again threatening the pawn. **11. Bd3 a5 12. Kb1** An amusing possibility here is 12. a3 a4! 13. axb4?? Nxb4 14. Qb1 Nb3 mate! **12. ... Qg6** Attacking the g pawn, which White cannot afford to give up, and also visualizing the coming advance by ...d5, after Ba6 has been played. **13. Rhg1 Ba6 14. Be3** Forcing an exchange of pieces in an attempt to relieve the pressure. The threat was ...d5! winning at least a pawn. **14. ... Nxd3 15. Qxd3 Bxc3 16. bxc3 d5!**

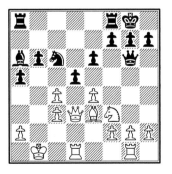

After 16. ... d5

Apparently simplifying, and leading to no immediate gain of material, but Black gains a strong attack, even without the queens, and White's pawn are still definitely weak after the exchange. **17. exd5 Qxd3+ 18. Rxd3 Bxc4 19. Rd2 Bxd5 20. Bxb6** Opening a file which becomes very useful for Black, but he must make the capture if he is to have any chance of equalizing. **20. … Rfb8 21. Rb2 a4** Threatening 22. … a3 23. Rb5 Bc4 winning. But not 21. … Bxf3 22. gxf3 Ne5 23. Bd4! and Black has nothing definite. **22. Bc7** Trying to exchange one rook, but it results in a loss of time. Still, there is hardly a good move left. If 22. Kh1 a3 23. Rbb1 Be4 24. Rb3 Bc2 25. Rb5 Ra6 26. Rc1 Bd3 wins. Or 22. a3 Bxf3 23. gxf3 Ne5 24. Bd4 Nc4! 25. Rxb8+ (Not 25. Rxg7+ Kf8 26. Rxb8+ Rxb8+ 27. Kc2 e5 wins a piece.) Rxb8+ 26. Kh2 e5 with a winning endgame. **22. … Rc8 23. Bf4 Na5** There is no good defense to the c pawn. If 24. Be5 f6 25. Bdd4 e5, etc. If 24. Bd2 Nc4 wins at least the exchange. Or 24. Rc2 Be4 wins. **24. Rc1** Seemingly overcoming all the difficulty, but now comes the surprising point, which allows Black to wind up with a pretty finish. **24. … Be4+ 25. Ka1 Nb3+!!** For if 26. axb3 axb3, followed by mate. And 26. Rxb3 would leave White with a hopeless ending. **0–1** Annotated by Kashdan in *Chess Review*, April 1936. (*The Gambit*, 1930)

123 Ahues (Germany)–Kashdan [D45]

Hamburg Olympiad, round 10, 1930 *[July 20]*

1. d4 Nf6 2. Nf3 e6 3. e3 d5 4. c4 Nbd7 5. Nc3 c6 6. cxd5 exd5 7. Bd3 Bd6 8. Qc2 0–0 9. 0–0 Re8 10. Re1 Nf8 11. Nd2 Ng6 12. Nf1 Nf4 13. Bf5 Bxf5 14. Qxf5 Qc8 15. Qxc8 Raxc8 16. Rd1 Ne6 17. Bd2 Nd7 18. Rac1 f5 19. Be1 Nf6 20. f3 Rcd8 21. Bf2 Rd7 22. Nd2 Bc7 23. Nb3 g5 24. Rc2 Kf7 25. Re2 Rde7 26. Red2 h5 27. Nc1 Ng7 28. Nd3 f4 29. e4 dxe4 30. Nxe4 Nxe4 31. fxe4 Rxe4 32. Nc5 Re2 33. Nxb7 g4 34. d5 Rxd2 35. Rxd2 g3 36. hxg3 fxg3 37. Kf1 gxf2 38. Rxf2+ Ke7 39. dxc6 Rf8 40. Rxf8 Kxf8 41. b4 Nf5 42. a4 Ne3+ 43. Ke2 Nd5 44. Nc5 Ke7 45. b5 Bb6 46. Ne4 Ke6 47. g3 Ke5 48. Kf3 Kd4 49. Nd6 Kc5 50. Nc8 Kb4 51. Ke4 Nc7 52. Ke5 Kxa4 53. Kd6 Nxb5+ 54. Kd7 Bf2 55. c7 Nxc7 56. Nxa7 Bxg3 57. Nc6 h4 58. Nd4 h3 59. Ne2 Be5 0–1 (*Brooklyn Daily Eagle*, August 28, 1930)

124 Kashdan–Hovind (Norway) [C28]

Hamburg Olympiad, round 11, 1930 *[July 21]*

1. e4 e5 2. Nc3 Nf6 3. Bc4 Nc6 4. d3 d6 5. f4 exf4 6. Bxf4 Be6 7. Bb5 a6 8. Ba4 b5 9. Bb3 Bxb3 10. axb3 Be7 11. Nge2 0–0 12. 0–0 Qd7 13. Ng3 Nd8 14. Nf5 Ne6 15. Be3 c6 16. Qf3 Ne8 17. d4 b4 18. Na4 Rb8 19. d5 cxd5 20. Nb6 Qb7 21. Nxe7+ Qxe7 22. Nxd5 Qb7 23. Ra4 N8c7 24. Rxb4 Qa8 25. Rc4 Rb7 26. Ne7+ Kh8 27. Nf5 Ne8 28. Rd1 Rd7 29. Bf4 Nxf4 30. Qxf4 d5 31. Rcd4 Nc7 32. Qg4 g6 33. Ne3 Rfd8 34. Qg5 Qa7 35. Qe5+ Kg8 36. Ng4 Ne8 37. Kh1 h5 38. Ne3 dxe4 39. Rxd7 Rxd7 40. Qxe8+ Kg7 41. Qxd7 1–0 (*The World* [New York], August 24, 1930)

125 Weenink (Holland)– Kashdan [D01]

Hamburg Olympiad, round 12, 1930 *[July 22]*

1. d4 Nf6 2. Nc3 d5 3. Bg5 Nbd7 4. Nf3 c6 5. e3 Qa5 6. Bxf6 Nxf6 7. Bd3 Ne4 8. Bxe4 dxe4 9. Nd2 Qg5 10. g3 Bg4 11. Ncxe4 Bxd1 12. Nxg5 Bxc2 13. 0–0 e6 14. Rfc1 Bg6 15. a3 0–0–0 16. Rc3 e5 17. Ngf3 exd4 18. Nxd4 Be7 19. b4 Kb8 20. N2b3 Bf6 21. Racl h5 22. h4 Be4 23. a4 Bd5 24. Nc5 g5 25. hxg5 Bxg5 26. b5 cxb5 27. Rb1 Bf6 28. Rxb5 Ka8 29. Rc1 h4 30. g4 Rhg8 31. f3 Bxd4 32. exd4 Bxf3 33. Kf2 Bc6 34. Rb4 Rxg4 35. Rel Rf4+ 36. Ke3 Rf3+ 37. Kd2 h3 38. d5 h2 39. Rh1 Rxd5+ 0–1 (*The Gambit*, September 1930, p. 240)

126 Kmoch (Austria)–Kashdan [C86]

Hamburg Olympiad, round 13, 1930 *[July 23]*

1. e4 e5 2. Nf3 Nc6 3. Bb5 a6 4. Ba4 Nf6 5. 0–0 Be7 6. Qe2 b5 7. Bb3 d6 8. c3 0–0 9. d4 Bg4 10. Rd1 Qc8 11. a4 b4 12. Be3 Rb8 13. Bc4 bxc3 14. Nxc3 exd4 15. Bxd4 Nxd4 16. Rxd4 Bxf3 17. gxf3 Qh3 18. Rd2 Nh5 19. Qf1 Qxf3

20. Be2 Qf4 21. Rad1 Nf6 22. Bxa6 Nxe4 23. Nxe4 Qxe4 24. Qc4 Qxc4 25. Bxc4 c6 26. Rc2 Rfd8 27. Bf1 c5 28. Bc4 Bf6 29. b3 Ra8 30. Re2 g6 31. Bd5 Ra7 32. Rde1 Kf8 33. Kg2 Be5! Despite being a pawn up, it is difficult to achieve a Black victory because of White's dominant d5 bishop and dangerous passed a4 pawn, but Black makes a good try 34. h3 h5 35. Ra2 Kg7 36. Ree2 Bc3? Black loses his direction. The a4 pawn advance should be held back by the rook, while the kingside pawns should be mobilized under cover of the e5 bishop. 37. Re3 Bb4 38. Rae2 From now on White controls the only open file, giving Black no winning chances. Rdd7 39. Re8 Kf6 40. f4 Bc3 41. Kf3 Ba5 Trading both rooks on e7 would only yield a draw at best, so Black plans to trade only a single rook. 42. R2e4 Rd8 43. Rxd8 Bxd8 44. Re8 Ba5 45. Re2 It seems that White is playing for a draw. With 45. Ke3, he could have started towards his passed pawn. g5 This creates a passed pawn, but it is a powerless one with Black's pieces sitting helplessly on the sidelines. 46. fxg5+ Kxg5 47. Rg2+ Kf6 47. ... Kh4 would have been met by 48. Rg7 resulting only in a draw. 48. Re2 Kf5 49. Re4 Bc3 50. Ke2! White finally finds the right path—activating his king to the queenside. Ba5 Black fails to return his bishop to e5. The White king could have been prevented from reaching b5 by playing Ra5 at any time. White is already better. 51. Kd3 Kg6 52. Kc4 Bc7? There have been many unnecessary moves by the bishop, but this one is the worst. Either 52. ... Bd8 or Bd2 was best to keep the fight alive. 53. Re7 f5 54. a5! It seems that Black did not expect this move. Now White can win automatically. Kf6 55. Rf7+ Ke5 56. a6 f4 57. Bb7 Bd8 58. Kb5 d5 59. Rd7 Bh4 60. Rxd5+ Ke6 61. Kb6 1–0 I assume that anyone playing first board in a chess olympiad would be happy with only one loss offset by 12 won games. Most likely the poor showing of the U.S. (they suffered a catastrophic 0–4 defeat by Austria) affected his performance in this game. A player plays not only for the team but also for himself. The analysis is by Benko from *Chess Life*, March 2006. The game with Desler in round 14 is not available. It was won by Kashdan. (*Hamburg*, 1930)

127 Sultan Khan (England)– Kashdan [C55]

Hamburg Olympiad, round 15, 1930 *[July 25]*

1. e4 e5 2. Nf3 Nc6 3. Bc4 Nf6 4. d3 Be7 5. Nc3 d6 6. h3 Na5 7. Bb3 Nxb3 8. axb3 0–0 9. Qe2 Re8 10. Bg5 h6 11. Bd2 c6 12. g4 Nh7 13. 0–0–0 Ng5 14. Rdg1 Nxf3 15. Qxf3 Bg5 16. Be3 a5 17. Kd1 b5 18. Bxg5 hxg5 19. Qg3 Re6 20. h4 a4 21. hxg5 axb3 22. Qh2 Kf8 23. Qh8+ Ke7 24. Qxd8+ Kxd8 25. cxb3 Ra1+ 26. Kd2 Rxg1 27. Rxg1 Rg6 28. f3 b4 29. Ne2 Rxg5 30. Rh1 Be6 31. Kc2 Rg6 32. Rh8+ Ke7 33. Rb8 c5 34. Rb7+ Kd8 35. Rb8+ Bc8 36. Ng3 Rf6 37. Nf5 g6 38. g5 Re6 39. Ne3 Kc7 40. Ra8 Kb7 41. Ra1 f6 42. Rg1 fxg5 43. Nd5 Bd7 44. Rxg5 Bc6 45. Ne3 Rf6 46. Rg3 Be8 47. Kd2 Rf8 48. Rh3 Bf7 49. Nc4 Kc6 50. Ke3 Ra8 51. f4 exf4+ 52. Kxf4 Ra1 53. Rg3 Rf1+ 54. Ke3 Kd7 55. Rg2 Ke7 56. e5 d5 57. Nd6 d4+ 58. Ke4 Bg8 59. Rxg6 Bh7 60. Nf5+ Rxf5 61. Kxf5 Bxg6+ 62. Kxg6 Ke6 63. Kg5 Kxe5 64. Kg4 Ke6 65. Kg5 ½–½ (*American Chess Bulletin*, September-October, 1930)

128 Kashdan–Flohr (Czechoslovakia) [B00]

Hamburg Olympiad, round 16, 1930 *[July 26]*

1. e4 Nc6 2. d4 d5 3. e5 Bf5 4. c3 e6 5. Ne2 Nge7 6. Ng3 Bg6 7. Bd3 Qd7 8. Qf3 b6 9. Nd2 Na5 10. h4 Bxd3 11. Qxd3 c5 12. b4 cxb4 12. ... c4 13. Qc2 Nec6 14. f4! would leave White with all the chances. 13. cxb4 Nc4 14. h5 After 14. Nxc4 dxc4 15. Qxc4 Rc8 followed by 16. ... Nc6 would give Black the initiative. 14. ... Rc8 15. h6! g6 16. Nf3 Nf5 17. a3 Qa4 18. Rb1 a5 19. Ne2 axb4 20. g4! bxa3 Reckoning the queenside pawns to be sufficient compensation, Flohr sacrifices the knight. 21. gxf5 gxf5 22. Rg1 b5 23. Nd2 Nxd2 There was nothing better, for White threatened to blockade the pawns by Nb3. 23. ... Bxh6 would have been met by 24. Nc3. 24. Bxd2 b4 25. Rg3! The immediate 25. Nc1 would have been answered by 25. ... Rxc1+ and 26. ... b3. 25. ... Rc4

26. Ncl Qa7 27. Nb3 Qc7 28. Ke2 Kd7 29. Rbgl Rc2 30. Rg8 Rxg8 31. Rxg8 Be7 Not 31. ... Bxh6? because of 32. Kdl!. 32. Qb5+ Qc6 33. Qb8 Qa6+ 34. Kdl Rc8 White's excellent defense has forced Black to simplify. 35. Rxc8 Qxc8 36. Qxc8+ Kxc8 37. Kc2 Kb7 38. Ncl Kb6 39. Kb3 Kb5 40. Na2 Bh4 The possibility of attacking his opponents pawns affords Black a slight chance. However, his attempts are foiled by accurate play. 41. Bel f6 42. Nxb4 fxe5 43. dxe5 Bg5 44. Nc2 Kc6 45. Nd4+ Kd7 46. Kxa3 Bxh6

After
46. ... Bxh6

The two extra pawns still ensure some counterplay. 47. Kb3 Bf4 48. Nf3 h5 49. Bc3 Bh6 50. Bb4 Bg7 51. Bd6 Bh6 52. Kc3 Bg7 53. Kd3 Bh6 54. Ke2 Bcl 55. Kfl Bb2 56. Bc5 Kc6 57. Bd4 Bcl 58. Kg2 Bf4 59. Be3 The exchange of bishops could have been avoided by 58. ... Bh6. In that event the White king would have penetrated on the kingside. 59. ... Bxe3 60. fxe3 d4! Black offers a pawn to make his king more active and in so doing almost obtains a draw. 61. exd4 Kd5 62. Kg3 Ke4 63. Ng5+! Kxd4 64. Kf4 Kd5 65. Nf3 Kc4 66. Kg5 Kd5 67. Kf6 f4 68. Nh4 68. Ng5 h4 69. Nxe6 f3 70. Nf4+ Ke4 71. Nh3 Ke3 72. Ng5 also wins. The accurately calculated text move leads to a spectacular but theoretical winning position. 68. ... Ke4 69. Kxe6 f3 70. Nxf3 Kxf3 71. Kf5! h4 72. e6 h3 73. e7 h2 74. e8Q Kg2 75. Kg4! After ...hl (Q) White continues 76. Qe2+ Kgl 77. Kg3. The game was awarded a special endgame prize. 1–0 (Chess Olympiads, by Földeák) The game with Marín of Spain in round 17 is not available. It was won by Kashdan.

129 Kashdan–Helling [B01]
Berlin Quadrangular, round 1, 1930
[August 8]

1. e4 d5 2. exd5 Qxd5 3. Nc3 Qa5 4. d4 e5 5. Nf3 Bg4 6. dxe5 Nc6 7. Bb5 Bb4 8. Qd3 Nge7 9. 0–0 0–0 10. Bxc6! bxc6 11. Ng5 Bf5 12. Qc4 h6 13. Nf3 Be6 14. Qe4 Rad8 15. Bd2 Bf5 16. Qc4! Bxc2 17. Ne4 Bxd2 18. Qxc2 Bf4 19. Nc5 Ng6? 20. Nb7 Qb4 21. Nxd8 Rxd8 22. e6 Rd5 23. Qxc6 Rh5 24. Qe8+ Kh7 25. exf7 Bxh2+ 26. Nxh2 Nf8 27. Rfel 1–0 (Deutsche Schachzeitung, September 1930)

130 H. Steiner–Kashdan [D36]
Berlin Quadrangular, round 2, 1930 *[August]*

1. d4 Nf6 2. c4 e6 3. Nf3 d5 4. Nc3 Nbd7 5. Bg5 c6 6. cxd5 exd5 7. e3 Be7 8. Bd3 0–0 9. Qc2 Re8 10. 0–0 Nf8 11. Ne5 Ng4 12. Bf4 Bd6 13. Nxg4 Bxg4 14. Bg3 Bxg3 15. hxg3 Qd6 16. Rael Rad8 17. Na4 h5 18. Nc5 Re7 19. Bf5 g6 20. Bxg4 hxg4 21. e4 Ne6 22. e5 Qc7 23. Nxe6 Rxe6 24. Qd1 c5 25. Qxg4 Qb6 26. Re2 cxd4 27. Rd1 Rde8 28. f4 d3+ 29. Rf2 Rc6 30. Rxd3 Rc2 31. Qf3 Rxb2 32. Rb3 Rbl+ 33. Kh2 Rxb3 34. axb3 Rc8 35. g4 Qd4 36. Qg3 Kg7 37. f5 Rh8+ 38. Kgl g5 39. e6 fxe6 40. Qc7+ Kf6 41. fxe6+ Kxe6 42. Qxb7 Qdl+ 43. Rf1 Rhl+ 44. Kxhl Qxfl+ 45. Kh2 Qf4+ 46. Khl Qe3 47. Qc6+ Ke5 48. Kh2 Qb6 49. Qd7 Qh6+ 50. Kgl a6 51. Qf5+ Kd6 52. Qc8 Qh7 53. Qxa6+ Ke5 54. Qe2+ Qe4 55. Kf2 Qxe2+ 56. Kxe2 Ke4 57. Kd2 Kd4 58. g3 Ke4 59. Ke2 ½–½ (Deutsche Schachzeitung, September 1930)

131 Sämisch–Kashdan [D51]
Berlin Quadrangular, round 3, 1930 *[August]*

1. d4 Nf6 2. c4 e6 3. Nc3 d5 4. Bg5 Nbd7 5. e3 c6 6. a3 Be7 7. Qc2 0–0 8. Nf3 a6 9. Rdl Re8 10. Bd3 dxc4 11. Bxc4 Nd5 12. Bxe7 Qxe7 13. Ne4 b5 14. Ba2 Bb7 15. 0–0 Rac8 16. Rcl N5f6 17. Ned2 e5 18. Ng5 Rf8 19. Bbl

After
19. Bb1

19. ... exd4 20. N×h7 dxe3 21. N×f8 exd2 22. N×d7 dxc1Q 23. N×f6+ Q×f6 24. R×c1 g6 25. Rd1 c5! 26. f3 c4 27. Qc3 Qb6+ 28. Kh1 Re8 29. h4 Re3 30. Qd2 Re5 31. Qf4 Qe6 32. B×g6!! Very pretty and strong. **32. ... f×g6 33. Rd8+ Kh7 34. Rf8??** Correct was 34. Qf8 after which Black has nothing better then Re1+ 35. Kh2 Qe5+ 36. f4 Rh1+ 37. K×h1 Qe1+ with a draw by perpetual check. **34. ... Bd5 35. Rf7+ Q×f7 36. Q×e5 a5 37. Qc3** And now White overstepped the time limit. **0–1** (*Deutsche Schachzeitung*, September 1930)

132 Helling–Kashdan [A45]

Berlin Quadrangular, round 4, 1930 *[August]*

1. d4 Nf6 2. e3 e6 3. Nd2 c5 4. Bd3 Nc6 5. c3 Qc7 6. Ngf3 d5 7. 0–0 Bd6 8. e4 cxd4 9. cxd4 Nb4 10. Bb1 dxe4 11. Nxe4 Nxe4 12. Bxe4 Bd7 13. Re1 0–0 14. Bxh7+ Kxh7 15. Ng5+ Kg6 16. h4 Bh2+ 17. Kh1 Bf4 18. Qg4 Bxg5 19. Qxg5+ Kh7 20. Bf4 Qd8 21. Qh5+ Kg8 22. Bd6 Nc2 23. Re5 f6 24. Bxf8 Qxf8 25. Rc1 fxe5 0–1 (*Deutsche Schachzeitung*, September 1930)

133 Kashdan–H. Steiner [C47]

Berlin Quadrangular, round 5, 1930 *[August]*

1. e4 e5 2. Nf3 Nc6 3. d4 exd4 4. Nxd4 Nf6 5. Nc3 Bb4 6. Nxc6 bxc6 7. Bd3 d5 8. exd5 cxd5 9. 0–0 0–0 10. Bg5 c6 11. Qf3 Be7 12. Rfe1 Rb8 13. Ne2 Rxb2 14. Nd4 Rb6 15. a4 c5 16. a5 Rd6 17. Nb5 Re6 18. Nxa7 Rxe1+ 19. Rxe1 Qxa5 20. Rxe7 Qa1+ 21. Bf1 Ba6 22. h3 Qxf1+ 23. Kh2 Ne4 24. Be3 Qb1

25. Qf5 Qb8+ 26. Qe5 ½–½ (*Deutsche Schachzeitung*, September 1930)

134 Kashdan–Sämisch [B85]

Berlin Quadrangular, round 6, 1930
[August 14]

1. e4 c5 2. Nf3 Nc6 3. d4 cxd4 4. Nxd4 Nf6 5. Nc3 d6 6. Be2 e6 7. 0–0 Be7 8. Be3 Bd7 9. f4 a6 10. Bf3 Qc7 11. Nb3 Rb8? 12. a4 Na5? 13. Nxa5 Qxa5 14. Qd2! Qc7 15. a5! Bc6

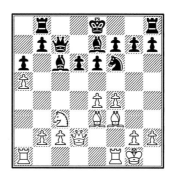

After
15. ... Bc6

White has a formidable grip on b6, and Black has no real counterplay. **16. Rfe1 0–0 17. Bb6 Qc8 18. Qf2 Nd7 19. Ba7 Ra8** Now White increases his advantage. **20. Nd5! exd5 21. exd5 Bf6 22. dxc6 bxc6 23. c3 d5** Black's pawn weaknesses will be his undoing. **24. Bd4 Qc7 25. g3 Rab8 26. b4 Rfd8 27. Bxf6 Nxf6 28. Qc5 Rd6 29. Re5 Re6 30. Rae1! Nd7?** A blunder, but the position had become untenable. **31. Rxe6! fxe6 32. Qe7 1–0** (*Deutsche Schachzeitung*, September 1928)

135 Kashdan–Orbach [C73]

Frankfort, round 1, 1930 *[September 8]*

1. e4 e5 2. Nf3 Nc6 3. Bb5 a6 4. Ba4 d6 5. Bxc6+ bxc6 6. d4 exd4 7. Nxd4 c5 8. Nf3 Be7 9. Qe2 Bg4 10. Nc3 Nf6 11. h3 Bxf3 12. Qxf3 0–0 13. 0–0 Nd7 14. Nd5 Bf6 15. Rb1 Re8 16. b4 cxb4 17. Rxb4 Rb8 18. Rxb8 Qxb8 19. Qg4 Qd8 20. Bh6 Nb6 21. Nxb6 cxb6 22. Rd1 Qc7 23. Rd2 Qc6 24. g3 g6 25. Qf4 Be5 26. Qe3 Bc3 27. Rd3 Bf6 28. Qd2 Re6 29. Rd5 Bg7 30. Bxg7

Kxg7 31. Qd4+ Kg8 32. c4 f6 33. f4 Kf7
34. f5 gxf5 35. exf5 Re2 36. Qh4 Re7
37. Qxh7+ Kf8 38. Qh8+ Kf7 39. Qh5+
Kf8 40. Qh4 Kf7 41. Kh2 b5 42. Qh5+
Kf8 43. Qh8+ Kf7 44. Rd3 Qe8
45. Qh7+ Kf8 46. Qh6+ 1–0 (*Deutsche
Schachzeitung*, October 1930)

136 Mannheimer–Kashdan [D30]
Frankfort, round 2, 1930 *[September]*

1. d4 Nf6 2. c4 e6 3. Nf3 d5 4. Bf4
This move is weak here. Better is 4. Nc3 Nbd7
5. Bf4, when Black has fewer threats. 4. ...
dxc4 The simplest course, gaining time in development while White is striving to recover
the pawn. 5. e3 Surer is Qa4+ and Qxc4.
Black's next move proves troublesome. 5. ...
Bb4+ 6. Nfd2 A strange looking move, and
certainly indicating something wrong in the
opening, if this retreat is necessary. But if
6. Nbd2 c3, and in each case Black can maintain
the pawn with a good game. 6. ... b5 7. a4
The start of a long-winded plan to regain the
pawn, which succeeds in the objective, but at a
considerable cost in time and development.
7. ... c6 8. axb5 cxb5 9. Bxb8 The point,
winning the a pawn. But he is forced to exchange his only developed piece, and Black
soon gets full control of the game. 9. ... Rxb8
10. Rxa7 Ba5! Threatening to win the exchange by ...Qb6. White's reply is forced.
11. Qf3 Qb6 12. Ra8 Rxa8 13. Qxa8
0–0! Simple development, but it involves a
threat which again wins time. White never gets
a moment to spare. Or a chance to think of his
kingside pieces. 14. Qf3 Bb7 15. Qf4 Ne4
The threat is now Bxd2+ 17. Nxd7 Qa5! White
has only one move to stave off immediate loss.
16. f3 Nxd2 17. Nxd2 Re8!

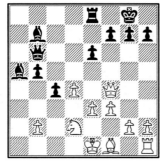

After
17. ... Re8

The last piece gets into action. The threat is
17. ... e5 19. dxe5 Rd8!. Against this plan, which
must open either the e or d file, White has no
good defense. 18. Qh4 e5 19. Qf2 No better
or worse than anything else. There is no help.
19. ... exd4 20. e4 f5! The last blow, which
opens up all the lines, and leads to a mating net
in a few moves. 21. Kd1 Bxd2 22. Kxd2 fxe4
23. fxe4 Qa5+ 0–1 Annotated by Kashdan.
(*Chess Review*, January 1936)

137 Kashdan–Pirc [D15]
Frankfort, round 3, 1930 *[September]*

1. d4 d5 2. c4 c6 3. Nf3 Nf6 4. Nc3
dxc4 5. e3 b5 6. Ne5 Bb7 7. b3 b4
8. Bxc4 (If Bxc3? then 9. Bxf7 mate! 8. ... e6
9. Na4 Nbd7 10. f4 Be7 11. Qf3 Qc7
12. Qh3 0–0 13. 0–0 c5 14. Bb2 Rad8
15. Bxe6 fxe6 16. Qxe6+ Kh8 17. Qxe7
Rde8 18. Nf7+ Rxf7 19. Qxf7 Bd5
20. Qxe8+ Nxe8 21. dxc5 Nef6 22. Bd4
Qc6 23. Rf2 Ne4 24. Rc2 Nd6 25. Re1
Be4 26. Rd2 Nf5 27. Bb2 Qg6 28. Ree2
If 28. Rxd7? then Qxg2 mate! 28. ... Qf7
29. Bd4 h5 30. Nb2 Nh4 31. Nc4 Qg6
32. Kh1 Nf5 33. Nd6 Nxd6 34. cxd6
h4 35. h3 a5 36. Kg1 Kg8 37. Bb2 Kf7
38. Re1 Qg3 39. Ree2 Bf3 40. Rf2 Be4
41. Bd4 Qg6 42. Bb2 Qf5 43. Rf1 Bc6
44. Bd4 g6 45. Rff2 Ke6 46. Rfe2 Qe4
47. Kh2 Qb1 48. Rb2 Qf5 49. Rbd2 Qe4
50. Re1 Qf5 51. Ree2 Bd5 52. Bb2 Nc5
53. Be5 g5 54. Rd4 g4 55. hxg4 Qb1
56. e4 Bc6 57. Rc4 Qd3 58. Rxc5 Qxe2
59. Rxc6 Qe3 ½–½ (*Deutsche Schachzeitung*,
October 1930)

138 Kashdan–G. Thomas [E00]
Frankfort, round 4, 1930 *[September]*

1. d4 Nf6 2. c4 e6 3. a3 d5 4. Nc3
Nbd7 5. Bg5 Be7 6. e3 0–0 7. Nf3 a6
8. cxd5 Nxd5 9. Bxe7 Qxe7 10. Nxd5
exd5 11. Bd3 Nf6 12. Qc2 Ne4 13. Rc1 c6
14. Bxe4 dxe4 15. Nd2 Re8 16. 0–0 Bf5
17. f4 Rad8 18. Nb3 Rd5 19. Nc5 Bc8
20. b4 Rh5 21. Qf2 Rd8 22. Na4 Rd6
23. Rc5 Rdh6 24. Rxh5 Rxh5 25. Rc1
Be6 26. Rc5 Rxc5 27. Nxc5 f5 28. h3

Bd5 29. Qg3 b6 30. Na4 a5 31. N×b6
a×b4 32. a×b4 Q×b4 33. Nd7 Qe7
34. Nc5 Qd8 35. Kh2 Kf7 36. Qe1 g5
37. f×g5 Q×g5 38. Qg3 Qe7 39. Qf4 Kg6
40. g4 f×g4 41. h×g4 Qh4+ 42. Kg2 Kg7
43. Nd7 h6 44. Qf8+ Kh7 45. Qf5+ Kg7
46. Ne5 Qg5 47. Qf4 Qe7 48. Kg3 Qg5
49. Nd7 Kg6 50. Nc5 Qe7 51. Qf5+ Kg7
52. Kf4 Qh4 53. Ne6+ B×e6 54. Q×e6
Qh2+ 55. K×e4 Qh1+ 56. Kf4 Qc1
57. Kf5 Qc2+ 58. Qe4 Qc1 59. Qe5+ 1–0
(*Deutsche Schachzeitung*, October 1930)

139 Nimzovitch–Kashdan [A06]
Frankfort, round 5, 1930 *[September]*

1. Nf3 Nf6 2. b3 d5 3. Bb2 c5 4. e3
Nc6 5. Bb5 Qb6 6. B×c6+ Q×c6 7. d3
g6 8. Nbd2 Bg7 9. Qe2 0–0 10. a4 Rd8
11. 0–0 b6 12. Rfe1 a6 13. e4 d×e4
14. N×e4 N×e4 15. B×g7 K×g7 16. Q×e4
Q×e4 17. R×e4 Ra7 18. Rae1 e6 19. Ne5
Bb7 20. R4e3 Bd5 21. f4 Rc7 22. Ra1
Rb8 23. Ree1 h5 24. Kf2 b5 25. a×b5
a×b5 26. Reb1 f6 27. Nf3 Rbb7 28. Nd2
Ra7 29. c4 Bc6 30. c×b5 B×b5 31. Ke3
Bc6 32. R×a7 R×a7 33. g3 Bd5 34. Rc1
Ra5 35. h3 e5 36. f×e5 f×e5 37. Ne4
B×b3 38. N×c5 Bd5 39. Ne4 Ra2
40. Rc7+ Kh6 41. Nf6 Bb3 42. h4 g5
43. Rc6 g×h4 44. g×h4 Ra5 45. Ke4 Bf7
½–½ (*Deutsche Schachzeitung*, October 1930)

140 Kashdan–Mieses [A25]
Frankfort, round 6, 1930 *[September]*

1. c4 e5 2. Nc3 Nc6 3. g3 Nf6 4. Bg2
Bb4 5. Nd5 Bc5 6. d3 N×d5 7. B×d5
Bb4+ 8. Bd2 B×d2+ 9. Q×d2 Qe7 10. e3
Qb4 11. Ne2 Q×d2+ 12. K×d2 Ne7
13. Bg2 d6 14. b4 Bd7 15. B×b7 Rb8
16. Bg2 R×b4 17. Rhb1 Rb6 18. a4 0–0
19. R×b6 a×b6 20. a5 b×a5 21. R×a5 Bc6
22. B×c6 N×c6 23. Ra6 Nb4 24. Ra4
Rb8 25. Nc3 Kf8 26. Ne4 c5 27. N×d6
Rd8 28. Nb7 R×d3+ 29. Ke2 Rc3
30. N×c5 R×c4 31. Nd3 Rc2+ 32. Kd1
N×d3 33. K×c2 N×f2 34. Kd2 h5
35. Ke2 Ng4 36. h3 Nf6 37. Ra5 Nd7
38. Kd3 g6 39. Ke4 Ke7 40. Kd5 Nb6+

41. Kc6 Nc4 42. Rc5 Nd2 43. R×e5+
Kf6 44. Kd5 Kg7 45. g4 Nf3 46. Re8
h4 47. Ra8 Ng1 48. Ra2 N×h3 49. Rh2
Ng5 50. R×h4 Kf6 51. Rh1 Ne6 52. Rf1+
Ke7 53. Ke5 Nc5 54. g5 Nd7+ 55. Kd5
Nb6+ 56. Kd4 Nd7 57. Ra1 Nf8
58. Ra7+ Kd6 59. Ra6+ Ke7 60. Ke5
Nh7 61. Ra7+ Kf8 62. Kf4 Kg7 63. Re7
Kf8 64. Re5 Kg8 65. Ke4 Kg7 66. Kd5
Nf8 67. Kd6 Nh7 68. Ke7 Kg8 69. Ra5
Kg7 70. e4 Kg8 71. Ra8+ Kg7 72. e5
N×g5 73. Rf8 Kh6 74. R×f7 Kh5 75. Rf1
Ne4 76. Re1 Nc3 77. e6 g5 78. Kf7 1–0
(*Deutsche Schachzeitung*, October 1930)

141 Colle–Kashdan [D12]
Frankfort, round 7, 1930 *[September]*

1. d4 Nf6 2. Nf3 d5 3. e3 Bf5 4. c4 c6
5. Nc3 e6 6. Bd3 B×d3 7. Q×d3 Nbd7
8. 0–0 Be7 9. e4 d×e4 10. N×e4 N×e4
11. Q×e4 Nf6 12. Qe2 0–0 13. Bd2 Qb6
14. Bc3 Bb4 15. Rab1 Rfd8 16. a3 B×c3
17. b×c3 Qa6 18. Ne5 c5 19. d×c5 Rac8
20. Rb5 Nd7 21. N×d7 R×d7 22. Rd1
Rcd8 23. R×d7 R×d7 24. Rb1 h6 25. h3
Q×a3 26. Qe5 Qa6 27. c6 Q×c6
28. Qb8+ Kh7 29. Q×a7 Q×c4 30. Qa5
Qe4 31. Qb4 Qf5 32. Qb5?? Rd1+ 0–1
(*Deutsche Schachzeitung*, November 1930)

142 Kashdan–Ahues [C87]
Frankfort, round 8, 1930 *[September]*

1. e4 e5 2. Nf3 Nc6 3. Bb5 a6 4. Ba4
d6 5. d4 Bd7 6. c3 Nf6 7. Nbd2 Be7
8. 0–0 0–0 9. Re1 Re8 10. Nf1 e×d4
11. c×d4 d5 12. e×d5 N×d5 13. Ne3 N×e3
14. B×e3 Nb4 15. B×d7 Q×d7 16. Qb3
Qd5 17. Q×d5 N×d5 18. Bd2 Bb4
19. R×e8+ R×e8 20. Re1 R×e1+ 21. B×e1
B×e1 22. N×e1 Nb4 23. a3 Nc6 24. Nf3
f6 25. Kf1 Kf7 26. Ke2 Ke6 27. Kd3 Kd5
28. h4 h5 29. Kc3 a5 30. b3 b6 31. Kd3
Nd8 32. Ng1 c6 33. Ne2 Ne6 ½–½
(*Deutsche Schachzeitung*, November 1930)

143 Sämisch–Kashdan [D52]
Frankfort, round 9, 1930 *[September]*

1. d4 Nf6 2. Nf3 e6 3. c4 d5 4. Bg5

Nbd7 5. Nc3 c6 6. e3 Qa5 7. Nd2 Bb4
8. Qc2 0–0 9. Be2 e5 10. 0–0 exd4
11. Nb3 Qc7 12. Nxd4 dxc4 13. Bxc4 Qa5
14. Nf3 Ne5 15. Nxe5 Qxe5 16. Bf4 Qe7
17. Bd3 h6 18. h3 Be6 19. Bh2 Rad8
20. e4 Nd7 21. Rfe1 Nc5 22. Bf1 Rd7
23. Rad1 Rfd8 24. Rxd7 Rxd7 25. f4
Bxa2 26. e5 Bb3 27. Qb1 Na4 28. e6
fxe6 29. Kh1 Nxc3 30. bxc3 Bxc3
31. Rc1 Bd2 32. Qxb3 Bxc1 33. Bc4 Kh8
34. Bxe6 Rd4 35. f5 Qb4 36. Qg3 Bf4
0–1 (*Deutsche Schachzeitung*, November 1930)

144 Kashdan–List [C79]
Frankfort, round 10, 1930 *[September]*

1. e4 e5 2. Nf3 Nc6 3. Bb5 a6 4. Ba4
d6 5. 0–0 Nf6 6. d4 b5 7. dxe5 dxe5
8. Qxd8+ Nxd8 9. Bb3 Bd6 10. Re1 Bb7
11. Nbd2 Ne6 12. c3 Ke7 13. Bc2 Nc5
14. b4 Ne6 15. Nf1 c5 16. Ne3 g6
17. Nd5+ Nxd5 18. exd5 Bxd5 19. bxc5
Bxc5 20. Nxe5 Rac8 21. Nd3 Bd6
22. Nf4 Bxf4 23. Bxf4 Rhd8 24. Be5 f6
25. Bd4 Kf7 26. Bb6 Rd7 27. Ba5 Nf4
28. Bb4 Be6 29. Red1 Rxd1+ 30. Bxd1
Nd3 31. Ba5 Nb2 32. Bb3 Bc4 33. Rb1
Re8 34. h3 Re2 35. Bb6 h5 36. Bc5 g5
37. Bd4 h4 38. Ra1 Rd2 39. Re1 Nd3
40. Re4 Bxb3 41. axb3 Rd1+ 42. Kh2
Nc1 43. b4 Nb3 44. Bb6 f5 45. Re2 Kf6
46. Re8 Nd2 47. Rd8 f4 48. g3 f3
49. gxh4 gxh4 50. Rd4 Kf5 51. Rxh4
Nf1+ 52. Kg1 Ne3+ 53. Kh2 Nf1+
54. Kg1 Ng3+ 55. Kh2 Ne4 56. Be3
Nxc3 57. Rf4+ Kg6 58. Rxf3 Nd5
59. Rg3+ Kf7 60. Bc5 Re1 61. Rg5 Nf6
62. f3 Nd7 63. h4 Nxc5 64. Rxc5 Rb1
65. Rf5+ Kg6 66. Rf4 Ra1 67. Rg4+ Kh6
68. Kg3 Ra4 69. Rd4 Kh5 70. Re4 Ra1
71. Re5+ Kg6 72. Kg4 Rg1+ 73. Kf4 Rb1
74. Re4 Kf6 75. Rd4 Rh1 76. Rd6+ Kg7
77. Kg5 Rg1+ 78. Kf5 Rb1 79. Rd4 Rg1
80. f4 Ra1 81. Rd6 Ra4 82. Kg5 Rxb4
83. Rxa6 Rb1 84. Ra7+ Kg8 85. Rb7 b4
86. Kg6 Rg1+ 87. Kf6 Rb1 88. h5 b3
89. h6 Rh1 90. Rb8+ Kh7 91. Rxb3
Rxh6+ 92. Kf7 Rh5 93. Kf6 Rh6+
94. Ke7 Ra6 95. Re3 Ra7+ 96. Kf6 Ra8
97. Re7+ Kg8 98. f5 Kf8 99. Rf7+ Kg8

100. Kg6 Ra6+ 101. Rf6 Ra7 102. Re6
Rg7+ 103. Kf6 Rf7+ 104. Ke5 Ra7
105. Kf6 Rf7+ 106. Kg5 Ra7 107. Rg6+
Kh7 108. Rh6+ Kg8 109. Rh1 Rg7+
110. Kf6 Ra7 111. Re1 Kf8 ½–½ (*Deutsche
Schachzeitung*, January 1931)

145 Przepiórka–Kashdan [E16]
Frankfort, round 11, 1930 *[September 18]*

1. d4 Nf6 2. Nf3 e6 3. c4 b6 4. g3 Bb7
5. Bg2 Bb4+ 6. Bd2 Qe7 7. 0–0 0–0

After
7. ... 0–0

8. Nc3? With 8. Bf4 White would achieve
a clear advantage 8. ... d5? 9. c5! bxc 10. a3 Ba5
11. dxc c6 12. Bd6 Qd8 13. Bxf8 Qxf8 14. b4
Bc7 15. Nd2 e5 16. e4! and White won (Znosko-
Borovsky–Thomas, Ramsgate 1929) Instead Black
must play 8. ... Bd6. 8. ... c5 9. Rc1 cxd4
10. Nxd4 Bxg2 11. Kxg2 Rc8 12. b3 Bc5
13. Nc2 Nc6 14. Be3 d5 15. cxd5 exd5
16. Nd4 Ba3 17. Rb1 Bb4 18. Ncb5 Ne5
19. Nf5 Qd7 20. Nbd4 Ne4 21. Rc1 Rc5
22. Nh4 Ng4 23. Qd3 Nxe3+ 24. fxe3
But not 24. Qxe3 because of Bd2. 24. ... g6
25. Nhf3 Re8 26. Rxc5 Nxc5 27. Qb5
Qxb5 28. Nxb5 Rxe3 29. Nxa7 Rxe2+
30. Rf2 Re3 31. Nb5 Nd3 32. Rc2 Kg7
Overlooking 32. ... Rxf3 33. Kxf3 Ne1+ followed
by 34. Nxc2. 33. Nbd4 Bc5 34. Rd2 Bb4
35. Rc2 h6 36. Kf1 Ne1 37. Nxe1 Rxe1+
38. Kg2 Bc5 39. Nf3 Rd1 40. Re2 f5
41. Re1 Rd3 42. Re6 g5 43. b4 Be3
44. Kf1 Ra3 45. Ke2 f4 46. gxf4 gxf4
47. Rd6 Rxa2+ 48. Kd3 Rf2 49. Nh4
Rd2+ 50. Kc3 h5 51. Nf5+ Kf7 52. h4
d4+! Forces a won pawn endgame. 53. Nxd4
Rxd4 54. Rxd4 Bxd4+ 55. Kxd4 Ke6
56. Ke4 f3 57. Kxf3 Ke5 58. Ke3 b5!

59. Kd3 Kd5 60. Ke3 Or 60. Kc3 Ke4.
60. ... Kc4 61. Kf4 Kxb4 62. Kg5 Kc5
63. Kxh5 b4 0-1 (*Deutsche Schachzeitung*,
January 1931)

146 Kashdan-Reich [B40]

Gyor, Hungary, round 1, 1930 *[October 2]*

1. e4 c5 2. Nf3 e6 3. d4 cxd4 4. Nxd4
Nf6 5. Bd3 Nc6 6. Nxc6 dxc6 7. 0-0
e5 8. Nd2 Bg4 9. Qe1 Bc5 10. Nc4 Qe7
11. Bd2 Nd7 12. b4 Bd4 13. c3 Bb6
14. Nxb6 axb6 15. Be3 b5 16. a3 Be6
17. f4 f6 18. f5 Bb3 19. Qh4 Qf7 20. Be2
Kd8 21. Qf2 Kc7 22. Rfc1 Ra6 23. Bd3
Rd8 24. Qb2 Nb6 25. Rcb1 Bc4
26. Bxb6+ Rxb6 27. Bc2 Ra6 28. Rd1
Rc8 29. Rd2 Raa8 30. Rad1 Qe7 31. Qc1
Rd8 32. Rxd8 Rxd8 33. a4 Rxd1+
34. Qxd1 bxa4 35. Bxa4 Qd7 36. Kf2
Qxd1 37. Bxd1 c5 38. bxc5 Kc6 39. g4
h6 40. h4 Kxc5 41. Kf3 Ba2 42. Be2
Bb1 43. Ke3 Kb6 44. Bd1 Kb5 45. Bb3
b6 46. Kf3 Bd3 47. Ke3 ½-½ (*Gyor* 1930)

147 H. Steiner-Kashdan [B13]

Gyor, round 2, 1930 *[October]*

1. e4 c6 2. d4 d5 3. exd5 cxd5 4. Bd3
Nf6 5. h3 With the double purpose of preventing a "pin" and affording a retreat for the
queen bishop when developed. 5. ... a6 6. Nf3
Nc6 7. c3 g6 Or 7. ... e6, to be followed by b5
and appropriate queenside fixing. 8. 0-0 Bg7
9. Bf4 0-0 10. Nbd2 Nh5 11. Bh2 Bh6
By this means Black gains control of f4, an important strategical point. 12. Re1 Bf4 13. Nf1
Qc7 14. Ne3 Be6 In instead 14. ... e6, this
would curtail the scope of the bishop badly.
15. Bxf4 Qxf4 16. g3 Qd6 He might play
16. ... Nxg3, sacrificing a piece for three pawns,
but it would be a case of taking chances.
17. Ng4 Nf6 18. Ng5? (*see diagram*)
White here goes astray. Nxf6+ was in order.
18. ... Nxg4 19. hxg4 Bd7 20. f4 Trying
vainly to stop a break in the center, which must
necessarily give Black the whip hand. 20. ... f6
21. Nh3 e5 22. Kg2 This king is the more exposed of the two and for that reason White balks
at initiating the pawn exchanges. 22. ... exd4

After
18. Ng5

23. cxd4 Nxd4 24. Bxg6 hxg6 25. Qxd4
Bxg4 26. Nf2 Bd7 With a clear pawn to the
good and the superior position, Black has the
game well in hand. 27. Ne4 Qe6 28. Nf2 If
28. Ng5 Qf5 29. Re7 Rac8, taking the sting out
of the seeming menace of White's tactics.
28. ... Qf7 29. Rh1 Kg7 30. Rae1 Rfe8
31. Nd3 Bf5 32. Nf2 Rac8 The lines of
communications are all in possession of Black.
33. g4 Rc4 34. Qd1 Be4+ 35. Nxe4
Rexe4 36. Rxe4 Rxe4 37. Rf1 Qe6 Estab-
lishing an absolutely invincible position. The
rest is merely routine, but instructively worked
out by Black. 38. Rf2 Re1 39. f5 He has no
choice. Any other course is equally futile. 39. ...
gxf5 40. gxf5 Rxd1 41. fxe6 Re1 42. Rc2
Kg6 43. Rc7 b5 44. Rc6 Kf5 45. Rxa6
Rxe6 46. Ra5 Re2+ 47. Kf3 Rxb2 48. a4
Rb3+ 49. Ke2 bxa4 50. Rxd5+ Ke4
51. Ra5 Ra3 52. Kd2 f5 53. Kc2 f4
54. Ra8 Ke3 55. Re8+ Kf2 56. Re4 f3
57. Kb2 Re3 58. Rxa4 Re2+ 0-1 (*American Chess Bulletin*, April 1931)

148 Kashdan-Boros [E11]

Gyor, round 3, 1930 *[October]*

1. d4 Nf6 2. c4 e6 3. Nf3 Bb4+ 4. Bd2
Bxd2+ 5. Qxd2 d6 6. Nc3 Qe7 7. g3 0-0
8. Bg2 Nc6 9. 0-0 e5 10. d5 Nd8 11. Nh4
Nh5 12. e4 g6 13. Rae1 f5 14. exf5 gxf5
15. f4 e4 16. Bh3 Ng7 17. Ng2 h5 18. Nb5
a6 19. Nd4 Bd7 20. Ne3 Rb8 21. Rc1
Rf6 22. Qa5 Rc8 23. c5 dxc5 24. Qxc5
Qxc5 25. Rxc5 b6 26. Rc3 c5 27. Rfc1
Rf8 28. Ndc2 Bb5 29. Na3 Nb7
30. Nac4 Rf6 31. b3 Rd8 32. Rd1 Bxc4
33. bxc4 Rdd6 34. Rb1 Nd8 35. Ra3 a5
36. Rab3 Kh7 37. Nd1 Ne8 38. Nc3 Nc7

39. Bxf5+! Rxf5 40. Nxe4 Rg6 41. Rxb6 Rxf4 42. Rxg6 Rxe4 43. Rd6 Re8 44. Rd7+ 1–0 (*Gyor* 1930)

149 Balogh–Kashdan [C73]
Gyor, round 4, 1930 *[October]*

1. e4 e5 2. Nf3 Nc6 3. Bb5 a6 4. Ba4 d6 5. Bxc6+ bxc6 6. d4 f6 Quite sound. Black's development is difficult, but White can hardly form an attack without the missing bishop. **7. 0–0 Ne7 8. Nh4 Be6 9. g3** If 9. f4 Bc4 10. Rf3 exf4, and he cannot recapture. 11. Rxf4 g5 12. Rxf6 gxh4 13. Qh5+ Ng6 14. Rxg6 Bf7 15. Re6+ Be7 wins the exchange. **9. ... g5** Venturesome, but in the spirit of the opening. Black must seek open lines. **10. Ng2 c5 11. d5** Exchanging leaves Black with the superior ending. **11. ... Bf7 12. h4** Here f4 was in order. The game might continue 12. ... gxf4 13. Bg7 c4! followed by c6. The text is relatively weak. **12. ... gxh4 13. Nxh4 Qd7 14. Kg2** If 14. Qf3 Bg7, followed by Bg6 and f5. **14. ... f5 15. f4** Going in for complications. Passive play will no longer serve. **15. ... fxe4 16. Nc3 Bg7 17. Qe2 Nxd5 18. Nxe4** If 18. Qxe4 c6, threatening Nxc3. **18. ... 0–0 19. fxe5 Bxe5 20. c4 Nb6 21. Bh6** It is do or die now. He cannot stop to defend pawns. **21. ... Bxc4 22. Rxf8+ Rxf8 23. Qh5 Bg7 24. Re1 Bxh6 25. Qxh6 Qg7 26. Qd2 Bxa2** Not so much for the third pawn, but it threatens Nc4 and Ne5. **27. Nc3 Bc4 28. Re4 d5 29. Rf4 d4**

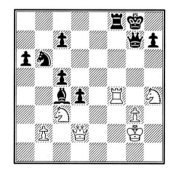

After
29. ... d4

30. Nf5 Interesting idea, but the sacrifice naturally fails. **30. ... dxc3 31. bxc3 Bd5+** Important. If 30. ... Qf6 31. Nh6+ wins the

queen. Or if 30. ... Qg5 31. Rg4. **32. Kh2 Qf6 0–1** Analysis by Kashdan. (*American Chess Bulletin*, November 1930)

150 Kashdan–Klein [B15]
Gyor, round 5, 1930 *[October]*

1. e4 c6 2. d4 d5 3. Nc3 Nf6 Inferior. It leads to a French Defense position, with White an important move ahead. **4. e5 Nfd7 5. Bd3** 5. e6 has been played here, but it is not very effective. White is preparing a general advance on the kingside. **5. ... e6 6. Nce2 c5 7. c3 Nc6 8. f4 Be7 9. Nf3 g6 10. 0–0 a6** h5 is necessary here, though Black's position is then none too solid. **11. g4 h5 12. h3 Nb6 13. Be3 c4 14. Bc2 Bd7 15. Ng3** Forcing a decision. If 15. ... h4 16. Nh1 followed by g5 Nf2, and Ng4. The pawn at h4 must soon fall. **15. ... hxg4 16. hxg4 Qc7 17. Kf2 0–0–0 18. Rh1 Rdf8 19. Qf1 Qd8 20. Qg2 Kb8 21. Rxh8** After the exchange of the major pieces, the break through at f5 should be decisive. **21. ... Rxh8 22. Rh1 Nc8 23. Rxh8 Qxh8 24. Qh2 Qxh2+ 25. Nxh2 b5 26. f5 gxf5 27. gxf5 a5** exf5 would leave Black with two weaknesses, yet it offered better chances. After f6 he is completely cramped and the White pieces enter at their leisure. **28. f6 Bf8 29. Nf3 Nd8 30. Bc1** To keep the bishop out of a3 later. It threatens Ng5, and if Bh6 Nxe6! **30. ... Be8 31. Nh5 Nb6 32. Ng7 Bc6 33. Ng5 b4 34. Nh7** Ba7 and Bg8 would also win. The text wins a pawn and allows no counter play. **34. ... Nd7 35. Nxf8 Nxf8 36. cxb4 a4** If axb4 Bd2 and the bishop gets on the right diagonal. Now it still requires a little maneuvering. **37. Bh6 Nd7 38. Nh5 Kb7 39. Nf4 Bb5 40. Ne2 Nc6 41. a3 Ka6 42. Ke3 Nb6** If Kb3 then not 43. Nc3 Ndxe5 44. Nxb5 Ng4+, but first 43. Bd1 Ka6 44. Nc3. **43. Nc3 Na7 44. Bf8 Be8 45. Bc5 Nb5** (*see diagram*)

46. Bxb6 Everything wins, but this is the quickest. The final position is a pleasure to play. **46. ... Nxc3 47. bxc3 Kxb6 48. Kf4 1–0** Annotated by Kashdan. (*American Chess Bulletin*, November 1930)

After
45. ... Nb5

151 Hoenlinger–Kashdan [D48]

Gyor, round 6, 1930 *[October]*

1. d4 Nf6 2. c4 e6 3. Nf3 d5 4. Nc3
c6 5. e3 Nbd7 6. Bd3 dxc4 7. Bxc4 b5
8. Bd3 a6 An old variation of doubtful value.
9. e4 c5 10. e5 cxd4 11. Nxb5 leads to difficult
complications. 9. Ne4 But this is tame and
only loses time. 9. ... c5 10. dxc5 Nxc5 11.
Nxc5 Bxc5 12. 0–0 Bb7 13. b3 13. a3 0–0
14. b4 would set up a symmetrical position with
Black a move ahead. The text leaves holes on
the queenside. 13. ... 0–0 14. Bb2 Qe7
15. Rc1 Rac8 16. Qe2 Ba3 17. Rfd1 Nd5
The knight will camp at c3. Black now stands
definitely better. 18. Bb1 Bxb2 19. Qxb2 b4

After
19. ... b4

20. Qe5 This loses the exchange. White is
playing for a grand combination. 20. ... Nc3
21. Rxc3 If at once 21. Bxh7+ Kxh7 22. Qh5+
Kg8 23. Ng5 Be4! 24. Rxc3 Bg6 wins. 21. ...
bxc3 22. Bxh7+ White has little choice,
though this time the sacrifice does not work.
22. ... Kxh7 23. Qh5+ Kg8 24. Ng5 Be4!
25. Nxe4 c2 The ending is now easily won.
26. Rc1 Rfd8 If Qa3 27. Nf6+ draws. The last
hope. 27. h3 Allowing a pretty finish. If 27. h4
Qa3 28. Ng5 Qxc1+ 20. Kh2 Rc7 wins. 27. ...

f5 28. Ng5 Qxg5! 29. Qxg5 Rd1+
30. Kh2 Rxc1 0–1 Annotation by Kashdan.
(*American Chess Bulletin*, November 1930)

152 Kashdan–Gereben [D64]

Gyor, round 7, 1930 *[October]*

1. d4 Nf6 2. c4 e6 3. Nc3 d5 4. Nf3
Nbd7 5. Bg5 Be7 6. e3 0–0 7. Rc1 c6
8. Qc2 Re8 9. a3 a6 10. cxd5 exd5
11. Bd3 Nf8 12. 0–0 Ne4 13. Bf4 Nxc3
14. Qxc3 Bd6 15. Bg3 Bxg3 16. hxg3
Re6 17. Rfe1 Rh6 18. e4 dxe4 19. Bxe4
Rd6 20. Rcd1 Ne6 21. Rd2 g6 22. Qe3
Nc7 23. Qh6 Qf8 24. Qh4 Be6 25. Bc2
h6 26. Re3 Rad8 27. Bb3 c5 28. Qe4
cxd4 29. Rxd4 Bxb3 30. Rxb3 Ne6
31. Rxd6 Qxd6 32. Qe3 Qd1+ 33. Kh2
b5 34. Rc3 Qb1 35. Rc6 Rd1 36. g4 h5
37. Rc8+ Kh7 38. Qc5 Rh1+ 39. Kg3
h4+ 40. Nxh4 Ng7 41. Nf3 Qd3 42. Qb8
Nh5+ 43. gxh5 Qf5 44. Rh8+ Kg7 45.
Qf8+ Kf6 46. Qd8+ Kg7 47. h6+ 1–0
(*Gyor* 1930)

153 Kashdan–Szijarto [C11]

Gyor, round 8, 1930 *[October]*

1. e4 e6 2. d4 d5 3. Nc3 Nf6 4. Bg5
dxe4 5. Nxe4 Be7 6. Ng3 c5 7. Nf3 Nc6
8. dxc5 Qa5+ 9. c3 Qxc5 10. Be3 Qd6
11. Qc2 0–0 12. Bd3 Ne5 13. Nxe5 Qxe5
14. 0–0 Qc7 15. Qe2 b6 16. a4 a5 17. Bd4
Bb7 18. Ne4 Nxe4 19. Bxe4 Bxe4
20. Qxe4 Rfd8 21. Rad1 Qc4 22. Qb7
Bc5 23. Bxc5 Qxc5 24. Rd7 Rxd7
25. Qxd7 Kf8 26. Rd1 Qe7 27. Rd6 Qxd7
28. Rxd7 Ke8 29. Rb7 Rd8 30. Kf1 Rd6
31. Ke2 g5 32. Rb8+ Ke7 33. Rh8 Rc6
34. Kd3 Rd6+ 35. Ke3 Rc6 36. Kd3
Rd6+ 37. Kc2 Rd5 38. Rb8 Rd6
39. Rb7+ Kf8 40. b4 axb4 41. cxb4 g4
42. Kc3 e5 43. a5 bxa5 44. bxa5 Rf6
45. Rb2 Rh6 46. Ra2 Ra6 47. Kc4 Ke7
48. Kb5 Ra8 49. Kc6 f5 50. a6 e4 51. a7
f4 52. Kb7 Rxa7+ 53. Rxa7 Kd6 54. Ra5
f3 55. gxf3 gxf3 56. Kb6 Ke6 57. Rc5
h5 58. h4 e3 59. fxe3 f2 60. Rc1 Kf5
61. Rf1 Kg4 62. Rxf2 Kxh4 63. e4 Kg3
64. Rf8 h4 65. e5 1–0 (*Gyor* 1930)

154 Mueller–Kashdan [C22]

Gyor, round 9, 1930 *[October 12]*

1. e4 e5 2. d4 exd4 3. Qxd4 Nc6
4. Qe3 Nf6 5. Bd2 Be7 6. Nc3 d5
7. exd5 Nxd5 8. Nxd5 Qxd5 9. c4 Qc5
10. 0-0-0 Bd7 11. Qxc5 Bxc5 12. Re1+
Be6 13. Be3 Be7 14. Nf3 0-0-0 15. Ng5
Bf5 16. a3 Bf6 17. b4 Bc3 18. Be2 Bxe1
19. Rxe1 Ne5 20. f4 Nd3+ 21. Bxd3 Rxd3
22. Nxf7 Re8 23. Ne5 Rc3+ 24. Kb2
Rc2+ 25. Kb3 Rxg2 26. Nf3 Be4 27. Bd2
Rxd2! After 28. Nxd2 follows Bc2+ winning
the exchange. 0–1 (*Gyor* 1930)

155 Kashdan–Lundin [C70]

Stockholm, round 1, 1930 *[October 20]*

1. e4 e5 2. Nf3 Nc6 3. Bb5 a6 4. Ba4
Bc5 One of the favorite defenses to the Ruy
Lopez at one time, but not so popular today.
Black has trouble in maintaining the center as
he must lose time with the bishop on White's
eventual d4. 5. 0-0 b5 If 5. ... Nf6 6. Nxe5!
Nxe5 7. d4 Nxe4 8. Re1 Be7 9. Rxe4 Ng6 10. c4
and White has the freer game. 6. Bb3 d6 7. c3
Nf6 7. ... Bb6 8. d4 Qe2 might have been better to avoid the necessity of exchanging pawns.
However, 9. a4 would prove annoying. 8. d4
exd4 Even here ...Bb6 could be played, and
Black can avoid any material loss by accurate
defense. If 9. dxe5 dxe5 10. Qxd8 Nxd8 11. Nxe5
Nxe4 12. Bd5 Bb7! 13. Bxe4 (the only way to
get the rook to e1) Bxe4 14. Re1 Bxg1! (not ...f5
15. Nd2 0-0 16. Nxe4 fxe4 17. Be3! wins the e
pawn) 15. Nc4+ (not 15. Ng6+ Ne6 16. Nxh8
Bd3 and Black will win the knight) Ne6 cxb6
17. Rxb1 and White has a very slight advantage,
though the position has been greatly simplified.
9. cxd4 Ba7 b6 seems a better square for the
bishop, though even in that event there is a
chance of Nc3 and Nd5 to attack it. White has
a definite edge already through the secure possession of the center. 10. Bg5 0-0 11. Bd5
Bb7 If 11. ... Bd7 12. e5! wins. After the text
this will not do as White's bishop will be "en
prise." 12. Nc3 Not 12. Qc1? Nxd4! 13. Nxd4
(evidently not 13. Bxb7 Ne2+! wins) Bxd5 with
a pawn ahead. The text threatens Rc1, as well as
e5. 12. ... h6 13. Bxf6 Qxf6 14. Rc1 Bb6

If 14. ... Nd8 15. Bxb7 Nxb7 16. Nd5 wins, or
14. ... b4 15. Ne2 and at least a pawn must fall.
15. Nxb5! axb5 16. Bxc6 Bxc6 17. Rxc6
Qe6 If 17. ... Rxa2 18. Qb3 Ra4 19. e5! Qd8
20. exd6 cxd6 21. Rc1 with a decisive advantage
in position. 18. Qe2 Rxa2 19. d5 Qe7
20. Re1 g5 This and the next move are very
risky, but Black feels his game is getting worse,
and he desires at all costs to get some counter
play. If 20. ... b4 21. Qc2 Bc5 22. e5 is strong.
21. h3 Not 21. Qxb5 g4 22. Nd2 Qf6! and
Black gets the attack. 21. ... f5! Leading to very
interesting play, in which White will have no
easy time in maintaining his game. 22. e5 Going in for the complications. If 22. exd6 Qxe2
23. Rxe2 Rxf5, Black would have rather the better of the ending. 22. ... g4

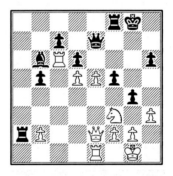

After
22. ... g4

23. exd6 The point of the defense. White
can sacrifice a piece, as he must regain the bishop
through the dangerous center pawns. Bad would
be 23. Nd2 g3! or 23. hxg4 fxg4 24. Nd2 Bxf2+,
etc. 23. ... Qg7 Trying to maintain his threats.
If 23. ... Qxe2 24. Rxe2 gxf3 25. Rec2! Ra1+
26. Kh2 and White should win. 24. Qe5! cxd6
As good as any, though White must come out
ahead in the resulting ending. If now 24. ... Qxe5
25. Nxe5 g3 26. Rxf2! 25. Qxg7+ Kxg7
26. Rxb6 gxf3 27. Rxb5 fxg2 28. Kxg2
White has come out of the melee just one pawn
ahead, but Black's remaining pawns are all weak,
and the advantage should be sufficient. 28. ...
Ra7 29. Kf3 Rf6 30. Rg1+ Rg6 The exchange of rooks simplifies White's task, but if
30. ... Kf7 31. Rb8, with some dangerous mating threats. 31. Rxg6+ Kxg6 32. Kf4 Rc7
33. Rb6 Rc4+ The best chance, as 30. ... Rd7
would be followed by b4 and b5, etc. 34. Ke3
Kg5 35. Rxd6 Rb4 36. f4+! Kh5 37. Rf6

Rxb2 38. d6 Rb1 39. Rxf5+ Kh4 Getting
into a mating net. 39. ... Kg6 was better, though
the pawns must win in any case. **40. Rd5 Rb8
41. d7 Rd8 42. Kf3 h5 43. Rd1! 1–0** Annotated by Kashdan. (*Chess Review*, March 1936)

156 Rellstab–Kashdan [D63]
Stockholm, round 2, 1930 *[October 21]*

**1. d4 Nf6 2. c4 e6 3. Nc3 d5 4. Bg5
Nbd7 5. e3 Be7 6. Nf3 0–0 7. Rc1 Re8
8. Bd3 dxc4 9. Bxc4 a6 10. Bd3 c5
11. 0–0 cxd4 12. Nxd4 Ne5 13. Bb1 Qa5
14. Qa4 Qxa4 15. Nxa4 Ned7 16. Nc3
Nb6 17. Rfd1 Bd7 18. Nf3 Red8 19. Ne4
Rac8 20. Nxf6+ gxf6 21. Bh6 Na4
22. Rxc8 Bxc8 23. Rxd8+ Bxd8**

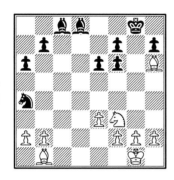

After
23. ... Bxd8

**24. b3 Nc3 25. Nd2 Bd7 26. a3 b5
27. Bd3 a5 28. e4 Be7 29. Nf3 Bxa3
30. Bd2 Bb2 31. Nd4 a4 32. bxa4 bxa4
33. Nc2 Nb1 34. Bb4 a3 35. Bc4 Ba4
36. Ne1 Nc3 37. Nd3 Bc2 38. f3 Bxd3
39. Bxd3 a2 0–1** (*L'Échiquier*, 1930, p. 1071)

157 Kashdan–Spielmann [C14]
Stockholm, round 3, 1930 *[October 22]*

**1. e4 e6 2. d4 d5 3. Nc3 Nf6 4. Bg5
Be7 5. e5 Nfd7 6. Bxe7 Qxe7 7. Qd2
0–0 8. Bd3 c5 9. Nb5 a6 10. Nd6 cxd4
11. f4 Nc6 12. Nf3 f6 13. Nxc8 Raxc8
14. exf6 Qxf6 15. 0–0 Qxf4 16. Bxh7+
Kh8!** But not 16. ... Kxh7 17. Ng5+ followed
by Rxf4. **17. Qxf4 Rxf4 18. Bd3 e5 19. Ng5
Rxf1+ 20. Rxf1 e4 21. Be2 Nce5 22. Bd1
Nf6 23. Ne6 d3 24. cxd3 Nxd3 25. g4
e3 26. g5 Ne4 27. Rf7 Ndf2 28. Be2
Nh3+ 29. Kg2 Nhxg5 30. Nxg5 Nxg5**

**31. Rxb7 Rf8 32. Bxa6 Rf2+ 33. Kg3
Ne4+ 34. Kg4 e2 35. Bxe2 Nf6+ 36. Kg3
Rxe2 37. a4 d4 38. Rb3 Kh7 39. h3 Kg6
40. Kf3 Rh2 41. Kf4 Nd7 42. a5 Rf2+
43. Kg3 Rf6 44. Ra3 Rd6 45. a6 d3
46. a7 d2 47. a8Q d1Q 48. Qe4+ Kh6
49. Qh4+ Qh5 50. Qf4+ Qg5+ 51. Qxg5+
Kxg5 52. Ra5+ Kh6 53. Rb5 Rd3+
54. Kg2 Nf6 55. Rf5 Rb3 0–1** (*L'Échiquier*,
1930, p. 1071)

158 Bogoljubow–Kashdan [D37]
Stockholm, round 4, 1930 *[October]*

**1. d4 Nf6 2. c4 e6 3. Nc3 d5 4. Nf3
Nbd7 5. Bf4** Weaker than 5. Bg5, in that it
makes it easier for Black to equalize, but the
move is quite playable, and a change from the
usual variations. **5. ... dxc4 6. e3** If 6. e4 Bb4
7. Qc2 b5 and Black can hold the pawn. **6. ...
Nd5** Gaining the advantage of two bishops,
for if 7. Bg3 Nxc3 8. bxc3 b5 is quite strong.
7. Bxc4 Nxf4 8. exf4 Nb6 9. 0–0 Be7
Inconsistent. Having played for the bishops,
Black should have taken the second one. 9. ...
Nxc4 10. Qa4+ regains the piece. But it is not
typical for Kashdan that he would not swap
bishop for knight. **10. Bb3 0–0 11. Re1 c5
12. dxc5 Nd7** A peculiar idea, based on the
plan of maintaining complications, and avoiding the exchange of pieces. When I played it, I
foresaw the necessary retreat on move 14, but
believed I would regain all the lost time. However, the simple ...Bxc5 was preferable and leads
to equality. **13. c6! bxc6 14. Nd4 Nb8** The
only move, as a sacrifice on e6 is threatened, as
well as Nxc6. If 14. ... Bb7 15. Nxe6 fxe6
16. Bxe6+ wins, or 14. ... Qc7 15. Nxe6 fxe6
16. Rxe6 regains the piece with a winning advantage. After the text Black plans ...Bb7 and ...c5
to command the long diagonal. **15. Na4** Preventing ...c5 because of 16. Qf3! or if 15. ... Bb7
16. Rc1 restrains Black's game. **15. ... Qd6
16. g3 Rd8 17. Nf3 Bb7** Continuing the
original plan, but underestimating the strength
of White's next move. Being behind in development, Black should have been content to simplify by 17. ... Qxd1 18. Raxd1 Rxd1 19. Rxd1 Kf8
etc., when the position is quite tenable. **18. f5!
c5** If 18. ... exf5 19. Ne5 Rf8 20. Qxd6 Bxd6

21. Nxf7! Rxf7 22. Re8+ Bf8 23. Rd1 with a winning attack. The text has a concealed threat which requires care on White's part. **19. fxe6 c4!** If 19. ... Qxd1 20. exf7+ Kf8 21. Raxd1 Bxf3?? 22. Rxd8+ Bxd8 23. Re8 mate. Or 21. ... Rxd1 22. Bxd1 protecting the knight and remaining a pawn ahead. **20. exf7+ Kf8 21. Bc2?** Not 21. Bxc4 Qxd1 22. Raxd1 Rxd1 23. Rxd1 Bxf3 wins. But the text also loses, due to the following forceful combination. Correct was 21. Qxd6 Rxd6 22. Bxh7! Bxf3 23. Rxe7! Kxe7 24. Re1+ wins. Or 21. ... Bxd6 22. Ng5+! Bd5 23. Rad1, with a winning endgame. Bogoljubow retreated, believing his position was still secure, but missing the point of the interpolation (Zugzwang) of c4. **21. ... Qf6 22. Nd2 Rxd2!!**

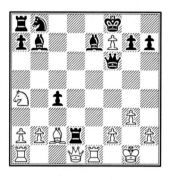

After
22. ... Rxd2

This sacrifice completely changes the picture, as White must give up a rook to avoid the mating threat. **23. Qxd2 Qf3 24. Be4** If 24. Kf1 Qg2+ 25. Ke2 Bf3+ 26. Ke3 Bg5+ wins. **24. ... Bxe4 25. Rxe4 Qxe4** Now with a piece for two pawns, Black's difficulties are purely of a technical nature. **26. Nc3 Qf5 27. Qe2 Nc6 28. Rd1 Rd8** Not 28. ... Ne5? 29. Rd5! Nf3+ 30. Kg2, and the piece is lost. **29. Rxd8+ Nxd8** Hoping for 29. ... Bxe8, as then 30. Qe8 is mate! **30. Qxc4 Nxf7 31. f4 g5** Opening lines for a quick entry. The text is stronger then exchanging by ...Qc5+, though that will also suffice. **32. fxg5 Bc5+ 33. Kg2 Qf2+ 34. Kh3 Nxg5+ 35. Kg4 Qf3+! 36. Kh4** 36. Kxg5 will not do because of ...Be7+ 37. Kh6 Qf6+, followed by mate next move. **36. ... Qf5 37. g4** There is nothing to be done. If 37. Qg4 Nf3+ 38. Kh3 Ng1+ wins the queen. **37. ... Bf2+ 38. Kh5 Qg6 mate 0–1** Analysis by Kashdan. (*Chess Review*, March 1936)

159 Stoltz–Kashdan [D48]
Stockholm, round 5, 1930 *[October]*

1. Nf3 Nf6 2. c4 c6 3. d4 d5 4. Nc3 e6 5. e3 Less aggressive than 5. Bg5, but it avoids the Cambridge Springs Defense and other counter attacks, by keeping the bishop on the queenside. **5. ... Nbd7 6. Bd3 dxc4 7. Bxc4 b5** The Meran Defense. Black wants to play ...c5 and fianchetto his c8 bishop. First he advances and supports the b pawn, to gain more space on that side. **8. Bd3 a6 9. 0–0** 9. e4 c5 10. e5 cxd4 11. Nxb5 Nxe5! leads to complications, in which Black can succeed in equalizing. **9. ... c5 10. Qe2 Bb7 11. Rd1 Qb6** 11. ... Qc7 is more accurate. Now White could play 12. a4 b4 13. a5! Qc7 14. Nb1 followed by Nbd2 and Nf4, gaining possession of several important squares. True, after 11. ... Qc7, the queen would later be disturbed by White Rc1, but it could then play Qb6 without danger. **12. Bc2** But this, with the idea of e4, is premature and loses time, as Black soon demonstrates. **12. ... Rd8** Preparing for White's advance. The text is stronger than the routine ...Be7. **13. e4 cxd4 14. Nxd4 Ne5!** If 14. ... Bc5 15. Ng3 with a good game. Now Black gains in development by forcing White's retreat. **15. Nf3** Ineffective is 15. Be3 Nc4! An interesting idea is possibly here 16. Ndxb5 Nxe3 17. Qxe3 Qxe3 18. Nc7+ Ke7 19. fxe3 Rc8 and the knight cannot escape. **15. ... Nxf3+ 16. Qxf3 Rxd1+ 17. Qxd1** If 17. Nxd1 Qc6 18. Nc3 Bg5 with advantage. But not 18. ... b4?? 19. Ba4 wins. **17. ... Bc5 18. Qe2 0–0** Black has a fine game, and the minor pieces are particularly well placed for an attack. But 18. ... e5 would have allowed White less chances, and might have been preferred. **19. e5?** Very tempting, as it seems that White will now gain initiative. But Black is better prepared to take advantage of the open lines. White should have developed with 19. Bf4 Rd8 20. Rd1, and played to equalize. **19. ... Qc6!** This is difficult to defend and shows how weak the White game is on the kingside. **20. Qf3 Qc7** 20. ... Qxf3 21. gxf3 Nd7 22. f4 Nb6 would be favorable to Black, in view of the opponents weak pawns. The text is played to see what White's intentions are. **21. Qg3** If 21. Qe2, there is nothing

better than Qc6 22. Qf3 Qxf3, etc., as before.
The text allows Black more forceful play. **21. ...
Nh5 22. Qd3 f5!**

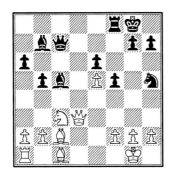

After
22. ... f5

Much stronger than ...g6 as Black welcomes
the exchange of pawns. **23. exf6** If 23. Qe2,
Black can win at least a pawn by ...Qc6 24. Qf1
b4! 25. Nd1 Bd4. Or 25. Ne2 f4! wins quickly.
If 23. Bd1? Qxe5 24. Bxh5 Qxe1+ 25. Qf1 Bxf2+
wins. **23. ... Nxf6** Now every Black piece is
trained directly against the king, and there are
any number of threats. White has succeeded in
isolating the e pawn, but that will hardly cut
much figure in this position. **24. Be3** Practically forced to defend the kingside, but it loses
a piece, due to the unfortunate grouping on the
c file. If 24. a3 Bxf2+ 25. Kxf2 Qxh2 would lead
to a winning attack, or simply 24. ... g6 threatening Ng4, and there is little White can do. If
24. Qe2 Qc6 25. Qf1 Ng4, and White must
bow. **24. ... Bxe3 25. Qxe3** If 25. fxe3 b4
followed by Be4, wins a piece. **25. ... b4
26. Qxe6+ Kh8 27. Ne4 Qxc2 28. Qd6**
The last desperate hope, but of course, the game
is gone. **28. ... Rc8 0–1** Analysis by Kashdan.
(*Chess Review*, March 1936)

160 Kashdan–Ståhlberg [C11]
Stockholm, round 6, 1930 *[October 27]*

**1. e4 e6 2. d4 d5 3. Nc3 Nf6 4. Bg5
dxe4 5. Nxe4 Be7 6. Bxf6 Bxf6 7. Nf3
Nd7 8. Nxf6+ Qxf6 9. Bc4 0–0 10. Qe2
Rd8 11. 0–0 b6 12. Ba6 Bxa6 13. Qxa6
c5!** With good play for Black. The game ended
in a draw but the rest of the moves have not
been found. **½–½** (*Tidskrift for Schack*, 1931,
p. 119)

161 Stoltz–Kashdan [B18]
Match Game #1, 1930 *[November]*

**1. e4 c6 2. d4 d5 3. Nc3 dxe4 4. Nxe4
Bf5 5. Ng3 Bg6 6. f4 e6 7. Nf3 Nf6
8. c3 c5? 9. Bb5+! Nc6 10. Qe2!** Threatening 11. f5. **10. ... Be7 11. dxc5 0–0 12. Be3
Qc7 13. 0–0 Nd5**

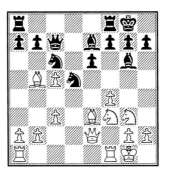

After
13. ... Nd5

**14. Bxc6 Qxc6 15. Ne5 Qc7 16. Nxg6
fxg6 17. Ne4 Nxf4 18. Bxf4 Rxf4 19. Rxf4
Qxf4 20. Nd6 Bxd6 21. Qxe6+ Kh8
22. cxd6 Rf8 23. h3 h6 24. d7 Qf2+
25. Kh1 Qh4 26. Qe8 Qd8 27. Re1 Kh7
28. a4 Qh4 29. Rd1 Qxa4 30. Re1 Qh4
31. b4 Qd8 32. c4 a6 33. c5 h5 34. Re6
Rf1+ 35. Kh2 Qg5 36. Qxg6+ Qxg6
37. Rxg6 Rf8 38. Rb6 1–0** (*Deutsche Schachzeitung*, December 1930)

162 Kashdan–Stoltz [C71]
Match Game #2, 1930 *[November]*

**1. e4 e5 2. Nf3 Nc6 3. Bb5 a6 4. Ba4
d6 5. d4 Bd7 6. c4** White wishes to avoid
well-known variations. However, it is doubtful
if the move can be recommended. **6. ... Nge7**
The exchange variation, that could follow if
Black had taken on d4 and it would have given
White the better game. **7. Nc3 Ng6 8. 0–0
Be7 9. Nd5 0–0 10. Nxe7+ Qxe7 11. d5
Nd8 12. Bc2** White now has the advantage
of the bishop pair, but as compensation Black
has the open f file. **12. ... f5 13. Bg5 Qe8
14. exf5 Bxf5 15. Nh4 Nxh4 16. Bxh4
Qg6! 17. Rc1 b6 18. Ba4** An attempt to keep
the bishop pair, which is immediately refuted.
To be considered was 18. b4. **18. ... Bd3
19. Re1 Rf4 20. Bxd8 Rxd8 21. Bc2 Bf5**

22. Bxf5 Qxf5 23. Qc2! Rf8 24. Qxf5 R8xf5 25. f3 Rd4 26. Red1 Rff4 27. b3 g5 28. h3 h5 29. Kf2 h4 30. Ke3 Kf7 31. Rxd4 Rxd4 ½–½ The remaining games from the match have never been found. (Contributed by Calle Erlandsson, from a Swedish newspaper)

163 Turover–Kashdan [D13]
New York, round 1, 1931 *[April 18]*

1. d4 d5 2. c4 c6 3. cxd5 cxd5 4. Nc3 Nf6 5. Nf3 Nc6 6. Qb3 e6 7. Bf4 a6 8. e3 Be7 9. Bd3 0–0 10. Rc1 b5 11. Ne5 Bb7 12. 0–0 Rc8 13. Nxc6 Bxc6 14. Rc2 Qd7 15. a3 Nh5 16. Be5 f6 17. Bg3 Nxg3 18. hxg3 f5 19. Rcc1 Bd6 20. f4 g5 21. Kf2 g4 22. Rfe1 Rb8 23. Na2 Rfc8 24. Nb4 Bb7 25. Be2 Rxc1 26. Rxc1 Rc8 27. Rxc8+ Qxc8 28. Qc2 Qd8 29. Nd3 h5 30. Nc5 Qe7 31. Nxb7 Qxb7 32. a4 Kf7 33. axb5 axb5 34. Qd3 b4 35. Qa6 Qc7 36. Bd1 Be7 37. Qd3 Bd8 38. b3 Qe7 39. Qf1 Kg6 40. Qh1 Qa7 41. Qf1 Qe7 42. Qd3 Kf7 43. Qf1 Qf6 44. Qh1 Qh8 45. Ke2 Bf6 46. Qe1 Be7 47. Bc2 Qc8 48. Bd3 Qa8 49. Qc1 Bf6 50. Kd2 Kg6 51. Qd1 Qh8 52. Kc1 Kf7 53. Qe1 h4 54. gxh4 Bxh4 55. g3 Bf6 56. Qf2 Qh1+ 57. Bf1 Qe4 58. Ba6 Be7 59. Bf1 Bf6 60. Be2 Kg6 61. Kd2 Qb1 62. Bd1 Qb2+ 63. Ke1 Qc3+ 64. Kf1 Qd2 ½–½ (*New York* 1931, Spanish Tournament Book)

164 Edward Lasker–Kashdan [D52]
New York, round 2, 1931 *[April 19]*

1. d4 d5 2. c4 c6 3. Nc3 Nf6 4. Nf3 e6 5. Bg5 Nbd7 6. e3 Be7 7. a3 a6 8. Qc2 dxc4 9. Bxc4 b5 10. Be2 Bb7 11. e4 c5 12. dxc5 Nxc5 13. Rd1 Qc7 14. e5 Nfe4 15. Bxe7 Qxe7 16. Rd4 Rc8 17. 0–0 0–0 18. Nxe4 Nxe4 19. Qd3 Nc5 20. Qe3 Na4 21. b3 Nc3 22. b4 Nxe2+ 23. Qxe2 Bd5 24. Qe3 Rc2 25. Rg4 f5 26. Nd4 Rc4 27. Rf4 g5 28. Rf3 f4 29. Qd2 Bxf3 30. Nxf3 Rd8 31. Qe2 h6 32. h3 Qh7 33. Rd1 Rxd1+ 34. Qxd1 Qc7 0–1 (*New York* 1931)

165 Kashdan–Dake [C11]
New York, round 3, 1931 *[April 21]*

1. e4 e6 2. d4 d5 3. Nc3 Nf6 4. Bg5 dxe4 5. Nxe4 Be7 6. Nc3 Nbd7 7. Nf3 0–0 8. Be2 b6 9. 0–0 Bb7 10. a4 a6 11. Bc4 Nd5 12. Bxe7 Qxe7 13. Nxd5 Bxd5 14. Qe2 Bxc4 15. Qxc4 c5 16. Rad1 Rfd8 17. Rfe1 cxd4 18. Rxd4 Nf6 19. Qc6 Rdc8 20. Qxb6 Rxc2 21. Rd2 Rxd2 22. Nxd2 Qe8 23. b3 Nd5 24. Qb7 Qc8 25. Qxc8+ Rxc8 26. Nc4 Kf8 27. Kf1 Ke7 28. Rd1 Rc5 29. Rd4 h5 30. Ke2 g5 31. Kd2 a5 32. Nb2 Kd6 33. Nc4+ Ke7 34. Ne5 Nf4 35. Nd3 Nxd3 36. Kxd3 g4 37. b4 axb4 38. Rxb4 Rc1 39. Rc4 Ra1 40. Rc7+ Kd6 41. Rc4 Kd5 42. Rf4 f5 43. Kc3 Rc1+ 44. Kb2 Rc8 45. Rb4 h4 46. a5 Ra8 47. Ra4 Kc5 48. Kc3 Ra6 49. f3 gxf3 50. gxf3 e5 51. h3 Kb5 52. Rb4+ Kc5 53. Rc4+ Kb5 54. Rb4+ ½–½ (*New York* 1931)

166 Kashdan–Santasiere [B18]
New York, round 4, 1931 *[April 22]*

1. e4 c6 2. d4 d5 3. Nc3 We prefer 3. exd5 cxd5 4. Bd3, etc. 3. ... dxe4 4. Nxe4 Bf5 The alternative is 4. Nf3. 5. Ng3 Bg6 6. Nf3 e6 7. Bc4 This seems rather pointless. The old-fashioned advance of the h pawn is not bad. 7. ... Nd7 8. 0–0 Bd6 9. Qe2 Ne7 10. Ne5 Nxe5 11. dxe5 Bc5 12. c3 Qc7 13. a4 a5 14. Kh1 Nf5 15. Nxf5 Bxf5 16. f4 h5 17. Be3 White's handling of the opening has been somewhat indifferent, hence he now seeks exchanges. 17. ... Qb6 18. Bxc5 Qxc5 19. Bd3 Bg4 20. Qc2 0–0–0 21. Rae1 If 21. h3? then Bxh3! 22. gxh3 Qd5+ followed by Qxd3 regaining the piece plus a pawn. 21. ... Rd7 22. Be2 Bf5 23. Qc1 h4 24. Rd1 Rxd1 25. Rxd1 Qf2 26. Qd2 h3 27. Bf3 hxg2+ 28. Bxg2 Qxd2 29. Rxd2 Rh4 30. Rf2 Kc7 Black seems to have a won endgame, but here and on the next move he wastes some time. 31. Kg1 g6 32. Bh1 Bd3 33. Kg2 Rg4+ 34. Kf3 Rg1 35. Ke3 Bc4 36. Bf3 Bb3 37. h4 Rg3 37. ... Bxa4 seems safe. 38. Rg2 Rxf3+

After
38. ... Rxf3

And here Black goes entirely astray, probably through miscalculation of the final ending moves. 38. ... Rxg3 39. Bxg3 Bxa4 is better. **39. Kxf3 Bd5+ 40. Kf2 Bxg2 41. Kxg2 Kb6** Whether Black can draw is now a matter of analysis, but the course he pursues is bad. **42. Kg3 Kc5 43. Kg4 Kc4 44. Kg5 Kb3 45. Kf6 Kxb2 46. Kxf7 b5 47. axb5 cxb5 48. h5!** Possibly, in his earlier calculation, Black overlooked this move and expected 48. Kxg3, in which case Black would queen first. **48. ... gxh5 49. f5 h4 50. fxe6 h3 51. e7 h2 52. e8Q h1Q 53. Qxb5+ Kxc3 54. e6 Qh7+ 55. Ke8 Qh8+ 56. Kd7 Qd4+ 57. Kc8 Qd6 58. Qd7 Qa6+ 59. Kc7 Kb2 60. Qd4+ Kb1 61. e7 Qe2 62. Kd8 a4 63. Qb4+ 1–0** Annotations by C. S. Howell. (*American Chess Bulletin*, May-June 1931)

167 H. Steiner–Kashdan [C13]
New York, round 5, 1931 *[April 23]*

1. e4 e6 2. d4 d5 3. Nc3 Nf6 4. Bg5 Be7 5. e5 Nfd7 6. h4 c5 7. Bxe7 Kxe7 8. Qg4 Kf8 9. Nf3 Nc6 10. dxc5 Ndxe5 11. Nxe5 Nxe5 12. Qg3

After
12. Qg3

12. ... Nd7 13. Qd6+ Qe7 14. Qxe7+

Kxe7 15. Na4 Nf6 16. Bb5 Bd7 17. Bxd7 Nxd7 18. Kd2 Rhc8 19. b4 b6! 20. cxb6 axb6 21. Nb2 Ra3! 22. Rh3 Rxh3 23. gxh3 Ne5 24. a4 Nf3+ Inferior is 24. ... Nc4+ 25. Nxc4 Rxc4 26. a5! **25. Kd3 Nxh4 26. c4 Nf3 27. cxd5 exd5 28. a5 Ne5+ 29. Kd2 bxa5 30. Rxa5 Nc6 31. Rb5 Rb8 32. Rxd5 Rxb4 33. Nd1 Rh4 34. Rd3 Ne5 35. Rg3 g6 36. Ne3 f5 37. f4!** Nf7 But not 37. ... Rxf4 because of Nd5+ winning the rook. **38. Ng2! Rh5 39. h4 Kf6 40. Rd3 h6 ½–½** (*New York 1931*)

168 Kashdan–Horowitz [A13]
New York, round 6, 1931 *[April 25]*

1. Nf3 Nf6 2. c4 e6 3. b3 d5 4. Bb2 Nbd7 5. g3 c6 6. Bg2 Be7 7. 0–0 0–0 8. Nc3 b6 9. e4 Bb7 10. d3 dxc4 11. dxc4 Qc7 12. Qe2 Rfd8 13. Rad1 Nf8 14. e5 Ne8 15. Nd4 a6 16. f4 c5 17. Nf3 Rxd1 18. Rxd1 Rd8 19. Kf2 Ng6 20. Rxd8 Qxd8 21. Ne4 Nf8 22. Ne1 Qd7 23. Qd3 Qxd3 24. Nxd3 Bc8 25. a3 a5 26. Ke3 f5 27. Nc3 g5 28. Na4 gxf4+ 29. gxf4 Bd8 30. Bc3 Kf7 31. b4 axb4 32. axb4 cxb4 33. Nxb4 Bd7 34. Nc6 Bxc6 35. Bxc6 Ng6 36. Bd4 Ng7 37. Bf3 Nh4 38. Bxb6 Bxb6+ 39. Nxb6 Nxf3 40. Kxf3 Ke7 41. Na4 Kd7 42. Nc5+ Kc6 43. Nd3 Ne8 44. Ke3 Nc7 45. Kd4 Na6 46. Ne1 Nc5 47. Nf3 Nd7 48. Kc3 Nf8 49. Kb4 Ng6 50. Nd4+ Kd7 51. Ne2 Kc6 52. c5 Ne7 53. Kc4 Nd5 54. Nd4+ Kd7 55. c6+ Ke7 56. Nxf5+! Kd8 57. Kc5 Nxf4 58. Nd4 1–0 (*New York 1931*)

169 Marshall–Kashdan [D61]
New York, round 7, 1931 *[April 26]*

1. d4 Nf6 2. Nf3 e6 3. c4 d5 4. Bg5 Nbd7 5. Nc3 c6 6. Qc2 Be7 7. e3 0–0 8. a3 Re8 9. Bd3 dxc4 10. Bxc4 Nd5 11. Bxe7 Qxe7 12. Rd1 Nxc3 13. Qxc3 b6 14. 0–0 Bb7 15. e4 c5 16. d5 exd5 17. Bxd5 Bxd5 18. exd5 Qd6 19. Nd2 Qxd5 20. Nc4 Qc6 21. Nd6 Red8 22. Rd3 Nf6 23. Rfd1 Rd7 24. Qc4 Qc7 25. h3 Kf8 26. b4 Rad8 27. Nb5 Qb8 28. Rxd7 Rxd7 29. Rxd7 Nxd7 30. bxc5

Nxc5 31. Qd5 Threatening 32. Nxa7 followed by 33. Qd8 mate! **31. ... a6 32. Nd6 Ne6 33. f4 Qc7! 34. Qa8+ Ke7 35. Nc8+ Kd7 36. f5 Nd8 37. Na7 Qb7 38. Nc8 Qxa8 39. Nxb6+ Kc6 40. Nxa8 Kb7 41. Kf2 Kxa8 42. Ke3 Kb7 43. f6 g6 44. Kf4 Ne6+ 45. Ke5 Kc6** 0–1 (*New York* 1931)

170 Kashdan–Fox [C71]
New York, round 8, 1931 *[April 28]*

1. e4 e5 2. Nf3 Nc6 3. Bb5 a6 4. Ba4 d6 5. d4 Bd7 6. c4 exd4 7. Nxd4 Nxd4 8. Bxd7+ Qxd7 9. Qxd4 Nf6 10. Nc3 Be7 11. 0–0 0–0 12. Bg5 Rfe8 13. Rad1 h6 14. Bc1 Qe6 15. b3 Bf8 16. Rfe1 c6 17. Bf4 Rad8 18. h3 g6 19. e5 Nh5 20. Bh2 dxe5 21. Qxd8 Rxd8 22. Rxd8 Qe7 23. Rb8 f6 24. Rd1 Ng7 25. Ne4 Kh8 26. Rd7! So if 26. ... Qxd7 then 27. Rxf8+ followed by Nxf6 mate! **26. ... Qb4 27. Bg3 Qe1+ 28. Kh2 Qxe4 29. Rxf8+ Kh7 30. Rff7 h5 31. Rxg7+ Kh6 32. h4 g5 33. hxg5+ fxg5 34. f3 Qe3 35. Rge7 g4 36. Rd6+** 1–0 (*New York* 1931)

171 Kashdan–Kupchik [D61]
New York, round 9, 1931 *[April 29]*

1. d4 Nf6 2. c4 e6 3. Nc3 d5 4. Nf3 Be7 5. Bg5 0–0 6. e3 Nbd7 7. Qc2 c6 8. a3 Re8 9. Bd3 dxc4 10. Bxc4 Nd5 11. Bxe7 Qxe7 12. Ne4 Nf8 13. 0–0 Rd8 14. Rad1 Bd7 15. Ba2 Be8 16. Qc5 Qc7 17. Rd2 f6 18. Ng3 Bf7 19. Rel Qb6 20. e4 Nf4 21. Qxb6 axb6 22. e5 f5 23. Nf1 N8g6 24. Ne3 Ne7 25. g3 Nfd5 26. Ng5 b5 27. Bb3 h6 28. Nxf7 Kxf7 29. Nxd5 Nxd5 30. Kf1 Rd7 31. Ke2 Rad8 32. Red1 Nb6 33. h3 Ke7 34. Rd3 Nc4 35. Bxc4 bxc4 36. R3d2 b5 37. f4 Ra7 38. Rc1 Rg8 39. h4 h5 40. Rc3 Kd7 41. Rdc2 Rga8 ½–½ (*New York* 1931)

172 Kevitz–Kashdan [A13]
New York, round 10, 1931 *[May 2]*

1. Nf3 d5 2. c4 e6 3. g3 d4 The advance of this pawn we believe to be Black's best line against the Reti with 2. c4, although recognizing the fact that many masters hold a different

opinion. The question is just when to make the advance. Kevitz opines that Black cannot play d4 on the second move, but 1. Nf3 d5 2. c4 d4 3. b4 (the line is supposed to be good for White) c5 4. Bb2 f6 and Black seems to have a playable game. **4. d3 c5 5. Bg2 Nc6 6. 0–0 Nf6 7. e3 e5 8. e4** This we do not understand. If White wishes to advance to e4, why not play 7. e4 and save a move? Moreover, the move blocks up the bishop on g2. We prefer 8. exd4. **8. ... g6** The fianchetto idea in this line does not appeal to us. **9. Ne1 Bg7 10. f4 Bg4 11. Nf3** And here we prefer 11. Bf3 followed soon by Ng2. **11. ... Qc8 12. Na3** The first and final move of this knight. However, it is difficult to find a first-class continuation for White. **12. ... 0–0 13. Qe1 Nh5 14. f5** Very tempting, but 14. Nc2 was probably safer. **14. ... Nb4 15. h3** White has no time to protect the d pawn. If 15. Qd2 gxf5 16. h3 fxe4 17. hxg4 exf3, etc. **15. ... Nxd3 16. Qd2 Bxf3 17. Bxf3 Nxc1** The simplest. If 17. ... Nxg3 18. Qxd3 Nxf1 19. Qxf1 and the issue is doubtful. **18. Bxh5 gxh5 19. f6?**

After 19. f6

A mistake. 19. Raxc1 would have given White drawing chances. After 19. f6 Qxh3 20. Qg5 Ne7+ 21. Kf2 Qxg3 22. Qxg3 Nxg3 23. fxg7, Kevitz had overlooked the fact that Black could play 23. ... Nxe4+ 24. Kf3 Ng5+, followed by 25. ... Kxg7. In this line if 23. Kxg3 Bh6, etc. **19. ... Qxh3! 20. fxg7 Qxg3+ 21. Kh1 Qh4+ 22. Kg1 Kxg7** Because White's knight is so thoroughly out of play, Black has time for this. The rest requires no comment. A highly interesting game. **23. Raxc1 Kh8 24. Rf3 Rg8+ 25. Kf1 Qh1+ 26. Ke2 Rg2+ 27. Rf2 Rxf2+ 28. Kxf2 Qh2+ 29. Ke1 Qg1+ 30. Ke2 d3+! 31. Kf3 Qg4+ 32. Kf2 Rg8**

33. Qxd3 Qf4+ 34. Qf3 Qd2+ 0–1 Annotation by C. S. Howell. (*American Chess Bulletin*, May-June 1931)

173 Capablanca–Kashdan [D61]
New York, round 11, 1931 *[May 3]*

1. Nf3 Nf6 2. c4 c6 3. d4 d5 4. Nc3 e6 5. Bg5 Nbd7 6. e3 Be7 7. Qc2 0–0 8. a3 Re8 9. Bd3 dxc4 10. Bxc4 Nd5 11. Bxe7 Qxe7 12. Ne4 Rd8 13. 0–0 Nf8 14. Rfe1 In the game with Kupchik, Kashdan played 14. Rad1. **14. ... b6** 15. Rac1 Bb7 16. Qe2 a5 17. Ne5 f6 18. Nf3 Kh8 19. Nc3 Nxc3 20. Rxc3 e5 21. Rd1 exd4 22. Rxd4 Rxd4 23. exd4 Qxe2 24. Bxe2 Re8 ½–½ (*New York 1931*)

174 Anderson (Denmark)– Kashdan [A47]
Prague Olympiad, round 1, 1931 *[June 11]*

1. d4 Nf6 2. Nf3 b6 3. e3 Bb7 4. Bd3 c5 5. 0–0 e6 6. Nbd2 Nc6 7. b3 Be7 8. Bb2 0–0 9. e4 cxd4 10. Nxd4 Nxd4 11. Bxd4 d5 12. e5 Ne4 13. Re1 f5 14. Nxe4 fxe4 15. Bf1 Bc5 16. c3 Qe7 17. b4 Bxd4 18. Qxd4 Rf5 19. Rad1 Raf8 20. Rd2 Qc7 21. g3 Rxe5 22. Bh3 Rf6 23. f4 Rh5 24. Bg4 e5 25. Qf2 Rhh6 26. f5 Qxc3 27. Rc2 Qxb4 28. Rc7 Rf7 29. Rec1 Rhf6 30. Bh5 g6 31. Qc2 Qd4+ 32. Kh1 gxh5 33. Rxb7 Rxb7 34. Qc8+ Kg7 35. Qxb7+ Rf7 36. f6+ Kg6 37. Qc8 Rxf6 38. Qg8+ Kh6 39. h4 Qe3 40. Rg1 Qf3+ 41. Kh2 Qg4 42. Qxd5 Rf2+ 43. Rg2 Rxg2+ 44. Kxg2 Qf3+ 45. Kh2 Qf2+ 46. Kh3 Qf5+ 47. Kh2 Kg7 48. a4 e3 49. Qb7+ Kf6 50. Qc6+ Ke7 51. Qc7+ Ke8 52. Qc6+ Qd7 53. Qh6 Qd2+ 54. Kh3 Qd1 55. Qe6+ Kd8 56. Qf6+ Kd7 57. Qf5+ Kd6 58. Qf6+ Kc5 59. Qxe5+ Kb4 60. Qb2+ Kc4 61. Qa2+ Kc5 62. Qa3+ Kc6 63. Kh2 Qd2+ 64. Kh3 e2 65. Qf3+ Kd6 66. Qa3+ Ke6 67. Qb3+ Ke7 0–1 (*Šachova Olympiade Praza*, 1931)

175 Kashdan–Mattison (Latvia) [E46]
Prague Olympiad, round 2, 1931 *[June]*

1. d4 Nf6 2. c4 e6 3. Nc3 Bb4 4. e3 0–0 5. Nge2 d5 6. a3 Be7 7. cxd5 exd5 8. Ng3 Re8 9. Bd3 c6 10. 0–0 Bd6 11. Nf5 Bf8 12. Qc2 g6 13. Ng3 Bg7 14. b4 Nbd7 15. Bd2 a5 16. Na4 axb4 17. axb4 b5 18. Nc5 Rxa1 19. Rxa1 Nxc5 20. bxc5 Qe7 21. Ra8 Be6 22. Ra6 Bd7 23. Ra7 Qe6 24. Ne2 Bh6 25. h3 Nh5 26. Qa2 f5 27. Qa5 Rc8 28. Qb6 Qe8 29. Qb7 Nf6 30. Nc3 Rb8 31. Qc7 Ra8 32. Na2 Rxa7 33. Qxa7 Qc8 34. Nb4 Ne4 35. Be1 Bg5 36. Qa6 Qxa6 37. Nxa6 Bd8 38. Kf1 Kf7 39. Ke2 Ke6 40. f3 Nf6 41. g4 Be8 42. Bg3 Bd7 43. Be5 Ba5 44. g5 Ng8 45. e4 fxe4 46. fxe4 Ne7 47. Nc7+ Bxc7 48. Bxc7 dxe4 49. Bxe4 Nd5 50. Bg3 Nc3+ 51. Kd3 Nxe4 ½–½ (Kashdan's scoresheet)

176 A. Steiner (Hungary)– Kashdan [C74]
Prague Olympiad, round 3, 1931 *[June]*

1. e4 e5 2. Nf3 Nc6 3. Bb5 a6 4. Ba4 d6 5. c3 f5 6. exf5 Bxf5 7. d4 e4 8. Ng5 Nf6 9. f3 d5 10. 0–0 Qd7 11. fxe4 Nxe4 12. Nxe4 Bxe4 13. Nd2 Bg6 14. Nf3 b5 15. Bb3 Be7 16. Ng5 h6 17. Nh3 0-0-0 18. a4 Kb7 19. Nf4 Be4 20. axb5 axb5 21. Qe2 Kb6 22. Nd3 Bxd3 23. Qxd3 Ra8 24. Rxa8 Rxa8 25. Qf3 Rd8 26. Re1 Bf6 27. Bf4 Na5 28. Bc2 Re8 29. Rxe8 Qxe8 30. Kf2 Qc6 31. Bh7 Nc4 32. Bc1 Qa8 33. Bd3 Qa1 34. Bxc4 bxc4 35. Qd1? Bg5 0–1 (*Magyar* 1931)

177 Kashdan–Flohr (Czechoslovakia) [E90]
Prague Olympiad, round 4, 1931 *[June]*

1. Nf3 Nf6 2. c4 g6 3. Nc3 Bg7 4. e4 d6 5. d4 0–0 6. Bd3 Nbd7 7. 0–0 e5 8. d5 Nc5 9. Bc2 a5 10. Nd2 Ne8 11. Nb3 f5 12. exf5 gxf5 13. f4 e4 14. Be3 b6 15. Nd4 Nf6 16. h3 Kh8 17. a3 Qe8 18. Ncb5 Na6 19. b4 Bd7 20. Ba4 Qf7 21. bxa5 bxa5 22. Rb1 Nc5 23. Bc2 Ne8 24. Qe2 Bf6 25. Kh2 Rg8 26. g3 Rg6 27. Rg1 Bd8 28. Rg2 Nf6 29. Rh1 Rb8 30. a4 h5 31. Bd2 Ra8 32. Bc3 Kh7

33. Re1 Be7 34. Nxc7 Rag8 35. Reg1 Rh6 36. Kh1 Rhg6 37. Ncb5 Nd3 38. Qe3 h4 39. gxh4 Rxg2 40. Rxg2 Rxg2 41. Kxg2 Nc5 42. Bxa5 Nh5 43. Be1 Bf8 44. Kh2 Bh6 45. Ne2 Qf6 46. Nbc3 Nd3 47. Bxd3 exd3 48. Qxd3 Nxf4 49. Nxf4 Bxf4+ 50. Kh1 Be5 51. a5 Qh6 52. Ne2 Bc8 53. Bg3 Qf6 54. Qe3 Bxg3 55. Qxg3 Qa1+ 56. Kg2 Qa2 57. Kf2 Qxc4 58. Qxd6 Qxh4+ 59. Qg3 Qc4 60. Qc3 Qh4+ 61. Kf1 Qd8 62. d6 Qe8 63. Qc4 Bd7 64. a6 Bb5 65. Qh4+ Kg6 66. Qe7 Qc6 67. Qe6+ Kg7 68. Qe5+ Kg6 69. Qe6+ Kg7 70. a7 1–0 (*Šachova Olympiade Praza*, 1931)

178 Alekhine (France)– Kashdan [D67]

Prague Olympiad, round 5, 1931 *[June]*

1. d4 Nf6 2. c4 e6 3. Nc3 d5 4. Bg5 Be7 5. e3 0–0 6. Nf3 Nbd7 7. Rc1 c6 8. Bd3 dxc4 9. Bxc4 Nd5 10. Bxe7 Qxe7 11. Ne4 Qb4+ 12. Qd2 Qxd2+ 13. Kxd2 Rd8 14. Rhd1 N7f6 15. Nxf6+ Nxf6 16. Bd3 Bd7 17. Ne5 Be8 18. g4 Nd7 19. Nc4 c5 20. Nd6 cxd4 21. Nxe8 Rxe8 22. exd4 Nf6 23. Rc7 Rab8 24. f3 Red8 25. Ke2 Nd5 26. Rc4 Nf4+ 27. Ke3 Nxd3 28. Rxd3 Rd7 29. Rdc3 f6 30. Rc7 Rbd8 31. f4 Kf7 32. Ke4 Ke7 33. Rxd7+ Rxd7 34. Rh3 h6 35. Ra3 a6 36. Rb3 Kd8 37. Rb6 Re7 38. a4 Kc7 39. a5 Re8 40. h4 Re7 41. g5 hxg5 42. fxg5 Re8 43. Kf4 Rd8 44. gxf6 gxf6 45. Rxe6 Rxd4+ 46. Kg3 Rd3+ 47. Kg4 Rd4+ 48. Kh5 Rf4 49. Re3 Rb4 50. Rh3 Kd6 51. Kg6 Ke7 52. h5 Rg4+ 53. Kf5 Rg5+ 54. Kf4 Kf7 55. Rb3 Rxa5 56. Rxb7+ Kg8 57. h6 Rh5 58. Rg7+ Kf8 59. Rb7 Rxh6 60. Kf5 Rh5+ ½–½ (*Šachova Olympiade Praza*, 1931)

179 Kashdan–Grünfeld (Austria) [C86]

Prague Olympiad, round 6, 1931 *[June]*

1. e4 e5 2. Nf3 Nc6 3. Bb5 a6 4. Ba4 Nf6 5. 0–0 Be7 6. Qe2 b5 7. Bb3 d6 8. a4 Bg4 9. c3 0–0 10. h3 Bd7 11. d4

Rb8 12. axb5 Rxb5 13. Bc4 Rb7 14. dxe5 Nxe5 15. Nxe5 dxe5 16. Rxa6 h6 17. Nd2 Bd6 18. Bd3 Re8 19. b4 Bf8 20. Nb3 Re6 21. Rxe6 Bxe6 22. Na5 Rb6 23. Be3 Qc8 24. Bxb6 cxb6 25. Nc4 b5 26. Nxe5 Qxc3 27. Nf3 Bxb4 28. Bxb5 Nh5 29. Qd3 Qc7 30. Rd1 Ba5 31. Nd4 Nf4 32. Nxe6 fxe6 33. Qf3 Qe5 34. Bf1 Bb6 35. g3 Nh5 36. Kg2 Nf6 37. Rc1 Qxe4 38. Rc6 Bd4 39. Bc4 Kf8 40. Rxe6 Qxf3+ 41. Kxf3 Bc5 42. Rc6 Nd7 43. Rc7 Ne5+ 44. Ke4 Bxf2 45. Rc8+ 1–0 (*Šachova Olympiade Praza*, 1931)

180 Kashdan–Vidmar (Yugoslavia) [B45]

Prague Olympiad, round 8, 1931 *[June]*

1. e4 c5 2. Nf3 Nc6 3. d4 cxd4 4. Nxd4 Nf6 Better than 4. ... d6, when 5. c4! Nf6 6. Nc3 would give White a stronger hold on the center and a definite advantage. 5. Nc3 e6 But here d6 was in order, to be followed by either ...e6 or ...g6. The text plans ...d5, which, however, Black can rarely play with safety in this opening. 6. Ndb5 a6? Forcing White's best move and leaving Black with a very restricted game. There is already only a choice of evils. If 6. ... d5? 7. exd5 exd5 8. Nxd5! Nxd5 9. Qxd5 Qxd5 10. Nc7+ with a pawn ahead. Or 6. ... Bb4 7. a3 (but not 7. Nd6+ Ke2! with a good game), Bxc3+ Nxc3, with advantage for White. Relatively best was 6. ... d6 7. Bf4 e5 8. Bg5 a6 9. Bxf6 gxf6 10. Na3 b5 11. Nd5, when the weakness of Black's pawns will tell against him. 7. Nd6+ Bxd6 8. Qxd6 Qe7 9. Bf4 White now has the two bishops and a considerable freer position, with Black's backward d pawn as another handicap for the second player. 9. ... Nh5 Forcing the exchange of queens which temporarily relieves the pressure. 10. Qxe7+ Kxe7 11. Be3 b5 12. 0–0–0 d6 13. Be2 Nf6 14. f3 Protecting the pawn against the threat of ...b4. White can afford to consolidate before proceeding with the attack. 14. ... Bb7 15. Rd2 Rhc8 Loss of time, as this rook will be needed at d8, but there is nothing constructive for Black to undertake. 16. Rhd1 Ne8 17. Bf4 Rd8 Forced. If ...Ne5? 18. Bxe5 dxe5 19. Rd7+ wins, or 17. ... e5 18. Nd5+ Kf8 19. Be3

and Black's weaknesses are still more pro-
nounced. **18. b3** To gain ground and place the
king on a better square before the breakthrough
by a4. **18. ... Rac8 19. Kb2 Nb8** With the
hope of doubling rooks on the c file for some
counter play, but he is allowed no time for this.
20. a4! The correct idea. Whether Black exchanges pawns or plays b4, he must open new
lines on the queenside for White's pieces, and
leave his pawns more vulnerable. **20. ... b4
21. Na2 Nc6 22. Bg5+** The bishop is going
to e3, but the text forces a slight additional weakness of the Black pawns. **22. ... f6 23. Be3
Nc7 24. Bb6!**

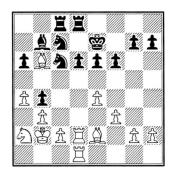

After
24. Bb6

A remarkable position. Black is in practically
complete "zugzwang." There is not a move with
any piece which does not lose at least a pawn.
24. ... Rd7 What is Black to do? If 24. ... Ba8
25. Bxc7 Rxc7 26. Bxa6. If 24. ... a5 25. Bb5,
and the a pawn must fall. On 24. ... e5 25. Bc4
maintains the grip. If 24. ... f5 25. exf5 exf5
26. f4, etc. On other moves of the kingside
pawns, White can wait until they are exhausted,
or take advantage of any further openings created. The move actually played also loses quickly.
**25. Bc5 Ne8 26. Nxb4 Ne5 27. Bb6 Ra8
28. a5** To exchange Black's only effective piece,
and clear the way for the White pawns. **28. ...
g6 29. Nd3 Nc6** A mistake due to time pressure, which costs the exchange. But in any case
it is only a matter of time for White's material
advantage to become decisive. **30. Nc5 1–0**
Annotated by Kashdan in *Chess Review*, April
1936. (*Šachova Olympiade Praza*, 1931)

181 Mikėnas (Latvia)–Kashdan [D53]

Prague Olympiad, round 9, 1931 *[June]*

**1. d4 Nf6 2. c4 e6 3. Nc3 d5 4. Bg5
Nbd7 5. e3 Be7 6. Nf3 dxc4 7. Bxc4 a6
8. 0–0 b5 9. Bd3 c5 10. Qc2 Bb7 11. Rfd1
Qb6 12. Rac1 0–0 13. Ne5 Rfe8 14. dxc5
Nxc5 15. Bxf6 Bxf6 16. Bxh7+! Kxh7
17. Qh5+ Kg8 18. Qxf7+**

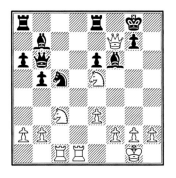

After
18. Qxf7

18. ... Kh7? The players agreed to a draw
here, but the correct move is Kh8. After the text
White could have won as follows: 19. Nd7!
Nxd7 20. Rxd7 Bc6 21. Ne4! Bxb2! (not Bxd7
as Nf6+ leads to mate) 22. Ng5+ Kh6 23. g4! g6
24. h4 Rh8 25. Qh7+ Rxh7 26. Rxh7 mate!
½–½ (Janowsky–Chajes, New York 1916)
(*Šachova Olympiade Praza*, 1931)

182 Kashdan–Christofferson (Norway) [C86]

Prague Olympiad, round 11, 1931 *[June]*

**1. e4 e5 2. Nf3 Nc6 3. Bb5 a6 4. Ba4
Nf6 5. 0–0 Be7 6. Qe2 b5 7. Bb3 d6
8. a4 Bg4 9. c3** But not 9. h3 as after 9. ...
Nd4 10. Qd1 Nxf3+ 11. gxf3 Bxh3 wins a pawn
and shatters the pawn structure on the kingside. **9. ... 0–0 10. h3 Bd7 11. d4 h6
12. Rd1 Qc8 13. Nbd2 Kh8 14. Nf1 Rb8
15. axb5 axb5 16. g4 h5 17. Ng5 hxg4
18. Nxf7+ Kh7 19. hxg4 Nxg4 20. f3 Be8
21. Ng5+ Bxg5 22. Bxg5 Nh6 23. Ng3
Kg6 24. Qg2 Kh7 25. Kf2 Bf7 26. Bxh6
Bxb3 27. Nf5 g6 28. Rh1 Rxf5 29. Bf8+
Kg8 30. Qxg6+ Kxf8 31. Rh8+ Ke7
32. Rxc8 1–0** (*Šachova Olympiade Praza*, 1931)

183 Sultan Khan (England)– Kashdan [D05]

Prague Olympiad, round 12, 1931 *[June]*

1. d4 d5 2. Nf3 Nf6 3. e3 e6 4. Nbd2

Nbd7 5. Bd3 c5 6. c3 Bd6 7. 0–0 0–0
8. e4 cxd4 9. cxd4 dxe4 10. Nxe4 Nxe4
11. Bxe4 Nf6 12. Bc2 b6 13. Re1 Bb7
14. Bg5 h6 15. Bh4 Rc8 16. Qd3 Ba6
17. Qxa6 Rxc2 18. Bxf6 Qxf6 19. Qxa7
Rfc8 20. Qb7 Qf4 21. Rab1 g5 22. h3
R8c6 23. Qd7 Kg7 24. Rbd1 h5 25. Qd8
g4 26. hxg4 hxg4 27. d5 Rc8 28. Qg5+
Qxg5 29. Nxg5 Bc5 30. Ne4 g3 31. Rf1
gxf2+ 32. Kh2 exd5 33. Rxd5 Rxb2
34. a4 Ra2 35. Nxc5 bxc5 36. Rf5 c4
37. Kg3 Rxa4 38. R1xf2 Rc7 39. Rc2 Kg6
40. Rf3 Kg5 41. Kf2 Ra5 42. Rfc3 Rf5+
43. Kg3 Rf4 44. Rb2 Rc5 45. Rb7 f6
46. Rg7+ Kf5 47. Rh7 Rc8 48. Re7 Rg8+
49. Kh3 Rh8+ 50. Kg3 Rhh4 51. Re8
Rhg4+ 52. Kh3 Re4 53. Rf3+ Rgf4
54. g4+ Kg6 55. Rxf4 Rxf4 56. Kg3 Rf1
57. Rg8+ Kf7 58. Rc8 Rc1 59. Kf4 c3
60. Kf5 Ke7 61. Ke4 Kd7 62. Rc4 Kd6
63. Kd3 Kd5 64. Ra4 Ke6 65. Ra5 Kf7
66. g5 ½–½ (*Šachova Olympiade Praza*, 1931)

184 Kashdan–Roselli (Italy) [A30]
Prague Olympiad, round 13, 1931 *[June]*

1. Nf3 Nf6 2. c4 e6 3. g3 b6 4. Bg2
Bb7 5. 0–0 c5 6. Nc3 Be7 7. d4 cxd4
8. Nxd4 Bxg2 9. Kxg2 0–0 10. b3 Nc6
11. Nf3 d5 12. cxd5 exd5 13. Bb2 Qd7
14. Rc1 Rfd8 15. Rc2 Rac8 16. Qb1 Qe6
17. Nb5 Ne4 18. Rxc6 Rxc6 19. Nbd4
Qc8 20. Nxc6 Qxc6 21. Rc1 Qb7 22. Qc2
Bc5 23. Nd4 Qd7 24. b4 Bxd4 25. Bxd4
f6 26. a4 Ng5 27. Be3 Ne6 28. f3 h6
29. Rd1 Kf7 30. b5 Qc7 31. Qf5 d4
32. Rc1 Qe5 33. Qxe5 fxe5 34. Bd2 Rd7
35. Bb4 Nc7 36. Rc6 Nd5 37. Bd2 Rc7
38. Rxc7+ Nxc7 39. Kf2 Nd5 40. Ke1
Ke6 41. Kd1 Nc7 42. Kc2 Kd5 43. Kd3
Ne6 44. e4+ dxe3 45. Bxe3 Nc5+
46. Bxc5 Kxc5 47. Kc3 Kd5 48. Kd3 Kc5
½–½ (*Šachova Olympiade Praza*, 1931)

185 Weenink (Holland)–
Kashdan [C42]
Prague Olympiad, round 14, 1931 *[June]*

1. e4 e5 2. Nf3 Nf6 3. Nxe5 d6 4. Nf3
Nxe4 5. c4 Be7 6. Nc3 Nxc3 7. dxc3

0–0 8. Qc2 Nd7 9. Bd3 h6 10. Be3 Nc5
11. Bxc5 dxc5 12. 0–0–0 Bd6 13. Bh7+
Kh8 14. Bf5 Qf6 15. Bxc8 Rfxc8 16. Kb1
a6 17. Rhe1 b5 18. Re4 Rab8 19. cxb5
axb5 20. Rde1 b4 21. c4 Ra8 22. b3 g6
23. Qb2 Qxb2+ 24. Kxb2 Kg7 25. h3
Rf8 26. R1e2 f5 27. Re6 g5 28. Ne5 Rf6
29. Rxf6 Kxf6 30. Nd3 h5 31. f3 Rg8
32. Kc2 g4 33. fxg4 hxg4 34. hxg4 Rxg4
35. Ne1 Kg5 36. Nf3+ Kf4 37. Nh2 Rh4
38. Nf1 Rh1 39. Rf2+ Kg5 40. Ne3 f4
41. Nd1 Kh4 42. Rf3 Rg1 43. Nf2 Rxg2
44. Kd3 Rg8 45. Rh3+ Kg5 46. Ne4+
Kg4 47. Rh1 Ra8 48. Rg1+ Kh3 49. Nxd6
cxd6 50. Ke4 Rxa2 51. Kxf4 Kh2
52. Rg6 Rb2 53. Rxd6 Rxb3 54. Rc6
Rb1 55. Rxc5 b3 56. Rb5 ½–½ (Dutch
magazine)

186 Kashdan–Bogoljubow
(Germany) [D52]
Prague Olympiad, round 15, 1931 *[June]*

1. d4 d5 2. c4 e6 3. Nc3 Nf6 4. Nf3
c6 5. Bg5 Nbd7 6. e3 Qa5 7. Nd2 Bb4
8. Qc2 0–0 9. Be2 dxc4 10. Bxf6 Nxf6
11. Nxc4 Qc7 12. 0–0 Rd8 13. Rac1 Be7
14. a3 Nd5 15. Ne4 Bd7 16. Bd3 Be8
17. Qe2 Nf6 18. b4 Nxe4 19. Bxe4 Rac8
20. f4 g6 21. Qf3 Bf8 22. g4 b6 23. Ne5
c5 24. g5 Qe7 25. bxc5 bxc5 26. d5
exd5 27. Bxd5 Bg7 28. Nc4 Kh8 29. Rb1
Rb8 30. Kh1 Qc7 31. e4 Bd4 32. f5 Rxb1
33. Rxb1 Rb8 34. Rf1 Kg8 35. fxg6 hxg6
36. h4 Rd8 37. h5 gxh5 38. g6 Rxd5
39. exd5 Qe7 40. gxf7+ Bxf7 41. Qf5
Kg7 42. Nd6 Qh4+ 43. Kg2 Bxd5+
44. Qxd5 ½–½ (*Šachova Olympiade Praza*,
1931)

187 Naegeli (Switzerland)–
Kashdan [E23]
Prague Olympiad, round 16, 1931 *[June]*

1. d4 Nf6 2. c4 e6 3. Nc3 Bb4 4. Qb3
c5 5. dxc5 Nc6 6. Nf3 Ne4 7. Bd2 Nxd2
8. Nxd2 f5 9. e3 0–0 10. Be2 Bxc5
11. Nf3 b6 12. 0–0 Bb7 13. Rad1 Rc8
14. Nb5 Qe7 15. a3 a6 16. Nc3 f4 17. e4
g5 18. h3 h5 19. Na4 g4 20. hxg4 hxg4

21. Nxc5 Qxc5 22. Rxd7 gxf3 23. Rxb7
Nd4! 24. Qxb6 Qxb6 25. Rxb6 fxe2
26. Re1 f3 0–1 (*Šachova Olympiade Praza*, 1931)

188 Kashdan–Vilardebó (Spain) [B29]

Prague Olympiad, round 17, 1931 *[June]*

1. e4 c5 2. Nf3 e6 3. Nc3 Nf6 4. e5
Nd5 5. Nxd5 exd5 6. d4 c4 7. c3 b5
8. Ng5 h6 9. Nh3 d6 10. exd6 Bxd6
11. g3 Nd7 12. Bg2 Nf6 13. 0–0 0–0
14. a4 b4 15. Nf4 Qa5 16. cxb4 Bxb4
17. Nh5 Nxh5 18. Qxh5 f5 19. Qg6 Rf6
20. Qe8+ Kh7 21. Bf4 Bb7 22. Qh5 Bc6
23. Be5 g6 24. Qe2 Rf7 25. Qc2 Rc8
26. f4 Rb7 27. Bf3 Bd2 28. Kh1 Rb3
29. Bd1 Qb4 30. Ra2 Re3 31. Bf3 Qb3
32. Qxd2 Rxf3 33. Rxf3 Qxf3+ 34. Kg1
Qd3 35. Qc1 Qb3 36. Ra3 Qb4 37. Kg2
Bd7 38. Qc2 Rc6 39. Qe2 Rb6 40. Re3
Qxb2 41. Bc7 Qxe2+ 42. Rxe2 Re6
43. Rxe6 Bxe6 ½–½ (*Šachova Olympiade
Praza*, 1931)

189 Erdely (Romania)–Kashdan [D52]

Prague Olympiad, round 18, 1931 *[June]*

1. d4 Nf6 2. c4 e6 3. Nc3 d5 4. Bg5
Nbd7 5. e3 c6 6. Nf3 Qa5 7. Nd2 Bb4
8. Qc2 0–0 9. Bh4 c5 10. Be2 cxd4
11. exd4 dxc4 12. Nxc4 Qd5 13. 0–0–0
Bxc3 14. bxc3 Qxg2 15. Bd3 Qh3 16. Bg5
b5 17. Nd6 Kh8 18. Rhg1 Qf3 19. Rg3
Qc6 20. Ne4 Nd5 21. Bd2 f5 22. Ng5
N7f6 23. Rdg1 Bd7 24. Kb2 Rac8
25. Nf3 Nh5 26. Ne5 Qd6 27. Rg5 Be8
28. Be2 b4 29. Bxh5 bxc3+ 30. Ka1 Nb4
31. Qb3 cxd2 32. Qb2 Nc2+ 0–1 (*Šachova
Olympiade Praza*, 1931)

190 Kashdan–Rubinstein (Poland) [D61]

Prague Olympiad, round 19, 1931 *[June 26]*

1. d4 d5 2. Nf3 Nf6 3. c4 e6 4. Nc3
Nbd7 5. Bg5 Be7 6. e3 0–0 7. Qc2 h6
8. Bf4 c5 9. cxd5 cxd4 10. exd4 Nxd5

11. Nxd5 exd5 12. a3 Re8 13. Be2 Nf6
14. Bc7 Bf5 15. Qxf5 Qxc7 16. 0–0 Qb6
17. Rab1 Rac8 18. Qd3 a6 19. Nh4 Ne4
20. Nf5 Bf6 21. Rfd1 Rc4 22. Qf3 Rcc8
23. Qg4 Kf8 24. Bf3 g6 25. Ne3 Bxd4
26. Nxd5 Bxf2+ 27. Kf1 Qb5+ 28. Be2
Qc6 29. g3 Ba7 30. Qf4 Kg7 31. Rbc1
Qe6 32. Bg4 Rxc1 33. Bxe6 Rxd1+
34. Ke2 Rd2+ 0–1 (*Šachova Olympiade Praza*,
1931)

191 Asztalos–Kashdan [C49]

Bled, round 1, 1931 *[August 23]*

1. e4 e5 2. Nf3 Nf6 3. Nc3 Nc6 4. Bb5
Bb4 5. 0–0 0–0 6. Bxc6 dxc6 7. d3 Re8
8. h3 b6 9. Nh2 Be6 10. Qe2 Qd7
11. Nd1 b5 12. b3 Qe7 13. Bb2 Nd7
14. Ne3 Bd6 15. Qh5 c5 16. a4 a6
17. axb5 axb5 18. Rxa8 Rxa8 19. Ra1
Rxa1+ 20. Bxa1 Qd8 21. Qd1 Nb8
22. Bb2 Nc6 23. Nf3 Nd4 24. Nd2 g6
25. c3 Nc6 26. Nd5 Qa8 27. Qa1 Qc8
28. Nf3 f5 29. Bc1 Kg7 30. b4! c4
31. dxc4 bxc4 32. Nd2 Ne7 33. Nxc4!
Nxd5 34. exd5 Bxd5 35. Nxd6 cxd6
36. Qa7+ Bb7? 37. c4 g5 38. b5 Kf6
39. Ba3 Qc7 40. Bxd6 Qxd6 41. Qxb7
Qd1+ 42. Kh2 Qd4 43. Qa6+ Kg7
44. Qa2 e4 45. Qe2? f4 46. c5 e3 47. c6
exf2 48. c7 Qe3 49. Qxe3 fxe3 50. c8Q
f1Q 51. Qc7+ Kg6 0–1 (*Bled* 1931)

192 Kashdan–Vidmar [D31]

Bled, round 2, 1931 *[August 24]*

1. d4 d5 2. c4 e6 3. Nc3 c6 4. Nf3
Nd7 5. e4 dxe4 6. Nxe4 Ngf6 7. Nc3
Bd6 8. Be2 0–0 9. Bg5 b6 10. 0–0 Qc7
11. Qc2 a6 12. Ne4 Nxe4 13. Qxe4 e5
14. Qh4 exd4 15. Bd3 f5 16. Be7 Bxe7
17. Qxe7 c5 18. Rae1 Ra7 19. Qe6+ Kh8
20. Bxf5 Nf6 21. Qe5 Qxe5 22. Rxe5
Bxf5 23. Rxf5 Re8 24. Re5 Rxe5
25. Nxe5 Re7 26. Re1 Kg8 27. Kf1 Nd7
28. Nxd7 Rxd7 29. Re6 Rb7 30. Re5
a5 31. Ke2 Kf7 32. Kd3 Rd7 33. f4 a4
34. g4 Re7 35. Rxe7+ Kxe7 36. Ke4 g6
37. h3 Kf6 38. Kd3 ½–½ (*Bled* 1931)

193 Colle–Kashdan [D05]
Bled, round 3, 1931 *[August 25]*

1. d4 d5 2. Nf3 Nf6 3. e3 c5 4. c3 The Colle System, made famous by this master, who employed it frequently. It is apparently backward development, but the idea is to play e4 very soon. It can lead to a surprisingly strong attack if Black does not defend properly. Nevertheless, it allows Black more choice and freedom than is usual in the Queen's Pawn Openings. **4. ... e6** If 4. ... Bg4 5. dxc5 and it is a Queen's Gambit with White a move ahead. He can probably hold the pawn safely. **5. Nbd2 Nc6 6. Bd3 Bd6 7. 0–0 0–0** 7. ... e5 is risky before Black has castled. There might follow 8. dxe5 Nxe5 9. Nxe5 Bxe5 10. e4! dxe4 11. Nxe4 Nxe4 12. Qa4+! Bd7 13. Qxa4 with a winning advantage. Or in this variation 10. ... 0–0 11. f4 Bc7 12. e5 with a strong attack. **8. dxc5 Bxc5 9. e4 Qc7 10. exd5** An interesting possibility which occurred in a "skittles" game is 10. Qe2 Bd7 11. e5 Ng4 12. Ng5? (best is 12. Bxh7+ Kxh7 13. Ng5+ Kg8 14. Qxg4 Qxe5 with a slight advantage to Black. *[But does not Qh4 threaten mate which can only be prevented by giving up the queen for the knight?–P.P.L.]* f5! 13. exf5ep?? Qxh2 mate! **10. ... exd5** 10. ... Nd5 11. Ne4 Be7 is sounder from the theoretical standpoint. Black chooses the isolated pawn, with the greater freedom for his pieces as compensation. **11. Nb3 Bb6 12. Qc2 Re8 13. Bg5 Ne4 14. Rae1 Bf5 15. Be3** Easing the pressure on the f pawn, and preparing to attack the center by Nd4 or Nh4. **15. ... Bg6** A simple looking retreat, but I took more time on this than any other move in the game, as I had to visualize the entire subsequent combination. Otherwise 15. ... h6 16. Nh4 Bh7 is more secure. **16. Nh4**

After
16. Nh4

Threatening to capture both bishops followed by Bxe4 winning a pawn. The move seemingly forces an abject retreat. **16. ... Nxf2!!** Certainly unexpected. The pawn is overprotected to the best taste of a Nimzovitch devotee, and there seems to be no drastic weakness in White's camp to justify this intrusion. I will admit when I first thought of the move, it appeared too fantastic to offer any real chances. But the pieces on both sides are exactly placed to create the maximum complications, and I knew my opponent would have a pretty problem in working out his proper defense. It is the sort of thing which cannot be analyzed to a decisive conclusion, but is worth trying over the board with the clock ticking, whatever the result may be in a post-mortem after the game. **17. Bxf2** The only move. Here are some of the variations that had to be looked into: (1) 17. Kxf2 Qf4+ 18. Nf3 Rxe3 19. Rxe3 Qxe3+ 20. Kg3 Bxd3 winning just about everything. (2) 17. Qxf2 Bxd3 with a pawn ahead. (3) 17. Rxf2 Bxe3 winning the exchange. (4) 17. Bxb6 Qxb6 18. Rxe8+ Rxe8 19. Bxg6 (not 19. Rxf2? Re1+ 20. Bf1 Bxc2) Ne4+ 20. Kh1 hxg6; with a pawn plus and the better position. (5) 17. Bxg6 Ng4! 18. Bxf2+ Kh1 19. g3 Nxd3; winning at least the exchange. Other commentators do not agree with this assessment. Kmoch gives the move 16. ... Nxf2!? and states that 16. ... Nf6 is correct. The text move is a brilliant idea, but is based on a miscalculation. Kashdan's miscalculation leads to a grand combination. After the sacrifice of a piece, Black obtains a very strong attack: however, with best play, White can in no way lose and might possibly even win. **17. ... Bxf2+ 18. Kxf2** Again forced to avoid material loss. **18. ... Qb6+ 19. Kg3** If 19. Kf3 Ne4+ 20. Rxe4 Rxe4; threatening ...Qe3+ or ...Qf6+, and White has little resource against the attack despite his extra piece. **19. ... Re3+ 20. Rxe3 Qxe3+ 21. Rf3 Qg5+** In my earlier analysis, I had first thought that I could play 21. ... Bxd3 22. Rxe3 Bxd3. But 22. Qxd3 destroys that elusion. White thus remains a piece ahead, but he is exposed to a lasting attack, which depends on the fact that the king is forced to a square in front of his pawns, from which he cannot secure a retreat. **22. Kh3 Ne5 23. Rg3 Qh6 24. Bf5?** This is weak, and the cause of White's later trouble.

Correct was 24. Bxg6 Nxg6 (if hxg6 25. Qd2! wins) 25. Rg4 Ne5 (there is nothing better) 26. Qe2 giving up the exchange. (But not Rg3 when g5 wins). Black would still retain enough attack to at least secure a draw. **24. ... Re8** If ...Bh5 25. Qd2! and White soon gets the upper hand. After the text he cannot try this, because of Bxf5+, and he finds himself with very few good moves. **25. Nd4 Bh5** Threatening g5, which White will find hard to prevent, as he no longer can oppose the queens. **26. Qf2 g5 27. Bxh7+** An interesting resource, and the best at his disposal. If 27. Qe3, NOT 27. g5+? 28. Bxg5 Bxg5 29. Rxg5+ and White wins, but 27. f6! threatening ...Kh8, and White has no time to untangle his pieces. **27. ... Kf8** If ...Qxh7 28. Rxg5+, or ...Kxh7 28. Qf5+ followed by Qxg5. But now the bishop must return. **28. Bf5 gxh4 29. Re3 Re7!** Threatening to win the exchange by Ng4! The text was important to avoid White playing Rxe7. **30. Re1** But this still loses the exchange through a neat rejoinder. There is no longer a defense. If 30. Nc2 Qg5 31. g3 Bg4+ 32. Bxg4 Nxg4 winning. **30. ... Bg4+! 31. Bxg4 Nd3 32. Qxh4 Nf4+** A little finesse which regains the pawn and leaves Black a full exchange ahead. **33. Kg3 Qxh4+ 34. Kxh4 Nxg2+ 35. Kg5 Rxe1 36. h4** White can still offer some resistance through the strength of the h pawn, but in the long run the material advantage must be decisive. **36. ... Ne3 37. Bf3 Nc4 38. Nf5 Rg1+ 39. Kf4 Rf1 40. Ne3 Rf2** Better than regaining the knights, as now the White pawns begin to fall. **41. Nd1 Rh2 42. h5 Nxb2 43. Ne3 Nd3+ 44. Kg3 Rxa2 45. Bxd5 Rb2 46. h6 Ne5 47. Kf4 Ng6+ 48. Ke4 b6 49. Nf5 Ne7** If 50. h7, of course ...Rh2. After the exchange of pieces, White is helpless against the march of the Black a pawn. **0−1** Annotations by Kashdan in *Chess Review*, February 1936. (*Bled* 1931)

194 Kashdan−Nimzovitch [A09]

Bled, round 4, 1931 *[August 27]*

1. Nf3 d5 2. c4 dxc4 3. Na3 Simpler is 3. e3, leading to the Q.G.A. position generally favorable to White. **3. ... c5** Avoiding the more complicated variations; 3. ... e5 4. Nxe5 Bxe5 5. Qa4+, etc. **4. g3** This is inferior, as it gives

Black time to build up a powerful center. This could be avoided by 4. Nxc4 Nc6 (if ...f6 5. d4! cxd4 6. Qxd4 with a powerful gain in development); 5. Nfe5 Nxe5 6. Nxe5 f3 7. Qa5+, and after the exchanges White has the endgame advantage with the two bishops. Also effective is 5. e3 f6? 6. d4!. **4. ... Nc6 5. Nxc4 f6!** Now ...e5 cannot be prevented, and Black gets good control of the mid-board. **6. Bg2 e5 7. d3 Be6 8. 0−0 Nge7 9. Nfd2** The start of an interesting knight maneuver, the point of which will be noted after move 12. White must find some compensation in the center before Black can complete and commence a promising kingside attack. **9. ... Nd5 10. Ne4 Be7 11. Ne3 Qd7 12. Nc3!** Thus gaining command of the important square d5. If Black takes either knight, followed by e5 or c5, and eventually d4. Otherwise Black must retreat, and he has no effective square. **12. ... Nb6 13. b3 Nd4 14. Ba3** Beginning an attack on the c pawn, which will gain a good deal of time for White later. **14. ... Rc8 15. Rc1 0−0 16. Ne4 Qb5 17. Qd2 f5** By driving the knight back relieves the queenside attack, and also threatens ...f4, which would be quite strong. **18. Nc3 Qd7 19. f4 exf4 20. gxf4** The White center pawns are not too strong, but the plan is to play e4 at the proper moment, and secure a supported passed pawn. **20. ... Rfd8 21. Kh1** A necessary precaution. Not 21. Nc4? Nxc4 22. bxc4 Bxc4 23. exb4 Nf3+ wins. **21. ... Kh8 22. Nc4 Bf6** If ...Nxc4 23. bxc4, followed by Nd5. Or 22. ... Nd5 23. Nxd5 Bxd5 24. e4 with a fine game. **23. Na5!** Threatening the b pawn, which is difficult to defend. If now 23. ... Nd5 24. Nxd5 Bxd5 25. e4 Be6 26. e5 and 27. Nxb7. Or 25. ... c6 26. Bxc5 will win. **23. ... Rc7 24. e3** This leads to no decisive result. Perhaps better was 24. Rfd1, defending the d pawn and preparing e3 or e4. **24. ... Nb5 25. Nxb5 Qxb5 26. Nxb7** *(see diagram)*

Again Rfd1 might have been preferred as the text gives Black too many chances. **26. ... Rxb7!** Very enterprising play leading to a surprisingly strong attack, which will require all White's resources to thwart. Also good was 26. Rxd3 Qf2 (not 27. Qe2, Rxb3!) c4, or 27. Qc2 Rxe3 28. Nxc5, in both cases leaving a difficult game with White having somewhat the advantage.

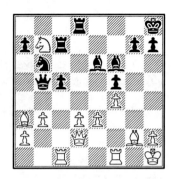

After
26. Nxb7

27. Bxb7 Nd5! The point of the sacrifice, gaining command of the long open diagonal. **28. Bxd5 Bxd5+ 29. Kg1 Qa6?** This was Nimzovitch's original idea. By attacking the bishop he gains time to swing the queen across to the kingside. But White has enough leeway to perfect his defense. Correct was 29. ... ba8! 30. h3 (if Rxc5 Qb7 with numerous threats to which there is no good defense), Qb7 31. Kh2 Rxd3! 32. Qc2 (if Qe2 Rxe3! or Qf2 Bh4!), Rc3 33. Qd2 Rd3, with a perpetual attack on the queen, thus forcing a draw. **30. Bxc5 Bh4 31. Rf2** The only defense, but quite satisfactory to White, who remains two pawns ahead after returning the exchange. **31. ... Bxf2+ 32. Kxf2 Qh6 33. Ke1 Qg6 34. Qf2 Qa6 35. Qe2** Reaching the correct square from which the queen can defend both sides of the board, and prepare for the eventual e4. **35. ... Bc6 36. Bd4 Rd6 37. Rc5** The inroad of the rook soon decides the game, as the attack on the Black king ties up his pieces. **37. ... Rg6 38. e4!** Stopping the check, and making everything secure. **38. ... fxe4 39. dxe4 Qb7 40. f5 Rd6 41. Qe3 Kg8** If ...Bxe4, 42. Re5 wins because of the mating threat. **42. Qc3 Bd7 43. Re5 Rc6 44. Bc5 Qc8 45. Re7** It is quite hopeless. If ...Qf8 46. Qc4+ Kh8 47. Rxd7 Rxc5 48. Qxc5 wins. Or 45. ... Rb6 46. Qc4+ Kh8 47. Bd4 Qxc4 48. bxc4 Rd6 49. Be5 Rd3 50. Ke2, and everything goes. **1–0** Annotations by Kashdan in *Chess Review*, February 1936. (*Bled* 1931)

195 Pirc–Kashdan [D28]
Bled, round 5, 1931 *[August 29]*

1. d4 d5 2. c4 dxc4 3. Nf3 e6 4. e3 a6 5. Bxc4 Nf6 6. 0–0 c5 7. Qe2 Nc6

8. Rd1 b5 9. dxc5 Qc7 10. Bb3 Bxc5 11. a4 b4 12. Nbd2 0–0 13. Bc2 Bb7 14. b3 Ne5 15. Bb2 Nxf3+ 16. Nxf3 Rfd8 17. h3 Ne4 18. Rac1 Nc3 19. Bxc3 bxc3 20. Qc4 Bd6 21. Qxc7 Bxc7 22. Rxd8+ Rxd8 23. Rd1 Rxd1+ 24. Bxd1 Kf8 25. Kf1 e5 26. Ne1 a5 27. f3 f5 28. Be2 Bb6 29. Nc2 Bd5 30. Bc4 Bxc4+ 31. bxc4 e4 32. Ke2 Ke7 33. fxe4 fxe4 34. Na1 Kd6 35. Nb3 Ke5 36. c5 Bd8 37. Kd1 Kd5 38. Kc2 Bg5 39. Nxa5 Kxc5 40. Kxc3 Bxe3 41. Nb3+ Kd5 42. Kc2 Ba7 ½–½ (*Bled* 1931)

196 Kashdan–Flohr [C76]
Bled, round 6, 1931 *[August 30]*

1. e4 e5 2. Nf3 Nc6 3. Bb5 a6 4. Ba4 d6 5. c3 g6 6. d4 Bd7 7. 0–0 Bg7 8. Be3 Nf6 9. dxe5 Nxe5 10. Nxe5 dxe5 11. Nd2 0–0 12. Bc2 Qe7 13. h3 Ne8 14. Qe2 Nd6 15. Rfe1 Rfe8 16. Rad1 b6 17. c4 Nb7 18. Nb1 b5 19. Nc3 c6 20. cxb5 axb5 21. a4 b4 22. Nb1 Be6 23. Nd2 Na5 24. b3 c5 25. Rb1 Nc6 26. Bd3 Nd4 27. Bxd4 exd4 28. Bb5 Red8 29. Qd3 Be5 30. Bc4 Bc8 31. Bd5 Ra7 32. Nc4 Bc7 33. Qf3 Kg7 34. Rbd1 h5 35. Qe2 Ra6 36. Rd3 Bb8 37. Nd2 Ra7 38. Bc4 f6 39. Nf3 Re8 40. Bb5 Rf8 41. Rdd1 Qd8 42. Qc2 Bd6 43. Bf1 Re7 44. g3 Be6 45. Nh4 Qe8 46. Bb5 Qf7 47. Bc4 Bxc4 48. bxc4 Ra7 49. f4 Rfa8 50. Ra1 Qe8 51. e5 fxe5 52. f5 e4 53. Rxe4 Re7 54. Rxe7+ Qxe7 55. fxg6 Qe3+ 56. Kh1 Qc3 57. Qb1 Rf8 58. Ra2 d3 59. Qd1 Bxg3 60. Nf3 Qf6 61. Kg2 Qxg6 62. a5 b3 63. Ra3 Bd6+ 64. Kf2 Qg3+ 65. Ke3 Bf4+ 0–1 (*Bled* 1931)

197 Bogoljubow–Kashdan [D63]
Bled, round 7, 1931 *[August 31]*

1. d4 d5 2. c4 e6 3. Nf3 Nf6 4. Bg5 Nbd7 5. e3 Be7 6. Nc3 0–0 7. Rc1 c6 8. a3 a6 9. cxd5 cxd5 10. Bd3 b5 11. 0–0 Bb7 12. Qb3 Ne4 13. Bf4 g5 14. Bg3 Nxg3 15. hxg3 f5 16. Ne2 Bd6 17. Qc2 Qf6 18. Nh2 h5 19. f4 g4 20. a4 b4 21. a5 Rfc8 22. Qa4 Qd8 23. Kf2 Rxc1

24. Nxc1 Qc7 25. Nb3 Bc6 26. Qa1 Qb7 27. Rc1 Bb5 28. Bxb5 Qxb5 29. Nf1 Kf7 30. Nfd2 Ra7 31. Rc8 Rc7 32. Rxc7 Bxc7 33. Qh1 Nf6 34. Qa1 Nd7 35. Qh1 Bxa5 36. Qxh5+ Ke7 37. Qg5+ Ke8 38. Qg6+ Ke7 39. Qg5+ Ke8 40. e4 dxe4 41. Nxe4 Qd5 42. Qg8+ Ke7 43. Qg7+ Kd8 44. Nec5 Nxc5 45. Qf8+ Kd7 46. Nxc5+ Kc7 47. Qe7+ Kc8 48. Ke3 Qxg2 49. Qxe6+ Kb8 50. Qd6+ Bc7 51. Nxa6+ Ka7 52. Nxc7 Qxg3+ 53. Kd2 Qf2+ 54. Kd3 Qf1+ 55. Kc2 Qc4+ 56. Kd2 g3 57. Qd7 g2 58. Ne6+ Kb8 59. Nc5 Qxc5 60. dxc5 g1Q 61. Qb5+ Kc8 62. Qxb4 Qf2+ 63. Kc3 Qe1+ 64. Kb3 Qd1+ 65. Ka2 Qd5+ 66. Ka3 Qd3+ 67. b3 Qf1 68. Qc4 Qa1+ 69. Kb4 Qe1+ 70. Ka4 Qe8+ 71. Ka3 Kc7 72. Qa6 Qb8 73. Qd6+ Kc8 74. Qe6+ 1–0 (*Bled* 1931)

198 Spielmann–Kashdan [D31]
Bled, round 8, 1931 *[September 2]*

1. d4 d5 2. c4 e6 3. Nc3 c6 4. e4 dxe4 5. Nxe4 Nd7 6. Nf3 Ngf6 7. Bd3 c5 8. dxc5 Nxc5 9. Nxc5 Bxc5 10. 0–0 0–0 11. Qe2 b6 12. Bd2 Qe7 13. Bc3 Bb7 14. a3 Rfd8 15. Rad1 Nd7? 16. b4 Bd6 17. Bxh7+ Kxh7 18. Qd3+ Kg8 19. Qxd6 Qxd6 20. Rxd6 Nf8 21. Rfd1 Rxd6 22. Rxd6 Rc8 23. Rd4 f6 24. Nd2 e5 25. Rd3 Ne6 26. g3 Rd8 27. Rxd8+ Nxd8 28. f3 Ne6 29. Kf2 Kf7 30. Ke3 Nf8 31. Ne4 Ke6 32. h4 Nd7 33. g4 a6 34. a4 Ba8 35. Ng3 a5 36. bxa5 bxa5 37. Bxa5 Bc6 38. Nf5 g6 39. Ng3 Bxa4 40. h5 gxh5 41. gxh5 Bb3 42. h6 Kf7 ½–½ (*Bled* 1931)

199 Kashdan–Maróczy [C01]
Bled, round 9, 1931 *[September 3]*

1. d4 d5 2. c4 e5 3. e3 exd4 4. exd4 Nf6 5. Nc3 c6 6. Nf3 Be7 7. Bd3 0–0 8. 0–0 dxc4 9. Bxc4 Nbd7 10. Re1 Nb6 11. Bb3 Nbd5 12. Bd2 Be6 13. Rc1 Re8 14. Na4 Nd7 15. h3 Rc8 16. Bc2 g6 17. a3 b5 18. Nc3 Nxc3 19. Bxc3 Nb6 20. Bb3 Nd5 21. Ne5 a6 22. Qf3 Bg5 23. Rc2

Kg7 24. Nxc6! Rxc6 25. Bxd5 Bxd5 26. Rxe8 Qxe8 27. Qxd5 Bf6 28. Qf3 Rc4 29. Qd3 Qc8 30. d5 Bxc3 31. Rxc3 Rxc3 32. bxc3 Qc4 33. Qxc4 bxc4 34. f4 1–0 (*Bled* 1931)

200 Alekhine–Kashdan [D52]
Bled, round 10, 1931 *[September 5]*

1. d4 Nf6 2. c4 c6 3. Nf3 d5 4. Nc3 e6 5. Bg5 Nbd7 6. e3 Qa5 7. Nd2 dxc4 From the theoretical standpoint this should be the best move. It forces the exchange of bishop for knight, leaving Black with the advantage in that respect. However, it involves a loss of time, and the development of the bishop at c8 is a source of difficulty. Whether White can make any capital of his early initiative is a question which has not been fully solved. 8. Bxf6 Nxf6 9. Nxc4 Qc7 10. Bd3 10. g3 has been played here, to fianchetto the bishop, and by pressure along the diagonal to restrain Black's c5. However the text looks more natural. 10. ... Be7 11. 0–0 0–0 12. Rc1 Rd8 To allow ...Bd7-e8 without interfering with this rook. The e1 square is the best for the bishop, where it can remain until a suitable line has been opened. Black's plan is to play c5 as soon as feasible, and White will use his command of the c file to keep the pawn back. 13. Qe2 Bd7 14. Ne5 Be8 15. f4 A doubtful move, as after the break in the center the pawn will be weakened. With White's next few moves he attempts to build up a kingside attack, but this should not be serious, as there is adequate defense for every point. 15. ... c5! This looks risky, but is quite playable, and from here on Black begins to get control of the game. 16. dxc5 If 16. Nb5 Qb6 or 16. Ne4 Nxe4 17. Bxe4 Qb6 18. Nc4 Qa6 and every thing is secure. Fortunately 16. Na4 will not do, as the bishop at e8 is already taking part in the fray. 16. ... Qxc5 Better than taking with the bishop, as the latter is needed for defense, whereas the queen easily avoids any attack. 17. Ne4 Qa5 18. Ng5 Rac8 Paying no attention to the kingside as there is no threat. Not 18. ... Qxa2; because of 19. Rc7. 19. a3 b5 A useful move which prevents Nc4 and secures a good square for the queen at b6. Black now commands most of the ground in the center

and on the queenside. **20. h3** This is hardly necessary, and leaves a bad weakness at his g3, which proves helpful to Black. White seems to have no definite plan at this point. **20. ... Qb6 21. Kh1** After his last move, Kh2 would have been a better choice for the king. **21. ... h6 22. Rxc8 Rxc8**

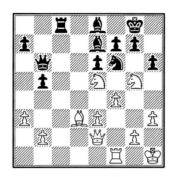

After
22. ... Rxc8

23. Ngf3 Better was 23. Ne4 Nd5 24. Re1. But White's pieces are all restricted, and Black might continue with 24. ... a5 followed by a4 or b4, to open new lines to attack. **23. ... Bc5 24. Nd4** Giving up the pawn at once, but it can hardly be held. If 24. e4 Nh5! wins at least a pawn. Or 24. Re1 Nd5!, etc. **24. ... Bxd4 25. exd4 Qxd4 26. f5** 26. Bxb5 would lose after ...Ne4! 27. Kh2 Bxb5 28. Qxb5 Nd2 followed by Qxf4+. The text is an attempt at counterplay which should prove fruitless. **26. ... Nh5** Forcing an exchange of pieces and simplify the game. **27. Qxh5 Qxe5 28. Qg4 exf5 29. Bxf5 Rc4 30. Qd1 Rf4** But this is carrying a good thing too far. The further exchanges bring on a queen ending, which is very difficult to win. Black actually has the better position, besides the pawn ahead and should continue to attack by 30. ... g6, followed by Rd4, or Bc6, etc. White's best chance lies in the removal of the lighter pieces. **31. Rxf4 Qxf4 32. Bd7 Bxd7 33. Qxd7 Qb8** Defending everything, but that is not enough. The main difficulty in the task is that there is no passed pawn, and to create one Black must expose his king, with all the danger of perpetual check. **34. Qd4 g6 35. a4 bxa4 36. Qxa4 Qb6** Exchanging the last pawn on the queenside would lead to a sure draw as there would be insufficient force to accomplish anything. Black's plan of campaign is to bring his king to the

queenside, and attempt to win the b pawn. Should White move his own king to the defense, then the pawn on the other wing can advance. The tactical difficulties of the plan are considerable, in avoiding the constant threat of perpetual check. **37. Qe8+ Kg7 38. Qe5+ Qf6 39. Qc5 a6** The best square for the pawn, where it can most easily be defended. **40. b4 Qf1+ 41. Kh2 h5 42. Qd4+ Kh7** The king cannot yet emerge, for if ...Kf8 43. Qh8+ Ke7 44. Qe5+, etc. would allow no escape. **43. Qe5 Qb5 44. Qf6 Kg8 45. Qd6 Qc4 46. Kg1 Kg7 47. Kf2 Qe6 48. Qb8 Kf6 49. Qb7** Checks at this stage would only aid Black in marching to the queenside. **49. ... Qc4 50. Ke3 Ke6 51. Qb6+ Kd7 52. Qb7+ Kd6 53. g3** White should have avoided this advance, which weakens the pawns, and gives Black a speedy opportunity to establish a passed pawn. However, the same result could have been achieved in any case by proper play. **53. ... g5 54. Qb8+ Ke7 55. Qh8 Qc1+ 56. Ke2 Qc4+ 57. Kf2 g4!** Giving up the a pawn but obtaining more than the equivalent in return. **58. Qxh5 Qd4+ 59. Ke2** He must leave the kingside. If 59. Kg2 Qe4+ 60. Kg1 Qe3+ 61. Kg2 Qf3+ 62. Kh2 Qf2+ 63. Kh1 Qf1+ 64. Kh2 Qxh3+! 65. Qxh3 gxh3 66. Kxh3 and counting will show that Black wins. **59. ... Qe4+ 60. Kd1 Qd3+ 61. Kc1 Qf1+!** This is the goal for which Black has struggled for so long, and the rest should have been easy. The checks are soon stopped, and the passed pawn ought to advance rapidly. BUT—**62. Kd2 Qg2+ 63. Kd1 Qf1+ 64. Kd2 gxh3 65. Qc5+** On continued checks the king would gain safety via f6 and g7, which the text prevents. **65. ... Ke6 66. Qc7 Kf6 67. Ke3 Qe1+ 68. Kf3**

After
24. Rd5

In order to approach the pawn with the king, and also to prevent the immediate exchange of queens. BUT—**68. ... Qe6??** A complete miscalculation, which at once throws away the fruits of very considerable labor. After three sessions, something over 12 hours all told, I had for the first time in my career obtained a clearly winning position against the World's Champion. And then to err on a simple matter of counting which every beginner is taught! White's 68th move b4 gained just enough time to draw in the resulting ending. The correct procedure was 68. ... Qd5+ 69. Kg3 Qg2+ 70. Kh4 h2 71. Qd3+ Kg7 72. Qd4+ f6! and now if 73. Qd7+ Kh6! or 73. Qa2+ Kg3!. After 68. ... Qd4+, if 69. Kf4 h2! 70. Qc2+ Kg7 and the pawn cannot be taken. Or 69. Ke3 f6 (threatening ...Qe5+); followed by Kg5 and the game should win easily enough. **69. Qc3+ Kg6 70. g4 Qf6+ 71. Qxf6+ Kxf6 72. Kg3 Ke5 73. Kxh3 Kd4 74. Kh4** Each side will succeed in queening. ½–½ Analysis by Kashdan in *Chess Review*, November 1936. (*Bled* 1931)

201 Kashdan–Kostić [A10]

Bled, round 11, 1931 *[September 6]*

1. Nf3 f5 2. c4 Nf6 3. Nc3 e6 4. g3 Bb4 5. Qc2 0–0 6. Bg2 Nc6 7. a3 Bxc3 8. Qxc3 d6 9. d4 Ne4 10. Qc2 Qf6 11. e3 a5 12. b3 e5 13. Bb2 Qe7 14. 0–0 Bd7 15. Rad1 exd4 16. exd4 Rae8 17. Rfe1 Qf7 18. d5 Nd8 19. b4 b6 20. Nd4 axb4 21. axb4 c5 22. dxc6 Nxc6 23. f3 Nf6 24. Rxe8 Qxe8 25. Nxc6 Bxc6 26. b5 Bb7 27. Rxd6 Qe1+ 28. Bf1 Bxf3 29. Bxf6 gxf6 30. Qf2 Qe5 31. Qxb6 Ba8 32. Qd4 Qe7 33. c5 f4 34. Qxf4 1–0 (*Bled* 1931)

202 Stoltz–Kashdan [D87]

Bled, round 12, 1931 *[September 7]*

1. d4 Nf6 2. c4 g6 3. Nc3 d5 This and the previous move constitute the Grünfeld Defense. It gives White the center, with the plan for Black of getting a later attack against the White pawns. **4. cxd5** 4. Qb3 was the move adopted in several games of the Alekhine–Euwe match. Other plausible continuations are 4. Nf3,

4. Bf3, or 4. Bg5. White generally gets the upper hand, as his pawn center is quite strong, and Black has difficulties in developing his queenside. **4. ... Nxd5 5. e4** This leaves a slight weakness at c3, but White has ample compensation in his freer game and easier development. **5. ... Nxc3 6. bxc3 Bg7 7. Bc4 c5 8. Ne2 0–0 9. Be3 Qc7 10. Rc1!** Black dare not exchange pawns, which would leave the White rook in full control of the file. **10. ... Nd7 11. 0–0 Rb8** To create a diversion on the queenside, and attempt to get some play ...e5 will not do because of 12. f4! No matter how Black exchanges he will lose time and weaken his position. **12. Bf4** This seemingly forceful move actually gives Black the one tempo he needs to work out his defense. Better was 12. f4 to be followed by f5 or e5 according to developments. **12. ... e5 13. Bg3** Threatening f4 to force open the long diagonal, with a winning position. But Black, by the attack on the other bishop, gains just enough time for his purpose. **13. ... b5 14. Bd5 Bb7!** The bishop must be exchanged. **15. f4 Bxd5 16. exd5 f6!**

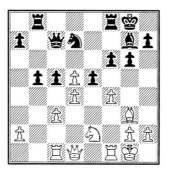

After
16. ... f6

The difference now is that the e pawn is securely protected. Black has thus safely challenged the center, and it is the White d pawn which will soon prove weak. **17. fxe5 fxe5 18. Rxf8+ Rxf8 19. Qb3** Threatening the b pawn as well as discovered check, but this is easily defended. Preferable was 19. dxe5 Bxe5 20. c4 with about an even game. **19. ... Qb6!** Now White is in difficulties. If 20. dxe5, of course ...c4+, a fitting reverse to White's threat on the last move. Or 20. dxc5 Nxc5, followed by ...Nd3+ wins. **20. Bf2 exd4 21. cxd4 c4** Now the game is definitely in Black's favor. The powerful queenside majority, coupled with the weakness of

White's pawns, must prove decisive. **22. Qh3 Rf5 23. Re1 b4** Better than ...Rxd5; whereupon 24. Nf4, with good attacking chances. **24. Ng3 Bxd4!** Forcing an exchange of pieces, which ends any White prospects of counterattack. **25. Nxf5** If 25. Bxd4 Qxd4+ 26. Kh1 Rf2, and White has no effective continuation. **25. ... Bxf2+ 26. Kh1** If 26. Kf1 Bxe1 threatening mate; 27. Nh6+ Kg7 28. Qxd7 Kxh6 29. Qh3+ Kg5! 30. Kxf2 Qd4 and will soon win without much trouble. **26. ... Bxe1 27. Ne7+ Kf8 28. Qxh7** The best chance. If 28. Qxd7 Qf6 29. Qd8+ Kf7 and the knight is lost because of the mate threat. **28. ... Qf6 29. Nxg6+ Ke8 30. h4** Only a momentary defense. To avoid mate White must exchange his remaining pieces, which of course is no salvation. **30. ... Bg3 31. Qg8+ Nf8 0–1** Annotated by Kashdan in *Chess Review*, February 1936. (*Bled* 1931)

203 Kashdan–Tartakower [D32]
Bled, round 13, 1931 *[September 9]*

1. d4 d5 2. c4 e6 3. Nc3 c5 4. cxd5 cxd4 5. Qxd4 Nc6 6. Qd1 exd5 7. Qxd5 Be6 8. Qxd8+ Rxd8 9. f3 Nb4 10. Kf2 Nc2 11. Rb1 Bc5+ 12. e3 Nh6 13. Bb5+ Ke7 14. g4 f5 15. g5 f4 16. gxh6 fxe3+ 17. Kf1 gxh6 18. b3 Rhg8 19. Rb2 Na3 20. Bc4 Nxc4 21. bxc4 Bxc4+ 22. Nge2 b5 23. Ke1 Bb6 24. Rg1 Rxg1+ 25. Nxg1 Ba5 26. Nge2 Rd3 27. Rc2 b4 28. Bb2 bxc3 29. Bxc3 Bxc3+ 30. Rxc3 Rxc3 31. Nxc3 Ke6 32. Nd1 Bxa2 33. Nxe3 Ke5 34. Ke2 h5 35. h4 Kf4 36. Kf2 Ke5 37. Nc2 Kf4 38. Ne1 a5 39. Nd3+ Kf5 40. Nc5 Ke5 41. Ke3 Kd5 42. Ne4 Kc4 43. f4 a4 44. f5 a3 45. Kd2 Kb4 46. f6 Bf7 47. Kc1 Bg6 48. Nd2 Kc3 49. Nb1+ Kb3 50. Nd2+ Kb4 51. Ne4 Kc4 52. Nd2+ Kd3 53. Nb3 The game could continue 53. ... Kc3 54. Na1 a2 55. f7 Bxf7 56. Nc2 Bg6 57. Na1+ Ka3 58. Nc2 Kb3 59. Na1+ Ka3 60. Kd2 Kb2 and Black wins. **0–1** (*Bled* 1931)

204 Kashdan–Asztalos [D60]
Bled, round 14, 1931 *[September 10]*

1. d4 d5 2. Nf3 Nf6 3. c4 e6 4. Nc3

Nbd7 5. Bg5 Be7 6. e3 0–0 7. a3 Re8 8. Rc1 c6 9. Bd3 dxc4 10. Bxc4 Nd5 11. Ne4 h6 12. Bxe7 Qxe7 13. 0–0 b6 14. Qe2 a6 15. Ne5 Bb7 16. Bd3 Rec8 17. Rc2 N5f6 18. Nxf6+ Nxf6 19. Rfc1 c5! 20. dxc5 Rxc5 21. Rxc5 bxc5 22. Qc2 Rc8 23. h3 Qc7 24. Nc4 Nd5 25. Qd2 Bc6 26. Na5 Bb5! 27. b4 Qb6 28. e4 Nf6 29. Qe3 Nd7 30. Bxb5 Qxb5! 31. Nb3 c4 32. Qc3 Nb6 33. Nc5 a5 34. f4 axb4 35. axb4 Rd8 36. Ra1 Ra8 37. Rxa8+ Nxa8 38. Kf2 Nb6 39. Ke3 Kh7 40. Qa3 Kg8 41. Kd2 Qc6 42. Qa7 Qd6+ 43. Kc2 f6 44. Qb7 e5 45. f5 Kh7 46. Qf7 Qd4 47. Qg6+ Kg8 48. Qe8+ Kh7 49. Qg6+ Kg8 50. Qg3 Qa1 51. Qc3 Qf1 ½–½ (*Bled* 1931)

205 Vidmar–Kashdan [D63]
Bled, round 15, 1931 *[September 12]*

1. d4 d5 2. c4 e6 3. Nf3 Nf6 4. Bg5 Nbd7 5. e3 Be7 6. Nc3 a6 7. Rc1 0–0 8. Qc2 dxc4 9. Bxc4 b5 10. Bd3 c5 11. Ne5! cxd4! 12. Nc6 Qe8 13. Nxe7+ Qxe7 14. Bxh7+ Kh8 15. Be4 Rb8 16. exd4 b4 17. Ne2 b3 18. axb3 Qb4+ 19. Bd2 Qxb3 20. Bc3 Nxe4 21. Qxe4 Bb7 22. Qh4+ Kg8 23. 0–0 Qd5 24. f3 a5 25. Qg3 Rfc8 26. Ra1 Ra8 27. Rfe1 a4 28. h4 Rc4 29. Qh3 Nf6 30. Qg3 Qf5 31. Nf4 Nd5 32. Nxd5 Bxd5 33. Ra3 Rac8 34. Re5 Qb1+ 35. Kh2 f6 36. Re1 Qc2 37. Kg1 Kf7 38. Rea1 Rh8 39. Qf2 Qxf2+ 40. Kxf2 Bc6 41. g3 Rh5 42. Ke3 Rf5 43. Rf1 Bb5 44. g4 Rd5 45. Rf2 Rc8 46. Ra1 g6 47. Kf4 g5+ 48. hxg5 Rxg5 49. Rh2 Rc4 50. Kg3 Rc8 51. Rh7+ Rg7 52. Rxg7+ Kxg7 53. d5 e5 54. g5 Rd8 55. Rd1 fxg5 56. Bxe5+ Kg6 57. Bc3 Rf8 58. Rd2 Rf5 59. d6 Bd7 60. Rd3 Kf7 61. Re3 Kg6 62. Be5 Rf8 63. Rd3 Rf5 64. Bc3 Kf7 65. Bd2 Ke6 66. Bb4 Kf7 67. Rc3 Kg6 68. Rc7 Rf7 69. Ba5 Kf5 70. Rc2 Ke6 71. Bc7 Rf5 72. Rh2 Kd5 73. Rh8 Kc6 74. Ra8 Kd5 75. Rb8 Ke6 76. Ra8 Kd5 77. Ra6 Ke6 78. Bd8 Bb5 79. Rb6 Kd7 80. Kg4 Rf4+ 81. Kxg5 Rxf3 82. Bf6 Bc6 83. Be5 Re3 84. Kf4 Rf3+ 85. Kg4 Re3 ½–½ (*Bled* 1931)

206 Kashdan–Colle [D02]
Bled, round 16, 1931 *[September 13]*

1. d4 d5 2. Nf3 Nc6 3. Bf4 Bg4 4. e3
e6 5. h3 Bxf3 6. Qxf3 Bd6 7. c3 Qf6
8. Nd2 Nge7 9. Bb5 0-0-0 10. Bxd6
Qxf3 11. Nxf3 cxd6 12. 0-0-0 a6
13. Bd3 h6 14. e4 Kd7 15. Rhe1 Rc8
16. Kb1 b5 17. e5 Na5? 18. exd6 Kxd6
19. Ne5 Rhf8 20. f4 Rc7 21. Re2 Nc8
22. Rde1 Nb6 23. g4 Na4 24. g5 Nc4
25. g6! Nxe5 26. Rxe5 fxg6 27. Rxe6+
Kd7 28. Rxa6 Rb7 29. Rxg6 Kc8 30. f5
b4? 31. Ba6 1-0 (*Bled* 1931)

207 Nimzovitch–Kashdan [C47]
Bled, round 17, 1931 *[September 14]*

1. e4 e5 2. Nf3 Nf6 3. Nc3 Nc6 4. a3
An odd move, but typical of Nimzovitch. He
liked to play a backward game, and would often
set up defensive formations with White. He
would open at times with 1. e3 or 1. b3, with
that idea. 4. ... d6 The normal move in the
Four Knights Game ...Bb4 has been prevented.
Black can turn it into a Scotch, with colors re-
versed, by ...d5. The text is slower, but quite
good. 5. Bc4 Inferior as Black can gain control
of the center by the following exchange. 5. d4
was in order, and would have retained a slight
initiative for White. 5. ... Nxe4! 6. Nxe4
6. Bxf7+ Kxf7 7. Nxe4 d5 would be better for
Black, who has the two bishops and real attacking chances, while his king is quite secure. 6. ...
d5 7. Bd3 dxe4 8. Bxe4 Bd6 9. d4 exd4
...Nxd4 would have prevented the doubling of
the pawns, but I did not consider the weakness
to be serious, and it is compensated by the active two bishops. 9. ... Nxd4 10. Nxd4 exd4
11. Qxd4 0-0 12. Be3 (but not 12. 0-0?? Bxh2+
wins), would have lead to perfect equality.
10. Bxc6+ bxc6 11. Qxd4 0-0 12. 0-0 c5
13. Qc3 Qd7 The queen obstructs the bishop,
but as the latter belongs at b7, that is no objec-
tion. Black wishes to be in a position for Qc6 or
Qf5 should the weak pawn be attacked. 14. Ne5
followed by Nc4 would have offered more prospects of equalizing. 14. b3 Bb7 15. Bb2 f6
16. Qd3 Rfe8 As the rook can be opened on
the open file, this only leads to a general ex-

change. Stronger was ...a5, when the threat of
...Ba6 and a4 would weaken White's pawns and
create targets for the bishops and rooks. 17. Rfe1
Rxe1+ 18. Rxe1 Re8 19. Kf1 Rxe1+
20. Nxe1 Qe6 Now Black threatens ...Bxh2
for if 22. g3 h5 and the bishop cannot be
trapped ...c4 followed by Ba6 is also a strong
possibility. 21. Qb5 Be4 22. h3 22. Qb8+
Kf2 23. Bxa7 Bxc2! 24. Nxc2 Qxb3, which
combination actually occurs on the next move.
Nimzovitch apparently did not realize the danger, but refrained from taking the a pawn because of Qd5. This would also be annoying, as
it threatens ...Bxh2 or Bxc2 or Qd1. 22. ...
Kf7 23. Qa6?

After
23. Qa6

This loses a pawn, and it is a curious oversight
for the man who was known as a keen tactician.
A defensive move such as 23. Qe2 was in order,
though Black always has the better winning
chances. 23. ... Bxc2! 24. Nxc2 Qxb3
25. Ne3 Qxb2 26. Qxa7 The game is still
far from easy. The extra pawn is doubled, and
White has an outside passed pawn, which may
become most dangerous. 26. ... Qb5+ The
plan is to combine the advance of the pawn
with direct threats against the king in order to
gain time. If 5. ... c4 27. a4 (but not 27. Nxc4
Qc1+) c3 28. Qd4 Qa2 29. Ke1 (better than
29. Qxc3 Qxa4 etc.) and it is difficult for Black
to make any headway. 27. Ke1 If 27. Kg1 Qb1+
28. Nf1 c4 29. Qd4 Qa1; and now White is tied
up, and can offer little resistance to the advance
of the c pawn. If then 30. Qd5+ Ke7 31. Qe4+
Kd8 32. Qa8+ Kd7 33. Qa4+ Ke7 etc. 27. ...
Be5 28. Kd2 The threat was 28. Bc3+ 29. Kd1
Qd3+ and mate in 2. 28. ... c4 29. Qa8 c3+
30. Ke1 Forced, for if 30. Kd1 Qd3+ 31. Ke1
Qd2+ 32. Kf1 c2 wins the knight. 30. ... Bf4

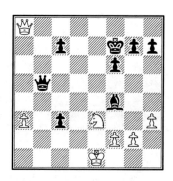

After
30. ... Bf4

30. c2 is very enticing, and if 31. Nxc2 Bc3+ forces mate, but, unfortunately, 31. Kd2 is a complete defense, after which the pawn cannot be saved. Another false try is 30. ... Qb1+ 31. Ke2 Qb2 32. Kf3 c2 33. Qd4+, and now wherever the king goes either Qe4+, Qc5+, or Qc6+ will win the advanced pawn. The idea of the text is to exchange the knight, which is well placed for defense. The resulting queen endgame requires exact play, but Black's advantage must prove sufficient to win. **31. Qe4** But not 31. Qd5+ Qxd5 32. Nxd5 c2! and the pawn queens. **31. ... Bxe3 32. fxe3** If 32. Qxf3 Qb1+ 33. Ke2 c2 wins, as White has no checks. **32. ... f5 33. Qc2 Qc5 34. Ke2 Ke7** Now threatening ...Qxa3, which at this point would have been answered by Qxf5+! Black's plan is to bring his king to the queenside, either winning the a pawn, or by protecting the c pawn, freeing the queen for action. **35. a4 Qc4+ 36. Ke1** If 36. Qd3 Qc6! 37. Kd1 (...c2 is threatened) Qxa4+; which would win with little further trouble. **36. ... Kd6 37. g4** In order to obtain a second passed pawn, but it gives Black an extra pawn on the h file, so hardly improves matters. There is little for White to do as his queen evidently must remain fixed. **37. ... fxg4 38. hxg4 Kc5 39. e4 Qd4** Stopping the pawn and threatening, curiously enough, to win the queen by 40. ... Qg1+ 41. Ke2 Qg2+; as either 42. Kd1 or 42. Kd3 would allow mate. **40. Ke2 Kb4** 40. ... Qd2+? would be a blunder because of 41. Qxd2+ cxd2 42. e5 Kd5 43. a5 and White wins. But the text puts White in "zugzwang," and he must lose one of his pawns. **41. g5 h5 42. gxh6 gxh6 43. Qb1+** There is nothing better, but now Black can easily avoid the checks, and the sequel requires little explanation. **43. ...**

Kxa4 **44. Qa2+ Kb4 45. Qb1+ Kc5 46. Qb7 Qd6 47. Qb3 Qd2+ 48. Kf3 c2 49. Qa3+ Qb4 50. Qa7+ Kb5 51. Qe3 Qb2 52. Qd3+ Kb6 53. Qd4+ Qxd4 0–1** Annotated by Kashdan in *Chess Review*, December 1936. (*Bled* 1931)

208 Kashdan–Pirc [D17]
Bled, round 18, 1931 *[September 16]*

1. d4 d5 2. c4 c6 3. Nc3 Nf6 4. Nf3 dxc4 5. a4 Bf5 6. Nh4 Bg6 To hold on to the c4 pawn, 6. ... Bd7 has been suggested. Also interesting is 6. ... g6 7. Nxf5 gxf5 8. e3 e6 9. Bxc4 Qc7 10. a5 Bg7 11. f3 Nbd7 12. e4 0–0 13. 0–0 Rfd8 14. Qe2 b5 etc. as in the postal game Ruester–Eliskases 1932. **7. Nxg6 hxg6 8. e3 e6 9. Bxc4 Nbd7 10. 0–0 Qc7 11. f4 Rd8 12. Qe2 Nb6 13. Bd3 g5! 14. g3 gxf4 15. gxf4 a5 16. Bd2 Bb4 17. Kh1 g6 18. Rac1 c5 19. e4 Qd7 20. d5 exd5 21. exd5+ Kf8 22. f5 Re8 23. Qf3 gxf5 24. Qxf5 Ng4 25. Bf4 c4 26. Qxd7 Nxd7 27. Bxc4 Ne3 28. Bb5 Nxf1 29. Bxd7 Re7 30. Bb5 Nxh2 31. Kg2 Ng4 32. d6 Re6 33. d7 Be7 34. Nd5 Bd8 35. Rc8 Kg7 36. Rxd8 Rxd8 37. Bc7 Rg8 38. Nf4 Re4 39. Kg3 Ne5 40. d8Q Rxd8 41. Bxd8 Nc4 42. Bxc4 Rxc4 43. Bxa5 Rxa4 44. Bc3+ Kf8 45. Kg4 Ke7 46. Kf5 Kd6 47. Be5+ Kc5 48. Nd3+ Kc4 49. Ke4 Ra6 50. Bc3 Rh6 51. Ne5+ Kb3 52. Nf3** If 52. Nxf7 then Rh2 followed by Rxb2. **52. ... Rh3 53. Bf6 Rg3 54. Nd4+ Kc4 55. Nf5 Rg6 56. Ne3+ Kb3 57. Bd4 Rd6 58. Bc3 Rc6 59. Kd3 Rd6+ 60. Ke2 Rh6 ½–½** (*Bled* 1931)

209 Flohr–Kashdan [D36]
Bled, round 19, 1931 *[September 17]*

1. d4 d5 2. c4 e6 3. Nc3 Nf6 4. Bg5 Nbd7 5. cxd5 exd5 6. e3 c6 7. Bd3 Be7 8. Qc2 0–0 9. Nf3 Re8 10. 0–0 Nf8 11. a3 Ne4 12. Bxe7 Qxe7 13. Bxe4 dxe4 14. Nd2 f5 15. b4 Be6 16. Ne2 Nd7 17. Rfe1 Rad8 18. Rab1 Nb6 19. Qc5 Qf7 20. Nf4 Ba2 21. Ra1 g5 22. Nh3 h6 23. f4 exf3 24. gxf3 Be6 25. Nf2 f4! 26. exf4 Qxf4 27. Nfe4 Rd5 28. Qc3 Bf7

29. Rad1 Red8 30. Nf1 R5d7 31. d5!
N×d5 32. R×d5 R×d5 33. Nf6+ Kf8
34. Nh7+ Kg8 35. Nf6+ Kf8 36. N×d5
R×d5 37. Qh8+ Bg8 38. Q×h6+ Kf7
39. Ng3 Qf6 40. Qh3 Kg6 41. Ne4 Qf4
42. Qc8 Qf7 43. Nc5 Rd2! 44. h4 Rd5
45. h5+ Kh6 If 45. ... K×h5? 46. h3+ Kg6
47. Re6+ Kg7 48. Qh6 mate! 46. Qe8 Rd1
47. Kf2 R×e1 48. Q×e1 K×h5 49. Qe5
Kg6 50. Kg3 b6 51. Ne4 Qf5 ½–½ (*Bled*
1931)

210 Kashdan–Bogoljubow [D75]
Bled, round 20, 1931 *[September 19]*

1. d4 Nf6 2. c4 g6 3. Nc3 Bg7 4. Nf3
0–0 5. g3 d5! 6. c×d5 N×d5 7. Bg2
N×c3 8. b×c3 c5 9. 0–0 Nc6 10. e3 Qa5
11. Qb3 Rb8 12. Nd2 Qc7! 13. Ba3 b6
14. d×c5? A mistaken combination. Instead
14. Qb5 has been recommended. 14. ... Ba6
15. Rfd1 b×c5 16. Qd5? Nb4 17. Qb3 Nd3
18. Qc2 Qa5 19. Nb1 c4 20. Bc1 Rb6
21. Na3 B×c3 22. Rb1 R×b1 23. N×b1 Be1
24. f4 Bf2+ 25. Kh1 Qh5 26. Nd2 B×g3
27. Nf3 B×h2 28. N×h2 Q×d1+ 29. Q×d1
Nf2+ 30. Kg1 N×d1 0–1 (*Bled* 1931)

211 Kashdan–Spielmann [D52]
Bled, round 21, 1931 *[September 20]*

1. d4 e6 2. c4 Nf6 3. Nf3 d5 4. Nc3
Nbd7 5. Bg5 c6 6. e3 Qa5 7. Qb3 Ne4
8. c×d5 N×g5 9. N×g5 e×d5 10. Bd3 Be7
11. Nf3 0–0 12. 0–0 Re8 13. Rfe1 Nf8
14. a3 Rb8 15. Qc2 Bg4 16. Ne5 Bh5
17. b4 Qd8 18. Be2 B×e2 19. N×e2 Bd6
20. Nf3 a6 21. Ng3 g6 22. e4 B×g3
23. h×g3 d×e4 24. R×e4 Qd5 25. Rae1
R×e4 26. R×e4 Ne6 27. g4 Rd8 28. Qd3
½–½ (*Bled* 1931)

212 Maróczy–Kashdan [B18]
Bled, round 22, 1931 *[September 21]*

1. e4 c6 2. d4 d5 3. Nc3 d×e4 4. N×e4
Bf5 5. Ng3 Bg6 6. Nf3 Nd7 7. Bd3 Ngf6
8. 0–0 e6 9. Qe2 Qc7 10. c4 B×d3
11. Q×d3 Bd6 12. Bd2 0–0 13. Bc3 Rad8
14. Qc2 b5 15. c5 Bf4? 16. a4! Rb8
17. a×b5 R×b5 18. Ra6 Ra8 19. Rfa1 Nb8

20. R6a4 Nd5 21. Ne2 Bh6 22. Ne5 g6
23. Nc4 Bf8 24. Bd2 Nd7 25. f4! f6?
Correct is Be7. 26. Qe4 c5 27. f×e5 f×e5
28. Nc3 N×c3 29. B×c3 Rbb8 30. Ra6
Rc8 31. Nb6 N×b6 32. c×b6 Qb7
33. R×a7 R×a7 34. b×a7 Ra8 35. Q×e5
R×a7 36. R×a7 Q×a7 37. Qe6+ Qf7
38. Q×c6 Qb3 39. h3 Kf7 40. d5 Be7
41. Qe6+ Kf8 42. Bg7+ K×g7 43. Q×e7+
Kh6 44. Qh4+ Kg7 45. Qd4+ Kf7 46. d6
Qc2 47. d7 Qc1+ 48. Kf2 Qc2+ 49. Kf3
Qc6+ 50. Kg3 Qc7+ 51. Qf4+ 1–0 (*Bled*
1931)

213 Kashdan–Alekhine [C48]
Bled, round 23, 1931 *[September 23]*

1. e4 e5 2. Nf3 Nc6 3. Nc3 Nf6 4. Bb5
Nd4 5. N×d4 e×d4 6. e5 d×c3 7. e×f6
Q×f6 8. d×c3 Bc5 9. Qe2+ Qe6 10. Bc4
Q×e2+ 11. K×e2 d6 12. Be3 B×e3
13. K×e3 Be6 14. B×e6 f×e6 15. f4 Rf8
16. Rhf1 Kd7 17. Rf3 Rae8 18. Raf1 Rf5
19. g4 Ra5 20. a3 Ra4 21. Rh3 h6 22. g5
h×g5 23. f×g5 Rg4 24. Rh5 e5 25. Rf7+
Re7 26. R×e7+ K×e7 27. h4 d5 28. Rh8
c5 29. Ra8 R×h4 30. R×a7 Rh3+ 31. Ke2
e4 32. R×b7+ Ke6 33. a4 d4 34. c×d4
c×d4 35. Rb5 Rh2+ 36. Kd1 Rh1+
37. Ke2 Rh2+ 38. Kd1 e3 39. a5 Rd2+
40. Kc1 d3 41. c×d3 R×d3 42. Rb8 Kd7
43. Rh8 Rd5 44. b4 Rd4 45. a6 e2
46. Rh1 R×b4 47. Re1 Ra4 48. R×e2
R×a6 49. Re5 ½–½ (*Bled* 1931)

214 Kostić–Kashdan [C43]
Bled, round 24, 1931 *[September 24]*

1. e4 e5 2. Nf3 Nf6 3. d4 e×d4 4. e5
Ne4 5. Q×d4 d5 6. e×d6 N×d6 7. Bg5
Nc6 8. Qe3+ Be7 9. B×e7 Q×e7
10. Q×e7+ N×e7 11. Nc3 Bg4 12. Be2
0–0–0 13. 0–0–0 Rhe8 14. Nd4 Bd7
15. Rhe1 c6 16. Nb3 Kc7 17. Nc5 Bc8
18. Bd3 Ng6 19. N3e4 N×e4 20. R×e4
b6 21. R×e8 R×e8 22. B×g6 h×g6
23. Nd3 Rh8 24. h3 Rh4 25. Re1 Be6
26. b3 Kd6 27. Kd2 c5 28. c4 a6 29. a4
b5 30. a×b5 a×b5 31. c×b5 B×b3 32. Kc3
Bd5 33. f3 Ra4 34. Re8 Ra3+ 35. Kc2

Bc4 36. Ne5 Bxb5 37. Nxf7+ Kd7
38. Rg8 c4 39. Ne5+ Kd6 40. f4 c3
41. Rc8 Ba4+ 42. Kd3 c2+ 43. Kd2 Ra1
44. Nc4+ Ke6 45. Nb2 Rd1+ 46. Ke3
c1Q+ 47. Rxc1 Rxc1 48. Nxa4 Rc2
49. Kf3 Kd6 50. g3!

After
50. g3

The saving move. If 50. ... Kc6 51. Kg4 Kb5
52. Kg5 Kxa4 53. Kxg6 draws. If instead of the
text 50. Nb6? follows Rc6 51. Na4 Rc4 52. Nb2
Rc3+! 53. Ke4 or 53. Kg4 Rc2 and Black, after
capturing the g2 pawn, wins easily. **50. ... Rc4
51. Nb2 Rc3+ 52. Kg4 Kd5 53. Nd1
Rb3 54. Nf2 Kd4 55. h4 Ke3 56. Nh3
Rb5 57. Ng5 Rb6 58. h5 Kd4 59. hxg6
Rxg6 60. f5 Rf6 61. Ne6+ Ke5 62. Nxg7
Rf7 ½–½** (Bled 1931)

215 Kashdan–Stoltz [D36]
Bled, round 25, 1931 [September 26]

**1. d4 d5 2. c4 e6 3. Nc3 Nf6 4. Nf3
Nbd7 5. cxd5 exd5 6. Bg5 Be7 7. e3
0–0 8. Qc2 c6 9. Bd3 Re8 10. 0–0 Nf8
11. Ne5 Ng4 12. Bxe7 Qxe7 13. Nxg4
Bxg4 14. Bf5** Stronger is 14. Rfe1 Rad8 15. Ne2
Rd6 16. Ng3 Rh6 17. Bf5 Qg5 18. Bxg4 Qxg4
19. h3 Qd7 20. b4! (Flohr–Euwe, Match Game
#1, 1932) **14. ... Bxf5 15. Qxf5 Rad8
16. Rfe1 Rd6 17. e4 dxe4 18. Rxe4 Re6
19. Rae1 Qd7 20. Rxe6 Rxe6 21. Rxe6
Qxe6 22. Qxe6 Nxe6 23. d5 cxd5
24. Nxd5 ½–½** (Bled 1931)

216 Tartakower–Kashdan [D35]
Bled, round 26, 1931 [September 28]

**1. d4 Nf6 2. Nf3 e6 3. c4 d5 4. Nc3
Nbd7 5. cxd5 exd5 6. Bf4 c6 7. e3 Be7**

**8. Bd3 0–0 9. Rc1! Re8 10. 0–0 Nf8
11. Ne5 Bd6 12. Bg3 Qe7 13. f4 Ng4
14. Re1 Nxe5 15. fxe5 Bc7 16. Qh5 Be6
17. Rf1 g6 18. Qh6 Nd7 19. Nb5! Bb8
20. Nd6 Bxd6 21. exd6 Qf8 22. Qf4 f5
23. Bh4 Nf6 24. h3! Ne4 25. Bxe4 dxe4
26. a4 Qf7 27. Be7 Bd7 28. g4 h5
29. Rc2 Kh7? 30. Qxe4! Rg8 31. Qe5
Qe6 32. Rcf2 Rg7 33. Kh2 Rag8 34. e4
fxg4 35. Qxe6 Bxe6 36. Rf6 Bc4 37. Rc1
Bd3 38. e5 Bf5 39. Bf8 Rd7 40. Be7 Re8
41. hxg4 Bxg4 42. Kg3 Bf5 43. Kf4 Kg7
44. Rg1 Bc2 45. Kg5 Bd3 46. Rd1 Bc2
47. Rdf1 Bf5 48. R1xf5! gxf5 49. Rg6+
Kh7 50. Rh6+ Kg8 51. Bf6! 1–0** (Bled
1931)

217 Kashdan–Menchik [C14]
Hastings, round 1, 1931 [December 28]

**1. e4 e6 2. d4 d5 3. Nc3 Nf6 4. Bg5
Be7 5. e5 Nfd7 6. Bxe7 Qxe7 7. Qd2
0–0 8. f4 c5 9. Nf3 Nc6 10. Rd1 a6 11. a4
f6 12. exf6 Nxf6 13. Be2 Ne4 14. Nxe4
dxe4 15. Ng5 Nxd4 16. 0–0 Bd7 17. a5
Rad8 18. Qe3 Nxe2+ 19. Qxe2 Bc6
20. Rxd8 Rxd8 21. Nxe4 Bxe4 22. Qxe4
Rd5 23. Qe3 Qd7 24. Re1 Rd1 25. Kf2
Rxe1 26. Qxe1 Qd4+ 27. Qe3 Qd5
28. Qd3 Kf7 29. g4 Qc6? 30. Qxh7 Qb5
31. Qh5+ Kf8 32. Qh8+ Kf7 33. Qh5+
Kf8 34. Qe5 Qxa5 35. Qb8+ Kf7
36. Qxb7+ Kf8 37. Qe4 Qd2+ 38. Kg3
Qc1 39. b3 Qg1+ 40. Kh3 Qf1+ 41. Kh4
Qf2+ 42. Kg5 Qxh2 43. Qxe6 Qf2** If
43. ... Qxc2 then 44. Qf5+ wins. **44. Qf5+
Ke8 45. Kg6 1–0** (American Chess Bulletin,
January 1932)

218 Yates–Kashdan [C42]
Hastings, round 2, 1931 [December]

**1. e4 e5 2. Nf3 Nf6 3. Nxe5 d6 4. Nf3
Nxe4 5. d4 d5 6. Bd3 Nc6 7. 0–0 Be7
8. c4 Nb4 9. cxd5 Nxd3 10. Qxd3 Qxd5
11. Re1 Bf5 12. Nc3 Nxc3 13. Qxc3 c6
14. Bd2 h6 15. Re5 Qd7 16. Rae1 Be6
17. R5e4 Bf6 18. Qa3 Be7 19. Qe3 0–0
20. Ne5 Qd5 21. Qg3 Bg5** Black must play
this to prevent the loss of the h pawn. **22. Bxg5**

hxg5 23. Nf3 But not 23. Qxg5 as f6 loses a piece. 23. ... g4 24. Re5 Qxa2 25. Ng5 f6 26. Rxe6 fxg5 27. R6e2 Rf4 28. h3 Raf8 29. hxg4 Qd5 30. Re7 Rxf2 31. Qxf2 Rxf2 32. Kxf2 Qxd4+ 33. Kg3 Qxb2 34. R1e3 Qd4 35. Re8+ Kh7 36. R3e5 Qf4+ 37. Kh3 b5 38. Rf5 Qc1 39. Ree5 b4 40. Rc5 Qe3+ 41. Kh2 b3 42. Rce5 Qd2 43. Re6 Qc1 44. Re7 b2 0–1 (*New York Sun*, 1931)

219 Kashdan–Flohr [B18]

Hastings, round 3, 1932 *[January]*

1. e4 c6 2. d4 d5 3. Nc3 dxe4 4. Nxe4 Bf5 5. Ng3 Bg6 6. Nf3 Nd7 7. Bd3 e6 8. 0–0 Ngf6 9. Re1 Qc7 10. c4 Bb4 11. Re2 Bxd3 12. Qxd3 0–0 13. c5 Ba5 14. Rb1 Qd8 15. b4 Bc7 16. Ne4 Nd5 17. g3 h6 18. b5 cxb5 19. Rxb5 b6 20. Rc2 a6 21. Rb1 bxc5 22. Nxc5 Nxc5 23. dxc5 Rb8 24. Rcb2 Rxb2 25. Bxb2 Qa8 26. Be5 Rd8 27. Qe4 Qc6 28. Bxc7 Qxc7 29. Rc1 Ne7 30. Ne5 Rd5 31. Nd3 Qb7 32. Qb4 Nf5 ½–½ (*American Chess Bulletin*, January 1932)

220 G. Thomas–Kashdan [C42]

Hastings, round 4, 1932 *[January]*

1. e4 e5 2. Nf3 Nf6 3. Nxe5 d6 4. Nf3 Nxe4 5. d4 d5 6. Bd3 Be7 The game Yates–Kashdan continued here with Nc6. 7. 0–0 0–0 8. c4 c6 9. Nc3 Nxc3 10. bxc3 dxc4 11. Bxc4 Bg4 12. Qd3 Nd7 13. a4 Qa5 14. Bf4 Bf5 15. Qe3 Rfe8 16. Rfe1 Nb6 17. Bb3 Nd5 18. Bxd5 cxd5 19. Qe5 Bd7 20. Qc7 Qxc7 21. Bxc7 f6 22. Rab1 Bc6 23. Nd2 Kf7 24. c4 Rac8 25. Bf4 g5 26. Bg3 dxc4 27. Nxc4 Red8 28. Na5 Rxd4 29. Nxc6 Rxc6 30. Rxb7 Re6 31. f4 gxf4 32. Bf2 Rxe1+ 33. Bxe1 Rxa4 34. Kf2 Ke6 35. Kf3 h5 36. Bf2 a6 37. Ba7 Bd6 38. Rh7 Ra3+ 39. Ke2 f3+ 40. gxf3 Ra2+ 41. Kf1 Rxh2 42. Bf2 Rh1+ 43. Kg2 Ra1 44. Rxh5 Ra2 45. Kf1 a5 46. Bd4 a4 47. Ra5 Be5 48. Be3 Bc3 49. Rc5 Bb4 50. Rb5 Bd6 51. Ra5 a3 52. f4 f5 53. Ke1 0–1 (*Times Literary Supplement*, 1932) The fifth round game

Sultan Khan–Kashdan was a draw. The game is not available.

221 Kashdan–Euwe [B03]

Hastings, round 6, 1932 *[January]*

1. e4 Nf6 Alekhine's Defense, which had quite a vogue in the 20's, but is infrequently seen today. The idea is to induce an early advance of White's pawns, which may become weak. But the loss of time through the knight moves is a serious handicap, and White should obtain the advantage. 2. e5 The most forceful move. If 2. Nc3 e5 turns into the Vienna Game, or d5 will also equalize. 2. ... Nd5 3. c4 Nb6 4. d4 d6 Essential at this point. Not 4. ... Nc6? 5. d5! Nxe5 6. c5 Nbc4 7. f4 winning a piece. 5. exd6 The simplest, maintaining a slight advantage in the possession of the center and generally freer game. 5. f4 leads to complications, after ...dxe5 6. fxe5 Nc6 7. Be3 Bf5, etc. The resulting position is more to Black's liking, and gives him good chances to play against the pawns. 5. ... exd6 6. Nf3 6. Nc3 is a shade better, to delay the favorable development of Black's queen bishop. However, the threats which Black builds up with his next few moves should not prove effective. 6. ... Bg4 7. h3 Bh5 8. Be2 Nc6 9. d5 Deliberately losing time to induce the exchange of bishop for knight. The continuation requires careful treatment and leads to interesting play. 9. 0–0 was a good alternative, as if then ...Bxf3 10. Bxf3 Nc4 11. Qe2+ wins. 9. ... Bxf3 Not ...Ne5? 10. Nxe5 Bxe2 11. Qxe2 dxe5 12. Qxe5+, etc. Retreating the knight is evidently inferior. 10. Bxf3 Ne5 11. Be2 Qh4 ...Nxc4? would lose a piece because of 12. Bxc4 Nxc4 13. Qa4+. But now the attack on the pawn becomes more acute. 12. 0–0! This was part of the plan started with the 9th move, and it is an important point that the pawn can still not be taken. If instead 12. b3 Qf6! with threats along the diagonal would be difficult to meet. 12. ... g5 13. Qc2 Rg8 14. Nd2 g4 15. hxg4 Nxg4 16. Qe4+? Up to this point White has obtained a clear positional advantage, which is jeopardized by this ill-considered move. Correct was at once 16. Nf3 Qh5 17. Bf4 0–0–0 (there is hardly anything better); 18. Nh2 f5 19. Bd3 when the pawn is lost. Black has no real attack

despite the menacing looking open file. The difference in the text move will be made apparent in the next note. **16. ... Be7 17. Nf3 Qh5 18. Bf4 f5!** The point is that 19. Qe6 will not do because of ...Rg6. The queen must retreat, and as a result White has lost two full moves, which naturally make the game more critical. **19. Qc2 0–0–0 20. Rfe1** Threatening Bd3. The weakness of Black's pawns is still an important factor, though the attack has gained in strength due to the extra tempos. **20. ... Nd7**

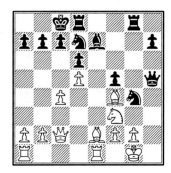

After
20. ... Nd7

Getting this piece in play and concealing a clever idea. **21. Nh2** If 21. Bd3 Nge5! 22. Nxe5 dxe5 23. Bxe5 Nxe5 24. Rxe5 Bd6! with a dangerous attack. **21. ... Qf7 22. Bd3 Nxh2** The exchange relieves White's game, and the two bishops soon take command of the situation. If 22. ... Rdc8 23. Nxg4 fxg4 24. Bh6 Re8 25. Bxf5! Rh8 26. Bg6 wins the exchange. Or 23. ... Rxg4 24. g3 Qg7 (if Rdg8 25. Bxf5! Rxf5 26. Be6 followed by Rxg1 wins) 25. Kf1, and the f pawn cannot be saved. **23. Bxh2 f4 24. Bf5 Rg5 25. Bh3** Now White's kingside is secure, and he is ready for effective play against the f pawn. The pressure on the K file and against the pinned knight becomes very useful. **25. ... f3 26. Qe4 Qg7?** An unsound sacrifice which loses off-hand. But there is no good reply. If ...Rg7 27. Bf4 (threatening Bh6 as well as Qxf3); fxg2 28. Bh6 Rg6 29. Qxe7 Qxe7 30. Rxe7 Rxh6 31. Kxg2. The threat then is Rae1 followed by doubling the rook on the seventh to which there is no adequate defense. **27. Qxe7 Rxg2+ 28. Kh1 Rg8?** Allowing a mate, but there is no good continuation, and the only alternative was to resign. **29. Qe8+ 1–0** Annotated by Kashdan. (*Chess Review*, December 1936)

222 Michell–Kashdan [D52]
Hastings, round 7, 1932 *[January]*

1. d4 Nf6 2. c4 e6 3. Nc3 d5 4. Bg5 Nbd7 5. e3 c6 6. Nf3 Qa5 7. Nd2 dxc4 8. Bxf6 Nxf6 9. Nxc4 Qc7 10. Be2 Be7 11. 0–0 0–0 12. Rc1 Rd8 13. Qb3 Bd7 14. Bf3 Be8 15. Rfd1 Rab8 16. g3 b5 17. Nd2 e5 18. d5 c5 19. Nce4 Nxe4 20. Nxe4 c4 21. Qc2 Qb6 22. h4 f5 23. d6 Bf8 24. Ng5 e4 25. Bxe4 fxe4 26. Qxe4 Bg6 27. Qd5+ Kh8 28. d7 Be7 29. Nf3 Bf6 30. Nd4 Rb7 31. h5 Rbxd7 32. Qf3 Bf7 33. h6 Bxd4 34. exd4 Qxh6 0–1 (*L'Échiquier*, December 1932)

223 Kashdan–Jackson [D17]
Hastings, round 8, 1932 *[January 6]*

1. d4 Nf6 2. c4 c6 3. Nc3 d5 4. Nf3 dxc4 5. a4 Bf5 6. Nh4 e6 7. Nxf5 exf5 8. e3 Bd6 9. Bxc4 0–0 10. Qf3 g6 11. h3! h5 12. 0–0 Nbd7 13. a5! Rc8 14. Re1 Re8 15. Bd2 Nf8? 16. e4 fxe4 17. Nxe4 N8h7 The text is more or less forced. If 17. ... Nxe4?? than 18. Qxf7+ leads to mate! 18. Ng5! Rc7 19. Rxe8+ Qxe8 20. Re1 Qf8 21. h4 Kg7 22. Bc3! Bb4 23. Qg3 Rd7? 24. Qe5 Bd6? 25. Nxh7 Bxe5 26. Nxf8 Rxd4 27. Rxe5 Rxc4 28. Re7 1–0 The ninth round game Stoltz–Kashdan was a draw. The score is not available. (*New York Sun*, 1932)

224 Kashdan–Milner-Barry [C78]
London, round 1, 1932 *[February 1]*

1. e4 e5 2. Nf3 Nc6 3. Bb5 a6 4. Ba4 Nf6 5. 0–0 Bc5 6. Nxe5 Nxe5 7. d4 Nxe4 8. Re1 Be7 9. Rxe4 Ng6 10. c4 0–0 11. Nc3 f5 12. Re2 f4 13. f3 d6 14. Bc2 Bf5 15. Bxf5 Rxf5 16. Qd3 Qd7 17. Nd5 Raf8 18. Nxe7+ Nxe7 19. Bd2 Nc6 20. Bc3 d5! 21. c5 g5 22. Rae1 R5f6 23. b4 R8f7 24. a4 Ne7 25. b5 axb5 26. axb5 Nf5 27. Re5 Ne3 A bold but not quite correct sacrifice. 28. Rxg5+ Rg7 29. Rxg7+ Qxg7 30. g3 Nf5 31. g4 h5 32. h3 hxg4 33. fxg4? A serious mistake which should cost the game. Necessary was 33. hxg4 Ne3 34. Bd2 with an easy defense.

33. ... Ne3 34. Bd2 N×g4? Black misses his chance. Instead he should play 34. Qh6 after which it seems White has no adequate defense. 35. h×g4 Qxg4+ 36. Kf2 Qh4+ 37. Ke2 f3+ 38. Kd1 f2 39. Rf1 Qg4+ 40. Kc2 Rf3 41. Be3 Qg2 42. Kd2 Rf8 After a series of forced moves for both sides Black finds the only move to win back his sacrificed piece. The position is very instructive. 43. Kd1! Ra8 44. R×f2 Ra1+ 45. Kc2 Ra2+ 46. Kb3 R×f2 47. B×f2 Q×f2 48. Qg6+ Kf8 49. Qh6+ Ke7 50. Qg5+ Ke6 51. Qe5+ Kd7 52. Q×d5+ Kc8 53. Qe6+ Kd8 54. Qg8+ Kd7 55. Qg4+ Kd8 56. Qg5+ Kd7 57. Qd5+ Ke7 58. c6 b×c6 59. b×c6 Qf4 60. Qc5+ Qd6 If 60. ... Ke6 then 61. Ka4 followed by b5 and e6 etc. Black is helpless. 61. Kc4 Ke6 62. Q×d6+ K×d6 63. d5 Ke7 64. Kc5 Ke8 65. Kb5 1–0 (*London 1932* with notes by Alekhine)

225 Buerger [i.e., Berger]– Kashdan [D65]
London, round 2, 1932 *[February 2]*

1. d4 d5 2. c4 e6 3. Nf3 Nf6 4. Bg5 Nbd7 5. Nc3 Be7 6. e3 0–0 7. Rc1 a6 8. c×d5 e×d5 9. Bd3 Re8 10. 0–0 c6 11. Qc2 Nf8 12. Rce1 Ne4 13. B×e7 Q×e7 14. Nd2 N×d2 15. Q×d2 Be6 16. Ne2 Rad8 17. Ng3 g6 18. b4 Nd7 19. Rb1 f5 20. a4 Nf6 21. Rfc1 Ne4 22. Qb2 Bd7 23. b5 a×b5 24. a×b5 h5 25. Nf1 Qf6 26. b×c6 b×c6 27. Nd2 N×d2 28. Q×d2 f4 29. e×f4 Q×d4

After
29. ... Q×d4

30. Rb4? Qf6 31. Qc2 Kg7 32. h3 c5! 33. Rb7 But not 33. Q×c4? because then follows Rc8 which then loses material for White.

33. ... c4 34. Bf1 Re7 35. Qd2 Bf5 36. Rb5 Red7 37. Ra5 Rd6 38. Qb4 Be6 39. Qc5? Q×f4 40. Rb1 Qf6 41. Ra7+ R8d7 42. Ra8 Bf7 43. Rc8 Re7 44. Rd1 Ra6 45. Rb1 Qd6 46. Qd4+ Qe5 47. Q×e5+ R×e5 48. Rb7 Kf6 49. f4 Re7 50. R×e7 K×e7 51. Rc7+ Ke8 52. Kf2 Ra3 53. Be2 Be6 54. Ke1 Kd8 55. Rc5 Kd7 56. Bd1 Kd6 57. Rb5 Kc6 58. Rb8 Ra1 59. Ke2 Bf5 0–1 (*London* 1932, with notes by Alekhine)

226 Kashdan–Koltanowski [C41]
London, round 3, 1932 *[February 3]*

1. e4 e5 2. Nf3 d6 3. d4 e×d4 4. N×d4 Nf6 5. Nc3 Be7 6. Bf4 0–0 7. Qd2 Re8 8. 0–0–0 Bf8 9. f3 Nbd7 10. g4 Ne5 11. Be2 a6 12. h4 b5? 13. h5 Be6 14. N×e6 f×e6? Loses a piece. 15. B×e5 d×e5 16. g5 Bd6 The knight is lost. 17. g×f6 Q×f6 18. Qe3 Qe7 19. Rd3 Red8 20. Qd2 1–0 (*London* 1932 with notes by Alekhine)

227 Kashdan–Tartakower [C17]
London, round 4, 1932 *[February 4]*

1. e4 e6 2. d4 d5 3. Nc3 Bb4 4. e5 c5 5. a3 c×d4 6. Q×d4 Nc6 7. Qg4 B×c3+ 8. b×c3 N×e5? 9. Q×g7 Qf6

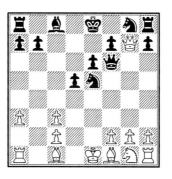

After
9. ... Qf6

White could win the exchange now with 10. Bh6! after which Black could not play Ng4 because of Bb5+ followed by Qf8 mate or Bg5. A nice trap to remember. 10. Q×f6? N×f6 11. Nf3! N×f3+ 12. g×f3 Bd7 13. c4 Bc6 14. c×d5 N×d5 15. Rg1 Ne7 16. Bb2 Rg8 17. R×g8+ N×g8 18. Bd3 f5 19. Ke2 Kf7 20. Rg1 Nf6 21. Be5 Rg8 22. Rg3 Nh5 23. Rh3 Kg6 24. Ke3 Rc8 25. Be2?

White has realized his advantage up to now. But here he could have increased it with 24. c4! The passive text gives Black the chance to keep the initiative. **25. ... Bd5 26. f4 Nf6 27. Bxf6 Kxf6 28. Bd3 Rc3 29. Rxh7 Rxa3 30. Rc7?** The decisive loss of time 30. h4 at once was necessary. If then 30. ... Ra1 31. h5 Rh1 32. Be2 with an even position. After the text move Tartakower exploits his disadvantage—until his unfortunate 44th move—in a very convincing manner. **30. ... a5 31. h4 a4 32. Kd2 Ra1 33. Bc4 Bxc4 34. Rxc4 a3 35. Kc3 b5 36. Rb4 Rf1 37. Kb3 Rxf2 38. Rxb5 Rxf4 39. Kxa3 Rxh4 40. Kb3 f4 41. c4 f3 42. Kc3 Rh1 43. Rb2 Kf5 44. Rc2 e5?** He could have won at once here with 44. Kf4 followed by Kg3. **45. c5 e4?** Even now 45. ... Kf4 still wins. **46. c6 e3 47. c7 Rh8 48. Kd3 e2 49. Kd2 Rc8 50. Ke1 Ke4 51. Kf2 Kd3 52. Rc6 Kd4 53. Rc1 Kd3 54. Rc6 Kd2 55. Rd6+ Kc3 56. Rc6+ Kd4 57. Rc1 Kd5 58. Kxf3 Rxc7 59. Re1 Rf7+ 60. Kxe2 Re7+ 61. Kd2 Rxe1 62. Kxe1 ½–½** A lucky escape for Kashdan. (*London* 1932 with notes by Alekhine)

228 Maróczy–Kashdan [C90]

London, round 5, 1932 *[February 5]*

1. e4 e5 2. Nf3 Nc6 3. Bb5 a6 4. Ba4 Nf6 5. 0–0 Be7 6. Re1 d6 7. c3 b5 8. Bb3 Na5 9. Bc2 c5 10. d4 Qc7 11. Nbd2 cxd4 12. cxd4 Nc6 13. d5 Nb4 14. Bb1 a5 15. a3 Na6 16. Nf1 0–0 17. Bd2 Nc5 18. Bc2 Bd7 19. Ng3 Rfc8 20. h3 Na4 21. Bxa4 bxa4 22. Rc1 Qb6 23. Rxc8+ Rxc8 24. Bc3 Ne8 25. Qd2 Ra8 26. Rd1 Bd8 27. Nf5 Bxf5 28. exf5 Nf6 29. Qc2 Qb5 30. Nd2 Nxd5 31. Ne4 Ra6? (*see diagram*)

32. Bxe5! A fatal surprise for Black. If 32. ... dxe5, then Qc8 wins at once. **32. ... Ne7 33. Rxd6 Rxd6 34. Bxd6 Qxf5 35. Qxa4 Kf8 36. Nc5 f6 37. Qc4 Ke8 38. Ne6 Kd7 39. Nxd8 Kxd6 40. Nb7+ Kd7 41. b4 axb4 42. axb4 Qd5 43. Nc5+ Kd6? 44. Qa6+ Ke5 45. Qe2+ Kd6 46. Qa6+ Ke5 47. Nd3+! Kf5 48. Qa7 Qd6 49. Qe3 Nd5 50. g4+ 1–0** (*London* 1932 with notes by Alekhine)

After
31. ... Ra6

229 Kashdan–Alekhine [D85]

London, round 6, 1932 *[February 6]*

1. d4 Nf6 2. c4 g6 3. Nc3 d5 4. cxd5 Nxd5 5. e4 Nxc3 6. bxc3 c5 7. Nf3 Bg7 8. Bb5+ Bd7 9. Bxd7+ Qxd7 10. 0–0 cxd4 11. cxd4 Nc6 12. Be3 0–0 13. Rc1 Rfc8 14. Qd2 b6 15. Rc2 e6 16. Rfc1 Ne7 17. Bh6 Rxc2 18. Rxc2 Rc8 19. Bxg7 Rxc2 20. Qxc2 Kxg7 21. Qc3 Qc6! 22. Qxc6 Nxc6 23. a3 f5 24. exf5 exf5 25. Kf1 Kf6 26. Ke2 Ke6 27. Ng5+ Kd5 28. Nxh7 Nxd4+ 29. Kd3 Ne6 30. g3 b5 31. f4 a5 32. Nf6+ Kd6 33. Kc3 Kc6 34. Kd3 Kd6 35. Kc3 Nd8 36. Nh7 Ne6 37. Nf6 ½–½ (*London* 1932)

230 Flohr–Kashdan [D48]

London, round 7, 1932 *[February 8]*

1. d4 d5 2. Nf3 Nf6 3. c4 c6 4. Nc3 e6 5. e3 Nbd7 6. Bd3 dxc4 7. Bxc4 b5 8. Bd3 a6 9. 0–0 c5 10. a4 b4 11. Ne4 Bb7 12. Nxc5 Nxc5 13. dxc5 Bxc5 14. Qe2 0–0? 15. e4 Be7 16. b3 Nd7 17. Bb2 Bf6 18. Bxf6 Qxf6 19. Rac1 Qf4 20. Rc4 a5 21. g3 Qb8 22. Rfc1 Ne5 23. Nxe5? Qxe5 24. Rc5 Qd4 25. R5c4 Qe5 26. Rc5 Qd4 ½–½ (*London* 1932)

231 Kashdan–G. Thomas [D52]

London, round 8, 1932 *[February 9]*

1. d4 Nf6 2. c4 e6 3. Nc3 d5 4. Nf3 Nbd7 5. Bg5 c6 6. e3 Qa5 7. Nd2 dxc4 8. Bxf6 Nxf6 9. Nxc4 Qc7 10. Bd3 Be7 11. 0–0 0–0 12. Rc1 Rd8 13. Qf3 Bf8 14. Rfd1 Qe7 15. c4! g6 16. Bf1 Bg7 17. e5

Ne8 18. Ne4 Bd7 19. a3 Rab8 20. b4 f5!
21. Nc5 Bf8 22. Nxd7 Rxd7 23. Na5 Nc7
24. Nb3 Qe8 25. Nc5 Bxc5 26. dxc5
Rhd8? 27. Rd6 a6 28. Bc4 Nd5 29. Rb1
Rc8 30. Qg3 Re7 31. h4 Qf7 32. f4 Kg7
33. Qf3 h6 34. a4 Nc7 35. Rbd1 Ne8
36. Qb3! Nc7 37. g3 Kh7 38. Kf2 Kg7
39. Qd3 Kh7 40. Rd8 Rxd8 41. Qxd8
Nd5 42. Bxd5 cxd5 43. b5 Rd7 44. Qb6
axb5 45. axb5 g5 46. hxg5 hxg5
47. Rh1+ Kg6 48. Ke2 Qe8 49. fxg5 Re7
50. c6 Qa8 51. Rh6+ Kg7 If Kxg5? he falls
into a mating net after Qe3+. 52. Qc5 Qa2+
53. Kf3 Rf7 54. Rf6 Qb3+ 55. Kg2 Qb2+
56. Kh3 bxc6 57. Qxc6 Qf2 58. Rxf7+
Kxf7 59. Qd7+ Kg6 60. Qxe6+ Kxg5
61. Qf6+ Kh5 62. Qf7+ Kh6 63. Qxd5
Kg5 64. Qd3 Kh5 65. b6 Qxb6
66. Qxf5+ Kh6 67. Qf6+ Qxf6 68. exf6
Kg6 69. Kg4 Kxf6 70. Kh5 Kg7 71. Kg5
1–0 (*London 1932*)

232 Sultan Khan–Kashdan [D04]
London, round 9, 1932 *[February 10]*

1. Nf3 d5 2. d4 Nf6 3. e3 c6 4. Bd3
g6 5. Nbd2 Bg7 6. b3 0–0 7. Bb2 Nbd7
8. 0–0 e5! 9. Nxe5 Nxe5 10. dxe5 Ng4
11. Nf3 Qe7 12. c4 dxc4 13. Bxc4 Nxe5
14. Nxe5 Bxe5 15. Bxe5 Qxe5 16. Rc1
Be6 17. Qe2 Rfe8 18. Rfd1 Rad8 19. h3
a5 20. Bxe6 Qxe6 21. Qb2 Rd5 22. Rxd5
Qxd5 23. Rc4 Re4 24. Rxe4 Qxe4
25. Qd2 a4 26. b4 h5 27. a3 Qb1+
28. Kh2 Qa1 29. Qd3 Kg7 30. Kg3 Qa2
31. Qd4+ Kg8 32. Qd8+ Kg7 33. Qd4+
Kg8 ½–½ (*London 1932*)

233 Kashdan–Menchik [D37]
London, round 10, 1932 *[February 11]*

1. d4 Nf6 2. c4 e6 3. Nf3 d5 4. Nc3
Nbd7 5. a3 Be7 6. Bf4 c5? 7. Nb5! 0–0
8. Bc7 Qe8 9. Nd6 Bxd6 10. Bxd6 cxd4
11. Bxf8 Kxf8 12. Nxd4 dxc4 13. e3 Nb6
14. a4 Qe7 15. a5 Nbd5 16. Nc2 Ne4
17. Qd4 f5 18. Bxc4 Ndf6 19. 0–0 Bd7
20. Rad1 Bc6 21. f3 e5 22. Qd3 Nc5
23. Qxf5 1–0 (*London 1932*)

234 Winter–Kashdan [D13]
London, round 11, 1932 *[February 12]*

1. d4 d5 2. c4 c6 3. cxd5 cxd5 4. Nc3
Nf6 5. Nf3 g6 6. Bf4 a6 7. Qb3 Nc6
8. e3 Na5 9. Qc2 Bg7 10. Bd3 0–0 11. h3
b5 12. 0–0 Bb7 13. Rfc1 Rc8 14. Qe2
Qb6 15. Rc2 Nc4 16. Rac1 Ne4 17. Bxe4
dxe4 18. Nd2 Nxd2 19. Qxd2 Rfd8
20. Qe2 Qe6 21. b3 f5 22. Nd1 Rxc2
23. Rxc2 Rc8 24. Rxc8+ Qxc8 25. Qd2
Kf7 26. Qc3 Qxc3 27. Nxc3 Bf6 28. Kf1
Ke6 29. Ke2 b4 30. Na4 Bc6 31. Nb6
Bb5+ 32. Ke1 g5 33. Bc7 h5 34. g3 Bg7
35. Nc4 Kd5 36. Nd2 Bf8 37. Ba5 e6
38. Bd8 g4 39. h4 Bd6 40. Kd1 Bd3
41. Kc1 Be2 42. Bf6 Bc7 43. Be7 e5
44. dxe5 a5 45. Bf6 Bb6 46. Bg5! Kxe5
47. Kc2 Kd5 48. Kc1 Bc7 49. Kc2 Kc6
50. Kc1 Be5 51. Kc2 Kb5 52. Kc1 a4
53. Kc2 Bc3 54. Kc1 Bd3 55. Kd1 Bb2
56. Be7 Bc3 57. Bg5 Ka6 58. Kc1 Bb5
59. Kc2 Bd7 60. Kc1 Be6 61. Kc2 Kb5
62. Kc1 Bxb3 63. Nxb3! axb3 64. axb3
Be1 65. Kd1 Bc3 ½–½ (*London 1932*)

235 Kashdan–H. Steiner [D05]
Pasadena, round 1, 1932 *[August 15]*

1. d4 Nf6 2. Nf3 d5 3. e3 e6 4. Bd3
Nbd7 5. Nbd2 Be7 6. Qe2 c5 7. c3 0–0
8. 0–0 b6 9. e4 dxe4 10. Nxe4 Bb7
11. Rd1 Qc7 12. Bg5 Rfe8 13. dxc5 Bxe4
14. Bxe4 Nxe4 15. Qxe4 Nxc5 16. Qc4
Bxg5 17. Nxg5 Qe7 18. Nf3 Red8
19. Nd4 Qh4 The best move driving the
White queen back. Had he played Rac8, White
would force an entrance with 20. b4. **20. Qe2
Rac8 21. a4 Qf6 22. b4 Nd7 23. Nb5
Nf8 24. Qe3** Protecting the c pawn, and
threatening Rxd8 followed by Nxa7. The object is to force a weakening advance of Black's
pawns. The advantage of the extra queenside
pawn is already telling. **24. ... a6 25. Nd6
Rb8** If 25. ... Rxc3 26. Ne4 Rxe3 27. Nxf6+
gxf6 28. fxe3 wins the exchange. **26. Rd2 Qe7
27. Rad1 Qc7 28. c4 Rd7 29. Qc3 h6
30. Ne4 Rxd2 31. Rxd2 Rc8 32. Nd6
Rd8 33. c5 Qc6 34. Qf3 Qxa4 35. Qxf7+
Kh7**

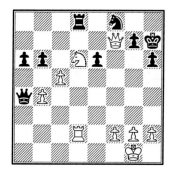

After
35. ... Kh7

But here it would appear, what with Black threatening mate and also the b4 pawn, that White has overplayed his hand, and is in some distress. But there is a hidden resource which makes everything right again. **36. h3** Stopping the mate. If now Qxb4 37. Ne4!! threatening mate in two by Nf6+ and also Rxd8. **36. ... bxc5 37. bxc5 Rb8 38. Kh2 Ng6 39. Re2** But not Qxe6 as Qf4+ wins the rook. **39. ... Rf8 40. Qxe6 Qf4+ 41. g3 Qd4 42. Qe3 Qxe3 43. fxe3 Ne5 44. Kg2 a5 45. Rc2 Nc6 46. Nb5 Rd8 47. Nd4 Nxd4 48. exd4 Rxd4 49. c6 Rd8 50. Kf3 a4 51. Ke4 a3 52. Ke5** Now he is in a position to advance c7 and then Kd6 ensures the victory. **52. ... Rd3 53. c7 a2 54. Rxa2 Rc3 55. Kd6 Rd3+ 56. Kc6 Rc3+ 57. Kb7 Rb3+ 58. Ka8 1–0** Analysis by Kashdan. The move order varies slightly with that of the tournament booklet. (*Chess Review*, January 1933)

236 Reinfeld–Kashdan [D18]
Pasadena, round 2, 1932 *[August 16]*

1. d4 d5 2. c4 c6 3. Nf3 Nf6 4. Nc3 dxc4 5. a4 Bf5 6. e3 e6 7. Bxc4 Nbd7 8. 0–0 Ne4 9. Qe2 Bb4 10. Bd2 Bxc3 11. Bxc3 Nxc3 12. bxc3 Qa5 13. e4 Bg4 14. Qe3 Bxf3 15. Qxf3 0–0 16. e5 Rfd8 17. Rfe1 Nf8 18. Rab1 Rab8 19. Ra1 Rd7 20. h4 Rbd8 21. h5 c5 22. dxc5 Qxc5 23. Re4 Rd2 24. Rae1 a6 25. Rg4 Qe7 26. Re3 Rb2 27. Qf4 Rd1+ 28. Kh2 Rbb1 29. Bd3 Rh1+ 30. Kg3 Rb2 31. Qf6 Qxf6 32. exf6 g6 33. hxg6 hxg6 34. Rb4 Rxb4 35. cxb4 Nd7 36. Be4 b6 37. Bb7 Rb1 38. Bxa6 Rxb4 39. Rf3 Rxa4 40. Bb5 Rd4 41. Bxd7 Rxd7 42. Rb3

Rd6 43. Kf4 g5+ 44. Kxg5 Rd5+ 45. Kf4 Rf5+ 46. Ke3 b5 47. g3 Re5+ 48. Kf4 Rc5 49. g4 Rc4+ 50. Ke5 Rc5+ 51. Kf4 Rc4+ ½–½ (Contributed by Ansel)

237 Kashdan–Fink [C60]
Pasadena, round 3, 1932 *[August 17]*

1. e4 e5 2. Nf3 Nc6 3. Bb5 Qf6 4. 0–0 Nd4 5. Nxd4 exd4 6. d3 b6 7. f4 Bb7 8. Nd2 0–0–0 9. Nf3 Ne7 10. Qe2 Ng6 11. e5 Qe6 12. Nxd4 Bc5 13. c3 a6 14. Bc4 d5 15. Bb3 Bxd4+ 16. cxd4 Ne7 17. Be3 h5 18. Rac1 Nf5 19. Rc3 Rh6 20. Rfc1 c6 21. Ba4 b5 22. Bd1 Rg6 23. Bf2 Rh8 24. a4 Rg4 25. Qd2 Qh6 26. axb5 axb5 27. Bxg4 hxg4 28. Bg3 b4 29. Rb3 Nxd4 30. Rxb4 Nf5 31. Kf2 d4 32. Rxb7! Nxg3 33. hxg3 1–0 (International Chess Congress, *Pasadena* 1932)

238 Kashdan–Dake [C71]
Pasadena, round 4, 1932 *[August 18]*

1. e4 e5 2. Nf3 Nc6 3. Bb5 a6 4. Ba4 d6 5. d4 b5 6. Bb3 Nxd4 7. Nxd4 exd4 8. Bd5 8. Qxd4? c5 leads to the Noah's Arc Trap. 8. ... Rb8 9. Bc6+ Bd7 10. Bxd7+ Qxd7 11. Qxd4 Nf6 12. 0–0 Be7 13. Rd1 Qc6 14. e5 dxe5 15. Qxe5 Qc5 16. Qe2 0–0 17. Nc3 Rfe8 18. Be3 Qf5 19. Qd3 Qxd3 20. Rxd3 Rbd8 21. Rad1 Rxd3 22. Rxd3 Rd8 23. Rxd8+ Bxd8 ½–½ (*Deutsche Schachzeitung*, 1932)

239 Fine–Kashdan [D35]
Pasadena, round 5, 1932 *[August 20]*

1. c4 Nf6 2. d4 e6 3. Nc3 d5 4. Nf3 Nbd7 5. cxd5 exd5 6. Bf4 c6 7. e3 Be7 8. Bd3 0–0 9. Qc2 Re8 10. h3 c5 11. dxc5 Nxc5 12. Bb5 Bd7 13. Bxd7 Qxd7 14. 0–0 Rac8 15. Rfd1 Nce4 16. Be5 Nxc3 17. bxc3 Qe6 18. Rab1 Nd7 19. Bf4 Nc5 20. Nd4 Qd7 21. c4 dxc4 22. Nb5 Nd3 23. Nc7 Red8 24. Qxc4 Qc6 25. Qxc6 bxc6 26. Bg3 h5 27. Na6 c5 28. Bc7 Rd5 29. Kf1 c4 30. Ke2 Ba3 31. Rd2 Rd7 32. Ba5 f6 33. Rc2 Rd5 34. Bc7 Nb2 35. Rcxb2 Bxb2 36. Rxb2 Rd7 37. Rc2 Rdxc7 38. Nxc7 Rxc7

39. Kd2 Kf7 40. Kc3 Ke6 ½–½ (California website)

240 Kashdan–O. Bernstein [D32]
Pasadena, round 6, 1932 *[August 21]*

1. d4 d5 2. c4 e6 3. Nc3 c5 4. cxd5 cxd4 5. Qa4+ Bd7 6. Qxd4 exd5 7. Qxd5 Nc6 8. Nf3 Nf6 9. Qd1 Bb4 10. Bd2 0–0 11. e3 Bg4 12. Be2 Bxf3 13. gxf3 Qe7 14. Qb3 Rfd8 15. a3 Ba5 16. Rd1 Rd7 17. Qc2 Re8 18. 0–0 Ne5 19. Ne4 Nxe4 20. fxe4 Rc7 21. Qa4 Bxd2 22. Rxd2 Rc4 23. Qxa7 Rxe4 24. Qb6 Qh4 25. f4 Ng4 26. Bxg4 Qxg4+ 27. Rg2 Qd7 28. Rg3 Qd2 29. Qxb7 Rxe3 30. Rxe3 Qxe3+ 31. Rf2 h5 32. Qf3 Qc1+ 33. Kg2 Re6 34. Qc3 Rg6+ 35. Kh3 Qg1 36. Qf3 Qb1 37. f5 Rg4 38. Re2 Qc1 39. Rg2 Rf4 40. Qg3 g6 41. Rf2 Rxf2 42. Qxf2 g5 43. Kg3 Qc7+ 44. Kh3 Qc4 45. Kg2 Qg4+ 46. Kf1 Qd1+ 47. Kg2 Qg4+ ½–½ (Kashdan's scoresheet)

241 Borochow–Kashdan [B40]
Pasadena, round 7, 1932 *[August 23]*

1. e4 c5 2. Nf3 e6 3. d4 cxd4 4. Nxd4 Nf6 5. Nc3 Bb4 6. Bd3 Nc6 7. Nxc6 dxc6 8. e5 Nd7 9. Qg4 Qa5 10. 0–0 Bxc3 11. bxc3 Qxe5 12. Bf4 Qxc3 13. Bd6 h5 14. Qg3 Qd4 15. Ba3 c5 16. Qh3 Qe5 17. Rad1 0–0 18. Rfe1 Qf6 19. Qxh5 g6 20. Qh6 b6 21. Re3 Bb7 22. Rg3 Qg7 23. Qxg7+ Kxg7 24. Bxg6 fxg6 25. Rxd7+ Rf7 26. Bb2+ Kf8 27. Rd6 Ke7 28. Be5 Be4 29. Ra3 Bxc2 30. Rxb6 axb6 31. Rxa8 Kd7 32. Ra7+ Ke8 33. Ra8+ Kd7 34. Ra7+ Ke8 35. Ra8+ Kd7 ½–½ (*Texas Chess*, November 1932)

242 Kashdan–Araiza [D52]
Pasadena, round 8, 1932 *[August 24]*

1. d4 Nf6 2. Nf3 d5 3. c4 e6 4. Nc3 c6 5. Bg5 Nbd7 6. e3 Be7 7. Qc2 c5 8. cxd5 Nxd5 9. Bxe7 Qxe7 10. Nxd5 exd5 11. dxc5 Qxc5 12. Qxc5 Nxc5 13. Rc1 b6 14. b4 Na6 15. Bb5+ Ke7 16. a3 Bb7 17. Nd4 Rac8 18. Kd2 g6 19. Nc6+ Kd6 20. Nxa7 Ra8 21. Bxa6 Bxa6 22. Nc6

Bc4 23. Nd4 Ra4 But not 23. ... Rxa3? 24. Rxc4! dxc4 25. Nb5 winning the rook. 24. Rc3 Rha8 25. Nc2 Re8 26. h4 Re5 27. Ne1 Re8 28. Rh3 f5 29. Rf3 Rea8 30. Nc2 b5 31. Rf4 Ke5 32. Kc1 h6 33. g4 fxg4 34. Rxg4 R4a6 35. Rf4 Rf6 36. Rg4 Raa6 37. f4+ Kf5 38. Rg3 Rf7 39. Nd4+ Kf6 40. Kb2 Rfa7 41. Rg1 Re7 42. Rg3 Rea7 43. Rg1 Re7 44. Nf3 Re4 45. Ne5 Kf5 46. Rd1 d4 47. Rxd4 Rxd4 48. exd4 Kxf4 49. Nxc4 bxc4 50. Rxc4 g5 51. hxg5 hxg5 52. d5+ Kf5 53. b5 Rb6 54. a4 g4 55. Kb3 g3 56. Kb4 Rh6 57. Rc1 Ke4 58. Kc5 Rh4 59. Re1+ Kf3 60. b6 g2 61. Rg1 Rh8 62. Rxg2 Rc8+ 63. Kd6 Kxg2 64. b7 Rb8 65. Kc7 1–0 (*Brooklyn Daily Eagle*, September 8, 1932)

243 Alekhine–Kashdan [D36]
Pasadena, round 9, 1932 *[August 25]*

1. d4 Nf6 2. c4 e6 3. Nc3 d5 4. Bg5 Nbd7 5. cxd5 exd5 6. e3 c6 7. Bd3 Be7 8. Qc2 0–0 9. Nge2 Re8 10. 0–0–0 Ne4 11. Bxe4 dxe4 12. h4 f5 13. Qb3+ Kh8 14. Nf4 Nf6 15. h5 h6 16. Qf7 Ng8 17. Ng6+ Kh7 18. Nxe7 Rxe7 19. Bxe7 Qxe7 20. Qxe7 Nxe7 21. d5 Bd7 22. dxc6 Bxc6 23. Rd6 Rc8 24. Rhd1 Ng8 25. Rd8 Rc7 26. Rf8 Nf6 27. Rdd8 Nxh5 28. Rxf5 Nf6 29. Kd2 Kg6 30. Rc5 Rf7 31. Rd6 Kh7 32. Rf5 Kg6 33. Ra5 a6 34. Nd5 Bxd5 35. Raxd5 Kh7 36. Rf5 Kg6 37. Rc5 Kh7 38. Ke2 g5 39. b4 Kg7 40. a4 Ng4 41. f3 exf3+ 42. gxf3 Nh2 43. f4 gxf4 44. exf4 Ng4 45. Kf3 Nf6 46. b5 Nd7 47. Rcd5 Nf6 48. Rf5 Kg6 49. Rc5 axb5 50. Rxb5 Rc7 51. Rbb5 Rf7 52. a5 Kg7 53. Rb5 Rc7 54. Rdb6 Rc3+ 55. Ke2 Rc4 56. Rxb7+ Kg6 57. f5+ Kg5 58. a6 Ra4 59. a7 Ne4 60. Ke3 1–0 The only game Alekhine ever won from Kashdan in serious competition. But Kashdan still took second place. (*International Chess Congress, Pasadena* 1932)

244 Kashdan–Reshevsky [E16]
Pasadena, round 10, 1932 *[August 27]*

1. d4 Nf6 2. Nf3 e6 3. c4 Bb4+ 4. Nbd2 b6 5. g3 Bb7 6. Bg2 0–0 7. 0–0

Bxd2 8. Qxd2 d6 9. b3 Nbd7 10. Bb2 Re8 11. Rad1 a5 12. Rfe1 Ra7 13. Nh4 Bxg2 14. Nxg2 d5 15. Nf4 a4 16. Rc1 axb3 17. axb3 Qe7 18. cxd5 exd5 19. Rc2 Nb8 20. Rec1 Rd8 21. Nd3 Ne8 22. Bc3 Nc6 23. Bb4 Nxb4 24. Nxb4 Raa8 25. Nc6 Qf6 26. Nxd8 Rxd8 27. Ra2 h6 28. Rca1 Qc6 29. Qc2 Qxc2 30. Rxc2 Kf8 31. Ra7 Rd7 32. Rc6 Ke7 33. f3 Rd6 34. Rxd6 Kxd6 35. Kf2 Nf6 36. Ke3 Nd7 37. Kd3 Nf8 38. e4 dxe4+ 39. fxe4 Ne6 40. b4 g6 41. b5 h5 42. h4 f6 43. Ra8 Ke7 44. Rg8 g5 45. hxg5 fxg5 46. d5 Nc5+ 47. Ke3 h4 48. Rxg5 hxg3 49. e5 1–0 (International Chess Congress, *Pasadena* 1932)

245 Factor–Kashdan [D46]
Pasadena, round 11, 1932 *[August 28]*

1. d4 Nf6 2. c4 c6 3. Nc3 d5 4. e3 e6 5. Nf3 Nbd7 6. Bd3 a6 7. a3 dxc4 8. Bxc4 b5 9. Bd3 c5 10. dxc5 Nxc5 11. Bc2 Qxd1+ 12. Nxd1 Bb7 13. b4 Nce4 14. Bb2 Be7 15. Rc1 0–0 16. Nc3 Nd6 17. Bd3 Rac8 18. 0–0 Nc4 19. Bxc4 Rxc4 20. Ne5 Rc7 21. Nxb5 Rxc1 22. Rxc1 axb5 23. Rc7 Rd8 24. h3 Rd1+ 25. Kh2 Bd6 26. Rxb7 Rd2 27. Bd4 Rxf2 28. Ra7 h5 29. Kg1 Ne4 30. g4 f6 31. Ra8+ Kh7 32. Nf7 Bh2+ 33. Kh1 Ng3 mate 0–1 (International Chess Congress, *Pasadena* 1932)

246 Kashdan (Manhattan)– Marshall (Marshall) [D52]
Metropolitan League Match, 1932 *[April 16]*

1. d4 d5 2. c4 e6 3. Nf3 Nf6 4. Nc3 Nbd7 5. Bg5 c6 6. e3 Qa5 The Cambridge Springs Defense, which usually leads to interesting play. 7. Nd2 Bb4 7. ... dxc4 is often played here to force the exchange of the bishop. I obtained a winning position with it against Dr. Alekhine in the Bled tournament (1931). 8. Qc2 0–0 9. Be2 Ne4 9. ... e5 has been tried here, but White castles, and if exd4 11. Nb3 Qc7 12. Nxd4 with advantage. 10. Ndxe4 dxe4 11. Bh4 e5 An interesting line and not at all bad, is g5 12. Bg3 f5. If now 13. h4 g5! followed

by e5. 12. 0–0 exd4 If ...f5 13. c5, followed by Bc4+ is strong. 13. Nxe4 Threatens to win a piece by a3. 13. ... f5 14. a3 fxe4 d3 is a striking possibility here. If 15. Bxd3 fxe4 16. axb4 exd3 wins a piece. But White plays 15. axb4 Qxa1 (best) 16. Bxd3 Qa6 17. c5 b5 18. Nd6, at least winning the exchange back, with the better game. 15. axb4 Qxb4 16. Qxe4 Playing for attack. 16. exd4 was sufficient for an advantage, White having two bishops and the weak king bishop to play for. 16. ... Nc5 He can hardly try to win pawns. If dxe3 17. Bd3 g6 18. Be7 wins. 17. Be7 Of course not 17. Qxd4, because of Nb3. If 17. Qe7 d3 is strong. The text leaves White with the better ending. 17. ... Nxe4 18. Bxb4 c5

After 18. ... c5

19. Bd3 Foreseen when Be7 was played. If now dxe3 20. fxe3 cxb4 21. bxd3, White wins at least a pawn. If 19. ... Nxf2 20. Bxc5 wins. 19. ... Re8 Best, to obtain opposite colored bishops. 20. Bxe4 Rxe4 21. Bxc5 Be6 Wrong. He could have escaped with only one pawn minus by dxe3 22. fxe3 Be6 23. Rxa7 Rc8! 24. Bd4 Bxc4 25. Rc1 Re7, etc. The win in that case would have been quite difficult. 22. Bxd4 Bxc4 23. Rfc1 Bd5 24. f3 Re7 25. Rxa7 Whereas, now it is a matter of a routine advance of the kingside pawns. The rest is simply a question of time. 25. ... Rd8 26. Ra5 Bc6 27. Kf2 h6 28. h4 Red7 29. Rcc5 Ra8 30. h5 Rad8 31. b4 Rd5 32. Rxd5 Rxd5 33. g4 Kf7 34. Rc5 g6 35. hxg6+ Kxg6 36. Rc1 h5 37. gxh5+ Rxh5 38. e4 Kf7 39. Ke3 Ke6 40. Rg1 Rh7 41. Rg5 1–0 At this stage time was up and Black sealed his move, but his position is hopeless and, barring an accident White must win. Annotated by Kashdan. (*American Chess Bulletin*, April 1932)

247 Araiza–Kashdan [C47]
Mexico City, round 1, 1932 *[October 6]*

1. e4 e5 2. Nf3 Nc6 3. Nc3 Nf6 4. d4
exd4 5. Nxd4 Bb4 6. Nxc6 bxc6 7. Bd3
d5 8. exd5 cxd5 9. 0–0 0–0 10. Bg5 c6
11. Qf3 Be7 12. Rae1 Rb8 13. Qe3 Bd6
14. Qxa7 Rxb2 15. Nd1 Rb4 16. h3 h6
17. Bd2 Rh4 18. Ba5 Qd7 19. Qxd7 Bxd7
20. Bc3 Ra8 21. Bxf6 gxf6 22. Ne3 Rha4
23. Nf5 Bf8 24. Re3 Rxa2 25. Rf3 c5
26. c3 Be6 27. Ng3 R8a3 28. Rc1 Ra1
29. Bb1 Kh8 30. Re3 Bd6 31. Ne2 Rb3
32. Bc2 Rxc1+ 33. Nxc1 Ra3 34. g4 Bf4
0–1 *(Mexico City 1932)*

248 Kashdan–Asiain [C26]
Mexico City, round 2, 1932 *[October 7]*

1. e4 e5 2. Nc3 Nf6 3. Bc4 Bc5 4. f4
d6 5. Nf3 Bg4 6. h3 Bxf3 7. Qxf3 Nc6
8. d3 Nd4 9. Qg3! Qe7 But not 9. ... Nxc2+
10. Kd2 Nxa1 11. Qxg7 and if 11. ... Rg8 then
Qxf7 mate! 10. fxe5 Qxe5 11. Bf4 Qe7
12. 0–0–0 Nh5 13. Qg4 Nxf4 14. Qxf4
0–0 15. Nd5 Qd8 16. Qg4 b5 17. Bb3 c6
18. Nf4 Nxb3+ 19. axb3 Be3+ 20. Kb1
Bxf4 21. Qxf4 a5 22. d4 b4 23. g4 a4
24. bxa4 Rxa4 25. b3 Ra3 26. Kb2 Qa5
27. Qxd6 Ra2+ 28. Kc1 Qg5+ 29. Kb1
Qa5 30. Kc1 Rd8 31. Qe7 Qa3+ 32. Kd2
But not 32. ... Rxd4+? 33. Ke3! Rf8 34. Rd8
wins. 32. ... Rb8 33. Rb1 Qa8 34. Rhf1
Ra7 35. Qc5 Ra5 36. Qc4 Qa7 37. Rf3
Rd8 38. Kd3 Re5 39. Ra1 Qe7 But not
Qxa1 as 40. Qxf7+ leads to mate! 40. Re3 Re6
41. Ra4 h6 42. Qxb4 c5 43. Qb5 cxd4
44. Rxd4 Red6 45. Rd5 Qe5 46. c4 Qa1
47. Qb4 Qf1+ 48. Kc2 Qf2+ 49. Qd2
Qf4 50. Re2 Qf6 51. e5 Qg6+ 52. Qd3
Qxd3+ 53. Kxd3 Rxd5+ 54. cxd5 Rxd5+
55. Kc4 Rd8 56. b4 Rc8+ 57. Kb3 Kf8
58. e6 Re8 59. e7+ Rxe7 60. Rxe7 Kxe7
61. Kc4 Kd6 62. Kb5 Kc7 63. Kc5 f6
64. Kd5 Kd7 65. h4 g6 66. h5 gxh5
67. gxh5 1–0 *(Mexico City 1932)*

249 Medina–Kashdan [D52]
Mexico City, round 3, 1932 *[October 8]*

1. c4 Nf6 2. Nf3 c6 This move is very

popular with Kashdan and even Alekhine has
used it. After that debut, Black has at his disposal the Slav Defense, the Capablanca variation
of the Queen's Gambit, and the Cambridge
Springs Defense. 3. d4 d5 4. Nc3 e6 5. Bg5
Nbd7 6. e3 Qa5 7. Nd2 Also to be considered here is 7. cxd5 Nxd5 8. Qb3 Bb4. 7. ...
Bb4 8. Qc2 0–0 9. Bh4 c5 This move was
played by Alekhine in the 7th game in his match
with Capablanca in 1927. The game continued
10. Nb3 Qa4 11. Bxf6 Nxf6 12. dxc5 Ne4 13. cxd5
Bxc3+ with advantage to White. 10. dxc5 Ne4
11. cxd5 Why not 11. Ndxe4 dxe4 12. Be7 Re8
13. Bd6. 11. ... exd5 12. Rc1 Ndxc5
13. Ndxe4 Nxe4 14. Bd3 This loses a pawn,
but there is nothing else. 14. ... Qxa2 15. 0–0
Bxc3 16. Bxe4 dxe4 17. Qxc3 Bd7
18. Qb4 Bc6 19. Rfd1 Qe6 20. Qd6 Qb3
21. Qd4 Rfe8 22. h3 a5 23. Qc3 Qe6
24. Qa3 a4 25. Rc3 h6 26. Rd6 Qe5
27. Rd4 Ra5 28. Bg3 Qh5 During the next
12 moves Black unsuccessfully attempts a direct
attack against the White king. 29. Bc7 Rg5
30. Bf4 Rg6 31. Kh2 Qe2 32. Bg3 Rg5
33. Qa1 Re6 34. Qc1 Reg6 35. Rd2 Qb5
36. Rdc2 Qd5 37. Rc5 Qe6 38. Rxg5
Rxg5 39. Rc5 f6 40. Rxg5 hxg5 41. Qc3
Qd7 42. Qb4 Qd3 43. Qe7 Qb3 44. Qa3
Qc2 45. h4 gxh4 46. Bxh4 Kf7 47. Qb4
b5 48. Qd6 g5 49. Bg3 Be8 50. Qd5+
Kg7 51. Qb7+ Kg6 52. Qe7 Bf7 53. Qb4
Qc4 Realizing that no headway can be made
until the queens are exchanged. [*White probably should not have exchanged queens.–P.P.L.*]
54. Qxc4 Bxc4 55. Bd6 Kf5 56. f3

After
56. f3

This move should have been delayed until
after Kg3. 56. ... Ke6 57. Bb4 exf3 58. gxf3
f5 59. Kg3 Be2 60. Bc3 Bd1 61. Bd2 Kf6

62. Bc3+ Kg6 63. Bb4 Kh5 64. Be7 Bb3
65. Kh3 Bd5 66. Kg3 Bc6 67. Kf2 Kg6
68. Kg3 Bb7 69. Bb4 Kf6 70. Bc3+ Kg6
71. Bb4 Bc8 72. Be7 Bd7 73. Bb4 Kf7
74. Ba5 Ke6 75. Bc3 Kd5 Kashdan's plan
is as follows: 1. To obtain a passed pawn on the
g file; 2. To blockade the White e pawn with
the bishop at e6; 3. To advance the queenside
pawn supported by the king at b3. 76. Bf6 g4
77. Kf4 Kc4 78. fxg4 fxg4 79. Be7 Kb3
80. Bf6 b4 81. Bd4 a3 82. bxa3 bxa3
83. e4 Kc2 84. e5 a2 85. Ke4 Kb1
86. Kf4 a1Q 87. Bxa1 Kxa1 88. Ke3 Kb2
89. Kd2 Kb1 90. Ke3 Kc1 91. Ke2 Kc2
92. Ke3 Kd1 93. Kf2 Be6 94. Ke3 Kc1
95. Ke2 Kc2 96. Ke3 Kd1 97. Kf2 Kd2
98. Kf1 Ke3 99. Kg2 Kf4 100. Kf2 g3+
101. Kf1 Kf3 0–1 Kashdan deserves credit
for working out the difficult win with bishops
of opposite colors against the promising young
Mexican player Medina, who refused to make
any serious mistakes throughout the entire contest. Analysis from *The Gambit* 1932. (*Mexico
City* 1932)

250 Kashdan–González [C86]
Mexico City, round 4, 1932 *[October 10]*

1. e4 e5 2. Nf3 Nc6 3. Bb5 a6 4. Ba4
Nf6 5. 0–0 Be7 6. Qe2 d6 7. c3 b5
8. Bc2 Bg4 9. h3 Bh5 10. d3 Rb8 11. g4
Bg6 12. Nh4 Qd7 13. f4 Nxe4 14. Nxg6
hxg6 15. dxe4 Rxh3 16. Kg2 Rh4 17. f5
gxf5 18. exf5 e4 19. Bxe4 Ne5 20. Bf3
g6 21. Bf4 gxf5 22. Bxe5 fxg4 23. Bd5
dxe5 24. Bxf7+ Kd8 25. Nd2 g3 26. Rh1
Qc6+ 27. Nf3 Rh2+ 28. Rxh2 gxh2
29. Qxe5 Bd6 30. Qh8+ Ke7 31. Qxb8
Kxf7 32. Qh8 Qe4 33. Qd4 Qe2+
34. Qf2 Qe4 35. Re1 Bc5 36. Qg3 1–0
(*Mexico City* 1932)

251 Vázquez–Kashdan [D94]
Mexico City, round 5, 1932 *[October 11]*

1. d4 Nf6 2. Nf3 g6 3. c4 Bg7 4. Nc3
d5 5. e3 0–0 6. Bd2 c6 7. Rc1 Ne4
8. Bd3 Nxd2 9. Qxd2 dxc4 10. Bxc4
Nd7 11. 0–0 e5 12. d5 Nb6 13. Bb3 cxd5
14. Nxd5 e4 15. Nxb6 Qxb6 16. Ng5

Bf5 17. Rc4 Rae8 18. Rb4 Qf6 19. h4 h6
20. Nxf7 Rxf7 21. Bxf7+ Qxf7 22. Rd1
Re7 23. Qd5 Qxd5 24. Rxd5 h5 25. b3
Kf7 26. Rd8 Bf6 27. g3 Rc7 28. Rd2 b5
29. Rxb5 Bg4 30. f4 exf3 31. Kf2 Bc3
32. Rdd5 Bb4 0–1 (*Mexico City* 1932)

252 Alekhine–Kashdan [C79]
Mexico City, round 6, 1932 *[October 12]*

1. e4 e5 2. Nf3 Nc6 3. Bb5 a6 4. Ba4
Nf6 5. 0–0 d6 6. c3 g6 7. d4 Bd7
8. Nbd2 b5 9. Bc2 Bg7 10. dxe5 dxe5
11. Nb3 Be6 12. Nc5 Bc4 13. Qxd8+
Nxd8 14. Re1 Nd7 15. Nxd7 Kxd7 16. a4
Nb7 17. b3 Be6 18. Ng5 Nc5 19. Rd1+
Kc6 20. Nxe6 Nxe6 21. b4 Rhd8 22. g3
Kb7 23. Be3 Rxd1+ 24. Bxd1 Bf8
25. Bb3 c6 26. h4 Bd6 27. Kg2 Bc7
28. axb5 axb5 29. Rxa8 Kxa8 30. Bxe6
fxe6 31. Bh6 Kb7 32. h5 Kc8 33. Kh3
Kd7 34. Bg7 Ke7 35. Kg4 Kf7 36. h6
Bb6 37. f3 Bc7 38. Bh8 Bd6 39. Bg7
Bc7 40. Bh8 Bd6 41. Kh4 Be7+ 42. Kh3
Bd6 43. Kg4 Bb8 44. Kg5 Bd6 45. Bf6
Bc7 46. Bh8 ½–½ (*Mexico City* 1932)

253 Kashdan–Brunner [B41]
Mexico City, round 7, 1932 *[October 14]*

1. e4 c5 2. Nf3 e6 3. d4 cxd4 4. Nxd4
a6 5. c4 Nf6 6. Nc3 d5 7. cxd5 exd5
8. Qa4+ Bd7 9. Qb3 Bc5 10. Be3 dxe4
11. Qxb7 Bxd4 12. Bxd4 Bc6 13. Qb4 a5
14. Qc5 Qe7 15. Nb5 Nd5 16. Qxe7+
Kxe7 17. Bxg7 Rg8 18. Be5 Rg5 19. Bg3
Bxb5 20. Bxb5 Ne3 21. Ba4 Nf5 22. Rc1
Na6 23. Rc4 Nxg3 24. hxg3 Re5
25. Rxh7 Nc5 26. Ke2 Rb8 27. b3 Rd8
28. Rh1 Red5 29. Rhc1 Kd6 30. Rd1
Ke5? 31. Rxc5 1–0 (*Mexico City* 1932)

254 Acevedo–Kashdan [D52]
Mexico City, round 8, 1932 *[October 15]*

1. d4 Nf6 2. c4 e6 3. Nf3 d5 4. Nc3
Nbd7 5. Bg5 c6 6. e3 Qa5 7. Bxf6 Nxf6
8. Nd2 Be7 9. Bd3 0–0 10. Qc2 Qc7
11. 0–0 Rd8 12. Rae1 dxc4 13. Nxc4 c5
14. f4 a6 15. dxc5 Bxc5 16. Ne4 Nxe4

17. Bxe4 f5 18. Bd3 b5 19. Ne5 Qb6
20. Rf3 Bb7 21. Rg3 Rac8 22. Qe2 Bd6
23. Kh1 Bxe5 24. fxe5 Rc5 25. b4 Rxe5
26. Qb2 Qc7 27. Rc1? Rxd3! 28. Rxg7+
Qxg7 0–1 (*Mexico City 1932*)

255 Kashdan–Lorrea [E16]

Mexico City, round 9, 1932 *[October 16]*

1. d4 Nf6 2. c4 e6 3. Nf3 b6 4. g3 Bb7
5. Bg2 Bb4+ 6. Nbd2 c5 7. a3 Bxd2+
8. Qxd2 cxd4 9. Qxd4 Nc6 10. Qc3 Qc7
11. 0–0 h6 12. b4 d6 13. Re1 Ne5
14. Nxe5 Bxg2 15. Nxf7 Qxf7 16. Kxg2
0–0 17. f3 Rac8 18. Qb3 d5 19. cxd5
Nxd5 20. Bd2 Qf6 21. Rac1 Qe5 22. e4
Rxc1 23. Rxc1 Qd4 24. Rc2 Nc7 25. Bf4
1–0 (*Mexico City 1932*)

256 Kashdan (Manhattan)– Fine (Marshall) [D18]

Metropolitan Chess League, 1933 *[April]*

1. d4 Nf6 2. c4 c6 3. Nc3 d5 4. Nf3
dxc4 5. a4 To prevent e5. White can also regain the pawn by 5. e3 b5 6. a4 b4 7. Na2 e6
8. Bxc4 Nbd7. **5. ...** Bf5 6. e3 e6 6. ... Na6
7. Bxc4 Nb4 8. 0–0 is frequently played here.
In spite of its appearance, the knight is not well
placed here. 7. Bxc4 Bb4 8. 0–0 0–0
9. Qb3 Qe7 10. Bd2 Nbd7? 11. Rfe1 h6
12. e4 Bh7 13. e5 Ne8 14. a5 Nc7 15. Ne4
But this exchange of bishops relieves Black's
game. Correct is Ra4! 15. ... Bxd2 16. Nfxd2
Rab8 17. Re3 c5 18. Nxc5 Nxc5 19. dxc5
Qxc5 20. Qa3 Qd4 21. Qc3 Rfd8 22. Nf3
Qxc3 23. Rxc3 Be4 24. Be2 Bc6 25. Rac1
Rd5 26. a6 Ne8 27. axb7 Bxb7 28. Ra3
a5 29. h3 Kf8 30. b3 Ke7 31. Rca1 Nc7

After
31. ... Nc7

Missing his chance. 31. ... Rc5 32. Rxa5 Rxa5
33. Rxa5 Bxf3 34. Bxf3 Rxb3 would probably
draw. 32. Bc4 Rd7 33. Rxa5 Bd5 34. Ra7
Nb5 35. Rxd7+ Kxd7 36. Ra5 Nc7
37. Bxd5 Nxd5 38. Ra7+ Nc7 39. Nd2
Nd4 was a bit better, though the text is quite
sufficient. 39. ... Rb6 40. Kf1 Rb8 41. Ke2
Rb5 42. f4 g5 43. g3 h5 44. Kf3 h4
45. gxh4 gxf4 46. Kxf4 Rb4+ 47. Kg3
White could have won more prettily by 47. Ne4
Kc6 48. Rxc7+! Kxc7 h5, etc. 47. ... Rb5
48. Nf3 Rxb3 49. h5 Kc6 50. h6 Rb8
51. Ng5 Rg8 52. Kh4 Kb6 53. Rxc7!
1–0 Analysis by Kashdan from *Chess Review*,
May 1933. (*New York Sun*, April 21, 1933)

257 Kashdan–Levin [C71]

Metropolitan Chess League, 1933

1. e4 e5 2. Nf3 Nc6 3. Bb5 a6 4. Ba4
d6 5. d4 b5 6. Bb3 Nxd4 7. Nxd4 exd4
8. Bd5 Rb8 9. Qxd4 Bd7 10. c3 Nf6
11. 0–0 Be7 12. Bb3 0–0 13. Bc2 Bc6
14. Bf4 Nd7 15. Nd2 Bf6 16. Qe3 Re8
17. a3 Qe7 18. Rfe1 Nc5 19. Qh3 Qe6
20. Qxe6 Nxe6 21. Be3 Rbd8 22. f4 Bb7
23. Rad1 Nf8 24. g3 Nd7 25. Bf2 Re7
26. Re2 Rde8 27. Rde1 g6 28. Bd4 c5
29. Bxf6 Nxf6 30. h3 Kg7 31. Kf2 Nd7
32. g4 f6 33. h4 c4 34. Nf3 Nc5 35. Nd2
h6 36. Re3 Bc6 37. R3e2 Ba8 38. Re3
Bb7 39. R1e2 Ba8 40. Re1 Bc6 41. R3e2
g5 42. hxg5 hxg5 43. fxg5 fxg5 44. Nf3
½–½ (*Brooklyn Daily Eagle*, May 4, 1933)

258 Kashdan–Willman [C49]

Manhattan Club Championship, 1932

1. e4 e5 2. Nf3 Nc6 3. Nc3 Nf6 4. Bb5
Bb4 5. 0–0 0–0 6. d3 d6 7. Bg5 Bxc3
8. bxc3 Qe7 9. c4 Bg4 10. c3 Nd8 11. h3
Bxf3 12. Qxf3 Ne6 13. Be3 Nc5 14. Bxc5
dxc5 15. Ba4 Rad8 16. Qe3 b6 17. Bd1
Nd7 18. Be2 Rfe8 19. g3 Nf8 20. Kh2
Rd6 21. f4 f5 22. Bf3 exf4 23. gxf4 Red8
24. Rad1 Qd7 25. Be2 fxe4 26. dxe4
Qe7 27. e5 Rxd1 28. Rxd1 Rxd1 29. Bxd1
Ne6 30. Bf3 Qh4 31. f5 If 31. Bd5 Qh6
preventing f5. 31. ... Qf4+ 32. Qxf4 Nxf4
33. Kg3 Nd3 34. e6 Kf8 35. Be4 Nb2

36. Bd5 Nd1 37. Kf4 Nxc3 38. Ke5 Ke7 39. a3 Nb1 40. a4 Nc3 41. Bc6 Na2 42. h4 Nb4 43. Be4 a6 44. h5 h6 45. f6+ gxf6+ 46. Kf5 c6 47. Kg6 Kxe6 48. Kxh6 Kf7 49. Kh7 b5 0–1 (*American Chess Bulletin*, December 1932.)

259 Schwartz–Kashdan [C79]
Manhattan Club Championship, 1933

1. e4 e5 2. Nf3 Nc6 3. Bb5 a6 4. Ba4 Nf6 5. 0–0 d6 6. c3 Be7 7. d3 0–0 8. Nbd2 b5 9. Bc2 d5 10. exd5 Qxd5 11. Qe2 Bg4 12. Re1 Rfe8 13. Nf1 Bxf3 14. Qxf3 Qxf3 15. gxf3 Bd6 16. Ng3 Ne7 17. Bd2 Ng6 18. Nf5 Bf8 19. Re2 Rad8 20. Rae1 c5 21. Bg5 Re6 22. Nh4 Rde8 23. Nxg6 hxg6 24. Bb3 Rd6 25. d4 cxd4 26. cxd4 Rxd4 27. Rxe5 Rc8 28. R1e2 Bd6 29. Bxf6 gxf6 30. R5e4 Rd3 31. Kg2 Kg7 32. R4e3 Rd4 33. Re4 Rxe4 34. fxe4 Rc5 35. h3 Be5 36. a4 bxa4 37. Bxa4 Rc4 38. Bd1 Rc1 39. Ba4 Rb1 40. b3 Kf8 41. Ra2 Bd4 42. Rc2 Ke7 43. Rd2 Bb6 44. Rc2 ½–½ (*American Chess Bulletin*, February 1933)

260 Denker–Kashdan [E16]
Manhattan Club Championship, 1932

1. Nf3 Nf6 2. d4 e6 3. c4 b6 4. g3 Bb7 5. Bg2 Bb4+ 6. Bd2 Qe7 7. 0–0 Bxd2 8. Qxd2 0–0 9. Nc3 d6 10. Ne1 Bxg2 11. Nxg2 Nbd7 12. e4 Rfd8 13. f4 Nf8 14. Qe2! e5 15. fxe5 dxe5 16. d5 Ng6 17. Ne3 Qc5 18. Kg2 Rac8 19. h4 c6 20. Rad1 cxd5 21. exd5! e4 22. b3 Re8 23. Nf5 Re5 24. Nb5 a6 25. Na7! Rc7 26. Nc6 Re8 27. Qb2 Rxc6 28. dxc6 Ne5 29. Rd6! Nfg4 30. Rf4 Ne3+ 31. Nxe3 Qxd6 32. Rxe4 Qxc6 33. Nd5 Nd3? 34. Qe2! Wins a piece. 34. ... Rxe4 35. Qxe4 He cannot save the piece and guard against 36. Ne7+ at the same time. 1–0 (Denker, *If You Must Play Chess*)

261 Kashdan–Asgeirsson
   (Iceland) [C41]
Folkestone Olympiad, round 1, 1933 *[June 12]*

1. e4 e5 2. Nf3 d6 The Philidor Defense,

a rarity in modern chess, being considered too backward and passive for successful play. **3. d4 exd4** This gives up the center without a struggle. Better is 3. ... Nf6 4. Nc3 Nbd7 5. Bc4 Be7 followed by 0–0, c6 and Qc7 etc. (The Hanham Variation), although here too Black is rather constricted. **4. Nxd4 Nf6 5. Nc3 Nc6 6. Bb5** It is now a variation of the Ruy Lopez which is favorable to White. Also good is 6. Be2, as later played. If then 6. ... d5? attempting to equalize, 7. Bb5! wins at least a pawn. **6. ... Bd7 7. 0–0 Nxd4 8. Qxd4 Be7** 8. ... Bxb5 9. Nxb5 a6 10. Nc3 Be7 would have been more consistent with Black's last move, but White's command of the center assures him a lasting advantage. **9. Be2** White's pieces being all freer than Black's, it is desirable to avoid unnecessary exchanges. **9. ... 0–0 10. b3** Hoping to command the long diagonal and play for a kingside attack. A good alternative is 10. Bf4 Re8 11. Rad1, with pressure on the center **10. ... Ne8 11. Ba3** An odd looking move, the plan being, after ...Bf6; to play for f4 and e5. Black avoids this, but at the expense of weakening his queenside pawns. A simpler line was 11. Nd5 Bf6 12. Nxf6+ Qxf6 13. Bb2. The two bishops would prove very strong in this type of position. **11. ... c6** Leaving the d pawn backward, but there is hardly any other method of getting his pieces in play. If 11. ... Bf6 12. Qd3 Bc6 13. f3, followed by Rad1 Nd4, etc. Black's knight would be quite out of play in this variation. **12. Rad1 Qa5 13. Bb2 Be6 14. Qe3 Bf6 15. f4** Allowing the exchange of queens, but White has all the better of the ending. If instead 15. Kh1 c5! 16. f4 Bd4 with a satisfactory game. **15. ... Qb6** If now ...c5 16. e5! would open all White's attacking lines very effectively. **16. Qxb6 axb6 17. a4 Rd8 18. Rd2 d5** Sooner or later necessary. as otherwise Black can hardly move a piece. It creates additional targets for attack, however. **19. exd5 Bxc3** Forced to avoid the isolation of the d pawn. **20. Bxc3 Rxd5 21. Rfd1 Nc7** At last the knight can move, but he is not to find a secure square. If ...Nd6 22. Bbb4 Rd8 23. Rxd5 cxd5 24. Bf3 Ne8 25. c4 Nc7 26. a5! b5 (if ...bxa5 27. Bxa5 Rd7 28. Bxc7 Rxc7 Bxd5 wins); 27. Bc5 Rd7 28. Bb6, and he must win the d pawn. The weakness of the knight, which is always subject to attack, is very apparent. **22. Be5 Na6** The knight must move. Not ...Rfd8 23. Rxd5 Nxd5 24. c4 winning a piece. **23. Rxd5 Bxd5 24. Bd4 Nc5 25. a5!**

After 25. a5

This does not win a pawn, but White obtains a pawn majority on the queenside, which, with the aid of the two bishops, soon becomes a decisive factor. **25. ... Ne6 26. Bxb6 Nxf4 27. Bf1 Be6 28. c4 f6 29. Rd6** A strong move, which obtains a passed pawn by force through the following exchange. **29. ... Kf7 30. a6 bxa6 31. Rxc6 Rc8 32. Rd6 Ke7 33. Rd2 Rc6 34. Bd4 Bc8** Allowing the immediate advance of the pawn, which could not be delayed for long, however. **35. b4 Ne6 36. Be3 Rd6 37. Ra2** Exchanging rooks would leave the Black king well posted. White can already visualize some mating threats later, with the combination of rook and both bishops. **37. ... Rd1 38. Kf2 Rb1 39. Bd2 39.** b5 could be played, but White wishes to drive the rook off first. **39. ... g5 40. Bd3 Rh1** Evidently not ...Rb3? 41. Bc2 wins. **41. h3 h5 42. b5** An attempt to shut the rook out by Bf1 would be unavailing because of 42. ... g4, threatening g3+. White need not be concerned with the kingside, but can go on with the strong passed pawn, which will be difficult to stop. **42. ... axb5 43. Bb4+** Placing Black in a quandary. If the king goes to the queenside, he will be exposed to attack; if he moves out of action, the pawn will advance more readily. **43. ... Kd8 44. cxb5 Nf4 45. Be4 Nxh3+!** (*see diagram*)

A clever idea. If 46. gxh3 Rh2+ 47. Bg2 Bxh3 48. Kg3 Rxg2+ 49. Rxg2 Bxg2 50. Kxg2 Kc7 would draw, since in order to win the Black pawns, White must give up his one pawn. How-

After 45. ... Nxh3

ever, White need not take the knight, which must lose time in moving again. **46. Ke3! f5** This drives the bishop to the strongest square, but the game is lost in any case. If ...Nf4 47. Ra7 Bd7 48. b6, etc. **47. Bc6 Nf4 48. Ra7 Nxg2+** This time it is desperation. White could easily take the knight, but prefers to maintain the mating threats. **49. Kf2 1–0** Annotated by Kashdan. (*Chess Review*, July 1936)

262 Fairhurst (Scotland)– Kashdan [D15]

Folkestone Olympiad, round 2, 1933 *[June 13]*

1. d4 Nf6 2. c4 c6 3. Nf3 d5 4. Nc3 dxc4 5. e3 b5 6. a4 b4 7. Na2 e6 8. Bxc4 Nbd7 9. 0–0 Bb7 10. Qe2 c5 11. Ne5 A suggestion of Bogoljubow's; a strong method of attack. **11. ... cxd4** To isolate the d pawn; but the opening of the king's file gives White too many chances. A line worth considering is 11. ... Nxe5 12. dxe5 Nd7 13. f4 Qc7 14. Rd1 0–0! White can do little on the queenside, whereas Black threatens b5 and Rb8, etc. **12. exd4 Bd5** Forced. If 12. ... Be7 13. Nxf7! Kxf7 14. Qxe6+ wins. **13. Bg5** If 13. Bb5 Be7 14. Bg5 0–0, and Black escapes. The text is the strongest. **13. ... Bxc4 14. Qxc4 h6** Forcing the issue. If 14. ... Rc8 15. Qa6, or 14. ... Be7 15. Nxb4 wins. **15. Bxf6 gxf6 16. Nc6** He cannot win a pawn. If 16. Nxd7 Qxd7 17. Nxb4 Rc8 18. Qb3 Rb8 wins a piece. **16. ... Qc7 17. Rfe1** Not 17. Nxb4 Bxb4 wins the knight. Black has thus succeeded in avoiding material loss, but there are worse things in store. White threatens Rxe6+, which seems to win by force. Black has a defense however, which shows the move to have been premature. Correct was 17. Rac1 a4 (to save the pawn) 18. Rfe1. White thus gains a clear move, which as will soon appear, would have made the attack decisive. **17. ... Nb6**

After
17. ... Nb6

18. Rxe6+ Extremely tempting, but it proves unsound. There was little choice, however. If 18. Qb5 a6 wins a piece. If 18. Qc2 b3!. His best was 18. Qc1 Nd5 (threatening Rc8) 19. Qc4 Nb6 with a draw by repetition of moves. **18. ... Kd7!** Best. If 18. ... fxe6 19. Qxe6+ Be7 20. Re1 Nc8 21. Nxb4 with a winning attack. After the text, the rook cannot escape because of the attack on the queen. Had White's queen rook been at c1, as indicated above, he could have won at once by Ne5+! **19. Qb5 fxe6** If 19. ... Kxe6 20. Re1+ Kd6 21. Qc5+ Kd7 22. Qf5+ Kxc3 23. c1+ Kb7 24. Qe4+ Kb8 25. Rxc7 Kxc7 26. a5. Black would have only two rooks for the queen, instead of three pieces as actually played, with no more than even chances. **20. Ne5+** If 20. Rc1 a6 21. Ne5+ Kd8 22. Qa5 Qb7 23. Nc6+ Ke8 and Black has an easy defense. **20. ... Kd8 21. Rc1 fxe5** Giving up the queen, but remaining with two rooks and a bishop, equivalent to a piece ahead. If now 21. ... Qb7 22. Nc6+ Ke8 23. Ne5+ would draw. **22. Rxc7 Kxc7 23. Nxb4 Bxb4 24. Qxb4 exd4 25. Qe7+ Kc6** If 25. ... Nd7 26. Qxe6 and White wins the d pawn as well. The king is quite safe in advancing, except that the possibility of perpetual check, which is White's only hope, is increased. **26. Qxe6+ Kc5 27. Qf5+** If 27. Qe5+ Nd5! 28. b4+ Kc4 29. Qe2+ d6! (not Kxb4 30. Qb5+ winning the knight in a less favorable position for Black) 30. Qe4+ Kc3 31. Qxd5 Rac8 32. Qe5+ Kc2 followed by Rad8 and the advance of the d pawn. White rightly avoids this variation, and plays to win the d pawn. **27. ... Nd5 28. Qc2+ Kd6 29. Qg6+ Ke5 30. Qh5+** Not 30. g3 Ra g8 31. f4+ Nxf4!

wins. The text forces Black to return to the other side. **30. ... Kd6 31. Qg6+ Kc5 32. Qc2+ Kb4 33. Qd2+ Kxa4 34. Qxd4+ Nb4 35. Qd1+ Ka5 36. Qh5+ Kb6 37. Qg6+ Nc6** At last Black is out of check, and the position has cleared. It is now a matter of getting the rooks into play, and either winning the pawns, or building up mating threats. **38. h4 Rad8 39. Qc2 Rhe8 40. Qb3+ Kc7 41. Qg3+ Rd6 42. Qc3 Re4 43. g3 a5 44. Kg2 Re2 45. g4 Rdd2 46. Qg7+ Kb6 47. Qxh6 Rxf2+ 48. Kg3 Rg2+ 49. Kf3 Rdf2+ 50. Ke3 Rxb2 51. g5 Rg4 52. g6 Rb3+ 53. Kf2 Ra4** The threat of mate forces the queen away from the support of the pawns. **54. Qc1 Rxh4 55. Qg1 Rh2+!** A pretty finish. If 56. Ke1+ Kb7 57. Qxh7 Rb8+ wins the queen. **0–1** Annotated by Kashdan. (*Folkestone 1933*)

263 Kashdan–Alekhine (France) [D41]

Folkestone Olympiad, round 3, 1933 *[June 14]*

1. d4 Nf6 2. c4 e6 3. Nf3 d5 4. Nc3 c5 5. cxd5 Nxd5 5. ... exd5 6. g3 Nc6 is the more usual form of this defense. The text is also sufficient to equalize. **6. Nxd5** This only helps Black's development. 6. e4 Nxc3 7. bxc3 would have given White a strong center. **6. ... Qxd5 7. Be3** An interesting move. The threat dxc5 forces Black's hand and prevents the normal continuation 7. ... Nc6. **7. ... Na6** If 7. ... cxd4 8. Qxd4 Qxd4 9. Nxd4 and White has gained time. Or 7. ... c4 8. g3 and White will gain the long diagonal. **8. g3** This allows Black to exchange with considerable gain in development through Bb4+. Better was 8. dxc5 Qxd1+ 9. Rxd1 Nxc5 10. g3, when White is about two moves ahead of the position actually obtained in the game. **8. ... cxd4 9. Qxd4 Bb4+ 10. Bd2 Qxd4 11. Nxd4 Bxd2+ 12. Kxd2 e5 13. Nf3** To gain time for e4, by attacking the pawn. The knight proves somewhat misplaced. on f3 however. If 13. Ng5 Ke7 14. Bg2 Rd8+ 15. Ke3 Bd7 16. Nf3 Nb4 17. Rac1 Bc6 with about an even game. **13. ... f6 14. e4 Nc5 15. Ke3 Bd7 16. Rc1 Rc8 17. b4** In order to effect the following exchange of bishops. But it weakens the queenside, where Black soon tries to effect an entry, 17. Be2 Ke7 18. Rc2 followed by doubling on either the c or d file would have equalized more easily. **17. ... Ne6 18. Bb5 Ke7 19. B×d7 K×d7 20. Kd2** To play 21. R×c8 R×c8 22. Rc1 and exchange both pairs of rooks. Black's reply prevents this. Stronger was 20. Rhd1+ Ke7 21. Ne1 Nd4 22. f4 Ke6 23. Nd3, with an even game. **20. ... Rc6 21. R×c6 K×c6 22. a4** Necessary to prevent Kb5, when the pawn would soon fall. **22. ... Rd8+ 23. Ke3 a5** After this pawn sacrifice Black can easily regain the pawn, but nothing more, and he has no real winning chances. There were more prospects with 23. ... Kb6 24. Rb1 Nd4 25. N×d4 R×d4; but 26. f4 gives White counter chances, and there is no way to break through. **24. b×a5 Nc5 25. Rc1 Rd3+ 26. Ke2 Ra3 27. Nd2 Ra2 28. Ke3 Kd6** 28. ... Ra3+ 29. Ke2 Ra2 would draw, as White has nothing better than Ke6. With the text Black plays for a win, but he comes nearer to losing. **29. Nc4+ Ke6 30. Nb6**

After 30. Nb6

30. ... Ra3+ He could have played N×e4 at once. See the diagram. If 31. K×e4? Ra6! 32. g4 g6 forces mate. But after 30. ... N×e4 31. Rc7! Black is not so well off. **31. Ke2 N×e4 32. Rc7 Nc3+**

After 32. ... Nc3

Best. This clears up the queenside, and succeeds in drawing. If 32. ... Nd6 33. R×g7 wins. But still not the tempting 33. R×h7 N×b7 34. a6 Nc5! 35. a7 N×a4 36. a8(Q) Nc3+ 37. Kd3 R×a8 38. N×a8 Nd5 wins. **33. Kf1 N×a4 34. N×a4** The exchange of knights is necessary. If 34. R×b7 Nc4 35. R×g7 R×a4 36. R×h7 Ra2, followed by Ne4 with annoying possibilities. **34. ... R×a4 35. R×b7 R×a5 36. R×g7 h5 37. Rh7** White must win a pawn, but it turns out that it is insufficient to win in the rook ending. **37. ... e4 38. Ke2 f5** Giving up the pawn at once, but it cannot be held. If 38. ... Re5 39. Ke3 Kd5 40. h4 Ke6 41. Kf4 Kd5 42. Ra7 Ke6 43. Ra6+ Ke7 44. Ra4 wins the pawn. **39. Rh6+** If at once 39. R×h4 Ra2+ 40. Kf1 Ra1+ 41. Kg2 Ra2, threatening e3 draws. **39. ... Ke5 40. R×h5 Ra2+ 41. Kf1 e3** Whereas now if 41. ... Ra1+ 42. Kg2 Ra2 43. g4! e3 44. R×f5+ Ke4 45. Rf8 e2 46. Re8+ Kd3 47. Kf3! wins. The text gives up a second pawn, which Black soon regains however, obtaining a drawn ending. Also good was 41. ... Kf6, as White can never free his king without exchanging pawns. **42. f×e3 Ke4 43. Kg1** If 43. h4 Ra3 regains the pawn with a position similar to that in the game. But not 43. ... Kf3? 44. R×f5+ K×g3 45. h5 wins. **43. ... Re2 44. Rh4+ Ke5 45. Rh8 Kf6 46. Rf8+ Kg6 47. Re8 Kf7 48. Rc8 R×e3 49. Kf2 Ra3 50. h4 Kf6 51. Rc6+ Kf7 52. Rc2 Rb3 53. Re2 Kf6 54. Re3 Rb4 55. Kf3 Ra4 56. Rb3 Rc4 57. Rb6+ Kf7 58. Rd6 Ra4** The White king cannot be advanced; if 59. Ke3 (to play Rd4) Re4+ 60. Kf3 (otherwise Rg4) Ra4, etc. If the h pawn advances, the Black king moves in front of it, and there is nothing further to do. ½–½ Annotated by Kashdan. (*Folkestone 1933*)

264 Tartakower (Poland)– Kashdan [A05]

Folkestone Olympiad, round 4, 1933 *[June 15]*

1. Nf3 Nf6 2. e3 d5 3. b3 A system frequently played by Nimzovitch. It reverses the various possible advances (c4, d4, etc.) till Black has declared himself. **3. ... g6 4. Bb2 Bg7 5. c4 d×c4 6. B×c4** 6. b×c4 c5 7. d4 gives White a strong center, though in practice his c pawn often becomes a weakness. **6. ... c5**

7. 0–0 0–0 8. d4 cxd4 9. Nxd4 a6 Better than 9. ... e5 10. Nb5 Nc6 11. Nd6 with advantage. **10. Nc3 b5 11. Be2 Bb7 12. Bf3 Ra7** A peculiar looking move, but it is the best method of getting the rook into play. The knight at b8 is best placed at home for the moment, to guard against Nc6. **13. Bxb7 Rxb7 14. Qf3 Rd7 15. Nc6** Losing time, by exchanging a centrally-placed piece for an undeveloped one. 15. Rad1, and if e5, 16. Nc6 was better. **15. ... Nxc6 16. Qxc6 Rd6 17. Qf3 Nd7** Black now has pressure on the long diagonal, due to the pinned knight. **18. Rad1 Nc5** 18. ... Ne5 19. Qe2 Nd3 20. Ba1 leads to nothing. The text threatens 19. ... b4 20. Na4 Nxa4, breaking up White's pawns. **19. Rxd6 Qxd6 20. Rd1 Qe6 21. Qe2 Rc8 22. Nd5 Ne4 23. Bxg7 Kxg7 24. Qb2+ f6 25. f3?** Overlooking the pretty knight move, which forces the win of a pawn. Black has a shade the better of the position, owing to the unstable position of the knight at d5. If 25. Nf4 Qf5 26. Rd5 e5 27. h3 (threatening to win the queen), Rc6 28. g4 Qc8, forcing an entrance by Rc2. **25. ... Nc3 26. Nxc3 Qxe3+ 27. Kh1 Rxc3 28. h3 b4 29. Qb1 e5 30. Re1 Qd3 31. Qxd3 Rxd3** The rook ending is easily won, as Black soon obtains a passed pawn. **32. Re2 Kf7 33. Rc2 Rc3 34. Rd2 Ke6 35. Kg1 f5 36. Kf2 g5 37. Ke2 a5 38. Kd1 e4 39. fxe4 fxe4 40. Rd8 Rg3**

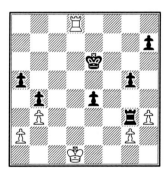

After
40. ... Rg3

The pawn ending is won after 40. ... Rd3+ 41. Rxd3 exd3, but the play has to be carefully timed. Best is 42. Kd2 Ke5 43. Kxe4 **41. Ra8 Rxg2 42. Rxa5 Kf6 43. Ke1 Rh2 44. Ra4 Kf5** 44. ... Rxh3 45. Rxb4 Rh1+ 46. Ke2 Rh2+ 47. Ke3 Rxa2 48. Rxe4 h5 was sufficient to win. With the text Black keeps all his kingside pawns.

45. Rxb4 Rxa2 46. Rb7 h5 47. Rf7+ Ke5 48. b4 Rh2 49. b5 Rxh3 50. b6 Rb3 51. b7 h4 52. Kf2 g4 53. Re7+ Kf4 54. Rf7+ Kg5 55. Re7 h3 The quickest, as the pawns can no longer be stopped. **56. Rxe4 Rb2+ 57. Ke2 h2 58. Rg4+ Kf5 59. Rxg3 Rb2+** 59. ... Rxb7 would also win. White resigned at this point, but he could conclude the game also with 60. Kg3 Rg2 mate. **0–1** Annotated by Kashdan. (*Folkestone 1933*)

265 Kashdan–Soultanbéieff (Belgium) [D16]
Folkestone Olympiad, round 5, 1933 *[June 15]*

1. d4 d5 2. c4 c6 3. Nc3 Nf6 4. Nf3 dxc4 5. a4 e6 6. e3 Nbd7 7. Bxc4 Bb4 8. 0–0 0–0 9. Qe2 Qa5! 10. Bd2! e5! 11. e4! exd4 12. Nxd4 Ne5 13. Ba2 Bg4!? 14. f3 Bc5 15. Be3 Bxd4 16. Bxd4 Be6!? 17. f4 Ned7 18. Bxe6 fxe6 19. Qc4 Rfe8 20. f5 Ne5! 21. Qb3 Qc7 22. fxe6 Neg4 23. g3 Qd6! 24. Rad1 Qxe6 25. Qxe6+ Rxe6 26. h3 Nh6 27. Bxf6 Rxf6 28. Rxf6 gxf6 29. Rd7 Rb8 30. Kf2? Much better is 30. a5! and if 30. ... Nf7 31. Na4 Ng5! 32. Nc5 b6. But better yet after Nf7 is 31. h4! Ne5 32. Rc7 Nd3 33. Na4. **30. ... Nf7 31. Ke2 a5 32. b3 h5 33. Re7 Ne5 34. Nd1 b5! 35. Ra7 bxa4 36. bxa4 Rb3 37. Rxa5 Rxg3 38. Nf2 ½–½** (*L'Échiquier*, 1933, p. 253)

266 Kashdan–Apscheneek [i.e., Apšenieks] (Latvia) [B38]
Folkestone Olympiad, round 6, 1933 *[June 16]*

1. e4 c5 2. Nf3 Nc6 3. d4 cxd4 4. Nxd4 g6 The correct order of moves is 4. ... Nf6 5. Nc3 d6 6. Be2 g6 to prevent c4, which gives White full control of the center. **5. c4 Bg7 6. Be3 Nf6 7. Nc3** The recommended continuation is Ng4 (Breyer's move). The game Kostić–Breyer, Gotenburg 1920, continued: 8. Nxc6 Nxe3 9. Nxd8 Nxd1 10. Nxd1 Kxd8 which is even. The game was eventually drawn. **7. ... d6 8. Be2 0–0 9. 0–0 Bd7 10. h3 a6** In the usual Sicilian position Black would now threaten b5. But the White pawn at c4 puts this, as well as d5, out of the question. **11. Qd2 Rc8 12. Rac1 Nxd4 13. Bxd4 Bc6 14. Qe3**

A bit better than either 14. f3 or Bf3, as White intends f4. **14. … Nd7 15. Bxg7 Kxg7 16. b4** White can advance on either side, all his pieces being better placed. **16. … b6 17. Rfd1** If 17. c5 dxc5 18. Bxa6 Ra8 19. b5 Nb8, with an even game. **17. … a5 18. a3 axb4 19. axb4 Ra8 20. Ra1 f5** This further weakens his game, 20. … Qc7, followed by Rxa1 and Ra8 might be tried. **21. Rxa8 Bxa8 22. exf5 gxf5 23. Nd5 Bxd5 24. Rxd5 f4 25. Qd4+ Ne5** There are no good moves. If 25. … Nf6 26. Rg5+ and Qxf4. Or if 25. Rf6 26. Bg4 (threatening Bxd7 and Qxb6) Nf8 27. Rg5 wins. **26. c5** 26. Rb5 would have won a pawn without allowing Black any counter chances. **26. … bxc5 27. bxc5 Qa5 28. cxd6 Qe1+ 29. Bf1 exd6 30. Rxd6 f3** The start of some interesting play, requiring accurate timing for attack and defense. **31. g4 Rf6 32. Rd5 Re6 33. Rd7+ Kg6** If 33. … Kg8 34. Ra7! threatening mate, and also Ra1, winning the queen. **34. Ra7** It is surprising that the Black queen would be lost after Ra1, in spite of the number of squares at her disposal. **34. … Rc6**

After
34. … Rc6

Threatening mate in three by …Qxf1+!! If now 35. Ra1 Qc3 and Black escapes. **35. Kh2!** Avoiding the mate, and also freeing the bishop for use in the attack. If 35. Qxf1 then it is mate in two. If 35. Kg5 then Kg3 wins. Black's reply allows a quick mate! **35. … Kf6 36. Qd8+ Ke6 37. Re7+ Kf6 38. Qf8+ 1–0** (*Folkestone 1933*)

267 Sultan Khan (England)– Kashdan [C47]
Folkestone Olympiad, round 7, 1933 *[June 17]*

1. e4 e5 2. Nf3 Nf6 3. Nc3 Nc6 4. d3

d5 5. Bg5 Bb4 6. Nd2 dxe4 7. dxe4 Be6 8. Bb5 h6 9. Bxf6 Qxf6 10. Nd5 Bxd5 11. exd5 Bxd2+ 12. Qxd2 0–0–0 13. Bxc6 bxc6 14. c4 cxd5 15. cxd5 Qa6 16. 0–0–0 Qxa2 17. Rhe1 Rd6 18. Rxe5 Rhd8 19. Qc3 Rxd5 20. Rexd5 Rxd5 21. Rxd5 Qxd5 22. Qxg7 Qc5+ 23. Kb1 Qxf2 24. Qxh6 Qxg2 25. Qf8+ Kb7 26. Qxf7 Qxh2 27. Qb3+ Kc8 28. Qe6+ Kd8 29. Qd5+ Qd6 30. Qa8+ Kd7 31. Qxa7 ½–½ In the next round the U.S.A. had the bye. The game in round 9 Kashdan played Grünfeld to a draw. This game is not available. (*American Chess Bulletin*, July-August 1933)

268 Kashdan–Andersen (Denmark) [E11]
Folkestone Olympiad, round 10, 1933 *[June 19]*

1. d4 Nf6 2. c4 e6 3. Nf3 Bb4+ 4. Nbd2 b6 5. a3 Bxd2+ 6. Qxd2 Bb7 7. g3 0–0 8. Bg2 Qe7 9. 0–0 d6 10. b4 Nbd7 11. Bb2 c5 12. Rfd1 Rad8 13. dxc5 dxc5 14. Qc3 Nb8 15. b5 Rxd1+ 16. Rxd1 Rd8 17. Re1 Qd7! 18. a4 a5! 19. h3 h6 20. Qc1 Ne8 21. Be5 Qe7 22. Rd1 Rxd1+ 23. Qxd1 Nd7 24. Bb2 Qd6 25. Qc2 f5! 26. Kh2 Be4 27. Qc3 Qd1 28. Ne5 Qxe2! 29. Bxe4 fxe4 30. Kg2 Ndf6 31. Bc1 Nd6 32. g4 Nf7 33. Be3 Nxe5 34. Qxe5 Qxc4 35. Qb8+ Kh7 36. Qxb6 Nd5 ½–½ (*Skakbladet*, 1933)

269 Rosselli (Italy)–Kashdan [E17]
Folkestone Olympiad, round 11, 1933 *[June 21]*

1. d4 Nf6 2. c4 e6 3. Nf3 b6 4. g3 The best reply to the Queen's Indian Defense, as it balances the pressure along the diagonal, and leaves White with slightly more control in the center. **4. … Bb7 5. Bg2 Be7** The alternative is …Bb4+, which leads to the exchange of bishops, but the text is quite good. **6. Nc3 0–0 7. Qc2 d5** The threat was e4 which should not be allowed. if 7. … c5 8. d5! exd5 9. Nh4 is advantageous to White, as the pawn on d5 greatly restricts Black's game. **8. Ne5** Seemingly strong, but the knight is not well placed, since its support, the pawn at d4, will soon be removed. Better was 8. cxd5 exd5 (or Nxd5 9. e4 is effective); 9. 0–0. If then 9. ... c5 10. dxc5 bxc5 11. Rd1, with pressure on the pawns. But 9. ... Ne4 is sufficient to equalize. **8. ... c5** Completely liquidating the center, which will allow Black to escape from any of the usual difficulties in this opening. **9. dxc5 Bxc5 10. 0–0 Qc8!** Protecting the bishop in order to free the d pawn. There is a concealed trap. If 11. cxd5 Nxd5 12. Nxd5? Bxf2+ wins the queen. **11. Bg5 dxc4** Allowing the breakup of the kingside formation, which leads to some tense play later. However, there is no actual danger, as White has no time to build up an attack. **12. Bxb7 Qxb7 13. Bxf6 gxf6 14. Nxc4 Nc6** If ...Nd7 15. Qe4 and Black must lose time if he does not wish to exchange queens. The text allows the entrance of the queen, relying on the next move as a sufficient counter. **15. Qe4 b5** White's attack had to be accurately calculated, but it just fails, and the knights are driven back with loss of time. **16. Qg4+ Kh8 17. Qf3 Be7** Not ...bxc4? 18. Qxf6+ Kg8 19. Qg5+ Kh8 20. Qxc5, with advantage. **18. Nd6**

After
18. Nd6

Feeling his hold on the game slipping, White plays for a draw by perpetual, which would follow if 18. ... Bxd6. But Black is not ready for such an end. **18. ... Qb6** The point of Black's 15th move is that the b pawn cannot be taken safely. **19. Ndxb5?** White misses the idea and loses a piece. 19. Naxb5 would also lose by a6 20. Nc3 Ne5 followed by ...Qxd6. Best was 19. Nde4 but Black would have the advantage after 19. ... f5. **19. ... a6 20. Na3** If 20. Nd6 Ne5 followed by ...Qxd6 as before. White had

expected to lose his pawn back, but had not realized the tangle that his knights would get into. **20. ... Ne5 21. Qf4** If 21. Qe3 Qxb2; and the knight still has no escape. 22. f4 fails because of Qxa3 23. Qxb2 fxe5? 24. Bc5. **21. ... Qxb2 22. Ne4** Unfortunately if 22. Nb1 Qxa1; and there is no other way for the knights to support each other. **22. ... Qxa3** After 23. Nxf6 Ng6 wins a second piece. If then 24. Qd4 Qb2 wins, and if 24. Qd4 e5 25. Qb6 Rab8 26. Qc6 Rfc8 27. Qf3 Qxf3 followed by Bxf6. **0–1** Annotations by Kashdan. (*Chess Review*, July 1936)

270 Kashdan–Mikėnas (Lithuania) [C42]

Folkestone Olympiad, round 12, 1933
[June 21]

1. e4 e5 2. Nf3 Nf6 3. Nxe5 d6 4. Nf3 Nxe4 5. Qe2 A favorite continuation of Dr. Lasker. It gains time, but leads to the exchange of queens, thus tending to simplify the game. 5. d4 d5 6. Bd3 etc., is also slightly in White's favor. **5. ... Qe7 6. d3 Nf6 7. Bg5 Qxe2+** If 7. ... Be6 8. Nd5! followed by 9. Nxe6 with advantage, inferior is 8. Nc3 h6! 9. Bxf6 (or 9. Bh4 g5 10. Bg3 Bg7) Qxf6 10. d4 Qe7! and Black retains the two bishops. **8. Bxe2 Be7 9. Nc3** White is now two moves ahead in development, but with the queens off this is only of slight importance. **9. ... Nc6 10. Nb5 Kd8** The king is not well placed here, as it interferes with the mobility of the rooks. Better was 10. ... Bd8. If then 11. Bxf6 gxf6; it is doubtful whether White can do much against the doubled pawns, whereas Black has some play on the open g file. **11. 0–0 a6 12. Nbd4 Nxd4 13. Nxd4 c5** This creates weaknesses on the queenside, of which White takes advantage later. 13. ... Nd5 would have equalized more readily. **14. Nf3 Be6 15. Bd2** The threat was Ng5, exchanging the useful bishop. **15. ... h6 16. b3** White's plan is to play d4, and he wishes to prevent the counter c4. He will then continue with c4 and d5, or if Black exchanges pawns the d pawn will be left backward. **16. ... Kd7** An indifferent move, which gives White just the time he needs to gain his objective. More accurate was 16. ... Rac8. If then 17. d4 c4! or 17. c4 d5, with an even game. **17. d4 Rhc8 18. c4 d5** Necessary to prevent d5, which would give White a far superior pawn formation. **19. dxc5 Bxc5** If ...dxc4 20. b4! and Black's c pawn would soon fall. **20. b4 Ba7 21. c5** The point of White's strategy. He has a pawn majority on the queenside, whereas Black's d pawn is weak. In addition, White has a strong post on d4 for the knight. **21. ... Ke7 22. Nd4 Bb8 23. Rac1 Be5 24. Bc3 Bf4 25. Rc2 Ne4 26. Bb2 a5** The best chance for counterplay. Otherwise White proceeds by driving back the pieces on the kingside, followed by a4, b5, etc. **27. g3 Be5 28. f3 axb4** Enterprising play. Black foresees that he will obtain three pawns for the piece, with reasonable chances in the ending. If 28. ... Nf6 29. b5 and White's position is much superior. **29. Nxe6 Rxa2 30. fxe4 Rxb2**

After
30. ... Rxb2

If ...Bxb2 31. Rb1 fxe6 (not ...Bd4+ 32. Nxd4, and the rook is protected); 32. Rcxb2 would win easily. Or 30. ... fxe6 31. Bxe5 Rxc2 32. Bd6+ Kd7 33. Bb5+ and wins. **31. Rxb2 Bxb2 32. exd5!** An unexpected counter sacrifice which leads to a surprising forced win. 32. Nf4 dxe4 would be doubtful, and offer Black good drawing chances. **32. ... fxe6 33. d6+ Ke8** If ...Kd8 34. Rf8+ Kd7 35. Rf7+ leads to the same position as in the game. **34. Bh5+!** Much stronger than the more obvious 34. Bb5+ Rc6; when White would have a difficult time because of the passed b pawn. **34. ... Kd7 35. Rf7+ Kc6** If ...Kd8 36. Bg4! Rxc5 37. Bxe6 Ke8 38. d7+ wins. Or 36. ... Bd4+ 37. Kg2 Bxc5 38. Bxe6 Bxd6 39. Rd7+ wins a piece. **36. Bf3+! Kb5** The point of the combination started with 32. exd5 is that now ...Kcc5 37. Rc7+ wins. Otherwise White obtains two connected passed pawns which cannot be stopped. **37. Rxb7+**

Kc4 **38. c6 1–0** Annotated by Kashdan. (*Folkestone 1933*)

271 L. Steiner (Hungary)– Kashdan [C86]

Folkestone Olympiad, round 13, 1933
[June 21]

1. e4 e5 2. Nf3 Nc6 3. Bb5 a6 4. Ba4 d6 5. c3 Nf6 6. Qe2 Be7 7. d4 Bd7 Better is 7. ... b5 8. Bc2 exd4 9. cxd4 Bg4 10. Be3 d5! (of course not 10. ... Nxe4 11. Bd5 wins) 11. e5 Ne4, with approximate equality. **8. 0–0 0–0 9. d5** Gaining considerable time, as Black will have difficulty in developing the knight. The text is better than Bb3, as played by Steiner against Alekhine. **9. ... Nb8** 9. ... Nd4 would lose a pawn by 10. cxd4 Bxa4 11. Nc3! (not 1. dxe5? Bb5 wins), Bd7 12. dxe5. **10. Bc2 c6 11. c4 cxd5 12. exd5** If 12. cxd5 Bb5 13. Bd3 Bxd3 14. Qxd3 Nbd7, and Black has more freedom than after the text. **12. ... Ne8 13. Ne1 f5 14. f4 e4 15. Be3 Bf6 16. Nc3 b5 17. Bb3** Best. White gains further ground after every effort of Black to get into play. Instead 17. cxb5 axb5 18. Nxb5 Bxb2 is quite agreeable for Black. **17. ... bxc4 18. Bxc4 Nc7 19. Nc2 Bb5** If 19. ... Nb5 20. Na4! Be8 21. Nb6 Ra2 22. a4 Nc7 23. Nd7! wins the exchange. **20. Nd4 Bxc4 21. Qxc4 Bxd4 22. Bxd4** The exchanges have only emphasized White's domination of the board. **22. ... Nd7 23. Qc6 Nf6 24. Bb6 Rf7 25. Rac1**

After
25. Rac1

25. ... Qd7 26. Qxd7 Here White could have earned his reward for his fine play by 26. Nxe4! fxe4 27. Bxc7 Qxc6 28. Rxc6 Nxd5 29. Bxd6, with a pawn ahead and an excellent position. If 26. ... Nfxd5 27. Bxc7 Nxc7 28. Nxd6 wins. The text also wins the e pawn, but not in as favorable a position. **26. ... Rxd7 27. Bxc7 Rxc7 28. Nxe4! Rac8** Of course not 28. ... Rxc1 29. Nxf6+ gxf6 30. Rxc1 with a won ending. The possession of the c file gives Black chances. **29. Rxc7 Rxc7 30. Nc3** After this Black succeeds in regaining the pawn. Best was 30. Nxd6 Nxd5 31. g3! (if 31. Nxf5 Rc2 32. Rf2 Rc1+ 33. Kg2 g6 34. Rd2, and White should still win. **30. ... Rc4 31. Re1 Rd4** If 31. ... Rxf4 32. Re6 wins. If now 32. Re6 Nxd5 33. Rxd6? Nxc3! winning a piece. **32. Kf2** With 32. g3 Nxd5 33. Nxd5 Rxd5 34. Rd2 White would still have a slight advantage, though the game should be drawn. But giving up the f pawn is risky, since White is left with a weakness in the d pawn. **32. ... Rxf4+ 33. Ke3 Rb4 34. b3 Ne4 35. Kd3** If 35. Nxe4 Rxe4+ 36. Kf2 Rd4 wins a pawn. **35. ... Nc5+ 36. Kc2 Kf7 37. Re3 h5 38. Ne2 Kf6 39. g3 h4 40. a3** An interesting variation is 40. Kc3 Rg4 41. h3 Rxg3! 42. Nxe3 hxg3. The pawn cannot be taken because of Ne4+, and the two passed pawns must win. **40. ... Re4** After the exchange of rooks, the Black king gains the center, which would suffice to win. **41. Rxe4 Nxe4 42. Kd3 Ke5 43. gxh4 Kxd5**

After
43. ... Kxd5

Loss of time, after which the following knight maneuver gives White some chances. 43. ... f4 44. Nd4 (or if 44. b4 f3 45. Nc1 f2 46. Ke2 Kxd5 wins easily) Nf2+ 45. Kc3 Ke4 46. Ne6 g6! 47. Nf8 f3 48. Nxg6 Ng4 49. Kd2 Nxh3 50. Ke1 Ke3 wins. The same possibility occurred later in the game, but then White could have defended himself. **44. Nf4+ Ke5 45. Ng6+ Kf6 46. Nf4 Nc5+ 47. Kc4 Ke5 48. Nh3 Nd7 49. b4 d5+ 50. Kd3 d4 51. a4 Nb6 52. Ng5** Winning the d pawn, after which it

is questionable whether Black can force a win. **52. ... Nxa4 53. Nf3+ Kd5 54. Nxd4 Nb2+ 55. Kc3 Nd1+ 56. Kd3 Nf2+ 57. Kc3 f4 58. Nf5 g6** If 58. ... Ke4 59. Nxg7 f3 60. h5 Ng4 61. Kd2 Nxh2 62. Ke1 Ke3 63. Nf5+ draws. **59. Ne7+ Ke4 60. Nxg6 f3 61. h5?** This loses. White must at once provide for the threat by 61. Kd2 Ng4 62. Ne7! Nxh2 63. Ke1 Ke3 64. Nf5+ as before, If 64. ... Kf4 65. Ne7 Kg3 66. Nf5+ Kg2 67. Ne3+ Kg1 68. Nd1 h5 draws. **61. ... Ng4 62. Kd2 Nxh2 63. h6** If 63. Ke1 Ke3 and the pawn cannot be stopped. With the text White also queens, but is left in a mating net. **63. ... f2 64. h7 f1Q 65. h8Q Nf3+ 66. Kc2 Nd4+ 67. Kb2 Qe2+** Black now mates in eight moves. **68. Ka3 Qd3+ 69. Ka4 Qb3+ 70. Ka5 Qd5+** If 71. Kb6 Qc6+ 72. Kh7 NNb5+, etc. **0−1** Annotations by Kashdan. (*Folkestone 1933*) In round 14 Kashdan played Ståhlberg to a draw. This game is not available.

272 Flohr (Czechoslovakia)− Kashdan [A18]
Folkestone Olympiad, round 15, 1933
[June 23]

1. c4 Nf6 2. Nc3 e6 3. e4 d5 4. e5 d4 5. exf6 dxc3 6. fxg7 cxd2+ 7. Bxd2 Bxg7 offers White no advantage. The Czechs needed an overwhelming victory in order to take first place and so they chose sharp variations in all four games. **6. bxc3 Qxf6 7. d4 b6 8. Nf3 Bb7 9. Be2 Nd7 10. 0−0 Bd6** 10. ... h6 was necessary. **11. Bg5 Qf5 12. Qa4 c6 13. c5! bxc5** In accepting this pawn sacrifice Black forfeits his chance to castle. Kashdan subsequently recommended 13. ... Bf4. **14. dxc5 Qxc5** 14. ... Bxc5 is answered by 15. Rfd1, while 14. ... Nxc5, then 15. Qd4. **15. Rfd1 Be7** But not 15. ... 0−0 16. Be3!. **16. Rxd7!** A brilliant stroke which keeps the Black king definitely in the center, exposed to a powerful attack (Kashdan). **16. ... Kxd7 17. Be3 Qa3** Taking the queen too far out of play. Better was Qf5 (Kashdan). **18. Qd4+ Ke8 19. Qxg7 Rf8 20. Ng5 Rd8 21. Bh5 Bxg5 22. Bxg5 Rd5 23. c4 Rxg5** He is forced to give back the exchange. However, White's attack remains very strong.

24. Qxg5 Kd7 25. Rd1+ Kc8 26. Bxf7 Kb8 27. Bxe6 Qxa2 28. Rd8+?

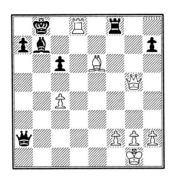

After
28. Rd8

28. Qe5+ Ka1 29. Qd4! was better, for the threat of Ra1 would force Black to play a6. **28. ... Kc7?** He could have defended himself satisfactorily with 28. ... Bc8!! White would then have no choice but to try advancing his king-side pawns after 29. Qe5+ Ka8 30. Rxc8+. If instead 29. ...Qb1+ 30. Kf2 Qb6+, while 29. h4 Rxd8 30. Qxd8 Qa1+ 31. Kh2 Qe5+ also wins for Black. These points were only discovered after the game had been published all over the world. The text move loses immediately. **29. Qe7+ Kb6 30. c5+ 1–0** (*Chess Olympiads*, by Földeák, page 96)

273 Fine (Marshall)–Kashdan [C42]

Metropolitan Chess League, 1934 *[April 21]*

1. e4 e5 2. Nf3 Nf6 3. Nxe5 d6 4. Nf3 Nxe4 5. Qe2 Qe7 6. d3 Nf6 7. Bg5 Qxe2+ 8. Bxe2 Be7 9. Nc3 h6 10. Bh4 Bd7 11. 0-0-0 Nc6 12. d4 0-0-0 13. Rhe1 Rde8 14. Bc4 Nd8 15. d5 g5 16. Bg3 Nh5 17. Be2 f5 18. Nd4 Nxg3 19. fxg3 Bf6 20. Rf1 Be5 21. Bb5 f4 22. Bxd7+ Kxd7 23. Nce2 fxg3 24. hxg3 Rhf8 25. c3 Bg7 26. Kd2 ½-½ (*American Chess Bulletin*, June 1934)

274 Goodman (Empire Chess Club)–Kashdan [D10]

Metropolitan Chess League, 1934

1. d4 Nf6 2. c4 c6 3. Nc3 d5 4. cxd5 cxd5 5. Qb3 e6 6. Bg5 Be7 7. e3 0-0 8. Bd3 Nc6 9. Rc1 a6 10. Nf3 h6 11. Bxf6

Bxf6 12. Bb1 Bd7 13. 0-0 b5 14. Ne2 Qb6 15. Nf4 Rfc8 16. Nd3 Na5 17. Qb4 Nc4 18. Nc5 Be8 19. Nd2 Nd6 20. Qc3 g6 21. Bd3 a5 22. a3 b4 23. Qb3 Be7 24. Rc2 Nb7 25. Nxb7 a4 26. Rxc8 Rxc8 27. Qd1 Qxb7 28. Qe2 Rc7 29. axb4 Qxb4 30. Nf3 Rb7 31. Rc1 Qxb2 32. Rc8 Kf8 33. g3 Qxe2 34. Bxe2 Bd6 35. Bd3 Ke7 36. Ra8 a3 37. Kg2 Rb3 38. Bf1 Rb2 39. Ra7+ Kf6 40. Ne5 Kg7 41. Nd3 Bb5 42. Nc5 Bxf1+ 43. Kxf1 a2 44. Kg2 Kf8 45. Ra8+ Ke7 46. Ra7+ Kd8 47. Kf3 Bxc5 48. dxc5 e5 49. h3 f5 50. g4 d4 **0–1** (*Brooklyn Daily Eagle*, April 19, 1934)

275 Palmi–Kashdan [C48]

Chicago, Western (Prelims), 1934 *[July 21]*

1. e4 e5 2. Nf3 Nf6 3. Nc3 Nc6 4. Bb5 Nd4 5. Nxd4 exd4 6. e5 dxc3 7. exf6 Qxf6! 8. dxc3 c6 9. Bd3 d5 10. 0-0 Bd6 11. Qh5? h6 12. Re1+ Be6 13. Bd2 0-0-0! 14. a4 g6 15. Qd1 g5 16. Be3 c5 17. Bf1 h5 18. b4 Be5 19. Ra3 d4 20. cxd4 cxd4 21. Bc1 g4 22. b5 h4 23. Bb2 Bxh2+! 24. Kxh2 g3+ 25. Kh1 h3 26. Rxg3 Qxf2 **0–1** (*Chess Review*, September 1934)

276 Kashdan–Ilsley [C45]

Chicago, Western (Prelims), 1934 *[July]*

1. e4 e5 2. Nf3 Nc6 3. d4 exd4 4. Nxd4 Nxd4? 5. Qxd4 d6 6. Nc3 Be6 7. Bf4 Ne7 8. Be2 Nc6 9. Qd2 Be7 10. Nd5 Bf6 11. c3 0-0 12. 0-0 Ne5 13. Bg3 Ng6? 14. Nxf6+ Qxf6 15. f4! Bc8 16. Rae1 Re8 17. Bd1 b6 18. Bb3 Ba6 19. Rf3 Bb7 20. Rfe3 Qe7 21. Qf2 Kh8 22. e5! dxe5 23. f5!! Nf8 24. Rxe5 Qd7 25. f6! Ng6 26. Re7!! **1–0** (*Chess Review*, September 1934)

277 Reshevsky–Kashdan [D48]

Chicago, Western (Prelims), 1934 *[July]*

1. d4 Nf6 2. c4 c6 3. Nf3 d5 4. Nc3 e6 5. e3 Nbd7 6. Bd3 dxc4 7. Bxc4 b5 8. Bd3 a6 9. a4 b4 10. Ne4 c5 11. 0-0 Bb7 12. Ned2 Be7 13. a5 0-0 14. Qe2 Qc7 15. Nc4 Rfd8 16. Nfe5 Nf8 17. Rd1

Ng6 18. Bxg6 hxg6 19. b3 cxd4 20. exd4
Nd5 21. Bd2 Bf6

After
21. ... Bf6

22. Rac1 Qe7 23. Nb2 Rac8 24. Na4
Bg5 25. Rxc8 Rxc8 26. Nc5 Bxd2
27. Qxd2 Nc3 28. Re1 Rd8 29. Qf4 Ba8
30. Nxa6 g5 31. Qg4 Qd6 32. Nc5 Qxd4
33. Qxd4 Rxd4 34. Nc4 Rd8 35. Nb6
Nd5 36. Ra1 Kf8 37. f3 Ke7 38. Kf2 Bc6
39. Na6 Kd6 40. Rd1 Bb7 41. Nxb4 Kc5
42. Nc2 Rh8 43. b4+ Kb5 44. Nxd5
Bxd5 45. Ne3 Bc6 46. Rc1 Rc8 47. Nc4
Kxb4 48. Nd6 Rc7 49. a6 f5 50. a7
Rxa7 51. Rxc6 Ra2+ 52. Kg3 Re2
53. Nf7 f4+ 54. Kh3 g4+ 55. Kxg4
Rxg2+ 56. Kxf4 Rxh2 57. Rxe6 Kc5
58. Rg6 Kd5 59. Rxg7 Ke6 60. Ne5 Ra2
61. Rg6+ Ke7 62. Kf5 Ra5 63. f4 Rb5
64. Re6+ Kf8 65. Kf6 Kg8 66. Kg6 Rb8
67. f5 Kh8 68. f6 Rg8+ 69. Kh6 1–0 (*Reshevsky on Chess*, Game 20)

278 Woods–Kashdan [C77]
Chicago, Western (Prelims), 1934 *[July]*

1. e4 e5 2. Nf3 Nc6 3. Bb5 a6 4. Ba4
Nf6 5. Qe2 b5 6. Bb3 Be7 7. c3 0–0
8. d4 exd4 9. cxd4 d5 10. e5 Ne4
11. 0–0 Bg4 12. Be3 f5 13. Rd1 Na5
14. Bc2 Nc4 15. Bc1 Qe8 16. b3 Nb6
17. Bb2 c5 18. h3 Bh5 19. Nbd2 c4
20. Nb1 a5 21. bxc4 Nxc4 22. Bc1 b4
23. Bb3 Rc8 24. a4 bxa3 25. Bxc4
Rxc4 26. Bxa3 a4 27. Qd3 Bxa3
28. Nxa3 Rc3 29. Qe2 Ng5 30. Rd3
Bxf3 31. Rxf3 Rxf3 32. gxf3 Qh5 33. h4
Qxh4 34. f4 Qxf4 35. Qe3 Nf3+ 36. Kf1
Qg4 37. Nc2 Rc8 38. Ne1 Nh2 mate
0–1 (Kashdan's scoresheet)

279 Kashdan–Jackson [B72]
Chicago, Western (Prelims), 1934

1. e4 c5 2. Nf3 Nc6 3. d4 cxd4
4. Nxd4 Nf6 5. Nc3 d6 6. Be2 g6 7. Be3
Bg7 8. h3 Bd7 9. Qd2 0–0 10. 0–0
Nxd4 11. Bxd4 Qc7 12. Bxf6 Bxf6
13. Nd5 Qc6 14. Rad1 Rfe8 15. Nxf6+
exf6 16. Bf3 Rad8? 17. e5! Qb5 18. exf6
Qxb2 19. Qxd6 Qb6 20. Qxb6 axb6
21. Bxb7 1–0 (Kashdan's scoresheet)

280 Denker–Kashdan [D18]
Chicago, Western (Finals), round 1, 1934
[July 27]

1. d4 Nf6 2. c4 c6 3. Nc3 d5 4. Nf3
dxc4 Black's idea as borne out by the following move is to avoid the usual difficulty experienced in developing the bishop at c8. It does not recommend itself because it leaves the queenside weak and permits White to gain time later with e4! 5. a4 Bf5 6. e3 Na6 7. Bxc4 Nb4
8. 0–0 e6 9. Qe2 Nbd5 10. Ne5 Bd6
11. f3 Nxc3 12. bxc3 Qc7 13. e4 Bg6
14. Bf4 Nd7 15. Nxg6 hxg6 16. e5 Be7
17. a5 0–0 18. g4 The beginning of a well calculated kingside assault. With the center under control, White takes advantage of Black's weakness on the open h file and the diagonal of the White bishop at c4. 18. ... Rfd8 19. Be3
Nf8 20. f4 c5 21. f5 cxd4 22. cxd4 Rac8
23. Rac1 Qd7 24. fxe6 fxe6 25. Qf3
Ba3 26. Rc2 Bb4 27. g5! Well played. The square g4 must be cleared to permit the queen to function on the diagonal h3–c8. White being engaged in carrying on a direct attack against his opponent's king can disregard Black's queenside activities. 27. ... Bxa5 28. Qh3 Rxc4
29. Rxc4 b5 30. Rcc1 Rc8 31. Rcd1 Bb6
32. Rf4 Rc3 (*see diagram*)

This permits White to bring off a combination to conclude the game. But there was no hope for Black. White threatened Rc1 to be followed by Ra4, etc. 33. Rxf8+ Kxf8 34. Qh8+
Ke7 35. Rf1 Qe8 36. Qxg7+ Kd8 37. Rf8
Rxe3 38. Qf6+ Kd7 39. Rxe8 Kxe8
40. Qxe6+ Kd8 41. Qd6+ Kc8 42. e6 1–0
Annotations by Denker. (*Chess Review*, September 1934)

After
32. ... Rc3

281 Belson–Kashdan [D52]
Chicago, Western (Finals), round 2, 1934
[July 27]

1. d4 d5 2. c4 e6 3. Nc3 Nf6 4. Bg5
Nbd7 5. e3 c6 6. Nf3 Qa5 7. Bxf6 Nxf6
8. Qc2 Bb4 9. Nd2 Ne4 10. Ndxe4 dxe4
11. Be2 f5 12. 0–0 Be7 13. f3 exf3
14. Bxf3 0–0 15. e4 e5 16. d5 Qc5+
17. Kh1 Qxc4 18. dxc6 bxc6 19. exf5
Bxf5 20. Qb3 Qxb3 21. axb3 Bd7
22. Rfe1 Bf6 23. b4 a6 24. Na4 Rfb8
25. Nc5 Be8 26. Nxa6 Rb6 27. Nc7
Rxa1 28. Rxa1 Bd7 29. b5 cxb5 30. Be4
Rb8 31. Ra8 Rxa8 32. Bxa8 Kf7 33. Be4
Bd8 34. Na6 g6 35. b4 Be7 36. Kg1 Bd6
37. Kf2 Bc8 38. Nc5 Bxc5+ 39. bxc5
Bf5 40. Bd5+ Ke7 41. Ke3 b4 42. h3
Be6 43. Be4 b3 44. Kd2 Bf5 45. Bxf5
gxf5 46. Kc3 Ke6 47. Kxb3 Kd5 48. Kb4
e4 49. Kb5 e3 50. c6 e2 51. c7 e1Q
52. c8Q Qb1+ 53. Ka5 Qa2+ 54. Kb6
Qb3+ 55. Ka5 Qa3+ 56. Kb5 Qd3+
57. Kb6 Qd4+ 58. Kb5 Qb2+ 59. Ka5
Qe5 60. Kb4 Qf4+ 61. Kb5 Qf1+
62. Kb4 Qb1+ 63. Ka5 Ke4 64. Qa8+
Kf4 65. Qf3+ Ke5 66. Qc3+ Kd5
67. Ka6 Qf1+ 68. Kb7 Ke4 69. Kc7 Kf4
70. g3+ Ke4 71. Qc6+ Ke3 72. Qc5+
Ke4 73. Qc6+ ½–½ (Kashdan's scoresheet)

282 Kashdan–Fine [A90]
Chicago, Western (Finals), round 3, 1934
[July 28]

1. d4 f5 2. c4 Nf6 3. g3 e6 4. Bg2
Bb4+ Taking advantage of White's second
move to exchange a piece which might otherwise be quite useful. 5. Bd2 Bxd2+ A good

alternative seems 5. ... Qe7 6. Nh3 0–0 7. 0–0
Bxd2 8. Qxd2 d6 9. Nc3 e5. 6. Qxd2 0–0
7. Nc3 d6 8. 0–0–0 In order to prevent
...e5, but White's king is not well placed now;
the same object could have been achieved more
simply with 8. Rd1, and if 8. ... Qe7 9. Nf3 e5?
10. dxe5 dxe5 11. Nd5! with advantage. 8. ...
d5 Changing his plan—evidently with a view to
opening a file on the queenside. 9. Nf3 c6
10. Ne5 Nfd7 11. cxd5 Nxe5 12. dxe5
cxd5 13. Kb1 Nd7? A blunder which loses
a pawn; 13. ... Nc6 was necessary, although after
14. f4 a6 (to prevent Nc3–b5–d6) 15. h3 Ne7
(15. ... Bd7 or 15. ... b5 would be answered by
Nxd5) 16. e3 followed by Nc3–e2–d4, Black
would have a difficult game. 14. Nxd5! Nxe5!
Of course if 14. ... exd5 15. Qxd5 and 16. e6.
15. Qc3! Nc6 There is nothing better in view
of the threatened Nc7. 16. Nb4 Qa5 The
exchange of queens is Black's only chance.
17. Nxc6 The alternative 17. Bxc6 bxc6
18. Nxc6 (not 18. Qxc6 Qxb4 19. Qxa8 Bb7
20. Qxa7 Bxh1 21. Rxh1 Qe4+) Qxc3 19. bxc3
Bb7 20. Rd6 Rf7 21. Rhd1 Rc7 would also involve some difficulties. 17. ... Qxc3 18. bxc3
bxc6 19. Bxc6 Rb8+ 20. Ka1 Ba6 21. Rd2
Better was e3; now the rook is tied up. 21. ...
Kf7 22. Ba4 Rfc8 23. Rc1 Rc5 24. Bb3
Rb6 25. e3 Kf6 26. Rd4 The ending has
become extremely difficult now; f4 was probably best. 26. ... g5 27. Rd7 Rb7 28. Rxb7
Bxb7 29. Kb2 And again f4 was in order.
29. ... g4 Creating a very slight chance for
himself, now that the h pawn and the f pawn are
fixed. 30. Rd1 Rc7 31. Rd6 Bc8 32. Rd4
Rg7 Obviously aiming at Rg7–g6–h6.
33. Ka3 Ke7 34. c4 e5 35. Rd5 e4
36. c5 Rg6 37. Ba4 Rh6 In his last moves
Fine has skillfully combined attack with defense. 38. c6 Rxh2 39. c7 Rxf2 40. Rd8
Bb7 41. Bc6 *(see diagram)*
The game is lost: if 41. Rb8 Ba6 42. Bb5 Rc2
43. Bxa6 Rxc7 44. Rb7 Rxb7 45. Bxb7 h5!
46. Ba6 h4 47. gxh4 g3 48. Bf1 f4 49. exf4 e3
and wins. 41. ... Rc2 42. Re8+ Kf7 43. c8Q
Bxc8 44. Rxc8 Rc3+ 45. Kb2 Rxe3
46. Rc7+ Kf6 47. Rxa7 Rxg3 48. a4
Rg2+ 49. Kb3 Rg1 50. Ra8 e3 51. Re8 f4
52. a5 Rc1 53. Bg2 Kg5 54. Kb2 White's
game is hopeless in any event. 54. ... f3

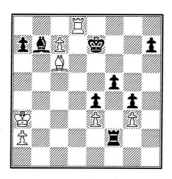

After
41. Bc6

55. Bxf3 gxf3 56. Rg8+ Kh6 57. Kxc1 f2
White resigned. **0–1** A weird finish to an interesting but by no means perfect game. The twenty year old Fine showed plucky and resourceful play. Annotated by Reinfeld. (*British Chess Magazine*, October 1934)

283 Kashdan–Dake [E80]
Chicago, Western (Finals), round 4, 1934
[July 29]

1. d4 Nf6 2. c4 g6 3. Nc3 Bg7 4. e4 d6
5. f3 Nbd7 6. Be3 e5 7. d5 a5 8. Qd2
h6 9. Bd3 Nc5 10. Bc2 Ng8 11. Nge2 b6
12. 0–0 f5 13. f4 Ne7 14. fxe5 dxe5
15. Bxc5 bxc5 16. Qe3 Qd6 17. Nb5
Qb6 18. Nec3 f4 19. Qf2 0–0 20. Na4
Qf6 21. Qxc5 g5 22. Nxc7 Rb8 23. g3
g4 24. d6 Ng6 25. Qd5+ Kh7 26. c5
Qg5 27. Qd2 Rb4 28. Rad1 Rd4 29. Qe2
fxg3 30. hxg3 Rf3 31. Qe1 Re3 32. Qf2
Rf3 33. Qe1 Re3 34. Qf2 Rf3 35. Qe1
½–½ (*Correspondence Chess League*, 1934)

284 Kashdan–Araiza [D61]
Chicago, Western (Finals), round 6, 1934
[July 30]

1. d4 Nf6 2. c4 e6 3. Nf3 d5 4. Nc3
c6 5. Bg5 Nbd7 6. e3 Be7 7. Qc2 0–0
8. Bd3 dxc4 9. Bxc4 Nd5 10. Bxe7 Qxe7
11. 0–0 Nxc3 12. Qxc3 b6 13. e4 Bb7
14. Rad1 Rfe8 15. Rfe1 Rac8 16. e5 b5
17. Bf1 Nb6 18. Nd2 b4 19. Qg3 c5
20. dxc5 Rxc5 21. Ne4 Bxe4 22. Rxe4
Rd5 23. Rde1 Red8 24. Rg4 g6 25. h4
Rd4 26. h5 Na4 27. Re3 Rxg4 28. Qxg4
Nxb2 29. Rb3 Nd1 30. Rg3 Nc3 31. Bd3
Qe8 32. Qxb4 Nd5 33. Qg4 Ne7

**34. hxg6 hxg6 35. Qg5 Qf8 36. Rh3
Rd7 37. Qh4 Qg7 38. Qa4 Rd8 39. Qxa7
Nd5 40. Qd4 Rb8 41. a4 Rb4 42. Qc5
Rb8 43. Qd6 Rc8 44. Ba6 Rf8 45. a5
1–0** (Kashdan's scoresheet)

285 McMurray–Kashdan [B12]
Chicago, Western (Finals), round 7, 1934
[July 31]

1. e4 c6 2. d4 d5 3. f3 dxe4 4. fxe4 e5
5. Nf3 exd4 6. Bc4 Bb4+ 7. c3 dxc3
8. Bxf7+ Ke7 9. Qb3 cxb2+ 10. Qxb4+
Kxf7 11. Bxb2 Nf6 12. Qb3+ Ke8
13. Nbd2 Na6 14. Ng5 Qe7 15. Ba3 c5
16. 0–0 Ng4 17. Nf7 Rf8 18. Nc4 Qe6
19. Rad1 Ke7 20. Rd6 Qxe4 21. Rdd1
Be6 22. Rfe1 Qf4 23. Qxb7+ Qc7
24. Ng5 Rf1+ 25. Kxf1 Qxb7 26. Nxe6
Kf6 27. Rd6 Kf7 28. Rd8 Qb5 29. Rxa8
Qxc4+ 30. Kg1 Qc3 31. Rxa7+ Kf6
32. Rf1+ Ke5 33. Bc1 Nb4 34. Ra3 Qc2
35. Re1+ Kd5 36. Rf3 Kc6 37. Ba3 Nd3
38. Ref1 Nge5 39. Rf5 Qxa2 40. Nxc5
Qxa3 41. Nxd3 Qxd3 0–1 (Kashdan's scoresheet)

286 Eastman–Kashdan [C86]
Chicago, Western (Finals), round 8, 1934
[July 31]

1. e4 e5 2. Nf3 Nc6 3. Bb5 a6 4. Ba4
Nf6 5. 0–0 Be7 6. Qe2 0–0 7. Bxc6
dxc6 8. Nxe5 Bd6 9. Nf3 Bg4 10. d4
Re8 11. e5 Bf8 12. Qd3 Nd5 13. a3 Qd7
14. Nc3 Rad8 15. Ne4 Ne7 16. c3 Ng6
17. Bg5 Rb8 18. Qe3 h6 19. Bf4 f5
20. Ned2 Ne7 21. e6 Qd8 22. c4 Ng6
23. Be5 Bxf3 24. Nxf3 Rxe6 25. Qc3
Qd7 26. Rfe1 Rbe8 27. Kf1 Qf7 28. Qb3
c5 29. Qc3 cxd4 30. Bxd4 c5 31. Be5
Qe7 32. Re3 f4 33. Re2 Nxe5 34. Rae1
Nxf3 35. Rxe6 Nxe1 36. Rxe7 Rxe7
37. h3 Kh8 38. Qd2 f3 39. gxf3 g6
40. Qd6 Kg7 41. Qxc5 Nxf3 42. Qd5 Rf7
43. b4 Ng5 44. Kg2 Re7 45. c5 Ne6
46. Kf1 g5 47. a4 Nf4 48. Qd4+ Kh7
49. b5 axb5 50. axb5 Ne6 51. Qd3+ Kg7
52. c6 bxc6 53. Qc3+ Kf7 54. Qf3+ Kg8
55. Qxc6 Kf7 56. Qf3+ Ke8 57. Qc6+

Kf7 58. Qf3+ Nf4 59. Qb3+ Re6 60. b6 Bd6 61. b7 Bb8 62. Qc4 Kf8 63. Qc8+ Re8 64. Qd7 Ne6 65. Qh7 Bf4 66. Qxh6+ Ke7 67. Qh7+ Kd6 68. Qc2 Rb8 69. Qc8 Ke7 70. f3 ½–½ (Kashdan's scoresheet)

287 Engholm–Kashdan [D05]
Chicago, Western (Finals), round 9, 1934 *[August 1]*

1. Nf3 d5 2. d4 Nf6 3. e3 e6 4. Bd3 c5 5. c3 Nc6 6. Nbd2 Bd6 7. Qe2 0–0 8. 0–0 Qc7 9. dxc5 Bxc5 10. e4 Bd7 11. e5 Ng4 12. Bxh7+ Kxh7 13. Ng5+ Kg8 14. Qxg4 Qxe5 15. Qh5 Qf5 16. g4 Qg6 17. Qxg6 fxg6 18. Ndf3 e5 19. h3 e4 20. Nh4 Rxf2 21. Rxf2 Rf8 22. Nhf3 Bxf2+ 23. Kxf2 Ne5 24. Be3 Nxf3 25. Kg2 Nxg5 26. Bxg5 Rf3 27. Re1 Rd3 28. Be3 a5 29. Kf2 Bb5 30. Rc1 Bc4 31. b3 Bb5 32. a3 Kf7 33. c4 dxc4 34. bxc4 Bc6 35. Ra1 Rc3 36. Bd2 Rxc4 37. Bxa5 Rc2+ 38. Kg3 g5 39. Rf1+ Kg6 40. Rf2 Rc1 41. Re2 Rg1+ 42. Kf2 Rh1 43. Re3 Rh2+ 44. Ke1 ½–½ (Kashdan's scoresheet) From the finals only the draw with Reshevsky is missing.

288 Kashdan–Araiza [C47]
Syracuse, round 1, 1934 *[August 13]*

1. e4 e5 2. Nf3 Nc6 3. d4 exd4 4. Nxd4 Nf6 5. Nc3 Bc5 6. Be3 Nxd4 7. Bxd4 Bxd4 8. Qxd4 d6 9. 0–0–0 Qe7 10. Bb5+ c6 11. Be2 Be6 12. Qxd6 Qxd6 13. Rxd6 Ke7 14. Rhd1 g5 15. f3 h5 16. g3 Rag8 17. a4 h4 18. g4 Ne8 19. R6d2 Nc7 20. Bc4 So if 20. ... Bxc4 then 21. Rd7+ regaining the piece. 20. ... Rd8 21. Rxd8 Rxd8 22. Rxd8 Kxd8 23. Bf1 Ke7 24. Kd2 Kd6 25. Ke3 Ke5 26. Nd1 b5 27. b3 bxa4 28. bxa4 c5 29. Nb2 f6 30. Bc4 Kd6 31. h3 Kc6 32. f4 Bxc4 33. Nxc4 Ne6 34. f5 Nf4 35. e5 fxe5 36. Nxe5+ Kd5 37. Nd3 Nxh3 38. c4+ Kd6 39. f6 Ke6 40. Nxc5+ Kxf6 41. Nd3 Ke6 42. Kf3 Kf6 43. Kg2 Nf4+ 44. Nxf4 gxf4 45. c5 Kg5 46. c6 1–0 (*New York Times*, August 26, 1934)

289 Seitz–Kashdan [C68]
Syracuse, round 2, 1934 *[August 14]*

1. e4 e5 2. Nf3 Nc6 3. Bb5 a6 4. Bxc6 dxc6 5. Nc3 f6 6. d4 exd4 7. Nxd4 c5 8. Nde2 Qxd1+ 9. Nxd1 Be6 10. 0–0 Ne7 11. Bf4 0–0–0 12. Ndc3 Nc6 13. Rfd1 Rxd1+ 14. Nxd1 Be7 15. a3 Rd8 16. Kf1 g5 17. Be3 Nd4 18. Nxd4 cxd4 19. Bd2 c5 20. f3 Bd6 21. g3 h5 22. Nf2 b5 23. Kg2 Kb7 24. Ba5 Rd7 25. Re1 Kc6 26. Nd3 c4 27. Nf2 Be5 28. Rb1 Kb7 29. Bd2 Kb6 30. h4 gxh4 31. f4 Bd6 32. f5 Bf7 33. gxh4 Be8 34. Kf3 Rg7 35. Bf4 Bc5 36. Bh6 Rh7 37. Bd2 Rg7 38. Bb4 Bc6 39. Re1 a5 40. Bxc5+ Kxc5 41. Kf4 Kd6 42. Rd1 Kc5 43. Re1 b4 44. axb4+ axb4 45. Re2 Rg1 46. e5 fxe5+ 47. Kxe5 Rg8 48. Kf4 Bd5 49. f6 Kd6 50. Kf5 Bf7 51. Ne4+ Kd5 52. Ng5 Bg6+ 53. Kf4 Rf8 54. Re5+ Kd6 55. Re6+ Kd5 56. Re5+ Kd6 57. Re6+ Kd5 ½–½ (*L'Échiquier*, 1934, p. 782)

290 Kashdan–Horowitz [D38]
Syracuse, round 3, 1934 *[August 14]*

1. d4 d5 2. c4 e6 3. Nc3 Nf6 4. Nf3 Nbd7 5. Bg5 Bb4 6. cxd5 exd5 7. Qb3 c5 8. a3 Bxc3+ 9. Qxc3 cxd4 10. Qxd4 0–0 11. e3 Qa5+ 12. b4 Qc7 13. Bd3 Ne4 14. Bf4 Qc6 15. 0–0 Ndf6 16. Rac1 Qa4 17. Qb2 Be6 18. Nd4 Qd7 19. Rc7 Qd8 20. Rxb7 Ne8 21. Nxe6 fxe6 22. Qe5 Qc8 23. Re7 Rf6 24. Bxe4 dxe4 25. Qxe4 Kf8 26. Qb7 Qxb7 27. Rxb7 Rf7 28. Rxf7+ Kxf7 29. Rd1 Ke7 30. e4 h6 31. Be3 e5 32. Rd5 Ke6 33. Ra5 Nd6 34. Ra6 Kd7 35. f3 Kc7 36. a4 Nc4 37. Rxa7+ Rxa7 38. Bxa7 Nb2 39. a5 Kc6 40. Bc5 h5 41. a6 1–0 (*New York Times*, August 17, 1934)

291 Kashdan–Monticelli [D61]
Syracuse, round 7, 1934 *[August 18]*

1. d4 d5 2. c4 e6 3. Nc3 Nf6 4. Bg5 Be7 5. e3 Nbd7 6. Nf3 0–0 7. Qc2 c6 8. Bd3 Re8 9. 0–0 h6 10. Bh4 a6 11. Rfd1 dxc4 12. Bxc4 b5 13. Bb3 Qb6

14. a4 Bb7 15. Qe2 b4 16. Nb1 c5
17. Nbd2 cxd4 18. exd4 a5 19. Nc4 Qa6
20. Nfe5 Bd5 21. Rac1 Rac8 22. Qe3
Nf8 23. Bxf6 Bxf6 24. Nd2 Qb7
25. Bxd5 Qxd5 26. Ndc4 Red8 27. b3
Ng6 28. Nxg6 fxg6 29. Qg3 g5 30. Rc2
Bxd4 31. Rcd2 e5 32. Nb6 Bxb6
33. Rxd5 Rxd5 34. Rf1 But not 34. Rxd5??
as after Rc1+ mate would follow. 34. ... Bd4
35. Qg4 Rdc5 36. g3 Kh8 37. Kg2 Rf8
38. Qe4 Rc3 39. Qd5 g4 40. Qe6 Rcf3
41. Qxg4 Rxb3 42. f4 Rc3 43. f5 Rc6
44. Qe4 Rb6 45. g4 b3 46. h4 b2 47. g5
Rfb8 48. Rb1 Rc8 49. Qd5 Rbc6
50. Qf7 Rc2+ 51. Kf3 R8c7 52. Qg6 e4+
53. Kxe4 Rc1 54. f6 gxf6 55. Qxh6+
Kg8 56. Qg6+ Kf8 57. Kxd4 1–0 (*L'Italia
Scacchistica*, 1934, p. 200)

292 Kashdan–Denker [D52]

Syracuse, round 9, 1934 *[August 20]*

1. d4 Nf6 2. c4 e6 3. Nc3 d5 4. Nf3
Nbd7 5. Bg5 c6 6. e3 Qa5 7. Nd2 Bb4
8. Qc2 Ne4 9. Ndxe4 dxe4 10. Bh4 0–0
11. Be2 f5 12. 0–0 e5 13. c5 Bxc3
14. bxc3 Nf6 15. Bc4+ Nd5 16. Qb3 Be6
17. Qxb7 Rac8 18. Qb3 Rc7 19. f3 exf3
20. Rxf3 h6 21. e4 fxe4 22. Rxf8+ Kxf8
23. Bd8 e3 24. Bxd5 e2 25. Bxe6 exd4
26. Qb8 1–0 (*Brooklyn Daily Eagle*, August 30,
1934)

293 Fine–Kashdan [D49]

Syracuse, round 13, 1934 *[August 13]*

1. d4 Nf6 2. c4 e6 3. Nc3 d5 4. Nf3
Nbd7 5. e3 c6 6. Bd3 dxc4 7. Bxc4 b5
8. Bd3 a6 9. e4 c5 10. e5 cxd4 11. Nxb5
Nxe5 12. Nxe5 axb5 13. 0–0 Qd5
14. Qe2 Rb8 15. Bf4 Bd6 16. Rac1 0–0
17. Nc6 Rb6 18. Bxd6 Qxd6 19. Na7
Bb7 20. Nxb5 Qd5 21. f3 Qxa2 22. Bc4
Qa5 23. Nxd4 Rd8 24. Qf2 Rbd6
25. Nb3 Qf5 26. Rfe1 h5 27. Qg3 Nd5
28. Nc5 Ba8 29. Ne4 Rb6 30. Qh4
Rdb8 31. Bxd5 exd5 32. Ng3 Qg6
33. Qxh5 Qxh5 34. Nxh5 Rxb2 35. Rcd1
Ra2 36. Ra1 Rbb2 37. Rxa2 ½–½ (*New
York Sun*, August 31, 1934; contributed by Jack
O'Keefe)

294 Reshevsky–Kashdan [D48]

Syracuse, round 15, 1934 *[August 24]*

1. d4 Nf6 2. c4 e6 3. Nc3 d5 4. Nf3 c6
5. e3 a6 6. Bd3 dxc4 7. Bxc4 b5 8. Bd3
Nbd7 9. a4 b4 10. Ne4 c5 11. 0–0 Bb7
12. Ned2 Be7 13. b3 cxd4 14. exd4 Nb6
15. Nc4 Nbd5 16. Bd2 0–0 17. Rc1 a5
18. Bb1 Qb8 19. Nce5 Qd6 20. Qe2 Rac8
21. Rxc8 Rxc8 22. Ng5 Nc3 23. Bxc3
bxc3 24. Bc2 Ba6 25. Nc4 Bxc4
26. bxc4 Qxd4 27. Bd3 Rd8 28. Rd1
Qc5 29. Ne4 Nxe4 30. Qxe4 g6 31. Bc2
Rxd1+ 32. Bxd1 Qd6 33. Qe2 Qd4 34. g3
Bc5 35. Bc2 Kg7 36. Kg2 f5 37. f4 Kf6
38. Kh3 Ke7 39. Kg2 Kd6 40. Kh3 Qe3
41. Qg2 Bb6 42. Qb7 Bc7 43. Qc8 Qf2
44. Bb3 Qb6 45. Qf8+ Kd7 46. Qg7+
½–½ (*New York Sun*, September 7, 1934)

295 Kashdan–Tholfsen [C10]

Syracuse, 1934 *[August]*

1. e4 e6 2. d4 d5 3. Nc3 dxe4 4. Nxe4
Nd7 5. Nf3 Be7 6. Bd3 Ngf6 7. c3 Unusual at this point, but probably the most accurate move. It provides for Black's two reasonable continuations. If 7. ... c5, as in the game,
White gains a pawn majority on the queenside,
and also has attacking chances. Or if 7. ... Nxe4
8. Bxe4 Nf6 9. Bc2! White continues with Bg5,
Qd3, etc., possession of the center giving him
the advantage. 7. ... c5 8. Nxc5 Nxc5
9. dxc5 Bxc5 10. 0–0 0–0 11. Bg5 h6
This is a weakening move, but it had to be played
very soon. 12. Bh4 Be7 13. Qe2 Qc7
14. Rad1 Rd8 To prepare for ...b6, which is a
dangerous move because of 15. Bxf6 Bxf6
16. Qe4. After the rook move, there is no longer
a mate threat. 15. Ne5 b6 16. Rfe1 Played
with the following sacrifice in mind. Also strong
was 16. Bxf6 Bxf6 17. Ng4 (not Qe4 Bb7, with
an easy defense). Now if ...Be7 or ...Qe7 18. Qe4
wins. Black could not avoid breaking up his
kingside. Bb7 *(see diagram)*

There is nothing better, as he must complete
his development. 17. Nxf7! A logical attack,
based on Black's weaknesses, and White command of the center files. However, Black has
many resources, which had to be carefully ex-

After
16. ... Bb7

amined. **17. ... Qc6** Best. If 17. Kxf7 18. Qxe6+ Kf8 19. Qxe6+ Kf8 20. Bxf6 Bxf6 (or ...gxf6) 21. Bc4 wins. Or if 17. ... Rxd3 18. Nxh6+ gxh6 19. Qxe6+ Kg7 20. Rxd3 and White has rook and three pawns for two minor pieces, plus an overwhelming attack. **18. Be4 Qxe4** If 18. ... Nxe4 19. Nxd8 and White is the exchange ahead, with little to fear. **19. Qxe4 Bxe4** Missing his best line. Black could have emerged even in material by 19. ... Nxe4 20. Nxd8 Bxh4! 21. Nxb7 Bxf2+ 22. Kf1 Bxe1 23. Rxe1 Rf8+ 24. Kg1. But now Black probably must lose a pawn, and White's position is sufficiently secure to give him excellent winning chances. **20. Nxd8 g5** The move Black was relying upon. If now 21. Nxe6, then 21. ... gxh4, White would have a rook and two pawns for the piece, but the strength of the bishops would make his task a very difficult one. **21. Rxe4** But this leads to a quick simplification, with White a pawn ahead, which suffices to win. **21. ... Nxe4** If either 21. ... Bxd8 or ...gxh4 22. Red4 and White remains the exchange ahead. **22. Nc6 Bc5 23. Bg3 Rf8 24. Rd8 Nxg3 25. Rxf8+ Kxf8 26. hxg3 a6** This allows the exchange of his last piece, but it only hastens the end, which is no longer in doubt. **27. Nb8 a5 28. Nd7+ Ke7 29. Nxc5 bxc5 30. Kf1 Kd6 31. Ke2 Kd5 32. b3 e5 33. Ke3 h5 34. f3 h4 35. gxh4 gxh4 36. a3 a4 37. bxa4 Kc4 38. Ke4 1–0** Annotations by Kashdan. (*American Chess Bulletin*, September-October 1934)

296 Reinfeld–Kashdan [C86]

Syracuse, 1934 [*August*]

1. e4 e5 2. Nf3 Nc6 3. Bb5 a6 4. Ba4 Nf6 5. 0–0 Be7 6. Qe2 b5 7. Bb3 d6

8. a4 Bg4 9. c3 0–0 10. axb5 axb5 11. Rxa8 Qxa8 12. Qxb5 Na5 13. Bc2 Nxe4 14. Bxe4 Qxe4 15. Qxa5 Qxb1 16. d3 Qxd3 17. Qxc7 Bxf3 And Black eventually won. **0–1** (*Practical Chess Openings*, p. 362)

297 Kashdan–Tenner [D38]

Manhattan Championship, round 1, 1934
[*October–December*]

1. d4 d5 2. c4 e6 3. Nc3 Nf6 4. Nf3 Nbd7 5. Bg5 Bb4 This only leads to the exchange of bishops. It is not as effective as the Cambridge Springs Defense, 5. ... c6 6. e3 Qa5, etc. **6. cxd5 exd5 7. Qb3 c5 8. Bd2** To force Bxc3, by threatening Nxd5. However 8. a3 would have been simpler, and equally effective. But not 8. dxc5 Qa5! when Black has the attack. **8. ... Bxc3 9. Bxc3 0–0 10. e3 c4 11. Qc2 Ne4 12. Be2 Qe7 13. 0–0 b5 14. Be1 f5 15. b3 Bb7 16. bxc4 bxc4 17. Rb1 Rfb8 18. Ba5 Bc6** An oversight which costs an important pawn. Qd6 was necessary, when White would double rooks, and maintain a slight advantage. **19. Bxc4! Qa3 20. Bb3 Qd6 21. Bc7! Qe6** A choice of evils. Of course, if Qxc7 22. Bxd5+ and White will be two pawns up. **22. Bxb8 Rxb8 23. Ba4 Rxb1 24. Rxb1 Bxa4 25. Qxa4 Nc3 26. Qxd7!** Notes by Kashdan. A neat finish. If 26. ... Qxd7 then Rb8+ Kf7 followed by 28. Ne5+. **1–0** (*American Chess Bulletin*, February 1935)

298 Kashdan–Kupchik [C11]

Manhattan Championship, 1934
[*October–December*]

1. e4 e6 2. d4 d5 3. Nc3 Nf6 4. Bg5 dxe4 5. Nxe4 Be7 6. Nc3 Nd5 7. Bxe7 Qxe7 8. Qd2 c6 9. 0–0–0 Nd7 10. Nf3 N7f6 11. Bd3 Nb4 12. Rhe1 Nxd3+ 13. Qxd3 Bd7 14. Ne5 0–0–0 15. Qg3 g6 16. Na4 Be8 17. Kb1 Qc7 18. Nc5 h5 19. Qf3 Nd5 20. c4 Nb6 21. Ne4 h4 22. c5 Nd5 23. Nd6+ Kb8 24. Nxe8 Rdxe8 25. Qxf7 Qxf7 26. Nxf7 Rhf8 27. Nd6 Re7 28. f3 Kc7 29. Re4 Rf4 30. Rde1 b6 31. g3 hxg3 32. hxg3 Rxe4 33. Rxe4 Nf6 34. Re2 Kd7 35. Nc4 bxc5

36. dxc5 g5 37. Kc2 Kc7 38. Ne5 Nd7
39. Nxd7 Kxd7 40. Kd3 Rf7 41. Ke3
Rf5 42. Rc2 a5 43. b3 g4 44. Rc4 Ke7
45. Rxg4 Rxc5 46. Kd3 Rb5 47. Re4
Kd6 48. f4 Rb8 49. g4 c5 50. Ra4 Ra8
51. Ke4 Ra7 52. g5 Ra8 53. g6 Ra7
54. f5 Ke7 55. Ke5 exf5 56. Kxf5 Kf8
57. Rh4 Kg8 58. Rh7 Ra8 59. Rc7 a4
60. Rxc5 axb3 61. axb3 Rb8 62. Rc3
Kg7 63. Rg3 Rb4 64. Ke5 Rb8 65. Kd4
Rd8+ 66. Kc3 Rc8+ 67. Kb2 Rb8
68. Rg4 1–0 (*Brooklyn Daily Eagle*, November 1, 1934)

299 Richman–Kashdan [C14]
Manhattan Championship, 1934
[October–December]

1. e4 e6 2. d4 d5 3. Nc3 Nf6 4. Bg5
Be7 5. e5 Nfd7 6. Bxe7 Qxe7 7. f4 0–0
8. Nf3 c5 9. Bd3 f6 10. 0–0 cxd4
11. Nxd4 fxe5 12. fxe5 Rxf1+ 13. Bxf1
Nxe5 14. Qh5 Ng6 15. Nxd5 Qd8
16. Bc4 exd5 17. Bxd5+ Kh8 18. Re1
Nc6 19. Nxc6 bxc6 20. Bf7 Qd4+
21. Kh1 Bg4 22. Qg5 Qf2 23. Rg1 Qxf7
24. Qxg4 Qxa2 25. Qd7 Qd5 26. Qb7
Re8 27. Qxa7 Nf4 28. Qf2 Nh3 0–1
(*American Chess Bulletin*, November 1934)

300 Kashdan–Willman [D66]
Manhattan Championship, 1934
[October–December]

1. d4 Nf6 2. c4 e6 3. Nf3 d5 4. Nc3
Nbd7 5. Bg5 Be7 6. e3 0–0 7. Rc1 c6
8. Bd3 a6 9. cxd5 cxd5 10. a4 Re8
11. 0–0 Nf8 12. Qe2 Bd7 13. Ne5 Rc8
14. Rc2 Bc6 15. Rfc1 N6d7 16. Nxc6
Rxc6 17. Bxe7 Qxe7 18. Na2 Rxc2
19. Qxc2 Nb6 20. Qb3 Nc8 21. Rc3 Nd6
22. Qc2 g6 23. Nc1 Nd7 24. Nb3 Nb6
25. Nc5 Rc8 26. g3 a5 27. h4 Nbc4
28. b3 Nb6 29. Qd2 Na8 30. Rc2 b6
31. Na6 Qd7 32. Qc1 Kf8 33. Kg2 Rxc2
34. Qxc2 Qc8 35. Qxc8+ Nxc8 36. Kf3
Ke7 37. Kf4 h6 38. g4 Nd6 39. f3 Ne8
40. g5 hxg5+ 41. hxg5 Nac7 42. Nxc7
Nxc7 43. Ke5 Ne8 44. Bc2 Nc7 45. Bd3
Ne8 46. Bb5 Nd6 47. e4 dxe4 48. fxe4

Nb7 49. Bc6 Nd6 50. d5 exd5 51. Kxd5
Nc8 52. e5 Na7 53. Bb7 Kd7 54. Ba6
Ke7 55. Be2 Kd7 56. Bg4+ Kc7 57. e6
fxe6+ 58. Kxe6 Nc6 59. Kf6 1–0 (*Brooklyn Daily Eagle*, December 13, 1934)

301 Platz–Kashdan [C42]
Manhattan Championship, 1934
[October–December]

1. e4 e5 2. Nf3 Nf6 3. Nxe5 d6 4. Nf3
Nxe4 5. Qe2 Qe7 6. d3 Nf6 7. Bg5
Qxe2+ 8. Bxe2 Be7 9. Nc3 h6 10. Bh4
Nc6 11. Nb5 Kd8 12. 0–0–0 g5 13. Bg3
Nh5 14. Rhe1 a6 15. Nbd4 Nxd4
16. Nxd4 Nxg3 17. hxg3 Bf6 18. Nb3 a5
19. c3 a4 20. Nd2 a3 21. d4 axb2+
22. Kxb2 Be6 23. Nb3 c6 24. Bf3 d5
25. Ra1 Kc7 26. a4 b6 27. Bd1 Rhb8
28. Bc2 c5 29. Kc1 c4 30. Nd2 b5
31. Nf3 g4 32. Ne5 bxa4 33. f4 gxf3
34. gxf3 Rg8 35. g4 Bg5+ 36. Kd1 a3
37. Ra2 Rgb8 38. Bh7 Rb2 39. Re2 Rxa2
40. Rxa2 Kd6 41. Bb1 Bf4 42. Re2 Rb8
43. Ba2 Rb2 44. Ke1 Rxe2+ 45. Kxe2
Bxe5 46. dxe5+ Kxe5 47. Ke3 Bd7
48. f4+ Kd6 0–1 (*Brooklyn Daily Eagle*, December 20, 1934)

302 Kashdan–Denker [D52]
Manhattan Championship, 1934
[October–December]

1. d4 Nf6 2. c4 e6 3. Nf3 d5 4. Nc3
c6 5. Bg5 Nbd7 6. e3 Qa5 7. Nd2 Bb4
8. Qc2 0–0 9. Be2 Ne4 10. Ndxe4 dxe4
11. Bh4 e5 In Syracuse in the same position
Denker played 11. ... f5 12. 0–0 e5 13. c5! Bxc3
14. bxc3 Nf6 15. Bc4+ Nd5 16. Qb3 winning a
pawn. 12. 0–0 exd4 13. Nxe4 If 13. exd4
g5 14. Bg3 f5 15. f4 leads to interesting play.
13. ... f5 14. a3 fxe4 14. ... d3 just fails. Then
not 15. Bxd3 fxe4 16. axb4 exd3! and wins, but
14. ... d3 15. axb4! Qxa1 16. Bxd3! Qa6 17. c5
b5 18. Nd6 Ne5 19. Be7 with a far superior
game. 15. axb4 Qxb4 16. exd4 Against Marshall, in 1932, I played 16. Qxe4 Nc5 17. Be7
obtaining the better ending. The text is also
strong. 16. ... Nf6 17. Rfd1 Bf5

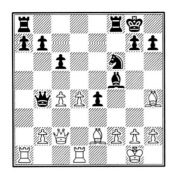

After
17. ... Bf5

18. Bg5 Planning h3 and Be3, followed by an advance of the center pawns. If 18. c5 Nd5 19. Ra4? e3 wins. **18. ... Ng4** Threatening ...Nxf2. If now 18. ... Ng4 19. c5 Nxf2! 20. Qc4+ Qxc4 21. Bxc4+ Kh8 22. Kxf2 Be6+ regains the piece. **19. Qd2** But this simple move wards off the attack, and leaves White in control of the important squares. **19. ... Qd6 20. Bf4 Qf6 21. h3 Nxf2** Black had planned this, but it proves unsound. However, there is no longer a good retreat. **22. Kxf2 Bxh3** If 22. ... Bd7 23. Kg3 and nothing happens. **23. gxh3 g5 24. Rg1 Kh8 25. d5** Playing to exchange queens, or command the long diagonal, which will break Black's attack. **25. ... cxd5 26. cxd5 Rac8** At once 26. Rae8 is better, but 27. Qc3 Re5 28. Bg4 etc., would still be sufficient. **27. Ra4 Rce8 28. Qc3 Re5 29. Bg4** The counter-attack, developed when his bishop reaches e6, proves the decisive factor. **29. ... gxf4 30. Be6** The threat is 31. Rxe4! Rxe4 32. Qxf6+ and 33. Rg8 mate. **30. ... h6 31. Rg6!** The quickest finish. Also good was 31. Rxe4 Rxe4 32. Rg8+! Kh7 33. Rxf8 Qxf8 (or 33. ... Qh4+ 34. Kf1 wins) 34. Qc2! regaining the rook. **31. ... e3+ 32. Kf3 Qxg6 33. Qxe5+ Kh7 34. Rxf4 Rxf4+ 35. Qxf4 1–0** (*American Chess Bulletin*, December 1934, p. 159)

303 Hassialis–Kashdan [E23]

Manhattan Championship, 1934
[October–December]

1. d4 Nf6 2. c4 e6 3. Nc3 Bb4 4. Qb3 c5 5. dxc5 Nc6 6. Nf3 Ne4 7. Bd2 Nxd2 8. Nxd2 f5 9. g3 Bxc5 10. Bg2 b6 11. 0–0 Bb7 12. e3 0–0 13. a3 Qc8 14. Nf3 Na5 15. Qa2 Be7 16. Rfd1 Rd8 17. b3 d5

18. Nd2 Bf6 19. Rac1 dxc4 20. Bxb7 Qxb7 21. bxc4 Rac8 22. c5 Qe7 23. Ne2 Rxc5 24. Rxc5 bxc5 25. Rc1 Rxd2 26. Qxd2 Nb3 27. Qc2 Nxc1 28. Qxc1 Qd6 29. Qc2 Kf7 30. Nf4 Be7 31. h4 Qa6 32. Qd1 g6 33. Qd7 c4 34. Qc7 Qxa3 35. Qxc4 Qd6 36. Qc8 Bf6 37. Qb7+ Qe7 38. Qa6 Be5 39. Nd3 Bd6 40. Qc8 Kg7 41. Qc3+ Kh6 42. Qd4 e5 43. Qd5 e4 44. Nc1 Qc7 45. Ne2 Be5 46. Kg2 Kg7 47. Qe6 Qd6 48. Qe8 a5 49. Qb5 Qc7 50. Qe8 Kf6 51. Qh8+ Ke6 52. Qe8+ Kd6 53. Qf8+ Kc6 54. Qe8+ Kb6 55. Qa4 Qc6 56. Qb3+ Ka6 57. Qd1 a4 58. Nd4 Qc4 59. Nc2 Qc3 60. Qe2+ Ka5 61. Qd1 Qd3 62. Qc1 Kb5 63. Qb1+ Qb3 64. Qf1+ Kb6 65. Qd1 Kc7 66. Qd2 Bc3 67. Qe2 a3 68. Nd4 Bxd4 69. exd4 Qf3+! 0–1 (*New York Sun*, December 15, 1934)

304 Kashdan–Simonson [D90]

Manhattan Championship, 1934 *[December]*

1. d4 Nf6 2. c4 c6 3. Nc3 d5 4. Nf3 g6 5. cxd5 Nxd5 If ...cxd5 6. e3, and Black's bishop at f8 will be misplaced with nothing to aim at. **6. e4** Exchanging was preferable, as this knight loses too much time. White already has firm control of the center. **6. ... Nb6 7. Be2 Bg7 8. Be3 Be6 9. 0–0 0–0–0** If ...Nc4 10. Bf4 Nxb2? 11. Qc2 Nc5 12. d5 wins a piece. **10. Qc1 Bc4 11. Bh6 Bxe2 12. Nxe2 N8d7 13. a4 Rc8 14. a5 Na8 15. Ng3 Nc7 16. Re1 Re8 17. Bxg7 Kxg7 18. Qg5 e6** As good as any. If now 19. Nh5+ Kg8 20. Qh6 gxh5 21. Ng5 Qf6! (Better than Nf8 22. Ra3 with a dangerous attack). **19. Qd2 f5 20. h4 Rf8 21. exf5 exf5 22. Qb4 Rb8 23. Ng5 Nf6 24. Qc5 h6 25. Nf3 a6 26. Re7+ Kg8 27. Ne5 Nfd5 28. Rd7 Qf6**

After
28. ... Qf6

29. Qc1! The winning move, the rook pawn must be defended, but some material loss can no longer be prevented. **29. ... f4 30. Ne4 Qf5 31. Nd6 Qe6 32. Ndf7** A remarkable position. With only one open file along which to operate, the White pieces have done a splendid job of sifting through the opponent's defenses. Black has nothing better than the coming sacrifice of the exchange. **32. ... Rxf7 33. Rxf7 Rf8 34. Rxf8+ Kxf8 35. Qc5+ Kg7 36. Re1 Nb5 37. Nf3 Qf6 38. Re8 Nd6 39. Rb8 Qe7 40. Ne5 Qc7 41. Ra8 Ne7 42. Nd3 Nf7** If 42. ... Nf5 43. Qe5+ Qxe5 44. dxe5 followed by Rb8. **43. Re8 Nf5 44. Qf8+ Kf6 45. Ne5 h5 46. Qg8** If 46. ... Nxh4, then 47. Rf8 wins. **1–0** Annotated by Kashdan. (*Chess Review,* January 1935)

305 Cohen–Kashdan [C42]
Manhattan Championship, 1934
[October–December]

1. e4 e5 2. Nf3 Nf6 3. Nxe5 d6 4. Nf3 Nxe4 5. d4 d5 6. Bd3 Be7 7. Nbd2 Nd6 8. Qe2 0–0 9. 0–0 Nc6 10. c3 Re8 11. Ne5 Bf8 12. f4 f6

After
12. ... f6

This is a crucial position. Black in playing f6 felt that White's best reply was 13. Nxc6 which would be met by bxc6 leaving Black with a good center formation and in possession of the open e file. White, however, has other ideas in mind. **13. Qh5! g6 14. Nxg6!!** White gives up a knight for three pawns, a practical equivalent since his pawn position has no weaknesses, and by doing so exposes Black's king and retains the initiative. **14. ... hxg6 15. Bxg6 Re7 16. Qxd5+ Be6 17. Qh5** Threatening 18. d5. **17. ... Rg7 18. f5 Bf7 19. Nf3 Ne7**

20. Nh4 This exchange is an error of judgment. Kashdan in his play shows a decided preference for bishops and tries whenever possible to win the "minor exchange" (trading knights for bishops). Correct was 20. ... Qe8! This forces an exchange of bishops since it threatens to win a pawn, and would help to free Black's game. White cannot answer with Bh6 because of 21. ... Rh7! 22. Bxh7+ Kxh7, etc. Neither can he play 21. Re1 because of 21. ... Ndxf5 22. Nxf5 Rxg6!. **20. ... Nxg6 21. fxg6 Bc4 22. Re1 Qd7 23. Bf4 Be6** This loses the exchange. However, there was little to be done. 23. ... Bd3 would have been met with Re3. **24. Bh6 Re8 25. Bxg7 Bxg7 26. Rf1 Bg4 27. Qh7+ Kf8 28. h3 Bf5 29. Nxf5 Nxf5 30. Rf2** White could win the knight at once with 30. g4, but this would allow Black counter chances with Qd6. **30. ... Qe6 31. Raf1 Qe3 32. Kh2 Qg3+ 33. Kh1 Re1 34. Rxf5 Rxf1+ 35. Rxf1 Qg5 36. h4 Qd5 37. h5 Qc4 38. Kg1 Qe6 39. h6 1–0** (*Chess Review,* December 1934, p. 226)

306 Kashdan–Horowitz [D38]
Manhattan Championship, 1934
[October–December]

1. d4 d5 2. c4 e6 3. Nc3 Nf6 4. Nf3 Nbd7 5. Bg5 Bb4 This generally amounts to a loss of time, as it is hardly good play to exchange the bishop for a knight. **6. cxd5 exd5 7. Rc1 c6 8. a3 Be7 9. e3 Nh5 10. Bxe7 Qxe7 11. Nd2** 11. Be2 f5 12. g3 etc. is a good form of development. The idea of the text is to restrain ...f5 for as long as possible. **11. ... Nf4 12. Qf3 Ng6 13. Bd3 Nf6 14. 0–0 0–0–0 15. Rfe1** This is not so much to play e4, as to allow Nf1 as a necessary defense later. White is preparing a general queenside advance. **15. ... Be6 16. Na4 Rae8 17. Nc5 Bc8 18. b4 Nh4** A time losing maneuver, but Black's knights are not well placed for his purposes. **19. Qe2 Nf5 20. Nf1 Nd6 21. f3** This might have been delayed until really needed. 21. a4 was preferable. **21. ... Nh5 22. Qc2 f5** At last. But White is now in readiness on the kingside, and goes forward with his own plans. **23. a4 b5** Badly weakening his pawns. 23. ... g5, etc., would have offered better prospects.

24. axb5 cxb5 25. Ra1 Nc4 26. Bxc4 bxc4 27. Ra5 Qf6 Giving up the pawn, which could not have been held long in any case. But he does not get enough for it. 28. Rxa7 f4 29. Qd2 fxe3 30. Rxe3 Nf4 31. Raa3 h6 32. Rxe8 Rxe8 33. Re3 Rf8 34. Ng3 It is now a question of getting the pieces on their proper squares, and advancing the b pawn. 34. ... Qb6 35. Ne2 Ng6 36. Qb2 Bf5 37. Nc3 Nf4 38. b5 Nd3

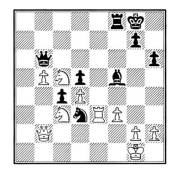

After
38. ... Nd3

39. Nxd5? Under time pressure, overlooking the loss of a piece. But strangely enough, it proves to be the quickest way to win owing to the strength of the passed pawn. Proper was 39. Nxd3 cxd3 (if 39. ... Qxd4 40. Nd1! wins a piece for White) 40. Nxd5 Qa5 41. Ne7+ Kh7 42. Nxf5 Rxf5 43. Qb1! remaining two pawns ahead. 39. ... Qxc5 40. dxc5 Nxb2 41. c6 Na4 42. b6 Kh7 There is nothing better. If 42. ... Nxb6 43. Nxb6 Rf6 44. Nd5! wins. 43. b7 Nc5 44. Ne7 Be6 Playing for a trap. But it loses quickly. The best chance was 44. ... Bd7 but after 45. cxd7 Nxb7 (45. ... Nxd7 46. Nc6 Nb8 47. Na5 wins easily) 46. Nc6 Nd8 47. Ne5 wins. (But not 47. Re8 c3! etc.) 45. c7 Avoiding the plausible 45. Rxe6 Nxe6 46. Nc8 c3 47. b8(Q) c2 48. Qb2 Nd4! threatening ...Rxc8 as well as ...Ne2+. White would have nothing better than 49. Nd6 leading to a drawn ending. 1–0 Analysis by Kashdan. (*American Chess Bulletin*, December 1934)

307 Kupchik–Kashdan [D35]
Manhattan Championship/Playoff, 1934
[December 23]

1. d4 Nf6 2. c4 e6 3. Nf3 d5 4. Nc3 c6 5. cxd5 exd5 6. Bg5 Be7 7. e3 0–0

8. Bd3 Ne4 Premature. I would prefer Nbd7. 9. Bxe4 Bxg5 10. Nxg5 Qxg5 11. h4 White capitalizes on Black's negligence and starts an attack. 11. ... Qe7 12. Bd3 f5 On the surface this move appears to meet White's attack effectively, but it actually hinders Black's development. 13. Qc2 g6 As a result of his preceding move he must further weaken the king's wing. 14. 0–0–0 Nd7 15. h5 Nf6 16. hxg6 hxg6 17. Ne2 Kg7 18. Nf4 Bd7 19. Rh3 g5 In an endeavor to prevent White's threat of Rg3. 20. Nh5+ Nxh5 21. Rxh5 Qf6 22. f4 White sacrifices a pawn in order to strengthen his attack. 22. ... gxf4 23. exf4

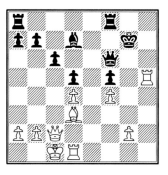

After
23. exf4

23. ... Qxd4 24. g3 Rf6 Rf7 would momentarily stave off White's persistent advance. 25. Rdh1 Qe3+ Black must control the e file in order to bring his king to a safer position. 26. Kb1 Kf7 27. Rh7+ Ke6 28. Qc3 d4 Preventing White from succeeding in his double threat of either Qxf6 or Re1. 29. Qc5! 1–0 Notes by Kupchik. Black has 29. ... Qxd3+, but after 30. Ka1 Black cannot guard against both mate threats, Qe5 and Qe7. Kupchik entered the game for the brilliancy prize and it decided the tournament in his favor after both had even scores in the tournament. While Kupchik won this game in the playoff, Kashdan defeated Kupchik in the tournament. See game 298. (*American Chess Bulletin*, February 1935)

308 Kashdan–Reinfeld
(Marshall C.C.) [E43]
Metropolitan Chess League, 1935

1. d4 Nf6 2. c4 e6 3. Nc3 Bb4 4. e3 b6 5. Bd3 Bb7 6. f3 c5 7. a3 cxd4 8. axb4 dxc3 9. bxc3 0–0 10. Ne2 d5 11. cxd5 exd5 12. 0–0 Nbd7 13. Nd4 Ne5 14. Be2

a6 15. Qe1 Qc8 16. Ra3 Nc4 17. Ra2 b5 18. Qh4 Ne8 19. Bd3 g6 20. f4 Ncd6 21. f5 Ne4 22. Bxe4 dxe4 23. Raf2 Qd8 24. Qh6 Qf6 25. Ne6!! fxe6 26. fxe6 1–0 (*Brooklyn Daily Eagle*, March 7, 1935)

309 Ratke–Kashdan [A13]
Milwaukee, Western (Prelims), 1935 *[July]*

1. Nf3 Nf6 2. b3 d5 3. Bb2 c5 4. e3 e6 5. c4 Nc6 6. Be2 d4 7. exd4 cxd4 8. Bd3 e5 9. Qe2 Qe7 10. Ba3 Qc7 11. Bxf8 Kxf8 12. 0–0 Bg4 13. Be4 Nxe4 14. Qxe4 f5 15. Qd5 Rd8 16. Qc5+ Qe7 17. Qxe7+ Kxe7 18. Re1 Kf6 19. Na3 e4 20. h3 Bxf3 21. gxf3 exf3 22. Kh2 Rhe8 23. Kg3 Ne5 24. Nb5 f4+ 25. Kh2 Nc6 26. Nc7 Re2 27. Rxe2 fxe2 28. Re1 d3 29. Nd5+ Rxd5 30. cxd5 Nd4 0–1 (Kashdan's score-sheet)

310 Kashdan–Kent [C41]
Milwaukee, Western (Prelims), 1935 *[July]*

1. e4 e5 2. Nf3 d6 3. d4 exd4 4. Nxd4 Nf6 5. Nc3 Be7 6. Bf4 0–0 7. Qd2 Nc6 8. 0–0–0 Be6 9. f3 Ne5 10. Be2 c6 11. Kb1 Qa5 12. Nd5! Qd8 13. Nxe6 fxe6 14. Nxe7+ Qxe7 15. Qxd6 Qxd6 16. Rxd6 Ng6 17. Be3 Rfe8 18. Rhd1 Kf7 19. a4 Ne7 20. g4 Rec8 21. Bc4 Ned5 22. exd5 cxd5 23. Bb5 Ke7 24. Bf4 a6 25. Bd3 Rc6 26. Rxc6 bxc6 27. Re1 Kd7 28. Be5 h6 29. h4 Rf8 30. a5 Ra8 31. g5 hxg5 32. hxg5 Ne8 33. Rh1 c5 34. Rh8 1–0 (Kashdan's scoresheet)

311 Kashdan–Holland [C17]
Milwaukee, Western (Prelims), 1935 *[July]*

1. e4 e6 2. d4 d5 3. Nc3 Bb4 4. e5 c5 5. Bd2 cxd4 6. Nb5 Bc5 7. b4 Be7 8. Qg4 g6 9. Nxd4 Nc6 10. Nxc6 bxc6 11. Nf3 h5 12. Qf4 Bd7 13. Bd3 Nh6 14. 0–0 Nf5 15. g3 Bf8 16. h4 Bh6 17. Ng5 Qe7 18. c4 f6 19. exf6 Qxf6 20. cxd5 cxd5 21. Rfe1 0–0 22. Rac1 Rac8 23. Rxc8 Rxc8 24. Bxf5 gxf5 25. Qd6 Bxg5 26. Qxd7 Rd8 27. Bxg5 Rxd7 28. Bxf6 Kf7 29. Be5 d4 30. Rd1 d3 31. f4 d2 32. Kf2 Rd3 33. b5 Ke7

34. Bb8 Rd7 35. a4 Rb7 36. Be5 a6 37. bxa6 Ra7 38. Rxd2 Rxa6 39. Ra2 Kd7 40. Ke3 Kc6 41. Kd4 Ra5 42. Kc4 Ra8 43. a5 Ra6 44. Rc2 Rxa5 45. Kb4+ Kb6 46. Bc7+ 1–0 (Kashdan's scoresheet)

312 Surgies–Kashdan [D05]
Milwaukee, Western (Prelims), 1935 *[July]*

1. d4 d5 2. Nf3 Nf6 3. e3 e6 4. Bd3 c5 5. c3 Nc6 6. Nbd2 Bd6 7. 0–0 0–0 8. dxc5 Bxc5 9. e4 Qc7 10. Qc2? Better is Qe2, for if 10. ... dxe4 11. Nxe4 Nxe4 12. Qxe4 f5 13. Qh4 with a fine game. **10. ... dxe4 11. Nxe4 Nxe4 12. Bxe4 f5 13. Bd3 e5** Whereas now Black has the better development, and a strong attack. **14. Bc4+ Kh8 15. Be3 Bd6** Better than exchanging bishops, as Black gains time for the advance of the pawns. **16. h3 e4 17. Ne1** If Nd4 Nxd4 18. cxd4 f5 followed by f3. Or 17. Ng5 Qe7 threatening h6. **17. ... f4 18. Bd2 Bf5 19. Qc1 f3 20. g4 Bxg4!**

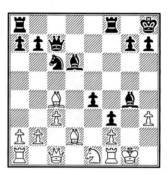

After
20. ... Bxg4

Quite sound, and the quickest way to force the win. **21. hxg4 Qd7 0–1** Annotated by Kashdan. (*Milwaukee* 1935)

313 Winkelman–Kashdan [D15]
Milwaukee, Western (Prelims), 1935 *[July]*

1. d4 d5 2. c4 c6 3. Nf3 Nf6 4. Nc3 Nbd7 5. cxd5 cxd5 6. Qb3 e6 7. Bf4 a6 8. e3 Be7 9. Rc1 0–0 10. Bd3 b5 11. h3 Bb7 12. 0–0 Rc8 13. a4 b4 14. Na2 Qa5 Threatening to win a pawn by Nb6 and Bc6. **15. Rxc8 Rxc8 16. Rc1 Rxc1+ 17. Nxc1 Ne4 18. Qc2 Qb6 19. Ne5 Nf8 20. f3 Nd6 21. Nb3 a5 22. Qc5 Bd8 23. Nxa5** Apparently winning a pawn, but only temporarily, as the continuation shows. **23. ... Qxc5**

24. dxc5 Bxa5 25. cxd6 f6 26. Ng4 e5 27. Nxe5? This is unwarranted. White gets three pawns for the piece, but they are all weak, and bound to fall soon. **27. ... fxe5 28. Bxe5 Kf7 29. Kf2 g6 30. g4 Nd7 31. Bf4 Nc5 32. Bb5 Ba6** The simplest, as after the exchange White's queenside pawns are left defenseless. **33. Bxa6 Nxa6 34. e4 dxe4 35. fxe4 Nc5 36. Ke3 Nxa4 37. Kd4 Nxb2 38. Bg5 Ke6 39. Kc5 b3 40. Be3 Nd3+ 0–1** Annotation by Kashdan. (*Milwaukee* 1935)

314 Kashdan–Santasiere [D92]
Milwaukee, Western (Finals), 1935 *[July]*

1. d4 Nf6 2. c4 g6 3. Nc3 d5 4. Nf3 Bg7 5. Bf4 0–0 6. cxd5 Winning a pawn, but at no great cost in development, e3 would suffice to give White a positional advantage. **6. ... Nxd5 7. Nxd5 Qxd5 8. Bxc7 Na6 9. Bg3** After this Black soon regains the pawn. It might have been held by 9. Bf4 Bf5 10. a3 Rac8 11. Bc1 followed by e3, etc. White's game would be none too easy. **9. ... Bf5 10. a3 Rac8 11. e3 Rc2 12. Bd3** If 12. b4 Qb3, threatening Bc3+, is too strong. **12. ... Rxb2 13. 0–0 Rc8 14. Rc1 Rc6 15. Bxf5 gxf5 16. Ne5 Bxe5 17. Bxe5 f6 18. Bf4 e6 19. Qh5** Starting a dangerous attack, which would succeed if White could get his rooks into action. Black plays well to counter the threat. **19. ... Qd7 20. Rcd1 Nc7 21. Bh6 Qf7 22. Qh3 Rbc2 23. f4**

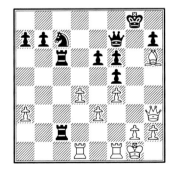

After
23. f4

Here the right idea was 23. f3. If then Rb2 24. e4 Rcc7 25. Kh1 Rxg2? 26. Rg1 wins. **23. ... Kh8 24. e4** If 24. Rf3 Rc1, etc. The text leads to interesting play, but Black has enough resources. **24. ... fxe4 25. f5 Nd5 26. Rde1**

exf5 27. Qxf5 Qg6 Returning the pawn but forcing an exchange after which the game is completely equalized. **28. Qxe4 Qxh6 29. Qxd5 Qf8 30. Qd7 Rc7 31. Qf5 Rd2 32. Rd1 Rcc2 33. Rxd2 Rxd2 34. Qa5 Rxd4 35. Qxa7 Rd7 36. Qb6 Kg7 37. Qe3 Qd6 38. Rb1 Re7 39. Qc3 b6 40. h3 ½–½** Annotations by Kashdan (*Milwaukee* 1935)

315 Dake–Kashdan [D36]
Milwaukee, Western (Finals), 1935 *[July]*

1. d4 Nf6 2. c4 e6 3. Nc3 d5 4. Bg5 c6 5. e3 Nbd7 6. cxd5 exd5 7. Bd3 Be7 8. Qc2 0–0 9. Nge2 Re8 10. h3 Ne4 11. Bxe7 Qxe7 12. Bxe4 dxe4 13. g4 Threatening to win a pawn by 14. Ng3 Nf6 15. g5, but this is easily prevented. **13. ... Nf6 14. Ng3 h6 15. 0–0–0** Leading to interesting play. Not so much because of possible kingside attacks as in the attempts of both sides to find strong posts for their pieces. **15. ... b5 16. Kb1 a5 17. Rc1 Bd7 18. Rhd1 Rac8 19. Nce2 Nd5 20. Nc3** Now 20. ... Nb4 21. Qe2 Nd3 22. Rc2 would lead to nothing, as the e pawn is left unprotected. **20. ... Nf6 21. Nce2? Nd5 22. Nc3? Nxc3+** Playing for a win, but in view of the hole at c5, and the e pawn, Black should perhaps have been content with the repetition of moves. **23. Qxc3 Be6 24. Nh5 f6 25. Nf4 Bf7 26. Qc5 Qd7 27. Qf5 Qd6** Exchanging queens would leave White with the more advantageous ending. **28. Rc5 Rc7 29. h4 a4 30. g5 fxg5 31. hxg5 g6 32. Qh3! h5 33. Rg1 Kg7 34. Qg3! Rd7** White threatened Nxh5+ winning the queen. **½–½** Annotated by Kashdan. (*Milwaukee* 1935)

316 Kashdan–Elo [D49]
Milwaukee, Western (Finals), 1935 *[July]*

1. d4 d5 2. c4 c6 3. Nc3 Nf6 4. Nf3 Nbd7 5. e3 e6 6. Bd3 dxc4 7. Bxc4 b5 8. Bd3 a6 9. e4 c5 10. e5 cxd4 11. Nxb5 Nxe5 12. Nxe5 axb5 13. Qf3 This move is coming into favor lately, and seems to give White the advantage. Less effective is 13. Bb5+ Bd7 14. Nxd7 Qa5+ followed by Qxb5 or 13. 0–0

Qd5 14. Qe2 Rb8, etc. **13. ... Bd7** An inferior defense, which gets him into serious trouble. Probably best is 13. ... Bb4 14. Ke2 Rb8 15. Nc6 Bb7 16. Bxb5 0–0 with some interesting play. **14. 0–0** 14. Nxd7 Nxd7 15. Bxb5 could be tried here, but there is no hurry about this, as Black soon finds he cannot save the b pawn. **14. ... Rb8** Trying to hold the pawn, as Nxd7 is threatened, but this at the expense of his kingside development. If 14. ... b4 15. Bg5 Be7 16. Bxf6 gxf6 17. Nxd7 Kxd7 18. Bb5 is unpleasant. **15. Bf4**

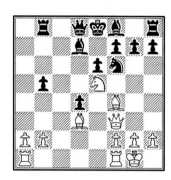

After
15. Bf4

15. ... Rc8 An unpleasant necessity. If 15. Bd6 16. Nxf7 wins. Or 15. ... Rb6 16. Rac1 Bd6 (the threat was 17. Nxf7 Kxf7 18. Bc7) 17. Nxd7 Nxd7 (Forced for if 17. ... Qxd7 18. Bxb5 Rxb5 19. Qa8+ wins.) 18. Bxd6 Rxd6 19. Qg3! which badly breaks up Black's game. **16. Nxd7 Qxd7 17. Qe2 Qa7** The pawn must finally go, for if 17. ... Rc5 18. Rac1 Rd5 19. Rc7 wins. **18. Bxb5+ Nd7 19. Rac1 Rxc1 20. Rxc1 Bc5** The only chance, but a piece must be lost. **21. b4 Bb6 22. Rc8+ Bd8 23. Bg5 0–0 24. Rxd8 1–0** Analysis by Kashdan. (*Milwaukee* 1935)

317 Ruth–Kashdan [D00]

Milwaukee, Western (Finals), 1935 *[July]*

1. d4 Nf6 2. Bg5 d5 3. Nd2 Nbd7 4. c4 e6 5. e3 Be7 6. cxd5 exd5 7. Rc1 0–0 8. Bd3 c6 9. Ne2 Making it easier for Black to free his game. 9. Qc2 is more accurate, to restrain Ne4. **9. ... Ne4 10. Bxe7 Qxe7 11. Bxe4 dxe4 12. Qc2 f5 13. h4 Nf6 14. Nf4 Be6 15. Nxe6 Qxe6 16. Qb3 Nd5 17. g3** If 17. Qxb7 Rfb8 18. Qxc6 Qxc6

19. Rxc6, and White is under considerable pressure from which he can hardly escape. **17. ... b5** To prevent Nc4 and Ne5, even at the expense of a backward pawn. **18. Rc5 Kh8 19. Ke2** Very risky, but if 19. 0–0 g5 20. hxg5 Rg8 with a dangerous attack. **19. ... Qg6** 19. ... f4 is tempting, but fails after 20. Rxd5! (not 22. exf4 Nxf4) Rxf2 23. Kxf2 Rf8+ 24. Ke1, and there is no sufficient continuation. **20. h5 Qg4+ 21. Ke1 Rf6 22. Rh4 Qg5**

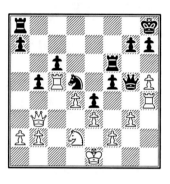

After
22. ... Qg5

23. Rxd5 Justified, as he obtains two pawns for the exchange, and also breaks the attack which Black has been building up. **23. ... cxd5 24. Qxd5 Rff8 25. Nxe4 Qe7 26. Nc5 Rad8 27. Qe6 Qc7** Black must avoid an exchange of queens to have winning chances. His problem is to find an open file for the rooks, which is difficult in view of the well placed knight. **28. Qa6 Rb8 29. Qa3 Rf6 30. Qd3 Qf7 31. b3 a5 32. a3 Rh6 33. Qe2 Qd5 34. Kd1** The correct idea. Whether White exchanges or not, his h pawn will be left weakened, and probably soon lost. **34. ... g5 35. hxg6 Rxh4 36. gxh4 hxg6 37. Kc2 a4 38. Kb2 axb3 39. Nxb3 Qh1 40. Qc2 Qxh4 41. Nc5 Qe7 42. f3 Kg7** Of course not 42. ... Qxe3 as then 43. Qh2+ wins. **43. e4 fxe4** Allowing two passed pawns, but they can be controlled, and Black's g pawn becomes a very effective weapon. **44. fxe4 g5 45. e5 Rf8 46. Qg2 Rf5 47. Qc6 Qf7** Now there are real threats, which will at least force the exchange of queens, after which Black's pawn can hardly be stopped. **48. Ne6+ Kh7 49. Qc7 Qxc7 50. Nxc7 g4 51. e6 g3** If 52.e7 then Rf2+ 53 K moves Re7 winning. **0–1** Analysis by Kashdan (*Milwaukee* 1935)

318 Kashdan–Fine [C90]
Milwaukee, Western (Finals), 1935 *[July 30]*

1. e4 e5 2. Nf3 Nc6 3. Bb5 a6 4. Ba4
Nf6 5. 0–0 Be7 6. Re1 b5 7. Bb3 d6
8. c3 Na5 9. Bc2 c5 10. d4 Qc7 11. Nbd2
Nc6 12. d5 Nd8 13. Nf1 0–0 14. h3 Ne8
15. g4 g6 16. Ng3 Ng7 17. Be3 f6 18. Qe2
Nf7 19. Kh2 Ng5 20. Ng1 Bd7 ½–½
(Fine's Notebook)

319 Kashdan–Belson [A29]
Milwaukee, Western (Finals), 1935 *[July]*

1. c4 Nf6 2. Nc3 e5 3. Nf3 Nc6 4. g3
Bb4 5. Nd5 Bc5 6. d3 h6 7. Bg2 0–0
8. 0–0 d6 9. a3 a5 10. Nd2 More accurate
was 10. Nxf6+ Qxf6 11. Nd2 getting to e4 with
gain of time. 10. ... Nxd5 11. Bxd5 Bh3
12. Bg2 Bxg2 13. Kxg2 a4 Planning to
place his knight on b3, but this does not prove
very fortunate. 13. ... d5 would have given Black
possession of the center. 14. Ne4 Nd4
15. Nxc5 dxc5 16. Bd2 Ra6 17. Bc3 Nb3
18. Rb1 Re8 19. Qc2 Rae6 Black is playing
for a kingside attack, but as matters turn out, his
knight is rather out of play, and the opening of
the lines will be to White's advantage. 20. f3
Qg5 21. e4 Rd6 22. Rbd1 h5 This only
weakens his position. In view of the coming f4,
Black should have adopted more defensive tactics. 23. f4 exf4 24. Rxf4 Rg6 25. Kh1
Black's threats are now over, and the superior
position of White's pieces begins to tell. 25. ...
Qe7 26. Rdf1 f6 27. Qe2 Rg5

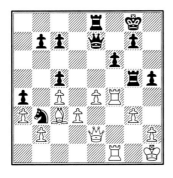

After
27. ... Rg5

Overlooking a pawn, but if 27. ... Rh6 28. Rh4
Qf7 29. g4 will win. **28. Rxf6! Nd4** Of course
if 28. ... gxf6 29. Bxf6 followed by Bxg5 wins

easily. 29. Bxd4 cxd4 30. R6f4 Qe6
31. Qf2 c5 32. Rf5 Rxf5 33. Qxf5 Qxf5
34. Rxf5 1–0 Resigns, as a second pawn must
go, after which the ending is hopeless. Analysis
by Kashdan. (*American Chess Bulletin*, July-August 1935)

320 Chevalier–Kashdan [D36]
Milwaukee, Western (Finals), 1935 *[July]*

1. d4 Nf6 2. c4 e6 3. Nc3 d5 4. Bg5
Nbd7 5. e3 c6 6. cxd5 exd5 7. Bd3 Be7
8. Qc2 0–0 9. Nf3 Re8 10. 0–0 Nf8
11. a3 g6 12. b4 a6 13. Rab1 Ne6 14. Bh4
Ng7 15. Ne2 Bf5 16. Bxf6 Bxf6 17. Ng3
Bxd3 18. Qxd3 Ne6 19. Rfc1 Bg7 20. Ne2
Qd6 21. Nc3 f5 22. g3 Re7 23. Na4 Rf8
24. Nc5 Nd8 25. a4 Nf7 26. b5 axb5
27. axb5 g5 28. bxc6 bxc6 29. Nb7 Qf6
30. Na5 Re6 31. Ne5 Nxe5 32. dxe5
Qxe5 33. Rxc6 f4 34. exf4 gxf4 35. Rd1
d4 36. Qc4 Rfe8 37. Nb3 Qe4 38. Rxe6
Qxe6 39. Qxe6+ Rxe6 40. Kg2 fxg3
41. hxg3 Rb6 42. Rd3 Rd6 ½–½ (*Brooklyn Daily Eagle*, August 15, 1935)

321 Simonson–Kashdan [D85]
Milwaukee, Western (Finals), 1935 *[July]*

1. d4 Nf6 2. c4 g6 3. Nc3 d5 4. cxd5
Nxd5 5. e4 Nxc3 6. bxc3 Bg7 7. Be3
0–0 8. Bc4 c5 9. Qd2 Nc6 10. Ne2 Qa5
11. Rd1 Rd8 12. f3 cxd4 13. cxd4 Qxd2+
14. Rxd2 b6 15. Kf2 Bb7 16. Rc1 Rac8
17. Rcc2 Na5 18. Bb5 Rxc2 19. Rxc2
Rc8 20. Rxc8+ Bxc8 21. d5 Be5 22. f4
Bc7 23. e5 f6 24. Bd4 fxe5 25. fxe5 a6
26. Bd3 b5 27. Ke3 Kf7 28. h4 e6
29. d6 Bd8 30. g3 Nc6 31. Bc3 Bb6+
32. Kf4 b4 33. Be4 Bd7 34. Bxc6 Bxc6
35. Bxb4 a5 36. Ba3 Bd5 37. Nc3 Bc6
38. Ne4 Bxe4 39. Kxe4 Ke8 40. Bc1 Bf2
41. Bf4 h5 42. Kf3 Bd4 43. Ke4 Bf2
44. Kf3 Bd4 45. g4 Kd7 46. Bg3 Bc3
47. gxh5 gxh5 48. Ke4 Bd2 49. a4 Bc3
50. Bf2 Bd2 51. Kd3 Bb4 52. Be3 Be1
53. Bd2 Bxh4 54. Bxa5 Bf2 55. Bc3 h4
56. Ke2 Bc5 57. a5 h3 58. Kf3 Bxd6
59. exd6 Kxd6 60. a6 ½–½ (*Los Angeles
Times*, August 15, 1935)

322 Factor–Kashdan [C54]

Milwaukee, Western (Finals), 1935 *[July 30]*

1. e4 e5 2. Nf3 Nc6 3. d4 exd4 4. Bc4 Bc5 5. c3 Nf6 6. cxd4 Bb4+ 7. Bd2 Bxd2+ 8. Nbxd2 d5 9. exd5 Nxd5 10. Qb3 Nce7 11. 0–0 0–0–0 12. Rfe1 Nb6 13. Bd3 Bf5 14. Rxe7 Bxd3 15. Rae1 Bg6 16. Nh4 Qxd4 17. Nxg6 hxg6 18. Nf3 Qd5 19. Rxc7 Qxb3 20. axb3 Rab8 21. Ng5 Nd5 22. Rd7 Nf6 23. Rde7 Nd5 24. Rd7 Nb6 25. Rc7 Nd5 ½–½ (*Chicago Checker & Chess Herald*; contributed by Jack O'-Keefe)

323 Kashdan–Reinfeld [D27]

Binghamton, round 1, 1935 *[August 19]*

1. d4 d5 2. c4 dxc4 3. Nf3 Nf6 4. Nc3 e6 5. e3 c5 6. Bxc4 a6 7. a4 Nc6 8. 0–0 Be7 9. Qe2 0–0 10. Rd1 Qc7 11. d5 exd5 12. Bxd5 Bg4 13. h3 Bh5 14. g4 Bg6 15. e4 Nb4 16. Bc4 Rad8 17. Bg5 Rxd1+ 18. Rxd1 Rd8 19. Rxd8+ Qxd8 20. Ne5 Ne8 21. Be3 Bd6 22. Nxg6 hxg6 23. f4 Qe7 24. e5 Bb8 25. Ne4 b5 26. axb5 axb5 27. Bxb5 Nf6 28. Bxc5 Ba7 29. Bxa7 Qxa7+ 30. Nf2 Nfd5 31. Qd2 Qc5 32. Be2 Nc2 33. Bf3 Nd4 34. Kg2 Nxf3 35. Kxf3 Qc4 36. Kg3 Kh8 37. Nd1 Qc5 38. Kf3 Qc4 39. Nf2 Kg8 40. Nd3 Qd4 41. Qe2 Nc7 42. Qe4 Qg1 43. Nf2 Qc1 44. b4 Ne6 45. h4 Qc3+ 46. Kg2 Nd4 47. f5 gxf5 48. gxf5 Nc6 49. e6 fxe6 50. fxe6 Ne7 51. Nd3 Qd2+ 52. Kf3 g6 53. Nf4 Qd1+ 54. Kf2 Qd2+ 55. Ne2 Qd6 56. Ke1 Qb6 57. Kd2 Qd6+ 58. Kc2 Qc7+ 59. Kb3 Qd6 60. Nd4 Kg7 61. Kc4 Qa6+ 62. b5 Qa4+ 63. Kc3 Qa3+ 64. Nb3 Kf6 65. b6 Qd6 66. b7 Qc7+ 67. Kb2 Nc6 68. Qxc6! Qxc6 69. b8Q Qxe6 70. Nd4 Qd5 71. Qf4+ Kg7 72. Kc3 Qc5+ 73. Kd3 Qa3+ 74. Ke2 Qa2+ 75. Kf3 Qd5+ 76. Kg3 Qd7 77. Qe5+ Kf7 78. Nf3 Kg8 79. Qf6 Qc7+ 80. Kg4 Qc2 81. Kg5 Kh7 82. Qe7+ Kg8 83. Kh6 1–0 (*Binghamton, NY*)

324 Lessing–Kashdan [D43]

Binghamton, round 2, 1935 *[August]*

1. d4 Nf6 2. c4 e6 3. Nc3 d5 4. Nf3 c6 5. Qc2 Nbd7 6. Bg5 h6 7. Bh4 Be7 8. e3 0–0 9. Rc1 a6 10. cxd5 exd5 11. Bd3 Re8 12. 0–0 Ne4 13. Bxe4 Bxh4 14. Bh7+ Kf8 15. Nxh4 Qxh4 16. Bd3 Qe7 17. Rfe1 Nf6 18. f3 Be6 19. Na4 Rad8 20. Nc5 Bc8 21. Qb3 Qc7 22. a4 Re7 23. Bb1 Rde8 24. Qc3 Kg8 25. b4 g6 26. b5 axb5 27. axb5 cxb5 28. Ne4 Qb6 29. Qc5 Re6 30. Nxf6+ Rxf6 31. Qxd5 Rd6 32. Qc5 Qxc5 33. Rxc5 Bd7 34. Kf2 Ra8 35. Bd3 Rb6 36. e4 Kf8 37. d5 Ra2+ 38. Re2 Ra3 39. Bb1 Ke7 40. e5 Kd8 41. Ba2 b4 42. e6 fxe6 43. dxe6 b3 44. Bxb3 Rbxb3 45. Rd5 Rd3 46. Rd2 Rxd2+ 47. Rxd2 Ke7 48. Rxd7+ Kxe6 49. Rxb7 Kf6 50. Rh7 h5 51. h4 Rb3 52. Kg3 Ra3 53. Rh8 Ra2 54. Rf8+ Kg7 55. Rf4 Rb2 56. Rc4 Kf6 57. Rc6+ Kf5 58. Rc5+ Kf6 59. Rg5 Ra2 60. Kh3 Ra3 61. Kg3 Ra2 62. Rb5 Rc2 63. Rb6+ Kf5 64. Rb8 Kf6 65. Rf8+ Kg7 66. Rf4 Rb2 67. Kh3 Rb3 68. g4 hxg4+ 69. Kxg4 Rb5 70. Rc4 Kf6 71. Rc6+ Kg7 72. Rc7+ Kf6 73. Rh7 Rb4+ 74. f4 Rb5 75. Rc7 Rb1 76. Rc6+ Kg7 77. Rc5 Rg1+ 78. Kf3 Rh1 79. Kg3 Rg1+ 80. Kf3 Rh1 81. Rg5 Rxh4 82. f5 Kf6 83. fxg6! Kg7! But not 83. ... Kxg5 84. g7 and the pawn cannot be stopped. 84. Kg3 Rh6 ½–½ (*Binghamton, NY*)

325 Kashdan–McCormick [D52]

Binghamton, round 3, 1935 *[August]*

1. c4 Nf6 2. Nf3 e6 3. Nc3 d5 4. d4 c6 5. Bg5 Nbd7 6. e3 a6 7. cxd5 exd5 After his last move, Black should probably recapture with the c pawn, followed by b5 and Bb7. Otherwise a6 is a lost move, and leaves holes on b6 and c5. 8. Bd3 Be7 9. Qc2 0–0 10. 0–0 Castling queenside is a possibility, but White's logical plan is to advance his pawns on that side for the eventual break at b5, and the king is better off on the other wing. 10. ... Re8 11. a3 Nf8 Not at once Ne4 when 12. Bxe4 wins a pawn. 12. b4 Ne4 13. Bxe7 Qxe7 14. Na4 Following out the plan of pressure on the queenside, 14. Bxe5 dxe5 15. Nd2 f5 is less effective, as Black can develop a strong attack. 14. ... Ng6 Better is 14. ... Bf5 15. Nc5 Rad8, which

completes Black's development. **15. Nb6** In order to exchange Black's bishop, which would end Black's attacking chance, and also leave his queenside pawns weaker after the coming of a4 and b5. **15. ... Bg4**

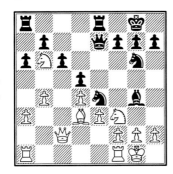

After
15. ... Bg4

An interesting idea, for if 17. Nxa8 Bxf3 and White is badly exposed. **16. Ne5!** But this is more than a sufficient reply. The threat is f3, as well as Nxa8. **16. ... Nxe5 17. dxe5 Ng5** Threatening Nf3+ with a winning attack. But White again has a resource which ensures a gain in material. **18. f4 Rad8 19. fxg5 Qxe5 20. Rae1 Qxg5 21. Bxh7+ Kh8 22. Bf5 Rxe3** Black is hoping to get enough pawns to make a fight against the piece, but this loses quickly. **23. Qd2** If either d4 or Rdd8, 24. Bxg4 wins another piece. **1–0** Analysis by Kashdan. (*American Chess Bulletin*, July-August 1935)

326 Bigelow–Kashdan [C14]
Binghamton, round 4, 1935 *[August]*

1. e4 e6 2. d4 d5 3. Nc3 Nf6 4. Bg5 Be7 5. e5 Nfd7 6. Bxe7 Qxe7 7. Qd2 0–0 8. 0–0–0 More usual is Rd1 or g3, with later castling on the kingside. The text is enterprising, and probably good, as Black's attack on the queen's wing is slow to get underway. **8. ... c5 9. f4 Nc6 10. Nf3 a6 11. g4** But this seems premature. 11. h4, and if f6 12. exf6 Qxf6 13. g3 is a sounder formation, with good attacking chances. **11. ... f6** The proper counter, White's pawns will now be weakened, because of the exposed position of the f file. **12. Bg2** This loses a pawn, but White foresees sufficient compensation through his better development. If 12. exf6 Qxf6 13. Ne2 Nb6 14. dxc5 Na4! with advantage for Black. **12. ... cxd4 13. Nxd4 Nxd4 14. Qxd4 fxe5 15. fxe5 Qg5+** Ac-

cepting the offer, but it is doubtful whether this is best. Simple development by 15. ... Rb8 followed by b5, etc., would have left the White e pawn permanently weak, without allowing much counterplay. **16. Kb1 Qxe5 17. Qb4** Best, as it holds several key squares, and makes it difficult for Black to get his queenside pieces out. **17. ... Nf6** There are a number of ways for Black to go wrong here. If b5 14. Nxd5 or Qc7 14. Qe7 wins. **18. g5** To open the g file, but it does not lead to enough. Better was 18. Rde1 Qg5 19. Bf3 threatening h4 which would be difficult to meet. **18. ... Qxg5 19. Rhg1 Qh5 20. Rd3 b5 21. Rg3 Ra7** After this Black is securely defended, and there is no compensation for the pawn minus. **22. Qc5 Raf7 23. Bf3 Qe5 24. Rg5 Qf4 25. Qf2 Nh5** The simplest. If 25. ... Ne4 26. Nxe4 dxe4 27. Qg2 threatens mate. The text forces an exchange of pieces, after which there is little for White to hope for. **26. Rxh5 Qxf3 0–1** Analysis by Kashdan. (*American Chess Bulletin*, July-August 1935)

327 Kashdan–Polland [C86]
Binghamton, round 5, 1935 *[August]*

1. e4 e5 2. Nf3 Nc6 3. Bb5 a6 4. Ba4 Nf6 5. 0–0 Be7 6. Qe2 d6 7. c3 0–0 8. d4 Bg4 9. d5 Nb8 10. h3 Bc8 11. c4 Ne8 12. g4 g6 13. Bh6 Ng7 14. Kh2 Nd7 15. Nc3 Nc5 16. Bc2 a5 17. Rg1 f6 18. Qe3 Rf7 19. Nd2 Nd7 20. Ne2 c6 21. f4 Qb6 22. Qxb6 Nxb6 23. f5 Bd7 24. dxc6 Bxc6 25. c5 dxc5 26. Bb3 a4 27. Bxf7+ Kxf7 28. Be3 Ne8 29. Rac1 Nd7 30. Ng3 Nc7 31. h4 Nb5 32. Rgf1 Nd4 33. g5 Kg7 34. Nf3 Bb5 35. Rf2 Bd6 36. Nd2 Rc8 37. Nc4 Bxc4 38. Rxc4 b5 39. Rc1 c4 40. Rcf1 c3 41. bxc3 Rxc3 42. Bd2 Rc2 43. fxg6 Kxg6 44. Be3 Rxf2+ 45. Rxf2 b4 46. h5+ Kf7 47. Kg2 b3 48. axb3 axb3 49. Bc1 Bb4 50. Bb2 Ne6 51. gxf6 Nf4+ 52. Kf3 Kxf6 53. Rf1 Ke6 54. Rb1 Nc5 55. Bc1 Nfd3 56. Be3 Kd6 57. Bxc5+ Nxc5 58. Ne2 Ba3 59. Nc3 Bb4 60. Rd1+ Kc6 61. Nb1 Ne6 62. Kg4 Nf4 63. Rd8 Kc5 64. Rh8 Kd4 65. Rxh7 Kxe4 66. Rb7 Nd5 67. Rxb4+! Nxb4 68. h6 1–0 (*Binghamton, NY*)

328 Barron–Kashdan [D48]
Binghamton, round 6, 1935 *[August]*

1. d4 Nf6 2. Nf3 e6 3. c4 d5 4. e3 Nbd7 5. Nc3 c6 6. Bd3 dxc4 7. Bxc4 b5 8. Bd3 a6 9. 0-0 c5 10. Ne4 Bb7 11. Nxf6+ Nxf6 12. dxc5 Bxc5 13. b3 0-0 14. Bb2 Qe7 15. Qe2 Rad8 16. Rad1 Nd5 17. Bb1 Rc8 18. Rc1 Ba3 19. Rxc8 Rxc8 20. Qd3 g6 21. Ba1 Bb4 22. Bd4 Nc3 23. a3 Ba5 24. b4 Be4 25. Qxe4 Nxe4 26. Bxe4 Bc7 27. g3 e5 28. Bc5 Bd6 29. Bb6 Rc3 30. Ra1 Kg7 31. Kg2 Qe6 32. Ba5 Bc7 33. Bxc7 Rxc7 34. Rd1 Rc3 35. Bd5 Qe7 36. Ra1 Qd6 37. Bb7 f5 38. a4 Rc7 39. axb5 Rxb7 40. bxa6 Ra7 41. b5 Qb4 42. Nxe5 Qxb5 0-1 *(Binghamton, NY)*

329 Goerlich–Kashdan [D10]
Binghamton, round 7, 1935 *[August]*

1. d4 d5 2. c4 c6 3. Nc3 Nf6 4. cxd5 cxd5 5. Bf4 e6 6. e3 a6 7. Bd3 b5 8. a3 Be7 9. Nf3 Bb7 10. 0-0 Nbd7 11. Rc1 0-0 12. Ne5 Rc8 13. Nxd7 Qxd7 14. Re1 Ne4 15. Nxe4 dxe4 16. Bb1 Bd5 17. Qd2 Rc4 18. Rxc4 bxc4 19. Bc2 Qb5 20. Qc3 h6 21. h3 Bd8 22. Bd6 Ba5 23. Bb4 Bxb4 24. axb4 Rb8 25. Rb1 Qxb4 26. Qxb4 Rxb4 27. Kf1 f5 28. g3 a5 29. Ke1 c3 30. bxc3 Rxb1+ 31. Bxb1 a4 32. Kd2 a3 33. Kc2 a2 34. Bxa2 Bxa2 35. Kb2 Bc4 36. Ka3 Kf7 37. Kb4 Bf1 38. c4 Bxh3 39. c5 Ke7 40. c6 Kd6 41. Kb5 Kc7 42. Kc5 Bg4 43. d5 exd5 44. Kxd5 g5 0-1 *(Binghamton, NY)*

330 Jaffe (Rice Progressive)–
Kashdan (Empire City) [D48]
Metropolitan Chess League, 1935

1. d4 Nf6 2. c4 e6 3. Nf3 d5 4. Nc3 c6 5. e3 Nbd7 6. Bd3 dxc4 7. Bxc4 b5 8. Bd3 a6 9. 0-0 c5 10. a4 b4 11. Ne4 Bb7 12. Nxc5 Nxc5 13. dxc5 Bxc5 14. b3 0-0 15. Bb2 Be7 16. Rc1 Qa5 17. Qe2 Ne4 18. Ne5 Rac8 19. Nc4 Qg5 20. f3 Nc5 21. Bc2 Rfd8 22. Bd4 Nd7 23. f4 Qh4 24. Na5 Ba8 25. Qxa6 Qg4 26. e4

Nc5 27. Bxc5 Bxc5+ 28. Kh1 e5 29. Bd1 Qh4 30. Bf3 Qxf4 31. Rc4 Qe3 32. Rfc1 Rc7 33. h3 h6 34. Qb5 Rdc8 35. Bg4 Bxe4 36. Bxc8 Rxc8 37. Qd7 f5! 38. Qxc8+ Kh7 39. Kh2 Qf4+ 40. Kh1 Qe3 41. Kh2

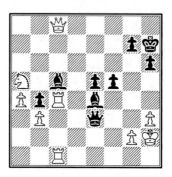

After
41. Kh2

Black has the advantage after 41. ... Qf4+ 42. Kh1 Qd2 43. R4c2 Bxc2 44. Qxc5, Qxc1+ etc., according to Fritz. Perhaps Black was in time trouble. ½–½ *(Chess Review, May 1936)*

331 Marshall (Marshall C. C.)–
Kashdan (Empire City) [D13]
Metropolitan Chess League, 1936

1. d4 d5 2. c4 c6 3. cxd5 cxd5 4. Nc3 Nf6 5. Nf3 e6 6. e3 a6 7. Bd3 Nbd7 8. 0-0 Be7 9. Qe2 b5 10. e4 dxe4 11. Nxe4 Bb7 12. Bg5 0-0 13. Rac1 Nxe4 14. Bxe7 Qxe7 15. Bxe4 Nf6 16. Bxb7 Qxb7 17. Rc5 Nd7 18. Rc2 Rac8 19. Rfc1 Nf6 20. h3 Rxc2 21. Rxc2 h6 22. b3 Rc8 23. Rc5 Nd7 24. Rc2 Rc7 25. Ne5 Qc8 26. Rxc7 Qxc7 27. Nxd7 Qxd7 28. Qe4 Qd6 29. Qa8+ Kh7 30. Qa7 ½–½ *(Brooklyn Daily Eagle, March 19, 1936)*

332 Kashdan–Simonson [C86]
New York, U.S. Championship, round 1, 1936 *[April 25]*

1. e4 e5 2. Nf3 Nc6 3. Bb5 a6 4. Ba4 Nf6 5. 0-0 Be7 6. Qe2 b5 7. Bb3 0-0 8. c3 d5 Sacrificing a pawn for a tricky attack, but it is hardly sound. The normal 8. ... d6 is quite good. 9. exd5 Nxd5 10. Nxe5 Nf4 Seemingly gaining time, but he has not counted on White's twelfth move, which completely re-

futes the idea. 10. ... Nxe5 11. Qxe5 Nf6 leads to a difficult game. A possibility then is 12. d4 Bd6 13. Qg5 Re8 14. Be3 Bxh2+ 15. Kxh2 Rxe3 16. Bxf7+ Kh8 (if 16. ... Kxf7 17. fxe3 wins, as the knight is pinned.) 17. Kg1 and White has retained the pawn plus. **11. Qe4 Nxe5**

After
11. ... Nxe5

12. d4! If 12. Qxa8 Qd3! threatening Bh3 and Ne2+ will win. The text is much stronger than taking either knight. **12. ... Nh3+** This and the next move are a desperate attempt to built up an attack at all cost. With Bb7 or Bd7 he would remain a pawn behind, with no compensation. **13. gxh3 Ng6** Slightly better was 13. ... Bxh3 14. dxe5 Bxf1 15. Kxf1, but Black has little to show for the lost material. **14. Qxa8 Bd6 15. f4 Qh4 16. Qf3 Bxh3 17. Qg3 Qh5 18. Re1 Qf5 19. Bc2** Forcing a simplification which ends up any hope of attack. **19. ... Qxc2 20. Qxh3 Bxf4** If 20. ... Nxf4 21. Bxf4 Bxf4 22. Qg2 wins. The text is no better, as White simply completes his development. **21. Na3 Qa4 22. Bxf4 Nxf4 23. Qf3 1–0** Annotated by Kashdan. (*American Chess Bulletin*, April 1936)

333 S. Bernstein–Kashdan [D21]
New York, U.S. Championship, round 2, 1936 *[April 26]*

1. d4 d5 2. Nf3 c5 3. c4 dxc4 4. Nc3 a6 5. dxc5 Qxd1+ 6. Kxd1 Nf6 7. Bg5 e6 8. e3 Bxc5 9. Bxc4 b5 10. Bd3 Nbd7 11. Rc1 Bb7 12. Bxf6 gxf6 13. Be4 0–0–0 14. Ke2 Kb8 15. Bxb7 Kxb7 16. Ne4 Be7 17. Rhd1 Nb6 18. Nd4 Rc8 19. Nb3 Nd5 20. Nec5+ Ka7 21. e4 Nb6 22. Nd3 Nc4 23. Nd2 Na5 24. Rxc8 Rxc8 25. Rc1 Nc6 26. Nb3 Kb6 27. Ke3 Rd8 28. f4

a5 29. Nd2 a4 30. Nf3 Na5 31. Nd2 Nb7 32. Nf3 Nd6 33. Nd2 f5 34. e5 Nb7 35. Nf3 Na5 36. Nd2 Rg8 37. Kf2 h5 38. Rc2 Bh4+ 39. g3 Be7 40. h4 Nc6 41. Nf3 Rd8 42. Ke2

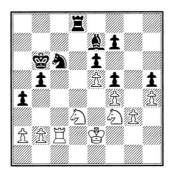

After
42. Ke2

42. ... Rxd3 43. Rxc6+ Kxc6 44. Kxd3 Kd5 45. Nd4 b4 46. b3 Bc5 47. Nc2 axb3 48. axb3 Bf2 49. Ne3+ Kc5 50. Nf1 Bd4 51. Ne3 Bc3 52. Nf1 f6 53. exf6 Bxf6 54. Ne3 Bd4 55. Nf1 Kd5 56. Ne3+ Kc5 57. Nf1 Bf2 58. Ke2 Bg1 59. Kd3 e5 60. fxe5 Kd5 61. Ne3+ Kxe5 62. Ke2 Ke4 63. Ng2 Kd4 64. Kd2 Bf2 65. Ke2 Bxg3 66. Ne3 f4 67. Nf5+ 0–1 (Scoresheet)

334 Kashdan–Horowitz [D26]
New York, U.S. Championship, round 3, 1936 *[April 27]*

1. d4 d5 2. c4 e6 3. Nc3 Nf6 4. Nf3 dxc4 5. e3 If 5. e4 Bb4 6. Bg5 c5! results in complications rather favorable to Black. **5. ... a6 6. Bxc4** Leading to a variation of the Meran Defense. 6. a4 is an alternative, but Black can equalize without trouble. **6. ... b5 7. Bd3 Bb7 8. 0–0 c5 9. Qe2 Nc6 10. dxc5 Bxc5 11. a3** The game now becomes very symmetrical, White retains a slight initiative up through this move. **11. ... 0–0 12. b4 Bd6 13. Bb2 Qe7 14. Rad1 Rad8 15. Rfe1** Indifferent, unless White intends e4, which could be effectively answered by Ne5. 15. Ne4 was the proper idea, as played next move. **15. ... Bb8 16. Ne4 Nxe4 17. Bxe4 f5** This play and the next move weaken Black's pawns. 17. ... Rxd1 18. Rxd1 Rd8 would have maintained equality. **18. Bb1 Rxd1 19. Rxd1 e5**

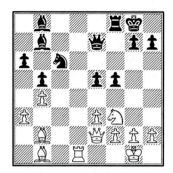

After
19. ... e5

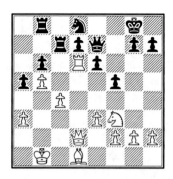

After
28. ... Nd8

20. e4! Preventing 20. ... e4, and leaving the Black e pawn backward and exposed to attack. **20. ... Nd4** An interesting attempt to get counter play, but it does not work out. If 20. ... f4 21. Ba2+ Kh8 22. Bd5 with considerable pressure in the center and on the queenside. **21. Nxd4 exd4 22. Bxd4 Bxe4** Losing the exchange, as Black's threats can be warded off. 22. ... fxe4 has a similar result, for 23. Bc5 Qe5 24. Ba2+ Kh8 25. f4! Qxf4 26. g3 wins. **23. Bc5 Qe5** If 23. ... Qc7 24. Bd6 or 23. ... Qh4 24. g3 Qh3 25. Bxe4 and in both cases Bxf8 follows. **24. f4! Qxf4 25. g3 Qf3?** A last attempt, which costs a piece, however. There was no longer any real hope. **26. Qxf3 Bxf3 27. Ba2+ Kh8 28. Rf1 1–0** Annotated by Kashdan. (*American Chess Bulletin*, May-June 1936)

335 Denker–Kashdan [E23]
New York, U.S. Championship, round 4, 1936 *[April 29]*

1. d4 Nf6 2. c4 e6 3. Nc3 Bb4 4. Qb3 c5 5. dxc5 Nc6 6. Nf3 Ne4 7. Bd2 Nxd2 8. Nxd2 f5 9. e3 Bxc5 10. 0–0–0 0–0 11. Nf3 b6 12. Be2 Qe7 13. Rd2 Bb7 14. Rhd1 Rfd8 15. a3 Rac8 16. Kb1 Qe8 17. Nb5 Na5 18. Qa2 a6 19. Nd6 Bxd6 20. Rxd6 Be4+ 21. Ka1 Bc2 22. b4 Bxd1 23. Rxd1 Nc6 24. Rd6 Qe7 25. Qd2 Rc7 26. Bd1 Rb8 27. Kb1 a5 28. b5 Nd8 (*see diagram*)

29. Ne5 Nf7 30. Nxf7 Kxf7 31. Ka2 Ke8 32. Be2 Kd8 33. a4 Rc5 34. f4 Kc7 35. Rd4 e5 36. fxe5 Rxe5 37. Bf3 Re8 38. h3 Rxe3 39. c5 Qxc5 40. Rxd7+ Kc8 41. Bd1 Qa3+ 42. Kb1 Qb4+ 43. Qxb4 axb4 44. Rd6 R8e6 45. Rd5 g6 46. Kb2 Kc7 47. Rd4 R3e4 48. Rd2 Rd6 49. Rc2+

Kd8 50. Bf3 Red4 51. Kb3 g5 52. Bc6 Rd3+ 53. Kxb4 R6d4+ 54. Rc4 g4 55. hxg4 fxg4 56. Be4 Rxc4+ 57. Kxc4 Rd2 58. g3 h5 59. Bg6 h4 60. gxh4 g3 0–1 (Scoresheet)

336 Kashdan–Hanauer [C86]
New York, U.S. Championship, round 5, 1936 *[April 30]*

1. e4 e5 2. Nf3 Nc6 3. Bb5 a6 4. Ba4 Nf6 5. 0–0 Be7 6. Qe2 This move of Alapin's has been rather popular of recent years as a variant to the routine Re1. However, if the soundness of Black's subsequent pawn sacrifice can be established, the text will have to be discarded. **6. ... b5 7. Bb3 0–0 8. c3 d5 9. d3 Bg4 10. h3 Bh5 11. g4 Bg6 12. g5 dxe4** If 12. ... exf3 13. Qxf3 and White wins a piece. **13. gxf6 exd3 14. Qe3 Bxf6 15. Nbd2 Qd7 16. Kg2 Rad8** This overprotects his d5 square to prevent the White bishop from coming to the defense. **17. Ne4 Be7 18. Bd2 Kh8 19. Rae1 f5** This regains the piece by the unusual circumstance of White's queen being stalemated in the middle of the board! **20. Nc5 Qd6 21. Ne6 f4 22. Nxf4 exf4 23. Qe6 Qxe6 24. Rxe6 Bd6 25. Ng5 Ne5** The rook is now cornered, and more exchanges forced; Black also supports his passed pawn. **26. Re1 Nc4 27. Bxc4 bxc4 28. Rb1 Bf5 29. Ree1 h6 30. Nf3 Rfe8** To avoid Ne5. By the following series of moves the White knight at d4 is also stalemated ! **31. Nd4 Bc8 32. f3 Bd7 33. b4** To prevent c5, which would win the knight. **33. ... Kg8 34. h4 Rxe1 35. Rxe1 Kf7 36. a4** (*see diagram*)

White offers the a pawn to get bishops of opposite colors (36. ... Bxa4 37. Nf5 but Black

After
36. a4

politely refuses. **36. ... Re8 37. Rb1 Rb8** To
play c5—a little trap. **38. Re1 Re8 39. Rb1
Kf6 40. Kf2 Rb8 41. Re1 Re8 42. Rg1 g5**
The winning plan is on the way: 1. Protect the
pawn on f4; 2. c5, forcing the exchange of rooks
or two passed pawns, or the win of the bishop
on d2. **43. Rh1 Kg6 44. hxg5 hxg5 45. a5
c5 46. bxc5 Bxc5 47. Re1** Forced because
of the threat of Re2. **47. ... Rxe1 48. Kxe1
Bd6 49. Bc1 Bc7 50. Ba3 Bxa5 51. Kd2
Kf6** Keeping the knight stalemated before the
final push. **52. Bc5 Bd8 53. Ke1 Be7
54. Bb6 Ke5 55. Kd2 Kd5 56. Ba5 g4
57. Bc7 g3 58. Bxf4 g2 59. Bh2 Bg5+
60. Ke1 Be3 0–1** Notes by Reinfeld and
Hanauer. (*American Chess Bulletin*, January 1937)

337 Factor–Kashdan [B29]
New York, U.S. Championship, round 6,
1936 *[May 2]*

**1. e4 c5 2. Nf3 Nf6 3. e5 Nd5 4. d4
cxd4 5. Qxd4 e6 6. Bd3 Nc6 7. Qe4
Ncb4 8. 0–0 Nxd3 9. Qxd3 Be7
10. Nbd2 Qc7 11. c4 Nf4 12. Qe4 Ng6
13. Re1 Rb8 14. Qd4 Bc5 15. Qd3 b6
16. Ne4 Bb7 17. Nxc5 Qxc5 18. b4 Qc7
19. Nd4 a6 20. Bd2 Rc8 21. Rac1 Nxe5
22. Qc3 f6 23. Bf4 0–0 24. Qg3 Qd6
25. Rxe5 Qxd4 26. Reel Rf7 27. Be3
Qb2 28. Qd6 Qxa2 29. Qxb6 Be4 30. b5
axb5 31. cxb5 Rxc1 32. Rxc1 Rf8 33. Qc7
Qd5 34. f3 Bd3 35. b6 Ba6 36. Ra1 Rc8
37. Qf4 Bb7 38. Qd4 Qxd4 39. Bxd4
Kf7 40. Ra7 Rc1+ 41. Kf2 Bc6 42. Ke3
e5 43. Kd2 Rb1 44. Be3 Ke6 45. Rc7
g5 46. Rc8 g4 47. fxg4 Bxg2 48. h4 Bf3
49. Rc4 f5 50. gxf5+ Kxf5 51. Rc5 h5
52. Rc1 Rxc1 53. Kxc1 Bb7 54. Kd2 d5**

**55. Bh6 d4 56. Bg7 Ke4 57. Ke2 Kd5
58. Kf3 e4+ 59. Ke2 Ba6+ 60. Kf2 Kc4
61. Bf6 Kd3 62. Ke1 e3 63. Kd1 Kc4
64. Kc2 d3+ 65. Kc3 d2 66. Kc2 Be2
0–1** (Scoresheet)

338 Kashdan–Fine [E23]
New York, U.S. Championship, round 7,
1936 *[May 3]*

**1. d4 Nf6 2. c4 e6 3. Nc3 Bb4 4. Qb3
c5 5. dxc5 Nc6 6. Nf3 Bxc5 7. e3 0–0
8. Be2 b6 9. 0–0 Bb7 10. a3 Qe7 11. Rd1
Rfd8 12. Bd2? d5 13. cxd5 exd5 14. Be1
d4 15. exd4 Nxd4 16. Nxd4 Bxd4 17. Bf1
Qe5 18. h3 h5 19. Rd2 Bc5 20. Rxd8+
Rxd8 21. Rd1 Rxd1 22. Qxd1 Bd6 23. g3
Bc5 24. Kh2 h4 25. Qd8+ Ne8 26. Qd2
Nd6 27. f4 hxg3+ 28. Bxg3 Qe3
29. Qxe3 Bxe3 30. a4 Bc1 31. b3 Bd2
32. Nb5 Nxb5 33. Bxb5 g6 34. Kg1 Bd5
35. Bc4 Bxc4 36. bxc4 Kg7 37. Kf2 Kf6
38. Ke2 Bc1 39. Kd1 Ba3 40. Ke2 Kf5
41. Kf3 Bd6 42. Bh2 g5 43. Bg1 Bxf4
44. c5 bxc5 45. Bxc5 a6 46. Bb6 Bd6
47. Bd8 Be5 48. Ba5 Bf6 49. Bb6 Be7
50. Ba5 Ke6 51. Kg4 f5+ 52. Kf3 Kd5
53. Bc7 Kc5 54. Ba5 Kc4 55. Bc7 Kb4
56. a5 Kc5 57. Bb6+ Kc6 58. Be3 Bd8
59. Bd2 Kb5 60. Kf2 f4 61. Bc3 Kc4!
62. Bd2 Be7 63. h4 gxh4 64. Bxf4 Bd8
65. Bd2 Kb5 66. Kg2 Bxa5 67. Bg5 Bb6
68. Bxh4 a5 69. Kf3 a4 70. Ke2 a3
71. Bf6 Kc4 72. Kd2 Kb3 73. Kc1 a2
0–1** (*Chess*, June 1936)

339 Kashdan–Reshevsky [C45]
New York, U.S. Championship, round 8,
1936 *[May 4]*

1. e4 e5 2. Nf3 Nc6 3. d4 This opening
has been played very seldom between masters
in recent tournaments. **3. ... exd4 4. Nxd4
Bc5 5. Be3 Qf6 6. c3 Nge7 7. Qd2 Bxd4**
The customary move is d5. **8. cxd4 d5 9. Nc3
dxe4** The natural-looking move is Be6. **10. d5
Ne5 11. Nb5 0–0 12. Nxc7** If 12. Bg5 Qb6
13. Bxe7 Re8 14. Qb4 Bd7 and Black has the
better game. **12. ... Rb8 13. Bxa7** Black's position, at a first glance, looks as though it were

lost, but this is merely a superficial observation. Black has sufficient attacking chances for the loss of material. **13. ... Bg4 14. Bxb8 Rxb8 15. Nb5** This isn't the best. Better would have been d6, followed by Nd5 and Ne3. This, however, would by no means stop the attack. **15. ... N7g6 16. Rc1 Nf4 17. Rc3 Ned3+ 18. Bxd3 exd3!**

After
18. ... exd3

19. 0–0? This loses immediately. The best here was 19. f3 Nxg2+ 20. Kd1 Qxf3+ 21. Kc1 Nf4 and Black stands much better. **19. ... Qg5 20. h4 Nh3+ 21. gxh3 Qxd2 22. hxg4 Qe2! 23. Rc4 d2 24. Rd4 Qxb5 25. Rd1 Re8 26. R4xd2 Re4 27. f3 Re2 28. Rc1 h5 29. Rcc2 Qb6+ 0–1** Annotations by Reshevsky. (*American Chess Bulletin*, May-June 1936)

340 Dake–Kashdan [D51]
New York, U.S. Championship, round 9, 1936 *[May 6]*

1. d4 Nf6 2. Nf3 e6 3. c4 d5 4. Bg5 c6 5. Nc3 Nbd7 6. cxd5 cxd5 7. e3 a6 8. Bd3 Be7 9. 0–0 b5 10. Qe2 Bb7 11. Rfc1 0–0 12. Rc2 Ne4 13. Bxe7 Qxe7 14. Nd2 Nd6 15. f4 Rfc8 16. Racl f5 ½–½ (Scoresheet)

341 Kashdan–H. Steiner [E46]
New York, U.S. Championship, round 10, 1936 *[May 7]*

1. d4 Nf6 2. c4 e6 3. Nc3 Bb4 4. e3 0–0 5. Qc2 d5 6. a3 Be7 7. Nf3 Nbd7 8. cxd5 exd5 9. Bd3 c6 10. 0–0 Re8 11. Bd2 Bd6 12. Rfe1 Nf8 13. h3 Ng6 14. b4 a6 15. Rab1 Bc7 16. a4 Qd6 17. b5 axb5 18. axb5 Bd7 19. Rec1 Bb8 20. Be1

Qe7 21. Na4 Rxa4 22. Qxa4 Ne4 23. bxc6 bxc6 24. Rb7 Qe6 25. Rcb1 Bd6 26. Ra7 h6 27. Ra8 f5 28. Rxe8+ Bxe8 29. Qc2 Ne7 30. Bb4 Bc7 31. Ra1 Ng6 32. Ra7 Bd8 33. Ra8 Bf6 34. Ba5 f4 0–1 (Scoresheet)

342 Treysman–Kashdan [E43]
New York, U.S. Championship, round 11, 1936 *[May 9]*

1. d4 Nf6 2. c4 e6 3. Nc3 Bb4 4. e3 b6 5. Be2 Ne4 6. Qc2 Nxc3 7. bxc3 Be7 8. Nf3 0–0 9. Bd3 h6 10. Be4 c6 11. 0–0 Ba6 12. Bh7+ Kh8 13. Bd3 c5 14. Rd1 cxd4 15. cxd4 Nc6 16. Bd2 Bb7 17. Rab1 d6 18. Bc3 Rc8 19. Qe2 Nb8 20. Nd2 Nd7 21. f4 f5 22. e4 fxe4 23. Bxe4 d5 24. Bf3 Rxf4 25. Qxe6 Nf8 26. Qe1 Qd7 27. g3 Rf6 28. Qe2 dxc4 29. d5 Rf7 30. Ne4 Bc5+ 31. Nxc5 Rxc5 32. Bg4 Qc7 33. Be5 Qe7 34. Be6 Nxe6 35. dxe6 Rf5 36. Rd7 Rcxe5 37. Qxe5 Rxe5 38. Rxe7 Bd5 39. Rxa7 Rxe6 40. Rb2 Rc6 41. Ra3 Be4 42. Rc3 Bd3 43. Kf2 Re6 44. Rc1 Kg8 45. a3 Kf7 46. Re1 Rc6 47. Ke3 Bf5 48. Kd4 c3 49. Rf2 Kg6

After
49. ... Kg6

50. g4 Bxg4 51. Rc1 Rd6+ 52. Kxc3 Kg5 53. Rg1 Kh4 54. Rf4 h5 55. Rg3 Rd1 56. Rf2 g5 57. Rd3 Rc1+ 58. Kb2 Rc6 59. Rd4 Kh3 60. Rd5 Kh4 61. Rd4 Kh3 62. a4 Be6 63. Rf3+ Kg2 64. Ra3 Bc4 65. Rd2+ Kg1 66. Rc3 Rc5 67. Rdc2 Be6 68. Rg3+ Kh1 69. Rxc5 bxc5 70. Rxg5 h4 71. a5 Kxh2 72. a6 Bc8 73. a7 Bb7 74. Kc3 h3 75. Kd2 c4 76. Ke3 c3 77. Kf2 c2 78. Rc5 Be4 79. Rxc2 Bxc2 80. a8Q Be4 81. Qa1 But

not 81. Qxe4 as that would be stalemate! **1–0**
(*Chess*, August 1936)

343 Kashdan–Adams [D08]
New York, U.S. Championship, round 12,
1936 *[May 10]*

1. Nf3 Nc6 2. d4 d5 3. c4 e5 4. dxe5
d4 5. Nbd2 Bb4 6. a3 Bxd2+ 7. Qxd2
Bg4 8. Qf4 Qd7 9. e3 Bxf3 10. gxf3
0-0-0 11. Qg3 Kb8 12. Bh3 Qe7 13. f4
f6 14. e6 g6 15. 0-0 f5 16. b4 Nf6
17. Bb2 Qxe6 18. Bg2 Rhe8 19. Bxc6
Qxc6 20. Bxd4 Ne4 21. Qg2 Qxc4
22. Rfc1 Qb3 23. Kh1 Qa4 24. f3 Nd6
25. Qc2 Qxc2 26. Rxc2 Nb5 27. Be5 Rd3
28. a4 Nd6 29. Rac1 Re7 30. Kg2 Ne8
But not 30. ... Rxe3?? as then would follow
31. Bxd6 fxd6 32. Rc8 mate! **31. Rc3 Rd2+
32. Kg3 Red7 33. R3c2 Rxc2 34. Rxc2
Rd3 35. Bd4 Ra3 36. a5 a6 37. Kh4 Rb3
38. Kg5 Rxb4 39. Kh6 Ra4 40. Kxh7
Rxa5 41. Kxg6 Rd5 42. h4 1-0** (Scoresheet)

344 Kevitz–Kashdan [D47]
New York, U.S. Championship, round 13,
1936 *[May 11]*

1. c4 e6 2. Nc3 d5 3. d4 Nf6 4. Nf3
Nbd7 5. e3 c6 6. Bd3 dxc4 7. Bxc4 b5
8. Bd3 b4 9. Ne4 Bb7 10. 0-0 Be7
11. Nxf6+ Bxf6 12. Qa4 a5 13. Be4 Qb6
14. Bd2 0-0 15. Rfc1 Rfc8 16. Rc2 Rc7
17. Rac1 Rac8 18. Be1 e5 19. Nxe5 Nxe5
20. dxe5 Bxe5 21. a3 Bd6 22. Rc4 c5
23. Bxb7 Qxb7 24. f3 h6 25. Bg3 Bxg3
26. hxg3 Qb6 27. Rd1 Qe6 28. Re4 Qc6
29. Qxc6 Rxc6 30. Rc4 bxa3 31. bxa3
Rb8 32. Rd3 Rb2 33. Rdc3 Ra2 34. a4
Rb6

After
34. ... Rb6

345 Kashdan–Kupchik [D67]
New York, U.S. Championship, round 14,
1936 *[May 13]*

1. d4 Nf6 2. c4 e6 3. Nc3 d5 4. Nf3
Nbd7 5. Bg5 Be7 The Orthodox Defense.
On the looks of things, Black gets a more backward game than in the Cambridge Springs or
Slav Defenses, and the text is about the least aggressive of Black's choices. But he has a sound
formation, with no real weaknesses, and White
has never demonstrated a lasting advantage if
properly continued. **6. e3 c6 7. Rc1 0-0
8. Bd3** Black waits for this move in order to
play dxc4 with gain of time. White can delay it
for a time by 8. Qc2 Re8 9. a3 a6 10. Bd3 but
the net result is about the same. **8. ... dxc4**
This temporarily yields the center, but Black re-
lies on the later ...e5, or ...c5 as an equalizing
measure. **9. Bxc4 Nd5** Black rightly tries to
exchange a piece or two, in order to free his
game. **10. Bxe7 Qxe7 11. 0-0 Rd8** More
consistent is 11. ... Nxc3 12. Rxc3 e5. If then
13. dxe5 Nxe5 14. Nxe5 Qxe5 15. f4 Qe4 with
an even game. Less good is 15. ... Qe7 16. f5! or
15. ... Qf6 16. e4 etc. Interesting is 13. e4 exd4
14. Qxd4 Re8 15. e5 and now ...Nxe5? will not
do because of 16. Nxe5 Qxe5 17. Re3! winning.
But 15. ... Nf8 followed by ...Be6 is sufficient.
12. Ne4 Now matters will be more difficult for
Black, as either ...e5, or ...c5 is answered by
Bxd5, isolating the d pawn. **12. ... N5f6** The
exchange now involves some loss of time, but
it is still Black's best plan. **13. Qc2** If 13. Ng3,

---

35. Rc2 Rxc2 36. Rxc2 Rb4 37. Rxc5
Rxa4 38. Rc8+ Kh7 39. Rc2 Ra1+
40. Kf2 a4 41. Ke2 a3 42. Kd3 h5
43. Kc3 g5 44. Kb3 Re1 45. Kxa3 Rxe3+
46. Kb2 g4 47. Rf2 Kg6 48. Kc2 gxf3
49. gxf3 Re1 50. Rh2 Rf1 51. f4 Rf3
52. Rh3 h4 53. Rxh4 Rxg3 54. Kd2 Kf5
55. Ke2 Ke4 56. f5+ Kxf5 57. Ra4 Kg5
58. Kf2 Rg4 59. Ra5+ f5 60. Ra8 Rb4
61. Ra3 Rf4+ 62. Kg3 Rg4+ 63. Kf3 Rh4
64. Ra8 Rh3+ 65. Kf2 Kg4 66. Rg8+
Kf4 67. Ra8 Rh2+ 68. Kf1 Kg4 69. Ra3
f4 70. Rb3 Ra2 71. Rc3 Ra1+ 72. Kf2
Rh1 73. Rb3 Rh2+ 74. Kf1 f3 75. Rb8
½–½ (Scoresheet)

or Nc3, ...c5 is effective. The text involves several queen moves, but accomplishes the object of delaying Black's break in the center. **13. ... Nxe4 14. Qxe4 Nf6** If here 14. ... c5 15. Rfd1 cxd4 16. Qxd4 with a marked advantage in development. Or 15. ... Nf6 16. Qe5 cxd4 17. Nxd4 and White has all the better of it. **15. Qc2 b6** Eventually necessary, but it creates weaknesses on the queenside, of which White can make good use. **16. Qe2 Nd7** To be able to retake with the knight after ...c5, dxc5. The move is sufficient evidence that Black did not gain time by driving the queen. **17. Rfd1 Bb7 18. Ba6 Bxa6 19. Qxa6 c5** At last! But White still has the superior game, because of his greater pressure on the queenside. **20. b3** A useful tempo. White wants his opponent to exchange pawns, as that will get his knight to a better post. The text move prevents 20. ... e5. **20. ... cxd4 21. Nxd4 Nc5 22. Qe2**

After
22. Qe2

22. ... Rac8? The most natural looking move, but here it is a mistake, which costs at least a pawn. Best was 22. Qb7, when White can establish his knight very strongly by 23. b4 Ne4 24. b5, followed by Nc6, with definitely better prospects for the endgame. **23. b4 e5** The point is that if 23. ... Ne4 24. Nc6! Rxd1+ 25. Qxd1 Qb7 26. Ne7+ wins. The text move is the only move to save the exchange. **24. Nf5 Qf6 25. Rxd8+ Rxd8 26. Nxg7 Kxg7** If the knight moves, 27. Nh5 and the Black king is too exposed. **27. bxc5 bxc5 28. Rxc5 Qd6** The best chance to obtain some counterplay but White can easily maintain the position. **29. Rc1 Qd2** Black has played well since losing the pawn, and has obtained some counter chances, but the following maneuver secures White's full defense. **30. Qg4+ Kf8 31. Qc4**

Now everything is defended, for if 31. Qd1+? 32. Rxd1 Rxd1+ 33. Qf1 etc. **31. ... Kg7 32. h4** This leads to some difficulty. 32. h3 would have been simpler, and more secure. **32. ... Rd6 33. Qc2** And here 33. Rc2 Qe1+ 34. Kh2 would have been more effective than the text, which loses some ground. **33. ... Qb4** The exchange of queens would lead to a fairly easy win in the ending. **34. Qf5** Now the strongest method, to force an exchange of pawns. But not 34. Qc5?? Rd1+! 35. Kh2 Qxh4 mate! **34. ... Qxh4 35. Qxe5+ Rf6 36. Rc2 Kg6 37. Rd2 Re6** Allowing an exchange, which makes things easier. But Black has little to do. If 37. ... h6 38. g3 Qb4 39. Qd4 to be followed by Qg4+, etc. **38. Rd6 Rxd6** If 38. ... Qc4 39. f4! threatening mate, and also f5+, wins the rook by force. **39. Qxd6+ f6 40. Qd3+ Kh6 41. Qd4** This forces the exchange of queens, or the gain of a second pawn, winning quickly in either case. **41. ... Qg5** If 41. ... Qxd4 42. exd4 Kg5 43. f3 Kf5 44. Kf2 wins. Now White can exchange by Qf4, but the capture is at least as strong. **42. Qxa7 Qb5 43. Qf7 Qe5 44. a4**

After
44. a4

44. ... f5 This allows a forced exchange of queens, but Black is hopelessly lost in any case, as there is no chance for a perpetual check. **45. Qf8+ Kg6 46. Qg8+ Kh6 47. Qg5+!** Very pretty. Black resigns as after 47. ... Kxg5 48.f4+ Kf6 49.fxe5+ Kxe5 50.Kf2 wins. Or 48. ... Qxf4 49.exf4+ Kxf4 50.a5, and the pawn cannot be stopped. **1–0** Annotated by Kashdan. (*Chess Review*, October 1936)

346 Morton–Kashdan [B13]
New York, U.S. Championship, round 15, 1936 *[May 16]*

1. e4 c6 2. d4 d5 3. exd5 Alternatives are 3. e5 Bf5 4. Bd3 Bxd3 5. Qxd3 e6 followed by ...c5, or 3. Nc3 dxe4 4. Nxe4 Bf5, or 4. ... Nf6, with an even game in every case. **3. ... cxd5 4. Bd3** More enterprising play is 4. c4, leading to complications after 4. ... Nf6 5. Nc3 Nc6 6. Nf3 Bg4 7. cxd5 Nxd5 8. Bb5 Qa5 9. Qb3 etc. With the text White seeks to restrain Black's queen bishop, and plays for simple development. **4. ... Nf6 5. c3** Delaying Nf3 until Black shuts in his bishop by ...e6. 5. ... Bg4 is playable anyway, but Black is quite content to develop the bishop on the queenside. **5. ... Nc6 6. Bf4 e6 7. Nd2 a6** Preparing for ...b5, which is useful either in supporting a knight at c4, or to start a queenside attack by b4. **8. Ngf3 b5 9. 0–0 Be7 10. Ne5 Bb7 11. Qe2** Preventing 11. ... Na5 (with the idea of ...Nc4) when 11. Bxb5+! axb5 12. Qxb5+ Nd7 13. b4 would win. **11. ... Nxe5 12. Bxe5** 12. dxe5 would not be favorable to White, as he cannot do much on the kingside, and Black would gain good squares for his pieces. **12. ... 0–0 13. f4**

After
13. f4

Planning a direct attack, but it doesn't turn out well. 13. Bg3 should have been played first, or 13. a3 to safeguard the other wing. **13. ... g6** 13. ... Nd7 is too risky because of 14. Bxh7+! Kxh7 15. Qh5+ Kg8 16. Bxg7!! Kxg7 17. Rf3 Bh4 this and Black's next move are practically forced 18. Qg4+ Bg5 19. fxg5 with a powerful attack for the piece. But after the text Black threatens ...Nd7 and ...f6, which compels the exchange of White's bishop. **14. Bxf6 Bxf6 15. Nb3 b4 16. Nc5 Bc8 17. Bxa6 bxc3 18. bxc3 Bxa6 19. Nxa6 Qa5 20. Nb4 Rfc8!** Black could have regained his pawn at once by 20. ... Bxd4+ 21. cxd4 Qxb4 but then White would have an easy game to defend by

Rfd1, Rd2, etc. Black's plan must be to win the pawn without exchanging his bishop, which will be very useful in further play. That this plan would prove feasible had to be foreseen when 15. ... b4 was played, and is the justification for the entire maneuver from that point. **21. Qd2** Not best. Not 21. Rfc1 Rxc3! 22. Rxc3 Bxd4+ wins. Or 21. Qb2 Qh3! 22. Qxh3 Rxh3 which will soon win both pawns. **21. ... Rc4 22. a3** A necessary precaution. If 23. Rfc1 Bxd4+ 24. cxd4 Qxb4! 25. Qxb4 Rxb4 26. Rd1 Raa4 wins the pawn. **22. ... Rac8 23. Rfc1 Qc7** Threatening ...Bxd4+, as well as Rxc3. **24. Na2**

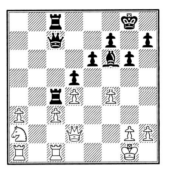

After
24. Na2

If 24. Na6 Bxd4+! 25. Qxd4 (evidently not 25. cxd4 Rxc1+ etc.) 25. ... Qb7 26. Qd2 Qxa6 and the threat of ...Qc6 and ...d4 will win the c pawn. **24. ... Qa7 25. Nb4** This loses quickly, but a pawn must fall, and Black's position will remain greatly superior. If 25. Qb2 Rxd4! 26. cxd4 Bxd4+ 27. Kh1 Bxb2 28. Rxc8+ Kg7; followed by ...Qxa3 and the two pawns are sufficient to decide. **25. ... Rxc3! 26. Rxc3** 26. Rd1 was better, but after 26. R8c4! the pawns begin to drop. The text loses at least the exchange. **26. ... Bxd4+ 27. Kh1 Bxc3 28. Qc2 Rc4** And White resigned, as ...Bxb4 as well as ...Bxa1 is threatened. **0–1** Annotated by Kashdan. (*Chess Review*, October 1936)

347 Kashdan–Morris [C10]
Philadelphia (Prelims), 1936 [*August*]

1. e4 e6 2. d4 d5 3. Nc3 dxe4 4. Nxe4 Nf6 5. Bd3 b6 5. ... Nbd7 was more to the point here, as Black gets into difficulties at once after the text. **6. Nxf6+ gxf6** If 6. ... Qxf6 7. Be4 c6 8. Nf3 h6 9. 0–0 as Black will hardly able to recover for his backwardness in develop-

ment. **7. Qf3 c6 8. Ne2 Bb7 9. 0–0 Nd7 10. Nf4 Qe7** This puts further difficulties in the harmonious completion of Black's development, but the "normal" 10. ... Qc7 could be answered by 11. Nh5 f5 12. Bxf5! exf5 13. Bg5 with a winning attack; or 11. ... Be7 12. Ng7+ Kd8 13. Qh5 and Black's game is hopeless. **11. a4 0–0–0**

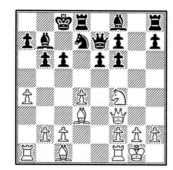

After 11. ...
0–0–0

Despite the storm signals indicated by White's last move, he "castles into it," since the king could not remain in the center very long anyway, e.g. after Re1. **12. a5 c5** The resultant opening up of the game is speedily ruinous for Black, but the alternative bottling up of the bishop on the diagonal would in the long run have proved intolerable. **13. Be4 Nb8 14. axb6 axb6 15. dxc5 bxc5 16. Be3 f5** 17. Bxc5 was threatened. **17. Bxb7+ Qxb7 18. Qe2 Bd6 19. Ra4 Rhg8 20. f3 Nc6 21. Nd3 Nd4** There was no longer any satisfactory defense. **22. Bxd4 cxd4 23. Rfa1 Bb8 24. Rc4+** If 24. ... Bc7 25. Nc5 wins the Queen: 25. ... Qxb2 26. Ra8+ Bb8 27. Na4+; or 25. ... Qb4 26. Ra8+ Bb8 27. Rxb8 Kxb8 28. Rb4 etc. **1–0** A pleasing game by Kashdan because of its directness and simplicity. (*Philadelphia* 1936)

348 Denker–Kashdan [A90]
Philadelphia (Prelims), 1936 *[August]*

1. d4 e6 2. c4 f5 3. g3 Nf6 4. Bg2 Bb4+ 5. Nd2 Nc6 6. Ngf3 0–0 7. 0–0 Qe8 8. d5 exd5 9. cxd5 Ne7 10. Nd4 Nfxd5 11. Nxf5 Nxf5 12. Bxd5+ Kh8 13. Bg2 c6 14. e4 Ne7 15. a3 Bc5 16. Nb3 Bb6 17. Bg5 h6 18. Bd2 d5 19. Bc3 dxe4 20. Bxe4 Bh3 21. Qd6 Ng8 White was threatening 22. Qxh6+ Kg8 23. Qxg7 mate!

22. Bg2 Bxg2 23. Kxg2 Qf7 24. Qd1 Rad8 25. Nd2 Bxf2 26. Qg4 Rxd2 27. Bxd2 Qd5+ 28. Kh3 Qxd2 29. Rad1 Qxb2 30. Rd7 Bc5 31. Rb1 Qf6 32. Rdxb7 Ne7 33. a4 Ng6 34. Rb8 Rxb8 35. Rxb8+ Kh7 36. Qe4 Qf1+ 37. Kg4 h5+! **0–1** (*Brooklyn Daily Eagle*, August 20, 1936)

349 Kashdan–Horowitz [A09]
Philadelphia (Finals), 1936 *[August]*

1. Nf3 d5 2. c4 d4 This move, sponsored by Rubinstein and Tarrasch, is the most aggressive reply at Black's disposal. Against 3. b4, the only logical attempt at refutation, he has 3. ... f6! which will enable him to set up a strong center. Kashdan therefore tries a simpler line. **3. g3 c5 4. Bg2 Nc6 5. 0–0 e5 6. e4 Bg4 7. h3 Be6 8. d3 f6** The position might now be regarded as a King's Indian Defense with colors reserved. **9. Na3 Qd7 10. Kh2 g5 11. Nc2 h5 12. Ng1 Nge7 13. Bd2 Ng6 14. a3 Bg4! 15. hxg4 hxg4+ 16. Nh3 Nf4!! 17. gxf4 exf4 18. f3**

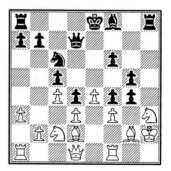

After
18. f3

18. ... gxh3 An attractive alternative here was 18. ... g3+ 19. Kg1 Rxh3 20. Bxh3 Qxh3 and although Black is a whole rook down, his attack can be warded off only with the greatest of difficulty. Thus if 21. Qe2 Kd7 22. Qg2 Qe6 23. Rfe1 Bg7 (not 23. ... Bd6 24. Qh1!) 24. Kf1 Rh8 25. Qg1 Rh2 26. Re2 Qh3+ winning the queen. However, there is a saving clause (as far as the mating attack is concerned) with 23. Qh1! Bg7 24. Qh2 Qf2 25. Kg2 Rh8 26. Qf5+ followed by 27. Rh1. The move actually adopted, however, is simple and strong. **19. Bh1 Ne5 20. Qe2 Bd6 21. Rg1 0–0–0** The immediate ...g4 would have been very strong, but Black can indulge in cat-and-mouse maneuvers since White's king cannot be rescued by flight to the center. **22. b4 b6 23. a4 Rh4 24. Be1 Rh7 25. Bd2 Rh4 26. Be1 Rhh8 27. Bd2 Rdg8 28. a5 g4!** At last! If now 29. fxg4, then f3, threatening to unmask the bishop along the diagonal, is decisive. **29. Bxf4 Nxf3+ 30. Bxf3 Bxf4+ 31. Kh1 g3!** Much stronger then ...gxf3. The threat of g2+ wins a rook. **32. Rxg3 Rxg3** Despite the propitiatory offer of the rook, Black's attack still persists. **33. axb6 Rhg8! 34. bxa7 Qxa7! 35. Bg4+ R8xg4 36. Qxg4+ Rxg4 37. Rxa7 Rg2** The previous exchanges have led to an easily won ending for Black. If now 38. Ra2 Rd2 wins. **38. Ne1 Rf2 39. Kg1 h2+ 40. Kxf2 h1Q 0–1** (*Philadelphia* 1936)

350 Kupchik–Kashdan [D36]
Philadelphia (Finals), 1936 *[August]*

1. d4 Nf6 2. Nf3 d5 3. c4 c6 4. Nc3 e6 5. cxd5 exd5 6. Bg5 Be7 7. e3 0-0 8. Bd3 Re8 9. Qc2 Nbd7 10. 0-0 Nf8 11. Rab1 g6 12. Ne5 Ne6 13. Bh4 Ng7 14. b4 a6 15. Na4 Nf5 16. Bg5 h6!? Not fearing any of the sacrificial combinations which might be tried here, although 17. Bxh6 Nxh6 18. Bxg6 looks very promising. **17. Bf4 Nh5 18. Bg3 Nhxg3 19. hxg3 Bd6 20. Nf3 h5! 21. Nc3 h4 22. g4 Ng7 23. g5 Bg4 24. Nh2 Bxh2+ 25. Kxh2 Qxg5 26. f4 Qf6 27. Rbe1 Bf5 28. Nd1 Re7 29. Nf2 Rae8 30. Bxf5 Qxf5 31. Qxf5 Nxf5 32. Ng4 Kg7 33. a4 Nxe3 34. Nxe3 Rxe3 35. Rb1 Rd3 36. b5 Rxd4 37. bxc6 bxc6 38. Rb6 Rxa4 39. Rxc6 Ra2 40. Rd6 Ree2 41. Rg1 Rf2 42. Rxd5 Rxf4 43. Kh3 Ra3+ 44. Kh2 Rf2 0–1** (*Philadelphia* 1936)

351 Kashdan–Mugridge [D15]
Philadelphia (Finals), 1936 *[August]*

1. d4 d5 2. c4 c6 3. Nc3 Nf6 4. Nf3 Ne4 5. e3 e6 6. Nxe4 dxe4 7. Nd2 f5 8. a3 Bd6 9. c5 Bc7 10. b4 0-0 11. Be2 Nd7 12. Nc4 b5 13. cxb6 axb6 14. Bb2 Nf6 15. 0-0 Nd5 16. Qc2 Bd7 17. Ne5 Rf6! Indirectly guarding the c6 pawn, for if 18. Nxc6 Bxh2+! **18. g3 Bxe5 19. dxe5 Rg6**

20. Bd4 Qg5 21. Rfb1 h5 22. a4 h4 23. Bf1 hxg3 24. hxg3 Kf7! 25. Bg2 Rh6 26. a5 Rah8 27. axb6 Rh2

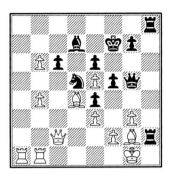

After
27. ... Rh2

28. Bxe4 Relatively the best chance. If 28. Ra7 Qh5 29. f3 (if Rxd7+ Ke8! 30. Qxc6 Rh1+ etc.) Rxg2+! 30. Qxg2 **28. ... Qh5 29. Kf1 fxe4 30. Qxe4 Rh1+ 31. Kg2 Rh2+ 32. Kf1 Rh1+** Here ...Qf5 would have won. **½–½** The game was abandoned as a draw here, both players having only a few seconds left. (*Philadelphia* 1936)

352 Kashdan–Polland [C86]
Philadelphia (Finals), 1936 *[August]*

1. e4 e5 2. Nf3 Nc6 3. Bb5 a6 4. Ba4 Nf6 5. 0-0 Be7 6. Qe2 d6 7. c3 0-0 8. d4 Bg4 9. d5 Nb8 10. c4 Nh5 11. h3 Bxf3 12. Qxf3 g6 13. Bc2 Bg5! 14. Nc3 Nd7 15. Ne2 Bxc1 16. Rfxc1 Qg5 17. Qg4 Qxg4 18. hxg4 Nhf6 19. g5 Nh5 20. b4 a5 21. a3 Nf4 22. Kf1 f6 23. Nxf4 exf4 24. gxf6 axb4 25. axb4 Kf7! 26. Ke2 Kxf6 27. Bb3 b6 28. Kd3 Ne5+ 29. Kd4 h5 30. Bd1 Rh8 31. Be2 g5! 32. Rh1 g4 33. c5 bxc5+ 34. bxc5 Kg5 35. Rhb1 h4 36. cxd6 cxd6 37. Rg1 Rhc8! Leaving White in a quandary; no matter how he plays, Black will seize the seventh rank with decisive effect. **38. Rgc1 h3 39. gxh3 gxh3 40. Rg1+ Kh4 41. Rxa8 Rxa8 42. Rg7 Ra2 43. Bf1 h2 44. Rh7+ Kg5 45. Bg2 Rxf2 46. Rxh2 Rc2** And mate or loss of rook cannot be prevented. **0–1** (*Philadelphia* 1936)

353 Denker–Kashdan [D52]
Philadelphia (Finals), 1936 *[August]*

1. d4 Nf6 2. Nf3 e6 3. c4 d5 4. Nc3

Nbd7 5. Bg5 c6 6. e3 Qa5 7. Nd2 Bb4
8. Qc2 0-0 9. Bh4 Ne4 10. Ncxe4 dxe4
11. Be2 e5 12. 0-0 exd4 13. Nxe4 dxe3
14. fxe3 Bc5 15. Nxc5 Qxc5 16. Bd3
Qxe3+ 17. Kh1 Qh6 18. Be7 Re8 19. Rae1
f6 20. Qf2 Qh5 21. Qg3 Qf7 22. Qh4
g5 23. Qe4 Nc5 24. Qxh7+ Qxh7
25. Bxh7+ Kxh7 26. Bxc5 Be6 27. b3
Kg6 ½-½ (Kashdan's scoresheet)

354 Kashdan-Fox [D16]
Philadelphia (Finals), 1936 *[August]*

1. d4 d5 2. c4 c6 3. Nc3 Nf6 4. Nf3
dxc4 5. a4 Nbd7 6. e4 e6 7. Bxc4 Bb4
8. Qc2 Qa5 9. 0-0 0-0 10. e5 Ne8
11. Ne4 Be7 12. Bd2 Qc7 13. a5 c5
14. Rfc1 b6 15. axb6 Qxb6 16. d5 exd5
17. Bxd5 Rb8 18. Neg5

After
18. Neg5

Black resigned here. The continuation might
be 18. ... Bxg5 19. Nxg5 g6 20. Nxf7! etc. **1-0**
(Kashdan's scoresheet)

355 S. Bernstein-Kashdan [B13]
Philadelphia (Finals), 1936 *[August]*

1. e4 c6 2. d4 d5 3. exd5 cxd5 4. Bd3
Nf6 5. h3 e6 6. Bf4 Qb6 7. Nf3 Qxb2
8. Nbd2 Qb6 9. 0-0 Be7 10. Rb1 Qd8
11. Ne5 0-0 12. Re1 b6 13. Qe2 Bb7
14. g4 Nc6 15. Nxc6 Bxc6 16. Bg3 Re8
17. Kh2 Bd6 18. Be5 Bxe5+ 19. dxe5 Nd7
20. Nf3 Nc5 21. Nd4 Nxd3 22. cxd3
Rc8 23. f4 Bd7 24. Rg1 Qe7 25. g5 Rc3
26. Rg2 Rec8 27. h4 Qa3 28. Rd1 Qa4
29. Nf3 Qxf4+ 30. Kh3 Bb5 31. Rg4
Qf5 32. Ne1 R8c4 **0-1** (Kashdan's scoresheet)

356 Shainswit-Kashdan [D37]
Poughkeepsie (N.Y. Championship), 1936
[September]

1. d4 Nf6 2. Nf3 e6 3. c4 d5 4. Nc3
Nbd7 5. e3 a6 6. a4 Be7 7. Bd3 dxc4
8. Bxc4 c5 9. 0-0 0-0 10. dxc5 Nxc5
11. Qe2 b6 12. e4 Bb7 13. e5 Nd5
14. Bxd5 exd5 15. Nd4 Qd7 16. f4 Rfe8
17. f5 Bf6 18. Ne6 fxe6 19. exf6 exf5
20. Qc2 g6 21. f7+ Qxf7 22. b4 Ne6
23. Bb2 Rad8 24. Rad1 d4 25. Ne2 Qf6
26. Rfe1 Re7 27. Qc4 Rc7 28. Qb3 Bd5
29. Qd3 Be4 30. Qh3 Rc2 31. Ba1 Qg5
32. Qg3 Qxg3 33. Nxg3 Rxg2+ 34. Kf1
Rxh2 **0-1** (*American Chess Bulletin*, September-October 1936)

357 Helms-Kashdan [D52]
Poughkeepsie (N.Y. Championship), 1936
[September]

1. Nf3 d5 2. d4 Nf6 3. c4 e6 4. Nc3
Nbd7 5. Bg5 c6 6. e3 Qa5 7. Bxf6 Nxf6
8. Nd2 Be7 9. Bd3 0-0 10. a3 Qc7
11. Rc1 Rd8 12. cxd5 exd5 13. h3 Re8
14. Qf3 Qd6 15. 0-0 Bd8 16. Rfd1 Bc7
17. Nf1 Bd7 18. Bf5 Bxf5 19. Qxf5 Ne4
20. Nxe4 Rxe4 21. Rc3 g6 22. Qf3 f5
23. g3 Rf8 24. h4 Re7 25. Qg2 Qf6
26. Nd2 h6 ½-½ (*American Chess Bulletin*,
September-October 1936)

358 Kashdan-Slater [B41]
Poughkeepsie (N.Y. Championship), 1936
[September]

1. e4 c5 2. Nf3 e6 3. d4 cxd4 4. Nxd4
a6 5. c4 Nf6 6. Nc3 Qc7 7. Bd3 d6
8. 0-0 Nbd7 9. Be3 Be7 10. Rc1 0-0
11. f4 Re8 12. Qf3 Bf8 13. Nb3 b6
14. Qh3 Bb7 15. Rce1 g6 16. Bd4 e5
17. fxe5 dxe5 18. Be3 Bg7 19. Re2 Nc5
20. Nxc5 bxc5 21. Nd5 Nxd5 22. cxd5
Qd6 23. Rc2 Rac8 24. Rfc1 Bf8 25. b4
c4 26. Rxc4 Rxc4 27. Rxc4 Qb8 28. Bc5
a5 29. a3 Ba6 30. Rc3 axb4 31. axb4
Bxd3 32. Qxd3 Bxc5+ 33. bxc5 Qa7
34. Rc1 Rb8 35. d6 Rb2 36. d7 **1-0** (*American Chess Bulletin*, September-October 1936)

359 Kashdan–Soudakoff [D18]
Poughkeepsie (N.Y. Championship), 1936
[September]

1. d4 d5 2. c4 c6 3. Nc3 dxc4 4. Nf3
Nf6 5. a4 Bf5 6. e3 e6 7. Bxc4 Bb4
8. 0–0 0–0 9. Bd2 c5 10. Qe2 Nc6
11. dxc5 e5 12. Rfd1 Qe7 13. h3 Be6
14. Bxe6 Qxe6 15. Nb5 Qb3 16. Bxb4
Qxb4 17. Qc2 Rad8 18. Racl Ne4 19. Nc3
Nxc3 20. Rxd8 Rxd8 21. Qxc3 Qxc3
22. Rxc3 Rd1+ 23. Kh2 f6 24. Rb3 Rd7
25. Ne1 Kf7 26. Kg3 Ke6 27. Kf3 Kd5
28. Rd3+ Ke6 29. Rxd7 Kxd7 30. Nc2
a5 31. Ke2 Nd8 32. Kd3 Kc6 33. Kc4
Ne6 34. b4 axb4 35. Nxb4+ Kd7
36. Kb5 Kc7 37. Nd5+ Kc8 38. c6 Nd8
39. cxb7+ Kxb7 40. Nb4 Ne6 41. a5
Nc7+ 42. Kc5 Ne8 43. a6+ Kb8 44. Kc6
Kc8 45. a7 Nc7 46. Nd5 Na8 47. Nb6+
1–0 (*American Chess Bulletin*, September-October 1936)

360 Kashdan–Carter [C47]
Poughkeepsie (N.Y. Championship), 1936
[September]

1. e4 e5 2. Nf3 Nc6 3. d4 exd4
4. Nxd4 Nf6 5. Nc3 Bb4 6. Nxc6 bxc6
7. Bd3 d6 8. 0–0 Bxc3 9. bxc3 0–0
10. Bg5 h6 11. Bh4 Re8 12. f4 Re6 13. e5
Bb7 14. exf6 gxf6 15. Qh5 Qf8 16. Rf3
Qe7 17. Qxh6 1–0 (*American Chess Bulletin*, September-October 1936)

361 Marshall–Kashdan [E11]
San Juan, 1936 *[November]*

1. d4 Nf6 2. c4 e6 3. Nf3 Bb4+ 4. Bd2
Qe7 5. Nc3 0–0 6. Qc2 d5 7. e3 Nbd7
8. a3 Bxc3 9. Bxc3 Ne4 10. Bd3 Nxc3
11. Qxc3 dxc4 12. Bxc4 c5 13. 0–0 b6
14. Bb5 Bb7 15. Bxd7 Qxd7 16. dxc5
Bxf3 17. gxf3 Rfc8 18. b4 bxc5 19. bxc5
Qd5 20. e4 Qg5+ 21. Kh1 Rxc5 22. Qe3
Qxe3 23. fxe3 Rc3 24. Rfe1 Rd8 25. Kg1
g6 26. a4 Rdd3 27. Rab1 Ra3 28. Rb4
Ra2 29. e5 Rdd2 30. h4 Rg2+ 31. Kh1
Rh2+ 32. Kg1 Rag2+ 33. Kf1 Rf2+
34. Kg1 Rhg2+ 35. Kh1 Rg3 36. f4 Ra2

37. Rb7 a5 38. h5 Rh3+ 39. Kg1 Rxh5
40. Rc1 Rxa4 41. Rc8+ Kg7 42. Re8 Rf5
43. Rxe6 g5 44. Ree7 gxf4 45. Kf2 fxc3+
46. Kxe3 Kg6 47. e6 Raf4 48. Ra7 Rf3+
49. Ke2 Rf2+ 50. Ke1 Rf1+ 51. Ke2
R5f2+ 52. Ke3 Rf6 53. Ke2 R1f5
54. exf7 h5 55. Re8 Rxf7 56. Rg8+ Kh6
57. Ra6+ R7f6 58. Raa8 Rg6 59. Rh8+
Kg5 60. Rh7 Kh4 61. Re7 Rg4 62. Rd8
Rb5 63. Rd1 Rb2+ 64. Kd3 Rb3+
65. Kc2 a4 66. Rd5 Rg2+ 67. Kc1 Rbg3
68. Ra5 a3 69. Ra4+ Kh3 70. Re5 h4
71. Ree4 Rg1+ 72. Kc2 R3g2+ 73. Kd3
Rg4 74. Ke2 Rxe4+ 75. Rxe4 a2 0–1
(*American Chess Bulletin*, November-December 1936)

362 Seitz–Kashdan [A46]
San Juan, 1936 *[November]*

1. d4 Nf6 2. Nf3 e6 3. g3 d5 4. Bg2 c5
5. c3 Nc6 6. 0–0 Be7 7. Nbd2 0–0
8. Re1 cxd4 9. cxd4 Qb6 10. e3 Bd6
11. Nb1 Bd7 12. Nc3 Rfc8 13. Bd2 Na5
14. Ne5 Be8 15. Na4 Bxa4 16. Qxa4 Nc4
17. Nxc4 dxc4 18. Qa5 ½–½ (*American Chess Bulletin*, November-December 1936)

363 Kashdan–Gotay [D16]
San Juan, 1936 *[November]*

1. d4 d5 2. c4 c6 3. Nc3 Nf6 4. Nf3
dxc4 5. a4 Nbd7 6. e4 e5? 7. dxe5 Ng4
8. e6! fxe6 9. Bxc4 Nde5 10. Qxd8+
Kxd8 11. Nxe5 Nxe5 12. Be2 c5 13. Bf4
Ng6 14. Rd1+ Ke7 15. Bg3 a6 16. h4 Kf7
17. a5 Be7 18. Bc7 Nxh4 19. Na4! b5
20. axb6 Bb7 21. Rxh4! Bxh4 22. Nxc5
Bc6 23. Rd6 1–0 (*Chess Review*, December 1936)

364 Kashdan–Cintrón [E22]
San Juan, 1936 *[November]*

1. d4 Nf6 2. c4 e6 3. Nc3 Bb4 4. Qb3
Nc6 5. Nf3 Ne4 6. e3 0–0 7. Bd3 d5
8. Qc2 f5 9. 0–0 Nxc3 10. bxc3 Bd6
11. Bd2 e5 12. cxd5 e4 13. dxc6 exf3
14. g3 Qe8 15. cxb7 Qh5 16. bxa8Q Be6
17. Qxf8+ Kxf8 18. Rfb1 Qg4 19. c4 h5

20. Bb4 h4 21. Bxd6+ 1–0 (*Los Angeles Times*, December 20, 1936)

365 Kashdan–Platz [D18]
Manhattan Championship, 1936

1. d4 Nf6 2. Nf3 d5 3. c4 c6 4. Nc3 dxc4 5. a4 Bf5 6. e3 Nbd7 7. Bxc4 e6 8. 0–0 Be7 9. Qe2 0–0 10. e4 Bg4 11. Rd1 Qa5 12. h3 Bh5 13. g4 Bg6 14. Ne5 c5 15. Nxg6 hxg6 16. e5 Nh7 17. d5 Nb6 18. dxe6 Nxc4 19. exf7+ Rxf7 20. Qxc4 Raf8 21. Nd5 Bh4 22. e6 Rf3 23. e7 Bxf2+ 24. Kg2 Rg3+ 25. Kh2 1–0 (*American Chess Bulletin*, November-December 1936)

366 Kashdan–Simonson [D62]
Manhattan Championship, 1936

1. d4 Nf6 2. c4 e6 3. Nc3 d5 4. Nf3 Nbd7 5. Bg5 Be7 6. e3 0–0 7. Qc2 c5 8. cxd5 Nxd5 9. Bxe7 Qxe7 10. Nxd5 exd5 11. Bd3 g6 12. dxc5 Nxc5 13. Rc1 Nxd3+ 14. Qxd3 Bf5 15. Qd4 Be4 16. 0–0 Bxf3 17. gxf3 Qg5+ 18. Kh1 Qf5 19. Kg2 Qg5+ 20. Kh1 Qf5 21. Kg2 Qg5+ 22. Kh1 Rac8 23. h4 Qf5 24. Kg2 Rc2 25. Rxc2 Qxc2 26. Rd1 Rc8 27. h5 gxh5 28. Qxd5 Qxb2 29. Rd4 Rc6 30. Rf4 Re6 31. Qd7 Qg7+ 32. Kh3 Rb6 33. Rf5 f6 34. Qe8+ Qf8 35. Qxh5 Rb1 36. Qg4+ Kh8 37. Kg2 Rb4 38. e4 Qg7 39. Qxg7+ Kxg7 40. Rc5 Kg6 41. Kg3 b6 42. Rc6 Ra4 43. Rc2 b5 44. Re2 Ra3 45. Kg2 Kg5 46. Rc2 b4 47. Rc5+ Kg6 48. Rc2 f5 49. Rc6+ Kf7 50. Rc5 f4 51. Rc2 Ke6 52. Kh3 h5 53. Kh4 Rxf3 54. Kxh5 Rc3 55. Rb2 a5 56. Kg4 Ke5 57. f3 Rc7 58. Rd2 Rg7+ 59. Kh4 ½–½ (*American Chess Bulletin*, November-December 1936)

367 Kupchik–Kashdan [D29]
Manhattan Championship, 1936

1. d4 e6 2. c4 Nf6 3. Nf3 d5 4. Nc3 c6 5. e3 Nbd7 6. Bd3 dxc4 7. Bxc4 b5 8. Bb3 Bb7 9. 0–0 a6 10. Qe2 c5 11. Rd1 Qb6 12. Bc2 Rd8 13. e4 cxd4 14. Nxd4 Ne5 15. Nf3 Nxf3+ 16. gxf3 Rxd1+

17. Nxd1 Bc5 18. Be3 0–0 19. Bxc5 Qxc5 20. Ne3 Nh5 21. Ng2 Qe5 22. Bd3 Rd8 23. Rd1 g6 24. b3 Nf4 25. Nxf4 Qxf4 26. Bc2 Rc8 27. Rd7 Bc6 28. Rd2 Be8 29. Qe3 ½–½ (*Brooklyn Daily Eagle*, January 7, 1937)

368 Kashdan–Simchow [D52]
Manhattan Championship, 1937 *[January]*

1. d4 e6 2. c4 d5 3. Nc3 Nf6 4. Nf3 c6 5. Bg5 Nbd7 6. e3 Qa5 7. Nd2 Bb4 8. Qc2 Ne4 Not the best, as he will be compelled to reinforce e4 by f5, after which the weakness created along the White diagonal a2 to g8 seriously compromises his game. Kashdan's exploitation of this weakness is artistic, forceful and instructive. 9. Ndxe4 dxe4 10. Bh4 f5 11. Be2 e5 12. 0–0 exd4 13. exd4 0–0 14. c5 Forcing 14. ... Bxc3 after which Black experiences difficulties anew because of the weak black squares. The stage is nearly set for the bishops to dominate the board. 14. ... Bxc3 15. bxc3 Nf6 16. Qb3+ Black must not be permitted to play Be6. 16. ... Kh8 17. Bg3 Qd8 18. Bd6 Re8 19. Bc4 Qd7 By such moves must he expurgate his past sins. Loss of the exchange was threatened. 20. Rfe1 b5 21. Be2 Nd5 22. a4 The position "goes on wheels" before Kashdan's simple and correct technique. The center is cleared of all resistance. 22. ... bxa4 23. Rxa4

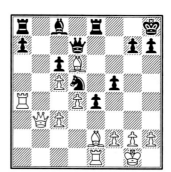

After
23. Rxa4

23. ... e3 Hastening the end in a rather frantic effort to gain counter play. An alternative not totally without merit is ...Qf7 with a kingside demonstration assisted by his pawn majority on that side. Quaintly Black adopts this procedure after first consigning his valuable ally,

the e pawn, to oblivion. **24. f4! Qf7 25. Bf3 Bd7 26. c4 Nf6 27. Rxe3 Ng4 28. Rxe8+ Rxe8 29. Be5 Qh5 30. Bxg4 Qxg4 31. h3 Qe2 32. Rxa7 Rxe5 33. dxe5 Be6 34. Qg3 1–0** (*Chess Review*, March 1937)

369 Schwartz–Kashdan [D78]
Manhattan Championship, 1937

1. d4 Nf6 2. Nf3 g6 3. c4 Bg7 4. Nc3 d5 5. g3 0–0 6. Bg2 dxc4 7. 0–0 c6 8. Ne5 Ng4 9. f4 Nxe5 10. dxe5 Qxd1 11. Rxd1 Na6 12. Be3 f6 13. exf6 Bxf6 14. Bd4 Bxd4+ 15. Rxd4 Be6 16. Rad1 Nc5 17. Bf3 Rac8 18. a4 Kf7 19. Kg2 Nb3 20. Re4 Rcd8 21. Rxd8 Rxd8 22. Re5 Nd2 23. g4 Nxf3 24. Kxf3 Rd2 25. f5 gxf5 26. gxf5 Bd7 27. Ne4 Rxb2 28. Ng5+ Kf6 29. Kf4 h6 30. h4 Rb6 31. Nf3 Rb4 32. e4 b6 33. Nd4 c3 34. Nxc6 c2 0–1 (*Brooklyn Daily Eagle*, January 7, 1937)

370 Tenner–Kashdan [C86]
Manhattan Championship, 1937

1. e4 e5 2. Nf3 Nc6 3. Bb5 a6 4. Ba4 Nf6 5. 0–0 Be7 6. Qe2 b5 7. Bb3 0–0 8. c3 d6 9. d4 Bg4 10. Be3 Na5 11. dxe5 dxe5 12. Nbd2 Nxb3 13. axb3 Bd6 14. c4 c6 15. Qd3 Qe7 16. h3 Bc8 17. Rfd1 Rd8 18. Nf1 Bb7 19. Ng3 g6 20. c5 Bxc5 21. Bxc5 Qxc5 22. Qxd8+ Rxd8 23. Rxd8+ Kg7 24. Rad1 a5 25. R1d2 a4 26. bxa4 bxa4 27. Kh2 Black won in 36 moves. **0–1** (*Brooklyn Daily Eagle*, January 14, 1937)

371 Cohen–Kashdan [D36]
Manhattan Championship, 1937

1. d4 d5 2. Nf3 Nf6 3. c4 e6 4. Nc3 c6 5. cxd5 exd5 6. Bg5 Be7 7. Qc2 0–0 8. e3 Ne4 9. Bxe7 Qxe7 10. Bd3 f5 11. 0–0 Be6 12. Ne5 Nd7 13. f4 Rf6 14. Rf3 Rh6 15. Raf1 Nxe5 16. fxe5 Qh4 17. Rh3 Qg5 18. Rff3 Rxh3 19. Rxh3 Qe7 20. Rf3 Rc8 21. Bxe4 fxe4 22. Rf1 c5 23. Qd2 cxd4 24. exd4 a6 25. Ne2 Rc6 26. Ng3 h6 27. Nf5 Qc7 28. Qf2 Rc2

29. Ne7+ Kh7 30. Qf8 Rc1 31. Qe8 Rxf1+ 32. Kxf1 Qc1+ 33. Ke2 Bg4+ 34. Kf2 Qf4+ 35. Ke1 Qe3+ 36. Kf1 Qe2+ 0–1 (*Brooklyn Daily Eagle*, December 9, 1937)

372 Denker–Kashdan [D05]
Manhattan Championship, 1937 *[January]*

1. d4 Nf6 2. Nf3 e6 3. e3 d5 4. Bd3 c5 5. c3 Nc6 6. Nbd2 Bd6 7. 0–0 0–0 8. dxc5 Bxc5 9. e4 Qc7 10. Qe2 Bd7 11. e5 Ng4 12. Bxh7+ Kxh7 13. Ng5+ Kg8 14. Qxg4 Qxe5 15. Ndf3 Qf5 16. Qxf5 exf5 17. Rd1 Ne7 18. Ne5 Rad8 19. Nxd7 Rxd7 20. Nf3 Nc6 21. Bf4 f6 22. h4 Kf7 23. Rd3 Rfd8 24. Rad1 b5 25. Be3 Be7 26. Nd4 Nxd4 27. Bxd4 f4 28. g3 Bd6 29. Kg2 fxg3 30. fxg3 Be5 31. Kf3 Ke6 32. a3 Rc8 33. Re3 Kd6 34. Rde1 Re7 35. Kg4 g6 36. Bxe5+ fxe5 37. Rf1 Rce8 38. Rf6+ Re6 39. Rxe6+ Rxe6 40. Kg5 e4 41. Re1 Ke5 42. g4 d4 43. cxd4+ Kxd4 44. Kf4 e3 45. Kf3 Rf6+ 46. Ke2 Rf2+ 47. Kd1 Kd3 0–1 (*Brooklyn Daily Eagle*, January 28, 1937)

373 Simonson–Kashdan [A20]
Manhattan Playoff, round 1, 1937

1. c4 e5 2. Nf3 e4 3. Nd4 Nc6 4. Nc2 d5 5. cxd5 Qxd5 6. Nc3 Qe6 7. g3 Nf6 8. Bg2 Bc5 9. b3 Bd7 10. Bb2 0–0 11. 0–0 Rfe8 12. Rc1 Ne7 13. Ne3 Bc6 14. Ncd5 Nfxd5 15. Rxc5 Rad8 16. Qc1 Nxe3 17. fxe3 Rd5 18. Rc4 Rd7 19. Qc3 f6 20. Qc2 Ng6 21. b4 Ne5 22. Bxe5 Qxe5 23. Bh3 Rf7 24. Rc5 Qd6 25. b5 Bd5 26. Rc1 c6 27. bxc6 Bxc6 28. a4 g6 29. a5 a6 30. Qa2 Kg7 31. R1c3 Rfe7 32. Qb2 Re5 33. Rxe5 Rxe5 34. Bc8 Rxa5 35. Qc1 Rb5 36. d4 exd3 37. exd3 Qd5 38. e4 Qd4+ 39. Kg2 f5? 40. Bxb7! Bxb7 41. Rc7+ Kf6 42. Rxb7 Rxb7 43. Qc6+ Ke5 44. Qxb7 Qxd3 45. Qe7+ Kd4 46. exf5 gxf5 47. Qxh7 Qe4+ 48. Kf2 Qc2+ 49. Kf3 Qc3+ 50. Kf4?? Qc1+! Black cannot avoid the loss of the queen, for if 51. Kxf5 Qc2+, or if 51. Kf3 Qf1 mate! **0–1** (*Chess Review*, March 1937)

374 Kashdan–Simonson [E23]
Manhattan Playoff, round 2, 1937

1. d4 Nf6 2. c4 e6 3. Nc3 Bb4 4. Qb3
c5 5. dxc5 Nc6 6. Nf3 Ne4 7. Bd2 Nxd2
8. Nxd2 f5 9. e3 0–0 10. a3 Bxc5 11. Be2
b6 12. 0–0 Bb7 13. Qc2 Rc8 14. Nf3
Bd6 15. Rad1 Bb8 16. Qd2 Rf7 17. Nb5
Ne5 18. Nxe5 Bxe5 19. f4 Bb8 20. Nd6
Bxd6 21. Qxd6 g5 22. Bf3 Bxf3 23. Rxf3
g4 24. Rf2 Rxc4 25. Qxe6 dxe6
26. Rxd8+ Rf8 27. Rfd2 Rxd8 28. Rxd8+
Kf7 29. Rd7+ Kf6 ½–½ (*American Chess
Bulletin*, January-February 1937)

375 Simonson–Kashdan [C79]
Manhattan Playoff, round 3, 1937

1. e4 e5 2. Nf3 Nc6 3. Bb5 a6 4. Ba4
Nf6 5. 0–0 d6 6. Re1 b5 7. Bb3 Na5
8. d4 Nxb3 9. axb3 Qe7 10. Nc3 c6
11. b4 Qc7 12. Bg5 Be7 13. h3 0–0
14. Qd3 h6 15. Bd2 Re8 16. Ne2 d5
17. Ng3 Nxe4 18. Nxe4 dxe4 19. Qxe4
exd4 20. Bf4 Qb7 21. Qxd4 Be6 22. Be5
Bf8 23. Re3 f6 24. Bf4 Rac8 25. Rae1
c5 26. Qd2 Bf7 27. Bd6 Rxe3 28. Rxe3
Bxd6 29. Qxd6 cxb4 30. Re7 Qc6
31. Qg3 Qxc2 32. Kh2 Qc5 33. Rd7 Re8
34. Rd6 Re6 35. Rd8+ Re8 36. Rd7
Re7 37. Qb8+ Be8 38. Rd8 Kf7 39. Qa8
½–½ Practically compelled by the conditions
of the contest to play a forcing game, inasmuch
as his rival was leading 1½–½. Albert Simonson invited complications in the third and final
game of the supplementary match with Isaac
Kashdan for the championship of the Manhattan Chess Club. With Kashdan at his best, difficulties naturally arose and Simonson found
himself two pawns down after 39 moves. It was
useless then to persist in the same tactics and
Kashdan's offer of a draw was readily accepted.
This ended it and Kashdan added the club title
to the state laurels he already had. It is worthy
of note that he has not lost a game in any of the
three tournaments—Poughkeepsie, San Juan
and Manhattan. (*Brooklyn Daily Eagle*, March 4,
1937)

376 Kashdan–Vistaneckis (Lithuania) [B56]
Stockholm Olympiad, round 1, 1937 *[July 31]*

1. e4 c5 2. Nf3 d6 3. d4 cxd4 4. Nxd4
Nf6 5. Nc3 Qc7 6. Bg5 Nbd7 7. Be2 a6
8. 0–0 b5 9. Qd2 e6 10. Rfe1 Be7 11. f3
0–0 12. a4 bxa4 13. Rxa4 Nc5 14. Ra2
Rb8 15. Kh1 h6 16. Be3 Rd8 17. Rb1 e5
18. Nf5 Bxf5 19. exf5 d5 20. Bxc5 Bxc5
21. Qd3 e4 22. fxe4 dxe4 23. Qh3 Bb4
24. Rf1 Bxc3 25. bxc3 a5 26. c4 Rd2
27. Qe3 Rbd8 28. Rfa1 Qe5 29. Rxa5
Qd4 30. R5a3 Qxe3 31. Rxe3 Rxc2
32. Kg1 Rdd2 33. Kf1 Rd4 34. g4 Nd7
35. Ra8+ Kh7 36. g5 Ne5 37. Rb3 Rc1+
38. Kf2 1–0 (*Nordish*)

377 Stoltz (Sweden)–Kashdan [A91]
Stockholm Olympiad, round 2, 1937
[August 1]

1. d4 e6 2. c4 f5 3. g3 Nf6 4. Bg2 Be7
5. Nh3 0–0 6. Nc3 d5 7. Qb3 c6 8. 0–0
Qb6 9. Rd1 Na6 10. Qxb6 It was perhaps
unwise of Stoltz to accept Kashdan's offer of a
queenless middlegame. 10. ... axb6 11. b3
Bd7 12. Nf4 Ne4 13. Na4 Bd8 14. f3 Nf6
15. Nc3 Bc7 16. Nd3 Rfd8 17. e4 c5
18. exd5 cxd4 19. Nb5 exd5 20. Nxc7
Nxc7 21. c5 Ne6 22. cxb6 Ra6 23. Bb2
Rda8 24. Nb4 Rxb6 25. Nc2 Rc6
26. Nxd4 Nxd4 27. Bxd4

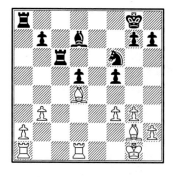

After
27. Bxd4

Things seem to be running White's way.
After the first skirmishes he has the two bishops,
the queenside majority and pawns grouped 3–2
against Black's 3–1–1. A new game begins.

27. ... Be6 28. a4 Kf7 29. Bf1 g5 30. b4 Rcc8 31. a5 Ne8 32. Be5 Ke7 33. h5 Nd6 34. b6 Rc6 35. Rdb1 Rb8 36. Bb5 Rc5 37. a6 d4 38. f4 gxf4 39. Bxf4 Bd5 40. Bd3 Be4 41. a7 Ra8 42. Re1 Rc6 43. Rab1 Kd7 44. Bxd6 Bxd3 45. Rbd1 Bc2 46. Rxd4 Rxd6 47. Rxd6+ Kxd6

After
47. ... Kxd6

The end of the battle of the majority finds Kashdan with B + R against B + P and that is a protected passed pawn on the seventh rank. Another game begins. 48. Rc1 Be4 49. Rc7 h5 50. Kf2 Bc6 51. Rf7 Kc5 52. Rxf5+ Kxb6 53. Rxh5 Rxa7 Another new game. 54. g4 Kc7 55. g5 Ra2+ 56. Ke3 Rg2 57. h4 b5 58. Kd3 b4 59. Kc4 Rg4+ 60. Kc5 b3 61. Rh6 Be8 62. Rb6 Bf7 63. Rf6 Bg8 64. Rf1 Rxh4 65. Rb1 Rg4 66. g6 Rxg6 67. Kb4 Rg2 68. Ka3 Kb6 69. Kb4 Rg4+ 70. Ka3 Kb5 71. Rh1 Ra4+ 72. Kb2 Ra2+ 73. Kb1 Bc4 74. Rh3 Kb4 75. Rg3 Rh2 76. Rf3 Ka3 0–1 Kashdan did not play in round 3 (*Stockholm* 1937)

378 Kashdan–Vuković
   (Yugoslavia) [E19]

Stockholm Olympiad, round 4, 1937
[August 2]

1. d4 Nf6 2. c4 e6 3. Nf3 b6 4. g3 Bb7 5. Bg2 Be7 6. 0–0 0–0 7. Nc3 Ne4 8. Qc2 Nxc3 9. Qxc3 d6 10. Qd3 f5 11. Qe3 Qc8 12. Bd2 Bf6 13. Bc3 Qe8 14. Rad1 Nd7 15. Rfe1 Be4 16. d5 e5 17. Rf1 Qg6 18. Qc1 Qh5 19. Kh1 Rae8 20. Ng1 Bg5 21. Bd2 Black calls the tune, but White has no worries. 21. ... Bxg2+ 22. Kxg2 f4 23. f3 Rf6 24. g4 Qf7 25. e4 fxe3 26. Bxe3 Bxe3 27. Qxe3 Nf8

28. Rf2 Ng6 29. Rdf1 Rf8 30. Ne2 Nf4+ 31. Nxf4 Rxf4 32. b3

After
32. b3

With all minor pieces gone, Black is still attacking. Yet he is quite unable to break White's position. 32. ... Qf6 33. h3 Qg5 The threat is Rxg4+ winning the queen. 34. Qd2 R8f6 35. Qe2 Qh4 36. Qe3 g5 37. Rd1 h5 38. Rdf1 e4 39. gxh5 The last reserve—and it's not enough. 39. ... Qxh5 40. fxe4 Qg6 41. Rf3 Qf7 42. Rxf4 gxf4 43. Qf3 Kf8 44. Kh2 Ke7 45. Rg1 Kd8 46. Rg5 1–0 (*Stockholm* 1937)

379 Kashdan–A. Steiner
   (Hungary) [E11]

Stockholm Olympiad, round 5, 1937
[August 2]

1. d4 Nf6 2. c4 e6 3. Nf3 Bb4+ 4. Bd2 Bxd2+ 5. Qxd2 b6 6. g3 Ba6 7. Qc2 c5 8. Bg2 Nc6 9. dxc5 bxc5 10. 0–0 0–0 In this variation, which Steiner knew very well, Black has good chances thanks to his play on the queenside and in the center. 11. Nbd2 Rb8 12. b3 Rb6 If 12. ... Qe7, White could exchange off his slightly passive knight by Ne4; now this would be met by 13. Nxe4 Nxe4 14. Qxe4 d5! 13. Rfe1 Nb4 14. Qc3 d6 15. a3 Nc6 16. Rab1 Qb8 17. Ng5 Rc8 18. Nde4 Nxe4 19. Bxe4 19. Nxe4 was better, though Black's position remains perfectly sound even then. 19. ... h6 20. Nf3 Bb7 21. Bc2 Qc7 22. Qd3 g6 23. h4 h5 24. Rbd1 Rd8 25. Qe3 Kg7 26. Rd2 e5 27. Kh2 Nd4 28. Nxd4 cxd4 29. Qg5 *(see diagram)*

He should have preferred 29. Qd3, to which Black would have replied 29. ... d5!. Now comes

After
29. Qg5

a great surprise. **29. ... Rxb3!!** 30. f4 If 30. Bxb3? then f6 and the queen is trapped. **30. ... d3 31. Rxd3 f6 32. Rxd6 fxg5 33. Rxg6+ Kf7 34. fxg5 Rf3** Black chooses a quick, vigorous finish. **35. exf3 Rd2+ 36. Kh3 Rxc2 0–1** (*Stockholm* 1937)

380 Guimard (Argentina)– Kashdan [D52]

Stockholm Olympiad, round 6, 1937
[August 3]

1. d4 Nf6 2. c4 e6 3. Nf3 d5 4. Nc3 Nbd7 5. Bg5 c6 6. e3 Qa5 7. Nd2 dxc4 8. Bxf6 Nxf6 9. Nxc4 Qc7 10. g3 Be7 11. Bg2 0–0 12. 0–0 Rd8 13. Qc2 Nd5 14. Rfc1 Bd7 15. a3 Be8 16. b4 Rac8 The beginning of a remarkable regrouping. 17. Ne4 b6 18. Qb3 Qb8 19. Rab1 Rc7 20. Rb2 Qc8 21. Ned2 c5 22. e4 cxd4 23. exd5 exd5 24. Rbc2 dxc4 25. Rxc4 Rxc4 26. Rxc4 Qe6 The smoke has cleared to reveal Kashdan with two bishops and a deadly extra center pawn. 27. Qb2 Bf6 28. Qc1 a5 29. bxa5 bxa5 30. a4 Be7 31. Bf1 Bb4 32. Qd1 d3 33. Re4 Qa2 34. Nc4 Bxa4 0–1 The U.S. had the bye in round 7. (*Stockholm* 1937)

381 Book (Finland)–Kashdan [C42]

Stockholm Olympiad, round 8, 1937
[August 5]

1. e4 e5 2. Nf3 Nf6 3. Nxe5 d6 4. Nf3 Nxe4 5. Qe2 Qe7 6. d3 Nf6 7. Bg5 Qxe2+ 8. Bxe2 Be7 9. Nc3 Bd7 10. d4 h6 11. Bh4 0–0 12. h3 Nc6 13. 0–0–0 a6 14. Rhe1 Rfe8 15. Bf1 b5 16. d5 Na5

17. b4 Nb7 18. g4 g5 19. Bg3 Bf8 20. Rxe8 Rxe8 21. a4! bxa4 22. Bxa6 Rb8 23. Nd4 Bg7 24. Nc6 Bxc6 25. dxc6 Nd8 26. b5 a3 27. Na2 Ne4 Better is 27. ... Ne6. 28. Bxd6! Bb2+ 29. Kb1 Nxc6 30. Bxc7 Nb4! 31. Bxb8?? 31. Rd3! wins for White. 31. ... Nc3+ 32. Nxc3 Bxc3 0–1 Contributed by Kalendovský. (*Sachovy Tyden* 1937, p. 144)

382 Baert (Belgium)–Kashdan [D15]

Stockholm Olympiad, round 9, 1937
[August 5]

1. d4 Nf6 2. Nf3 d5 3. c4 c6 4. Nc3 Nbd7 5. cxd5 cxd5 6. Bf4 e6 7. e3 a6 8. Bd3 Be7 9. 0–0 0–0 10. h3 b5 11. Rc1 Bb7 12. Ne5 Rc8 13. Qf3 Nb6 14. Ne2 Ne4 15. Rxc8 Nxc8 16. Rc1 Ncd6 17. Nc6 Bxc6 18. Rxc6 Qa5 19. Bxd6 Qe1+ 20. Kh2 Nd2 21. Bxh7+ Kxh7 22. Qh5+ Kg8 23. Ng3 Bxd6 24. Rxd6 Qxf2 25. Qe2 Qxe2 26. Nxe2 Rc8 27. Rxa6 Rc2 28. Ra8+ Kh7 29. b4 Nc4 30. Nf4 g5 31. Nd3 Nxe3 32. a4 Rxg2+ 33. Kh1 Ra2 34. a5 Nf5 35. Ne5 f6 36. Nc6 Nh4 37. a6 Nf3 0–1 (Contributed by Holmgren, Sweden)

383 Kashdan–Zinner (Czechoslovakia) [C86]

Stockholm Olympiad, round 10, 1937
[August 5]

1. e4 e5 2. Nf3 Nc6 3. Bb5 a6 4. Ba4 Nf6 5. 0–0 Be7 6. Qe2 b5 7. Bb3 d6 8. c3 Na5 9. Bc2 c5 10. d3 0–0 11. h3 Nc6 12. Re1 Qc7 13. Nbd2 Nd8 14. a4 Rb8 15. axb5 axb5 16. Nf1 Ne6 17. d4 Nh5 18. Be3 Nef4 19. Qd2 g5 20. Ng3 Ng7 21. Nf5 Nxf5 22. exf5 f6 23. d5 Bd7 24. g3 Nxh3+ 25. Kg2 g4 26. Nh2 h5 27. f3 Ng5 28. fxg4 Nf7 29. gxh5 Kh7 30. Nf3 Rg8 31. Nh4 Bf8 32. Ng6 Bh6 33. Rh1 Bxe3 34. Qxe3 Ra8 35. h6 Rxa1 36. Rxa1 Qb7 37. Rd1 Ng5 38. Qe2 Be8 39. b3 Bf7 40. c4 Ra8 41. Rd2 b4 42. Rd1 Ra2 43. Nf8+ Kh8 44. Rd2 Qa8 45. Ne6 Qg8 46. g4 Be8 47. Bd1 Rxd2

48. Qxd2 Nxe6 49. dxe6 Bc6+ 50. Kg3 Qd8 51. g5 1–0 (*Stockholm* 1937)

384 Frydman (Poland)– Kashdan [E36]

Stockholm Olympiad, round 11, 1937
[*August 7*]

1. d4 Nf6 2. c4 e6 3. Nc3 Bb4 4. Qc2 d5 5. a3 Bxc3+ 6. Qxc3 0–0 7. Bg5 h6 8. Bxf6 Qxf6 9. Nf3 c6 10. e3 Nd7 11. cxd5 exd5 12. Bd3 Re8 13. 0–0 Qd6 14. b4 Nf6 15. Ne5 Ne4 16. Qc2 f6 17. Ng6 Bf5 18. Nf4 Qd7 19. Rfc1 a6 20. a4 Rac8 21. Qa2 g5 22. Nh5 Qf7 23. Bxe4 Bxe4 24. Ng3 Bg6 25. Qd2 Qd7 26. Rc5 h5 27. Ne2 h4 28. h3 Bf5 29. f3 Kf7 30. Rac1 Qe7 31. e4 Bd7 32. R5c3 dxe4 33. Re3 f5 34. fxe4 fxe4

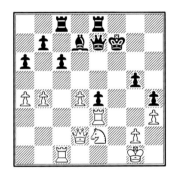

After
34. ... fxe4

Kashdan has succeeded to the extent of winning a pawn—a passed pawn but isolated. Somehow or other that pawn has to win the game, but how? 35. Rc5 Qf6 36. Nc3 Bf5 37. Re5 Rxe5 38. dxe5 Rd8 39. Qf2 Qxe5 40. Rxe4 Rd1+ 41. Nxd1 Qxe4 42. Ne3 Kg6 43. Nxf5 Qxf5 Frydman has deliberately gone for the queen ending for, with the Black king not too well shielded, it will be fiendishly difficult for Black to make headway. There is even a possibility of the 50-move rule coming into operation. Kashdan has no intention of offering a draw. Such an idea would not have occurred to him, 44. Qb6 Qd7 45. a5 Qe7 46. Qd4 Kf7 47. Qf2+ Ke8 48. Qd4 Qe6 49. Qh8+ Kd7 50. Qg7+ Qe7 51. Qd4+ Kc8 52. Kh1 Kb8 53. Qb6 Qe1+ 54. Kh2 Qe5+ 55. Kh1 Qb5 56. Qd8+ Ka7 57. Qe7 Qd5 58. Kg1 Kb8 59. Kf2 Kc8

60. Ke3 Qb3+ 61. Kd2 Qd5+ 62. Ke3 Qb3+ 63. Kd2 Qb2+ 64. Kd3 Qb1+ 65. Kd4 Qb2+ 66. Kd3 Qb1+ 67. Kd4 Qa1+ 68. Kc4 Qf1+ 69. Kc3 Qc1+ If 69. ... Qxg2, White gives perpetual check. All Black maneuvers are inhibited by this possibility. 70. Kb3 Qd1+ 71. Kc3 Qd8 72. Qe6+ Kc7 73. Qe5+ Kd7 74. Qf5+ Kd6 75. Qg6+ Ke5 76. Qg7+ Ke4 77. Qxb7 Qd3+ 78. Kb2 Qb5 79. Qh7+ Ke3 80. Qa7+ Ke2 81. Qd4 Kf1 82. Kc3 Kxg2 Accomplishing the mission begun to move at move 72. 83. Qg4+ Kh2 84. Qf3 Qe5+ 85. Kc2 Qd6 86. Qf2+ Kxh3 87. Qf1+ Kg4 88. Qe2+ Kf5 89. Qxa6 Qxb4 90. Qc8+ Kf4 91. a6 Qc4+ 92. Kb2 Qb4+ 93. Kc2 Qc5+ 94. Kb2 Qb6+ 95. Kc2 Qf2+ 96. Kb3 Qe3+ 97. Kc2 h3 Bravo! After 54 moves of king and queen, Black at last advances a pawn. 98. Qb8+ Kg4 99. a7 Qf2+ 100. Kb3 h2 101. Qc8+ Kg3 102. Qb8+ Qf4 103. a8Q h1Q 104. Qxf4+ gxf4 And a new queen ending begins, the old queens being worn out. 105. Qg8+ Kf2 106. Qf8 Qd5+ 107. Ka4 f3 108. Qf6 Ke2 109. Qb2+ Qd2 110. Qe5+ Kf1 111. Qc5 Qf4+ 112. Ka5 f2 113. Qxc6 Kg1 114. Qg6+ Kh2 115. Qh7+ Kg3 116. Qd3+ Kh4 117. Qf1 Qd2+ 118. Ka6 Kg3 119. Kb7 Qe3 120. Kb8 Kh2 The arrival of queen #5 can no longer be delayed. 0–1 (*Stockholm* 1937)

385 Paulsen (Denmark)– Kashdan [D73]

Stockholm Olympiad, round 12, 1937
[*August 7*]

1. d4 Nf6 2. Nf3 g6 3. c4 Bg7 4. Nc3 d5 5. Qb3 c6 Kashdan typically plays a solid system, not yet trying to force White's hand in any way. 6. g3 The most active line for White is 6. cxd5; he can also continue actively with 6. Bf4 or more quietly with 6. e3. Paulsen prefers the fianchetto as a logical way of increasing pressure against d5. 6. ... 0–0 7. Bg2 Ne4 Black begins the simplification which is necessary in order to ease the cramp of his queenside. 8. cxd5 Nxc3 9. bxc3 cxd5 10. 0–0 Nc6 11. Bf4 Now it remains for Black to complete the development of his queenside before

beginning to make trouble on the half open c file with a backward pawn for a target. **11. ... Na5 12. Qb4 b6 13. Ne5 Bb7 14. Rfe1 Rc8 15. Rac1 Re8 16. Qb1 f6** Black has been gently taking over the initiative and now he starts to open up, shifting the White minor pieces and clearing the center so that his own bishops—especially the black-square one—can exert their latent power; a model example of what had been called hyper modernism ten years before. **17. Nf3 e5 18. dxe5 fxe5 19. Bg5 Qd7** At this point, with his pawn-islands grouped 2–2–2 against White's 4–1–1, Kashdan was probably contemplating an endgame with confidence, but this is where Paulsen seizes a chance to hit back, challenging for his share of the central terrain and leaving Black also with an isolated pawn. **20. e4! dxe4 21. Nd2 e3!** Eliminating the white-square bishops and remorsely approaching the endgame, though there are complications still to come. **22. Bxe3 Bxg2 23. Kxg2 Qd5+ 24. Ne4 Nc4** The square this knight has been eyeing ever since move 11. **25. Rcd1 Qc6 26. f3 h6 27. Qb3!** White has a crafty scheme in mind; Black hastens to unpin the knight. **27. ... Kh7**

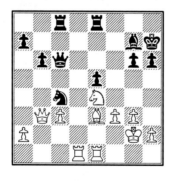

After
27. ... Kh7

28. Bc5!? Into the quicksand. This is the sort of reaction which Kashdan's infuriatingly "correct" play is liable to provoke. Paulsen cuts the defense line so that 28. ... bxc5 can be answered by 29. Qxc4 splitting the Black pawns and remaining with a splendid central knight against the bishop. Kashdan, however, proves more than a match for him in the complications, and Black emerges not only with an extra piece but with a mating attack in the bargain. **28. ... Qe6!** Leaving the bishop stranded, with nothing better to do then return along its orig-

inal diagonal to f2. **29. Ba3?** On this square, protected only by the queen, the bishop is only a liability. **29. ... a5! 30. Rd3 a4! 31. Qb4** The queen cannot desert the bishop, and if 31. Qxa4 the queen and bishop would be skewered by Ra8. **31. ... Bf8!** Skewering the same two pieces diagonally instead of orthogonally; the bishop is lost for only a pawn. The game finishes, however, not with an ending after all, but a short, sharp slugging match. **32. Qxa4 Bxa3 33. Rd7+ Re7 34. Qa7 Rxd7 35. Nf6+ Kh8 36. Nxd7 Rd8 37. Nxe5** Paulsen has a quick eye for the overloaded piece—the Black queen at move 35, and now the Black knight; but it is wasted ingenuity—he has a king! **37. ... Nxe5 38. Qxa3**

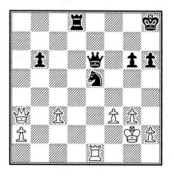

After
38. Qxa3

White has actually acquired two pawns for the piece, but his days are numbered. **38. ... Rd2+ 39. Kh1 Nxf3!!** Finishing beautifully. White is invited to die gloriously either by 40. Rxe6 Rxh2 mate, or by 40. Qf8+ Kh7 41. Qxf3 Qxe1+ and mate next move. **40. Qa8+ Kg7 41. Qa7+** Again 41. Qxf3 allows mate in two. **41. ... Qf7** The appropriate finish would be 42. Re7 Rxh2 mate. **0–1** This is "not" the work of a "mere" endgame technician. (*Stockholm* 1937)

386 Kashdan–Prins (Holland)
[C61]
Stockholm Olympiad, round 13, 1937
[August 9]

1. e4 e5 2. Nf3 Nc6 3. Bb5 Nd4 4. Nxd4 exd4 5. 0–0 Ne7 6. Qe2 c6 7. Bc4 d6 8. d3 Be6 9. Bxe6 fxe6 10. f4 Qd7 11. Nd2 g6 12. e5 Nd5 13. Ne4 0–0–0 14. Bd2 Be7 15. c4 dxc3 16. bxc3

dxe5 17. fxe5 Rhf8 18. d4 Rf5 19. g4 Rxf1+ 20. Rxf1 Rf8 21. Rxf8+ Bxf8 22. Qf3 Qg7 23. Ng5 Kd7 24. Nxh7! Be7 25. Ng5 b5 26. Ne4 g5 27. Kg2 c5 28. c4 bxc4 29. Qa3 Qg6 30. Qxa7+ Ke8 31. Qa4+ Kf7 32. Qc2 cxd4 33. Nd6+ Bxd6 34. Qxg6+ Kxg6 35. exd6 Nf6 36. a4 c3 37. Bc1 d3 38. Kf3 Nxg4 39. d7 Ne5+ 40. Ke3 Nxd7 41. Kxd3 Nc5+ 42. Kxc3 Nxa4+ 43. Kd4 Kf5 44. Ke3 Nc3 45. Kf3 e5 46. Bd2 Nd5 47. Be1 Nf6 48. Bd2 Ng4 49. Kg3 Nf6 50. Kf3 Ne4 51. Be3 g4+ ½–½ (Dutch chess magazine)

387 Kashdan–Mezgailis (Latvia) [D56]

Stockholm Olympiad, round 14, 1937
[August 10]

1. d4 Nf6 2. c4 e6 3. Nc3 d5 4. Nf3 Be7 5. Bg5 h6 6. Bh4 0–0 7. e3 Ne4 8. Bxe7 Qxe7 9. Qc2 Nxc3 10. Qxc3 c6 11. Bd3 Nd7 12. 0–0 Rd8 13. Rfd1 Nf8 14. b4 Bd7 15. e4! dxc4 16. Bxc4 Be8 17. e5 Rd7 18. a3 Ng6 Black needs to get this move in right away. If he dallies with 18. ... Rad8, White has time to play 19. Bd3! meeting 19. ... Ng6 with 20. Bxg6. This would leave Kashdan with a great knight against a very poor bishop. 19. g3 Qd8 20. Qe3 Ne7 21. Bd3 Nd5 22. Qe4 g6 23. Rac1 a5 24. b5 Rc7 25. bxc6 Rxc6 26. Qe1 Qe7 27. Qd2 Kg7 28. Qb2 Rac8 29. Rxc6 Rxc6 30. Rc1 Qc7 31. Rxc6 Qxc6 32. Nd2 b5 33. Ne4 b4 34. Nd6 Qa4 35. axb4 axb4 36. Nxe8+ Qxe8 37. Bc4 Qa4 Mezgailis has succeeded in outplaying his famous opponent, but beating him is another matter. 38. Kg2 Qa3 39. Qb3 Nb6

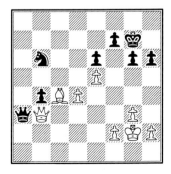

After
39. ... Nb6

White can hold after 39. ... Qxb3 40. axb3 Ne7 41. Kf3! Nc6 42. Ke4 Na5 43. Bd1 40. Bxe6 fxe6 41. Qxe6 Qa8+ 42. f3 Nd5 43. Qd7+ Kh8! 44. e6 Qa2+ 45. Kh3 Ne3 If Black wanted to keep playing he had to try 45. ... Kf6 46. Qf7 Ng8 47. Qxg6 Qd5. 46. Qd8+ Kg7 47. Qc7+ Kg8 ½–½ (*Inside Chess*, November 1998)

388 Raud (Estonia)–Kashdan [D53]

Stockholm Olympiad, round 15, 1937
[August 10]

1. d4 Nf6 2. c4 e6 3. Nc3 d5 4. Bg5 Nbd7 5. e3 Be7 6. Nf3 a6 7. a3 dxc4 8. Bxc4 c5 9. dxc5 Nxc5 10. Qxd8+ Bxd8 11. 0–0 b5 12. Be2 Bb7 13. Rad1 Rc8 14. Nd4 Bc7 15. Bxf6 gxf6 16. Bf3 Bxf3 17. Nxf3 Ke7 18. Nd4 Be5 19. f4 Bb8 20. Rd2 Nb7 21. Na2 Rhd8 22. Rfd1 Rd6 23. Nc3 f5 24. e4 fxe4 25. Nxe4 Rdd8 26. g3 Ba7 27. Nc3 Rxd4 28. Rxd4 Rc4 29. Ne2 Rc2 30. b4 Rxe2 31. Kf1 Bxd4 32. Kxe2 Bb2 33. Rd3 Nd6 34. Kd2 Nc4+ 35. Kc2 Bxa3 36. Kb3 Bb2 37. g4 Bc1 38. f5 e5 39. Rd1 Bd2 40. Ra1 e4 41. Kc2 e3 42. Kd3 Bxb4 43. Rxa6 Bc5 44. Ke2 Ne5 45. g5 b4 46. Ra5 Kd6 47. h4 Kd5 48. h5 b3 49. Rb5 Kc4 50. Rb7 Bb4 51. Rc7+ Bc5 52. Rb7 Bd4 53. Rc7+ Kd5 54. h6 0–1 (Contributed by Holmgren, Sweden)

389 Alexander (England)– Kashdan [C73]

Stockholm Olympiad, round 16, 1937
[August 12]

1. e4 e5 2. Nf3 Nc6 3. Bb5 a6 4. Ba4 Nf6 5. 0–0 d6 6. Bxc6+ The most forcing line against the Steinitz Deferred. Inferior would be 6. d4? b5 7. Bb3 Nxd4 8. Nxd4 exd4 9. Qxd4? c5 and Black wins a piece. Not often that you see Kashdan parting with his bishop. 6. ... bxc6 7. d4 Nd7 8. b3 Be7 9. Bb2 f6 The Strongpoint Defense. Black has the two bishops and seemingly has nothing to fear. 10. Nh4 White is threatening 11. Nf5 or 11. Qh5+ and so Black has to weaken his pawn structure. 10. ... g6 11. Qe2 f5?

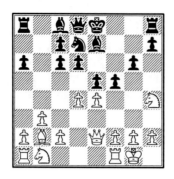

After
11. ... f5

12. dxe5! Sacrificing his knight for a crushing attack. **12. ... Bxh4 13. e6 Nf6 14. Qc4!** This sets up many threats—Qc6+ as well as threats against the bishop at e5 or exf5; also Black cannot castle because of 15. e7+. **14. ... c5! 15. e5 Ng4!** So that after 16. exd6 Qxd6 Black will be threatening mate at h2 and so will have time to conserve the piece. But another shock awaits him. **16. Qd5! Rb8 17. exd6 Bb7 18. d7+ Kf8 19. Qc4 Bf6 20. Bxf6 Nxf6** Kashdan is playing accurately. For if 20. ... Qxf6 would have lost after 21. Qxc5+ etc. **21. Qxc5+ Kg7 22. Nc3 Ng8! 23. Rad1?! h6!!**

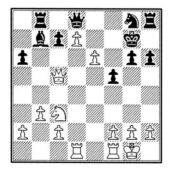

After
23. ... h6

The only move. If Alexander had foreseen this ingenious move, he would have prefaced this move with 23. Qe5+ Nf6 and only then 24. Rad1 Qe7 25. Qxc7, after which White has a winning attack. **24. Rfe1** Dr. Euwe pointed out after the game 24. e7!! Nxe7 25. Rfe1! Nc6 26. Nd5 Rf8 27. Ne7 Rf6 28. Nxc6 Rxc6 29. Qd4+ Rf6 30. Re8. **24. ... Ne7 25. Qe5+ Kh7 26. Na4 Rf8 27. f4 Rg8! 28. Nc5 g5! 29. Nxb7 Rxb7 30. c4 gxf4 31. Qxf4 Rg6 32. Qh4!** Threatening 33. Qxe7+! Qxe7 34. d8=Q. **32. ... Rb8! 33. Re5 Qf8 34. Qf2 Rd8 35. Qc5 c6 36. Rf1!** White is fighting

to keep his attack alive. He is threatening 37. Rexf5! Nxf5 38. Qxf8 Rxf8 39. e7 Nxe7 40. Rxf8. **36. ... Qg7! 37. Re2 Rg8 38. g3 Rxg3+!** Accepting of the rook leads to mate. **39. Kh1 Rg6 40. Qb6 Rxe6! 41. Rg1! Rxe2!! 42. Rxg7+ Rxg7 43. h4?** The final mistake. After 43. h3 Black would have had to settle for a perpetual. **43. ... Re1+ 44. Kh2 Re2+ 45. Kh3 f4! 46.** d8=Q leads to Rg3 mate! **0–1** (*Stockholm* 1937)

390 Napolitano (Italy)–Kashdan [D52]
Stockholm Olympiad, round 17, 1937
[August 12]

1. d4 Nf6 2. Nf3 e6 3. c4 d5 4. Nc3 Nbd7 5. Bg5 c6 6. e3 Qa5 7. Nd2 Bb4 8. Qc2 0–0 9. Bxf6 Nxf6 10. Be2 Qc7 11. 0–0 Rd8 12. Rfd1 Bd7 13. Rac1 Be7 14. Bf3 Be8 15. a3 dxc4 16. Nxc4 c5 17. dxc5 Qxc5 18. Ne4 Nxe4 19. Bxe4 Rxd1+ 20. Qxd1 Rd8 21. Qe1 b6 22. b4 Qh5 23. Bf3 Qg5 24. Nd2 Qe5 25. Nc4 Qf6 26. h3 g6 27. Nd2 Qb2 28. Nc4 Qa2 29. Be2 b5 30. Ra1 Qc2 31. Rc1 Qa4 32. Ne5 Qxa3 33. Nd3 Rxd3 34. Bxd3 Qxd3 35. Rc8 Kf8 36. Qa1 f6 37. Qxa7 Kf7 38. f4 Qd2 39. Rc7 Qd6 40. Rc8 Bc6 41. Rc7 Be4 42. Qc5 Qxc5 43. bxc5 e5 44. c6 exf4 45. exf4 Ke6 46. Rc8 Kd6 47. c7 Bb7 48. Rh8 Kxc7 49. Rxh7 Kd6 50. Kf2 b4 0–1 (Kashdan's scoresheet)

391 Kashdan–Asgeirsson (Iceland) [A40]
Stockholm Olympiad, round 18, 1937
[August 13]

1. d4 b5 2. e4 Bb7 3. Bd3 Nf6 4. Qe2 e6 5. Bg5 Be7 6. Nd2 a6 7. a4 Nc6 8. c3 b4 9. f4 h6 10. Bh4 Qc8 11. Ngf3 bxc3 12. bxc3 Na5 13. 0–0 c5 14. Rac1 Qc7 15. e5 Nd5 16. Bg3 g6 17. Ne4 c4 18. Bc2 Nb6 19. Nd6+ Bxd6 20. exd6 Qc6 21. Qe5 Threatening both 22.Qxa5 and 22.Qxh8, hence Black resigns. **1–0** (Contributed by Holmgren)

392 Cohen Kashdan [D36]
Manhattan Championship, round 1, 1937
[December]

1. d4 d5 2. Nf3 Nf6 3. c4 e6 4. Nc3
c6 5. cxd5 exd5 6. Bg5 Be7 7. Qc2 0–0
8. e3 Ne4 9. Bxe7 Qxe7 10. Bd3 f5
11. 0–0 Be6 12. Ne5 Nd7 13. f4 Rf6
14. Rf3 Rh6 15. Raf1 Nxe5 16. fxe5 Qh4
17. Rh3 Qg5 18. Rff3 Rxh3 19. Rxh3
Qe7 20. Rf3 Rc8 21. Bxe4 fxe4 22. Rf1
c5 23. Qd2 cxd4 24. exd4 a6 25. Ne2
Rc6 26. Ng3 h6 27. Nf5 Qc7 28. Qf2
Rc2 29. Ne7+ Kh7 30. Qf8 Rc1 31. Qe8
Rxf1+ 32. Kxf1 Qc1+

After
32. ... Qc1

33. Ke2 (After 33. Kf2 Qxb2+ 34. Kg3 Qc3+
35. Kf2 Qxd4+ 36. Ke2 Qd3+ 37. Kf2 Qd2+
38. Kg3 Qe3+ 39. Kh4 Qg5 mate, Fritz) 33. ...
Bg4+ 34. Kf2 Qf4+ 35. Ke1 Qe3+ 36. Kf1
Qe2+ 0–1 (*Brooklyn Daily Eagle*, December 9,
1937)

393 Denker–Kashdan [D61]
Manhattan Championship, 1937
[December]

1. d4 Nf6 2. c4 e6 3. Nc3 d5 4. Nf3
Nbd7 5. Bg5 c6 6. e3 Be7 7. Qc2 0–0
8. Bd3 dxc4 9. Bxc4 Nd5 10. Bxe7 Qxe7
All this is part of the Orthodox Defense, one of
the safest methods of threatening this opening.
Black gives up the center, but he can enforce
...e5 or ...c5 at the proper moment. 11. 0–0
Nxc3 12. Qxc3 b6 Not at once 12. ... c5
13. Bb5! cxd4 14. Qxd4 and White has gained
considerable ground. If then 14. ... e5 15. Qe4!
with annoying threats. 13. e4 Bb7 14. Rad1
Rfd8 15. Rfe1 Rac8 16. Bb3 Nf6 17. Qe3

c5 18. dxc5 Rxc5 19. Rxd8+ Qxd8
20. Qf4? This loses time. 20. Nd2 was essential to defend the k pawn, when the game would
be about even. 20. ... Qc7! 21. Rd1 Pretty, but
it hardly helps matters. If 21. Qxc7 Rxc7 22. Nd2
21. ... h6 22. Qxc7 Rxc7 23. e5 Bxf3
24. gxf3 Nh5 25. Kg2 g5 26. h4 Rc5
27. hxg5 hxg5 28. Rd8+ Kg7 29. Ra8
Nf4+ 30. Kg3 Rxe5 31. Rxa7 Re1 32. Rb7

After
32. Rb7

Allowing a forced mate. But if 32. Kh2 Rf1
33. Rb7 Rxf2+ 34. Kg1 Rxf3 35. Rxb6 g5 wins
easily. 32. ... Rh1 33. Bc2 If 33. Rxb6 f5 followed by ...Rh3 mate. 33. ... Kf6 34. Rxb6
Rh3+ Black announced mate in four here:
35. Kg4 Rh2 36. Rxe6+ fxe6 37. any Rg2 mate.
0–1 Notes by Kashdan. (*Chess Review*, February
1938)

394 Kashdan–Simonson [C17]
Match: Game 3, 1938

1. e4 e6 2. d4 d5 3. Nc3 Bb4 4. e5 c5
5. Bd2 Nc6 6. Qg4 Kf8 7. dxc5 d4
8. Ne4 Bxd2+ 9. Nxd2 Nxe5 10. Qg3
Nc6 11. 0–0–0 Nge7 12. Ngf3 Nf5
13. Qf4 f6 14. g4 e5 15. Nxe5 fxe5
16. Qf3 Qf6 17. gxf5 Qxf5 18. Re1 Be6
19. Qxf5+ Bxf5 20. Bg2 Rc8 21. Bxc6
Rxc6 22. Rxe5 Bg6 23. Nb3 Rf6 24. Rf1
1–0 (*New York Sun*, March 26, 1938)

395 Simonson–Kashdan [D15]
Match: Game 4 (Final) 1938

1. Nf3 d5 2. d4 Nf6 3. c4 c6 4. Nc3
dxc4 5. e3 b5 6. a4 b4 7. Na2 e6 8. Bxc4
Nbd7 9. b3 Bb7 10. Bb2 c5 11. 0–0 Be7
12. dxc5 Bxc5 13. Qe2 0–0 14. Rfd1 Qe7

15. a5 a6 16. Ne1 Nb8 17. Nd3 Nc6 18. Bxf6 gxf6 19. Bxe6 fxe6 20. Qg4+ Kh8 21. Nxc5 Rg8! 22. Qxe6 Rxg2+! 23. Kf1 Qxc5! 24. Qxf6+ Rg7 25. Rd7 Qb5+ 26. Ke1 Qg5 27. Qxg5 Rxg5 28. Ke2 Rb8 0–1 (*New York Times*, March 30, 1938)

396 Kashdan (Manhattan)– Fine (Marshall) [D80]

Metropolitan League Match, 1938 *[March 12]*

1. d4 Nf6 2. c4 g6 3. Nc3 d5 4. Bg5 Ne4 5. cxd5 Nxg5 6. h4 Ne4 7. Nxe4 Qxd5 8. Nc3 Qa5 9. h5 Bg7 10. Qd2 Nc6 11. e3 Bf5 12. h6 Bf6 13. e4 Nxd4 14. exf5 0–0–0 15. Bd3 Nb3 16. axb3 Qxa1+ 17. Nd1 e5 18. fxe6 Rhe8 19. Ne2 Rxe6 20. Rh3 Be7 21. Qc2? Bb4+ 22. Kf1 Rc6 23. Nec3 Bxc3 24. bxc3 Rxc3 25. Qe2 Rxb3 26. Rf3 Qd4 27. Bc2 Rxf3 28. Qxf3 Qc4+ 29. Qe2 Qh4 30. Qf3 Qxh6 31. Qxf7 Qh1+ 32. Ke2 Qxg2 33. Ne3 Qh3 34. Bb3 Qh5+ 35. Kf1 a6 36. Qe7! Qb5+ 37. Bc4 Qe8 38. Qxh7 Kb8 39. Qh4 Rd6 40. Qf4 Qd8 41. Kg2 Rd4 42. Qf7 Qg5+ 43. Kf3 Rd6 44. Ke2 Rf6 45. Qe8+ Ka7 46. Qe4 Qf4 47. Qg2 Rb6 48. Bd3 Rb2+ 49. Bc2 g5 50. Qd5 g4 51. Qg2 a5 52. Kd3 Qd6+ 53. Ke2 Qd4 54. Qg3 c6 55. Qc7 Qb4 56. Kd3 a4 57. Nd1 a3! 58. Nxb2 a2! 59. Nc4 a1Q 0–1 (*Chess Review*, April 1938)

397 Marshall (Marshall)– Kashdan (Manhattan) [A29]

Metropolitan League Match, 1938 *[May 21]*

1. c4 e5 2. Nc3 Nf6 3. g3 d5 4. cxd5 Nxd5 5. Bg2 Be6 6. Nf3 Nc6 7. 0–0 Nb6 8. d3 Be7 9. Be3 0–0 10. d4 exd4 11. Nxd4 Nxd4 12. Bxd4 c5 13. Be3 Qc8 14. Qc2 Bf5 15. Qc1 Bh3 16. Bg5 Bxg2 17. Kxg2 Qc6+ 18. Kg1 Rfe8 19. Bxe7 Rxe7 20. Rd1 Rae8 21. Qf4 Re6 22. Rac1 Nd7 23. Rd5 b5 24. Rcd1 Ne5 25. Rd8 h6 26. R1d5 Ng6 27. Qb8 b4 28. Rxc5! Qxc5 29. Rxe8+ Kh7 30. Rc8 Qa5 31. Qb5 Qxb5 32. Nxb5 Rxe2 33. Nxa7 Rxb2 34. Nc6 Rc2 35. h4 h5 36. f4 f6

37. Kf1 Nh8 38. Ne7 Rxa2 39. Rb8 Rb2 40. Rb5 Kh6 41. Nf5+ ½–½ (*Brooklyn Daily Eagle*, June 2, 1938)

398 Santasiere–Kashdan [A06]

New York, U.S. Championship, round 1, 1938 *[April 2]*

1. Nf3 d5 2. b4 An opening with which I have occasionally experimented; the idea behind it is to obtain a majority of pawns in the center, if Black exchanges his c pawn for the b pawn. Kashdan treats this surprise opening and soon (as played) obtains the better game. 2. ... e6 3. Bb2 Nf6 4. a3 a5 5. b5 c5 The advance has its disadvantages; it leaves the White b pawn strongly entrenched and renders weakness on his own b6. 6. e3 Nbd7 7. c4 dxc4 8. Bxc4 Be7 9. Qc2? White develops pieces, indulges in a superficial knight maneuver and strives desperately a la hyper-modern to hold back the d pawn; whereas here the simple 9. d4 (if 9. ... cxd4 10. Bxd4 or Nxd4) challenges the center, reserves the possibility of d2 for the knight and allows White to complete an easy and splendid development. 9. ... Qc7 10. Nc3 b6 11. Ne2 Bb7 12. Ng3 Bd6 13. Rd1 0–0–0 It was far safer and better for Black than for White to castle on the queenside. 14. Be2 To avoid the pin after d4, but d4 was nevertheless necessary at once. 14. ... h5 15. Ng5 Now this is the only chance and White must lose a pawn. 15. ... h4 16. N3e4 Nxe4 17. Nxe4 Bxh2 18. Bf3 Be5 19. d4 At last—the good you might have wrought! 19. ... cxd4 20. Qxc7+ Bxc7 21. Bxd4 f6 22. Rc1 Kb8

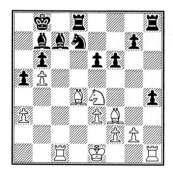

After 22. ... Kb8

23. Ke2 Inviting quick and fatal complications and preferable to a certain, if slower, death.

23. ... e5 24. Bb2 f5 25. Ng5 e4 26. Nf7
Neither 26. Bxe4 Bxe4 27. f3 Bd5 nor 26. Ne6
Nc5 27. Nxd8 Bxd8 could save the game.
**26. ... exf3+ 27. gxf3 Rh7 28. Nxd8
Bxd8 29. Rcd1 g5 30. Rhg1 h3 31. Be5+
Nxe5 32. Rxd8+ Kc7 33. Rg8 Bxf3+
34. Kd2 Bd5 35. Rc1+ Nc4+ 0–1** Anno-
tated by Santasiere. (*American Chess Bulletin*,
May-June 1938)

399 Kashdan–Horowitz [D30]
New York, U.S. Championship, round 2,
1938 *[April 3]*

1. d4 d5 2. Nf3 e6 3. c4 c5 4. cxd5
exd5 5. g3 Nc6 6. Bg2 Nf6 7. 0–0 Be7
8. dxc5 Bxc5 9. Nbd2 0–0 10. Nb3 Bb6
11. Nfd4 Ne4 12. Be3 Qf6 13. Rc1 Re8
14. Nxc6 bxc6 15. Bd4 Qh6 16. Nc5
Nxc5 17. Bxc5 Bg4 18. Bf3 Bxf3 19. exf3
Re6 20. Kg2 Qf6 21. Qb3 Re2 22. Rc2
Rxc2 23. Qxc2 Re8 24. b4 h6 25. a4
d4 26. Rd1 Rd8 27. Bxb6 axb6 28. a5
bxa5 29. bxa5 Qd6 30. a6 c5 31. a7 Qb6
32. Rc1 Qxa7 33. Qxc5 Qd7 34. Qc7 Kf8
35. Qxd7 Rxd7 36. f4 Ke7 37. Kf3 f5
38. Ke2 Ra7 39. Kd3 Ra2 40. Rc7+ Kf6
41. Rc6+ Kf7 ½–½ (Kashdan's scoresheet)

400 Cohen–Kashdan [C99]
New York, U.S. Championship, round 3,
1938 *[April 4]*

1. e4 e5 2. Nf3 Nc6 3. Bb5 a6 4. Ba4
Nf6 5. 0–0 Be7 6. Re1 b5 7. Bb3 d6
8. c3 Na5 9. Bc2 c5 10. d4 Qc7 11. Nbd2
0–0 12. h3 cxd4 13. cxd4 Nc6 14. d5
Nb4 15. Bb1 a5 16. Nb3 a4 17. Bd2
Nbxd5 18. exd5 axb3 19. Qxb3 Qc4
20. Qxc4 bxc4 21. Bg5 Rb8 22. Nd2
Ba6 23. b3 cxb3 24. axb3 Bb7 25. Bxf6
Bxf6 26. Ra5 Ba8 27. Be4 Bd8 28. Ra6
f5 29. Bd3 e4 30. Bc4 Bc7 31. Nb1 Bb7
32. Ra4 Bb6 33. Nc3 Rfe8 34. Nb5
Rbd8 35. Na7 f4 36. Kf1 Re7 37. f3 Be3
Fritz prefers here 37. ... Bxa7 38. Rxa7 e3.
38. Nc6 Bxc6 39. dxc6+ Kf8 40. Bd5
exf3 41. gxf3 g6 42. Rea1 Kg7 43. Rb4
Kf6 44. Rb7 Rde8 45. Ra4 Rc8 46. Re4
Rxe4 47. fxe4

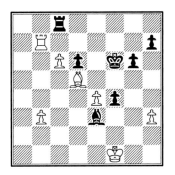

After
47. fxe4

47. ... f3? 48. Rf7+ Ke5 49. Rxf3 Bb6
50. Ke2 Kd4 51. b4 Rc7 52. Kd2 Ra7
53. Kc2 g5 54. Rf6 Rg7 55. Rxd6 h5
56. Bf7+ Kxe4 57. Bxh5 Ke5 58. Rd3
Rc7 59. Bf3 Rh7 60. Bg4 Rc7 61. Bd7
Ra7 62. Kb3 Ra1 63. Kc4 Bc7 64. Rd5+
Kf6 65. Bg4 Rb1 66. Kb5 Bg3 67. Rf5+
Ke7 68. Rxg5 Bd6 69. Rc5 Kd8 70. Rc4
Kc7 71. Bd7 Rh1 72. Re4 Rb1 73. h4 Rh1
74. Be8 Rf1 75. Bg6 Rg1 76. Be8 Rf1
77. h5 Rf5+ 78. Kc4 Bf8 79. Kb3 Rf3+
80. Ka4 Rf5 81. Bg6 Rf6 82. b5 Rf3
83. Ka5 Bc5 84. h6 Ra3+ 85. Ra4 Rf3
86. Rc4 Ra3+ 87. Ra4 Rf3 88. h7 Rf8
89. b6+ Bxb6+ 90. Kb5 Rb8 91. Re4
Bd4+ 92. Kc4 Bf6 93. Re8 Rb2 94. Be4
Rd2 95. Re6 Ba1 96. Re7+ Kb6 97. Rb7+
Ka6 98. c7 Rc2+ 99. Kd3 Rc3+ 100. Ke2
Rc4 101. Rb4 Rxc7 102. Ra4+ 1–0 A
marathon game which is most instructive. Black
seems to get an edge with the exchange of queens,
but White defends sturdily and soon has the
advantage. But the position is uncommonly
difficult, and Black puts up a magnificent struggle. (*Chess Review*, July 1938)

401 Kupchik–Kashdan [E02]
New York, U.S. Championship, round 4,
1938 *[April 8]*

1. d4 Nf6 2. c4 e6 3. g3 d5 4. Bg2
dxc4 5. Qa4+ Nbd7 6. Nf3 c6 7. Qxc4
Bd6 8. 0–0 0–0 9. Nc3 e5 10. Bg5 exd4
11. Qxd4 Bc5 12. Qd3 h6 13. Bf4 Nb6
14. Qc2 Qe7 15. Rad1 Nbd5 16. Be5 Bg4
17. Bd4 Bxd4 18. Rxd4 Nxc3 19. bxc3
Rfe8 20. h3 Be6 21. Rfd1 c5 22. R4d2
Rad8 23. Rxd8 Rxd8 24. Rxd8+ Qxd8
25. Nd2 b5 26. Nb3 Qc7 27. e4 a5

28. Bf1 a4 29. Nd2 Qa5 30. a3 b4 31. Nb1 Bb3 32. Qd3 Ba2 33. cxb4 cxb4 34. axb4 Qxb4 35. Nc3 Be6 36. Nd5 Bxd5 37. exd5 Ne4 38. Qc2 g6 39. Bc4 Nd6 40. Ba2 a3 41. Bb3 Qe1+ 42. Kh2 Qe5 43. Qc5 Qb2 44. Qb6 Kh7 45. Qxd6 Qxf2+ 46. Kh1 Qf3+ 47. Kh2 Qxb3 48. Qe7 Qb2+ 49. Kg1 a2 0–1 (Kashdan's scoresheet)

402 Morton–Kashdan [C01]

New York, U.S. Championship, round 5, 1938 *[April 8]*

1. e4 e6 2. d4 d5 3. exd5 exd5 4. Bd3 Nf6 5. Nc3 Nc6 6. Nge2 Nb4 7. 0–0 Be7 8. Ng3 Nxd3 9. Qxd3 0–0 10. Re1 c6 11. Bf4 Re8 12. Re2 Bf8 13. Rae1 Rxe2 14. Rxe2 Be6 15. Bg5 h6 16. Bd2 Qc7 17. Nd1 Re8 18. Ne3 Qc8 19. Kf1 Ne4 20. Be1 f5 21. f3 Nd6 22. Nd1 Qd7 23. Bd2 Qf7 24. Bc1 f4 25. Nh1 Bf5 26. Qd2 Nc4 27. Qe1 Rxe2 28. Qxe2 Qg6 29. Bxf4 Bxc2 30. Nhf2 Kh7 31. g3 Bf5 32. Kg2 Nd6 33. Ne3 Bb1 34. a3 Nf5 35. Nxf5 Bxf5 36. Qe5 Qf7 37. g4 Bb1 38. Kg3 g5 39. Bd2 Bg7 40. Qe1 Bg6 41. Qe3 Qf6 42. Bc3 c5 43. Qc1 cxd4 44. Bd2 Qe5+ 45. Kg2 Qe2 46. Qd1 Qxd1 47. Nxd1 Bc2 48. Nf2 d3 49. Bc1 b6 50. Kf1 d2 51. Bxd2 Bxb2 52. Bb4 Be5 53. h3 Kg7 54. Bd2 Bb2 55. Bb4 Kf7 56. Ke2 a5 57. Bd6 Bd4 58. Bc7 Bc5 59. Kd2 Bh7 60. Nd1 Bxa3 61. Bxb6 Bb4+ 62. Nc3 Bb1 63. Bd4 Ba2 64. Ke3 Bb3 65. f4 a4 66. f5 a3 67. Ne2 Bc4 68. Ng1 a2 0–1 (Kashdan's scoresheet)

403 Kashdan–Reinfeld [D15]

New York, U.S. Championship, round 6, 1938 *[April 9]*

1. d4 Nf6 2. c4 c6 3. Nc3 d5 4. Nf3 dxc4 5. e3 b5 6. a4 b4 7. Na2 e6 8. Bxc4 Be7 9. 0–0 0–0 10. Qe2 c5 11. Rd1 Nbd7 12. e4 Bb7 13. dxc5 Bxc5 14. Ne5 Qc7 15. Nxd7 Nxd7 16. Bg5 Nb6 17. Bd3 Qe5 18. Bh4 Nxa4 19. Rd2 Nb6 20. Nc1 a5 21. Nb3 a4 22. Bg3 Qg5 23. h4 Qe7 24. Nxc5 Qxc5 25. Rc2 Qa5

26. Qe3 Rfc8 27. Bc7 Rxc7 28. Rxc7 Nd5 29. exd5 Qxc7 30. dxe6 fxe6 31. Qxe6+ Kf8 32. Bxh7 Qe7?? 33. Qg8 mate 1–0 (Contributed by Ansel)

404 S. Bernstein–Kashdan [D52]

New York, U.S. Championship, round 7, 1938 *[April 10]*

1. d4 Nf6 2. c4 e6 3. Nc3 d5 4. Bg5 Nbd7 5. e3 c6 6. Nf3 Qa5 7. cxd5 Nxd5 8. Qd2 Bb4 9. Rc1 0–0 10. Bd3 e5 11. 0–0 exd4 12. exd4 N7f6 13. Rfe1 Be6 14. Re5 Ng4 15. Re2 h6 16. Bh4 Rae8 17. Bb1 Ngf6 18. Re5 Nd7 19. Rh5 f5 20. Rxh6 gxh6 21. Qxh6 N5f6 22. Qg6+ Kh8 23. Ne4 fxe4 24. Qh6+ Nh7 25. Ng5 Bf5 26. g4 Rf6 0–1 (Kashdan's scoresheet)

405 Kashdan–Polland [D10]

New York, U.S. Championship, round 8, 1938 *[April 13]*

1. d4 d5 2. c4 c6 3. Nc3 dxc4 4. e4 e5 5. Nf3 exd4 6. Bxc4! White by slight transposition of moves has reached the position Alekhine held in the 6th game of the World Championship in 1937 with Dr. Euwe. If 6. ... dxc3 White continues with 7. Bxf7+ Ke7 8. Qb3. But later this sacrifice was refuted by Alekhine himself. In his book he states that this combination is certainly very tempting and, especially over the board , extremely hard to refute. The refutation given in ECO is as follows: 6. Bc4? dxc3 7. Bxf7+ Ke7 8. Qb3 cxb2 9. Bxb2 Qb6! 10. Ba3 c5 11. Bxg8 Rxg8 which is in Black's favor. There are other moves for White but they all favor Black. **6. ... Bc5** Dr. Euwe played 6. ... b5? after which 7. Nxb5! followed. This was already recommended by Eliskases but Dr. Euwe apparently was not familiar with it. **7. Ne5 Qf6 (see diagram)**

It appears that at this point dxc3 is feasible. **8. Nxf7 dxc3 9. 0–0 Be6 10. Bg5! Qxg5** If 10. ... Qxf7? 11. Qd8 mate! If 10. ... Qd4 simply 11. Bxe6. **11. Nxg5 Bxc4 12. Qh5+ g6 13. Qh3 cxb2 14. Rad1** Quicker than 14. Qc8+. Polland could have spared the gallery the rest. **14. ... Na6 15. Qc3 Bxf1 16. Kxf1 b1Q 17. Rxb1 1–0** (*Chess*, May 14, 1938)

After
7. ... Qf6

406 Kashdan–Treysman [C13]
New York, U.S. Championship, round 9,
1938 *[April 14]*

1. e4 e6 2. d4 d5 3. Nc3 Nf6 4. Bg5
Be7 5. e5 Nfd7 6. h4 This gambit variation
was introduced into master practice for the first
time by Dr. Alekhine at Mannheim in 1914. The
last tournament before World War I. 6. ... c5
Spielmann adopted this move at Baden-Baden
in 1925. Other defenses are 6. ... h6 and 6. ... a6.
It is not advisable to accept the gambit. 7. Bxe7
Kxe7 8. Qg4 Kf8 9. dxc5 Bogoljubow continued here with 9. Nf3. Kashdan's variation
appears to break open the f file effectively. 9. ...
Nc6 10. 0–0–0 Ndxe5 11. Qg3 Qe7 12. f4
Nd7 13. f5 Qxc5 If 13. ... exf5 14. Nxd5!.
Now Kashdan rushes a rook on to the open file.
14. fxe6 fxe6 15. Nf3 Nf6 16. Bd3 Bd7
17. Rhf1 White hits out straight at Black's weak
defenses and his opponent appears to have few
resources. 17. ... Rc8 18. Ng5 Nb4
19. Nxh7+ Rxh7 20. Bxh7 d4

After
20. ... d4

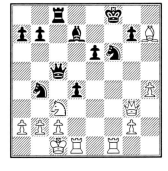

21. Rxf6+! There is no time to be wasted;
the one who wins is who gets there first. 21. ...
gxf6 22. Qg8+ Ke7 23. Qg7+ Kd8 Obviously not 23. ... Kd6 as 24. Ne4+ would follow.

24. Qxf6+ Qe7 If 24. ... Kc7 25. Qxd4.
25. Qxe7+ Kxe7 26. Rxd4 Two passed
pawns to the good, White has an easy win. The
rest needs no comment. 26. ... Nc6 27. Rg4
Ne5 28. Rg7+ Kf6 29. Rg5 Rh8
30. Ne4+ Ke7 31. Rxe5 Rxh7 32. g3 Rf7
33. Kd2 Rf1 34. Rh5 Bc6 35. Rh7+ Kf8
36. Ng5 e5 37. h5 Rf2+ 38. Ke1 Rh2
39. h6 Kg8 40. Rg7+ Kf8 41. Ne6+ Ke8
42. h7 1–0 (*Chess*, May 14, 1938)

407 Hanauer–Kashdan [A29]
New York, U.S. Championship, round 10,
1938 *[April 15]*

1. c4 e5 2. Nc3 Nf6 3. g3 d5 4. cxd5
Nxd5 5. Bg2 Be6 6. Nf3 Nc6 7. 0–0 Be7
8. d4 Nxc3 9. bxc3 e4 10. Ne1 f5 11. f3
exf3 12. Bxf3 0–0 13. Bf4 Na5 14. Nd3
c6 15. e4 fxe4 16. Bxe4 Bd5 17. Qf3 Nc4
18. Rae1 Rf7 19. Qh5 g6 20. Qe2 Qd7
21. Bxd5 cxd5 22. Bh6 Bf8 23. Rxf7
Qxf7 24. Rf1 Qd7 25. Bxf8 Rxf8
26. Rxf8+ Kxf8 27. Ne5 Qe6 28. Qf3+
Kg8 29. Nxc4 dxc4 30. Kf2 Qd7 31. Ke3
b5 32. Kd2 Kg7 33. Qe4 a5 34. Qe5+
Kf7 35. Qf4+ Kg7 36. Qe5+ Kf7
37. Qf4+ Kg8 38. Qb8+ Kg7 ½–½ (*New
York Times*, April 16, 1938)

408 Simonson–Kashdan [D18]
New York, U.S. Championship, round 11,
1938 *[April 16]*

1. Nf3 d5 2. d4 Nf6 3. c4 c6 4. Nc3
dxc4 5. a4 Bf5 6. e3 e6 7. Bxc4 Bb4
8. 0–0 0–0 9. Ne5 Nbd7 10. Qb3 Bd6
11. f4 Rb8 12. Bd2 Nb6 13. Be2 Ne4
14. Nxe4 Bxe4 15. Bf3 Bxf3 16. Rxf3 c5
17. Qd3 cxd4 18. exd4 Nd5 19. Rh3 f5
20. Re1 Bxe5 21. Rxe5 Qd7 22. b3 Rbc8
23. g4 g6 24. gxf5 Rxf5 25. Rf3 Qc6
26. Rf2 Rcf8 27. Qe4 R8f6 28. Rxf5
Rxf5 29. Re2 Kf7 30. h3 Qd6 31. Rf2
Qe7 32. Kg2 Qh4 33. Rf3 g5 34. Be1
Qh5 35. fxg5 Qxg5+ 36. Bg3 Qh5
37. Rxf5+ Qxf5 38. Qe2 h5 39. Kh2 h4
40. Be5 Nf4 41. Qf3 ½–½ (*New York Times*,
April 19, 1938)

409 Kashdan–Shainswit [B02]

New York, U.S. Championship, round 12, 1938 *[April 17]*

1. e4 Nf6 2. e5 Nd5 3. c4 Nb6 4. d4 d6 5. exd6 cxd6 6. Nc3 g6 7. Be3 Bg7 8. Be2 0–0 9. Nf3 Bg4 10. Rc1 Nc6 11. b3 f5 12. Ng5 Qd7 13. d5 Nd8 14. f3 h6 15. Bxb6 hxg5 16. Bf2 Bh5 17. g4 fxg4 18. fxg4 Nf7 19. 0–0 Ne5 20. gxh5 gxh5 21. Ne4 Bh6 22. Be3 Qh3 23. Qd2 1–0 (*Brooklyn Daily Eagle*, April 19, 1938)

410 Fine–Kashdan [E06]

New York, U.S. Championship, round 13, 1938 *[April 18]*

1. d4 Nf6 2. c4 e6 3. Nf3 d5 4. g3 The Catalan System, which was one of my favorites in the period 1938 to 1942. In effect White is playing a Grünfeld Defense in reverse. There are so many transpositions possible that it requires a very thorough knowledge of the opening to play it properly. **4. … Be7** More aggressive is 4. … c5, but Kashdan was always a cautious player. **5. Bg2 0–0 6. 0–0 c5** Now this allows White to obtain a strong initiative. **7. cxd5 Nxd5** 7. … exd5 transposes to the unfavorable Tarrasch Defense to the Queen's Gambit. **8. e4 Nb6 9. Nc3 cxd4 10. Nxd4 Bf6 11. Ndb5 Nc6 12. Be3 Nc4 13. Bc5 Qxd1 14. Raxd1 Rd8 15. Rxd8+ Bxd8 16. b3 Bb6 17. Na4 Bxc5 18. Nxc5 N4e5 19. f4 Nd7 20. Nxd7 Bxd7 21. Rd1**

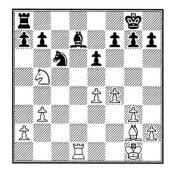

After 21. Rd1

21. … Be8 22. Nd6 Rb8 23. e5 Kf8 24. a3 Ke7 25. b4 a6 26. Rc1 f6 27. Rc5 fxe5 28. fxe5 Bd7 29. Nxb7 Rxb7 30. Bxc6 Rc7 31. Bc4 Rxc5 32. bxc5 h6 33. Kf2 Kd8 34. Ke3 Kc7 35. Kd4 a5

36. Bd3 Be8 37. Bc4 Bd7 38. Bb3 Bc8 39. Ba4 Bb7 40. Kc4 Ba6+ 41. Bb5 Bb7 42. Kb3 Bf3 1–0 Annotated by Fine. (*Lessons from My Games*)

411 Suesman–Kashdan [C33]

New York, U.S. Championship, round 14, 1938 *[April 20]*

1. e4 e5 2. f4 exf4 3. Bc4 Nf6 4. Nc3 c6 5. Qf3 Bb4 6. Nge2 Qe7 7. d3 d5 8. exd5 Bg4 9. Qf2 Bxc3+ 10. bxc3 0–0 11. d6 Qxd6 12. 0–0 b5 13. Bb3 Bxe2 14. Qxe2 Qc5+ 15. Kh1 Qxc3 16. Bd2 f3 17. Qe3 Ng4 18. Qf4 Nf2+ 19. Kg1 Nxd3 20. cxd3 Qxd3 21. Bb4 Na6 22. Bxf8 Rxf8 23. Rad1 Qg6 24. Rxf3 Kh8 25. Bxf7 Qc2 26. Bb3 Qc5+ 27. Kh1 Rc8 28. Qd6 h6 29. Qxc5 Nxc5 30. Rf7 a5 31. Re1 Nd3 32. Ref1 g5 33. R1f6 1–0 (By Suesman from his booklet)

412 Kashdan–Reshevsky [E03]

New York, U.S. Championship, round 15, 1938 *[April 21]*

1. Nf3 d5 2. d4 Nf6 3. c4 e6 4. g3 dxc4 5. Qa4+ Nbd7 6. Bg2 a6 7. Qxc4 c5 8. 0–0 b5 9. Qd3 Bb7 10. a4 b4 11. Nbd2 cxd4 12. Qxd4 Bc5 13. Qh4 0–0 14. b3 Nd5 15. Qxd8 Rfxd8 16. Bb2 Nc3 17. Rfe1 Rac8 18. Rac1 Nf6 19. e3 Ba7 20. Nc4 Nce4 21. Ng5 Bd5 22. Nxe4 Nxe4 23. Red1 f6 24. Kf1 Kf8 25. Bd4 Bxd4 26. Rxd4 Nd2+ 27. Rxd2 Bxg2+ 28. Ke1 Rxd2 29. Kxd2 Bd5 30. Kd3 e5 31. e4 Be6 32. Rc2 Ke7 33. Nd2 Rxc2 34. Kxc2 Kd6 35. Kd3 Kc5 36. Ke3 g6 37. Kd3 f5 38. f3 f4 39. gxf4 exf4 40. h4 h6 41. a5 Bd7 42. Kc2 Kd4 43. Nc4 Be6 44. Nd2 Ke3 45. Kd1 Kf2 46. Kc2 Ke2 47. Kc1 h5 48. e5 g5 49. Ne4 gxh4 50. Ng5 h3 51. Nxe6 h2 52. Nxf4+ Kxf3 0–1 (*Chess*, June 1938)

413 Kashdan–Dake [D79]

New York, U.S. Championship, round 16, 1938 *[April 22]*

1. d4 Nf6 2. c4 g6 3. Nf3 Bg7 4. g3

0–0 5. Bg2 c6 6. 0–0 d5 7. cxd5 cxd5
8. Nc3 Nc6 9. Ne5 Nxe5 10. dxe5 Ng4
11. Nxd5 Nxe5 12. Bg5 Nc6 13. Nxe7+
Nxe7 14. Qxd8 Rxd8 15. Bxe7 Re8
16. Ba3 Rxe2 17. Rad1 Bf5 18. Bxb7 Rb8
19. Bf3 Rc2 20. g4 Be6 21. Bd5 Bxg4
22. Rb1 Bd4 23. Bb3 Rd2 24. Kg2 Be2
25. Rfe1 Rb5 26. Be7 Rf5 27. Bh4 Bxf2
28. Bxf2 Bd3 29. Rbd1 Rfxf2+ 30. Kg3
Rg2+ 31. Kf4 Rdf2+ 32. Ke3 Bb5
33. Rd8+ Kg7 34. Ra8 a6 35. Ra7 Rxh2
36. Rc1 Rf5 37. Rcc7 Rhf2 38. Bc2 R5f4
39. a4 Bf1 40. b3 g5 41. Bd1 Rh2 42. b4
Rh3+ 43. Kd2 Bc4 44. Kc1 Rh1 45. Kc2
g4 46. b5 axb5 47. axb5 Bxb5 48. Bxg4
Rxg4 49. Rxf7+ Kg8 50. Rf2 Re1 51. Kd2
Re8 52. Rb7 Bc6 53. Rb1 Rg3 54. Rb4
Ra8 55. Rb2 Rf8 56. Rh2 Rg2+
57. Rxg2+ Bxg2 58. Ke3 Bh3 59. Rh2
Bg4 60. Ra2 h5 0–1 (By Dake from his
book *Grandmaster From Oregon*)

414 Kashdan–Mitchell [B60]

Boston, U.S. Open, section 3, round 1,
1938 [*July*]

1. e4 c5 2. Nf3 Nc6 3. d4 cxd4 4. Nxd4
Nf6 5. Nc3 d6 6. Bg5 h6 7. Bh4 e6
8. Be2 Be7 9. 0–0 0–0 10. Bg3 a6
11. Qd2 Nxd4 12. Qxd4 b5 13. Rfd1 Ne8
14. a4 bxa4 15. Nxa4 Bb7 16. c4 f5
17. exf5 Rxf5 18. Bg4 Rf6 19. Qe3 Nc7
20. Nc5 Bc8 21. Ne4 Rf8 22. Nxd6 Bd7
23. Nb7 Qc8 24. Bxc7 Qxc7 25. Rxd7
If now Qxd7 then 26. Bxe6+ winning the
queen, hence Black resigns. 1–0 (*Chess Review*,
November 1938)

415 Epstein–Kashdan [A20]

Boston, U.S. Open, section 3, round 2,
1938 [*July*]

1. c4 e5 2. Nf3 e4 3. Nd4 Nc6 4. Nxc6
dxc6 5. d4 exd3 6. Qxd3 Qxd3 7. exd3
Bf5 8. d4 0–0–0 9. Be3 Nf6 10. f3 Bb4+
11. Kf2 Rhe8 12. a3 Be1+ 13. Kxe1 Rxe3+
14. Kf2 Rb3 15. Nd2 Rxb2 16. Rd1 Rxd4
17. Ke3 c5 18. g4 Bc2 19. Rc1 Ra2
20. Nb1 Bxb1 21. Rxb1 Rxa3+ 22. Kf2
Rf4 0–1 (*Brooklyn Daily Eagle*, July 14, 1938)

416 Kashdan–Barron [C26]

Boston, U.S. Open, section 3, round 3, 1938

1. e4 e5 2. Nc3 Nf6 3. Bc4 Be7 4. d3
h6? 5. f4 Nc6 6. Nf3 d6 7. 0–0 0–0 8. f5
Na5 9. Qe2 Nxc4 10. dxc4 c6 11. Kh1
Bd7 12. Be3 White peruses a leisurely course,
evidently under the impression that the center
is blocked for good. Correct was 12. g4! and if
Nxg4 13. Rg1 regaining the pawn with a strong
attack. 12. ... Qc7 13. Rad1 Rad8 14. Rg1
d5! Black brings off a surprisingly strong positional sacrifice of a pawn, rather than waiting for
g4. 15. cxd5 cxd5 16. Nxd5 Nxd5 17. Rxd5
Bc6 18. Rxd8 Rxd8 19. Bd2 a6 20. c4
b5 21. Bc3 f6 22. b3 bxc4 23. Qxc4+
Kh7 24. Re1 Qb7 25. Bd2 Bb5 26. Qe6
Bc5 27. b4 Bf2 28. Rc1 Qxe4 29. Be1
Bxe1 30. Rxe1 Qxb4 Black has played very
well and has a won game. 31. Rc1 Qf4 32. Re1
Re8 Winning a second pawn. The rest should
be easy. 33. Qd5 Qxf5 34. Rd1 Qf4 35. Qc5
e4 36. Nd4 Bd3 Even stronger was 36. Rd8!
But the text also wins. 37. Qc6 Rb8 38. Ne6
Qg4 39. Rg1 e3 Simpler was Rb1. 40. Qd6
Re8??

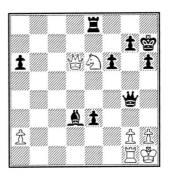

After
40. ... Re8

A blunder that loses the game. Correct was
40. ... Be4 41. Qxb1 and now black has a perpetual with Bxg2+, but 41. Qxe6 would eventually win for Black. 41. Qxd3+ Kg8
42. Nd4 Re4 43. h3 Qh4 44. Nf3 Qf4
45. Qxa6 f5 46. Qg6 Ra4 47. Rd1 Ra8
48. Rd7 1–0 (*Boston* 1938)

417 Lyman–Kashdan [C55]

Boston, U.S. Open, section 3, round 5,
1938 [*July*]

1. e4 e5 2. Nf3 Nc6 3. Bc4 Nf6 4. d4

exd4 5. e5 d5 6. Bb5 Ne4 7. Nxd4 Bd7
8. Bxc6 bxc6 9. 0–0 Be7 10. f3 Nc5
11. f4 Ne4 12. f5 c5 13. Ne2 c6 14. Nbc3
Nxc3 15. bxc3 0–0 16. f6 gxf6 17. Bh6
Re8 18. Qd3 Kh8 19. exf6 Bxf6 20. Qf3
Bg5 21. Qh5 Bxh6 22. Qxh6 Rxe2
23. Rxf7

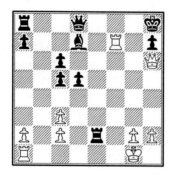

After
23. Rxf7

The position looks hopeless for Black at first
sight (if 23. ... Qg8 then 24. Qf6+ wins.) But
Kashdan who is defending cleverly, has a resource which must have been seen some moves
back. 23. ... Rxg2+ 24. Kh1 Bf5 25. Rxf5
Rg6 26. Qf4 Qd6 27. Qxd6 Rxd6
28. Rf7 Rg6 29. Rg1! Rxg1+ 30. Kxg1 Rb8
31. Rxa7 Rb1+ 32. Kf2 Rb2 33. Ke3!
Rxc2 34. Kd3 Rxh2 35. Ra6 c4+ 36. Kd4
Rd2+ As will be seen, Black temporary material superiority is meaningless; White gives up
his rook for the rook pawn and is just able to
draw with a lone pawn against the Black rook.
37. Kc5 Kg7 38. Rxc6 h5 39. Re6 h4
40. Re1 Kg6 41. Ra1 h3 42. a4 h2 43. a5
Ra2! 44. Rh1 Rxa5+ 45. Kd4 Ra2
46. Kxd5 Kf5 47. Kxc4 Kf4 48. Kd5
Rd2+ 49. Kc5 Kg3 50. c4 Kg2 51. Rxh2+
Kxh2 52. Kb6 Rb2+ 53. Kc6 Kg3 54. c5
Kf4 55. Kd7 Rd2+ 56. Ke6 Rc2 57. Kd6
Rd2+ 58. Ke6 Rh2 59. c6 Rh6+ 60. Kd7
Rh7+ ½–½ (*Boston* 1938)

418 Kashdan–Collins [B73]

Boston, U.S. Open, section 3, round 6,
1938 *[July]*

1. e4 c5 2. Nf3 d6 3. d4 cxd4 4. Nxd4
Nf6 5. Nc3 g6 6. Be2 Bg7 7. Be3 Nc6
8. 0–0 0–0 9. h3 Bd7 10. Qd2 Rc8
11. Nb3 a6 12. f4 Qc7 13. Bf3 Na5

14. Nxa5 Qxa5 15. Rad1 Rfd8 16. Qf2
Rxc3 17. bxc3 Qxc3 18. Bd4 Qc8 19. e5
1–0 (*Los Angeles Times*, October 16, 1938)

419 Barnes–Kashdan [C83]

Boston, U.S. Open, section 3, round 7,
1938 *[July]*

1. e4 e5 2. Nf3 Nc6 3. Bb5 a6 4. Ba4
Nf6 5. 0–0 Nxe4 6. d4 b5 7. Bb3 d5
8. dxe5 Be6 9. c3 Be7 10. Nbd2 0–0
11. Re1 Nc5 12. Bc2 d4 13. cxd4 Nxd4
14. Nxd4 Qxd4 15. Qe2 Rfd8 16. Nf3
Qc4 17. Be3 Qxe2 18. Rxe2 Bg4 19. h3
Bh5 20. g4 Bg6 21. Bxg6 hxg6 22. Nd4
Rd5 23. Rc2 Bf8 24. Nc6 Nd7 25. Racl
Re8 26. Kg2 f6 27. exf6 gxf6 28. Bf4
Bd6 29. Bxd6 Rxd6 30. Na5 c5 31. Nb7
Rc6 32. Nxc5 Rec8 33. b4 a5 34. a3
Kf7 35. Rc3 Nxc5 36. h4 axb4 37. axb4
R6c7 38. Rxc5 Rxc5 After the trade of both
rooks, followed by the simplification of the
pawn situation, both sides queen and White
will have a pawn advantage not sufficient to win.
½–½ (*Boston Post*)

420 Santasiere–Kashdan [E01]

Boston, U.S. Open, Finals, round 1, 1938
[July]

1. Nf3 d5 2. g3 c5 3. Bg2 Nc6 4. d4
Nf6 5. 0–0 e6 6. c4 cxd4 7. Nxd4 Qb6
8. Nxc6 bxc6 9. Nc3 Be7 10. cxd5 exd5
11. Na4 Qb5 12. Be3 0–0 13. Qc2 Re8
14. Racl Bg4 15. Nc3 Qa6 16. Rfd1 Bb4
17. Bf1 Rac8 18. Qd3 Qb7 19. a3 Bf8
Kashdan allows his preference of the bishops
to get the better of him. A much better chance
was 19. ... Bxc3 20. Qxc3 c5. 20. b4 Be6
21. Na4 Nd7 22. Nc5 Nxc5 23. Bxc5
Bxc5 24. Rxc5 Bd7 25. Rdc1 Re7 26. e3
Rce8 27. Bg2 Qb8 28. Qd4 Rd8 29. Rd1
Rc8 30. h4 h6 31. Bf3 Qb6 32. Kg2
Rb8 33. Rdc1 Be8 34. Qf4 Rd8 35. Rd1
Re6 36. Qd4 Rb8 37. Rdc1 Re7 38. R1c3
Rd8 39. Rc2 Rb8 40. Rd2 Re6 41. Rdc2
Rd8 42. Rd2 Rd7 43. Qc3 Rd8 44. Rd4
Re7 45. Bd1 Re6 46. Bc2 Rdd6 47. h5
Qd8 48. Qd3 g6 49. Rh4 Kh7 50. Qd4
Qf6 51. Qxf6 Rxf6 52. Ba4 Rde6 53. Rd4

gxh5 54. Rh4 Kg7 55. Rxh5 Re7 56. Rh4 Kf8 57. Rd4 Rb7 58. e4! Opening up the fifth rank and the d file for his rooks, and also making available a new diagonal (f3–a8) along which to menace the c pawn. 58. ... dxe4 59. Rxe4 Bd7 Rxe8 was threatened. 60. Rec4 Rb6 61. Rc3 Ke7 62. Ra5! a6 63. Bd1 Rd6 64. Be2 Bc8 65. Rac5 Be6 66. f3 Bd7 67. Kf2 Re6 68. Ra5 Bc8 69. g4 Rd6 70. Bd3 Kd8 71. Be4 Kc7 72. Rh5 Rb5 73. Rcc5 Rf6 74. Ke3 Rb8 75. Bd3 Kb6 76. Rh2 Bd7 77. Re5! An interesting finesse. White threatens to establish a rook on e7. 77. ... Re8 78. Rxe8 Bxe8 79. Rh5 Bd7 80. Ra5 Bc8 81. Be4 Be6 82. Rc5 Bd7 83. Kd4 Rd6+ 84. Ke5 Re6+ 85. Kf4 Rd6 86. Bf5 Be8 87. Ke5 Kc7 88. Ra5 f6+ 89. Kf4 Kb7 90. Ke3 h5 91. gxh5 Bxh5 92. Bd3 Bf7 93. Bxa6+ Kb6 94. Bd3 Bd5 95. Be4 Bb3 96. Rc5 Ba4 97. Kf4 Bb3 98. Kf5 Bf7 99. a4 Be8 100. a5+ Ka6 101. Rc3 Bd7+ 102. Kf4 Rd4 103. Rd3 Rxd3 104. Bxd3+ Kb7 The ending is still difficult, as White must be aware of a too far reaching reduction of forces. 105. Bf5 Be8 106. Be6 Bg6 107. Ke3 Kc7 108. Kd4 Kd6 109. Bc4 Bf5 110. Bd3 Bh3 111. a6 Kc7 112. Kc5 Bg2 113. Be4 Bf1 114. Bxc6 Bxa6 115. b5 Bc8 116. b6+ Kb8 117. Kd6 Bh3 118. f4 Bg4 119. Ke7 f5 120. Kf6 Bh3 121. Ke5 Kc8 122. Bf3 Kb8 123. Bd5 Kc8 124. Be6+ Kb7 125. Bxf5 Bf1 126. Be6 Bd3? Exhausted by the lengthy battle Black finally blunders. 126. ... Kxb6 was somewhat better, but White would still win with 127. f5. 127. Kd4 For White has time for Kc5. Both players deserve credit for their tenacity. 1–0 (Boston 1938)

421 Kashdan–Collins [D18]
Boston, U.S. Open, Finals, round 2, 1938
[July]

1. d4 d5 2. c4 c6 3. Nc3 dxc4 4. Nf3 Nf6 5. a4 Bf5 6. e3 e6 7. Bxc4 Nbd7 8. 0–0 Bd6 9. Qe2 Ne4 10. Nxe4 Bxe4 11. Nd2 Bg6 12. f4 0–0 13. e4 h6 A game Reinfeld–Collins (U.S. Championship 1938 Prelims) continued: 13. ... Bc7 14. f5! exf5 15. exf5 Re8 16. Ne4! Bxh2+?! 17. Kh1!! Bc7 (if

Qh4 18. Bg5!! wins) 18. Bg5! Nf6 19. Bxf6 gxf6 20. fxg6 hxg6 21. Nf6+ 1–0. 14. a5 a6 15. Kh1 Bb4 16. Nb3 Nf6 17. Bd3 Qe7 18. g4 Rfe8 19. Qg2 Kh8 20. f5 exf5 21. gxf5 Bh7 22. e5 Nd5 23. f6 gxf6 24. Bxh7 Kxh7 25. Bxh6! Rg8 If now 25. ... Kxh6? 26. Qh3+ and it is mate in two. But 25. Qe4+ would have left White with a clear winning position. 26. Qh3 Qe6 27. Rf5 Rg6 28. Bf8+ Kg8 29. Bxb4

After
29. Bxb4

29. ... Nxb4 Black misses the reply which would have turned the tables which is 29. ... Nf5!!. 30. exf6 Re8 31. Nc5! Qe2 32. Raf1! Re3 33. R5f3 Rxf3 34. Qxf3 Qxb2 35. Qe4 Nd5 36. Qxg6+! fxg6 37. f7+ Kh7 38. f8Q 1–0 (Boston 1938)

422 Kashdan–Jaffe [D44]
Boston, U.S. Open, Finals, round 3, 1938
[July]

1. d4 Nf6 2. c4 e6 3. Nc3 d5 4. Nf3 c6 5. Bg5 dxc4 6. e4 Qb6 7. Qc2 Nbd7 8. Bxc4 h6 9. Be3 Be7 10. 0–0 0–0 11. a3 Qc7 12. e5 Nd5 13. Bd2 Nxc3 14. bxc3 c5 15. Qe4 cxd4 16. Bd3 g6 17. cxd4 Kg7 18. Nh4 Bxh4 19. Qxh4 Rh8 20. Rfc1 Qb8 21. Rc3 g5 22. Qg3 Nb6 23. Bxg5 Kf8 24. Bf6 Rg8 25. Qh4 Bd7 26. Bh7 Nd5 27. Bxg8 Nxc3 28. Qxh6+ Ke8 29. Bxf7+ 1–0 (Boston Post)

423 Moskowitz–Kashdan [E36]
Boston, U.S. Open, Finals, round 4, 1938
[July]

1. d4 Nf6 2. c4 e6 3. Nc3 Bb4 4. Qc2 d5 5. a3 Bxc3+ 6. Qxc3 0–0 7. Bg5 h6

8. Bh4 c5 9. e3 g5 10. Bg3 Ne4 11. Qc2
Qa5+ 12. Kd1 Bd7 13. b3 cxd4 14. Bd3
dxe3 15. Bxe4 dxe4 16. fxe3 Na6 17. Ne2
Rfd8 18. Kc1 Nb4 19. Qc3 Nd3+ 20. Kb1
Qxc3 21. Nxc3 f5 22. Ra2 Rac8 23. Rc2
Bc6 24. Rf1 Kg7 25. Ka2 Kg6 26. b4 e5
27. Be1 Nxe1 28. Rxe1 b6 29. Kb2 Rd3
30. b5 Ba8 31. Nd1 Rcd8 32. Nf2 Rd2
33. Kc3 Rxc2+ 34. Kxc2 h5 35. g3 Rc8
36. Kb3 f4 37. exf4 exf4 38. gxf4 gxf4
39. Nxe4 Bxe4 40. Rxe4 Rf8 41. Kc3 f3
42. Re1 Kf5 43. Rc1 Kg4 44. Kd2 Kh3
0–1 (*Boston Post*)

424 Morton–Kashdan [D95]
Boston, U.S. Open, Finals, round 5, 1938
[July]

1. d4 Nf6 2. c4 g6 3. Nc3 d5 4. Nf3
Bg7 5. e3 0–0 6. Qb3 e6 7. Bd2 Nc6
8. cxd5 exd5 9. Rc1 Ne7 10. Ne5 c6
11. Be2 Nf5 12. 0–0 Nd6 13. Rfd1 Nfe4!
14. Be1 Re8 15. Nxe4 Nxe4 16. Nd3 Nd6
17. Nc5 f5! 18. Rc2 Qe7 19. Bb4 a5!
20. Be1 f4 21. Na4 Bf5 22. Rc3 b5!
23. Nb6 Nc4!!

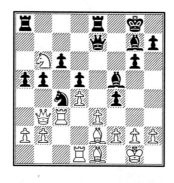

After
23. ... Nc4

24. a4! Nxb6 25. Rxc6 fxe3 26. Bxb5
exf2+ 27. Bxf2 Nd7 28. Qxd5+ Qf7
29. Qxf7+ Kxf7 30. Rc7 Red8 31. Bh4
Bf6 32. Bxf6 Kxf6 33. Rf1 Ke7 34. Re1+
Kd6 35. Rc6+ Kd5 36. Re7 h5 37. Kf2
Rf8 38. Kg3 Rfd8 39. Kh4 Re8 40. Rxe8
Rxe8 41. Ra6 Re4+ 42. Kg5 Rxd4 43. h3
Nc5 44. Rxa5 Ke6 45. Be8 Ne4+
46. Kh6 Kf6 47. Ra6+ Nd6 48. Rb6 h4!
49. a5 Rd5! 50. Kh7 Bd3 51. b3 Rh5+
52. Kg8 Ke7 53. a6 Nxe8 54. a7 Be4!
0–1 An outstanding game full of complica-

tions. Black might easily have gone astray despite his material superiority, but he plays the
ending with consummate skill. (*Chess Review*,
October 1938)

425 Kashdan–Shainswit [D62]
Boston, U.S. Open, Finals, round 6, 1938
[July]

1. d4 d5 2. c4 e6 3. Nc3 Nf6 4. Nf3
Nbd7 5. Bg5 Be7 6. e3 0–0 7. Qc2 c5
8. cxd5 Nxd5 9. Bxe7 Qxe7 10. Nxd5
exd5 11. Be2 cxd4 12. Nxd4 Ne5 13. 0–0
Be6 14. Nxe6 Rfc8 15. Qb3 fxe6 16. Rac1
Nf7 17. Rc3 Nd6 18. Rfc1 Rxc3 19. Rxc3
Rf8 20. Bd3 Qf6 21. Rc2 Qe5 22. Qa4
a6 23. Qb4 g6 24. h3 Rf7 25. Qb6 Ne4
26. Rc8+ Kg7 27. f4 Qf6 28. Bxe4 dxe4
29. Rc7 Kh6 30. Rxb7 Rxb7 31. Qxb7
a5 32. Qxe4 1–0 (*New York Sun*, July 30, 1938)

426 Polland–Kashdan [D49]
Boston, U.S. Open, Finals, round 7, 1938
[July]

1. c4 Nf6 2. Nf3 e6 3. Nc3 d5 4. d4 c6
5. e3 Nbd7 6. Bd3 dxc4 7. Bxc4 b5
8. Bd3 a6 9. e4 c5 10. e5 cxd4 11. Nxb5
Nxe5 12. Nxe5 axb5 13. 0–0 Qd5
14. Qe2 Rb8 15. Bg5 Be7 16. f4 0–0
17. Rf3 h6 18. Rh3 Bb7 19. Rf1 Rfc8
20. Bxf6 Bxf6 21. Ng4 Kf8 22. Nxf6
gxf6 23. Rxh6 Ke7 24. b3 Rc3 25. Rh5
f5 26. Rxf5 Qxg2+ 27. Qxg2 Bxg2
28. Re1 Bh3 29. Rxb5 Rg8+ 0–1 (*Chess Review*, October 1938)

427 Kashdan–Horowitz [D31]
Boston, U.S. Open, Finals, round 8, 1938
[July]

1. c4 e6 2. Nc3 d5 3. cxd5 exd5 4. d4
c6 5. Nf3 Bd6 6. e4 dxe4 7. Nxe4 Bb4+
8. Bd2 Bxd2+ 9. Qxd2 Nf6 10. Nxf6+
Qxf6 11. Bc4 0–0 12. 0–0 Nd7 13. Rfe1
Nb6 14. Bb3 Bf5 15. Qf4 Rad8 16. Qe5
Qxe5 17. Rxe5 Bd7 18. Rd1 Nc8 19. h3
h6 20. Rc1 Rfe8 21. d5 Ne7 22. dxc6
Nxc6 23. Rxe8+ ½–½ (*American Chess Bulletin*, July-August 1938)

428 Kashdan–Blumin [D61]

Boston, U.S. Open, Finals, round 9, 1938
[July]

1. d4 Nf6 2. c4 e6 3. Nc3 d5 4. Bg5
Be7 5. Nf3 Nbd7 6. e3 0–0 7. Qc2 c6
8. Bd3 dxc4 9. Bxc4 h6 10. Bh4 a6
11. 0–0 b5 12. Be2 Bb7 13. Rfd1 Qb6
14. e4 Rfe8 15. e5 Nd5 16. Bxe7 Nxc3
17. Qxc3 Rxe7 18. b4 Qd8 19. Nd2 Nb6
20. Nb3 Nd5 21. Qd2 Ra7 22. Rac1 Rc7
23. Bf3 Ba8 24. Rc5 Rc8 25. Rdc1 Rd7
26. a3 Ne7 27. Be4 Nd5 28. g3 Kf8
29. Qc2 Kg8 30. Qe2 Qg5 31. h4 Qd8
32. R5c2 Ra7 33. Qf3 Qe7 34. Kh2 Qd8
35. Rc5 Rd7 36. Qe2 Qe7 37. Na5 Rdc7
38. Qd2 Qd7 39. Qd3 Qd8 40. R1c2 Qe7
41. Rc1 Qd8 42. Qf3 Qe7 43. Bd3 g6
44. h5 Qg5 45. Be4 Qxh5+ 46. Qxh5
gxh5 47. Bxd5 exd5 48. Kh3 Kg7
49. Kh4 f6 50. exf6+ Kxf6 51. Kxh5 Kf5
52. Re1 Kf6 53. Rc3 Rg8 54. Rf3+ Kg7
55. Re6 Rf7 56. Rg6+ Kf8 57. Rxf7+
Kxf7 58. Rxg8 Kxg8 59. Kxh6 1–0
(*Boston* 1938)

429 Dahlstrom–Kashdan [C01]

Boston, U.S. Open, Finals, round 10, 1938
[July]

1. e4 e6 2. d4 d5 3. exd5 exd5 4. Bd3
Nf6 5. Nf3 Nc6 6. 0–0 Bg4 7. Re1+ Be7
8. c3 0–0 9. Bg5 h6 10. Bh4 Re8
11. Nbd2 Nh5 12. Bg3 Nxg3 13. hxg3
Qd6 14. Qc2 Bf6 15. Bf5 Bxf5 16. Qxf5
Ne7 17. Qd3 Qb6 18. Nb3 Ng6 19. Re2
Rxe2 20. Qxe2 a5 21. Nc5 Qc6 22. Re1
b6 23. Nd3 Qd6 24. Qd2 c5 25. Nf4
Nxf4 26. gxf4 c4 27. g3 b5 28. Re2 b4
29. Ne5 Rb8 30. Qc2 b3 31. Qb1 bxa2
32. Qxa2 Bd8 33. Qa4 Bc7 34. Nd7 Ra8
35. Nc5 Kf8 36. Nd7+ Kg8 37. Nc5 Kf8
38. Nd7+ Kg8 ½–½ (*Boston Post*)

430 Rosenzweig–Kashdan [C45]

Boston, U.S. Open, Finals, round 11, 1938
[July]

1. e4 e5 2. Nf3 Nc6 3. d4 exd4 4. Nxd4
Bc5 5. Be3 Qf6 6. c3 Nge7 7. Bc4 Bb6

8. Nxc6 Bxe3 9. 0–0 Qxc6 10. Bd5 Qb6
11. fxe3 Nxd5 12. Qxd5 Qxe3+ 13. Kh1
0–0 14. Na3 d6 15. Nc2 Qc5 16. Nd4
Qxd5 17. exd5 Bd7 18. Rf4 Rae8 19. Raf1
Re5 20. c4 f6 21. h3 Rfe8 22. b3 Re1
23. Kg1 Kf7 24. a4 R8e3 25. Rxe1 Rxe1+
26. Kf2 Rb1 27. Re4 c5 28. Nb5 Rb2+
29. Kf1 Bxb5 30. axb5 Rxb3 31. Re6 Rb4
32. Rxd6 Ke7 33. Re6+ Kd7 34. Re4 a6
35. bxa6 bxa6 36. Ke2 a5 37. Kd3 Rb6
38. Kc2 a4 39. Re3 Rb4 40. Kc3 f5
41. Kd3 g5 42. g3 Rb3+ 0–1 (*Boston* 1938)

431 Kashdan–Horowitz [C86]

U.S. Open, Playoff Match, round 1, 1938
[October 15]

1. e4 e5 2. Nf3 Nc6 3. Bb5 a6 4. Ba4
Nf6 5. 0–0 Be7 6. Qe2 b5 7. Bb3 0–0
8. c3 d6 9. d4 Bg4 10. Rd1 Qe8 11. h3
Bh5 12. g4 Bg6 13. Nh4 Na5 14. Nxg6
hxg6 15. Bc2 Nh7 16. a4 Ng5 17. axb5
axb5 18. Kg2 Ne6 19. d5 Nf4+ 20. Bxf4
exf4 21. Bd3 Nc4 22. Rxa8 Qxa8
23. Bxc4 bxc4 24. Qxc4 Qb7 25. b4 Ra8
26. Nd2 Ra3 27. Nf3 Bf6 28. Nd4 Qa7
29. Qc6 Kh7 30. Nf3 Ra2 31. Rf1 Qa3
32. Qxc7 Bh4! 0–1 (*Chess Review*, November
1938)

432 Horowitz–Kashdan [D15]

U.S. Open, Playoff Match, round 2, 1938
[October]

1. Nf3 d5 2. d4 Nf6 3. c4 c6 4. Nc3
dxc4 5. e3 b5 6. a4 b4 7. Na2 e6 8. Bxc4
Nbd7 9. 0–0 Bb7 10. Qe2 c5 11. Rd1
Qb6 12. e4! First played by Fairhurst against
Reshevsky at Hastings in 1937. It gives White
excellent attacking chances. 12. ... cxd4 If
...Nxe4 13. d5! or ...Bxe4 Ne5! and in either
case White's superior development will tell.
13. Nxd4 Bc5 14. Be3 In the game referred
to, Fairhurst played 14. Nb3! 0–0 15. Nxc5 Nxc5
16. Be3 with advantage, as the pin of the knight
proved serious. The text is less forceful. 14. ...
0–0 15. Nc1 Now the pawn can be taken, but
White would have little to show for the pawn.
15. ... Bxe4 16. Ncb3 Bxd4 17. Bxd4 Qb8
18. Bb5 Probably stronger was 18. Nc5 Nxc5

19. Bxc5 Rc8 (if ...Rd8 20. Rxd8+ Qxd8 21. Bxb4) 20. Bd6, and the queen may get into trouble. **18. ... Bd5 19. Nc5 Nxc5 20. Bxc5 Rc8** Now the queen file is blocked, and if 21. Bxb4?, a6 wins. **21. Racl Qf4 22. Be3 Qe5 23. f3 a5 24. Qf2 Bb3 25. Rel Rxcl 26. Rxcl Nd5 27. Bd4 Qg5 28. Rel Rc8 29. h4 Qg6 30. Be5 Rc2 31. Re2 Rxe2** As it turns out the ending cannot be won, despite the pawn ahead, in view of the strength of the White bishops. But it is difficult for Black to make any headway without exchanging. **32. Qxe2 Qc2 33. Qxc2 Bxc2 34. Kf2 f6 35. Bd6 Kf7** If 35. ... Nb6 36. Bc7 Nxa4 37. Bxa4 Bxa4 38. Bxa5, and will draw with opposite colored Bishops. Or 36. ... Bxa4 37. Bxb6 Bxb5 38. Bxa5, with the same position. **36. Bc6** But this is inaccurate, and loses. Correct was 36. Bc5, to be followed by Bc6, Bxd5, and Bb6. **36. ... Nb6 37. Bc7 Nc4** The point. Black can retain the pawn plus, without allowing opposite colored bishops. **38. Bb5 Nxb2 39. Bxa5 Bxa4**

After
39. ... Bxa4

39. ... b3 is tempting, but after 40. Ke2 Nd1 41. Kd2 Bf5 42. Bc3! b2 43. Bxb2 Nxb2 44. a5 and White will have the winning chances. **40. Bxa4?** This was White's last chance. 40. Be2! Bd7 (...b3? 41. Bc3 Nd1+ 42. Bxd1 b2 43. Bxb2, and draws); 41. Bxb4. **40. ... Nxa4 41. Bxb4 Nb6** The following ending is quite instructive. Black must obtain a passed pawn, and keep at least one other pawn in order to win. The superior defensive power of the bishop increases the difficulty. **42. f4 Nd5 43. Bd2 g6 44. g4 e5 45. fxe5 fxe5 46. Kf3 Ke6 47. h5 Nf6** If 47. ... gxh5 48. gxh5 Kf5 49. h6, the game could not be won, as Black could never win the h pawn without losing his e pawn, and the latter alone cannot be forced through.

48. hxg6 hxg6 49. Bg5 Nd7 50. Ke4 Nc5+ 51. Ke3 Kd5 52. Be7 Na4 The plan is to play the knight to c4. If then Kd3, e4+ Kc3 Ne5 g5 Nf3 followed by Ke3 and Kf5. There is no defense to this maneuver. **53. Bf6 Nb2 54. Kf3 Nc4 55. Be7 Kd4 56. Kg3** Hoping for Kh4 and Kg5, but this is easily thwarted. **56. ... Nd2 57. Kh4 Nf3+ 58. Kg3 Ke3 59. Bc5+ Ke2** More accurate was ...Nd4, and if 60. Kh4 Kf4. **60. Bd6 Ke3** The proper square for the king. **61. Bc7 e4 62. Bb6+ Nd4 63. g5 Kd3 64. Kf4 e3 65. Ba5 Ne6+** Forcing the king back, or winning the second pawn. But a simpler win was e2 66. Bel Nc2 67. Bf2 d1(Q) 68. Bxd1 Nxd1 69. Ke4 Ng2 70. Kf3 Nh4. **66. Ke5 Nxg5 67. Kf6 Nf3**

After
67. ... Nf3

The key square. White's reply is forced. **68. Bb6 Nd4 69. Bc7** Allowing the advance of the second pawn. **69. ... g5** If 70. Kxg5 then Ne6+ wins the bishop and the game. **70. Bg3 Ne2** For g5 follows, winning the bishop. **0–1** Annotated by Kashdan. (*Chess Review*, November 1938)

433 Kashdan–Horowitz [D63]

U.S. Open, Playoff Match, round 3, 1938
[October]

1. d4 d5 2. c4 e6 3. Nc3 Nf6 4. Bg5 Be7 5. Nf3 0–0 6. e3 a6 7. Rc1 Nbd7 8. a3 dxc4 9. Bxc4 b5 10. Ba2 c5 11. 0–0 Bb7 12. Qe2 Ne4 13. Bxe7 Qxe7 14. Rfd1 c4 15. Bb1 Ndf6 16. Nd2 Nxc3 17. Rxc3 Rfd8 18. f4 Rac8 19. Qf2 Nd5 20. Rc2 c3 21. Ne4 cxb2 22. Nc5 Nb6 23. Nxb7 Qxb7 24. Rxc8 Rxc8 25. Qxb2 Na4 26. Qf2 Nc3 27. Rf1 Nxb1 28. Rxb1 Qe4 29. Re1 Rc2 30. Re2 Rc1+ 31. Re1 Qb1

32. Kf1 Qd3+ 33. Qe2 Qxa3 34. Rxc1
Qxc1+ 35. Kf2 Qc4 36. Qh5 Qd5 37. Qe2
a5 38. Qc2 Qc4 39. Qe4 Qd5 40. Qc2 g6
41. g4 a4 42. Qc3 Qh1 43. g5 Qxh2+
44. Kf3 Qh1+ 45. Kg3 Qa8 46. Qa3 Qf8
47. Qa1 a3 48. e4 b4 49. Qa2 Qa8 50. d5
exd5 51. exd5 b3 0–1 (*Chess Review*, November 1938)

434 Horowitz–Kashdan [C90]
U.S. Open, Playoff Match, round 4, 1938
[November]

1. e4 e5 2. Nf3 Nc6 3. Bb5 a6 4. Ba4
Nf6 5. 0–0 Be7 6. Re1 b5 7. Bb3 d6
8. c3 Na5 9. Bc2 c5 10. a4 b4 11. d4 Qc7
12. h3 0–0 13. Nbd2 Bd7 14. Nf1 Rfc8
15. d5 Rab8 16. Ng3 c4 17. Nf5 Bxf5
18. exf5 bxc3 19. bxc3 Nb3 20. Rb1 Nxc1
21. Rxc1 Qc5 22. Ng5 Qxd5 23. Ne4
Qxd1 24. Nxf6+ gxf6 25. Rexd1 Rc5
26. Rb1 Rxb1 27. Rxb1 d5 28. Rb7 Kf8
29. Rb8+ Kg7 30. Kf1 Bd6 31. Rd8 Bc7
32. Rc8 Bb6 33. Rxc5 Bxc5 34. a5 Kf8
35. Ba4 Ke7 36. Bc6 Kd6 37. Bb7 Ba3
38. Bxa6 Bb2 39. Bc8 Bxc3 40. a6 Bd4
41. Ke2 e4 42. Bb7 Bb6 43. g3 Ke5
44. Bc6 d4 45. Kd2 d3 46. Kc3 Bxf2
47. Kxc4 Kxf5 48. Kd5 d2 49. Ba4 Ba7
50. Bc2 h5 51. Bxe4+ Kg5 52. Bf3 h4
53. gxh4+ Kxh4 54. Ke4 Kxh3 55. Kf5
½–½ (*Chess Review*, December 1938)

435 Kashdan–Horowitz [A29]
U.S. Open, Playoff Match, round 5, 1938
[November 19]

1. c4 Nf6 2. Nc3 e5 This move turns the
game into an inverted Sicilian, which White
plays with a move more than Black has at his
disposal in the corresponding opening. Instead
Black could play g6 or e6 or c6, steering into
variations of the Queen's Gambit, but White
could answer e4 and in this way obtain earlier
attacking chances than usual in those variations. 3. Nf3 Here to e4 would be more aggressive. 3. ... Nc6 4. g3 White could also
play d4, in answer to which Black would either
exchange pawns and continue with Bb4 or ad-

vance the e pawn. 4. ... d5 5. cxd5 Nxd5
6. Bg2 Nb6 7. 0–0 Be7 8. d3 0–0 9. Be3
f5 Black would naturally try for an attack on
the kingside, where he has more territory, while
White will attempt to bring pressure to bear on
b7, either by playing his knight to c5 via a4, or
by running his a pawn up. To combat the latter
plan Black would play Be6 before advancing his
f pawn. 10. Na4 Bf6 11. Nd2 Nd4 Enables
fortifying the b pawn with c3. 12. Nc5 c6
13. Rc1 Qe7 14. a4 Rd8 15. a5 Nd5
16. Bxd4 exd4 17. Nf3 17. a6 would have
been answered with b6 and c5. But the text
seems aimless. Re1 or Nb3 might have been considered. The latter would have maintained pressure in the long diagonal. After the text move
Black obtains the better game by freeing his
queenside pawns from that pressure. He then
controls the greater part of the board and has
two bishops to work with. 17. ... b6! 18. Na4
c5 19. Nd2 Which shows that the knight
should have stayed there to begin with. 19. ...
Rb8 20. axb6 axb6 21. Bxd5+ To give up
the bishop must have been a hard decision. But
without the exchange White could not obtain
any elbow room on the queenside his only
chance for counterplay. 21. ... Rxd5 22. b4!
Black cannot take the pawn because White
would reply 23. Nxb6! Rc5 24. Nxc8 Rbxc8
25. Rxc5 and 26. Qb3+ with a good game.
22. ... Be6 23. bxc5 bxc5 24. Nb3 No
doubt White considered the possibility that
Black might give up the c pawn and attack with
f4. Perhaps he did not dare play f4, restricting
considerably Black's mobility for the moment,
because Black might press the attack with g5
and in the long run two bishops usually are
much stronger then two knights when the game
can be opened by pawn exchanges. 24. ... f4!
A powerful shot which opens lines for the
bishop on e6 and the rook, and which is
certainly preferable to the defensive Rb5.
25. Nbxc5 fxg3 26. hxg3 He cannot take
the pawn with the f pawn because Black would
play Bg5 followed by Be3+, forcing the White
king into the white diagonal into which Black
might then maneuver his queen's bishop. 26. ...
Bh3 27. Re1 Re5 28. Qc2 Bg5 29. Rb1
Rf8 30. Ne4 Rxe4! 31. dxe4 Be3!!

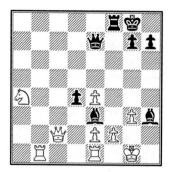

After
31. ... Be3

While White, of course, had expected the sacrifice of the exchange he probably did not foresee this additional bishop sacrifice. His reply should lose the game. In order to draw he must accept the sacrifice. After 32. fxe3 Qd6 he can save the day with 33. Qb3+. Then if Black interposes the bishop, he has time to protect his g pawn by 34. e5! Qxe5 35 **32. Rf1? Qe5 33. Kh2 Qh5 34. e5! Qxe5 35. exd4 Bxf1 36. Rxf1 Rxf2+ 37. Rxf2 Bxf2 38. Nd3 Be3 39. Nb4 Kf7 40. Nc2 Ke6 41. Nxe3 dxe3 42. Kg2 Ke5 43. Kf3 h5 ½–½** The game was played on November 19, which is Kashdan's birthday. (Mitchell's *Guide to Chess*)

436 Horowitz–Kashdan [A28]

U.S. Open, Playoff Match, round 6, 1938
[November]

1. c4 e5 2. Nc3 Nf6 3. Nf3 Nc6 4. d4 exd4 5. Nxd4 Bb4 6. e3 0–0 7. Be2 Ne4 8. Qc2 Re8 9. 0–0 Nxc3 10. bxc3 Bf8 11. Rb1 b6 12. Rd1 Bb7 13. f3 g6 14. e4 Qe7 15. Bf1 Bg7 16. Bf4 Ne5 17. Bg3 d6 18. Qa4 h5 19. Bf2 a5 20. Kh1 Qf6 21. Qc2 Rad8 22. Nb5 Qe7 23. Qd2 Kh7 24. Be3 Qd7 25. Qc2 f5 26. exf5 Nxf3 27. fxg6+ Kh8 28. Bd4 Qg4 29. Qf2 Nxd4 30. Nxd4 Qxg6 31. Bd3 Be4 32. Bxe4 Rxe4 33. Rb5 Rf8 34. Qd2 Ref4 35. Qe2 Rf2 36. Qxh5+ Qxh5 37. Rxh5+ Kg8 38. Kg1 Rxa2 39. Ne6 Rf7 40. Rg5 Kh7 41. Rg3 Bh6 42. Rf1 Rxf1+ 43. Kxf1 a4 44. Nxc7 a3 45. Ne8 Bf4 ½–½ (*Chess Review*, December 1938)

437 Kashdan–Horowitz [D63]

U.S. Open, Playoff Match, round 7, 1938
[December 4]

1. d4 d5 2. c4 e6 3. Nc3 Nf6 4. Bg5 Nbd7 5. e3 Be7 6. Nf3 0–0 7. Rc1 h6 This looks wrong at this point. It creates a weakness and allows White to take a stronger diagonal with the bishop. 7. ... c6 or 7. ... a6 are more usual. **8. Bf4 c5** If now 8. ... c6 9. c5!, since Black no longer can play the equalizing move ...e5. The text is risky, but the only way to gain any freedom. **9. cxd5 exd5** This leaves the d pawn weak with no compensation. Better was 9. ... Nxd5. If then 10. Nxd5 exd5 11. Bd3 Qa5+; or 11. ... c4 followed by ...Bb4+, with good chances. White's best might be 10. Bg3 Nxc3 11. bxc3, with about an even game. **10. Bd3 b6 11. 0–0 Bb7 12. Ne5** From this point White aims directly for the kingside, where he has definitely greater mobility. **12. ... Nxe5 13. dxe5 Ne4 14. Qh5** Stronger than 14. Bxe4 dxe4 15. Qc2 Qd3 16. Qa4, when ...Qa6! would save the threatened e pawn. **14. ... Nxc3** The exchange only accentuates White's advantage on the king's wing. Better was 14. f5, to be followed by Qe8. **15. bxc3 Bg5** The threat was 16. Bxh6 gxh6 17. Qxh6 with a winning attack. **16. Bg3 Qe8 17. f4 Be7 18. Qf5!** The most forceful, as it creates further weaknesses. 18. f5 f6! would lead to nothing for White. **18. ... g6 19. Qh3 Kh7 20. f5** Now this move is the prelude to a quick break-through. The immediate threat is 21. Bf4 h5 22. fxg6 fxg6 23. Qxh5+. **20. ... Bg5 21. Bf4 Bxf4 22. Rxf4 Qxe5**

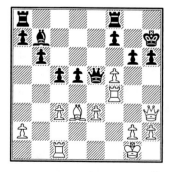

After
22. ... Qxe5

23. Rcf1 White could win material by 23. fxg6+ fxg6 24. Bxg6+! Kxg6 25. Qg3+ Kh7

26. Rf7+ Rxf7 27. Qxe5, but Black could still put up a strong resistance in the ensuing endgame. The text, threatening both fxg6+ and Rh4, is even more effective. **23. ... Kg8** A sorry retreat, but there is nothing better. If 23. ... Bc8 24. fxg6+ fxg6 25. Rxf8! Bxh3 26. R1f7+ wins. 23. ... Rg8 would allow a sparkling finish: 24. fxg6+ fxg6 25. Rh4 Qg5 26. Rf7+ Rg7 27. Rxh6+ Qxh6 28. Bxg6+!! Kxg6 29. Qf5 mate! **24. fxg6 fxg6 25. Qxh6 Qxe3+?** This loses quickly. Best was 25. ... Qg7 when 26. Qxg7+ Kg7 27. Rxf8 Rxf8 28. Rxf8 Kxf8 29. Bxg6 would be a won ending. Or 26. Qg5 would maintain the attack. **26. Kh1 Rxf4** If 26. ... Rf6 27. Bxg6 Rxf4 28. Bh7+! Kh8 (or ...Kf7 29. Rxf4+ wins) 29. Bf5+ Kg8 30. Be6+. **27. Qxg6+ Kf8 28. Qd6+ Kg8 29. Rxf4 Qe1+** If 29. ... Qxd3; it is mate in five beginning with 30. Qe6+. The text only delays matters a bit. **30. Bf1 Re8 31. Qg6+ Kh8 32. Qh6+ Kg8 33. Rg4+** After 33. ... Kf7 34. Rg7+ Kf8 35. Qh8 mate. **1–0** Annotated by Kashdan. (*Chess Review*, January 1939)

438 Horowitz–Kashdan [A50]
U.S. Open, Playoff Match, round 8, 1938
[December]

1. d4 Nf6 2. c4 g6 3. Nf3 Bg7 4. g3 b6
5. Bg2 Bb7 6. 0–0 0–0 7. Nc3 Ne4
8. Qc2 Nxc3 9. Qxc3 c5 10. Be3 Nc6
11. Qd2 cxd4 12. Nxd4 Qc8 13. Racl Ne5
14. f3 Rd8 15. b3 d6 16. Bf2 Qd7 17. e4
e6 18. h3 Nc6 19. f4 Rac8 20. Rcd1
Nxd4 21. Bxd4 Bxd4+ 22. Qxd4 b5
23. cxb5 Qxb5 24. Rd2 Qc5 25. Rfd1
Qxd4+ 26. Rxd4 Rc2 27. R1d2 Rxd2
28. Rxd2 Kf8 29. Rc2 Ke7 30. Kf2 Rd7
31. Ke3 f6 32. Bf1 Kd8 33. Bb5 Rg7
34. g4 f5 35. Bd3 fxe4 36. Bxe4 Bxe4
37. Kxe4 Rb7 38. Rc6 Kd7 39. Ra6 Rb4+
40. Ke3 Rb7 41. Kd3 Ke7 42. g5 Kd7
43. h4 Ke7 44. Ke3 Kd7 45. b4 Ke7
46. a3 Kd7 47. Ke2 Ke7 48. Kf3 Kd7
49. b5 Ke7 50. a4 Kd7 51. Ke3 Rc7
52. Kd3 Ke7 53. Kd4 Kd7 54. a5 Rb7
55. Kc4 Rc7+ 56. Kb4 Rb7 57. Ka4 Kc7
58. Kb4 Kd7 59. Kc3 Kc7 60. Kc4 Kd7
61. Kb4 Kc7 62. h5 gxh5 63. Rc6+ Kd7
64. Rc3 Rb8 65. b6 axb6 66. a6 Rc8

67. Rh3 Kc6 68. Rc3+ Kd7 69. Rh3 Kc6
70. Re3 Kd7 71. Kb5 Rc5+ 72. Kxb6
Rc6+ 73. Kb5 Rc1 74. Ra3 Rb1+ 75. Kc4
Rc1+ 76. Kb4 Rb1+ 77. Kc4 Rc1+ 78. Kd4
Rc8 79. Rb3 Rc1 80. Rb8 Ra1 81. Rh8
Kc6 82. Re8 Kd7 83. Rh8 ½–½ (*Chess Review*, January 1939)

439 Kashdan–Horowitz [C86]
U.S. Open, Playoff Match, round 9, 1938
[December]

1. e4 e5 2. Nf3 Nc6 3. Bb5 a6 4. Ba4
Nf6 5. 0–0 Be7 6. Qe2 b5 7. Bb3 d6
8. a4 Bg4 9. c3 0–0 10. h3 Bh5 11. g4
Bg6 12. d3 Na5 13. Bc2 Nd7 14. d4 c6
15. Rd1 Qc7 16. Nbd2 Rfe8 17. Nf1 f6
18. Ne3 Bf7 19. d5 Bf8 20. b4 Nb7
21. Bb2 Nb6 22. a5 Nc8 23. dxc6 Qxc6
24. Nd5 Ne7 25. c4

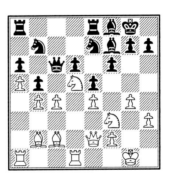

After
25. c4

25. ...Nxd5 Not 25. ... bxc4 26. Ba4! Also not 25. ... Qxc4 26. Qxc4 bxc4 27. Nc7! 26. cxd5 Qd7 27. Bd3 h5 28. Nh2 hxg4 29. Qxg4 Qxg4+ 30. Nxg4 Rec8 31. Racl Be8 32. Ne3 Bd7 33. Kg2 Kf7 34. Be2 g6 35. Bg4 Ke7 36. Kf3 Bh6 37. Bxd7 Kxd7 38. Rg1 Bxe3 39. Kxe3 Rxcl 40. Bxcl Rg8 41. Kf3 Nd8 42. Be3 Nf7 43. h4 g5 44. hxg5 Nxg5+ 45. Bxg5 fxg5 46. Rh1 Rf8+ 47. Kg3 g4 48. Rh7+ Kc8 49. Ra7 Rf4! 50. Rxa6 Rxe4! Not 50. ... Kc7 51. Rc6+ Kd7 52. Rb6 Rxe4 53. Rxb5 wins. 51. Rxd6 Rxb4 52. Rg6 Kd7 53. a6 Ra4 54. Rh6 b4 55. Kxg4 b3+ 56. Kf5 b2 57. Rb6 Rxa6 58. Rxb2 Kd6 59. Rb3 Ra8! 60. f3 Rf8+ ½–½ White did not make the most of his opportunities in the middle game and ending. (*Chess Review*, January 1939)

440 Horowitz–Kashdan [D65]
U.S. Open, Playoff Match, round 10, 1938
[December]

1. d4 Nf6 2. c4 e6 3. Nf3 d5 4. Nc3
Nbd7 5. Bg5 Be7 6. e3 0–0 7. Rc1 a6
8. cxd5 exd5 9. Bd3 c6 10. Qc2 Re8
11. 0–0 Nf8 12. Ne5 Ng4 13. Bxe7 Qxe7
14. Nxg4 Bxg4 15. Na4 Rad8 16. Bf5
Bxf5 17. Qxf5 Rd6 18. Nc5 Rf6 19. Qd3
Qc7 20. Rc3 Ng6 21. Rb3 Rb8 22. Qd2
Nh4 23. e4 Rg6 24. Rg3 dxe4 25. Nxe4
Rd8 26. Rd1 Nf5 27. Rd3 Ne7 28. Nc3
Nd5 29. Nxd5 Rxd5 30. Re1 h6 31. Re8+
Kh7 32. Qe3 Qd6 33. Qe7 Qxe7
34. Rxe7 Re6 35. Rxe6 fxe6 36. Kf1 e5
37. Rb3 exd4 38. Rxb7 d3 39. Ke1 Re5+
40. Kd2 Re2+ 41. Kxd3 Rxf2 42. g3
Rxh2 43. Ke3 Rc2 44. b4 Rxa2 45. Rb6
Kg6 46. Rxc6+ Kf5 47. Kf3 Ra3+
48. Kg2 g5 49. Rc5+ Ke4 50. Kh3 Ra4
51. Rc6 h5 52. Rh6 Kf5 53. Rc6 Ra3
54. Rc5+ Kf6 55. Rc6+ Ke7 56. Rc5 h4
57. Rxg5 hxg3 58. b5 ½–½ (*Chess Review*,
January 1939)

441 Levin–Kashdan [A29]
Manhattan vs. Philadelphia, 1939

1. c4 e5 2. Nc3 Nf6 3. g3 d5 4. cxd5
Nxd5 5. Bg2 Nb6 6. Nf3 Nc6 7. 0–0
Be7 8. d3 0–0 9. Be3 f5 10. Na4 Bf6
11. Rc1 Kh8 12. Nd2 Nd4 13. Nc5 c6
14. b4 Nd5 15. a3 Nb5 16. Nc4 Nxe3
17. fxe3 Bg5 18. Rc2 a5 19. bxa5 Nd6
20. a6 b6 21. Nb7 Nxb7 22. axb7 Bxb7
23. Nxe5 Bxe3+ 24. Kh1 Qc7 25. Nxc6
Rxa3 26. d4 Qd6 27. d5 Rfa8 28. Rb2
f4 29. gxf4 Bxf4 30. e4 Qh6! 31. h3
Rxh3+? 32. Bxh3 Qxh3+ 33. Kg1 Be3+
34. Rbf2 Qg3+ 35. Kh1 Bxf2 36. Qh5
Rf8 37. e5 Ba6 38. Rd1 Be2! Bf3+ is the
threat. If 39. Qxe2 then Qh3 mate! **0–1** (*New
York Post*, June 24, 1939)

442 Kashdan–Denker [D77]
Hamilton, New York State Championship,
1939

1. d4 Nf6 2. c4 g6 3. Nf3 Bg7 4. g3 d5
5. Bg2 0–0 6. 0–0 Na6 7. Nc3 dxc4

8. Qa4 c5 9. dxc5 Bd7 10. Qxc4 Rc8
11. Rd1 Nxc5 12. Ne5 Nce4 13. Qb3 Nxc3
14. bxc3 Qc7 15. Nxd7 Nxd7 16. Qxb7
Qxb7 17. Bxb7 Rc7 18. Bg2 Nb6 19. Bf4
Rxc3 20. Rac1 Rxc1 21. Rxc1 Rc8
22. Rxc8+ Nxc8 23. Be3

After
23. Be3

23. ...Bc3! 24. Bb7 Nb6 25. Bc5 e5
26. e3 f5 27. Ba6 Kf7 28. Bd6 Nd7
29. Bc4+ Kf6 30. Kf1 e4 31. Ke2 Ba5
32. Ba3 Bc3 ½–½ (Denker, *If You Must Play
Chess*)

443 Kashdan–Platz [D63]
Hamilton, New York State Championship,
1939

1. d4 d5 2. c4 e6 3. Nc3 Nf6 4. Bg5
Nbd7 5. e3 Be7 6. Nf3 0–0 7. Rc1 a6
8. b3 b6 9. Bd3 Bb7 10. 0–0 c5 11. Qe2
Ne4 12. Bxe7 Qxe7 13. Rfd1 Rfd8 14. Bb1
Nxc3 15. Rxc3 Rac8 16. cxd5 exd5
17. Rdc1 g6 18. Bd3 b5 19. dxc5 Rxc5
20. Rxc5 Nxc5 21. Nd4 Nxd3 22. Qxd3
Qe4 23. Qxe4 dxe4 24. Kf1 Rc8
25. Rxc8+ Bxc8 26. Ke2 Kf8 27. Kd2
Ke7 28. Kc3 Kd6 29. Kb4 h5 30. Ka5
Kc7 31. Nc2 g5 32. Nb4 f5 33. g3 h4
34. gxh4 gxh4 35. Nxa6+ Bxa6 36. Kxa6
Kc6 37. b4 h3 38. a3 A rare knight vs bishop
endgame that Kashdan wins with the knight.
1–0 (*Brooklyn Daily Eagle*, September 7, 1939)

444 Kashdan–Blumin [C86]
Hamilton, New York State Championship,
1939

1. e4 e5 2. Nf3 Nc6 3. Bb5 a6 4. Ba4
Nf6 5. 0–0 Be7 6. Qe2 b5 7. Bb3 d6

8. c3 Na5 9. Bc2 c5 10. d4 Qc7 11. d5
Bd7 12. Nbd2 0–0 13. Rd1 h6 14. Nf1
Qc8 15. h3 Nh7 16. Ng3 Nb7 17. Be3
Qd8 18. Nf5 Bf6 19. g4 Ng5 20. Kg2
Nxf3 21. Qxf3 Kh7 22. Rh1 Bg5 23. h4
Bxe3 24. Qxe3 Rh8 25. Raf1 Qf8 26. g5
h5 27. f4 Re8 28. Rf2 exf4 29. Qxf4 Re5
30. Rhf1 Qe8 31. Nxg7! Kxg7 32. Qxf7+
Qxf7 33. Rxf7+ Kg8 34. Rf8+ Kg7
35. R1f7+ Kg6 36. Rf6+ Kg7 37. R8f7+
Kg8 38. Rxd7 Na5 39. Rfxd6 Re8 40. b3
1–0 (*New York Sun*, September 9, 1939)

445 Kashdan–Mott-Smith [C86]
Hamilton, New York State Championship,
1939

1. e4 e5 2. Nf3 Nc6 3. Bb5 a6 4. Ba4
Nf6 5. 0–0 Be7 6. Qe2 b5 7. Bb3 d6
8. a4 Bg4 9. c3 0–0 10. h3 Na5 11. Bc2
Be6 12. axb5 axb5 13. d4 Bc4 14. Bd3
Nd7 15. Nbd2 Bxd3 16. Qxd3 c6 17. b4
Nb7 18. Rxa8 Qxa8 19. dxe5 Nxe5
20. Nxe5 dxe5 21. Qd7 Re8 22. Qxc6
Nd6 23. Qd5 Qxd5 24. exd5 Rc8
25. Bb2 e4 26. Ra1 f5 27. Ra7 Bf6
28. Rd7 Be5 29. Kf1 Ra8 30. Ke1 Ra2
31. Bc1 f4 32. Re7 Bxc3 33. Kd1 Bxb4
Black here missed the continuation 33. ...e3
34. fxe3 followed with 35. Nc4, etc. attacking
the rook. 34. Nxe4 Nxe4 35. Rxe4 Bc5
36. Bxf4 Rxf2 37. d6 Rxf4 38. Rxf4
Bxd6 39. Rd4 Be7 40. Rd7 Kf7 41. Rb7
h5? [*It seems that after 41 ... b4 the game would be
a draw–P.P.L.*] 42. Rxb5 g6 43. Rb6 Bf6
44. Ke2 Kg7 45. Kf3 Kf7 46. Ke4 Kg7
47. Kd5 Kf7 48. Rb7+ Kg8 49. Ke6 Bc3
50. Rc7 Bd4 51. Rc4 Bb2 52. Kd5 Bf6
53. Rc8+ Kg7 54. Rc7+ Kg8 55. Ke4
Kf8 56. Kf4 Kg8 57. g4 hxg4 58. Kxg4
Kf8 59. Kf4 Kg8 60. Rb7 Kf8 61. Ke4
Kg8 62. Kd5 Bc3 63. Ke6 Bd4 64. Rf7
Bc3 65. h4 Bb2 66. Rf2 Bc3 67. Rf3
Bd4 68. Rf4 Bc3 69. Rc4 Bb2 70. Rg4
Kh7 71. Kf7 Kh6 72. Rxg6+ Kh5 73. Rg2
Ba1 74. Rh2 Be5 75. Rh1 Bd4 76. Ke6
Bb6 77. Kf5 Bc5 78. Rc1 Be3 79. Rc4
Bd2 80. Ke4 Be1 81. Rc1 Bd2 82. Rd1
Bh6 83. Rd6 Bf8 84. Rd1 Bh6 85. Rh1
Bd2 86. Kf3 Bc3 87. Rc1 Bb2 88. Rc2

Bf6 89. Kf4 Be7 90. Rd2 Bf6 91. Rd7
Bc3 92. Kg3 1–0 (*Brooklyn Daily Eagle*, November 16, 1939)

446 Kashdan–Florido [C00]
Havana, Cuba, 1940 *[January]*

1. e4 e6 2. c4 c5 3. Nf3 Nc6 4. d4
cxd4 5. Nxd4 Bc5 6. Nb3 Nf6 7. Nxc5
Qa5+ 8. Nc3 Qxc5 9. Be3 Qa5 10. Qd2
0–0 11. Be2 a6 12. 0–0 Re8 13. a3 Qc7
14. b4 b6 15. f4 d6 16. Bf3 Bb7 17. Rfd1
Ne7 18. Rac1 Rad8 19. Qc2 Nc8 20. Qe2
Qb8 21. Bf2 Bc6 22. Rd2 Ne7 23. Rcd1
Ng6 24. Qe3 b5 25. cxb5 axb5 26. Qb6
Qxb6 27. Bxb6 Rc8 28. g3 Bd7 29. Rd3
Rc6 30. Bf2 Rc4 31. Be1 Bc6 32. Rxd6
Bxe4 33. Be2 Rc6 34. Nxe4 1–0 (Kashdan's scoresheet)

447 Kashdan–Alemán [C86]
Havana, 1940 *[January]*

1. e4 e5 2. Nf3 Nc6 3. Bb5 a6 4. Ba4
Nf6 5. 0–0 Be7 6. Qe2 b5 7. Bb3 d6
8. a4 Bd7 9. c3 Na5 10. Bc2 c5 11. axb5
axb5 12. d4 Nc6 13. Rxa8 Qxa8 14. dxc5
dxc5 15. Qxb5 Nd4 16. Qd3 Nxc2
17. Qxc2 Bc6 18. Nbd2 Nxe4 19. Nxe5
Nxd2 20. Qxd2 Bd5 21. Re1 0–0
22. Nd7 Bxg2 23. Nxf8 Bh3 24. f4 Qf3
25. Qe2 Qxe2 26. Rxe2 Kxf8 27. c4 1–0
(Kashdan's scoresheet)

448 González–Kashdan [D85]
Havana, 1940 *[January]*

1. d4 Nf6 2. c4 g6 3. Nc3 d5 4. cxd5
Nxd5 5. e3 Bg7 6. Qb3 Nb6 7. Nf3 0–0
8. Be2 Nc6 9. 0–0 Be6 10. Qd1 Qd7
11. Ne4 Rfd8 12. Nc5 Qc8 13. Bd2 Bc4
14. Rc1 Bxe2 15. Qxe2 e5 16. dxe5 Nxe5
17. Bc3 Nxf3+ 18. Qxf3 c6 19. Bxg7 Kxg7
20. Rfd1 Qc7 21. b3 Qe7 22. b4 Rxd1+
23. Rxd1 a5 24. a3 axb4 25. axb4 Nd5
26. e4 Nf6 27. Qc3 Kg8 28. f3 b6
29. Nd3 Rc8 30. Rc1 Nd7 31. Qd4 c5
32. Qd5 Rd8 33. Qc4 Ne5 34. Nxe5
Qxe5 35. bxc5 bxc5 36. Qxc5 ½–½
(Kashdan's scoresheet)

449 Kashdan–Mora [C26]
Havana, 1940 *[January]*

1. e4 e5 2. Bc4 Nf6 3. Nc3 Bc5 4. d3
d6 5. f4 Ng4 6. f5 h5 7. Nh3 Qh4+
8. Kf1 Be3 9. Nd5 Bxc1 10. Qxc1 Kd8
11. Qg5+ Qxg5 12. Nxg5 Nh6 13. h3 c6
14. Ne3 Ke7 15. g4 Nd7 16. a4 Nf6
17. Nf3 Nd7 18. g5 Ng8 19. Ke2 Kf8
20. Raf1 Ne7 21. Nh4 Nb6 22. Bb3 d5
23. a5 Nd7 24. exd5 cxd5 25. f6 gxf6
26. gxf6 Nc6 27. Bxd5 Rh6 28. Bxc6
bxc6 29. Nc4 Ba6 30. Rf5 Bxc4 31. dxc4
Re8 32. Rd1 Nc5 33. Ke3 Nb7 34. b4
Re6 35. c5 Ke8 36. Rg5 Rhxf6 37. a6
Nxc5 38. bxc5 Rf4 39. Nf5 Rg6
40. Rxh5 f6 1–0 (Kashdan's scoresheet)

450 Kashdan–Paz [C14]
Havana, round 5, 1940 *[January]*

1. e4 e6 2. d4 d5 3. Nc3 Nf6 4. Bg5
Be7 5. e5 Nfd7 6. Bxe7 Qxe7 7. Qd2 a6
8. f4 c5 9. Nf3 Nc6 10. g3 b5 11. Ne2
Nb6 12. b3 Bb7 13. Bh3 g6 14. 0–0 Rc8
15. Rf2 Nd7 16. Re1 cxd4 17. Nfxd4 Nc5
18. Bg2 Nxd4 19. Nxd4 Ne4 This creates
a weak pawn for Black. So far the whole play is
characteristic of the French Defense, White is
playing on the kingside, Black on the queenside.
20. Bxe4 dxe4 21. b4 A very important
move. It threatens Nb3 followed by Nc5, and
stops b4, which would give great mobility to
Black. 21. ...Rd8 22. c3 Qc7 23. Qe3 h5
24. h4 0–0 25. Kh2 Kg7 26. Ref1 Rc8
27. f5! Bd5 If 27. ... Qxc3 then 28. Qg5 Qxd4
29. fxe6, threatening 30. Rxf6 and e7. 28. Qg5
Qd8 29. fxe6 Qxg5 30. hxg5 fxe6
31. Rxf8 Rxf8 32. Rxf8 Kxf8 33. a3 e3
34. Kg1 Ke7 35. Nc2 e2 36. Kf2 Bc4
37. Ne3 Bd3 38. Ng2 Bc4 39. Nf4 Kd7
40. Nxg6 Ke8 41. Nf4 Kf7 42. Nxh5 Kg6
43. Nf4+ Kxg5 44. Nxe2 Kf5 45. Ke3
Kxe5 46. Nf4 Kf5 47. Nd3 The threat is
Nc5 winning another pawn. 1–0 (British Chess
Magazine, July 1940)

451 Koltanowski–Kashdan [D05]
Havana, round 7, 1940 *[January]*

1. d4 Nf6 2. Nf3 e6 3. e3 d5 4. Bd3

c5 5. c3 Nbd7 6. Nbd2 Be7 7. 0–0 0–0
8. Qe2 b6 9. e4 dxe4 10. Nxe4 cxd4
11. Nxd4 Bb7 12. Rd1 Qc8 13. Bg5 Re8
14. Nxf6+ Nxf6 15. Bxf6 Bxf6 16. Be4
a6 17. Nf3 Qc7 18. Rd3 Rad8 19. Bxb7
Qxb7 20. Rad1 Rxd3 21. Rxd3 g6
22. Qd1 Qc8 23. Rd7 Rd8 24. Rxd8+
Qxd8 25. Qxd8+ Bxd8 26. Kf1 Kf8
27. Ke2 Ke7 28. Kd3 Kd6 29. b4 e5
30. Nd2 f5 31. f3 Bc7 32. c4 Kc6 33. h3
Bd6 34. Kc3 Be7 35. a3 Kd7 36. Kd3
Ke6 37. Nb3 h5 38. Nd2 Kd7 39. Nb3
Kc6 40. Nd2 Bf8 ½–½ (Koltanowski,
Chessnicdotes)

452 Planas–Kashdan [D36]
Havana, round 9, 1940 *[January]*

1. d4 Nf6 2. c4 e6 3. Nf3 d5 4. Nc3
Nbd7 5. Bg5 c6 6. cxd5 exd5 7. e3 Be7
8. Bd3 0–0 9. 0–0 Re8 10. Qc2 Nf8
11. a3 g6 12. b4 a6 13. Bxf6 Bxf6 14. Na4
Bg7 15. Nc5 Qe7 16. Rab1 f5 17. a4 Nd7
18. b5 Nxc5 19. dxc5 axb5 20. axb5 Ra3
21. bxc6 bxc6 22. Nd4 Bxd4 23. exd4
Qh4 24. Rb4 f4 25. f3 Qe7 26. Bxg6
hxg6 27. Qxg6+ Kf8 28. Qh6+ Kg8
29. Qg6+ ½–½ (*Chess Review*, March 1940)

453 Kashdan–Kupchik [C42]
New York, U.S. Championship, round 1,
1940 *[April 27]*

1. e4 e5 2. Nf3 Nf6 3. Nxe5 d6 4. Nf3
Nxe4 5. d4 d5 6. Bd3 Be7 7. 0–0 0–0
8. c4 Nf6 Perhaps 8. ... c6 was preferable, all
the more since Black's later Nc6 turns out to
be of little value. 9. Nc3 Nc6 But here 9. ...
dxc4 10. Bxc4 Nbd7 to be followed by Nb6 and
Nd5 was definitely better. 10. c5! Leaving
Black with a terrible cramped game. 10. ... Bg4
11. Be3 Qc8 12. Re1 Re8 13. h3! Be6
White's last move forced Black to renounce
one of the bishop's two diagonals. Thus 13. ...
Bh4 maintains the pin, but then 14. Bb5 is very
awkward. 14. a3 Nb8 Bravely admitting that
the development of the queen's knight was
wrong. Black is in a terrible quandary, for if 14. ...
a6 15. b4 followed by the usual queenside advance is strong; while if 14. ... a5 15. Bb5 is again

annoying. The text avoids these difficulties, but the harm done to Black's development is irreparable. **15. Qc2 c6** ...h6 would prevent the following move, but would weaken the kingside. **16. Ng5 g6** Not h6 17. Nxe6 (17. ... Qxe6 18. Bxh6) 18. Bg6 and Black's e pawn is not long for this world. **17. Nxe6 Qxe6 18. Bg5**

After
18. Bg5

18. ... Qd7 Black is burdened with one disagreeable situation after another. If 18. ... Qc8? (in order to make way for the queen knight), there follows 19. Rxe7 Rxe7 20. Bxf6 etc. **19. Re3 Bd8 20. Qe2 Rxe3 21. Qxe3 Nh5 22. Re1 Bxg5 23. Qxg5 Ng7 24. Re7 Qd8** The exchanges of the last few moves have failed to eliminate the pressure. White now wins a pawn, while Black still struggles with his development. **25. Qf6 Qf8 26. Rxb7 Ne6 27. b4 Qg7 28. Qxg7+ Kxg7 29. Ne2 a5 30. b5 cxb5** Now White has a passed c pawn, and the d pawn cannot last long. **31. Bxb5 Na6 32. Bxa6** Kashdan exchanges a bishop for a knight! There must be reason! **32. ... Rxa6 33. Rd7** There is a reason. Now the d pawn falls, leaving White two connected passed pawns to the good. **33. ... Ra8 34. Rxd5 Rb8 35. c6 Rb2 36. Re5 Nc7 37. Nc3 1–0** An admirably clear and simple game by Kashdan. Black had no real chance after getting so cramped a position in the opening. Annotated by Reinfeld (*Chess Review*, June-July 1930)

454 Fine–Kashdan [D30]
New York, U.S. Championship, round 2, 1940 *[April 28]*

1. d4 d5 2. c4 c6 3. Nf3 Nf6 4. e3 e6 5. Nbd2 Ne4 6. Nxe4 dxe4 7. Nd2 f5 8. f3 Bd6 9. g3 exf3 10. Nxf3 Nd7

11. Qb3 c5 12. Bg2 0–0 13. 0–0 Qe7 14. Bd2 Nf6 15. Rad1 Ne4 16. Bc3 b6 17. Nd2 Nxd2 18. Rxd2 Bb7 19. Qd1 Bxg2 20. Kxg2 Rad8 21. Qf3 Qc7 22. b3 Rf7 23. Rfd1 Bf8 24. a4 Qb7 25. a5 cxd4 26. exd4 Qxf3+ 27. Kxf3 bxa5 28. Bxa5 Rb8 29. Rb1 Bb4 30. Ra2 Bxa5 31. Rxa5 Rfb7 32. Kf4 Kf7 33. Ke5 Rd7 34. b4 Rbd8 35. Rd1 Rb8 36. Rda1 Rbb7 37. b5 Rbc7

After
37. ... Rbc7

38. Ra6 Rxc4 39. Rd6 Rb7 40. Rxe6 Rxb5+ 41. d5 Re4+ 42. Kd6 Rb6+ 43. Kc5 Rbxe6 44. dxe6+ Rxe6 45. Rxa7+ Kf6 46. Kd4 Re2 47. h4 Re4+ 48. Kd3 Rg4 49. Ra6+ Kf7 50. Ke3 h5 51. Kf3 g6 52. Ra7+ Kf6 53. Ra6+ Kg7 54. Ra7+ Kh6 55. Ra6 Re4 56. Ra7 ½–½ (*U.S. Championship*, New York 1940)

455 Kashdan–Seidman [D78]
New York, U.S. Championship, round 3, 1940 *[April 29]*

1. d4 Nf6 2. c4 g6 3. Nf3 Bg7 4. g3 0–0 5. Bg2 c6 6. 0–0 d5 7. Nbd2 Nbd7 8. b3 e5 9. dxe5 Ng4 10. cxd5 cxd5 11. Bb2 Ngxe5 12. Qc2 Nxf3+ 13. Nxf3 Nf6 14. Rac1 Be6 15. Nd4 Rc8 16. Qd3 Qd7 17. Nxe6 fxe6 18. Bh3 a6 19. Qe3 Kf7 20. Qb6 Rc6 21. Rxc6 Qxc6 22. Qe3 Rc8 23. Rc1 Qd7 24. Bxe6+! 1–0 (*U.S. Championship*, New York 1940)

456 Simonson–Kashdan [D45]
New York, U.S. Championship, round 4, 1940 *[May 1]*

1. d4 d5 2. c4 c6 3. Nc3 Nf6 Avoiding

the two-edged 3. ... dxc4 4. e4 e5 5. Bxc4 exd4 6. Nf3?! **4. e3** Nf3 would transpose into the normal Slav Variation. **4. ... e6 5. Qc2** And this is altogether an experiment with nothing to recommend it but its novelty (a factor which must not be under-estimated). **5. ... Nbd7 6. Nf3** Interesting would be 6. f4 first, but Black will obtain counterplay with 6. ... c5! **6. ... a6** Forcing the issue. Now White has five tactical possibilities—i.e. (in order of worth) A. 7. cxd5, followed ultimately by a pawn advance on the queenside, B. 7. b3; C. 7. Bd3; D. 7. a4; E. 7. c5. The last is refuted at once by 7. ... e5. **7. a4?** This accomplishes nothing much and negatively, leaves a bad "hole" at his b4. **7. ... Bb4** The pin means nothing; the move is a hasty reaction to White's poor move. More substantial was simply 7. ... c5, so that if this pawn is taken(as in the game) Black can at least gain a tempo. **8. Bd3 dxc4 9. Bxc4 c5 10. dxc5 Qc7 11. 0–0 0–0 12. e4 Bxc5** He had probably intended 12. ... Nxc5, but this would now allow an immediate 13. e5. **13. Qe2 b6** Must White permit e5? Kashdan, however, may have judged this advance to be not without weakness (the pawn has problems of protection). The text seems a trifle slow, and while 13. e5 instead is bad (yielding d5), 13. Ne4, followed by Bd2, looks quite good. **14. e5 Ng4 15. Bf4 Bb7** Threatening Bxf3. **16. Ne4** Inviting complications, since black threatened Bxf3, as well as Nd5. But 16. Rfe1 (over-protection) impresses one as a move worthy for the "long term." **16. ... Ngf6 17. Nxc5 bxc5 18. Ng5 Qc6 19. f3 Nh5 20. Bd2 g6 21. g4** Don't forget for a minute that it requires courage to make an un-conservative move against a Kashdan. It is sometimes a good (if not only) way to win (or lose). **21. ... Ng7 22. Bc3 Nb6 23. Ne4 Ne8**

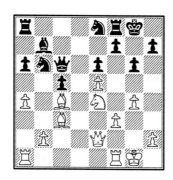

After
23. ... Ne8

24. Rad1? Simonson has been conducting his attack with great skill and even success, but this move is a serious tactical error. The loss of the pawn is immaterial, but the switch in diagonals of the White queen bishop is a bad conception. He should have played 24. b3. **24. ... Nxa4 25. Ba5 Nb6 26. Nf6+ Nxf6 27. exf6 Nxc4 28. Qxc4 e5 29. Bc3** Too late, he realizes his mistake. Now the tables are turned and Black forces the pace, since he is a pawn ahead. **29. ... Rfe8 30. Rde1 Rad8** Better than capturing the f pawn, when he would have to yield in return both his own f pawn and the e pawn. **31. Bxe5** He has no time for 31. g5, because 31. ... Qd5 is threatened. **31. ... h6 32. h4 Qd5 33. Qf4 Kh7** Both kings are sort of punch drunk (what kind of punch?), but Black has a very slight advantage in the superior mobility of his rooks. **34. h5 g5 35. Qf5+**

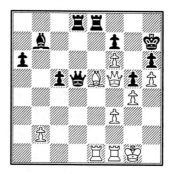

After
35. Qf5

35. ... Kh8 White's attack has petered out; the White queen cannot very well move, especially in view of the Black threat of doubling on the e file. Best for White now seems 36. Bc7, so that if 36. ... Qxf5 37. gxf5 Rc8 38. Re7! But Simonson uncovers an amazing blunder (time pressure?) which soon loses. **36. Rd1 Qxd1 37. Rxd1 Rxd1+ 38. Kf2 Rd2+ 39. Kf1 Kg8 40. Bc3 Rd5 41. Qc2 Bc6** To threaten 42. ... Bb5+. **42. Kf2 Bb5 43. Qb3** How helpless a queen can sometimes be! Here her mobility is at the zero level. **43. ... Re2+ 44. Kg3 Rd3 0–1** Simonson deserved a better fate. His conceptions were, for the most part, positive and constructive. But Kashdan's greater defensive skill must not be under-rated. Annotations by Santasiere. (*American Chess Bulletin*, May 1940) For the game in round 5 against Wolliston his opponent did not appear. This was likely a mixup as to when the game was to start.

457 Green−Kashdan [A95]

New York, U.S. Championship, round 6, 1940 *[May 2]*

1. d4 f5 2. g3 Nf6 3. Bg2 e6 4. Nf3 Be7 5. 0−0 0−0 6. c4 d5 7. Nc3 c6 8. b3 Qe8 9. Ne5 Nbd7 10. Nd3 Ne4 11. Bb2 Bf6 12. e3 a5 13. Qc2 Kh8 14. Rae1 Nxc3 15. Bxc3 dxc4 16. bxc4 e5 17. Nb2 Qh5 18. f4 e4 19. a4 b6 20. Rf2 Ba6 21. Bf1 Qf7 22. Bd2 Be7 23. Rg2 Nf6 24. Be2 Rfb8 25. h3 h5 26. Rc1 Bc8 27. Nd1 Bd7 28. Rb1 Qe8 29. Nf2 c5 30. Ra1 cxd4 31. exd4 Bb4 32. Be3 Rc8 33. Qb3 Qf7 34. d5 Rab8 35. Nd1 Bc5 36. Bf1 Qe7 37. Be2 Qd6 38. Kh1 Bxe3 39. Qxe3 Qc5 40. Ra3 Kg8 41. Nb2 Kf7 42. h4 Ng4 43. Bxg4 hxg4 44. Rd2 Qxe3 45. Rxe3 Ke7 46. Kg1 Kd6 47. Kf2 Kc5 48. Rb3 ½−½ (*U.S. Championship*, New York 1940)

458 Kashdan−Denker [B62]

New York, U.S. Championship, round 7, 1940 *[May 3]*

1. e4 c5 2. Nf3 Nc6 3. d4 cxd4 4. Nxd4 Nf6 5. Nc3 d6 6. Bg5 e6 7. Be2 Be7 8. 0−0 0−0 9. Kh1 d5 10. exd5 Nxd5 11. Nxc6 bxc6 12. Bxe7 Qxe7 13. Qd4 Rb8 14. Nxd5 cxd5 15. b3 Rb4 16. c4 Rd8 17. Qe5 Ba6 18. Rad1 Qd6 19. Qc3 Qc5 20. Qe5 Qd6 21. Qxd6 Rxd6 22. Bf3 Kf8 23. Rfe1 Bb7 24. Rd3 Ba8 25. Red1 Rb8 26. Kg1 Rbd8 27. Kf1 Ke7 28. Ke1 Bb7 29. b4 Rc8 30. cxd5 Rcd8 31. Ra3 Ba6 32. dxe6 Rxe6+ 33. Re3 Rxe3+ 34. fxe3 Rc8 35. Kd2 Bb5 36. Rc1 Rxc1 37. Kxc1 Kd6 38. Kc2 f5 39. Kc3 Ke5 40. Kb3 g5 41. a4 Bd3 42. b5 h5 43. Kb4 g4 44. Ba8 f4 45. exf4+ Kxf4 46. a5 Ke3 47. b6 axb6 48. axb6 Ba6 49. Kc5 h4 50. Bc6 Kf2 51. h3 gxh3 52. gxh3 Kg3 53. Bd7 Bb7 54. Kd6 Bg2 55. Bc6 Bxc6 56. Kxc6 Kxh3 57. b7 Kg2 58. b8Q h3 59. Qb2+ Kg1 60. Qd4+ 1−0 (*U.S. Championship*, New York 1940)

459 S. Bernstein−Kashdan [D13]

New York, U.S. Championship, round 8, 1940 *[May 5]*

1. d4 d5 2. c4 c6 3. cxd5 Deliberately choosing a line which leaves Black with a rather lifeless position. (White does not have very much play either!) 3. ... cxd5 4. Nc3 Nf6 5. Nf3 e6 6. Bf4 a6 7. e3 Be7 8. Bd3 b5 9. 0−0 0−0 10. Ne5 Bb7 11. a4 b4 12. Nb1 Aiming of course for c5 via d2−b3. 12. ... Nbd7 13. Nd2 Nxe5 14. Bxe5 Nd7 15. Bg3 Rc8 16. a5! To fix the enemy queenside pawns. 16. ... Nb8 17. Nb3 Qd7 18. Qe2 Rc6 19. Rfc1 Rfc8 20. Nc5! At this point I was feeling quite snug, in view of Kashdan's well known partiality for bishops. 20. ... Bxc5 21. dxc5 Qe7 The capture of the pawn would leave his knight hanging. 22. Qh5 g6 Kashdan's subsequent skillful play renders this weakening of his dark squares innocuous. 23. Qe2 e5! 24. e4 d4 Allowing less counterplay than after 24. ... Rxe5 25. Rxe5 Qxc5 26. exd5 (26. Bxe5? dxe4) Qxd5 27. f3 etc. Black rightly judges that there is no hurry about winning the c pawn. White of course is striving to open lines for his bishops. 25. f4 exf4 26. Bxf4 Rxc5 27. Rxc5 Qxc5 28. Rc1 Qf8 29. Rf1! Qc5 I never learned whether this move indicated willingness to draw (I assumed it was merely a device to gain clock time—that's why I refrained from Rc1 etc.) If 29. ... Nc6 30. Bxa6. 30. Qf2 Nd7 31. Bh6 f6! 32. g4 This "attacking" move prevents 32. ... Qh5! 32. ... Qe5 33. Bd2 Nc5 34. Bc4+ Kg7 35. Bf4 Qe7 Not 35. ... Qxe4 36. Bh6+! 36. e5 What else? He is still trying to break through with his bishop pair. 36. ... fxe5 37. Bd2 Ne6!! The move White had not foreseen! If 38. Bxb4 (seemingly very strong) Black responds 38. ... Ng5! threatening mate! 38. Bxe6 White's last hope rests in the bishops of opposite colors. 38. ... Qxe6 39. h3 b3 40. Kh2 Qe7 41. Bb4 Qe6 42. Kg3 If 42. Bd2 Rd8 followed by 43. ... e4. 42. ... Kg8 43. Bd2 Bd5 44. Bh6 Qe7 (The threat was 45. Qf8+ Rxf8 46. Rxf8 mate!) 45. h4 Bf7! 46. Re1 Qd6 47. Rf1 Bc4 48. Rc1 Qe6 49. Qd2 Qf7 50. Qb4 e4 51. Bf4 h5 52. Qd6

After
52. Qd6

52. ... Qe6? Too eager to simplify—52. ...
d3 was the move. Now White escapes with a
draw. **53. Qxe6+ Bxe6 54. Rxc8+ Bxc8
55. gxh5 gxh5 56. Be5 d3 57. Bf4 Kf7
58. Bd2 Ke6 59. Kf4 Bb7 60. Bb4 Kd5
61. Ke3 Ke5 62. Be7 Kf5 63. Bg5 Kg4
64. Kd2** ½–½ Annotations by Bernstein.
(Bernstein, *Combat*)

460 Kashdan–Shainswit [D66]
New York, U.S. Championship, round 9,
1940 *[May 6]*

1. d4 Nf6 2. Nf3 d5 3. c4 e6 4. Nc3
Nbd7 5. Bg5 Be7 6. e3 0–0 7. Rc1 c6
8. Bd3 a6 9. 0–0 b5 10. cxd5 cxd5
11. a4 b4 12. Nb1 Bb7 13. Nbd2 Qb6
14. Nb3 a5 15. Ne5 Bd6 16. Nxd7 Nxd7
17. Bb5 Nb8 18. Nc5 Bc8 19. e4 dxe4
20. Nxe4 f5 21. Nxd6 Qxd6 22. Qf3 Ra7
23. Bf4 Qb6 24. Qg3 Bd7 25. Bc7 Qb7
26. Bd6 1–0 (*U.S. Championship*, New York
1940)

461 Littman–Kashdan [C99]
New York, U.S. Championship, round 10,
1940 *[May 9]*

1. e4 e5 2. Nf3 Nc6 3. Bb5 a6 4. Ba4
Nf6 5. 0–0 Be7 6. Re1 b5 7. Bb3 d6
8. c3 Na5 9. Bc2 c5 10. d4 Qc7 11. Nbd2
0–0 12. h3 cxd4 13. cxd4 Nc6 14. d5
Nb4 15. Bb1 a5 16. a3 Na6 17. Bd3 Bd7
18. Nf1 Nc5 19. Qe2 Nxd3 20. Qxd3
Rfc8 21. Ne3 Nh5 22. Bd2 Nf4 23. Qb1
Qb7 24. b4 axb4 25. Bxb4 Bf8 26. Kh2
Rc7 27. Ng1 Qc8 28. Qd1 g6 29. g3 Nh5
30. Qf3 Bc7 31. Ne2 Qf8 32. Rac1 Rac8
33. Rc3 Rxc3 34. Nxc3 Ng7 35. Qe2

Rb8 36. Rf1 f5 37. f4 exf4 38. Rxf4 Bg5
39. Rf3 Qe7 40. exf5 Re8 41. Qf1 Nxf5
42. Nxf5 gxf5 43. Kh1 Qe5 44. Kg2 Rc8
45. Qd3 Rc4 46. Rf2 Rd4 47. Qf3 Rd2
48. h4 Rxf2+ 49. Kxf2 Bd2 50. Ne2
Bxb4 51. axb4 Kg7 52. Qf4 Qxf4+
53. gxf4 Kf6 54. Ke3 Kg6 55. Kf2 Kf6
56. Nd4 h6 ½–½ (*U.S. Championship*, New
York 1940)

462 Kashdan–Hanauer [E44]
New York, U.S. Championship, round 11,
1940 *[May 11]*

1. d4 Nf6 2. c4 e6 3. Nc3 Bb4 4. e3
b6 5. Nge2 Bb7 6. a3 Be7 7. Ng3 h5
8. d5 h4 9. Nge2 e5 10. e4 d6 11. f3 a5
12. Be3 Na6 13. Nc1 Nc5 14. Nd3 Nxd3+
15. Bxd3 Nh5 16. Qd2 Nf4 17. Bxf4 exf4
18. Ne2 Bg5 19. h3 Qf6 20. Bc2 0–0
21. Nd4 Qe5 22. 0–0 Bf6 23. Rad1 Qg5
24. Ba4 Bc8 25. Kh1 Be5 26. Bc6 Rb8
27. b4 Ba6 28. Bb5 Ra8 29. Bxa6 Rxa6
30. Nb5 axb4 31. axb4 Qe7 32. Rc1 Rfa8
33. Rc2 Qd7 34. Rfc1 Ra4 35. Kg1 R8a6
36. Rb1 Ra8 37. Nd4 Ra1 38. Rbc1 Qa4
39. Nc6 f6 40. Rxa1 Qxa1+ 41. Rc1 Qa3
42. Nxe5 fxe5 43. Qc3 Qa2 44. c5 bxc5
45. bxc5 dxc5 46. Qxc5 Qb2 47. Qxc7
Kh7 48. Qc3 Qb6+ 49. Kh1 Qd6 50. Qc5
Qf6 51. Qc6 Qxc6 52. Rxc6 Re8 53. Kg1
Kg8 54. Kf2 Kf7 55. Ke2 Ra8 56. Re6
Ra2+ 57. Kf1 Ra1+ 58. Ke2 Ra2+ 59. Kd3
Rxg2 60. Rxe5 Rg3 61. Rf5+ Ke7
62. Rxf4 Rxh3 63. Kd4 g5 64. Rf5 Rg3
65. Ke5 h3 66. d6+ Kd7 67. Rf7+ Kc6
68. d7 Kc7 69. Ke6 Rg1 70. Rf8 Rd1
71. Rc8+ 1–0 (*U.S. Championship*, New York
1940)

463 Polland–Kashdan [D79]
New York, U.S. Championship, round 12,
1940 *[May 12]*

1. d4 Nf6 2. c4 g6 3. Nf3 Bg7 4. g3
0–0 5. Bg2 c6 6. 0–0 d5 7. cxd5 cxd5
8. Nc3 Nc6 9. Bf4 Ne4 10. Rc1 Qa5
11. a3 Be6 12. Ne5 Nxe5 13. Bxe5 Nxc3
14. Rxc3 Bxe5 15. dxe5 Rac8 16. Rd3
Qc7 17. Bxd5 Bh3 18. Bg2 Bxg2 19. Kxg2

Qxe5 20. Qd2 Rc6 21. Rd1 Rfc8 22. Re3
Qf6 23. Rf3 Qe6 24. Re3 ½–½ (*U.S.
Championship*, New York 1940)

464 Kashdan–Reshevsky [C86]
New York, U.S. Championship, round 13,
1940 *[May 13]*

1. e4 e5 2. Nf3 Nc6 3. Bb5 a6 4. Ba4
Nf6 5. 0–0 Be7 6. Qe2 b5 7. Bb3 d6
8. a4 Bg4 9. c3 0–0 10. h3 Bh5 A fateful decision. 10. ... Bd7 would give the bishop
better prospects, for as the game goes, the
bishop is eventually driven to g6, where is plays
a rather passive role. 11. d3 Na5 12. Bc2 c5
13. axb5 axb5 14. g4 Bg6 15. Nbd2 Qc7
16. Nh4 A plausible idea which, however, allows a powerful counterstroke. If however
16. Rd1 (intending to bring the knight on d2 to
e3) there might follow 16. ... Nd7 (permanently
preventing Nh4) 17. Nf1 Nb6 and Black stands
well. 16. ... d5! 17. Ndf3 dxe4 18. dxe4 c4
19. Nf5 Nb7 20. Rxa8 Rxa8 20. Bg5 was
a promising alternative to the simplifying text.
However, Kashdan is indulging in his favorite
strategy of obtaining bishops for knights.
21. Nxe7+ Qxe7 22. Nh4 Nc5 23. Nf5
Bxf5 Permitting White to achieve his ambi-
tion and leading to play of great delicacy and
complexity. 24. exf5 e4!

After
24. ... e4

25. Rd1 Better was 25. f3, leaving Black
nothing better than the defensive 25. ... Re8; if
25. f3 Nd3 26. g5 Nh5 27. Qxe4 Qxe4 28. fxe4
Ng3 29. Bxd3! cxd3 30. Rd1 Ra1 31. Rxd3 Rxc1+
32. Kg2 regaining the piece because of the mating threat. 25. g5 would have been satisfactorily answered by 25. ... Nd5 26. Rd1 (26. f3 e3!
27. h4 Ra1) 26. ... Nd3 27. Bxd3 exd3 28. Qg4

Ra1—in either event with a splendid game for
Black. 25. ... Re8 26. Rd4 This assures the
rook some freedom before it can be blocked by
Nd3. 26. ... h6 27. Be3 Nd3 28. Bxd3
This capture is inevitable, as the knight is too
strongly posted to be here indefinitely. 28. ...
cxd3!? According to Fritz, exd3 is preferred
over cxd3. 29. Qd1 Nd7 30. Kg2 Nb6
31. Qb3 This is one of the counterchances allowed by Black's 28th move. The b pawn cannot
be held. 31. ... Nc4 32. Qxb5 Nxe3+
33. fxe3 h5? An inexactitude: Black should
have played 33. ... Rd8, which would have led to
the same kind of ending as actually arises, except
that Black's king would have had a more secure
shelter. 34. f6! Alertly played. 34. ... gxf6
35. Qxh5 Rd8 36. Qa5 Black was threatening 36. ... d2. 36. ... Rxd4 37. cxd4 Forced,
as 37. exd4?? e3 would lose in a few moves.
37. ... Qb7 Beginning an extraordinarily
difficult and exciting struggle. The question is
whether Black can support the advance of his
passed pawn and at the same time repulse White's
efforts to secure a perpetual check. 38. Qd8+
Kg7 39. g5! f5! After 39. ... fxg5 the game
would at once be drawn: 40. Qxg5+ Kh7
41. Qh5+ Kg7 42. Qg5+ Kf8 43. Qd8+, etc.
40. Kf2 Qxb2+ 41. Kg3 Qb7 Black has no
choice: to play d2 would allow White to draw by
Qf6+ etc. 42. Kf2 But not 42. Qf6+ Kg8
43. Qd8+ Kh7 44. Qf6 d2 45. Qxf5+ Kg8 and
the pawn must queen. 42. ... Kh7 43. h4?
To prevent Black's next move, White should
have played 43. Qf6, Black would then have no
convincing continuation, for if 43. ... d2 44. Ke2
or Qb2+ 45. Kg3 and the Black queen must retreat; or 43. ... Qc7 44. Qxf5+ Kg7 45. Qxe4
etc. 43. ... f4!? Creating two passed pawns—
and a severe headache for White! A good alternative was 43. ... Qb2+ 44. Kg3 Qe2 (taking advantage of the momentary freedom allowed by
White's last move) 45. g6+ Kg7 46. gxf7 Qxe3+
47. Kg2 Qf3+ 48. Kh2 Kxf7 and Black has excellent winning chances. It must be borne in mind
that both players were in terrific time pressure
hereabouts. 44. exf4 Black was threatening
44. ... Qb2+ 45. Kg1 Qc1+ 46. Kg2 Qd2+ 47. Kh1
Qe1+ 48. Kg2 Qg3+ and at last picking up the
pawns with check. 44. ... d2 45. Ke2 e3
Threatening an immediate catastrophe with

...Qb5+. **46. Qf6 Kg8 47. Qd8+ Kh7 48. Qf6 Qc7!** But not 48. ... Qb5+ 49. Kxe3 d1(Q) 50. Qxf7+ and White draws with a queen down! After the text threatens 49. ... Qc4+ (preventing perpetual check!) 50. Kxe3 d1(Q) and wins. **49. g6+! fxg6 50. h5!** Simpler than 50. d5?! Qc4+ 51. Kxe3 d1(N)+! (not d1(Q)? 52. Qe7+ and White draws) 52. Kd2! Qxd5+ 53. Ke1 Nb2! 54. Qxb2 Qh1+ and Black wins both remaining White pawns and remains with some winning chances. **50. ... Qc4+ 51. Kxe3 d1Q 52. Qe7+ Kh6** After 52. ... Kg8 White draws with 53. Qe8+ Kg7 54. Qe7+! Qf7 55. h6+! Kg8 56. h7+! Qxh7 57. Qe8+ Kg7 58. Qe7+ Kh8 (58. ... Kh6 59. Qg5+, but not 59. Qh4+ which loses to Qh5!) 59. Qf8+ Qg8 60. Qh6+. **53. Qg5+ Kg7**

After
53. ... Kg7

54. Qxg6+?? Throwing away the draw—very excusable, after what White has gone through. Correct was 54. Qe7+ Qf7 55. h6+ transposing into the drawing line indicated above. **54. ... Kf8 55. Qd6+ Ke8** Had Kashdan found the right method on move 54, it would have confirmed the correctness of his intuitive judgment on move 43, although the latter move would still deserve censure because of the practical difficulties which it involved. One should always select the clearest line (43. Qf6!) in order to simplify one's problems. **0–1** Annotations by Reshevsky. (*Reshevsky on Chess*)

465 Adams–Kashdan [C14]
New York, U.S. Championship, round 14, 1940 *[May 15]*

1. e4 e6 2. d4 d5 3. Nc3 Nf6 4. Bg5 Be7 5. c5 Nfd7 6. Bxe7 The latest analysis purports to show a favorable game for White

by 6. h4 (the Alekhine Chatard Attack), but I am not over-familiar with this line, and besides, that Kashdan permits it does not speak highly in its favor. **6. ... Qxe7 7. Bd3** 7. Qd2 or 7. f4 is more usual, but I am convinced that 7. Bd3 is the strongest move, though it opens Black to extreme complications, if he chooses. **7. ... a6 8. Nce2 c5 9. c3 Nc6 10. Qd2 0–0 11. f4 f5 12. Nf3 b5 13. 0–0 Bb7** Throughout the game Black suffers from the ineffectiveness of his queen bishop, a characteristic of this opening. **14. h3 c4** Slower but more deadly from the alternative 14. ... cxd4. The attacks on both sides are slow in developing, but as usual in such cases fireworks are promised when they finally culminate. **15. Bc2 b4 16. g4 g6 17. Ng3 a5 18. gxf5 gxf5 19. Kh2 Kh8 20. Rf2** Providing for Rg1 before Black can play a4 and b3. **20. ... Rg8 21. Rg1 a4 22. Rfg2 a3 23. Ng5 Raf8** Sacrificing the b pawn, but to resolve the queenside pawn situation by 23. ... bxc3 would leave White free to continue his attack on the kingside via Nxe6 followed by Bxf5 etc. **24. cxb4**

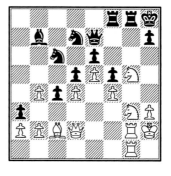

After
24. cxb4

24. ... h6 This move has been criticized because it forces White into an apparently sound sacrifice. Yet if Black had not made this move, White would simply have consolidated his pawn at b4, and then have played for the ending with a pawn to the good. Of course, if 24. ... Nxb4 25. Nxf5 exf5 26. Qb4! **25. Nxe6 Qxe6 26. Bxf5 Qe7** Not 26. ... Rxf5 27. Nxf5 Rxg2+ 28. Qxg2 Qxf5 and the queen mates. **27. Bxd7 Qxd7 28. b5 Nd8** Relatively better was 28. ... Ne7 29. f5 Nxf5 30. Nh5 Rxg2+ 31. Qxg2 Qxb5! 32. b3! Qd7 (32. ... cxb3? 33. Nf6 and if 32. ... Bc8 then 35. Qd2) 33. f6 Qf7 34. b4 Bc8 35. Qd2 etc. with intriguing possibilities. **29. f5**

Qh7 30. e6 Now White's pawns become irresistible. 30. ... axb2 31. Qxb2 h5 32. Qe2 h4 33. e7 Re8 34. Qe5+ Qg7 35. f6 Qf7 36. Nf5 1–0 Annotations by Adams. (*Chess Review*, June-July 1940) Kashdan had the bye in round 15.

466 Kashdan–Pinkus [D74]

New York, U.S. Championship, round 16, 1940 *[May 18]*

1. d4 Nf6 2. c4 g6 3. Nf3 Bg7 4. g3 d5 5. cxd5 Nxd5 6. Bg2 0–0 7. 0–0 c6 8. Nbd2 Nb6 9. Nb3 Na6 10. Bf4 Be6 11. Qc1 Re8 12. Rd1 Qc8 13. Na5 Bd5 14. Qb1 Nc4 15. Nxc4 Bxc4 16. Qc2 Be6 17. a3 Rd8 18. Rac1 Nc7 19. e4 Ne8 20. Qa4 Bg4 21. Rd2 Bxf3 22. Bxf3 e5 23. dxe5 Rxd2 24. Bxd2 Bxe5 25. Bc3 Bxc3 26. Rxc3 Qd7 27. Kg2 Ng7 28. Rc1 Ne6 29. Rd1 Qe7 30. Qb3 Re8 31. Qe3 c5 32. Kg1 Nd4 33. Bg2 b6 34. f4 Rd8 35. Kf2 Ne6 36. Rd5 Nd4 37. Rxd8+ Qxd8 38. Bf1 Qd7 39. Qd3 Kg7 40. Bg2 Qe6 41. Qd2 Qb3 42. h4 Nc2 43. Qc1 Qd3 44. f5 Nd4 45. f6+ Kxf6 46. Qg5+ Ke6 47. Qd5+ Ke7 48. Qb7+ Kf6 49. Qxa7 Qd2+ 50. Kg1 Ne2+ 51. Kh2 Qd6 52. e5+ Qxe5 53. Qxb6+ Kg7 54. Qb3 c4 55. Qxc4 Qxg3+ 56. Kh1 Qf2 57. Kh2 f5 58. Qb4 Qg1+ 59. Kh3 Qe3+ 60. Kh2 f4 61. Qb7+ Kh6 62. Qf3 Qg1+ 63. Kh3 Qe1 64. Qg4 Ng1+ 65. Kh2 Qe3 66. a4 Ne2 67. a5 Qg1+ 68. Kh3 Qe3+ 69. Kh2 Nd4 70. a6 Nf5 71. Qf3 Qd4 72. Kh3 Ne3 ½–½ (*U.S. Championship*, New York 1940)

467 Reinfeld–Kashdan [C68]

New York, U.S. Championship, round 17, 1940 *[May 19]*

1. e4 e5 2. Nf3 Nc6 3. Bb5 a6 4. Bxc6 dxc6 5. d4 exd4 6. Qxd4 Qxd4 7. Nxd4 Bd7 8. Nc3 0–0–0 9. Be3 Bb4 10. 0–0–0 Bxc3 11. bxc3 Re8 12. Nb3 b6 [12. ... Rxe4?? 13. Rxd7 Kxd7 14. Nc5+] 13. Bd4 f6 14. f3 c5 15. Bf2 Ne7 16. Nd2 Be6 17. Kb2 Nc6 18. Nf1 Rd8 19. Ne3 Rxd1 20. Rxd1 Rd8 ½–½ (*U.S. Championship*, New York, 1940)

468 Cruz–Kashdan [C56]

Hamilton, New York State Championship, round 1, 1941 *[August 17]*

1. e4 e5 2. Nf3 Nc6 3. Bc4 Nf6 4. d4 exd4 5. 0–0 Nxe4 6. Re1 d5 7. Bxd5 Qxd5 8. Nc3 Qa5 9. Nxe4 Be6 10. Neg5 0–0–0 11. Nxe6 fxe6 12. Rxe6 Bd6 13. Bg5 Rdf8 14. Qe2 h6 15. Bd2 Qf5 16. Qe4 Qxe4 17. Rxe4 Bc5 18. a3 a6 19. b4 Bb6 20. a4 Rf5 21. Rae1 Kd7 22. R1e2 Rhf8 23. Ne1 R8f7 24. Nd3 Re7 25. g4 Rxe4 26. Rxe4 Rf6 27. f4 Re6 28. Rxe6 Kxe6 29. Kg2 Ne7 30. Kf3 Nd5 31. h4 g6 32. Nf2 Nf6 33. Ne4 Ne8 34. Ng3 Nf6 35. f5+ gxf5 36. gxf5+ Kf7 37. Bxh6 c6 38. Ne4 Nd5 39. Bd2 Bd8 40. Nd6+ Kf8 41. Nxb7 Bxh4 42. Nc5 Nb6 43. Ke4 Ke7 44. a5 Nc4 45. Bc1 Nd6+ 46. Kf4 Kf6 47. Ne4+ Nxe4 48. Kxe4 Be1 49. Bb2 Bxb4 50. Bxd4+ Kf7 51. Bb6 Bd6 52. Kd4 Kf6 53. Bc5 Bg3 54. Bb4 Bf2+ 55. Ke4 Bg3 56. Bc3+ Kf7 57. Kd4 Bd6 58. Kc4 Be7 59. Bb4 Bh4 60. Kc5 Be7+ 61. Kc4 Bh4 62. Bd6 Bd8 63. Be5 Be7 64. Bd4 Bd6 65. Bc5 Bg3 66. c3 Kf6 67. Bd4+ Kxf5 68. Kc5 Bc7 ½–½ (*New York State Bulletin*, August 1941)

469 Kashdan–Willman [E43]

Hamilton, New York State Championship, round 2, 1941 *[August 17]*

1. d4 Nf6 2. c4 e6 3. Nc3 Bb4 4. e3 b6 5. Be2 Ne4 6. Qc2 Bb7 7. Bf3 Bxc3+ 8. bxc3 f5 9. Ne2 0–0 10. 0–0 d6 11. a4 Nd7 12. a5 Ndf6 13. a6 Bc6 14. Nf4 Qe8 15. Rd1 g5 16. Nd3 g4 17. Be2 Ng5 18. Nf4 Be4 19. Bd3 h5 20. c5 bxc5 21. dxc5 e5 22. Bxe4 fxe4 23. Ne2 Qf7 24. cxd6 cxd6 25. Ba3 Ne8 26. Ng3 Rc8 27. Nxe4 Nxe4 28. Qxe4 Rxc3 29. Qd5 Qxd5 30. Rxd5 Rc6 31. Bb4 Rb6 32. Bd2 Kf7 33. Rda5 Rb2 34. R5a2 Rxa2 35. Rxa2 Nc7 36. e4 Rb8 37. Kf1 Ke6 38. Be3 Rb1+ 39. Ke2 Nb5 40. Kd3 Kd7 41. Kc4 Kc6 42. Kd3 Rb4 43. Ra1 Nd4 44. Ra5 Rb1 45. Bxd4 Rd1+ 46. Ke3 Rxd4 47. f3 Rd1 48. Kf2 Rd2+ 49. Kg3 gxf3 50. gxf3 h4+ 51. Kxh4 Rxh2+

52. Kg4 Rg2+ 53. Kf5 ½–½ (*New York State Bulletin*, August 1941)

470 Shainswit–Kashdan [D79]

Hamilton, New York State Championship, round 3, 1941 [*August 18*]

1. Nf3 d5 2. g3 Nf6 3. Bg2 g6 4. 0–0 Bg7 5. d4 0–0 6. c4 c6 7. cxd5 cxd5 8. Nc3 Nc6 9. Ne5 Be6 10. Nxc6 bxc6 11. Bf4 Qc8 12. Na4 Bh3 13. Be5 Qf5 14. Nc5 Rfc8 15. Qd3 Qh5 16. Bxf6 Bxf6 17. Bxh3 Qxh3 18. f4 Qf5 19. e3 e6 20. Qxf5 gxf5 21. Rac1 Be7 22. Rf2 Rab8 23. b3 Bxc5 24. Rxc5 Rb5 25. Rfc2 Rxc5 26. Rxc5 Kf8 27. Ra5 Rc7 28. Kf2 Ke7 29. h3 h5 30. Kf3 Kd6 31. g4 hxg4+ 32. hxg4 fxg4+ 33. Kxg4 f6 34. Kf3 e5 35. fxe5+ fxe5 36. dxe5+ Kxe5 37. Rc5 Kd6 38. b4 Rh7 39. a3 Rh3+ 40. Ke2 Rh7 ½–½ (*New York State Bulletin*, August 1941)

471 Kashdan–Hewlett [C13]

Hamilton, New York State Championship, round 4, 1941 [*August 19*]

1. e4 e6 2. d4 d5 3. Nc3 Nf6 4. Bg5 Be7 5. e5 Nfd7 6. h4 c5 7. Bxe7 Kxe7 8. Qg4 Kf8 9. dxc5 Nxe5 10. Qg3 Nbc6 11. 0–0–0 Qe7 12. f4 Nd7 13. Nf3 Qxc5 14. f5 d4 15. fxe6 Nf6 16. e7+ Kxe7 17. Qc7+ Kf8 18. Nxd4 g5 19. Nxc6 bxc6 20. Qd8+ Kg7 21. Qxf6+ If 21. ... Kxf6 22. Ne4+. 1–0 (*New York State Bulletin*, August 1941)

472 Kashdan–Denker [B74]

Hamilton, New York State Championship, round 6, 1941 [*August 20*]

1. e4 c5 2. Nf3 Nc6 3. d4 cxd4 4. Nxd4 Nf6 5. Nc3 d6 6. Be2 g6 7. Be3 Bg7 8. 0–0 0–0 9. Nb3 Be6 10. f4 Na5 11. f5 Bc4 12. Bd3 d5 13. e5 Nxb3 14. exf6 Bxf6 15. axb3 Bxd3 16. Qxd3 d4 17. fxg6 dxc3 18. gxf7+ Rxf7 19. bxc3 Qxd3 20. cxd3 Bxc3 21. Rxa7 Rd8 22. Rxf7 Kxf7 23. Rxb7 Rxd3 24. Kf2 Be5 25. h3 Rc3 26. b4 Bd6 27. b5 Ke6 28. b6 Rc2+ 29. Kf3 Rc3 30. Ke4 Rc2

31. Kf3 Rc3 32. Kf2 Rc2+ 33. Kf1 Rc3 34. Bd4 Rc4 35. Be3 Rc3 36. Bd2 Rb3 37. Ke2 Rb2 38. Kd3 Bc5 39. Ba5 Rxg2 40. Rc7 Rg3+ 41. Kc4 Bxb6 42. Bxb6 Rxh3 43. Bc5 Rh4+ 44. Kd3 Rh3+ 45. Ke4 Rh4+ 46. Ke3 Rh5 47. Rxe7+ Kd5 48. Rc7 Rh3+ 49. Kd2 Rh2+ 50. Kd3 Rh1 51. Be3 Rd1+ 52. Ke2 Rh1 53. Kf3 Rh3+ 54. Kf4 Rh4+ 55. Kf5 Rh5+ 56. Kg4 Rh1 57. Bf2 Rh6 58. Bh4 Kd6 59. Ra7 Ke5 60. Kg5 Rg6+ 61. Kh5 Rg1 62. Rxh7 Kf5 63. Rf7+ Ke6 64. Rf3 Rg8 65. Bg5 Ke5 66. Kg4 Ke4 67. Re3+ Kd4 68. Re2 Rf8 69. Bf4 Kd3 70. Re1 Rf7 71. Kf3 Rh7 72. Rd1+ Kc4 73. Ke4 Rh4 74. Rc1+ Kb4 75. Ke5 Kb5 76. Be3 Rh3 77. Bd4 Rh5+ 78. Kd6 Rh6+ 79. Kd5 Rh5+ 80. Be5 Ka5 81. Kd4 Kb4 82. Kd5 Rg5 83. Rb1+ Ka5 84. Kd6 Ka4 85. Bd4 Rb5 86. Ra1+ Kb3 87. Bc5 Kc4 88. Rc1+ Kd3 89. Kd5 Ra5 90. Rh1 Ra8 91. Rh3+ Ke2 92. Re3+ Kd2 93. Rb3 Ke2 ½–½ (*New York State Bulletin*, August 1941)

473 Fine–Kashdan [E00]

Hamilton, New York State Championship, round 7, 1941 [*August 21*]

1. d4 Nf6 2. c4 e6 3. g3 Bb4+ 4. Bd2 Bxd2+ 5. Nxd2 0–0 6. Bg2 Nc6 7. Ngf3 d6 8. 0–0 e5 9. e3 Ne8 10. dxe5 dxe5 11. Ne4 Bf5 12. Nh4 Qxd1 13. Rfxd1 Bg4 14. f3 Be6 15. b3 f5 16. Nc5 Bc8 17. f4 e4 18. g4 g6 19. gxf5 gxf5 20. Kf2 Nd6 21. Bf1 b6 22. Na4 Be6 23. Nc3 Ne7 24. Rd2 Kf7 25. Rc1 a5 26. Na4 Rad8 27. Rcd1 Nb7 28. Rxd8 Rxd8 29. Rxd8 Nxd8 30. c5 bxc5 31. Nxc5 Bc8 32. Ng2 Nec6 33. Ne1 Ke7 34. Nc2 Kd6 35. Na4 Nb4 36. Nd4 Nxa2 37. Bh3 Nc1 38. Nxf5+ Bxf5 39. Bxf5 h6 40. Bxe4 Nxb3 41. Bc2 ½–½ (*New York State Bulletin*, August 1941)

474 Seidman–Kashdan [C86]

Hamilton, New York State Championship, round 8, 1941 [*August 21*]

1. e4 e5 2. Nf3 Nc6 3. Bb5 a6 4. Ba4 Nf6 5. 0–0 Be7 6. Qe2 b5 7. Bb3 d6

8. a4 Bg4 9. c3 0–0 10. Rd1 b4 11. d4
Qb8 12. Bc4 Na5 13. Nbd2 Nxc4
14. Nxc4 exd4 15. cxd4 Re8 16. h3 Bh5
17. Bf4 d5 18. exd5 Nxd5 19. Bh2 Bd6
20. Nce5 Qb7 21. Qc4 Bxe5 22. dxe5
Bxf3 23. gxf3 c6 24. Kh1 Re6 25. Rg1
Ne7 26. Qe4 g6 27. Rad1 Qb6 28. f4
Qxf2 29. Bg3 Qa7 30. Bh4 f5 31. Qxb4
Nd5 32. Qd4 Qxd4 33. Rxd4 Rb8
34. Rg2 Rb3 35. Kh2 Kf7 36. Rc2 Ke8
37. Re2 Kd7 38. Kg2 Re8 39. Bf2 Ke6
40. Rc2 Kd7 41. Rdc4 Reb8 42. Rxc6
Nxf4+ 43. Kf1 Rxb2 44. Rd6+ Ke8
45. Rc7 Rb1+ 46. Be1 Rd8 47. Rxa6 Nd3
48. Rxh7 Rxe1+ 49. Kg2 Nxe5 50. Rh8+
Ke7 51. Rh7+ Nf7 52. Ra7+ Kf6
53. Rhxf7+ Kg5 54. Rfd7 Rde8 55. Rd2
Ra1 56. a5 Re3 57. Kh2 Raa3 58. Rg2+
Kh6 59. h4 Rh3+ 60. Kg1 Rxh4 61. Ra6
Ra1+ 62. Kf2 Ra2+ 63. Kg1 Rxg2+
64. Kxg2 Ra4 65. Ra8 Kg5 66. a6 Kg4
67. a7 Ra2+ 68. Kf1 g5 69. Ke1 f4 70. Kf1
f3 71. Ke1 Kg3 0–1 (*New York State Bulletin*,
August 1941)

475 Kashdan–Reshevsky [D95]

Hamilton, New York State Championship,
round 9, 1941 *[August 22]*

1. c4 Nf6 2. Nc3 d5 3. d4 g6 4. Nf3
Bg7 5. e3 0–0 6. Qb3 c6 7. Bd2 dxc4
8. Bxc4 Nbd7 9. 0–0 Nb6 10. Be2 Bf5
11. Rfd1 Ne4 12. Nxe4 Bxe4 13. Ba5 Qd5
14. Qb4 Qd6 15. Qxd6 exd6 16. Nd2
½–½ (*New York State Bulletin*, August 1941)

476 Kashdan–Santasiere [B14]

Hamilton, New York State Championship,
round 11, 1941 *[August 23]*

1. c4 c6 2. e4 d5 3. exd5 cxd5 4. d4
Nf6 5. Nc3 e6 6. Nf3 Be7 7. c5 0–0
8. Bd3 b6 9. cxb6 Qxb6 10. 0–0 Ba6
11. a3 Rc8 12. Na4 Qb7 13. b4 Bxd3
14. Qxd3 Qa6 15. Qxa6 Nxa6 16. b5 Rc4?
17. Nb2 Nc7 18. Nxc4 dxc4 19. a4 Ncd5
20. Ne5 c3 21. Nc6 Bd6 22. a5 Nb4
23. Nxb4 Bxb4 24. Ba3 Bxa3 25. Rxa3
Nd5 26. g3 Rb8 27. Rb3 Kf8 28. Rc1
Ke7 29. Kf1 Kd6 30. Ke2 g5 31. Kd3 h5

32. Ra1 Rb7 33. b6 axb6 34. axb6 f5
35. Ra8 g4 36. Rh8 Nf6 37. Kxc3 Ne4+
38. Kd3 Nxf2+ 39. Kc4 Kc6 40. Rh6
Ne4 41. d5+ Kd7 42. dxe6+ 1–0 (*New York
State Bulletin*, August 1941)

477 Pilnik–Kashdan [C43]

Metropolitan Chess League, 1942 *[March]*

1. e4 e5 2. Nf3 Nf6 The rarely seen Petroff or Russian Defense, a great favorite with
Kashdan, Marshall and Hitler!! 3. d4 Nxe4
4. Bd3 d5 5. Nxe5 Be7 And not Bd6, as
Levy learned recently following his sad affair
with Almgren. We must not forget that Black
should defend in an opening. 6. 0–0 0–0
7. c4 Nc6! 8. cxd5 Nxe5 9. Bxe4 Ng6
White has gained a pawn, but he has doubled,
isolated queen pawns—a situation to make anyone with an isolani complex faint five times!
10. Nc3 f5 11. Bd3 Bd6 Not 11. ... f4, because of 12. Qh5. 12. f4 Qf6 13. Bc4 a6
14. a4 Bd7 15. Be3 Rfe8 16. Qd3 Re7
17. Rae1 Rae8 18. g3 In order to be able to
play Bf2. Now Kashdan, who has the initiative
will bring his inactive knight into play via h8.
18. ... Nh8 19. b4 A superficial demonstration which accomplishes nothing. Meaningful
was Bf2, after which he should quickly exchange
about five of those bad rooks. 19. ... Nf7
20. b5 a5 21. Bf2 g5!

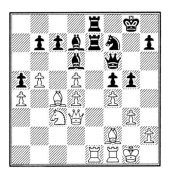

After
21. ... g5

Black uses his gained time to press forward.
22. Re5 More whipped cream without vita-
mins. Since he cannot maintain his lovely post,
he is merely giving Black more time to prepare.
It was best here to yield a pawn and achieve
equality—Thus: 22. Rxe7 Rxe7 23. Re1 Rxe1
24. Bxe1 gxf4 25. Ne2! fxg3 26. Bxg3. 22. ...

gxf4 23. gxf4 Nh6 24. Kh1 Ng4 25. Bg3 Kh8 26. Rxe7 Rxe7 27. Rf3 Qh6 28. Kg2 Rg7 29. h3 Nf6 30. Kh2 Ne4! 31. Ne2 Be8 32. Re3 Bh5 33. Rxe4 fxe4 34. Qxe4 Re7 0–1 Annotations are by Santasiere. According to the annotator, Kashdan had not played a serious game in seven months. (*American Chess Bulletin*, March-April, p. 35, 1942)

478 Hanauer (Marshall)– Kashdan (Manhattan) [C97]
Metropolitan Chess League, 1942 *[April 4]*

1. e4 e5 2. Nf3 Nc6 3. Bb5 a6 4. Ba4 Nf6 5. 0–0 Be7 6. Re1 b5 7. Bb3 d6 8. c3 Na5 9. Bc2 c5 10. d4 Qc7 11. h3 0–0 12. Nbd2 Bd7 13. Nf1 Rac8 14. dxe5 dxe5 15. Ne3 c4 16. Nd5 Nxd5 17. exd5 f6 18. d6 Qxd6 19. Qe2 Nc6 20. Be3 Qc7 21. Rad1 Be6 22. Nh4 f5 23. Qh5 e4 24. f3 Bf7 25. Qxf5 Bxh4 26. Qxe4 Bg6 27. Qxh4 Bxc2 28. Rd5 Rcd8 29. Rxd8 Rxd8 30. Qf2 Rd1 31. Rxd1 Bxd1 32. Qd2 Qd8 33. Bd4 Ba4 34. Qe3 Qe7 35. Kf2 Qxe3+ 36. Kxe3 Bc2 0–1 (Kashdan's scoresheet)

479 Kashdan–Pilnik [A52]
New York, U.S. Championship, round 1, 1942 *[April 10]*

1. d4 Nf6 2. c4 e5 3. dxe5 Ng4 4. Bf4 Nc6 5. Nf3 Bb4+ 6. Nc3 Qe7 7. Qd5 Bxc3+ 8. bxc3 f6 9. exf6 Nxf6 10. Qd3 d6 11. g3 0–0 12. Bg2 Ne4 13. 0–0 Bf5 14. Nh4 g6 15. Nxf5 gxf5 16. Rab1 Rab8 17. Rb2 Kh8 18. Rfb1 b6 19. Qd5 Qe8 20. Be3 Ne7 21. Qd4+ Nf6 22. Bh6 Rf7 23. Bg5 Neg8 24. Bd5 c5 25. Bxf7 cxd4 26. Bxe8 dxc3 27. Rc2 Rxe8 28. Bf4 Rc8 29. Rxc3 d5 30. Rbc1 Re8 31. Be3 Ne7 32. Bd4 Kg7 33. Re3 1–0 (*New York Times*, April 12, 1942)

480 Kashdan–Horowitz [D60]
New York, U.S. Championship, round 2, 1942 *[April 11]*

1. d4 d5 2. c4 e6 3. Nc3 Nf6 4. Nf3 Nbd7 5. Bg5 Be7 6. e3 0–0 7. Bd3 dxc4 8. Bxc4 a6 9. e4 b5 10. Bd3 Bb7 11. Qe2 Re8 12. 0–0 c5 13. e5 Nd5 14. Ne4 Qb6 15. Bxe7 Rxe7 16. Nxc5 Nxc5 17. dxc5 Qxc5 18. Rac1 Qb4 19. a3 Qg4 20. h3 Qh5 21. Be4 Rd8 22. Rfd1 Red7 23. Kh2 Qh6 24. Qd2 Qxd2 25. Rxd2 Kf8 26. Nd4 Nf4 27. Bxb7 Rxb7 28. Nf5! So if 28. ... Rxd7 29. Rc8 leads to mate. And if 28. ... exf5 29. Rxd8 loses the exchange. 28. ... Nd5 29. Nd6 Rb6 30. Rdc2 f6 31. Rc8 Rb8 32. Rxd8+ Rxd8 33. Rc6 Ra8 34. Ne4 fxe5 35. Nc5 a5 36. Rxe6 Re8 37. Nd7+ Kf7 38. Rxe5 Rxe5 39. Nxe5+ Kf6 40. Nc6 a4 41. Kg3 Nb6 42. Nd4 Nc4 43. Nxb5 Nxb2 44. Kf4 Ke6 45. Ke4 Nd1 46. f4 h5 47. g4 hxg4 48. hxg4 Kf6 49. g5+ Kg6 50. Kf3 Nb2 51. Kg4 Nc4 52. f5+ Kf7 53. Kf4 Ke7 54. Ke4 Nd2+ 55. Ke3 Nc4+ 56. Kd4 Nd2 57. Ke5 Nf3+ 58. Kf4 Nd2 59. g6 Nc4 60. Kg5 Ne5 61. Nc3 Nf3+ 62. Kf4 Ne1 63. Nd5+ Kf8 64. Nb4 Ke7 65. Nd5+ Kf8 66. Nb4 1–0 (*Los Angeles Times*, May 10, 1942)

481 Seidman–Kashdan [C80]
New York, U.S. Championship, round 3, 1942 *[April 12]*

1. e4 e5 2. Nf3 Nf6 3. d4 Nxe4 4. Bd3 d5 5. dxe5 Nc5 6. 0–0 Be7 7. Nc3 c6 8. Nd4 Nxd3 9. Qxd3 0–0 10. f4 f5 11. Nb3 Na6 12. Be3 b6 13. Rad1 Nc5 14. Nxc5 bxc5 15. Na4 Qa5 16. Qa3 d4 17. Bd2 Qb5 18. b3 Be6 19. c4 dxc3 20. Nxc3 Qb7 21. Qc1 c4 22. bxc4 Bxc4 23. Rf2 Bh4 24. g3 Be7 25. Be3 Rfd8 26. Rb2 Rxd1+ 27. Nxd1 Qa6 28. Rc2 Ba3 29. Qd2 Bd5 30. Rc3 Be4 31. Qd7 Bb4 32. e6 Qxa2 33. Bd2 Bxc3 34. Nxc3 Qc4 35. Nxe4 fxe4 36. Be3 Rb8 37. Kg2 Qe2+ 38. Bf2 Qf3+ 39. Kh3 Qh5+ 40. Kg2 e3 41. Bxe3 Rb2+ 42. Bf2 Qd5 43. Kh3 Qxd7 44. exd7 Rd2 45. Bxa7 Rxd7 46. Be3 Kf7 0–1 (*Christian Science Monitor*, June 27, 1942)

482 Green–Kashdan [E49]

New York, U.S. Championship, round 5,
1942 *[April 15]*

1. d4 Nf6 2. c4 e6 3. Nc3 Bb4 4. a3
Bxc3+ 5. bxc3 b6 6. f3 d5 7. cxd5 exd5
8. e3 0–0 9. Bd3 Ba6 10. Bxa6 Nxa6
11. Ne2 c5 12. 0–0 Re8 13. Qd3 Qc8
14. Bb2 c4 15. Qd2 Nc7 16. Rae1 Nb5
17. Ng3 Nd6 18. Qc2 Qc6 19. Re2 Re6
20. Rfe1 Rae8 21. a4 g6 22. Ba3 a5
23. Bxd6 Qxd6 24. e4 Qc6 25. e5 Nd7
26. Rb1 Nb8 27. f4 f6 28. Qd1 fxe5
29. fxe5 Na6 30. Rf2 Rf8 31. Rxf8+ Kxf8
32. Qf3+ Ke8 33. Rf1 Kd8 34. Ne2 Nc7
35. Qf8+ Re8 36. Qa3 Qd7 37. h3 Kc8
38. Rf6 Kb7 39. Nf4 g5 40. Rd6 Qf7
41. Ne2 Re6 42. Rd8 Re8 43. Rd6 Re6
44. Rd8 Qe7 45. Qxe7 Rxe7 46. h4 b5
47. axb5 gxh4 48. Rd6 a4 49. Rf6 Nxb5
50. Rf3 a3 51. Nc1 Nc7 52. Na2 Rg7
53. Kh2 Kc6 54. Rf1 Kb5 55. Rb1+ Ka4
56. Rb7 Ne6 57. Rb4+ Ka5 58. Rb8 Nf4
59. Ra8+ Kb6 60. Rxa3 Rxg2+ 61. Kh1
h3 62. Nb4 Nh5 63. Nxd5+ Kb7 0–1
(*American Chess Bulletin*, January 1943)

483 Kashdan–Altman [C78]

New York, U.S. Championship, round 6,
1942 *[April 17]*

1. e4 e5 2. Nf3 Nc6 3. Bb5 a6 4. Ba4
Nf6 5. 0–0 b5 6. Bb3 Be7 7. a4 Rb8
8. axb5 axb5 9. Qe2 d6 10. c3 0–0 11. d4
exd4 12. cxd4 Bg4 13. Be3 Qe8 Better is
13. ... d5. 14. h3 Bxf3 15. Qxf3 Ra8
16. Nc3 Na5 17. Bc2 c5 18. dxc5 dxc5
19. e5 Nd7 20. Nxb5

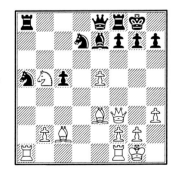

After
20. Nxb5

20. ... Nxe5? 21. Qe4 After 21. ... Ng6
22. Nc7 wins the exchange, hence Black resigns.
1–0 (*Los Angeles Times*, May 3, 1942)

484 Levy–Kashdan [C29]

New York, U.S. Championship, round 7,
1942 *[April 18]*

1. e4 e5 2. Nc3 Nf6 3. f4 d5 4. exd5
e4 5. d4 Bb4 6. Bb5+ Bd7 7. Bc4 Bg4
8. Qd2 0–0 9. h3 Bf5 10. Nge2 Nbd7
11. a3 e3 12. Qd1 Bxc3+ 13. Nxc3 Nb6
14. Bd3 Nfxd5 15. 0–0 Bxd3 16. Qxd3
Re8 17. Nxd5 Nxd5 18. c4 Qh4 19. Qe2
Nxf4 20. Qf3 e2

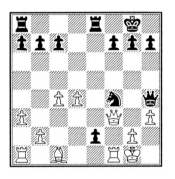

After
20. ... e2

[20. ... Nxg2 21. Qxf7+ Kh8 22. Kxg2 e2
23. Be3 exf1Q+ 24. Rxf1 Qe4+ 25. Rf3 Rf8]
21. Bxf4 exf1Q+ 22. Rxf1 Re1 23. Rxe1
Qxe1+ 24. Kh2 c6 25. d5 cxd5 26. cxd5
Qe7 27. d6 Qd7 28. Qd5 Rc8 29. Qd3
h6 30. Qg3 Qe6 31. h4 Rc4 32. b3 Rd4
33. b4 Qf5 34. Be5 Rg4 35. Qc3 Rxh4+
36. Kg1 f6 37. Bg3 Re4 38. Qd2 Re8
39. Qd4 Rc8 40. Bf4 g5 41. Bd2 b6
42. Bc3 Kf7 43. a4 Rd8 44. b5 Qc5 0–1
(Contributed by Andy Ansel)

485 Kashdan–Denker [D37]

New York, U.S. Championship, round 8,
1942 *[April 19]*

1. d4 Nf6 2. c4 e6 3. Nc3 d5 4. Nf3
Nbd7 5. g3 Bb4 6. Bg2 dxc4 7. Qa4
Nd5 8. Bd2 0–0 9. e4 Bxc3 10. bxc3
N5b6 11. Qc2 h6 12. 0–0 Re8 13. Bf4
Nf8 14. Nd2 Bd7 15. a4 a5 16. Ra3 Ng6
17. Be3 Bc6 18. Rfa1 f5 19. f3 Qd7
20. Qa2 Kh7 21. Nxc4 Nxa4 22. Nd2

b5 23. c4 Nb6 24. cxb5 Bxb5 25. Rxa5
Rxa5 26. Qxa5 f4 27. Bf2 Ra8 28. Qc3
Qc6 29. Qb2 Rxa1+ 30. Qxa1 Qc2
31. Qb1 Qxd2 32. Qxb5 Qd1+ 33. Qf1
Qc2 34. Bh3 e5 35. Bf5 fxg3 36. hxg3
exd4 37. Qb5 Qc1+ 38. Kg2 Qg5 39. f4
Qf6 40. Bxd4! If now 40. ... Qxd4 then
41. Bxg6+ Kxg6? 42. Qf5 mate! **40. ... Qf7**
41. Bxb6 cxb6 42. Qxb6 h5 43. Bxg6+
Qxg6 44. Qxg6+ Kxg6 45. Kh3 Kh6
46. Kh4 g5+ 47. fxg5+ Kg6 48. e5 1–0
(*British Chess Magazine*, August 1942)

486 Kashdan–H. Steiner [C78]

New York, U.S. Championship, round 10,
1942 *[April 22]*

1. e4 e5 2. Nf3 Nc6 3. Bb5 a6 4. Ba4
Nf6 5. 0–0 b5 6. Bb3 Be7 7. a4 Rb8
8. axb5 axb5 9. Qe2 0–0 10. c3 d5 11. d3
d4 12. cxd4 Bg4 13. d5 Nd4 14. Qd1 Nh5
15. Be3 Nxf3+ 16. gxf3 Bh3 17. Re1 Bb4
18. Nc3 Nf4 19. Bxf4 exf4 20. Kh1 Rb6
21. Rg1 Bxc3 22. bxc3 Qh4 23. Rg2 Rh6
24. Qg1 Bxg2+ 25. Qxg2 Rg6 26. Qf1
Qh5 27. Bd1 Rc8 28. Ra5 c6 29. dxc6
Rgxc6 30. c4 Rc5 31. d4 Rg5 32. c5 h6
33. Rxb5 Ra8 34. Rb1 Ra6 35. d5 Rag6
36. c6 Qh3 37. Be2 Rg2 38. Qg1 Rxg1+
39. Rxg1 Rxg1+ 40. Kxg1 Qc8 41. Bb5
Qc7 0–1 (*Golden Treasury of Chess*, Game 538)

487 Kashdan–Baker [B92]

New York, U.S. Championship, round 12,
1942 *[April 25]*

1. e4 c5 2. Nf3 d6 3. d4 cxd4 4. Nxd4
Nf6 5. Nc3 a6 6. Be2 Qc7 7. 0–0 b5
8. f4 b4 9. Nd5 Nxd5 10. exd5 g6 If
10. ... Bb7 11. Bf3 Qc5 12. a3! and White's superior development soon tells. **11. Be3 Bb7**
12. Bf3 Bg7 13. Qd2 a5 14. a3! Breaking
the formation that Black has so laboriously con-
structed. **14. ... Na6 15. axb4 Nxb4 16. c3**
(*see diagram*)

16. ... Nxd5? Best is 16. ... Na6, although
White would have the advantage according to
Fritz. **17. Bxd5** For if 17. ... Bxd5 18. Nb5 Qc6
19. Qxd5 Qxd5 20. Nc7+ wins. **1–0** Annotated
by Kashdan. (*Chess Review*, October 1942)

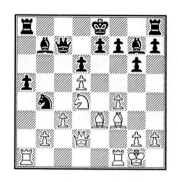

After
16. c3

488 Kashdan–Reshevsky [A34]

New York, U.S. Championship, round 14,
1942 *[April 28]*

1. c4 Nf6 2. Nc3 d5 3. cxd5 Nxd5
4. g3 c5 5. Bg2 Nc7 6. Nf3 Nc6 7. 0–0
e5 8. d3 Be7 9. Be3 0–0 10. Rc1 Rb8
11. Na4 b6 12. b4 Nxb4 13. Nxe5 Bf6
14. Nc6 Nxc6 15. Bxc6 Nd5 16. Bd2 Qd6
17. Bb5 Nc7 18. Bf4 Be5 19. Bxe5 Qxe5
20. Bc6 Be6 21. Nc3 Nd5 22. Bxd5 Bxd5
23. Nxd5 Qxd5 24. Qa4 Rb7 25. Rfd1
Re7 26. e3 Rc8 27. Rc4 Qf3 28. Rd2 h5
29. Qc2 Rd8 30. h4 Red7 31. Qb3 Qd5
32. a4 Qe6 ½–½ (*United States Chess Federation Chess Tournaments, 1942, 1943, 1944*)

489 Chernev–Kashdan [D93]

New York, U.S. Championship, round 15,
1942 *[April 29]*

1. d4 Nf6 2. c4 g6 3. Nc3 d5 4. Bf4
Bg7 5. e3 0–0 6. Nf3 c6 7. Qb3 dxc4
8. Bxc4 Nbd7 9. 0–0 Nb6 10. Be2 Be6
11. Qc2 Nbd5 12. Be5 Bf5 13. Qb3 Qb6
14. Nxd5 Nxd5 15. Bc4 Rfd8 16. Bxg7
An unnecessary exchange, which only helps
Black. 18.Rfe1 was stronger. **16. ... Kxg7**
17. Rac1 f6 18. Bxd5 Rxd5 19. Qa3 Re8
20. Qc3 And here 20.Rc4 was more effective.
After the text Black gets the better ending.
20. ... Qa5 21. a3 Qxc3 22. Rxc3 Rb5
23. b4 a5 24. bxa5 Rxa5 25. Re1 Rea8
26. e4 Bg4 27. Ree3 Rd8 (*see diagram*)
Threatening ...Bxf3 and Rxd4. **28. Rb3** Inadequate because of the unusual mating attack
which follows the exchange of pawns. If 28. Rc4
e5 29. dxe5 Rd1+ 30. Ne1 (Not Re1? as Bxf3
wins) 30. ... Rxa3! and the two passed pawns

After
27. ... Rd8

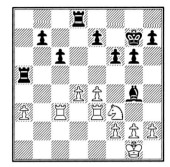

should decide. **28. ... Bxf3 29. gxf3 Rxd4 30. Rxb7** Completely unaware of the fatal threat. Black could now announce mate in seven. **30. ... Rd1+ 31. Kg2 Rg5+ 32. Kh3 Rdg1 33. Rxe7+ Kh6 0–1** Annotated by Kashdan. (*Chess Review*, May 1942)

490 Reshevsky–Kashdan [D83]
U.S. Championship, Playoff Match,
round 1, 1942 *[October 7]*

1. d4 Nf6 Kashdan almost invariably adopts the Orthodox Defense to the QGD. The opening reveals that he has come well armed with prepared variations. **2. c4 g6 3. Nc3 d5 4. Bf4 Bg7 5. e3 0–0!? 6. Qb3 c5!** This is obviously what he had up his sleeve. 6. ... c6 is theoretically good enough to equalize; one main line runs 7. Nf3 dxc4 8. Bxc4 Nbd7 9. 0–0 Nb6 10. Be2 Bf5! with an excellent game, a line which, incidentally, occurred in the game Kashdan–Reshevsky, Hamilton 1941. The simplest refutation (and perhaps the only one) of Black's sacrifice is 7. cxd5 cxd4 8. exd4 Nbd7 9. Be2 Nb6. Eventually White will give back the pawn with d6 and secure the better position. **7. dxc5 Ne4 8. cxd5 Qa5 9. Nge2** He must guard against ...e5. **9. ... Nxc5** There is nothing better. If 9. ... e5 10. dxe6 e.p. Bxe6 11. Qa4 will sweep queens off the board, bringing down the curtain on Black's attack. **10. Qd1** Up to this point they had been following a game Capablanca–Flohr, AVRO, 1938. Reshevsky's move is undoubtedly an improvement over Capa's 10. Qc4, when 10. ... e5 is a powerful reply. **10. ... e5** So that if 11. Bg3 Bf5 12. Nc1 e4 with strong pressure. But there is a surprise in store for him. **11. Bg5! f6** Loses a valuable tempo. 11. ... Ne4 at once yields the same attack. **12. a3!**

Much better than 12. Bh4 g5 13. Bg3 Bf5 14. Nc1 Nbd7 etc. Despite his predilection for bishops, Kashdan cannot afford to try 12. ... fxg5 13. b4 Qc7 14. bxc5 Qxc5 15. Ne4 with a strategically won game. **12. ... Ne4 13. Bh4 g5 14. Bg3 f5 15. f3**

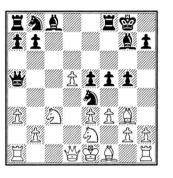

After
15. f3

The natural reply now is 15. ... Nxg3, and if then 16. Nxg3 e4 17. Rc1 fxe4 18. fxe4 **15. ... Nxc3 16. Nxc3 f4 17. Bf2 e4 18. Rc1 Bf5** A timid continuation which hands over the initiative to White. The most energetic was 18. ... fxe3 19. Bxe3 exf3 20. gxf3 Re8 21. Kf2 RxB! 22. KxR Qb6+ 23. Ke2 Bf5 24. Na4 (forced) Qd6 and despite his pawn and the exchange minus Black has excellent chances because the White king is almost as exposed as a sheep among a pack of wolves. **19. Be2 exf3 20. gxf3 fxe3 21. Bxe3 Nd7 22. 0–0 Rae8 23. Bd4 Ne5 24. Kh1 a6** This shows that Black's attack has petered out; all he can do is wait for the counter blows. **25. d6 Kh8 26. b4**

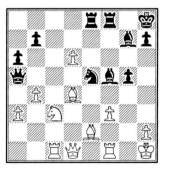

After
26. b4

Gives Black a new lease on life. An easy win is not to be found, e.g., 26. Na4 Qd5, or 26. Qd2 Rd8, with adequate defenses on 26. Qb3 Qd8 27. Qxb7 Qxd6. White has not made much progress because of the exchange of pawns is just what the defender wants in such cases. But 26. Ne4 would maintain White's superiority with good prospects of increasing it. **26. ... Qd8??** The losing mistake. After 26. ... Qxa3 Black would have excellent chances. 27. Nd5, threatening to win the queen, would be met by 27. ... Qa2 26. Bc3 Rd8. Other moves are even less promising for White. However, Reshevsky points out that he would have played after 27. ... Qa2 28. Bc4! Nxc4 29. Bxg7+ Kxg7 30. Qd4+ Ne5 31. Ne7 Qe6 32. Rfe1 regaining the piece with a strong attack. **27. Nd5 g4** Desperation. On 27. ... Qxd6 28. Bc3 wins, while if 27. ... Nc6 28. Bb6 Qd7 29. Ne7! Nxe7 30. Rc7 wins neatly. **28. Nc7 gxf3 29. Bxf3** Reshevsky concludes beautifully. **29. ... Nxf3 30. Bxg7+ Kxg7 31. Nxe8+ Qxe8 32. Rc7+** There are still traps to be avoided; if he takes the knight ...Be4 will be most annoying. **32. ... Kg8 33. Re7 Qg6** Another pretty variation is 33. ... Qc6 34. Qxf3! Qxf3 35. Rxf3 Be4 36. Rxe4 Rxf3 37. d7 Rd3 38. Re8+ and wins. **34. Qd5+ Kh8 35. Rxf3 1–0** Black lost by overstepping the time limit, but as has been pointed out, if he had had a thousand years he could not have saved himself. Annotated by Reuben Fine. (*Reshevsky–Kashdan Match 1942*, 1942)

491 Kashdan–Reshevsky [C75]

U.S. Championship, Playoff Match, round 2, 1942 *[October 10*

1. e4 e5 2. Nf3 Nc6 3. Bb5 a6 4. Ba4 d6 The Steinitz Defense Deferred. This is infrequently seen, but quite sound. **5. c3 Bd7 6. d4 Nge7** More normal is 6. ... g6 and later ...Nf6. The text makes no effort to challenge White's center. **7. Bb3** Forcing Black's reply, to prevent 8. Ng5. However, it is questionable whether White gains anything. **7. ... h6 8. Be3 Ng6 9. Nbd2 Qf6** A strong move which gives Black control of the kingside. White decides to let him have it and hustles over to the other wing. **10. Qe2 Be7 11. 0–0–0 Nf4 12. Bxf4 Qxf4 13. Kb1 Na5** Weak, as the knight runs into trouble on this square. A direct pawn advance, by 13. ... a5, or 13. ... b5, was more logical. **14. Bc2 0–0 15. Nf1** Threatening Ne3 and either Nd5 or Nf5, when the Black queen would be seriously embarrassed. White's

hold on the center is beginning to be felt. **15. ... Bb5 16. Bd3 f5**

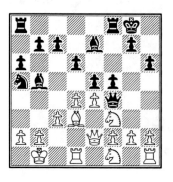

After
16. ... f5

Based on a fallacious idea, though the move is sufficient to equalize. An alternative was 16. ... Bxd3 17. Qxd3 exd4 18. cxd4 Nc6. If then 19. Ne3? Nb4 wins the e pawn. Or 19. a3 Rae8 20. Ne3? Bd8 with advantage. However, White could continue (after 18. ... Nc6) 19. g3 Qf6 20. h4 to be followed by g4 with excellent prospects. **17. dxe5** The are enough ways to go wrong: A. 17. exf5 Bxd3+ 18. Qxd3 e4 wins a piece; B. 17. Bxb5 axb5 18. exf5 Qxf5+ 19. Qc2 Qxc2 20. Kxc2 e4 followed by Rxf2+; C. 17. Ng3 Bxd3+ 18. Qxd3 fxe4 19. Qxe4 (If 19. ... Nxe4 d5 and then e4 wins) Qxe4 20. Nxe4 d5 followed by ...e4 wins. **17. ... Bxd3+ 18. Qxd3 fxe4?** But this loses. 18. ... Qxe4 was essential, leading to an even ending. **19. Qd5+ Kh8 20. Rd4** Black must have overlooked the pin, which wins at least a pawn. If 20. Qxa5 exf3 21. g3 Qf5+ 22. Ka1 b6 followed by ...Qxe5. **20. ... dxe5** This only makes matters worse. After 20. ... Nc6 21. Rxe4 Qf7, Black has no compensation for the pawn, but there would still be drawing chances. **21. Nxe5** Threatening a "family" check at g6. Inferior would be 21. Rxe4 Rfd8! 22. Rxf5 (not 22. Qxe4?? Rd1+ 23. Kc2 Qc1 mate) Rxd5, and Black is out of the woods. **21. ... Rf6 22. Rxe4** 22. Qxa5 could be played, but Black would have some chances after 22. ... c5 23. Rd5 Qxf2. Best would then be 24. Ng3 Qxg2 25. Rd7. The text leads to clearer play. **22. ... Qxf2 23. Qxa5 Rb6 24. Nd3 Qxg2 25. Ng3** Now everything is safeguarded, and the extra piece must win without much difficulty. Black has only about five minutes left on which to make his remaining twenty moves. **25. ... Bd6 26. Re2 Qc6 27. Ne5 Qe8**

28. Qd5 Threatening Nf7+ which forces the following exchange. **28. ... Bxe5 29. Qxe5 Qg6+ 30. Qf5 Qd6 31. Rhe1 Rg8 32. Re8 Qg6 33. Rxg8+ Kxg8 34. Qxg6 Rxg6 35. Re7 Rc6 36. Kc2** The king is all-important in any ending and it is never too early to get him out. Now Black has less than 30 seconds to go! **36. ... g6 37. Kd3 h5 38. Ne4 a5 39. Kd4 a4 40. Ke5 Rb6** Seizing the opportunity for counter-play. Black is putting up the best fight possible, though in a hopeless cause. **41. Rxc7 Rxb2 42. Kf6 Rb6+** Mate was threatened by 43. Rc8+ Kh7 44. Ng5+. **43. Kg5 Kf8 44. a3 Rb3 45. Kxg6 Ke8** Reshevsky just succeeded in making his 45 moves under the time limit. If 45. ... Rxa3 46. Nf6 and Rf7 mate cannot be avoided. A typical formation with rook and knight. **46. Rxb7 Rxa3 47. c4** The passed pawn, combined with the mating threats, must decide in a few moves. If 47. ... Ra1 48. c5 Rc1 49. Kf6 a3 50. Nd6+ Kd8 51. c6! (the quickest way), Rxc6 52. Ke6 and Black must give up the rook. **1–0** Annotations by Kashdan. (*Chess Review*, November 1942)

492 Reshevsky–Kashdan [D81]
U.S. Championship, Playoff Match,
round 3, 1942 *[October 17]*

1. d4 Nf6 2. c4 g6 3. Nc3 d5 4. Qb3 dxc4 5. Qxc4 Be6 6. Qd3 On 6. Qb5+, follows ...Nc6! 7. Nf3 Nd5 and if 8. Qxb7? Ncb4. If 8. Nxd5 Bxd5 9. Qxb7? Nxd4! and again if 8. e4 Ndb4 with good prospects, e.g. 9. d5 Nc2+, etc. **6. ... Bg7 7. e4** Obtaining a strong grip on the center. **7. ... c6 8. Nf3 0–0 9. Be2 Ne8! 10. 0–0 Nd6 11. Qc2** If 11. b3, in order to prevent Bc4, then Black frees his game by ...c5 12. d5 Bg4, or if 12. e5 cxd4. **11. ... Bc4 12. Bf4 Bxe2 13. Qxe2 Qb6 14. Rad1 Qa6** Black's idea is to drive White's queen off the e file, where it serves to back up the advance of the center pawns. **15. Rd3!** To maintain the queen in its present position and at the same time retain prospects for the Black rook on either wing. **15. ... Nd7** Finally, Black completes his development. However, White's position is superior. **16. e5 Nb5 17. Ng5!** Compelling the reply, and hence weakening Black's kingside pawn formation. White now threatens

18. e6, whereas e6 immediately produces no appreciable results. Thus if 17. e6 Nxc3 18. bxc3 fxe6 19. Qxe6+ Kh8 20. Re3 Rxf4 21. Qxd7 with approximate equality. **17. ... Nxc3 18. bxc3 h6 19. Ne4 c5!** Enabling the Black queen to exercise control over the third rank, where it may be needed for protection of the kingside. It also tends to reduce the force of White's center. **20. Rfd1** So that the queen is free for action. **20. ... cxd4 21. cxd4 Rac8 22. Qd2!** The action starts. **22. ... Rfd8 23. h4** 23. Bxh6, though enticing accomplishes little, Black continues with 23. ... Nxe5 24. dxe5 Rxd3 25. Qxd3 Qxd3 26. Rxd3 Bxh6 27. g3 Rc2 with even chances. **23. ... Kh7 24. h5! g5**

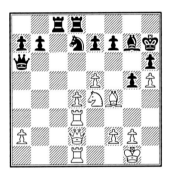

After
24. ... g5

If 24. ... gxh5 25. Qe2 Qg6 26. Rg3 Qf5 27. Ng5+! with excellent attacking chances, thus 27. ... hxg5 28. Rxg5 Qxf4? 29. Qxh5+ Kg8 30. Qh6 wins. **25. Bg3** Interesting and tempting here is the sacrifice of the bishop for two pawns. But Black appears to have adequate defenses against all of the possible threats: 25. Bxg5 hxg5 26. Nxg5+ Kg8 27. e6! Nf8! 28. exf7+ Kh8, and White has three pawns for the piece, Black's game is to be preferred. Later Reshevsky discovered 28. h6! and if then 28. ... Bxh6 29. Rh3! Bxg5 30. Qxg5+ Ng6 31. Re1 with an overwhelming position for White. **25. ... Rc4 26. f4 f5 27. Nc3 gxf4 28. Bxf4** If 28. Qxf4, either ...e6 or Qe6 suffices. **28. ... e6?** *(see diagram)*

Definitely bad as it cuts off Black's queen from the king's wing. Yet it is difficult to find an adequate continuation: 28. ... Nc5 29. dxc5 Rxd3 30. Qxd3 Rxf4 31. Qxa6 bxa6 32. Rd7! Rc4 33. Nd5 Rxc5 34. Nf6+! exf6 35. fxe6 with good winning chances. However, Fine suggests Nb6 as quite promising, although it may not be

After
28. ... e6

enough to save Black. Alekhine gives Qe6! with an eventual Nc5 as given Black at least equal chances. **29. Rg3 Nf8 30. Rxg7+ Kxg7 31. Bxh6+ Kh7 32. Qg5 Rd7 33. Bxf8 Rxc3 34. Qg6+ Kh8 35. Qe8! Rcc7** [In *Chess Life* for January 1977 it was pointed out that Black still had a resource here by playing 35. ... Rg3! Then the continuation would be 36. Be7+ Kh7 37. Qxd7 Rxg2+! 38. Kh1 Rh2+ 39. Kxh2 Qe2+ 40. Kg1 with a perpetual. And if after 37. ... Rxg2+ 38. Kxg2 Qe2+ 39. Kg3+ Qe3+ 40. Kh4 Qf4+ 41. Kh3 Qg4+ 42. Kh2 Qe2+ 43. Kg1 Qxd1+ 44. Kf2 Qd2+ also ending with a perpetual.] **36. Be7+ Kg7 37. Qf8+ Kh7 38. Qf7+ 1–0** Analysis by Reshevsky. (*Chess Review*, November 1942)

493 Kashdan–Reshevsky [C71]

U.S. Championship, Playoff Match,
round 4, 1942 *[November 15]*

1. e4 Both masters stick to their favorites. Everybody who has ever played Reshevsky knows that he is still experimenting for a good defense to e4. Formerly he used to try the French, Sicilian, Alekhine's; nowadays he sticks to e5, but has not found a fully satisfactory line against the Ruy Lopez. Psychological considerations of this kind are of the utmost value in a championship match. **1. ... e5 2. Nf3 Nc6 3. Bb5 a6 4. Ba4 d6 5. c4** In the second game he tried 5. c3, but the outcome of the opening evidently did not please him. **5. ... Bd7 6. Nc3** 6. d4 may be more accurate, since Black can now reply 6. ... Nd4. **6. ... Nf6** The fianchetto defense has often been tried here, but invariably with bad results. E.g., the famous encounter Keres–Alekhine, Margate 1937, ran 6. ... g6 7. d4 Bg7 8. Be3 Nf6 9. dxe5 dxe5 10. Bc5! Nh5

11. Nd5 Nf4 12. Nxxf4 exf4 and now 13. 0–0! is overwhelming. **7. d4 exd4 8. Nxd4 Nxd4?** Why this haste to exchange developed pieces? Indicated was 8. ... Be7, followed by 9. ... 0–0. **9. Bxd7+ Qxd7 10. Qxd4 Be7 11. 0–0 0–0** Kashdan has secured a position which is ideal for White in the Ruy Lopez; he has the definite advantage of a pawn at e4 vs. a pawn at d6, which yields his pieces more room. His plan is to increase his superiority by an attack; thus he will fianchetto his bishop, concentrate on the kingside, always taking good care to prevent the liberating d5. Black on the other hand, will try to counter the various threats by safeguarding his king and instituting a counter-advance on the queenside. In the past, games with this type of position have definitely been nullified because it was so slight. Kashdan introduces an ingenious new idea at a latter point which will surely prove to be a permanent strengthening of White's attack. **12. b3 Rfe8 13. Bb2 Bf8 14. Rad1** Nimzovitch's principle of "overprotection" (though it was certainly not consciously applied). The point is that by stopping ...d5 in so many different ways the mobility of all White's pieces is enhanced. **14. ... Re6 15. Rfe1 Rae8 16. f3**

After
16. f3

He overdefends the e pawn in order to maneuver his knight to the kingside, preferably to f5. **16. ... Kh8??** A pointless move which is rather hard to understand. Reshevsky's plan is to safeguard his king by shifting his knight to d7, then playing ...f6, after which his counter-action on the queenside can commence. Yet even for this plan (which he actually carries out) the king was better placed at g8. Perhaps he felt uncertain about what to do (yes, even grand masters are often faced with that dilemma!) and wanted to see what Kash would do. In any case, the loss of time was positionally fatal. It is an established principle that the best way to counteract a fianchettoed bishop is to fianchetto your own. Thus here the normal move for Black would have been 16. ... g6. If then 17. Nd5 Bg7 18. Nf4 Nh5 19. Qd2 Nxf4 Black has nothing to fear; likewise 17. Qa7 Qc8 18. Nd5 Bg7 19. Nxf6+ Bxf6 20. Bxf6 Rxf6 21. c5 dxc5 22. Qxc5 Rc6 is good enough for a draw. **17. Ne2 Qc8 18. Qf2 Nd7 19. Nd4 R6e7 20. Qg3 f6 21. Nf5 Re6 22. h4 b5 23. cxb5 axb5 24. h5 Qa6 25. a3 c5 26. Rd5 Ne5 27. Red1 Nf7 28. Qh4 Ne5? 29. f4 Nf7**

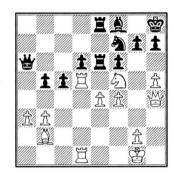

After
29. ... Nf7

On 29. ... Nd7 30. h6 g6 31. Ng3 Black's game is likewise hopeless. **30. h6 g6 31. Bxf6+ Kg8 32. Ng3 Bxh6 33. Bb2 Bg7 34. f5 Bxb2 35. fxe6 Rxe6 36. Qg4** Kashdan's play is splendid. Despite his material advantage he must be careful, for if Black were able to consolidate his position the win would be fearfully difficult, perhaps impossible. After this powerful queen move the remainder is virtually forced. If e.g. 36. ... Qc8 in reply 37. Nf5! and if 37. ... Ne5 38. Rxe5! dxe5 39. Ne7+ wins the queen, while on other moves 38. Nxd6 pulls Black's game apart at the seams. **36. ... Re8 37. Qd7 Rd8 38. Qe7 Rf8 39. Rf1 Be5 40. Rd3 Qc8 41. Rdf3 Qe8 42. Rxf7 Qxe7 43. Rxe7 Bxg3 44. Rxf8+ Kxf8 45. Rb7 c4 46. bxc4 1–0** This game is of great didactic interest. It demonstrates in a very convincing way the dangers of positions with a limited field of action (although without a weakness) and also a way to take advantage of this drawback. It was a defeat (but also a victory) that was well deserved. (*107 Great Chess Battles*)

494 Reshevsky–Kashdan [E29]
U.S. Championship, Playoff Match, round 5, 1942 *[November 29]*

1. d4 Nf6 2. c4 e6 3. Nc3 Bb4 4. a3 Bxc3+ 5. bxc3 c5 6. e3 0–0 7. Bd3 Nc6 8. Nf3 d6 9. Qc2 e5 10. d5 Ne7 11. 0–0 Kh8 12. Ne1 Ne8 13. f4! exf4 14. exf4 g6 15. Nf3 Bf5 16. Bxf5 Nxf5 17. g4 Nh6! 18. f5! Nxg4 19. h3! Ne5! 20. Nxe5 dxe5 21. Bh6 Rg8 22. f6 g5? 23. Qf5 Rg6 24. Bf8 Nd6! 25. Bg7+ Kg8 26. Qxe5

After
26. Qxe5

26. ... Qd7? 27. Rae1 h5? 28. Qe7 Qxe7 29. Rxe7 Rd8 30. Rfe1 Kh7 31. Kg2 g4 32. R1e5 gxh3+ 33. Kxh3 Rg1 34. Rxh5+ Kg6 35. Ree5 Rh1+ 36. Kg4 Ne4 37. Rxh1 Nf2+ 38. Kf4 1–0 (*Chess Review*, January 1943)

495 Kashdan–Reshevsky [C97]
U.S. Championship, Playoff Match, round 6, 1942 *[December 6]*

1. e4 e5 2. Nf3 Nc6 3. Bb5 a6 4. Ba4 Nf6 5. 0–0 Be7 Enough of experimentation. This time he reverts to an old favorite. **6. Re1 b5 7. Bb3 d6** It would be interesting to see the Marshall line, 7. ... 0–0, followed by ...d5, tried again in an important game. **8. c3 Na5 9. Bc2 c5 10. d4 Qc7** All book so far— and a book the pages of which have been fingered a million times. Kashdan now adopts a line recommended in MCO, but neglects to consider the improvements that have been found since that was published. **11. h3** This is all right, but not in conjunction with his next move. White plays a4 to force some weakness on the Black queenside: if he wishes to play it at all, he must

do so now. The reason will soon be evident. **11. ...
0–0 12. a4** Leads to more simplification at
best, which is exactly what Black wants. He
should adopt the routine build-up with Nbd2,
Nf1, g4, Ng3, etc. The move which Kashdan
adopts is given in MCO, with a continuation
from the game Keres–Reshevsky, Stockholm
1937. A year later, against me in the AVRO tournament, Reshevsky bettered his play considerably. Kashdan was apparently unaware of the
latter game. **12. ... Bd7!** Against Keres Reshevsky replied 12. ... b4 and after 13. cxb4 cxb4
14. Nbd2 the weakness of the center eventually
proved fatal. 12. ... Rb8? is bad because the exchanges win a pawn for White (this is not the
case on White's 11th move). The significance of
the text lies in the fact that Black need not relax
his threats on White's center. **13. Nbd2?** The
alternative 13. axb5 axb5 14. dxe5, or 14. d5
leaves Black with no real problems because the
open a file guarantees him counter-play. Thus
13. a4 is seen to be a pure waste of time. **13. ...
cxd4 14. cxd4 Rfc8 15. axb5 Qxc2
16. Qxc2** White prefers to exchange queens,
even though Black's rook comes strongly placed,
because the two bishops might otherwise yield
Black a strong attack. **16. ... Rxc2 17. Rxa5
Bxb5 18. Ra1** Not 18. dxe5? dxe5 19. Nxe5?
because of Bb4, winning at least the exchange.
18. ... Rac8 So that if now 19. dxe5 dxe5
20. Nxe5 Bb4 21. Nef3 22. Rxe4 Rxc1+ 23. Rxc1
Rxc1+ and the two bishops would offer excellent winning chances. **19. b3 Bf8** A fuzzy
move which dissipates Black's minute advantage. 19. ... Nd7 would keep White tied up for
awhile. If e.g. 20. Ba3? exd4 21. e5 Nxe5! etc.
with good prospects. **20. dxe5 dxe5 21. Ba3**
The opportunity White has been waiting for.
21. ... Bxa3 22. Rxa3 Rc1 This exchange
also eases White's game. 22. ... Nd7, followed
by f6, ...Nc5 was harder to meet. Reshevsky may
have been in time pressure here. **23. Rxc1
Rxc1+ 24. Kh2 Rc2 25. Ra1** To get his king
back. **25. ... Kf8 26. Kg1 Nd7** (*see diagram*)
  27. Nc4 A liquidation maneuver, to compel
a quick draw. **27. ... Bxc4** All too willing.
27. ... f6 was still more promising. **28. bxc4
Rxc4 29. Rxa6 Rxe4 30. Ra7 Ke7
31. Ng5 Rd4** He must defend either the

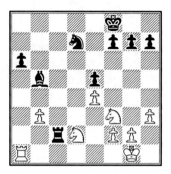

After
26. ... Nd7

g pawn or the f pawn. On 31. ... Rf4 32. Nxh7
f6 33. Nf8 draws at once. **32. Nxh7!** Nicely
calculated. **32. ... f6 33. g4 Kf7 34. g5 f5**
34. ... Kg6 would be met by 35. Rxd7+!; and
34. ... Kg8 by 35. g6. **35. Kf1 Rd6** He has no
good tempo moves. On a king move the variations above still hold. **36. g6+** Forcing the conclusion. **36. ... Rxg6** On 36. ... Kxg6 37. Rxd7!
White would suddenly come out on top.
37. Rxd7+ Kg8 38. Re7 Kxh7 Or 38. ... e4
39. Re5. **39. Rxe5** ½–½ (Fine, *Reshevsky–
Kashdan Match 1942*)

496 Reshevsky–Kashdan [E34]
U.S. Championship, Playoff Match,
round 7, 1942 *[December 13]*

  **1. d4 Nf6 2. c4 e6 3. Nc3 Bb4 4. Qc2
d5 5. cxd5 Qxd5 6. Nf3 c5 7. Bd2 Bxc3
8. Bxc3 Nc6 9. e3 0–0 10. Rd1 Qxa2!
11. dxc5 Nd5 12. Be2 Ncb4 13. Qd2 Nxc3
14. Qxc3 Nd5 15. Qd2 b6! 16. cxb6
axb6 17. 0–0 Bb7 18. Rc1 Rfc8 19. Ne5
Nf6? 20. Nc4! Qb3? 21. Qd4!**

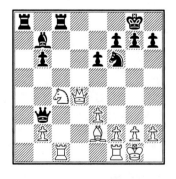

After
21. Qd4

  **21. ... Rc6 22. Nd6 Rxc1 23. Rxc1 Qd5
24. Qxd5 Bxd5 25. Rc8+ Rxc8 26. Nxc8
Kf8 27. Nxb6 Bb7 28. f3 Ke7 29. Kf2**

Ne8 30. Nc4 f6 31. Ke1 e5 32. Kd2 Nc7
33. Bd3 h6 34. Na5 Bc8 35. Bc4 Kd6
36. Kc3 Nd5+ 37. Bxd5 Kxd5 38. e4+
Ke6 39. Nc4 Ba6 40. Ne3? h5 41. Kb4
g6 42. Kc5 f5 43. b4? fxe4 44. fxe4
Bd3 45. b5 Bxe4 46. g3 Bf3 47. h3 Bh1
48. b6 Ba8 49. Nc4 Kf5 50. Kd6 h4?
51. gxh4 e4 52. Ke7 Bc6 53. Kf7 Bd5+
54. Kg7 Ba8 55. Kh6! Bc6 56. Na5 Bd5
57. b7 Bxb7 58. Nxb7 e3 59. Nc5 Ke5
60. Nd3+ Ke4 61. Ne1 Kf5 62. Kg7 e2
63. Nc2 1–0 (*Chess Review*, January 1943)

497 Kashdan–Reshevsky [C86]
U.S. Championship, Playoff Match,
round 8, 1942 *[December 15]*

1. e4 e5 2. Nf3 Nc6 3. Bb5 a6 4. Ba4
Nf6 5. 0–0 Be7 Reshevsky sticks to the defense which worked for him in the sixth game.
This Kashdan decides to vary. 6. Qe2 b5
7. Bb3 d6 The gambit with 7. ... 0–0 8. c3
d5!? is interesting; a definite appraisal of its mer-
its and demerits is not yet available. 8. a4 Bg4
9. c3 0–0 10. h3 Probably best: he controls
the bishop to stick to one side or the other. The
capture of the pawn with 10. axb5 axb5 11. Rxa8
Qxa8 12. Qxb5 is not profitable because of
12. ... Na7. 10. Rd1 is also good. 10. ... Bd7
The most usual. On 10. ... Bh5 11. g4! Bg6
12. d3 is quite strong. 11. d4 Qc8 The strength
of White's set-up is due to the fact that Black
does not have the time to get his queen knight
out of the way and hit at the White center with
c5. Black's last move is designed to get the
queen off the explosive d file and keep the
threat of Bxh3 alive. 12. Rd1 b4 Normally
Black does everything he can to avoid this weakening advance; here he has little choice. The alternative 12. ... exd4 13. cxd4 Na5 14. Bc2 c5
15. e5 is much worse. 13. cxb4 Not the most
energetic. 13. Nbd2–f1 and eventually Ne3–d5
or f5, is routine and leaves Black with many
difficult problems to solve. Another good choice
for this type of position is 13. a5! to continue
with Bc4 and pressure against the a pawn. Kashdan's move is inferior because it allows too
much simplification, which is always the goal
of the defender in a cramped position. 13. ...
exd4 14. Nxd4 Nxb4 15. Nc3 c5! He

takes immediate advantage of the opportunity
to secure counterplay. The backward d pawn is
of minor importance because will not be able to
attack it easily. 16. Nf3 16. Nf5 looks good,
but would be met by 16. ... Bxf5 17. exf5 Re8!
with adequate counterplay; for if 18. Qf3 c4,
while if 18. Qc4 d5! with a sufficiently free game
in both cases. 16. ... Be6 Again seizing the opportunity to free his game by exchanges. 17. Bc4
Bxc4 18. Qxc4 Qe6 19. Qxe6 Leads to
nothing, but he had no strong alternative. On
19. b3 Qxc4 20. bxc4 Rfe8 Black's position is
adequate largely because of his powerful knight
at b4. 19. ... fxe6 20. e5 Splits Black's pawns
again. On 20. Ng5 instead, after 20. ... e5 the
strong square d4 which would be exploited with
...Nc2–d4, effectively nullifies the weakness of
the d pawn. 20. ... dxe5 21. Nxe5 Nfd5
22. Ne4 Rfd8 23. Bg5 Bxg5 24. Nxg5
Nf4 Reshevsky, as usual defends himself in-
geniously. Active counterplay provides enough
compensation for the weakness of his scattered
pawns. 25. g3 Ne2+ 26. Kg2 Nd4

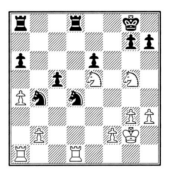

After
26. ... Nd4

27. Rac1 Looks natural yet yields nothing because Black's knights are too firmly entrenched.
There is no alternative which really means something, though with another line he would not
drift into a position which might be lost, as happens after the text. E.g. 27. Nc4 h6 28. Ne4 Nb3
29. Rb1 Rd4! with equality. 27. ... Rd5 28. Re1
After this he has no winning chances left at all,
and could very well have lost. 28. f4 was better:
28. ... Nb3 29. Rxd5 exd5 30. Rd1 retains some
slight possibilities for White, though in view of
Black's strong center pawn the game should end
in a draw. 28. ... h6 29. Ngf3 Nxf3
30. Kxf3 Rf8+ 31. Kg2 Rxe5 He is satisfied
with a draw. 31. ... Rd2 32. Nf3 Rxb2 33. Rxe6

Nd3 gives him some winning chances. **32. Rxe5 Nd3 33. Rexc5 Rxf2+ 34. Kg1 Nxc5 35. Rxc5 Rxb2 36. Rc6 a5 37. Rc5 Ra2 38. Rxa5 e5 39. Rxe5 Rxa4 ½–½** (Fine, *Reshevsky–Kashdan Match 1942*)

498 Reshevsky–Kashdan [D93]
U.S. Championship, Playoff Match,
round 9, 1942 *[December 20]*

1. d4 Nf6 2. c4 g6 3. Nc3 d5 4. Qb3 c6
In the fifth game Kashdan tried 4. ... dxc4 and drifted into a bad position, though he did not choose the strongest line. Here he reverts to a less promising, but safer, continuation—hardly good policy in view of the state of the score at the time. **5. Nf3 Bg7 6. Bf4 0–0 7. e3 dxc4** Black must either strengthen the center and prepare ...c5, or play for exchanges. 7. ... e6 is inferior in view of White's dominating bishop at f4. **8. Bxc4 Nbd7 9. 0–0 Nb6 10. Be2 Be6** Reshevsky has tried 10. ... Bf5 on several occasions with good results. Black's strategy is to compel so many exchanges that even if White eventually forces the advance e4 (inevitable in the long run) the reduced material will deprive the center pawns of their significance. **11. Qc2 Nbd5 12. Be5 Bf5** So far the game has been all book, but here Reshevsky varies, to avoid further exchanges. On the routine 13. Qb3 Qb6 equalizes. **13. Qd2 Nxc3 14. Qxc3** 14. bxc3 is by no means devoid of merit. **14. ... Ne4 15. Qb4 f6!** To get the two bishops, which might possibly give him the better of it eventually. 15. ... Bxe5 16. Nxe5 Nd6 would probably draw in the long run, but is too passive. **16. Bg3 Qd7 17. Rfd1 Kh8** Prevents d5, for if the king remains on the diagonal, d5! cxd5 could be answered by Rxd5! (Bc4). However, 17. ... Nxg3 18. hxg3 Be6 would serve the same purpose and get the queen bishop into a safer position. **18. Nd2 Nxg3 19. hxg3 Rfd8 20. Rac1 Bf8 21. Qc3 Bg4** Exchanging the better bishop. A more logical plan—though one which would involve more risk—is the preparation of an attack on the h file with ...g5, Bg6, h5, Kg7, e6 Be7 and eventually Rh8 and h4. **22. Qc4 Bxe2 23. Qxe2 e6 24. Ne4 Qf7 25. Nc5**

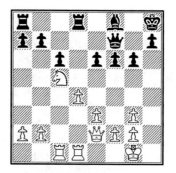

After
25. Nc5

There is not much left for either side. The minority advance on the queenside by White is useless here because of the absence of a potential Black weakness at d5. White controls a little more terrain, but exchanges will easily neutralize that. **25. ... e5** To mobilize his queenside majority. However, he cedes White an impregnable post for his knight at e4. A simpler way to maintain the equilibrium was 25. ... Bcc5. If then 26. dxc5 Qe7; if 26. Rxc5 Rd6 27. b4 Rad8 28. b5 e5, with full equality in both cases. Interesting is 25. ... Rd6; then 26. Qc4! Rad8 27. Qb3 maintaining the pressure for White. **26. dxe5 fxe5 27. b3 Rd5!** Best. If White does not exchange, Black will secure a formidable position on the d file. **28. Rxd5** And yet he might well have preferred the more complicated 28. Ne4 Rad8 29. Rc1 to continue with f3 Kf2 Rh1 and attacking possibilities. However, Black could then advance his queenside pawns and undoubtedly secure counter-chances. In view of the two point lead, Reshevsky simplifies. **28. ... cxd5 29. Nd3 Bg7 30. e4 Rd8 31. exd5 Qxd5 32. Nb2 e4 33. Nc4 Bd4**

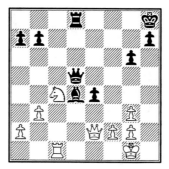

After
33. ... Bd4

After this powerful centralization the bishop is no longer out of the game and Black's prospects are about as good as White's, though he must watch his exposed king position. **34. Ne3 Qe5 35. Ng4?** 35. g4 is far better, though 35. ... Qg5 would be an adequate reply. **35. ... Qe7** Much stronger is 35. ... Qxg3 36. Qxe4 Bb6 and Black, rid of his only weakness, has all the positive chances. **36. Re1 Re8 37. Qc4 Qg7 38. Qd5 h5 39. Ne3 Bb6 40. Nc4 Qc3 41. Rxe4** If 41. Re2 e3! is no improvement. **41. ... Rxe4 42. Qxe4 Qa1+ 43. Kh2 Bxf2** The remainder is simple enough. White has perpetual check (because of the exposed Black bishop), rejects it in the hope that he may do better, drifts into an inferior position, and is finally compelled to take the draw. **44. Qe8+ Kg7 45. Qd7+ Kg8** Now Black avoids the draw. Perhaps White will exchange queens, then Black would probably win because his king can get to the center more quickly. **46. Qc8+ Kh7 47. Qd7+ Qg7 48. Qe6 Bd4 49. Nd6 b6 50. Ne4 Kh6 51. Nd6 Kh7** Black has little to say in the matter. 51. ... Qf6? 52. Qxf5 Bxf6 53. Nc8 would cost him a pawn. **52. Ne4 Kh6 53. Nd6 ½–½** (Fine, *Reshevsky–Kashdan Match 1942*)

499 Kashdan–Reshevsky [D93]
U.S. Championship, Playoff Match, round 10, 1942 *[December 24]*

1. d4 Nf6 2. c4 g6 3. Nc3 d5 4. Bf4 Bg7 5. e3 c6 6. Nf3 0–0 7. Qb3 dxc4 8. Bxc4 Nbd7 9. 0–0 Nb6 10. Be2 Be6 11. Qc2 Nbd5 12. Be5 Bf5 13. Qb3 Qb6 14. Bc4 Nxc3 15. bxc3 Ne4 16. Qa3 Bxe5 17. Nxe5 Qc7 18. Rad1 Nd6 19. Bb3 a5! 20. Qc1 a4 21. Bc2 c5 22. Bxf5 Nxf5

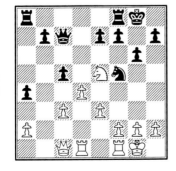

After
22. ... Nxf5

23. e4 cxd4! 24. Ng4? Nd6 25. Rxd4 Rac8 26. Ne3? Nb5 27. Rc4 Qe5 28. f4

Qe6 29. f5 Qb6 30. Rxc8 Rxc8 31. c4 Nd6 32. Kh1 Nxe4 33. Nd5 Qd6 34. fxg6 hxg6 35. Qb1 Rxc4 36. Qxb7 Nf2+ 37. Kg1 Ng4! 38. Nxe7+ Kg7 39. Qb2+ f6 0–1 (*Chess Review*, February 1943)

500 Reshevsky–Kashdan [D15]
U.S. Championship, Playoff Match, round 11, 1942 *[December 27]*

1. d4 d5 2. c4 c6 3. Nf3 Nf6 4. Nc3 dxc4 5. e3 b5 6. a4 b4 7. Na2 e6 8. Bxc4 Nbd7 9. 0–0 Bb7 10. Qe2 c5 11. Rd1 cxd4 12. Nxd4 Bc5 13. Nb3 Be7 14. a5 0–0 15. Bd2 Qb8 16. a6 Bd5 17. Bxd5 exd5! 18. Nd4 Qb6 19. Nc1 Nc5 20. Ncb3 Rfd8 21. Na5 Rdc8 22. Rdc1 Bf8 23. Nab3 Nfe4 24. Be1 Nxb3 25. Nxb3 Nc5 26. Nd4 Ne6 27. Nb3 Rc7 28. Rxc7 Nxc7 29. Qd3 Rd8 30. Qd4 Qb8 31. h3 Ne6 32. Qd3 Qe5 33. Nd4 Nxd4? 34. Qxd4 Qxd4 35. exd4 Rc8 36. Ra5 Rc2? 37. Rxd5 Rxb2 38. Rd7!

After
38. Rd7

38. ... Rb1 39. Kf1 b3 40. Rxa7 g6 41. Rb7 Ra1 42. Rxb3 Rxa6 43. Rb8 Kg7 44. Ke2 Ra2+ 45. Kd3 Ra3+ 46. Bc3 Bd6 47. Rb2 Be7 48. Kc4 Ra4+ 49. Kb5 Ra1 50. d5+ Kf8 51. Kc6 Ra8 52. Be5 Rc8+ 53. Bc7 Bf6 54. Rb8 Rxb8 55. Bxb8 Bd4 56. Bd6+ Kg7 57. Bc5 1–0 (*Chess Review*, February 1943)

501 Edward Lasker (Marshall)– Kashdan (Manhattan) [D18]
Metropolitan Chess League, 1944 *[March]*

1. d4 Nf6 2. c4 c6 3. Nc3 d5 4. Nf3 dxc4 5. a4 Bf5 6. e3 e6 7. Bxc4 Bb4

8. 0–0 0–0 9. Ne5 Nbd7 10. f4 Nb6
11. Bd3 Nbd5 12. g4 Bxd3 13. Qxd3 c5
14. Na2 a5 15. e4 Nb6 16. Nxb4 axb4
17. dxc5 Qxd3 18. Nxd3 Nxa4 19. Re1
Rfd8

After
19. ... Rfd8

20. c6! bxc6 21. Nxb4 Nc5 22. Rxa8
Rxa8 23. Nxc6 Nxg4 24. b4 Nd3 25. Rd1
Ngf2 26. Rd2 Nh3+ 27. Kg2 Nhxf4+
28. Kf3 Ra1 29. Bb2 Rb1 30. Ne5? Rxb2
31. Rxb2 Nxb2 32. Kxf4 f6 33. Nc6 Kf7
34. Ke3 e5 35. Na5 Ke6 36. Kd2 Na4
37. Nc4 Kd7 38. Kc2 Kc6 39. Kb3 Nb6
40. Na5+ Kb5 41. Nb7 g6 42. Nd6+ Kc6
43. Ne8 Nd7 44. Kc4 f5 45. exf5 gxf5
46. b5+! Kb6 47. Nd6 f4 48. Kd5 f3
49. Nc4+ Kxb5 50. Ne3 f2 51. Ke4 Kc5
52. Nf1 Kc4 53. Ne3+ Kb3 54. Kf3 Kc3
55. Kxf2 Kd3 56. Nd5??

After
56. Nd5

The decisive error according to Lasker. **56. ...
e4 57. Ke1 Kd4 58. Nf4 Ke3 59. Ng2+
Kf3 60. Kf1 Ne5 61. Nh4+ Ke3 62. Nf5+
Kd3 63. h3 e3** Threatening 64. ... e7+ fol-
lowed by ...Nf3. **64. Ng3 Nf3 65. Ne2 Kd2
66. Nf4 h5 67. Ng2 h4 68. Nf4 Ng5!**
White is in Zugzwang! **69. Ng2 e2+ 70. Kg1
Nxh3+ 71. Kh2 Ng5 0–1** Annotations by
Horowitz. (*Chess Review*, March 1944)

502 Kashdan–Platz [D36]
Manhattan Championship, 1944

**1. d4 d5 2. c4 e6 3. Nc3 Nf6 4. Bg5
Nbd7 5. cxd5 exd5** The well-known trap is
now 6. Nxd5? Nxd5! 7. Bxd8 Bb4+ 8. Qd2 and
after 8. ... Bxd2+ Black wins a piece. **6. e3 Be7
7. Bd3 0–0 8. Qc2 c6 9. Nf3 Re8 10. 0–0
Nf8 11. Rab1 Bg4 12. Ne5 Bh5 13. b4
N6d7 14. Bxe7 Qxe7 15. Nxd7 Qxd7
16. b5 Bg6 17. bxc6 Qxc6** Rather than accept the backward and weak c pawn, he plays
this which leads to the almost immediate loss of
a pawn, but then goes on to put up a magnificent fight. **18. Bxg6 Nxg6 19. Qb3 Red8
20. Rfc1 b6 21. Nb5 Qd7 22. Rc7 Qg4**
This counter attack is the only hope. **23. f3**
Giving his opponent his opportunity. leading to
an easily won game was 23. Qd1! and if Qg5
24. Qf3. **23. ... Qg5 24. f4 Qg4 25. Nxa7
Nh4 26. Rb2 Nf3+ 27. Kf2** If 27. Kh8?
Nxh2! 28. Kxh2 Qh4+ 29. Kg1 Qe1+ 30. Kh2
Rd3 winning. **27. ... Nxd4! 28. Qxb6** Not
28. exd4? Qxf4+ picking up the rook! **28. ...
Qh4+ 29. Kf1 Ne6 30. Rcc2 Qxh2
31. Nc6 Re8 32. Rd2 d4**

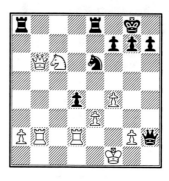

After
32. ... d4

Dr. Platz has fought superbly, but here, in severe time pressure, unfortunately brings his opponent's knight back into play. The immediate
32. ... Nxf4! would have won, for if exf4
33. Qh1+ Qg1 34. Re1+ or if 33. Ne7+ Kf8 (but
not Rxe7 34. Qb8+ Re8 35. Qxf4) **33. Nxd4
Nxf4 34. Nf3 Qh1+ 35. Ng1** A lucky horse!
**35. ... Rac8 36. Rdc2 Rcd8 37. Rd2 Rc8
38. Rdc2 Rxc2 39. Rxc2 Nd5** Black lost
on time. The game should probably have been
a draw here after 40. Qd4 Nf6 (and not Nxe3+?
41. Qxe3!) White's king is exposed—but he has

a strong passed pawn. **1–0** Annotations by Santasiere. (*American Chess Bulletin*, August 1944, p. 129.)

503 Jackson–Kashdan [C33]
Manhattan Championship, 1944

1. e4 e5 2. f4 exf4 3. Be2 d5 4. exd5 Nf6 5. c4 c6 6. d4 cxd5 7. Bxf4 Bb4+ 8. Nc3 0–0 9. Nf3 dxc4 10. 0–0 Bxc3 11. bxc3 Be6 12. Bg5 Nbd7 13. Qc2 h6 14. Bh4 Qa5 15. Bxf6 Nxf6 16. Ne5 Rac8 17. Rf3 Ng4 18. Nxg4 Bxg4 19. Rg3 Qf5 20. Qxf5 Bxf5 21. Rf1 Be4 22. Re3 f5 23. Re1 Rc7 24. Bf3 Bxf3 25. gxf3 Kf7 26. Re5 g6 27. Kf2 Rd8 28. Rb1 b6 29. a4 Re7 30. f4 Rd6 31. h4 h5 32. Ke3 Rc7 33. d5 a5 34. Kd4 Rc8 35. Re6 Rxe6 36. dxe6+ Kxe6 37. Rxb6+ Kf7 38. Rb5 Re8 Here Black overstepped the time control, though White should win anyway though not easily. **1–0** (*American Chess Bulletin*, January 1945)

504 D. Byrne–Kashdan [D70]
Manhattan Championship, 1944

1. d4 Nf6 2. c4 g6 3. f3 d5 4. cxd5 Nxd5 5. e4 Nb6 6. Be3 Bg7 7. Nc3 0–0 8. Rc1 Nc6 9. d5 Ne5 10. Bc5 Re8 11. Bxb6 axb6 12. Qc2 e6 13. Be2 exd5 14. Nxd5 Nc6 15. Bc4 b5 16. Bb3 Be6 17. Ne2 Bxd5 18. Bxd5 Nb4 19. Qb3 Nxd5 20. exd5 Qg5 21. Kf2 Rxe2+! 22. Kxe2 Re8+ 23. Kd1 Qxg2 24. Re1 Rxe1+ 25. Kxe1 Qg1+ After 26.Kd2 Bh6+ wins the rook. **0–1** (*Chess Review*, February 1945)

505 Kashdan–Pinkus [E28]
Manhattan Championship, 1944

1. d4 Nf6 2. c4 e6 3. Nc3 Bb4 4. a3 Bxc3+ 5. bxc3 0–0 6. e3 d6 7. Nf3 Nc6 8. Be2 e5 9. 0–0 Qe7 10. a4 Re8 11. Ba3 Nd7 12. Re1 a5 13. Nd2 b6 14. Rb1 Bb7 15. Bf3 Nd8 16. Bxb7 Nxb7 17. e4 Qf6 18. Nf1 Qe6 19. Ne3 Nf6 20. f3 Rad8 21. Qc2 Rd7 22. Re2 Nh5 23. Nd5 Nf4 24. Nxf4 exf4 25. Qd3 f6 26. Rbe1 Nd8 27. Bc1 g5 28. g3 fxg3 29. hxg3 Qh3

30. Rg2 Nf7 31. Be3 Rde7 32. Bf2 Qd7 33. Ra1 g4 34. f4? Rxe4 35. Rh2 f5 36. Rh5 Qe6 37. Kg2 h6 38. Rb1 Qg6 39. Rhh1 R8e6 40. Rb5 Re8 41. Rd1 ½–½ (Contributed by Larry Parr)

506 Kashdan–Shipman [B74]
Manhattan Championship, 1944

1. e4 c5 2. Nf3 d6 3. d4 cxd4 4. Nxd4 Nf6 5. Nc3 g6 6. Be2 Bg7 7. 0–0 Nc6 8. Be3 0–0 9. Nb3 Be6 10. f4 Na5 11. f5 Bc4 12. Bd3 Nxb3 13. axb3 Bxd3 14. cxd3 a6 15. Qf3 Nd7 16. d4 Rc8 17. Rad1 b5 18. Qh3 b4 19. Nd5 a5 20. Bg5 Nf6 21. fxg6 hxg6 22. Qxc8! **1–0** (*Brooklyn Daily Eagle*, December 1, 1944)

507 Kashdan–Camarena [C17]
Hollywood, round 1, 1945 *[July 28]*

1. e4 e6 2. d4 d5 3. Nc3 Bb4 4. e5 c5 5. Bd2 cxd4 6. Nb5 Bxd2+ 7. Qxd2 Nc6 8. Nf3 Nh6 9. Bd3 0–0 10. 0–0 f5 11. exf6 Ng4?

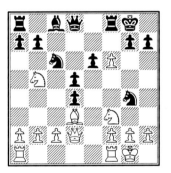

After
11. ... Ng4

Black has several good choices here according to Fritz. The most logical is Rxf6. But e5 may be the best. **12. fxg7 Rxf3? 13. gxf3 e5? 14. fxg4 Qh4 15. f3 1–0** (*Hollywood* 1945)

508 Cruz–Kashdan [C50]
Hollywood, round 2, 1945 *[July 29]*

1. e4 e5 2. Nf3 Nc6 3. Bc4 Nf6 4. d3 Cruz bypassed the various intricate lines arising from the Max Lange Attack on his fourth move when he played d3 instead of d4. He got into the Canal Variation, noted for center play. 4. ... Bc5 5. Nc3 d6 6. Bg5 h6 7. Bxf6

Qxf6 8. Nd5 Qd8 9. c3 a6 10. d4 exd4
11. Nxd4

After
11. Nxd4

Cruz left the books with the text, when exd4
was proper. Even then Kashdan could not do
much with his queenside counterplay. He forced
a passed pawn and in spite of a daring exchange
by White which left him with double isolated
pawns on the e file. Black could not make any
headway nor is it easy to see where he could
have improved his play. **11. ... 0-0 12. 0-0
Nxd4 13. cxd4 Ba7 14. Qd3 c6 15. Ne3
b5 16. Bb3 c5 17. Bd5 Rb8 18. dxc5 dxc5
19. Qc3 c4 20. a4 Bc5 21. axb5 axb5
22. b3 Qb6 23. Nc2 cxb3 24. Qxb3 b4
25. Ne3 Bxe3 26. fxe3 Be6 27. Rfd1 Rfe8
28. Rd4 Re7 29. h3 Rbe8 30. Rxb4 Qd6
31. Bxe6 Rxe6 32. Rf1 R8e7 33. Rd4 Qg3
34. Rf3 Qg6 35. Qb8+ Re8 36. Qb7
Rxe4 37. Rxe4 Rxe4 38. Qb8+ Kh7
39. Qb3 Re7 40. Qd5 Qb1+ ½-½** (*Hollywood* 1945)

509 Kashdan-W. Adams [C84]
Hollywood, round 3, 1945 *[July 30]*

**1. e4 e5 2. Nf3 Nc6 3. Bb5 a6 4. Ba4
Nf6 5. 0-0 Be7 6. d4 exd4 7. Re1** The
Strong Point Variation is one of the most popular lines in the Ruy Lopez. Here Kashdan
leaves Alekhine-Keres, Kemeri 1937, which continued 7. e5 Ne4 8. Re1 etc. which equalizes.
Even 8. ... 0-0 is satisfactory according to PCO,
p. 364. The text is a noteworthy innovation
which seemingly forces 8. ... Ne8. **7. ... 0-0
8. e5 Ne8 9. Nxd4 Nxd4 10. Qxd4 d5
11. c4** Questionable as it relieves the center
tension rapidly. White must be aware of 11. ... b5
12. Bb3 c5 and c4 (Noah's Ark trap). Instead ei-

ther Nc3 or c3 seem strong. **11. ... dxc4
12. Qxc4 Be6** 12. ... b5 is answered by Qe4.
13. Qe4 Qd5 Apparently afraid of 14. Bc2
with the disruption of his kingside, Adams hopes
to trade queens. **14. Qxd5 Bxd5 15. Nc3
Be6 16. Be3 c5 17. Red1 Nc7 18. Bd7
Rfd8 19. Bxe6 Nxe6 20. Nd5 Bf8
21. Nb6 Rxd1+ 22. Rxd1 Rd8 23. Rxd8
Nxd8 24. Kf1** White has a tangible advantage since his king can reach the center quickly.
Adams obligingly assists him by wasting time.
24. ... Nc6 25. f4 Nb4 Beginning a series
of time-wasting maneuvers which accomplish
nothing. Here 25. ... f6? 26. exf6 gxf6 27. Nd7
wins a pawn. But he might try Be7 then f6,
however White reaches the center before Black
in any event. **26. a3 Nc2 27. Ke2 Be7
28. Bf2 Na1 29. Kd3 Nb3 30. Kc4 Nd2+
31. Kd5 Nb3 32. Nc8**

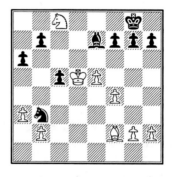

After
32. Nc8

The helpless Black king watches from the
sidelines as the pawn wins a piece. A nice ending. **32. ... Bf8 33. f5 Na5 34. e6 fxe6+
35. fxe6 Nc6 36. Bh4 1-0** (*Hollywood* 1945)

510 H. Steiner-Kashdan [D63]
Hollywood, round 4, 1945 *[July 31]*

**1. d4 Nf6 2. Nf3 e6 3. Bg5 Be7 4. c4
0-0 5. Nc3 d5 6. e3 Nbd7 7. Rc1 c6
8. a3** 8. a3 is held in low esteem even though
Fine believes it playable. The line in PCO continues: 8. ... Ne4 9. Bxe7 Qxe7 10. Bd3 Nac3
11. Rxc3 dxc4 12. Rxc4! e5. The reply 8. ... Re8
is inferior, as played in Botvinnik-Kan, 1934,
9. Bf4 h6 10. Bd3 dxc4 11. Bxc4 b5 12. Ba2.
**8. ... a6 9. Qc2 Re8 10. Bd3 dxc4
11. Bxc4 Nd5 12. Bxe7 Qxe7 13. Ne4
N5f6 14. Ba2 Nxe4 15. Qxe4 c5 16. 0-0**

cxd4 17. exd4 Qd6 18. Rfd1 Rd8 19. Qh4 Nf6 20. Ne5 b5 21. f4 Bb7 22. Rc3 Rac8 23. Rxc8 A better try was 23. Rg3 in spite of Ne4 in reply. The rook exchange gave Black control of the c file with subsequent infiltration which won a pawn easily. 23. ... Rxc8 24. f5 Rc2 25. fxe6 Rxg2+ 26. Kf1 fxe6 27. Qh3 Nd5! After 28. Qxg2 follows Ne3+ and if Kxg2 then Nf5+. 28. Qf3 White's game has hung by a thread until Black exchanges queens with good possibilities in the ending. 28. ... Qf8 29. Qxf8+ Kxf8 30. Kxg2 Ne3+ 31. Kg3 Nxd1 32. Bxe6 Nxb2 33. Nd7+ Ke7 34. Nc5 Bc6 35. d5 Be8 36. Nxa6 Nc4 37. Bf5 g6 38. Bd3 Nxa3 39. Nb4 Kd6 40. Kf4 Kc5 41. Na6+ Kxd5 42. Kg5 Kd4 White might have resigned here as a piece is lost by force. The faint hope of liquidation of the kingside pawns resulting in an ending of knight and bishop against a lone knight without pawns kept Steiner playing with dogged determination. White played the rest of the game close to the best but resourceful and accurate play by Black was too much for him. 43. Nb4 Kc3 44. Bxb5 Nxb5 45. Nd5+ Kd4 46. Nf6 Nd6 47. Nxh7 Ke5 48. h4 Ne4+ 49. Kh6 Kf5

After
49. ... Kf5

The try Nf8 fails against 50. ... g5! The rest was sheer futility! One of Kashdan's best games of the tournament and an ending worthy of careful study. 50. Kg7 Kg4 51. Nf8 Kh5 52. Kh7 Nd6 53. Kg7 Nf5+ 54. Kf6 Nxh4 55. Ne6 Ba4 56. Nf4+ Kh6 57. Nd3 Nf3 58. Nb4 Bd7 59. Nd3 g5 60. Nc5 g4 0–1 (*Hollywood* 1945)

511 Kashdan–Reshevsky [C91]
Hollywood, round 6, 1945 *[August 2]*

1. e4 e5 2. Nf3 Nc6 3. Bb5 a6 4. Ba4 Nf6 5. 0–0 Be7 6. Re1 b5 7. Bb3 d6 8. c3 0–0 9. d4 Bg4 10. d5 Na5 11. Bc2 c6 12. dxc6 Qc7 13. h3 Be6 14. Ng5 Bc8 15. Nd2 Qxc6 16. Nf1 h6 17. Nf3 Be6 18. Ng3 Nh7 19. Nf5 An aggressive move designed to stop f5 and force Black to defend. The bishop cannot be saved from exchange. 19. ... Rfe8 20. Nxe7+ Rxe7 21. Nh4 Nc4 22. Qf3 Kh8 23. Nf5 Ree8 24. h4 Rad8 25. a4 d5 26. exd5 Bxd5 27. Qg3 Qf6 28. axb5 axb5 29. b3 Nd6 30. Nxd6 Qxd6 31. Ba3 Qc7 32. Bb4 Qc6 33. Ra7 e4 34. Rc7 Qa6 35. Kh2

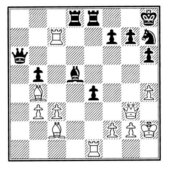

After
35. Kh2

At this point White did not know how to continue the attack. According to Fritz he could have continued with 35. c4 bxc4 36. bxc4 Bxc4 37. Bc3 Rg8 38. Rxe4 Be6 39. gxf6, etc. 35. ... Nf6 36. Be7 Rc8 37. Rxc8 Rxc8 White has made a dangerous penetration. 37. Bxg6 Qxf6 38. Bxe4 Re8 39. f3 favors White but the relentless time clock decides in favor of Reshevsky at a time when the game is far from settled across the board. 0–1 (*Hollywood* 1945)

512 Araiza–Kashdan [A29]
Hollywood, round 7, 1945 *[August 7]*

1. c4 e5 2. Nc3 Nf6 3. g3 d5 4. cxd5 Nxd5 5. Bg2 Be6 6. Nf3 Nc6 7. d3 Be7 8. 0–0 Nb6 9. Be3 0–0 10. Na4 Nd5 11. Bc5 Bd6 12. Nd2 Qe7 13. Bxd6 cxd6 14. Nc3 Nxc3 15. bxc3 f5 16. Qa4 f4 17. Rab1 Rac8 18. Rb2 Rc7 19. d4 exd4 20. cxd4 d5 21. e4 dxe4 22. Bxe4 Bh3

23. Re1 Qf6 24. Nf3 Re7 25. Bd5+ Kh8
26. Rxe7 Qxe7 27. Bxc6 bxc6 28. Qxc6
Bc8 29. g4 Bxg4 30. Qd5 Bh3 31. Rb1
h6 32. Re1 Qf6 33. Qh5 Be6 34. Ne5
Bxa2 35. Qg4 Rd8 36. Ra1 Bg8 37. Qxf4
Qxf4 38. Ng6+ Kh7 39. Nxf4 Rxd4
40. Ne2 Rd7 41. Nc3 Bc4 42. Ra5 a6
43. Rc5 Bd3 44. f3 Rd4 45. Ra5 Rc4
46. Ra3 Rb4 47. Kf2 Bc4 48. Ne4 Rb2+
49. Kg3 Rb3 50. Ra5 Be2 51. Kf2 Rb2
52. h4 Bb5+ 53. Kg3 Rc2 54. Nd6 Bf1
55. Ne4 Rc6 56. Ra1 Bb5 57. Kf4 Rc7
58. Nd6 Rd7 59. Ke5 Re7+ 60. Kd4 Rd7
61. Ke5 Re7+ 62. Kd4 Be2 63. f4 Kg6
64. Ra5 Kf6 65. Ne4+ Kf7 66. Nc5 Ra7
67. Ne4 Rd7+ 68. Ke5 Re7+ 69. Kd4
Ke8 70. f5 Kd8 71. Nc5 Ra7 72. Ne6+
Kc8 73. Rc5+ Kb8 74. Ke5 Bg4 75. Nd8
Rd7 76. Nc6+ Kb7 77. Ke6 Rd1 78. Kf7
Kb6 79. Rc4 Bxf5 80. Kxg7 h5 81. Ne5
Rg1+ 82. Kf6 Rf1 83. Kg5 Kb5 84. Rf4
Rxf4 85. Kxf4 Bh7 86. Ke3 Kb4 87. Kd4
Bf5 88. Nc6+ Kb3 89. Kc5 Kc3 90. Kb6
Kd3 91. Ne7 Be6 92. Kxa6 Ke3 93. Kb6
Kf4 94. Kc6 Kg4 95. Kd6 Bb3 96. Ke5
Kxh4 97. Kf4 Bc2 98. Nd5 Kh3 99. Ne3
Bd3 100. Kg5 h4 101. Ng2! ½–½ (*Holly-
wood* 1945)

513 Kashdan–Fine [B02]

Hollywood, round 8, 1945 [*August 5*]

1. e4 Nf6 2. e5 Nd5 3. c4 Nb6 4. d4 d6
5. exd6 Qxd6 Can it be that Fine's long association with Emanual Lasker has resulted in
a weakness for psychological moves?! The text is
demonstrably bad. 6. Nc3 6.Be3 (not 6. c5
Qe6+) Qd8 7. Bd3 g6 8. f3 Bg7 9. Nc3 0–0
10. h3 is also good as in Zubarev–Grünfeld,
Moscow 1925 (PCO). 6. ... Qd8 7. Nf3 Bg4
8. c5 He advances the pawn after all, but
under less favorable circumstances. If now 8. ...
Nd5 9. Qb3 Nxc3 (9. ... Bxf3 10. Qxb7 leads to
similar variations) 10. Qxb7 Bxf3 11. gxf3 Qxd4
(11. ... Qd5! Aidan Woodger) 12. Be3 Qd5 13. c6!
wins. Hence Fine replies carefully. 8. ... N6d7
9. h3 Bh5 10. g4 Bg6 11. Bg2 c6 12. Bf4
e6 13. 0–0 Be7 14. Qe2 A superfluous routine move. 14. b4 at one would have saved useful time. 14. ... 0–0 15. b4 Na6 16. b5 Nb4

17. bxc6 bxc6 18. Qd2 Qc8 19. Nb5 Nd5
20. Nd6 Qa6 21. Bg3 Bd8 22. Rfd1 Qa4
23. Nb7 Qa6 24. Nxd8 Kashdan jumps at
the opportunity to obtain two bishops for two
knights. However, his endgame position will be
slightly inferior because of the rapidity with
which Black can double rooks on the d file.
Consequently it would have been more prudent
to play 24. Nd6; Black would then have hardly
anything better than a draw be repetition. 24. ...
Rfxd8 25. Nh4 N7f6 26. Nxg6 hxg6
27. a4 Rd7 28. Bf1 Qc8 29. Qa5 Ne4
30. Bh2 Qd8

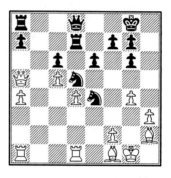

After
30. ... Qd8

31. Qxd8+ Hardly in the spirit of the position. White seems to be entirely unaware of the
danger of his d pawn, or else he is counting too
heavily on his two bishops. More aggressive and
full of possibilities where the bishops come in
to their own, would be the following sacrifice:
31. Qa6 N5c3 32. Qxc6 Nxd1 (Better is 32. ...
Rc8! according to Aidan Woodger) 33. Rxd1! a
likely continuation is 33. ... Nc3 34. Rc1 Rc8
35. Qa6 Ne4 36. f3 Rxd4 37. c6 Qf8 38. Qxc8
Qxc8 39. Rb1!! and wins. 31. ... Raxd8
32. Bg2?! Missing his last chance. 32. f3
would still have given him a chance to regroup
his pieces and hold his game together. From
now on White's position becomes steadily more
helpless in the face of Fine's pitilessly accurate
play. 32. ... Ndc3 33. Re1 Rxd4 34. Be5
Rc4 35. Bxc3 Nxc3 36. Bxc6 Rxc5
37. Bg2 Rd2 38. a5 If instead 38. Kf1 Rc4
39. Rac1 Rf4 40. f3 Nd5 and White's position
is a sorry mess. 38. ... Ne2+ 39. Kf1 Nf4
40. Rec1 Rxc1+ 41. Rxc1 Ra2 Winning still
another pawn, for if 42. Rc5?? Ra1+ forces mate.
42. Rc8+ Kh7 43. Kg1 Rxa5 White's resignation is now in order. The rest is played me-

rhodically by Fine. **44. Kh2 g5 45. Bc6 Ng6 46. Be4 f5 47. Bc2 Nf4 48. Bb3 Ra3 49. Rb8 g6 50. Rb7+ Kg8 51. f3 a5 52. Kg3 a4 53. Bc4 Rc3 54. Rb4 Rc2 55. Bf1 Nd5 56. Rb8+ Kg7 57. h4 f4+ 58. Kh3 Rf2 59. Rb7+ Kf6 60. h×g5+ K×g5 61. Bg2 a3 0–1** Analysis by Denker. (*Chess Review*, January 1946)

514 Rosetto–Kashdan [D96]
Hollywood, round 9, 1945 *[August 7]*

1. d4 Nf6 2. c4 g6 3. Nc3 d5 4. Nf3 Bg7 5. Qb3 c6 6. c×d5 N×d5 7. e4 N×c3 8. b×c3 0–0 9. Ba3 b6 10. Bc4 Ba6 11. 0–0 B×c4 12. Q×c4 Re8 13. Rfd1 Qc8 14. Ng5 e6 15. e5 Qa6 16. Qb3 c5 17. Ne4 Nc6 18. Nd6 Red8 19. f4 Rab8 20. Rd2 Bf8 21. Nb5 c4 22. Qb2 B×a3 23. N×a3 b5 24. Nc2 Ne7 25. Rf1 Qb6 26. Ne3 Nd5 27. N×d5 R×d5 28. Rf3 a5 29. a3 Qc6 30. Qc2 Rd7 31. Kf2 Rdb7 32. h3 Qd5 33. Kg3 b4 34. a×b4 a×b4 35. c×b4 R×b4 36. Rc3 Rb3 37. Kh2 R×c3 38. Q×c3 Rb3 39. Qc2 c3 40. Re2 Rb2 41. Qd3 R×e2 42. Q×e2 Q×d4 43. Kg3 Qc5 44. Qe1 c2 45. Qc1 Qc3+ 46. Kf2 Qd3 47. Ke1 Qc3+ 48. Ke2 Kf8 49. Kf2 Ke8 50. Ke2 h5 51. h4 Ke7 52. g3 Ke8 53. Kf2 Kd7 0–1 (*Hollywood* 1945)

515 Kashdan–Horowitz [D28]
Hollywood, round 10, 1945 *[August 8]*

1. d4 d5 2. c4 d×c4 3. Nf3 Nf6 4. e3 e6 5. B×c4 c5 6. 0–0 a6 7. Qe2 Nc6 8. Rd1 b5 9. d×c5 Qc7 10. Bd3 Nb4 11. a4 N×d3 12. Q×d3 b4 13. c6 Be7 But not 13. ... Q×c6?? **14. Qd8 mate! 14. Qc2 0–0 15. b3 Bd7 16. Nd4 Rac8 17. Nd2 B×c6 18. N×c6 Q×c6 19. Nc4 Ne4 20. Bb2 Nc5 21. Rac1 Rfd8 22. Bd4 f6 23. h3 Qe4 24. B×c5 Q×c2 25. R×d8+ R×d8 26. R×c2 Rd1+ 27. Kh2 B×c5 28. Kg3 Rd3 29. Rb2 Kf7 30. Kf3 e5 31. Ke2 e4 32. Nd2 f5 33. Rc2 Rd5 34. Rc4 Ke6 35. g4 g6 36. g×f5+ g×f5 37. f3 e×f3+ 38. N×f3 h6 39. Ne1 Re5 40. Nd3 R×e3+ 41. Kd2 Ba7 42. Rc6+ Kd5 43. R×a6 Ke4 44. Re6+ Kf3 45. Ne1+ Kf2 46. Nd3+** Kf3 **47. R×e3+ B×e3+ 48. Ke1 f4 49. a5 Kg3 50. Kf1 K×h3 51. N×b4 Kg3 52. Nd5 Bd4 53. Ne7 Kf3 54. Nf5 Ba7 55. b4 Ke4 56. b5 Kd5 ½–½** (*Hollywood* 1945)

516 Broderman–Kashdan [D30]
Hollywood, round 11, 1945 *[August 9]*

1. d4 Nf6 2. c4 e6 3. Nf3 d5 4. Bg5 Nbd7 5. e3 c6 6. Nbd2 Be7 7. Bd3 0–0 8. 0–0 c5 9. Rc1 b6 10. e4 d×e4 11. N×e4 c×d4 12. N×d4 Bb7 13. Ng3 h6 14. Be3 Qc8 15. Bb1 Rd8 16. Qe2 Bf8 17. a3 g6 18. Qc2 Bg7 19. f3 a6 20. Qf2 Qc7 21. Rfd1 Rac8 22. Ba2 e5 23. Nb3 Bf8 24. Nd2 a5 25. Nde4 N×e4 26. f×e4 Bc5 27. Rf1 B×e3 28. Q×e3 Qc5 29. Rc3 Nf8 30. b4 Q×e3+ 31. R×e3 a×b4 32. a×b4 Ne6 33. Ref3 Nf4 34. h4 Rd2 35. R1f2 Rcd8 36. h5 g×h5 37. c5 b×c5 38. N×h5 R×f2 39. R×f2 c×b4 40. N×f4 e×f4 41. R×f4 Rd7 42. e5 Bd5 43. B×d5 R×d5 44. R×b4 R×e5 45. Kf2 Kg7 46. Rb3 Kg6 47. Ra3 h5 48. Rb3 Re4 49. Ra3 Kg5 50. Rb3 h4 51. Ra3 Kg4 52. Rb3 Rf4+ 53. Kg1 Ra4 54. Kf2 Ra2+ 55. Kg1 f5 56. Rc3 Ra1+ 57. Kf2 Ra2+ 58. Kg1 f4 59. Rb3 Re2 60. Ra3 Re3 61. Ra8 h3 62. Rg8+ Kf5 63. Rf8+ Ke4 64. Re8+ Kd3 65. Rf8 Re4 66. g×h3 Ke2 67. Kg2 Ke3 68. Ra8 Rd4 69. Re8+ ½–½ (*Hollywood* 1945)

517 Pilnik–Kashdan [C74]
Hollywood, round 13, 1945 *[August 11]*

1. e4 e5 2. Nf3 Nc6 3. Bb5 a6 4. Ba4 d6 5. c3 Nf6 6. Qe2 Bd7 7. 0–0 g6 8. d4 Qe7 9. Bg5 Bg7 10. Nbd2 h6 11. B×f6 B×f6 12. d5 Nd8 13. B×d7+ Q×d7 14. Nc4 0–0 15. Ne3 a5 16. Ne1 b6 17. Nd3 Nb7 18. g3 Bg7 19. Kg2 f5 20. f3 h5 21. e×f5 g×f5 22. f4 e4 23. Nf2 Qf7 24. Nh3 Nc5 25. Ng5 Qg6 26. h4 a4 27. a3 Bf6 28. Nc2 Kg7 29. Rad1 Kh6 30. Nb4 Qe8 31. Rde1 Kg6 32. Qc4 Qd7 33. Re3 Rae8 34. Qe2 Re7 35. Rh1 Ree8 36. Rd1 Rh8 37. Rh1 Qc8 38. Qb5 Qb7 39. Rhe1 Re7 40. Qc4 B×g5 41. h×g5 Nb3 42. Nc6 Reh7 43. R×e4!

After
43. Rxe4

Pilnik cracks the defense with a neat rook sacrifice which forced concessions within a few moves. **43. ... Nc5 44. Re6+ Nxe6 45. Rxe6+ 1–0** (*Hollywood 1945*)

518 Kashdan–Kotov [B85]
USA–USSR Match, round 1, 1945
[September 1]

1. e4 c5 2. Nf3 d6 3. d4 cxd4 4. Nxd4 Nf6 5. Nc3 a6 6. Be2 Qc7 7. 0–0 e6 8. f4 Nc6 9. Kh1 Be7 10. Bf3 0–0 Reaching the normal position of the Scheveningen Variation. White's overall plan is: 1. to maintain control of the center; 2. To prevent d5 and any undue expansion by Black on the queen's wing; 3. to institute a vigorous advance on the kingside, beginning with g4. The measure of his success will depend on his ability to execute this. **11. Nb3** The idea of the text move is to prevent Black from enforcing ...d5, for White's queen move bears down on that square, and also to avoid the exchange of knights. The latter thought is based on White's intention to attack. For aggression generally calls for expandable force and reserve. However, the move has its drawbacks. For it enables Black to advance on the queenside. There are two alternative lines, one starting with 11. a4 and the other with 11. g4. **11. ... b5 12. Be3 Bb7 13. Qe1 Rac8** Not 13. ... Na5 (heading for c4) on account of 14. Nxa5 Qxa5 15. e5 and Black loses material. **14. Qf2 Nd7 15. Rad1 Na5** It now develops that I could not complete my plan of 16. Bc1, hold the queenside intact and presume the kingside assault. For the immediate threat of 15. ... b4 calls for a change in tactics. **16. Nxa5** 16. a3 fails not so much on account of ...Nxb3 and the consequent doubled pawns but because

of ...Nc4 17. Bc1 Nxa3. **16. ... Qxa5 17. a3 b4 18. axb4 Qxb4 19. Bc1 Nc5 20. e5** Black's queenside initiative has not only deferred White's contemplated kingside advance, it has halted it in its tracks. Now the only chance for any play is a breakthrough in the center. The positional continuation 20. Rd4 Qb6 21. Rfd1 Rfd8 leaves White without a satisfactory reply to the threat of ...Bf6 and ...Bxc3, which would unhinge support in the center. **20. ... Bxf3 21. Qxf3 Qb8 22. Qg3 dxe5 23. fxe5** The isolated pawn has compensatory advantages in that it exerts a bind on Black's position and controls important squares. **23. ... f5!**

After
23. ... f5

Fixing the isolated pawn. For on 24. fxe6ep Qxg3, Black's position is superior. **24. Rd4** The text move could almost be reached by the process of elimination. For instance, there is no point to say 24. h4–5–6, for Black counters at the proper moment with ...g6 and the White h pawn becomes a target. Nor is the overprotection of the e pawn with Rde1–e2 and Rfe1 a delightful prospect. For Black can penetrate on the d file. **24. ... Rfd8 25. Rfd1 Rxd4 26. Rxd4 Rd8** Black pares down as he rates his endgame chances superior, mainly on account of the isolated pawn. **27. Qe3 Nd7 28. Qe2 Nc5** 28. ... a5 29. Rd1 and Black can continue with ...Qxe5 on account of 30. Rxd7; nor does 29. Nxe5 lead to anything after 30. Re1. **29. Rxd8+** If 29. Qe3, repeating the position, Black might play 29. ... a5. But 29. Qd1 appears more forceful. **29. ... Qxd8 30. Be3 Qb8** Simultaneously attacking the e pawn and the b pawn. **31. Bxc5 Bxc5 32. Qxa6 Qxe5** Despite material equality Black's chances are better. He can create mating threats and his center pawns are free to advance. **33. Qe2** Hoping to ex-

change and avert the mating threats. **33. ...
Qd6 34. Qd1 Qf4 35. Ne2 Qf2 36. Nc1
Bd6** Here the game was adjourned. **37. Qe2?**
A mental aberration. But anything can happen
after 15 hours of play the previous day. Nd3 was
probably best here. **37. ... Qf4!** Threatening
the knight and mate. **38. Qxe6+** Perhaps there
is still a 50–50 chance. After all, Black has two
squares to go to and he might choose the wrong
one. **38. ... Kf8** After 39. Qc8+ Ke7 40. Qb7+
Kf6 his checks have petered out, hence White
resigns. **0–1** Annotations by Kashdan. (*Chess
Review,* December 1945)

519 Kotov–Kashdan [D93]
USA–USSR Match, round 2, 1945
[September 3]

**1. d4 Nf6 2. c4 g6 3. Nc3 d5 4. Nf3
Bg7 5. Qb3** Sharpest, White's pressure on
the d pawn prevents the liberating ...c5 for some
time to come. **5. ... c6 6. Bf4 0–0 7. e3
dxc4** A preconceived plan to give Black a measure of freedom and play for all of his forces at
the expense of relinquishing the center. Another more tedious development is 7. ... e6 followed by ...b6, the fianchetto of the queen
bishop and the eventual ...c5. This method does
not give up the center. **8. Bxc4 Nbd7 9. 0–0
Nb6 10. Be2 Be6 11. Qc2 Nbd5 12. Be5
Bf5 13. Qb3 Qb6** Thus far as in Capablanca–Flohr, Semmering 1937. This has been
appraised as equal. **14. Nd2 Qxb3 15. Nxb3
Rad8**

After
15. ... Rad8

The position is simplified, but it is a long way
to equality for Black. The strong White bishop
on the h2–b8 diagonal secures White an appre-

ciable advantage and, with help from the other
pieces, it allows him to develop a decisive of-
fensive (Kotov). **16. Na5 Bc8 17. Bf3 h5**
There is no real justification for this advance
which is the prelude to some minor tactical
threats which are easily parried. Instead 17. ...
Ne8, is a better plan. **18. h3 Nh7 19. Bh2
Ng5 20. Bd1 c5 21. Bb3 Nxc3 22. bxc3
b6** Kashdan wrongly gives up the two bishops.
Black could put up a more stubborn resistance by 22. ... Ne4 (Kotov). **23. Nc6 Rd7
24. f3 Ba6** In any event, Black's position is
difficult. But this aggravates his weakness by
permitting the following move which removes
Black's best bishop. **25. Nb8! Rxb8 26. Bxb8
Bxf1 27. Kxf1 Ne6 28. Rb1 cxd4** Black
wrongly opens the c file, however, also after
28. ... Nd8 29. Ba4 Rb7 30. Bg3, Black's position remains difficult—Kotov. **29. cxd4 Rb7
30. Bg3 b5 31. Rc1 a5 32. Rc8+ Kh7
33. Ke2 a4 34. Bxe6 fxe6 35. Rb8** Par-
ing down to a bishop ending with Black's
chronic structural weakness foreshadowing the
end. **35. ... Rxb8 36. Bxb8 b4 37. Kd3
Bh6 38. f4 g5 39. g4 hxg4 40. hxg4
gxf4 41. exf4**

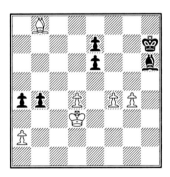

After
41. exf4

I adjourned the game here, but soon convinced myself of the futility of further resistance. This is how I reasoned about the position: Black can hold out for a while, but with no
hope of success. The winning process may be
reduced as follows: 1. White plays Kc4, winning
a pawn on the queenside; 2. White plays Be5,
reducing Black's bishop to immobility; 3. White
plays his king to d7, eventually forcing the win
of the remaining Black pawns. **1–0** Annotations by Kashdan and Kotov. (*Chess Review,* December 1945)

520 Santasiere–Kashdan [C36]
Metropolitan Championship, 1946 *[June]*

1. e4 e5 2. f4 exf4 3. Nf3 d5 4. exd5 Nf6 5. Nc3 Nxd5 6. Nxd5 Qxd5 7. d4 Nc6 In his "The Romantic King's Gambit in Games and Analysis," published in 1992 by *Chess Digest*, Santasiere gives 7. ... Be7 as better. 8. Bxf4 Bg4 9. Bxc7 Rc8 10. Bg3 Bxf3 11. Qxf3 Qe6+ 12. Qe2! Qxe2+ 13. Kxe2 Nxd4+ 14. Kd1 Nxc2 15. Bb5+ Kd8 16. Rc1 Nd4 17. Rxc8+ Kxc8 18. Bd3 Bb4 In his "Confidential Chess Lessons" James Schroeder suggests 18. ... Kd7! which threatens ...Bd6 leading to a draw after 19. Be5 Bc5 20. Bxg7 Rg8. **19. Rf1 f6 20. Kc1 Ba5 21. Kb1 Bc7 22. Rc1 Nc6 23. Bf2 Be5?** Overlooking the pin. Black needs to play either 23. ... g6 or ...Kb8. **24. Bxa7 Bxh2 25. b4 Bc7 26. Bf5+ Kd8 27. Rd1+ Ke8 28. Rd7?**

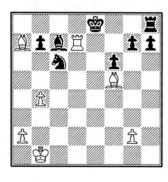

After
28. Rd7

With 28. Bd7+ Kf8 29. Bxc6 bxc6 30. Rd7 he could have won a piece. **28. ... Bd8 29. Rxb7 Nxa7 30. Rxa7 g6 31. Be6 f5 32. a4 Rf8 33. a5 Rf6 34. Bd7+ Ke7 35. Bc8+ Ke8 36. b5 Rd6 37. Ra6 Ke7 38. b6 Rd4 39. b7 Rb4+ 40. Kc2 Bc7 41. Ra8** Santasiere planned the very cute line 41. ... Kd6 42. a6 Kc6 43. a7 Rxb7 44. Bxb7+ Kxb7 45. Rc8! **1–0** (*Chess Correspondent*, September-October 1948, and *Chess Life*, August 2001)

521 Kashdan–S. Bernstein [D75]
Metropolitan Championship, 1946 *[June 29]*

1. Nf3 Nf6 2. c4 d5 3. cxd5 Nxd5 4. d4 g6 5. g3 Bg7 6. Bg2 0–0 7. 0–0 c5 8. dxc5 Na6 9. c6 bxc6 10. Nd4 Bd7 11. e4 Nf6 12. Nc3 Rb8 13. e5 Nd5

14. Qe2 Nxc3 15. bxc3 Qc8 16. Bf4 Rb6 17. Rab1 Qb7 18. Rxb6 Qxb6 19. e6 Be8 20. exf7+ Rxf7 21. Rd1 Nc5 22. Nf3 Na4 23. Be5 Nxc3 24. Bxc3 Bxc3 25. Ng5 Bf6 26. Nxf7 Bxf7 27. Qc2 c5 28. Bd5 Bd4 29. Bxf7+ Kxf7 30. Qb3+ Qxb3 31. axb3 Ke6 32. Rc1 Kd5 33. Kf1 e5 34. Ke2 a5 35. Rc4 e4 36. f3 exf3+ 37. Kxf3 h6 38. g4 Be5 39. h3 Bd6 40. Ke3 Be5 41. Kd3 Bg3 42. Re4 h5 43. gxh5 gxh5 44. Ra4 Be1 45. Rf4 1–0 (Kashdan's scoresheet)

522 Pinkus–Kashdan [C83]
Metropolitan Championship, 1946 *[June]*

1. e4 e5 2. Nf3 Nc6 3. Bb5 a6 4. Ba4 Nf6 5. 0–0 Nxe4 6. d4 b5 7. Bb3 d5 8. dxe5 Be6 9. c3 Be7 10. Nbd2 0–0 11. Re1 Nc5 12. Nd4 Nxd4 13. cxd4 Nxb3 14. Nxb3 a5 15. Qc2 Qd7 16. Bd2 Bf5 17. Nc5 Qc8 18. Qc1 c6 19. Bg5 Bxc5 20. Qxc5 Qe6 21. Re3 Rfe8 22. Rae1 Qd7 23. h3 Re6 24. Rg3 Rae8 25. Kh2 Rg6 26. Rc1 a4 27. Bf4 Rxg3 28. Bxg3 Re6 29. Qb6 h6 30. b3 axb3 31. axb3 Kh7 32. Ra1 Re8 33. Ra7 Qe6 34. Qc5 Qg6 35. f3 h5 36. Qc1 Rc8 37. b4 Be6 38. Qd2 Kg8 39. Bh4 Qf5 40. Be7 Kh7 41. Ra3 Re8 42. Bg5 Bd7 43. Ra7 Be6 44. Bf4 Rg8 ½–½ (Contributed by Larry Parr)

523 Kotov–Kashdan [E47]
USA–USSR Match, round 1, 1946
[September 13]

1. d4 Nf6 2. c4 e6 3. Nc3 Bb4 4. e3 0–0 5. Bd3 c5 6. a3 Ba5 7. Nge2 cxd4 8. exd4 d5 9. 0–0 dxc4 10. Bxc4 a6 11. Bg5 b5 12. Bd3 Bb7 13. Ne4 Nbd7 14. Rc1 h6 15. Bh4 Bc7 16. Nxf6+ Nxf6 17. Bxf6 gxf6 He must allow the doubling of the pawns, as otherwise the bishop is hanging. 18. Qd2 Kg7 19. Nf4 f5 20. Rfe1 Rc8 21. Qe3 Rg8 22. f3 Qh4 23. g3 Bxf4 24. Qxf4 Qxf4 25. gxf4 Bxf3 26. Kf2 Bd5 27. Rg1+ Kf6 28. Rxc8 Rxc8 29. Kc3 Bb7 30. h4 Bd5 31. Ke2 Be4 32. Ke3 Bxd3 33. Kxd3 a5 34. h5 b4 35. axb4

axb4 36. Ra1 Rg8 37. Kc4 Rg2 38. Rb1
Rd2 39. b3 Rf2 40. Kxb4 Rxf4

After
40. ... Rxf4

Black has a healthy extra pawn. White's only
chance of saving himself lies in his strong passed
pawn on b3, supported from behind by the rook.
White quickly brings this pawn into action.
41. Kc5! Rf3! 42. b4 Ke7 Again the best
move. The other continuation, 42. ... Rc3+
43. Kd6 f4 44. b5 Kf5 45. b6 Rc8 46. b7 Rb8
47. Kc7 Rxb7+ 48. Rxb7! entails the risk of losing for Black. **43. b5 Rc3+ 44. Kb6 f4
45. Ka7 Ra3+ 46. Kb8 f3 47. b6 Kd7
48. b7 f6 49. Rc1 e5 50. dxe5?** A mistake.
He should play 50. Rc7+! Ke6 51. Rc6+ Kf5 and
only now 52. dxe5 with a draw. The fact is that
without an exchange on e5, Black would not
have the important f6 square, which is necessary
for the winning maneuver. **50. ... fxe5
51. Rc7+ Ke6 52. Rc6+ Kf5** 52. ... Kf7! was
the correct move, with which Kashdan could
have won. Kotov gives this analysis as follows:
Black reciprocates the opponent's mistake and
does not exploit the free f6 square for a win by
52. ... Kf7! 53. Rc7+ Kf6 54. Rc6+ Kg5. On
52. ... Kf7, no good is 53. Kc7 Ra7 54. Kd6
Rxb7 55. Kxe5 Re7+! and Black wins. **53. Kc7
Ra7 54. Rxh6 e4 55. Rh8 e3 56. Rf8+
Kg4 57. h6 e2**

After
57. ... e2

Kashdan had reckoned on this position, as-
suming that he would queen first and give a
winning check with the queen on the seventh
rank. A disappointment awaited him when
White demonstrated the following study-like
draw—Kotov. **58. Re8 f2 59. h7 f1Q
60. Rg8+ Kf5**

After
60. ... Kf5

Now we can appreciate the damage done by
52. ... Kf5. Had the King moved back to f7,
Black would have been unable to execute the
maneuver whereby he places his rook in back
of the passed pawn and supports the advance of
the passed rook pawn; or if he did carry out this
maneuver, he would have lost precious time.
But, under time pressure conditions, this was
not an easy position in which to come to such
grave decision quickly. **61. Rf8+** This is the
point! It is bad for Black to move his king onto
the e file, since on this follows 62. h8(Q). With
the following move he submits to the draw, but
White still tries to play for the win—Kotov.
**61. ... Kg4 62. h8Q Qc1+ 63. Kb8 Rxb7+
64. Kxb7 Qb1+ 65. Kc7 Qc2+ 66. Kb7
Qe4+ 67. Kb6 Qe6+ 68. Kc5 Qe7+
69. Kd4 Qd6+ 70. Kc4 Qa6+ 71. Kb3**
½–½ (*Chess Review*, November 1946). Additional analysis by Kotov. (Kotov, *Grandmaster at
Work*)

524 Kashdan–Kotov [B17]
USA–USSR Match, round 2, 1946
[September 15]

1. e4 c6 2. d4 d5 3. Nc3 dxe4 4. Nxe4
Nd7 5. Nf3 Ngf6 6. Ng3 e6 7. Bd3 Be7
8. 0–0 c5 9. c3 0–0 10. Qe2 b6 11. Re1
Bb7 12. Ne5 cxd4 13. cxd4 Nd5 14. Bd2
Bb4 15. Rac1 Bxd2 16. Qxd2 N7f6 17. a3

Qd6 18. Ne4 Nxe4 19. Bxe4 Rac8 20. b4
h6 21. h4 Rxc1 22. Rxc1 Rc8 23. Rxc8+
Bxc8 24. Qc2 Qc7 25. Qc6 Qd8 26. Qa8
Qc7 27. Nc6

After
27. Nc6

27. ... Qb7? The correct move is either Kf8
or Kh8. But even then Kashdan has the advantage. **28. Ne7+!** For if 28. ... Qxe7 29. Qxc8+
Qf8 30. Bh7+! wins the queen. A witty finish.
1–0 (*Chess Review*, November 1946)

525 Kashdan–H. Steiner [E49]

New York, U.S. Championship, round 1,
1946 *[October 26]*

1. d4 Nf6 2. c4 e6 3. Nc3 Bb4 4. e3
0–0 5. Bd3 d5 6. a3 Bxc3+ 7. bxc3 c5
8. cxd5 exd5 9. Ne2 Nc6 10. 0–0 Re8
11. Ng3 b6 12. a4 Qc7 13. Re1 Bb7
14. Ba3 Ne7 15. a5 Ng6 16. a6 Bc8
17. Bb5 Rd8 18. f3 h5 19. Qd2 h4
20. Nf1 Bf5 21. Rac1 c4 22. Qf2 Bd3
23. Nd2 Rac8 24. Kh1 Kh7 25. e4 dxe4
26. Nxe4 Bxe4 27. fxe4 Ng4 28. Qg1
Nf4 29. Rc2 Rh8 30. e5 Kg8 31. Re4
Nh5 32. Rxg4 Ng3+ 33. Rxg3 hxg3
34. h3 Qd8 35. Bd6 Qh4 36. Qe3 Rh6
37. Rc1 Rh5 38. Bd7 Rd8 39. e6 fxe6
40. Bxg3 Qg5 41. Qxg5 Rxg5 42. Bxe6+
1–0 (*U.S. Championship* 1946)

526 A. Sandrin–Kashdan [B84]

New York, U.S. Championship, round 2,
1946 *[October 27]*

1. e4 c5 2. Nf3 d6 3. d4 cxd4 4. Nxd4
Nf6 5. Nc3 e6 6. Be3 a6 7. Be2 Qc7
8. 0–0 Be7 9. Qd2 0–0 10. f4 b5 11. Bf3
Bb7 12. a4 b4 13. Nce2 Nxe4 14. Qxb4

d5 15. Qe1 Nd7 16. Bxe4 dxe4 17. a5
Rab8 18. Kh1 Nf6 19. Ra4 Rfc8 20. c4
Nd7 21. b3 Nc5 22. Ra2 Nd3 23. Qg3 g6
24. Nc2 Bf6 25. Ba7 Ra8 26. Bb6 Qd7
27. Qe3 Bg7 28. Nc1 e5 29. fxe5 Nxe5
30. h3 f5 31. Nd4 Rf8 32. Nde2 h6
33. Rd2 Qf7 34. g4 Nf3 35. Rdd1 f4
36. Qc5 e3 37. Rd5 Rac8 38. Qd6 Bxd5
39. cxd5 Be5 40. Qe6 Qxe6 41. dxe6
Nd2 42. Re1 f3 43. e7 Rfe8 44. Bxe3
Ne4 45. Nd3 fxe2 46. Nxe5 Rxe7
47. Bf4 g5 **0–1** (*U.S. Championship* 1946)

527 Kashdan–Horowitz [D49]

New York, U.S. Championship, round 3,
1946 *[October 28]*

1. d4 d5 2. c4 c6 3. Nc3 Nf6 4. Nf3 e6
5. e3 Nbd7 6. Bd3 dxc4 7. Bxc4 b5
8. Bd3 a6 9. e4 c5 10. e5 cxd4 11. Nxb5
axb5 12. exf6 Qb6 13. 0–0 gxf6 14. Qe2
b4 15. Rd1 Bc5 16. a4 h5 17. Bf4 Kf8
18. Bg3 e5 19. Rdc1 Ba6 20. Qe4 Ra7
21. Bb5 Be7 22. Nh4 Nc5 23. Qe2 Nb3
24. Bxa6 Nxc1 25. Rxc1 Qxa6 26. Nf5
So if 26. ... Qxe2? then 27. Rc8+ Bd8 28. Rxc8
mate! 26. ... d3 27. Qe3 Rd7 28. Bh4 d2
29. Rd1 Qd3 30. Qxd3 Rxd3 31. Kf1 Ke8
32. Ke2 Rd5 33. Rxd2 Rxd2+ 34. Kxd2
Kd7 35. Ne3 Ke6 36. b3 Rd8+ 37. Kc2
Rd4 38. g3 Bc5 39. h3 Rd7 40. Nd1 Bd4
41. g4 hxg4 42. hxg4 Rc7+ 43. Kd2 Rd7
44. Ke2 Bc3 45. Ne3 Rd2+ **0–1** (*U.S.
Championship* 1946)

528 Pinkus–Kashdan [B17]

New York, U.S. Championship, round 4,
1946 *[October 29]*

1. e4 c6 2. d4 d5 3. Nc3 dxe4 4. Nxe4
Nd7 5. Nf3 Ngf6 6. Ng3 e6 7. Bd3 Be7
8. 0–0 0–0–0 9. Qe2 c5 10. Rd1 Qc7 11. c4
Rd8 12. b3 cxd4 13. Nxd4 Nc5 14. Bc2
b6 15. Bb2 Bb7 16. Nb5 Qc6 17. f3 a6
18. Nd4 Qc7 19. b4 Ncd7 20. a3 Nf8
21. Rac1 Bd6 22. Nf1 Bf4 23. Rb1 Rac8
24. Bb3 Ng6 25. g3 Be5 26. Rbc1 Ba8
27. c5 b5 28. Ne3 Qb7 29. Kf2 h5
30. Rd2 h4 31. Nf1 hxg3+ 32. hxg3 Qc7
33. Rcd1 Nh5 34. Nxe6 Bxg3+ 35. Kg1

fxe6 36. Bxe6+ Kh7 37. Bxc8 Rxc8
38. Rd7 Qf4 39. R1d4 Qe5 40. Re4 Qf5
41. Nxg3 Qxd7 42. Nxh5 Bxe4 43. fxe4
Qh3 44. e5 Re8 45. c6 Qf5 46. Ng3 Qg5
47. Qf3 Nf4 48. Kf1 Ne6 49. Ke1 Rf8
50. Qd3+ Qg6 51. Ne4 Rf4 52. Qh3+
Kg8 53. Nd2 Qg1+ 54. Nf1 Qf2+ 0–1
(*U.S. Championship* 1946)

529 Kashdan–Suesman [D27]
New York, U.S. Championship, round 5,
1946 *[October 30]*

1. d4 d5 2. c4 dxc4 3. e3 e6 4. Nf3
Nf6 5. Bxc4 c5 6. 0–0 a6 7. a4 Nc6
8. Qe2 Qc7 9. Nc3 Be7 10. h3 0–0
11. Rd1 Rd8 12. d5 exd5 13. Bxd5 Nb4
14. Bb3 Rxd1+ 15. Bxd1 Bd7 16. e4 Rd8
17. Bb3 Be8 18. Bg5 Nh5 19. e5 h6
20. Be3 Nd3 21. Nd5 Rxd5 22. Bxd5
Nhf4 23. Qd2 Nxd5 24. Qxd3 Nb4
25. Qe2 Bc6 26. Bf4 Bd5 27. Rc1 Bb3
28. Qd2 Qc6 29. a5 Qb5 30. Be3 Bd5
31. Ne1 Kf8 32. Nc2 Nd3? 33. Na3 1–0
(*U.S. Championship* 1946)

530 DiCamillo–Kashdan [E00]
New York, U.S. Championship, round 6,
1946 *[October 31]*

1. Nf3 Nf6 2. c4 e6 3. g3 d5 4. d4 c6
5. Nbd2 Nbd7 6. Bg2 Be7 7. 0–0 0–0
8. b3 Ne4 9. Nxe4 dxe4 10. Ne5 f5
11. Nxd7 Qxd7 12. Bf4 Rd8 13. Be5 a5
14. Qc2 a4 15. c5 Bf6 16. Rad1 axb3
17. axb3 Qf7 18. Bd6 Bd7 19. e3 Ra6
20. Ra1 Rda8 21. Qc3 Qe8 22. Rfb1 Ra2
23. Rxa2 Rxa2 24. Ra1 Qa8 25. Rxa2
Qxa2 26. Qb4 Qa7 27. Bc7 Be8 28. Qa4
Qxa4 29. bxa4 Bh5 30. Bf1 Kf7 31. Bc4
g6 32. Kf1 Ke7 33. Ke1 Kd7 34. Bb8 Bd8
35. Ba7 Ba5+ 36. Kf1 Bd1 37. Bb6 Bxb6
38. cxb6 Bxa4 39. Ke1 Bb5 40. Bb3 Kd6
41. Kd2 e5 42. dxe5+ Kxe5 43. Kc3 c5
44. Bf7 g5 45. Bg8 h6 46. Bf7 g4
47. Bg8 Kd6 48. Bf7 Bd7 49. Bb3 Bc8
50. Ba4 Be6 51. Kb2 Bd7 52. Bb3 Bb5
53. Kc3 Kc6 54. Be6 Be2 55. Bxf5 Bf3
56. h3 gxh3 57. Bxh3 Kxb6 58. Bf5 Kc6
59. Bg6 b5 60. Be8+ Kb6 61. Bg6 Ka5

62. Kb3 Kb6 63. Kc3 Kc7 64. Be8 b4+
65. Kc4 Kd6 66. Bf7 Bg4 67. Bg6 Be6+
68. Kb5 Kd5 69. Ka4 Bg4 70. Kb3 Bd1+
71. Kb2 c4 72. Bf7+ Kc5 73. Bg6 c3+
74. Kc1 Ba4 75. Bxe4 b3 76. f4 Kb4
77. Bd3 b2+ 78. Kb1 Ka3 79. f5 Bb3
0–1 (*U.S. Championship* 1946)

531 Kashdan–Isaacs [C41]
New York, U.S. Championship, round 7,
1946 *[November 1]*

1. e4 e5 2. Nf3 d6 3. d4 Nf6 4. Nc3
Nbd7 5. Bc4 Be7 6. 0–0 0–0 7. h3 c6
8. a4 Qc7 9. Ba2 h6 10. Be3 Kh7 11. Qd2
exd4 12. Bxd4 Ne5 13. Nh2 Be6 14. Bxe6
fxe6 15. f4 Nf7 16. Qe2 e5 17. fxe5 Nxe5
18. Rad1 a6 19. b3 Rae8 20. Rf2 Bd8
21. Nf1 Ng6 22. Qd3 Qa5 23. b4 Qc7
24. Ng3 Ne5 25. Qf1 g6 26. Be3 Nfd7
27. a5 Bh4 28. Nce2 Rxf2 29. Bxf2 Rf8
30. Qe1 Nc4 31. Nd4 Rf6 32. Nf3 Bxg3
33. Bxg3 Nce5 34. Nxe5 Nxe5 35. Qc3
Qe7 36. Qd4 Nf7 37. Be1 Ne5 38. c4 Qf7
39. Bc3 Re6 40. c5 dxc5 41. bxc5 Qe7
42. Kh1 g5 43. Qf2 Qf7 44. Qf5+ Qxf5
45. exf5 Re8 46. Re1 1–0 (*U.S. Championship* 1946)

532 Fink–Kashdan [B85]
New York, U.S. Championship, round 8,
1946 *[November 2]*

1. e4 c5 2. Nf3 d6 3. d4 cxd4 4. Nxd4
Nf6 5. Nc3 e6 6. Be2 a6 7. a4 Be7
8. 0–0 Nc6 9. Be3 0–0 10. f4 Qc7
11. Qe1 Bd7 12. Qg3 Rfc8 13. f5 Kh8
14. fxe6 fxe6 15. Nf3 d5 16. Qxc7 Rxc7
17. Bb6 Rcc8 18. exd5 exd5 19. Rad1
Nb4 20. Ne5 Be6 21. Bd3 Ng4 22. Nxg4
Bxg4 23. Rde1 Bf6 24. Rf4 Nxd3
25. cxd3 Bd7 26. Nxd5 Bxb2 27. Bd4
Bxd4+ 28. Rxd4 Bc6 29. Nb6 Re8
30. Rxe8+ Rxe8 31. Kf2 Rf8+ 32. Kg3
Kg8 33. Nd5 Re8 34. Nb6 Re2 35. Nd5
Kf7 36. h3 Ra2 37. Nb4 Rxg2+ 38. Kf4
Be8 39. Rc4 Ke6 40. Re4+ Kd7 41. Rd4+
Kc7 42. Nd5+ Kc6 43. Ne7+ Kb6
44. Rb4+ Ka7 45. Nc8+ Kb8 46. Nb6
Bc6 47. Ke5 a5 48. Rf4 Ka7 49. Nc4

Rg5+ 50. Rf5 Rxf5+ 51. Kxf5 Bxa4
52. Nxa5 Bd7+ 53. Ke5 Bxh3 54. d4
Kb6 55. Nc4+ Kc7 56. d5 b5 57. d6+
Kd7 58. Nb6+ Kd8 0–1 (*U.S. Championship*
1946)

533 Kashdan–Ulvestad [C82]
New York, U.S. Championship, round 9,
1946 *[November 3]*

1. e4 e5 2. Nf3 Nc6 3. Bb5 a6 4. Ba4
Nf6 5. 0–0 Nxe4 6. d4 b5 7. Bb3 d5
8. dxe5 Be6 9. c3 g6 10. Nbd2 Nc5
11. Qe2 Bg7 12. Bc2 0–0 13. Nb3 Nxb3
14. Bxb3 Re8 15. Bf4 Na5 16. Nd4 Qd7
17. Rfe1 c5 18. Nxe6 Qxe6 19. Qe3 Nxb3
20. axb3 Rac8 21. Rad1 Red8 22. h3 Rd7
23. Rd2 Bf8 24. Red1 Be7 25. Bg5 d4
26. cxd4 cxd4 27. Qf4 Bxg5 28. Qxg5
Rcd8 29. Rd3 Rd5 30. f4 Kg7 31. Kh2
h6 32. Qg3 Qf5 33. Qf3 g5 34. g3 Kh7
35. fxg5 Rxe5 36. Qxf5+ Rxf5 37. Kg2
hxg5 38. Rxd4 Re8 39. R1d2 Re3 40. b4
Rb3 41. h4 gxh4 42. Rxh4+ Kg6
43. Rd6+ f6 44. Rxa6 Rg5 45. Rf4
Rxb2+ 46. Kh3 Rf5 47. Rg4+ Kf7
48. Rh4 Rb3 49. Rb6 Rg5 50. Rg4 Rh5+
51. Kg2 Rf5 52. Rb7+ Ke6 53. Rb6+
Kf7 ½–½ (*U.S. Championship* 1946)

534 Kowalski–Kashdan [E35]
New York, U.S. Championship, round 10,
1946 *[November 4]*

1. d4 Nf6 2. c4 e6 3. Nc3 Bb4 4. Qc2
d5 5. cxd5 exd5 6. Nf3 0–0 7. e3 c6
8. Bd3 Re8 9. 0–0 Nbd7 10. a3 Bd6
11. b4 a6 12. Re1 Nf8 13. h3 Bc7 14. Bb2
Ng6 15. Rac1 Be6 16. a4 Qd6 17. b5 Nh5
18. bxa6 Nh4 19. Ne5 bxa6 20. Qe2 g6
21. Nb1 Qd8 22. Rxc6 Bxe5 23. dxe5
Bxh3 24. gxh3 Qg5+ 25. Qg4 Nf3+
26. Kh1 Qxg4 27. hxg4 Nxe1 28. Bxa6
Ng7 29. Nd2 Re6 30. Rxe6 Nxe6
31. Bb5 Rc8 32. Ba3 Rc2 33. Bb4 Nc5
34. Bxc5 Rxc5 35. Nb3 Rc2 36. Kg1
Nf3+ 37. Kg2 Nxe5 38. Nd4 Ra2
39. Kg3 Kf8 40. Nc6 Nxc6 41. Bxc6
Ke7 42. Bxd5 Rxa4 43. g5 Ra5 44. e4
Rxd5 0–1 (*U.S. Championship* 1946)

535 Kashdan–Rubinow [C18]
New York, U.S. Championship, round 11,
1946 *[November 5]*

1. e4 e6 2. d4 d5 3. Nc3 Bb4 4. e5 c5
5. a3 Bxc3+ 6. bxc3 Ne7 7. Qg4 Nf5
This and the next move set up Black's most secure defense. In time, however, White can open
lines for an attack on the kingside. Black must
look for counterplay on the other wing. **8. Nf3**

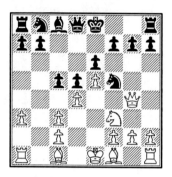

After
8. Nf3

8. ... h5 An offhand game won by the annotator continued: 8. ... cxd4 9. cxd4 Qc7 10. Bd3!
Qc3+ 11. Ke2 Qxa1 12. Bxf5 exf5 13. Qxg7 Rf8
14. Qxf8+! Kxf8 15. Bh6+ and Rxa1. **9. Qf4**
Qa5 10. Bd2 c4 11. Be2 Qa4 12. Ra2
Tying up the rook, but all White's other pieces
are ready for action on the kingside as soon as
an opening is created. **12. ... Nc6 13. Nh4**
Nce7 14. Nxf5 exf5 If Black plays 14. ...
Nxf5 White still plays 15. Qg5 g6 16. Qf6 and
eventually g4. **15. Qg5 g6 16. Qf6 Rg8**
17. h3 White will keep the king in the center
and open a file for the king's rook. Black's resources are already very limited. **17. ... Qb5**

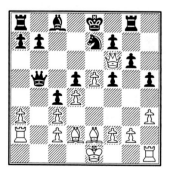

After
17. ... Qb5

Threatening ...Qb1+ and hoping for 18. 0–0
when b5 would be more difficult for White.

There is a much stronger reply, however. If instead, Black played Qc6 18. Bf3! Be6 19. Bg5 leads to a position similar to the game. **18. Bg5! Nc6 19. Kd2 Be6 20. g4 hxg4 21. hxg4 Qb6** If 21. ... fxg4 22. Rh7 threatening Bxg4! to which there is no good defense. **22. gxf5 Bxf5** 22. ... gxf5 allows 23. Bh5 threatening Qxe6+, and after 23. ... Kd7 24. Bxf7 wins. **23. Rh7** on 23. Rh8 Rxh8 24. Qxh8+ Kd7 25. Qxa8 Qb1 with some counterchances. The text move forces the issue. **23. ... Qc7** What else? If 23. ... Be6 24. Bg4! or 23. ... Rf8 24. Bh6 wins. **24. Rh8 Rxh8** He must lose material. If 24. ... Ne7 25. Qxe7 Qxe7 26. Rxh8, winding up a piece ahead. **25. Qxh8+ Kd7 26. Qxa8 Qb6 27. Ra1 Nxd4 28. Qf8** The quickest way to defeat Black's desperate efforts. **28. ... Ne6 29. Qe7+ Kc8 30. Rh1 1–0** Annotations by Kashdan. (*Chess Review*, February 1947)

536 Levin–Kashdan [E19]
New York, U.S. Championship, round 12, 1946 *[November 6]*

1. d4 Nf6 2. Nf3 e6 3. c4 b6 4. g3 Bb7 5. Bg2 Be7 6. 0–0 0–0 7. Nc3 Ne4 8. Qc2 Nxc3 9. Qxc3 Be4 10. Qe3 d5 11. Rd1 Nc6 12. Ne5 Nxe5 13. dxe5 Bxg2 14. Kxg2 Qd7 15. Qf3 Rfd8 16. Bf4 c6 17. Racl Rac8 18. h4 b5 19. c5 f6 20. Qg4 Rf8 21. b4 a5 22. a3 Rf7 23. h5 Rcf8 24. Rf1 d4 25. exf6 Rxf6 26. Bg5 Qd5+ 27. Kg1 Rxf2 28. Rxf2 Rxf2 29. Kxf2 Bxg5 30. Rg1 Be3+ 31. Kf1 Bxg1 32. Kxg1 axb4 33. axb4 Qe5 34. Qf3 Qc7 35. Kg2 Qd7 36. Qf4 Qd5+ 37. Qf3 Qd7 38. Qf4 h6 39. g4 d3 40. exd3 Qxd3 41. Qb8+ Kh7 42. Qe8 Qe4+ 43. Kg3 e5 44. Qf7 Qe3+ 45. Qf3 Qe1+ 46. Kh3 e4 ½–½ (*U.S. Championship* 1946)

537 Kashdan–Drexel [C10]
New York, U.S. Championship, round 13, 1946 *[November 7]*

1. e4 e6 2. d4 d5 3. Nc3 Nf6 4. Bg5 dxe4 Giving White control of the center. Either 4. ... Be7 or 4. ... Bb4 are preferable. 5. Nxe4 Nbd7 6. Nxf6+ Nxf6 7. Nf3 h6

8. Bh4 Be7 9. Bd3 0–0 10. Qe2 Stronger than 10. 0–0, when Black could reply 10. ... b6 and 11. ... Bb7 with reasonable development. Now 10. ... b6 will not do because of 11. Bxf6 Bxf6 12. Qe4! another point in favor of 10. Qe2 is that the possibility of castling queenside, with a direct kingside attack to follow remains open. **10. ... Qd5?** The only discernible point to this move is that 11. 0–0–0 Qxa2. But after a few simple moves, White gains still more time and soon has an overwhelming advantage in development. **11. 0–0 c5 12. c4 Qh5 13. dxc5 Qxc5 14. a3 a5 15. Ne5** Preventing ...Bd7. Black soon finds that he had no good way of developing his queenside. Incidentally, if 15. b4 Black must not exchange pawns, but 15. ... Qc7 is safe. **15. ... Rd8 16. Rad1 b6** Finally this seems playable since if 17. Bxf6 Bxf6 18. Qe4 Bb7 the mating threat no longer exists. **17. Be4!**

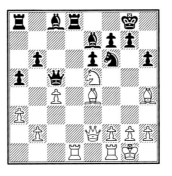

After 17. Be4

17. ... Rxd1 But something new has been added. If 17. ... Nxe4 18. Bxe7 Qxe7 19. Nc6 wins. Of course, if 17. ... Qxe5? 18. Bh7+ nets the queen. **18. Rxd1 Ra7** Now if 18. ... Nxe4 19. Qxe4 R any 20. Bxe7 Qxe7 21. Nc6 followed by 22. Rd8, either mates or wins the queen. The text also loses quickly. Best was 18. ... Ra6 19. Nc6 a4, although White would have a marked advantage after 20. Nxe7+ Qxe7 21. Bf6. **19. Nc6 Rd7 20. Rxd7 Bxd7 21. b4** The poor queen is in for a cruel buffeting which costs a piece. **21. ... axb4 22. axb4 Qd6 23. Bg3 e5 24. Bxe5 Qe6 25. Bd5** An oddly symmetrical formation; all four bishops help to surround the queen. **25. ... Qg4 26. Nxe7+ Kf8 27. Qxg4 Nxg4 28. Bd6 Ke8 29. c5 bxc5 30. bxc5 Nf6 31. Bf3 Bb5 32. c6 Ba6 33. Nf5 1–0** Annotations by Kashdan. (*Chess Review*, February 1947)

538 Kashdan–Santasiere [E43]
New York, U.S. Championship, round 14,
1946 *[November 8]*

1. d4 Nf6 2. c4 e6 3. Nc3 Bb4 4. e3
b6 5. Be2 Bb7 6. Bf3 Ne4 7. Qc2 Bxc3+
8. bxc3 f5 9. Ne2 0–0 10. 0–0 d6 11. g3
Qe7 12. Bg2 Nd7 13. f3 Ng5 14. h4 Nf7
15. Nf4 g5 16. hxg5 Nxg5 17. Kf2 Qf7
18. Nh3 Nxh3+ 19. Bxh3 Kh8 20. Rh1
Qf6 21. Bd2 Rf7 22. Bg2 Rg8 23. Rh3
Qg6 24. Rah1 f4 25. Qxg6 fxe3+
26. Bxe3 Rxg6 27. Rh6 Rxh6 28. Bxh6
Nf6 29. Bf4 Ba6 30. Bf1 Kg8 31. Ke3
Bb7 32. Rh4 Ba6 33. Bd3 d5 34. c5
Bxd3 35. Kxd3 bxc5 36. dxc5 Nd7
37. Rg4+ Rg7 38. Rxg7+ Kxg7 39. Bxc7
Nxc5+ 40. Kd4 Nb7 41. c4 dxc4
42. Kxc4 a6 43. Kd4 Kf6 44. g4 Ke7
45. Ke5 Kf7 46. Bb6 Ke7 47. Bf2 Na5
48. Bh4+ Kf7 49. Be1 Nc6+ 50. Kd6
Nd4 51. f4 Nf3 52. Bg3 Nd2 53. Kc6
Ne4 54. Be1 h6 55. a4 Nf6 56. g5 hxg5
57. fxg5 Ne4 58. Kb6 Nxg5 59. Kxa6
Ke8 60. a5 Kd7 61. Kb6 Ne4 62. a6 Nd6
63. Bg3 Nc8+ 64. Kb7 Kd8 65. Be5 Kd7
66. Bh2 Kd8 67. Kc6 Na7+ 68. Kd6 Kc8
69. Kc5 Kd7 70. Bb8 Nc8 71. Be5 Kd8
72. Kc6 Ne7+ 73. Kb7 Nc8 74. Bf4 Kd7
75. Kb8 Ne7 76. Bg5 Nc8 77. Bf6 Kc6
½–½ (*U.S. Championship* 1946)

539 Kramer–Kashdan [D19]
New York, U.S. Championship, round 15,
1946 *[November 9]*

1. Nf3 Nf6 2. c4 c6 3. d4 d5 4. Nc3
dxc4 5. a4 Bf5 6. e3 e6 7. Bxc4 Bb4
8. 0–0 0–0 9. Qe2 Ne4 10. Bd3 Nxc3
11. bxc3 Bxd3 12. Qxd3 Be7 13. a5 Qc7
14. Ba3 c5 15. Rfb1 Nd7 16. Qc4 Rab8
17. Ne1 Qxa5 18. dxc5 Qc7 19. Nd3 b6
20. c6 Bxa3 21. Rxa3 Rbc8 22. Nb4 Ne5
23. Qd4 Nxc6 24. Nxc6 Qxc6 25. Rd1
a5 26. c4 h6 27. g3 Rb8 28. Rc3 b5
29. c5 b4 30. Rc4 b3 31. Qb2 a4
32. Rg4 g6 33. Qf6 Qe8 34. Rh4 h5
35. Qf3 b2 36. Rb1 Qb5 0–1 (*U.S. Championship* 1946)

540 Kashdan–Denker [B74]
New York, U.S. Championship, round 16,
1946 *[November 10]*

1. e4 c5 2. Nf3 d6 3. d4 cxd4 4. Nxd4
Nf6 5. Nc3 g6 6. Be2 Bg7 7. 0–0 0–0
8. Be3 Nc6 9. Nb3 Be6 10. f4 Qc8 11. h3
Rd8 12. Nd4 d5 13. e5 Ne4 14. Nxc6
bxc6 15. Nxe4 dxe4 16. Qe1 f6 17. exf6
exf6 18. Rd1 f5 19. Rxd8+ Qxd8 20. b3
Bd4 21. Qf2 Bxe3 22. Qxe3 Qb6 23. Kf2
Rd8 24. Qxb6 axb6 25. Ke3 Kf7 26. a4
Ra8 27. Rd1 Ke7 ½–½ (*U.S. Championship*
1946)

541 Adams–Kashdan [B56]
New York, U.S. Championship, round 17,
1946 *[November 11]*

1. e4 c5 2. Nf3 Nc6 3. d4 cxd4
4. Nxd4 Nf6 5. Nc3 d6 6. h3 e6 7. g4
a6 8. Bg2 Qc7 9. Be3 Be7 10. Qe2 Nxd4
11. Bxd4 e5 12. Be3 Be6 13. f4 exf4
14. Bxf4 Nd7 15. 0–0–0 Ne5 16. Nd5
Bxd5 17. exd5 0–0 18. Bxe5 dxe5
19. Be4 Bg5+ 20. Kb1 Qd6 21. h4 Bf4
22. Qd3 g6 23. h5 Kg7 24. Qh3 h6
25. g5 Bxg5 26. Rdg1 f5 27. hxg6 Qxg6
28. Bf3 e4 29. Bh5 Qf6 30. Qh2 f4
31. Rxg5+ hxg5 32. Be8 Rfxe8 33. Qh7+
Kf8 34. Rh6 Qf7 35. Qh8+ Ke7 36. Qc3
Kd7 37. Qc5 Qf8 38. Qb6 Qxh6
39. Qxh6 e3 40. Qh7+ Kd6 41. Qg6+
Kxd5 42. Qxg5+ Kc6 43. Qf6+ Kd7
44. Qf7+ Re7 45. Qd5+ Kc7 46. Qc5+
Kd7 47. Qf5+ Kc6 48. Qf6+ Kd7
49. Qf5+ Ke8 50. Qg6+ Kd8 51. Qd6+
Ke8 52. Qg6+ Kd8 53. Qd6+ Rd7
54. Qf8+ Kc7 55. Qxf4+ Rd6 56. Qf7+
Rd7 57. Qf4+ Rd6 58. Qf7+ Rd7
59. Qf4+ Rd6 ½–½ (*U.S. Championship* 1946)

542 Kashdan–Rothman [C13]
New York, U.S. Championship, round 18,
1946 *[November 12]*

1. e4 e6 2. d4 d5 3. Nc3 Nf6 4. Bg5
Be7 5. e5 Nfd7 6. h4 c5 7. Bxe7 Kxe7
8. Qg4 Kf8 9. dxc5 Nc6 10. 0–0–0 b6
11. Nf3 bxc5 12. Rh3 h5 13. Qf4 Qb6

14. Bb5 Ne7 15. Ng5 Nf5 16. Bd3 g6
17. Nb5 Rb8 18. b3 Qa5 19. a4 c4
20. Bxf5 gxf5 21. Qd4 a6 22. Nd6 cxb3
23. Rxb3 Rxb3 24. cxb3 Nc5 25. b4
Nb3+ 26. Kb2 Qxa4 27. Qc3 Nc5
28. Qxc5 Qxd1 29. Nxf5+ 1–0 (*U.S.
Championship* 1946)

543 Reshevsky–Kashdan [D13]

New York, U.S. Championship, round 19,
1946 *[November 13]*

1. d4 Nf6 2. c4 c6 3. Nf3 d5 4. cxd5
cxd5 5. Nc3 e6 6. Bf4 a6 7. e3 Be7
8. Bd3 b5 9. Rc1 Bb7 10. a4 b4 11. Nb1
Nc6 12. Nbd2 0–0 13. 0–0 Nh5 14. Be5
f6 15. Ng5 Qe8 16. Bxh7+ Kh8 17. Bb1
fxe5 18. Nxe6 exd4 19. Nxf8 Bxf8
20. exd4 Nf6 21. Re1 Qh5 22. Qxh5+
Nxh5 23. Nf3 Nf6 24. Re6 Rc8 25. Bf5
Ne7 26. Rxc8 Nxc8 27. Ne5 Kg8
28. Ng6 Nd6 29. Bh3 Nc4 30. b3 Na5
31. Rb6 Kf7 32. Nxf8 Kxf8 33. Rxb4
Bc6 34. Rb6 Be8 35. Rxa6 Nxb3 36. a5
Ke7 37. Re6+ Kd8 38. a6 Kc7 39. a7
Kb7 40. Rb6+ 1–0 (*U.S. Championship* 1946)

544 Goodman–Kashdan [E35]

Metropolitan Chess League, 1946

1. d4 Nf6 2. c4 e6 3. Nc3 Bb4 4. Qc2
d5 5. cxd5 exd5 6. Bf4 6 Bg5 is inferior because of 6. ... Qd6 7. e3 Ne4 8. Bf4 Qg6. 6. ...
0–0 7. e3 Nc6 8. Bd3 Bd6 9. Bxd6
Qxd6 10. a3 a6 11. Nge2 Bg4 12. Ng3
Rae8 13. 0–0 g6 An excellent defensive move.
White can now forget about Bf5, exchanging
Black's bishop and further weakening his b
pawn. 14. h3 Bc8 15. Rac1 Re7 16. Na4
Rfe8 17. b4 Kg7 18. b5 axb5 19. Bxb5
Bd7 Not 19. ... Qxa3 20. Bxc6 bxc6 21. Nc5
and Black's queen is in trouble. 20. Qc5
20. Nc5? is answered by 20. ... Nxd4!. 20. ...
Qe6 21. Qc3 Nd8 22. Bxd7 Qxd7
23. Nc5 Qd6 24. a4 h5 25. Nd3 h4
26. Ne2 Ne4 27. Qc2 c6 28. Ne5 Qf6
29. Nf4 Ne6 30. Nfd3 Qf5 31. Qe2 f6
32. Nf3 g5 33. Nh2 Nxd4? In terrific time
pressure Black embarks on an unsound sacrifice. 34. exd4 Nc5 35. Ne5? Returning the

favor. Winning would be 35. Qxe7+! Rxe7
36. Nxc5 with a rook and two knights for the
queen. 35. ... Nb3 36. Qd3 Qxd3
37. Nxd3 Nxc1 38. Rxc1 White has two
knights for a rook and a pawn enough to win,
but the road has many pitfalls. 38. ... Re2
39. Nf3 Ra2 40. Rb1 Re7 41. Nc5 Kg6
42. Ne1? b6 43. Ncd3 Rxa4 44. Rxb6
Rxd4 45. Rxc6 Rc4 46. Rd6 Rc1 47. Kf1
Rd1 48. f4 Re3 49. Ne5+ Kg7 50. Rd7+
Kf8 51. N5f3 gxf4 52. Kf2 Ke8 53. Rh7
d4 54. Nc2 Rxf3+! 55. Kxf3 d3! 56. Ne3!
Re1 57. Nc4 f5! 58. Nd2 Rd1 59. Kxf4
Rxd2 60. Ke3 ½–½ Annotations by Goodman. The match was between the Brooklyn
Chess Club and the Manhattan Chess Club.
(*Chess Correspondent*, September 1946)

545 Hanauer (Marshall)– Kashdan (Manhattan) [A29]

Metropolitan Chess League, Board 3, 1947
[May 10]

1. c4 e5 2. Nc3 Nf6 3. g3 d5 4. cxd5
Nxd5 5. Bg2 Nb6 6. Nf3 Nc6 7. d3 Be7
8. a4 a5 9. Be3 0–0 10. Bxb6 cxb6
11. 0–0 Be6 12. Rc1 f5 13. e3 Qd7
14. Nb5 Rac8 15. Rxc6! bxc6 16. Nxe5
Qb7 17. Nxc6 Rxc6 18. Nd4 Bd7
19. Qb3+ Kh8 20. Qd5 Rfc8 21. Qf7
Rf6 22. Qxe7 Qc7 23. Qa3 Qc5 24. Qa2
Qb4 25. Ra1 f4 26. gxf4 ½–½ (Contributed by Dale Brandreth from a copy of the
scoresheet)

546 Collins–Kashdan [E48]

Metropolitan Chess League, 1947

1. d4 Nf6 2. c4 e6 3. Nc3 Bb4 4. e3
0–0 5. Bd3 d5 6. Nge2 Nc6 7. 0–0 dxc4
8. Bxc4 e5 9. d5 Ne7 10. e4 Ng6 11. f3
Bc5+ 12. Kh1 a6 13. Qd3 Nh5 14. Be3
Qd6 15. Rac1 Nhf4 16. Nxf4 Nxf4
17. Qd2 Bxe3 18. Qxe3 Bd7 19. Ne2 Ng6
20. Ng3 Ne7 21. Rfe1 Rfc8 22. Bb3 c5
23. dxc6 Nxc6 24. Bd5 Be6 25. Red1
Bxd5 26. Rxd5 Qb4 27. b3 g6 28. Rdc5
Rd8 29. h4 Qd2 30. Qxd2 Rxd2
31. R5c2 Rad8 32. Nf1 Rxc2 33. Rxc2
Rd1 34. Kg1 Ra1 35. a4 Rb1 36. Rc3 Nd4

37. Rc5 Nxb3 38. Rd5 Kg7 39. Kf2 Kf6 40. Rd6+ Ke7 41. Rb6 Nd2 42. Rxb1 Nxb1 43. Ke3 Nc3 44. a5 Kd6 45. Kd3 Nb5 46. Kc4 Nd4 47. Nd2 f6 48. g3 f5 49. exf5 gxf5 50. g4 Nc6 51. gxf5 Nxa5+ 52. Kd3 Ke7 53. Ne4 Nb3 54. Kc4 Nd4 55. f6+ Ke6 56. Ng5+ Kxf6 57. Nxh7+ Kg6 58. Ng5 Nf5 59. Ne4 Nxh4 60. Nc5 b5+ 61. Kb4 Nxf3 62. Nxa6 Nd4 63. Kc3 Kf5 64. Kd3 Kf4 65. Nc5 b4 66. Kc4 b3 67. Kc3 e4 0–1 (*American Chess Bulletin*, March-April, 1947)

547 Weinstock–Kashdan [A29]
Metropolitan Chess League, 1947

1. c4 Nf6 2. Nc3 e5 3. g3 d5 4. cxd5 Nxd5 5. Bg2 Nb6 6. Nf3 Nc6 7. d3 Be7 8. 0–0 0–0 9. Be3 Kh8 10. Rc1 f5 11. Na4 f4 12. Bc5 Bd6 13. Bxd6 cxd6 14. a3 Bg4 15. Nxb6 Qxb6 16. Qd2 d5 17. Rxc6 bxc6 18. Nxe5 Be6 19. gxf4 Rab8 20. b4 c5 21. bxc5 Qxc5 22. e4 dxe4 23. Bxe4 Qxa3 24. Qe2 Bf5 25. Qh5 Bxe4 26. dxe4 Rf6 27. f5 Rc8 28. Ng6+ Kg8 29. e5 Rfc6 30. e6 Rc1 31. e7 Rxf1+ 32. Kxf1 Qd3+ 33. Kg2 Qd5+ 0–1 (*American Chess Bulletin*, March-April, 1947)

548 Kashdan–K. Smith [C83]
Corpus Christi, U.S. Open, round 2, 1947
[August]

1. e4 e5 2. Nf3 Nc6 3. Bb5 a6 4. Ba4 Nf6 5. 0–0 Nxe4 6. d4 b5 7. Bb3 d5 8. dxe5 Be6 9. c3 Be7 10. Nbd2 White's problem is to dislodge the knight at e4 without allowing his opponent much counterplay. 10. ... 0–0 11. Bc2 Nxd2 Innocently falling in line with White's scheme. Much to be preferred is 11. ... f5, putting up a fight for his well-posted knight. If 12. exf6 e.p. Nxf6, Black has compensation in the open f file. 12. Qxd2! Stronger than 12. Bxd2 which allows d4 in reply. 12. ... Na5 Black is daydreaming. Better is 12. ... f6 and if 13. Qd3 f5 to ease his burden on the kingside. 13. Qd3 g6 14. Bh6 (*see diagram*)
Also powerful is 14. Nd4! A game between

After
14. Bh6

Broadbent and van Doesburgh (England–Holland match, 1938) continued 14. ... c5 15. Nxe6 fxe6 16. h4 Bxh4 17. Qh3 Kg7 18. g3 Bg5 19. f4 Bh6 20. Rf2 Bxf4 21. Bxf4 1–0. 14. ... Re8 15. Nd4 Bf8 16. Bxf8 Rxf8 17. f4 c5 18. Nxe6 fxe6 19. Qg3! Having in mind 20. Bxg6 hxg6 21. Qxg6+ Kh8 22. Rf3 followed by mate. 19. ... Qe7 Ra7 offers a better defense. 20. Rf3! Renewing the menace of 21. Bxg6! hxg6 22. Qxg6+ Qg7 23. Qxe6+ winning. 20. ... Rf7 Had Black played 19. ... Ra2, he could parry the threat without recourse to this awkward move. 21. h4 Kf8 Black is floundering. 21. ... Rg7 presents White with more problems. 22. Qg4 Nc6 Now it is too late for 22. ... Rg7 for then 23. h5 gxh5 24. Qxh5 and f5 is irresistible. 23. h5 gxh5 24. Qxh5 d4

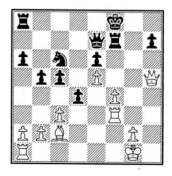

After
24. ... d4

Clearly patient defense is not Black's dish. Proper is 24. ... Kg8 to circumvent the potential threat on the back rank. The text allows a precise and pretty finish. 25. Bg6! Rg7 The rook must abandon its protection of the file. Obviously if 25. ... hxg6?? 26. Qh8 mate! 26. Be4! The bishop would not have this tempo move but for Black's impetuous ...d4 move. 26. ... Rc8 27. f5 Nxe5 If 27. ... exf5 28. Qxf5+ drops the rook at c8. 28. f6 Nxf3+

29. Qxf3 For White wins a piece. **1–0** (*Chess Review*, December 1947)

549 Aleman–Kashdan [B84]

Corpus Christi, U.S. Open, round 4, 1947
[August]

1. e4 c5 2. Nf3 d6 3. Nc3 Nf6 4. d4 cxd4 5. Nxd4 e6 6. Be2 a6 7. Bg5 Be7 8. 0–0 Qc7 9. a4 0–0 10. Qd2 Nc6 11. Nb3 b6 12. Qe3 Bb7 13. Qg3 Kh8 14. Rad1 Rfd8 15. Be3 Nb4 16. Bd3 Nxd3 17. cxd3 Bc6 18. Nd4 Be8 19. f4 Qb7 20. Qf3 b5 21. axb5 axb5 22. g4 b4 23. Nce2 e5 24. fxe5 dxe5 25. Nf5 Bf8 26. Bg5 Ra6 27. h4 Rc8 28. h5 Ng8 29. Kh1 Rc2 30. Bc1 Ba4 31. Rd2 Qd7 32. Rfd1 Rxd2 33. Rxd2 Rc6 34. b3 Bxb3 35. d4 Bc4 36. Bb2 f6 37. d5 Ra6 38. g5 b3 39. h6 g6 40. Ne3 Bxe2 41. Rxe2 Ba3 42. gxf6 Nxh6 43. Bxe5 Nf7 44. Bc3 Qc7 45. Ng4 b2 46. Re1 Bb4 47. Bxb4 Ra1 48. Qb3 Qc1 49. Kg2 b1Q 50. Qxb1 Qxb1 51. Rxb1 Rxb1 52. Bc3 Kg8 53. Kf2 h5 54. Ne5 Rb3 55. Bd4 Nxe5 56. Bxe5 Kf7 57. Ba1 Ra3 58. Bd4 Rd3 59. Ba1 h4 **0–1** (*American Chess Bulletin*, September-October 1947)

550 Kashdan–Yanofsky [C13]

Corpus Christi, U.S. Open, round 7, 1947
[August]

1. e4 e6 2. d4 d5 3. Nc3 Nf6 4. Bg5 Be7 5. e5 Nfd7 6. h4 c5 7. Bxe7 Kxe7 8. Qg4 A variation of the Alekhine–Chatard Attack. 8. f4, maintaining a strong center is the book move. The text move aims to capitalize on Black's early move of the king. **8. ... Kf8 9. dxc5 Nxe5 10. Qg3** White has deliberately rid himself of the center pawns to open lines for attack. **10. ... Ned7 11. 0–0–0 Nc6 12. f4 Ne7** The attempt to bolster the king position results in loss of time. 12. ... Nxc5 is correct. If then 13. f5 Qf6 14. fxe6 Bxe6, Black's development is advanced and he can institute a strong counter attack against the White king. **13. h5 Nxc5 14. h6 g6 15. Nf3 a6** Again, Black's timing is faulty. 15. ... Bd7, followed by Rc8, institutes a powerful counter. **16. Qf2 Nd7**

Black's vacillating policy hinders his chances. **17. Qd4 f6 18. g4 Qb6 19. Re1** White can afford to exchange queens. For after 19. ... Qxd4 20. Nxd4, he must recover the pawn with superior prospects. **19. ... Nc6 20. Qd2 Nc5 21. Kb1** To prevent 21. ... d4 22. Nxd4 Nxd4 23. Qxd4 Nb3+ winning the queen. **21. ... Kf7**

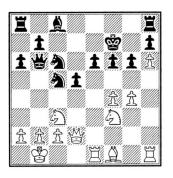

After
21. ... Kf7

There is no good defense against the threats of f5 and g5 which would perforate Black's king position. **22. f5! Ne7 23. Qd4 gxf5** Not 23. ... e5 24. Rxe5 fxe5 25. Nxe5+ Ke8 26. Nc4 dxc4 27. Qxh8+ followed by Bxc4, with excellent chances for the sacrificed piece. **24. gxf5 Nxf5 25. Qg4 Rg8 26. Qh5+ Rg6 27. Rg1 d4** It is unwise for Black to open the position until he has use of all his forces. Under the circumstances, 27. ... Bd7 is better. **28. Nd1 Bd7 29. Bc4** Made possible by Black's 27th move. **29. ... Bb5** This loses but it is doubtful that the position could be held. **30. Qxf5 Bxc4 31. Ne5+ Ke8 32. Nxc4 Qb4** If 32. ... Rxg1 33. Qh5+ Ke7 34. Nxb6 Rxe1 35. Nxa8 and wins. **33. Rxg6 Qxe1 34. Rg8+ Kd7 35. Rg7+ Kc6 36. Qf3+** Now that the knight is guarded and White is a piece to the good, Black's continued effort is futile. **36. ... Kb5 37. b3 Rb8 38. Kb2 a5 39. Qf4 e5 40. Qxf6** If 40. ... Qxd1 41. Qxb6 mate! **1–0** Annotations by Horowitz. (*Chess Review*, November 1947)

551 Ulvestad–Kashdan [A50]

Corpus Christi, U.S. Open, round 8, 1947
[August]

1. d4 Nf6 2. c4 c6 3. Bf4 d5 4. e3 e6 5. a3 Bd6 6. c5 Bc7 7. Nf3 Nbd7 8. b4 0–0 9. Bd3 Re8 10. Nbd2 e5 11. dxe5

Nxe5 12. Nxe5 Bxe5 13. Bxe5 Rxe5
14. Nb3 Qc7 15. Be2 Bd7 16. 0–0 Rae8
17. Nd4 Rg5 18. Re1 Re4 19. g3 Bh3
20. Ra2 h5 21. Nf3 Rg6 22. Bd3 Bg4
23. Be2 h4 24. Nd2 hxg3 25. hxg3
Rxe3! 26. Nf1 Rxe2 27. Raxe2 Ne4
28. Qd3 Bxe2 29. Rxe2 Re6 30. Nh2
Qe7 31. Re3 Ng5 32. Ng4 Rxe3 33. Nxe3
Nf3+ 34. Kf1 Qe5 35. Nc2 Ng5 36. Nd4
Ne6 37. Nxe6 Qxe6 38. f3 Qh3+ 39. Ke2
Qxg3 40. Qf5 Qc7 41. Kd3 g6 42. Qf6
Qd7 43. Kd4 Qf5 44. Qd6 Qxf3
45. Qb8+ Kg7 46. Qxb7 Qe4+ 47. Kc3
d4+ 48. Kb3 Qd5+ 0–1 (*Chess Life*, September 20, 1947) In the ninth round Santasiere
with Black answered with the Alekhine's Defense.
The game was drawn in 23 moves. The game is
not available.

552 Whitaker–Kashdan [C68]

Corpus Christi, U.S. Open, round 11, 1947
[*August*]

1. e4 e5 2. Nf3 Nc6 3. Bb5 a6 4. Bxc6
dxc6 5. Nc3 Bc5 6. 0–0 Qe7 7. d4 exd4
8. Nxd4 Bd7 9. Nf5 Qf8 10. Qf3 0–0–0
11. a3 g6 12. Ne3 f5 13. exf5 gxf5 14. Ne2
Ne7 15. b4 Bd6 16. Nc4 Ng6 17. Nxd6+
Qxd6 18. Bf4 Nxf4 19. Nxf4 Kb8
20. Rad1 Qf6 21. g3 Bc8 22. c4 Rxd1
23. Rxd1 Rd8 24. Rxd8 Qxd8 25. Qd3
Qf6 26. Qe3 b6 27. c5 Kb7 28. Kg2 Qf7
29. h4 Qc4 30. cxb6 cxb6 31. Qe7+ Kb8
32. Qxh7 Qe4+ 33. Kh2 Qf3 34. Nh3
c5 35. Qh6 cxb4 36. axb4 Ka7 37. Qf4
Qd1 38. Ng1 Bb7 39. Qxf5 Qf1 40. f3
Qf2+ 41. Kh1 Qxg3 42. Qf6 Qg4 43. Qe7
Qf5 44. Kh2 a5 45. bxa5 bxa5 46. Kg3
a4 47. Qe3+ Ka6 48. Ne2 Bc8 49. Qh6+
Ka7 50. Nd4 Qh3+ 51. Kf2? This loses a
piece. 51. ... Qh2+ 52. Ke3 Qe5+ 53. Kd3
Ba6+ 54. Kc3 Qc5+ 55. Kb2 Qxd4+
56. Ka3 Bb5 57. Qh7+ Kb6 58. Qc2
Qxh4 59. Qe4 Qf6 60. Qe3+ Ka6 61. Qc1
Qd6+ 62. Ka2 Qd5+ 63. Ka1 Qd4+
64. Qb2 Qc5 65. Qf6+ Bc6 66. f4 a3
67. Qe5 And Black mates in three moves with
67. ... Qc1+ 68. Ka2 Bd5+ 69. Qxd5 Qb2 mate.
0–1 (*Chess Life*, December 5, 1947)

553 Kashdan–Wade [D19]

Corpus Christi, U.S. Open, round 13, 1947
[*August*]

1. d4 d5 2. c4 c6 3. Nc3 Nf6 4. Nf3
dxc4 5. a4 Bf5 6. e3 e6 7. Bxc4 Bb4
8. 0–0 0–0 9. Qe2 Bg4 A parting of the
ways, 9. ... Ne4 is also frequently played here.
10. h3 Bh5 11. Rd1 Nbd7 12. e4 Qe7
13. g4 Bg6 14. Bg5 Up to this point everything is well explored territory. 14. e5 Nd5
15. Ne4 has been tried here, giving White a
strong attack which, however, is not without
risks. Kashdan's simple development move,
which retains the tension in the center, seems
very good. 14. ... h6 15. Bh4 e5 16. d5
Rad8 17. Nd2 What to do? White's kingside
attack can hardly make headway. So he prepares
for queenside action but first wisely over-pro-
tects the e pawn. 17. ... Rfe8 18. a5 Nf8
19. a6 Bxc3 Black suddenly finds the queenside embarrassingly weak, White threatens
20. Bxf6 gxf6 21. axb7 Qxb7 22. dxc6 Qxc6
23. Bb5. Part of Black's problem is that he never
got his full share of the center, in fact it may
well be that 9. ... Bg4 is theoretically inadequate
for that very reason. 20. bxc3 N8h7 This
loses material. But no better is 20. ... Rb8
21. axb7 Qxb7 22. Bxf6 gxf6, etc. There is no adequate defense. The text at least gives Black
some tactical chances. 21. axb7 Qxb7
22. dxc6 Qxc6 23. Bb5 Qxc3 24. Bxe8
Rxd2!

After
24. ... Rxd2

The sacrifice is the only thing that keeps Black
alive. In fact it nearly turns the tide. White
wisely elects to return some material to regain
the initiative. 25. Qxd2 Qxh3 26. Qe3
Qxh4 27. Rd8 Nxe4 This allows White to

finish artistically. But there was no salvation anyway. **28. Bxf7+ Kxf7 29. Rxa7+ Kf6 30. Ra6+ Ke7 31. Qa7+! Kxd8 32. Qb8+ Ke7 33. Qxe5+ Kd7 34. Qxg7+ 1–0** Annotations by Marchand. (*Chess Life*, November 5, 1947)

554 Najdorf–Kashdan [D19]
New York–La Plata Match, 1947 *[November 2]*

1. d4 Nf6 2. c4 c6 3. Nf3 d5 4. Nc3 dxc4 5. a4 Bf5 6. e3 e6 7. Bxc4 Bb4 8. 0–0 0–0 9. Qe2 Ne4 10. Bd3 Nxc3?! 11. bxc3 Bxc3 12. Bxf5! exf5 The rook cannot be captured because of 13. Bc2 with the threats of Qd3 and Ba3 insure gain of material. **13. Rb1 Qc8 14. Ba3 Rd8 15. Ng5! Qd7** It is essential to guard against f7 with the threats of Qc4 and Qh5. **16. Qh5! h6 17. Nf3 b6 18. Rfc1 Ba5** The unlucky bishop retires but too late to save the game. **19. Nh4 f4 20. Nf5!**

After
20. Nf5

The best move of the game. **20. ... Re8** Necessary to prevent Ne7+ **21. Qg4 f6 22. Qxf4 Na6 23. Qg4 Kh7 24. Rxc6 Rac8 25. Rd6 Qf7 26. Nxg7!** Black's game crumbles like an ancient ruin. The knight cannot be captured because Rd7 would win the queen. The rest is technique. **26. ... Red8 27. Nh5 f5 28. Qh4 Rxd6 29. Bxd6 Bb4 30. Nf6+ Kg7 31. Be5 Bf8 32. h3 Qg6 33. a5 f4 34. Ne4+ Kh7 35. Qxf4 1–0** Annotations by Marchand. (*Chess Life*, December 5, 1947)

555 Kashdan–Jenkins [B70]
Baltimore, U.S. Open, round 1, 1948 *[July 5]*

1. e4 c5 2. Nf3 d6 3. d4 cxd4 4. Nxd4 Nf6 5. Nc3 g6 6. Be2 Bg7 7. 0–0 0–0 8. Nb3 Nc6 9. f4 Bd7 10. Kh1 a6 11. Bf3

Qc7 12. Be3 Rac8 13. g4 e6 14. Qd2 Rfd8 15. Qf2 Qb8 16. Bb6 Rf8 17. Rad1 Ne8 18. e5 d5 19. Nc5 Rc7 20. Bxc7 Qxc7 21. Bxd5 Bc8 22. Bg2 Qb6 23. Nd7 Qxf2 24. Rxf2 Bxd7 25. Rxd7 f5 26. g5 h6 27. Rxb7 Nd8 28. Rd7 Nf7 29. h4 hxg5 30. hxg5 Bh8 31. Nd5 Bg7 32. Ne7+ Kh7 33. Bb7 Bh8 34. Rh2+ Kg7 35. c4 1–0 (*U.S. Open* 1948)

556 Nash–Kashdan [C81]
Baltimore, U.S. Open, round 2, 1948 *[July]*

1. e4 e5 2. Nf3 Nc6 3. Bb5 a6 4. Ba4 Nf6 5. 0–0 Nxe4 6. d4 b5 7. Bb3 d5 8. dxe5 Be6 9. Qe2 Be7 10. Rd1 0–0 11. c4 bxc4 12. Bxc4 Bc5 13. Be3 Bxe3 14. Qxe3 Qb8 15. Bb3 Na5 16. Nbd2 Nxd2 17. Rxd2 Nxb3 18. axb3 Qb7 19. Rc2 Rfc8 20. Rc5 c6 21. Rac1 a5 22. Nd4 Bd7 23. Qc3 Ra6 24. Ra1 Rca8 25. Raxa5 Rxa5 26. Rxa5 c5 27. Nf3 d4 28. Rxa8+ Qxa8 29. Qc1 h6 30. h3 Bc6 31. Qxc5 Bxf3 32. gxf3 d3 33. Kg2? Qd8 34. Qc1 d2 35. Qd1 Qd3 36. b4 Kf8 37. b5 Ke8 38. b6 Kd8 39. f4 g6 40. h4 h5 41. f5 gxf5 42. f4 Kc8 43. Kf2 Kb7 44. Kg2 Kxb6 45. Kg1 Kc5 46. Kh2 Kb4 47. Kg2 Qd4 48. b3 Qxf4 0–1 (*U.S. Open* 1948)

557 Kashdan–Bain [D74]
Baltimore, U.S. Open, round 3, 1948 *[July]*

1. d4 Nf6 2. c4 g6 3. Nf3 Bg7 4. g3 0–0 5. Bg2 d5 6. cxd5 Nxd5 7. 0–0 c6 8. e4 Nb6 9. h3 Be6 10. Nc3 Na6 11. Ne2 Qd7 12. Nf4 Bc4 13. Re1 Nc7 14. Be3 Rfd8 15. b3 Ba6 16. Qc2 Rac8 17. Rad1 Ne6 18. Nd3 Bxd3 19. Qxd3 c5 20. d5 c4 21. bxc4 Nxc4 22. Qb3 Nf8 23. Bxa7 b5 24. Bd4 Ra8 25. Bxg7 Kxg7 26. Nd4 Rdb8 27. e5 Ra3 28. Qb1 Kg8 29. Nc6 Rb6 30. Qb4 Rb7 31. e6 Qd6 32. exf7+ Kxf7 33. Qxd6 Nxd6 34. Nd8+ Kf6 35. Nxb7 1–0 (*U.S. Open* 1948)

558 Pilnik–Kashdan [E32]
Baltimore, U.S. Open, round 4, 1948 *[July]*

1. d4 Nf6 2. c4 e6 3. Nc3 Bb4 4. Qc2

b6 5. e4 Bxc3+ 6. bxc3 d6 7. Bd3 e5 8. Ne2 0-0 9. 0-0 Nc6 10. c5 bxc5 11. dxc5 dxc5 12. Ba3 Qe7 13. Ng3 Be6 14. Bb5 Nb8 15. f4 exf4 16. Rxf4 Nbd7 17. Raf1 Ng4 18. Qe2 Nge5 19. Qh5 h6 20. Nf5 Bxf5 21. exf5 Rab8 22. Qe2 Qf6 23. Bc1 c6 24. Ba4 c4 25. Bc2 Rfe8 26. Qf2 c5 27. Qg3 Nd3 28. Bxd3 cxd3 29. Qxd3 Ne5 30. Qg3 Red8 31. Re4 Nd3 32. Be3 Rb2 33. a4 Rc2 34. Bxh6 Qxh6 35. Rh4 Nc1 36. Qh3 Ne2+ 37. Kh1 Rc1 38. g3 Rxf1+ 39. Qxf1 Qe3 0-1 (U.S. Open 1948)

559 Pavey-Kashdan [A11]

Baltimore, U.S. Open, round 5, 1948 *[July]*

1. Nf3 d5 2. c4 c6 3. b3 Nf6 4. g3 g6 5. Bb2 Bg7 6. Bg2 0-0 7. 0-0 a5 8. d3 a4 9. Nbd2 Re8 10. Qc2 Na6 11. a3 axb3 12. Nxb3 dxc4 13. Qxc4 Be6 14. Qc2 Qd7 15. Ng5 Bd5 16. e4 Bxb3 17. Qxb3 e5 18. Bh3 Qe7 19. f4 Nc5 20. Qc2 exf4 21. gxf4 Na4 22. Be5 Qc5+ 23. Qf2 Qxf2+ 24. Kxf2 Nc5 25. Rfd1 h6 26. Nf3 Nfd7 27. Bxg7 Kxg7 28. Bxd7 Nxd7 29. Rdc1 c5 30. Rcb1 c4 31. Rxb7 Nc5 32. Rc7 Nxd3+ 33. Ke3 Rac8 34. Rxc8 Rxc8 35. Ne5 Nxe5 36. fxe5 c3 37. Rc1 c2 38. Kd2 Rc4 39. Rxc2 Rxe4 40. Ra2 Rxe5 41. a4 Ra5 42. Kc3 f5 43. Kb4 Ra8 44. a5 Kf6 45. a6 Ke5 46. Kc5 f4 47. Re2+ Kf5 48. Kb6 f3 49. Re7 Rf8 50. a7 f2 51. a8Q Rxa8 52. Rf7+ Kg4 53. Rxf2 Rc8 54. Rg2+ Kh5 55. Kb5 g5 56. Kb4 Kh4 57. Re2 g4 0-1 (U.S. Open 1948)

560 Kashdan-Kramer [D28]

Baltimore, U.S. Open, round 6, 1948 *[July]*

1. c4 Nf6 2. Nc3 e6 3. Nf3 d5 4. d4 dxc4 5. e3 c5 6. Bxc4 Nc6 7. 0-0 a6 8. Qe2 b5 9. Bb3 Bb7 10. Rd1 Qc7 11. d5 exd5 12. Nxd5 Nxd5 13. Bxd5 Be7 14. b3 0-0 15. Bb2 Rfd8 16. e4 Nb4 17. Bxb7 Qxb7 18. a3 Nc6 19. Rd5 Rxd5 20. exd5 Na5 21. Rd1 Rd8 22. Qe3 Bf8 23. Qe4 h6 24. Ne5 Nxb3 25. Qf3 Nd4 26. Bxd4 Qxd5! 27. Qg3 cxd4 28. f4 d3

29. Nxd3 Qb3 30. Qf3 Bxa3 31. f5 Be7 32. Qe2 Bf6 33. g3 Bd4+ 34. Kg2 Qd5+ 35. Qf3 Qxf3+ 36. Kxf3 Bf6 37. Ke3 Bg5+ 38. Ke4 a5 39. Rb1 Rb8 40. Ne5 b4 41. Nc6 Rb5 42. Nd4 Rb6 43. Kd5 Bf6 44. Nc6 b3 45. Kc5 Rxc6+ 46. Kxc6 a4 47. Kb5 a3 48. Rxb3 a2 0-1 (U.S. Open 1948)

561 Ulvestad-Kashdan [C45]

Baltimore, U.S. Open, round 7, 1948 *[July]*

1. e4 e5 2. Nf3 Nc6 3. d4 exd4 4. Nxd4 Nf6 5. Nxc6 bxc6 6. Bd3 d5 7. exd5 cxd5 8. 0-0 Be7 9. Bb5+ Bd7 10. Bxd7+ Qxd7 11. b3 0-0 12. Bb2 Qf5 13. Nd2 Rad8 14. Nf3 c5 15. Qd3 Ne4 16. Rae1 Bf6 17. Bxf6 Qxf6 18. c4 Nc3 19. Re5 Nxa2 20. cxd5 Nb4 21. Qc4 Qd6 22. Rd1 h6 23. h3 Rfe8 24. Rxe8+ Rxe8 25. Rc1 Rc8 26. Qg4 Rd8 27. Qc4 Rc8 28. Qg4 ½-½ (U.S. Open 1948)

562 Kashdan-Adams [C86]

Baltimore, U.S. Open, round 8, 1948 *[July]*

1. e4 e5 2. Nf3 Nc6 3. Bb5 a6 4. Ba4 Nf6 5. 0-0 Be7 6. Qe2 b5 7. Bb3 d6 8. a4 Bg4 9. c3 0-0 10. h3 Bxf3 11. Qxf3 Na5 12. Bc2 c5 13. d3 b4 14. Nd2 bxc3 15. bxc3 d5 16. g4 d4 17. c4 Ne8 18. Qg3 Bd6 19. Nf3 Nc7 20. Nh4 Ne6 21. Ng2 g5 22. Bd2 Nc6 23. Rab1 a5 24. Qf3 Nb4 25. Bb3 Rb8 26. Rfd1 Rb6 27. Kf1 Qe7 28. Ke2 Rfb8 29. Bxb4 Rxb4 30. Bc2 Rxb1 31. Rxb1 Rxb1 32. Bxb1 Qb7 33. Bc2 Qb2 34. Kd1 Qa1+ 35. Ke2 Qh1 36. Bd1 Be7 37. Qg3 Nf4+ 38. Nxf4 gxf4 39. Qf3 Qg1 40. Bc2 Bh4 41. Bd1 Kg7 42. Bc2 Kg6 43. Bb3 Kg5 44. Bc2 Bg3 45. fxg3 Qh2+ 46. Kf1 Qxc2 47. h4+ Kf6 48. gxf4 Qc1+ 49. Kg2 exf4 50. e5+ Ke7 51. Qb7+ Kf8 52. Qc8+ Kg7 53. Qf5 ½-½ (U.S. Open 1948)

563 Bisguier-Kashdan [C77]

Baltimore, U.S. Open, round 9, 1948 *[July]*

1. e4 e5 2. Nf3 Nc6 3. Bb5 a6 4. Ba4 Nf6 5. Qe2 Be7 6. c3 b5 7. Bc2 d5 8. d4

Bg4 9. exd5 Rxf3 10. Qxf3 Qxd5
11. Qxd5 Nxd5 12. dxe5 Nxe5 13. 0–0
0–0–0 14. Nd2 Bc5 15. Ne4 Bb6 16. Bg5
f6 17. Bh4 Nf4 18. a4 Kb7 19. Rfd1 Nc4
20. b3 Nb2 21. Rdb1 Nbd3 22. axb5
axb5 23. Bd1 c6 24. Bg3 Rhe8 25. Bf3
f5 26. Ng5 h6 27. Bxf4 Nxf4 28. Nh3
Nxh3+ 29. gxh3 Rd3 30. Kg2 Re6
31. Bh5 g6 32. Rd1 Rxc3 33. Rd7+ Bc7
34. Bf3 Rxb3 35. Rh7 g5 36. Rd1 Kb6
37. Rf7 g4 38. hxg4 fxg4 39. Bxg4 Rg6
40. h3 h5 41. Rdd7 hxg4 42. Rxc7
gxh3+ 43. Kf1 h2 0–1 (*U.S. Open 1948*)

564 Kashdan–Evans [E19]

Baltimore, U.S. Open, round 10, 1948 *[July]*

1. d4 Nf6 2. Nf3 e6 3. c4 b6 4. g3 Bb7
5. Bg2 Be7 6. 0–0 0–0 7. Nc3 Ne4
8. Qc2 Nxc3 9. Qxc3 f5 10. Rd1 Bf6
11. Qe3 Be4 12. Bd2 Re8 13. Bc3 d6
14. Ne1 Bxg2 15. Nxg2 Nd7 16. Qf3 Qe7
17. Nf4 Bg5 18. d5 Bxf4 19. Qxf4 Qf7
20. dxe6 Rxe6 21. Rd5 Rf8 22. Qf3 Nc5
23. b3 Ne4 24. Re1 Ng5 25. Qg2 Rfe8
26. Kf1 Ne4 27. Bb2 a5 28. f3 Nc5
29. Qf2 R8e7 30. Kg1 Qe8 31. Kf1 Re3
32. Rdd1 R3e6 33. Rd5 Re3 ½–½ (*U.S. Open 1948*)

565 Pinkus–Kashdan [B24]

Baltimore, U.S. Open, round 11, 1948 *[July]*

1. e4 c5 2. Nc3 Nc6 3. g3 g6 4. Bg2
Bg7 5. Nge2 d6 6. 0–0 Nf6 7. d3 0–0
8. h3 Ne8 9. Be3 Nd4 10. Rb1 Rb8 11. f4
a5 12. g4 e6 13. Ng3 f5 14. exf5 exf5
15. g5 Nc7 16. Nce2 Re8 17. Bf2 Be6
18. Nxd4 cxd4 19. Ne2 Bxa2 20. Ra1 Bd5
21. Nxd4 Bxg2 22. Kxg2 Ne6 23. Nxe6
Rxe6 24. Qf3 d5 25. c3 Ra8 26. Rfe1
Raa6 27. Bc5 Rac6 28. Qf2 Qe8 29. Kf1
Rxe1+ 30. Rxe1 Re6 31. Rxe6 Qxe6
32. Bd4 Bf8 33. Be5 Qc6 34. Bd4 Qe6
35. Be5 Qc6 36. Bd4 Bd6 37. Qe3 Kf7
38. Be5 Bc5 39. Bd4 Bd6 40. Be5 Be7
41. Bd4 Qb5 42. Qe2 a4 43. h4 Bd6
44. Qd2 Ke8 45. Kg2 Kd7 46. Kg3 ½–½ (*U.S. Open 1948*)

566 Kashdan–McCormick [C82]

Baltimore, U.S. Open, round 12, 1948
[July 17]

1. e4 e5 2. Nf3 Nc6 3. Bb5 a6 4. Ba4
Nf6 5. 0–0 Nxe4 6. d4 b5 7. Bb3 d5
8. dxe5 Be6 9. c3 Bc5 10. Nbd2 0–0
11. Bc2 Nxf2 12. Rxf2 f6 13. exf6 Qxf6
14. Qe2 Rae8 15. Nf1 Bxf2+ 16. Qxf2
Ne5 17. Bd1 Bg4 18. Be3 Bxf3 19. Bxf3
Nxf3+ 20. gxf3 Qxf3 21. Qxf3 Rxf3
22. Re1 c5 23. Kg2 Rf5 24. Bf2 Rxe1
25. Bxe1 d4 26. cxd4 cxd4 27. Bf2 d3
28. Be3 b4 29. Bd2 a5 30. Ne3 Rf6
31. Kg3 Kf7 32. Nc4 Rf1 33. Nxa5 Ra1
34. Bxb4 Rxa2 35. Nc4 Ke6 36. Bc3
Kd5 37. Nd2 Ra6 38. Kf4 Rh6 39. Nf3
Kc4 40. Bxg7 Rg6 41. Bc3 Rg2 42. Nd2+
Kd5 43. h4 h5 44. Ke3 Rg3+ 45. Nf3
Rh3 46. b3 Kc5 47. Bd2 Kd5 48. Be1
Kd6 49. Ke4 Kc5 50. Bd2 Rg3 51. Ne5
Kb5 52. Be1 d2 53. Bxd2 Rxb3 54. Bg5
Kc5 55. Be7+ Kb6 56. Kf4 Kc7 57. Kg5
Rb5 58. Bf6 Kd6 59. Kxh5 Ke6 60. Kg6
1–0 (*U.S. Open 1948*)

567 Siff–Kashdan [E36]

Manhattan Masters, round 5, 1948

1. d4 Nf6 2. c4 e6 3. Nc3 Bb4 4. Qc2
d5 5. a3 Be7 6. cxd5 exd5 7. Bf4 c6
8. h3 0–0 9. e3 Re8 10. Bd3 Nbd7
11. Nf3 Nf8 12. Ne5 Bd6 13. 0–0 Ne6
14. Bh2 g6 15. Nf3 Ng7 16. Bxd6 Qxd6
17. Rfc1 Bf5 18. Nd2 Re7 19. b4 Rae8
20. Rab1? Bxh3! 21. gxh3 Rxe3!

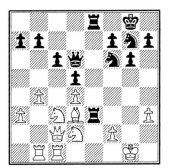

After
21. ... Rxe3

The point of the first sacrifice. **22. Bf1!** The
best defense! **22. ... Nf5! 23. fxe3 Qg3+**

24. Bg2 Qxe3+ 25. Kh1 Ng3+ 26. Kh2 Qf4

After
26. ... Qf4

Threatening mate in four. **27. Nf3? Re2!! 28. Nxe2? Nxe2+ 29. Kh1 Nh5 30. Qd2 Nhg3+ 31. Kh2 Nf1+ 32. Kh1 Qh2+!** White resigns as 33. ... N/8g3 mate follows. **0–1** One of the best games played by Kashdan. (*Chess Review*, October 1948)

568 Pinkus–Kashdan [B23]
Manhattan Masters, round 7, 1948

1. e4 c5 2. Nc3 d6 3. g3 Nf6 4. Bg2 Nc6 5. Nge2 Nd4 6. 0–0 g6 7. d3 Bg7 8. Nxd4 cxd4 9. Ne2 Qb6 10. c3 dxc3 11. bxc3 0–0 12. Be3 Qa6 13. h3 Bd7 14. Qd2 Rfc8 15. Rab1 Rab8 16. f4 Qa5 17. Rb4 Rxc3! 18. Rb3 Rc5 19. Rd1 Qxd2 20. Rxd2 Ra5 21. g4 b6 22. d4 Rc8 23. g5 Ne8 24. Kf2 e6 25. h4 Bb5 26. Bh3 Bc4 27. Rc3 b5 28. h5 Rb8 29. h6 Bf8 30. d5 exd5 31. exd5 Rxa2 32. Rxa2 Bxa2 33. Bxa7 Ra8 34. Bd4 Bxd5 35. f5 gxf5 36. Bxf5

After
36. Bxf5

36. ... Be6 37. Bb1 b4 38. Rc1 Rc8 39. Re1 d5 40. Nf4 Rc4 41. Be5 Rc6

42. Bb2 Nc7 43. Nh5 Ne8 44. Nf4 Nc7 45. Bd3 Bd6 46. Kf3 Bxf4 47. Kxf4 Na6 48. Ra1 Nc5 49. Bf5 Rc8 50. Bb1 Nd7 51. Ra7 Rc4+ 52. Ke3 Nf8 53. Rb7 Bc8 54. Rb8 Ne6 55. Bd3 d4+ 56. Kd2 Rc6 57. Rxb4 Nxg5 58. Bxd4 Nf3+ 59. Ke3 Nxd4 60. Kxd4 Kf8 61. Rb8 Ke7 62. Bxh7 Ba6 63. Bg6! The game was given up as a draw. The game could continue 63. ... Rxg6 64. h7 Rh6 65. h8 Rxh8 66. Rxh8 which should lead to a draw. ½–½ (Contributed by Larry Parr)

569 Kashdan–A. Sandrin [B32]
South Fallsburg, U.S. Championship, round 1, 1948 *[August 11]*

1. e4 c5 2. Nf3 Nc6 3. d4 cxd4 4. Nxd4 d5 5. Bb5 dxe4 6. Nxc6 Qxd1+ 7. Kxd1 a6 8. Ba4 Bd7 9. Nc3 Bxc6 10. Bxc6+ bxc6 11. Nxe4 e5 12. Ke2 f5 13. Ng5 Nf6 14. b3 Be7 15. Ne6 Kf7 16. Ng5+ Ke8 17. Nf3 e4 18. Nd4 Nd5 19. Nxf5 Bf6 20. Bd2 Bxa1 21. Rxa1 Kf7 22. Nd6+ Kg6 23. Nxe4 Rhe8 24. f3 Rad8 25. Re1 Nf6 26. Ke3 h5 27. Ba5 Rd7 28. Kf2 Nxe4+ 29. fxe4 Kf7 30. Re3 Re5 31. Be1 Re6 32. Bc3 Rde7 33. Kf3 g5 34. h3 Kg6 35. Re2 Re8 36. e5 Rf8+ 37. Ke3 h4 38. Kd4 Rd8+ 39. Kc4 Rd1 40. Rf2 Rd8 41. Bd4 Kg7 42. a4 Rd7 43. b4 1–0 (*U.S. Championship* 1948)

570 Platz–Kashdan [C48]
South Fallsburg, U.S. Championship, round 2, 1948 *[August 12]*

1. e4 e5 2. Nf3 Nc6 3. Nc3 Nf6 4. Bb5 Nd4 5. Nxe5 Bc5 6. Nd3 Bb6 7. e5 Nxb5 8. Nxb5 Ne4 9. Qg4 Ng5 10. f4 Ne6 11. f5 Qg5 12. Qe4 d5 13. exd6 0–0 14. fxe6 Bxe6 15. Ne5 cxd6 16. d4 Qh5 17. Nxd6 Rad8 18. h4 Rxd6 19. g4 f5 20. gxh5 fxe4 21. c3 Rd5 22. Rf1 Rxf1+ 23. Kxf1 h6 24. Bf4 Bf7 25. Re1 Bxh5 26. Rxe4 Rd8 27. Kg2 Rf8 28. Kg3 Rf5 29. Nd7 g5 30. hxg5 hxg5 31. Bd6 Bd1 32. Re5 Rf3+ 33. Kg2 Rd3 34. Be7 Rd2+ 35. Kf1 Rd1+ 36. Kf2 Rd2+ 37. Ke1 Rd1+ ½–½ (*U.S. Championship* 1948)

571 Kashdan–Shainswit [B17]

South Fallsburg, U.S. Championship, round 3, 1948 *[August 13]*

1. e4 c6 2. d4 d5 3. Nc3 dxe4 4. Nxe4 Nd7 5. Bd3 Ngf6 6. c3 Nxe4 7. Bxe4 Nf6 8. Bc2 Bg4 9. Ne2 e6 10. 0–0 Bd6 11. Qe1 Qc7 12. Ng3 0–0–0 13. h3 Bh5 14. Nxh5 Nxh5 15. b4 Bh2+ 16. Kh1 Bf4 17. Bb2 Rhe8 18. Qe2 Nf6 19. Qf3 e5 20. g3 Bh6 21. Rfe1 exd4 22. cxd4 Rxe1+ 23. Rxe1 Bd2 24. Re2 Bxb4 25. d5 Kb8 26. Be5 Bd6 27. Bxf6 gxf6 28. dxc6 Qxc6 29. Be4 Qc1+ 30. Kg2 Be5 31. Bxb7 Rd6 32. Be4 Qc7 33. Qb3+ 1–0 (*U.S. Championship* 1948)

572 Heitner–Kashdan [A15]

South Fallsburg, U.S. Championship, round 4, 1948 *[August 14]*

1. Nf3 Nf6 2. c4 g6 3. b3 Bg7 4. Bb2 0–0 5. g3 Re8 6. Bg2 Nc6 7. d4 d5 8. Nbd2 dxc4 9. Nxc4 Bf5 10. 0–0 Qc8 11. Re1 Rd8 12. Rc1 Bh6 13. e3 Nb4 14. Ba3 Nxa2 15. Bxe7 Nxc1 16. Bxd8 Qxd8 17. Qxc1 c6 18. Qa3 Bf8 19. Qb2 a5 20. Nfe5 Qc7 21. Ra1 Nd7 22. Nxd7 Bxd7 23. Ra2 Be6 24. Qc2 Bb4 25. Ra1 Rc8 26. f4 f6 27. Kh1 Rd8 28. Rd1 Qf7 29. Bf3 a4 30. Be2 b5 31. Nd2 axb3 32. Qxc6?? Bd5+ 0–1 (*U.S. Championship* 1948)

573 Kashdan–Shipman [D02]

South Fallsburg, U.S. Championship, round 5, 1948 *[August 15]*

1. Nf3 d5 2. g3 Nc6 3. d4 Bf5 4. Bg2 e6 5. 0–0 Nf6 6. a3 Bd6 7. c4 dxc4 8. Nbd2 Na5 9. Nxc4 Nxc4 10. Qa4+ c6 11. Qxc4 0–0 12. Nh4 Bg6 13. Nxg6 hxg6 14. e4 Nd7 15. Be3 e5 16. Rad1 Qc7 17. f4 exd4 18. Bxd4 c5 19. Be3 Nb6 20. Qc2 c4 21. Qf2 Na4 22. Rc1 Rac8 23. Bh3 Nc5 24. Rxc4 b5 25. Rcc1 Nd3 26. Rxc7 Nxf2 27. Bxc8 Bxc7 28. Kxf2 Rxc8 29. Rc1 Kf8 30. Ke2 Ke7 31. Bxa7 Kd7 32. Bd4 f6 33. e5 f5 34. Bb6 Bxb6 35. e6+ Kxe6 36. Rxc8 Bd4 37. b3 1–0 (*U.S. Championship* 1948)

574 Suraci–Kashdan [C82]

South Fallsburg, U.S. Championship, round 6, 1948 *[August 16]*

1. e4 e5 2. Nf3 Nc6 3. Bb5 a6 4. Ba4 Nf6 5. 0–0 Nxe4 6. d4 b5 7. Bb3 d5 8. dxe5 Be6 9. c3 Bc5 10. Nbd2 0–0 11. Bc2 Nxf2 12. Rxf2 f6 13. exf6 Qxf6 14. Nf1 Bxf2+ 15. Kxf2 Ne5 16. Ne3 c5 17. Nxd5 Qh4+ 18. Kg1 Nxf3+ 19. gxf3 Rad8 20. Be4 Kh8 21. b3 Bxd5 22. Bxd5 Rfe8 23. Be3 Rxe3 24. c4 bxc4 25. bxc4 Rb8 26. Qd2 Qg5+ 27. Kh1 Qe5 28. Qc1 Re2 29. f4 Qh5 30. Bg2 Rbb2 31. Qd1 Qe8 32. Bf3 Rxh2+ 33. Kg1 Qe3+ 0–1 (*U.S. Championship* 1948)

575 Kashdan–Hesse [D37]

South Fallsburg, U.S. Championship, round 7, 1948 *[August 17]*

1. d4 Nf6 2. c4 e6 3. Nc3 d5 4. Nf3 Be7 5. e3 0–0 6. Bd3 c5 7. 0–0 dxc4 8. Bxc4 a6 9. Qe2 b5 10. Bd3 Nbd7 11. Rd1 Qc7 12. Bd2 Bb7 13. Rac1 c4 14. Bc2 e5 15. e4 Bd6 16. Bg5 exd4 17. Rxd4 Bf4 18. Bxf4 Qxf4 19. Rcd1 Ne5 20. Nxe5 Qxe5 21. f4 Qc5 22. Kh1 Rae8 23. e5 g6 24. Qf2 Ng4 25. Qg3 Rd8 26. Ne2 Rxd4 27. Rxd4 Qb4 28. Qxg4 Qe1+ 29. Ng1 Qf2 30. Rd7 Bc8 31. Be4 Bxd7 32. Qxd7 Qxb2 33. e6 fxe6 34. Qxe6+ Kg7 35. Qxa6 Rxf4 36. Qa7+ Rf7 37. Qc5 Qxa2 38. Qxb5 Qb3 39. Qe5+ Kh6 40. Bd5 Rf5 41. Qd4 Qb4 42. Bxc4 Qe1 43. h3 Qe5 44. Qh4+ Rh5 45. Qd8 Rf5 46. Nf3 Qg3 47. Qd2+ Kg7 48. Nd4 Re5 49. Ne6+ Kf6 50. Qd8+ Kf5 51. Qf8+ Ke4 52. Qa8+ Ke3 53. Qa3+ Kf2 54. Qb2+ Ke1 55. Qc1+ After 55. ... Kf2 56.Qf1+ Ke3 57.Qe2 mate! 1–0 (*U.S. Championship* 1948)

576 Ulvestad–Kashdan [E12]

South Fallsburg, U.S. Championship, round 8, 1948 *[August 18]*

1. d4 Nf6 2. c4 e6 3. Nf3 b6 4. Bg5 Bb7 5. Nbd2 Be7 6. Qc2 h6 7. Bh4 Nc6 8. e3 0–0 9. a3 a5 10. Be2 d5 11. 0–0

Ne4 12. Nxe4 Bxh4 13. Nxh4 Qxh4
14. cxd5 exd5 15. Nc3 Rad8 16. Nb5
Rd7 17. Qf5 Rfd8 18. Bd3 g6 19. Qf3
Nb8 20. Rfd1 Ba6 21. Rac1 c6 22. Nc3
Bxd3 23. Rxd3 Rd6 24. Na4 Nd7
25. Qe2 Re6 26. Qc2 h5 27. Rc3 Rc8
28. b4 axb4 29. axb4 b5 30. Nc5 Nxc5
31. Rxc5 Qe7 32. h3 Rd8 33. Ra1 Qb7
34. Qa2 Rb8 35. Rc3 Qe7 36. Qb2 Rd8
37. Rca3 Kg7 38. Qc3 g5 39. Ra6 Rdd6
40. Ra8 g4 41. Rc8 g3 42. Raa8 gxf2+
43. Kxf2 Qh4+ 44. Ke2 Rg6 45. Rg8+
Kh6 46. Rh8+ Kg7 47. Rag8+ Kf6
48. Qe1 Qxe1+ 49. Kxe1 Kg5 50. Re8
½–½ (*U.S. Championship* 1948)

577 Kashdan–Evans [D31]
South Fallsburg, U.S. Championship,
round 9, 1948 *[August 19]*

1. d4 d5 2. c4 e6 3. Nc3 c6 4. Nf3
dxc4 5. e3 b5 6. a4 Bb4 7. Be2 Bb7
8. 0–0 a6 9. Ne5 f6 10. Nf3 Nd7 11. Bd2
Nh6 12. Nxb5 cxb5 13. Bxb4 Kf7 14. b3
cxb3 15. a5 Bd5 16. Nd2 Rc8 17. Nxb3
Bc4 18. Rc1 Bxe2 19. Qxe2 Re8 20. Rxc8
Qxc8 21. Rc1 Qd8 22. Rc6 Nb8 23. Rd6
Qc8 24. Nc5 Kg8 25. Qa2 Kf7 26. Rb6
Nf5 27. h3 Nc6 28. Bd2 Nb8 29. Bb4
Nc6 30. Bc3 Nb8 31. e4 Nh4 32. Qb3
Re7 33. Bb4 Nc6 34. d5 Nxb4
35. dxe6+ Ke8 36. Qxb4 Rc7 37. Nxa6
Rc1+ 38. Kh2 Rh1+ 39. Kg3! But not
39. Kxh1 Qc1+ 40. Kh2 Qf4+ leads to a draw by
perpetual. 1–0 (*U.S. Championship* 1948)

578 Rubinow–Kashdan [C47]
South Fallsburg, U.S. Championship,
round 10, 1948 *[August 20]*

1. e4 e5 2. Nf3 Nc6 3. Nc3 Nf6 4. d4
exd4 5. Nd5 Nxd5 6. exd5 Nb4 7. Bc4
b5 8. Bb3 Qe7+ 9. Kd2 g6 10. Qe1 Bb7
11. Nxd4 a6 12. d6 cxd6 13. Kc3 Bg7
14. Bg5 Bxd4+ 15. Kxd4 Nc6+ 16. Kc3
Qe5+ 17. Qxe5+ dxe5 18. Rad1 Rc8
19. Rd6 Nd4+ 20. Kd3 Bxg2 21. Rg1 Bc6
22. Rxd4 d5 23. Bf6 e4+ 24. Ke3 0–0
25. c3 Rfe8 26. Bxd5 Bxd5 27. Rxd5
Rc6 28. Rd8 Rxd8 29. Bxd8 f5 30. Rd1

Kf7 31. Bg5 Ke6 32. Rd8 h5 33. h4 Ke5
34. Rd7 Ke6 35. Rg7 Kd5 36. Rf7 Ke5
37. Bf4+ Ke6 38. Rc7 Rb6 39. Kd4 b4
40. c4 b3 41. a3 a5 42. Kc5 1–0 (*U.S.
Championship* 1948)

579 Kashdan–H. Steiner [D41]
South Fallsburg, U.S. Championship,
round 11, 1948 *[August 21]*

1. d4 Nf6 2. Nf3 e6 3. c4 d5 4. Nc3 c5
5. cxd5 Nxd5 6. e4 Nxc3 7. bxc3 cxd4
8. cxd4 Bb4+ 9. Bd2 Bxd2+ 10. Qxd2
0–0 11. Be2 b6 12. 0–0 Bb7 13. Qe3
Nc6 14. Rac1 Rc8 15. Rfd1 Re8 16. Bd3
Qe7 17. Bb1 Qb4 18. e5 Ne7 19. Ng5 h6
20. Bh7+ Kh8 21. Rb1 Qc3 22. Qxc3
Rxc3 23. Ne4 Rcc8 24. Nd6 Kxh7
25. Nxb7 Rc2 26. Nd6 Rf8 27. a3 Nd5
28. Rdc1 Ra2 29. Ra1 Rxa1 30. Rxa1 f6
31. Rc1 fxe5 32. dxe5 Rf4 33. Rd1 Ne7
34. g3 Ra4 35. Rd3 g5 36. Rf3 Nd5
37. Kg2 g4 38. Rb3 Kg6 39. h3 h5
40. hxg4 hxg4 41. Rd3 a6 42. Rb3 Rd4
43. Kf1 b5 44. Ke2 Kg7 45. Ne8+ Kf8
46. Nd6 Ke7 47. Rd3 Ra4 ½–½ (*U.S.
Championship* 1948)

580 Kashdan–James [C82]
South Fallsburg, U.S. Championship,
round 12, 1948 *[August 22]*

1. e4 e5 2. Nf3 Nc6 3. Bb5 a6 4. Ba4
Nf6 5. 0–0 Nxe4 6. d4 b5 7. Bb3 d5
8. dxe5 Be6 9. c3 Bc5 10. Nbd2 Nxd2
11. Qxd2 0–0 12. Qd3 Ne7 13. Nd4 Qd7
14. Bc2 g6 15. Bg5 Nf5 16. Rae1 Rfc8
17. Nxe6 Qxe6 18. Kh1 c6 19. g4 Ng7
20. Qg3 Be7 21. Bc1 Rf8 22. f4 f5
23. exf6 Qxf6 24. f5 Bd6 25. Qh3 g5
26. Be3 Rae8 27. Bd4 Be5 28. Bc5 Bd6
29. Bxd6 Qxd6 30. f6 Rxf6 31. Rxe8+
Nxe8 32. Qxh7+ Kf8 33. Qh6+ Kf7
34. Bg6+ Ke7 35. Qxg5 Nc7 36. Bh5 b4
37. Qg7+ Kd8 38. Rxf6 1–0 (*U.S. Championship* 1948)

581 Santasiere–Kashdan [B72]
South Fallsburg, U.S. Championship,
round 13, 1948 *[August 24]*

1. e4 c5 2. Nf3 d6 3. d4 cxd4 4. Nxd4 Nf6 5. Nc3 g6 6. h3 Bg7 7. Be3 Nc6 8. Qd2 0–0 9. 0–0–0 a6 10. g4 Nd7 11. Be2 Re8 12. Nxc6 bxc6 13. Bd4 Bxd4 14. Qxd4 Qb6 15. f4 Qxd4 16. Rxd4 Nc5 17. Rd2 a5 18. h4 Bb7 19. h5 Ne6 20. hxg6 hxg6 21. f5 Ng5 22. Bd3 Kg7 23. Rdh2 Rh8 24. Rxh8 Rxh8 25. Rxh8 Kxh8 26. Kd2 Kg7 27. Ke3 Kf6 28. Na4 gxf5 29. gxf5 Ke5 30. c4 d5 31. cxd5 cxd5 32. exd5 Bxd5 33. Nc5 Kd6 34. Na4 Bxa2 35. Kf4 f6 36. Nc3 Bb3 37. Nb5+ Kc5 38. Nc3 Nf7 39. Bb1 Nd6 40. Ne2 Nc4 41. Nc1 a4 42. Nd3+ Kd6 43. Nc1 Nxb2 44. Nxb3 axb3 45. Ke3 Kc5 0–1 (*U.S. Championship* 1948)

582 Kashdan–Almgren [C86]
South Fallsburg, U.S. Championship, round 14, 1948 *[August 25]*

1. e4 e5 2. Nf3 Nc6 3. Bb5 a6 4. Ba4 Nf6 5. 0–0 Be7 6. Qe2 b5 7. Bb3 0–0 8. c3 d5 9. exd5 Nxd5 10. Nxe5 Nxe5 11. Qxe5 c6 12. d4 Bd6 13. Qh5 g6 14. Qh6 Re8 15. Bg5 f6 16. Bh4 Be6 17. Bg3 Bf8 18. Qd2 h5 19. Na3 Kh7 20. Rae1 Bh6 21. f4 Qd7 22. Nc2 Bf5 23. Ne3 Be4 24. h3 Qg7 25. Nxd5 cxd5 26. Bc2 f5 27. Bxe4 fxe4 28. Qe2 Rf8 29. Kh1 Qc7 30. Qe3 Qd7 31. Bh2 Rf6 32. Rf2 Raf8 33. Refl a5 34. Qe2 R6f7 35. g4 hxg4 36. hxg4 b4 37. cxb4 axb4 38. f5 gxf5 39. gxf5 Rxf5 40. Qg4 e3 41. Rxf5 e2 42. Qxe2 Rxf5 43. Qd3 Kg6 44. Be5 Bf8 45. Kg2 Be7 46. Kh3 Kg5 47. Qg3+ 1–0 (*U.S. Championship* 1948)

583 Howard–Kashdan [C82]
South Fallsburg, U.S. Championship, round 15, 1948 *[August 26]*

1. e4 e5 2. Nf3 Nc6 3. Bb5 a6 4. Ba4 Nf6 5. 0–0 Nxe4 6. d4 b5 7. Bb3 d5 8. dxe5 Be6 9. c3 Bc5 10. Nbd2 0–0 11. Bc2 Nxf2 12. Rxf2 f6 13. exf6 Qxf6 14. Qf1 Rae8 15. Nb3 Bxf2+ 16. Qxf2 Bg4 17. Bg5 Qf7 18. Qh4 Qh5 19. Qxh5 Bxh5 20. Rf1 Bxf3 21. gxf3 Ne5 22. Nd2 c5 23. Kg2 h6 24. Be3 Nd3 25. Bxd3

Rxe3 26. Bc2 c4 27. Kf2 Re5 28. Re1 Rxe1 29. Kxe1 Kf7 30. Nf1 Ke6 31. Ke2 a5 32. Ke3 g5 33. b3 Ke5 34. a3 Rf4 35. b4 axb4 36. axb4 d4+ 37. cxd4+ Rxd4 38. Nd2 Rh4 39. Nf1 Rd4 40. Nd2 c3 41. Ne4 Rxb4 42. Nxc3 Rc4 43. Kd3 Rh4 44. Nxb5 Rxh2 45. Bb3 Kf4 46. Nd4 h5 47. Ne6+ Kf5 48. Ke3 h4 49. Nc5 h3 50. Be6+ Kg6 51. Ne4 Kh5 52. Bg4+ Kg6 53. Nf2 Rg2 54. Bxh3 Rg1 55. Bg4 Ra1 56. Nd3 Ra3 ½–½ (*U.S. Championship* 1948)

584 Kashdan–Whitaker [D36]
South Fallsburg, U.S. Championship, round 16, 1948 *[August 27]*

1. d4 d5 2. c4 e6 3. Nc3 Nf6 4. Bg5 Nbd7 5. cxd5 exd5 6. e3 c6 7. Bd3 Be7 8. Qc2 Nf8 9. Nf3 Ne6 10. Bh4 g6 11. 0–0 0–0 12. a3 a5 13. h3 Nh5 14. Bxe7 Qxe7 15. Na4 Ng5 16. Nxg5 Qxg5 17. Nb6 Rb8 18. Nxc8 Rbxc8 19. b4 axb4 20. axb4 f5 21. Be2 f4 22. Bxh5 Qxh5 23. exf4 Rxf4 24. Ra7 Rc7 25. b5 Qf5 26. Qxf5 gxf5 27. bxc6 Rxc6 28. Rxb7 Rxd4 29. Ra1 Rdc4 30. Raa7 Rc8 31. Rg7+ Kf8 32. Rxh7 Kg8 33. Rhd7 R4c5 34. Kh2 f4 35. h4 Rc2 36. f3 1–0 (*U.S. Championship* 1948)

585 Adams–Kashdan [C30]
South Fallsburg, U.S. Championship, round 17, 1948 *[August 28]*

1. e4 e5 2. Nc3 Nf6 3. Bc4 Bc5 4. f4 d6 5. Nf3 Nc6 6. d3 Bg4 7. Na4 Nd4 8. Nxc5 dxc5 9. c3 Nxf3+ 10. gxf3 Bh5 11. Rg1 Nd7 12. Qe2 exf4 13. Bxf4 Qh4+ 14. Bg3 Qf6 15. Bxc7 Rc8 16. Bg3 Bxf3 17. Qe3 Bh5 18. Kd2 0–0 19. Raf1 Qe7 20. a3 Nb6 21. Ba2 Rfd8 22. Rf5 Bg6 23. Be5 c4 24. Bd4 Bxf5 25. Rxg7+ Kf8 26. Qh6 Ke8 27. exf5 Kd7 28. Rxh7 Rg8 29. Qh3 Qg5+ 30. Kd1 Rce8 31. Rxf7+ Kc8 32. f6+ Kb8 33. Qf3 Qg2 34. Rxb7+ Kc8 35. Qxg2 Rxg2 36. f7 Rf8 37. Rxa7 Rxb2 38. Bxb6 Rxb6 39. Ra8+ Rb8 40. Rxb8+ Kxb8 41. Bxc4 Kc7 42. Bd5 Kd6 43. c4 Ke7 44. Kc2 Rh8 45. a4

Rxh2+ 46. Kc3 Ra2 47. Kb4 Rb2+
48. Ka3 Rd2 49. a5 Rxd3+ 50. Kb4 Rd1
51. a6 Ra1 52. Kb5 Rb1+ 53. Kc6 Ra1
54. Kb7 Rb1+ 55. Ka8 Rb6 56. a7 Rb4
57. c5 1–0 (*U.S. Championship* 1948)

586 Kashdan–Poschel [D57]
South Fallsburg, U.S. Championship,
round 18, 1948 *[August 29]*

1. d4 d5 2. c4 e6 3. Nc3 Nf6 4. Bg5
Be7 5. e3 0–0 6. Nf3 h6 7. Bh4 Ne4
8. Bxe7 Qxe7 9. cxd5 Nxc3 10. bxc3
exd5 11. Bd3 Nc6 12. 0–0 Qd6 13. Rb1
b6 14. Nd2 Re8 15. e4 dxe4 16. Bxe4
Rb8 17. Qf3 Na5 18. Rfe1 Be6 19. d5 Bd7
20. Bc2 Re5 21. Rxe5 Qxe5 22. Qd3 g6
23. Nf3 Qd6 24. Qd4 c6 25. c4 cxd5
26. cxd5 Rd8 27. Qh4 Rc8 28. Bd3
Qxd5 29. Ba6 Rc5 30. Qxh6 Qxa2
31. Re1 Nc6 32. Bc8 Rh5 33. Qc1 Rc5
34. Qh6 Rh5 35. Qc1 Bxc8 36. Re8+
Kh7 37. Qxc6 Qa1+ 38. Re1 Rc5 39. Qe8
Qf6 40. h4 Bg4 41. Ng5+ Kg7 42. Nxf7
Rc7 43. Ng5 Bf5 44. g3 Qd6 45. Kh2
Rd7 46. Ne6+ Bxe6 47. Rxe6 Qd3
48. Rxg6+ Qxg6 49. Qxd7+ Qf7
50. Qd2 a5 51. Kg2 Qb3 52. Qd4+ Kg6
53. Qd6+ Kg7 54. h5 a4 55. g4 a3 56. g5
a2 57. h6+ Kh7 58. Qe7+ Kg6 59. Qf6+
Kh5 60. h7 Qd5+ 61. Kh2 a1Q 62. h8Q+
1–0 (*U.S. Championship* 1948)

587 Kramer–Kashdan [E19]
South Fallsburg, U.S. Championship,
round 19, 1948 *[August 30]*

1. d4 Nf6 2. Nf3 e6 3. c4 b6 4. g3 Bb7
5. Bg2 Be7 6. 0–0 0–0 7. Nc3 Ne4
8. Qc2 Nxc3 9. Qxc3 f5 10. Ne1 Bxg2
11. Nxg2 Bf6 12. Rd1 Nc6 13. e3 e5 14. c5
Kh8 15. b4 bxc5 16. bxc5 Rb8 17. a3
Qe8 18. Ra2 exd4 19. exd4 Qe4 20. Be3
Rb1 21. Rad2 Rfb8 22. Rd3 Rxd1+
23. Rxd1 Rb1 24. Rxb1 Qxb1+ 25. Ne1
Nxd4 26. Bxd4 Bxd4 27. Qxd4 Qxe1+
28. Kg2 Qe6 29. h4 Kg8 30. Kh2 a6
31. Qf4 d6 32. Qb4 Qd7 33. Qc4+ d5
34. Qxa6 d4 35. c6 Qe6 36. Qb7 Qe5
37. a4 f4 38. Qc8+ Kf7 39. Qd7+ Kf6

40. a5 fxg3+ 41. fxg3 Qe2+ 42. Kh3 Qf1+
43. Kh2 Qf2+ 44. Kh3 Qf1+ 45. Kh2
Qe2+ 46. Kh3 d3 47. a6 d2 48. Qd8+
Kf5 49. Qd5+ Kf6 50. Qd8+ Kf7
51. Qxc7+ Kg6 52. Qd6+ Kf5 53. Qf4+
Kg6 54. Qg5+ Kf7 55. Qf5+ Ke7
56. Qd7+ ½–½ (*U.S. Championship* 1948)

588 Kashdan–Raizman [B74]
New York–Paris Cable Match, 1948
[December 19]

1. e4 c5 2. Nf3 d6 3. d4 cxd4 4. Nxd4
Nf6 5. Nc3 g6 6. Be2 Bg7 7. 0–0 0–0
8. Be3 Nc6 9. Nb3 a6 10. f4 b5 11. Bf3
Bb7 12. Qe1 Qc7 13. Rd1 Nd8 14. Qf2
Nd7 15. e5! dxe5 16. Bxb7 Qxb7 17. Na5
Qc8 18. Nd5 Re8 19. fxe5 Bxe5 20. Bb6
Threatening Bxd8 followed by Qxf7+ 20. ...
Nxb6 21. Nxb6 Qb8 22. Nxa8 Qxa8
23. c3 Qb8 1–0 The game was adjudicated
a win for White. (*Chess*, February 1949)

589 Kashdan–Bisguier [C86]
New York International, round 1, 1948
[December 23]

1. e4 e5 2. Nf3 Nc6 3. Bb5 a6 4. Ba4
Nf6 5. 0–0 Be7 6. Qe2 b5 7. Bb3 0–0
8. c3 d5 9. exd5 Nxd5 10. Nxe5 Nxe5
11. Qxe5 Bb7 12. d4 a5 13. Be3 Ra6
14. Bc2 Re6 15. Qh5 g6 16. Qh3 Nxe3?
This leads to a mere recapture of the pawn
whereafter Black's tremendous attack quickly
peters out. Much stronger, leaving White with
hardly any chance for escaping defeat, is 16. ...
Bg5! 17. fxe3 Bg5 18. e4 Bxe4 19. Bxe4
Rxe4 20. Na3 Qd5 21. Qd3 c6 22. Nc2
Rfe8 23. b3 Re2 24. Rf2 Rxf2 25. Kxf2
Re4 26. Kg1 Qe6 27. Kf2 Qf5+ 28. Kg1
Qe6 29. Kf2 Qf5+ 30. Kg1 ½–½ (*New York
International* 1948–49)

590 Pilnik–Kashdan [B71]
New York International, round 2, 1948
[December 24]

1. e4 c5 2. Nf3 d6 3. d4 cxd4 4. Nxd4
Nf6 5. Nc3 g6 6. f4 Bg7 7. e5 dxe5
8. fxe5 Ng4 9. Bb5+ Nc6 10. Nxc6

Qxd1+ 11. Nxd1 a6 12. Ba4 Bd7 13. h3
Nh6 14. Nxe7 Bxa4 15. Nd5 Rd8 16. c4
Nf5 17. Bg5 Rd7 18. N1c3 Bc6 19. 0-0-0
h5 20. Nc7+ Kf8 21. Rxd7 Bxd7 22. Rd1
Bxe5 23. Rxd7 h4 24. Ne4 Nd4
25. Rd8+ Kg7 26. Ne8+ Kh7 27. N4f6+
Bxf6 28. Nxf6+ Kg7 1-0 (*New York International* 1948-49)

591 Kashdan–Denker [D02]
New York International, round 3, 1948
[December 25]

1. d4 Nf6 2. Nf3 g6 3. g3 Bg7 4. Bg2
0-0 5. 0-0 d5 6. Ne5 Ng4 7. Nxg4
Bxg4 8. h3 Bc8 9. c3 c6 10. Nd2 Nd7
11. e4 dxe4 12. Nxe4 Nf6 13. Nc5 Nd7
14. Ne4 Nf6 15. Nxf6+ Bxf6 16. Bf4 Be6
17. Re1 Qd7 18. Kh2 Rfd8 19. Qe2 Rac8
20. Qe3 b6 21. Be5 Bxe5 22. Qxe5 Qd6
23. Qe3 Kg7 24. h4 h5 25. b3 b5
26. Rad1 Rc7 27. Bf1 Bg4 28. Rd2 Qf6
29. Qe5 Qxe5 30. Rxe5 e6 31. Rc5

After
31. Rc5

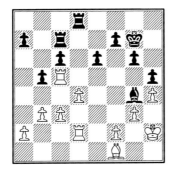

31. ... Bf3? After this move Black is definitely lost. Instead there are two alternatives that hold promise of holding the game: first 31. ... Rb8, second 31. ... d5 32. Bg2 Rd6, but not 32. ... RxR? 33. PxR e5 34. Rd6 Bd7 35. f4! which gives White a great advantage. 32. Bxb5 e5 33. Bf1 exd4 34. cxd4 Rcd7 35. Bg2 Bxg2 36. Kxg2 Rxd4 37. Rxd4 Rxd4 38. Rxc6 Rd7 39. Ra6 Rb7 40. Kf3 Re7 41. b4 Kf8 42. b5 Rb7 43. a4 Re7 44. Kf4 Kg7 45. Rc6 Kf8 46. Rc2 Re6 47. a5 Re7 48. b6 axb6 49. axb6 Rb7 50. Rc6 Kg7 51. Ke5 Rd7 52. Rc2 Rd1 53. Rb2 Re1+ 54. Kd5 Rd1+ 55. Kc5 1-0 (*New York International* 1948-49)

592 H. Steiner–Kashdan [E49]
New York International, round 4, 1948
[December 26]

1. d4 Nf6 2. c4 e6 3. Nc3 Bb4 4. e3
0-0 5. a3 Bxc3+ 6. bxc3 d5 7. Bd3 c5
8. Ne2 Qc7 9. cxd5 exd5 10. 0-0 Nc6
11. Ng3 Re8 12. Nh5 Ng4 13. Nf4 Nf6
14. f3 Ne7 15. g4 Ng6 16. Ng2 h6
17. Bd2 Bd7 18. Be1 Rac8 19. h4 Nf8
20. Ra2 Ne6 21. Rb2 b6 22. Kh1 Qd6
23. Ra2 b5 24. Rg1 Rb8 25. f4 Ne4
26. Bxe4 dxe4 27. Bg3 cxd4 28. cxd4
Rbc8 29. Qe1 Nf8 30. f5 Qd5 31. Rb2
Qc4 32. Qf2 f6 33. g5 fxg5 34. hxg5
hxg5 35. Be5 Rc6 36. Nh4?! Nh7!
37. Ng6 Qf7 38. Bh2 Qxf5 39. Qxf5
Bxf5 40. Ne5 Rc3 41. Rxb5 Rxe3
42. Ra5 Re2 43. Nc4 Bg6 44. Rg2? Rxg2
45. Kxg2 e3 46. Re5 Rxe5 47. Bxe5 e2
48. Kf2 Bd3 49. Ne3 Nf6 50. d5 Kf7
51. a4 a6 52. a5 g4 53. Ke1 Bb5
54. Bxf6 Kxf6 55. Nxg4+ Kf5 56. Ne3+
Ke5 57. Kd2 Ke4 58. Nc2 Kxd5 59. Ke3
Kc5 60. Kd2 Bc4 0-1 (New York International 1948-49)

593 Kashdan–Kramer [D19]
New York International, round 5, 1948
[December 28]

1. Nf3 Nf6 2. c4 c6 3. Nc3 d5 4. d4
dxc4 5. a4 Bf5 6. e3 e6 7. Bxc4 Bb4
8. 0-0 0-0 9. Qe2 Bg4 10. Rd1 Qe7
11. e4 Nbd7 12. Bg5 h6 13. Bh4 e5 14. d5
Rfd8 15. a5 Bxc3 16. bxc3 Nf8 17. h3
Bh5 18. g4 Bg6 19. Qe3 Rd7 20. dxc6
bxc6 21. Rxd7 N8xd7 22. Rd1 Qe8
23. Rd6 Qb8 24. Rxc6 Bxe4 25. Ra6
Bb7 26. Rxf6 gxf6 27. Qd3 Nf8 28. Bxf6
Bxf3 29. Qxf3 Qb1+ 30. Kh2 Rc8
31. Bd5 Nd7 32. Be4 Qc1 33. Qf5 Qf4+
34. Qxf4 exf4 35. Bd4 Nc5 36. Bf5 Ne6
0-1 (*New York International* 1948-49)

594 Najdorf–Kashdan [D74]
New York International, round 6, 1948
[December 29]

1. d4 Nf6 2. c4 g6 3. g3 Bg7 4. Bg2 d5

5. cxd5 Nxd5 6. Nf3 0–0 7. 0–0 Na6
8. e4 Nb6 9. Nc3 Bg4 10. d5 Qd7 11. a4
Bh3 12. a5 Bxg2 13. Kxg2 Nc4 14. Qe2
Ne5 15. Nxe5 Bxe5 16. Rd1 Bg7 17. Qc4
Rfd8 18. Be3 Qd6 19. Rac1 e6 20. Nb5
exd5 21. exd5 Qe7 22. b3 Rd7 23. Bf4
g5 24. Bxc7 Nxc7 25. d6 Rxd6 26. Nxd6
Ne6 27. Qd5 Rd8 28. Qxb7 Rd7 29. Qd5
Rd8 30. Qb7 Rd7 31. Rc8+ Bf8 32. Qd5
Nc7 33. Nf5 Nxd5 34. Nxe7+ Rxe7
35. Rxd5 1–0 (*New York International* 1948-
49)

595 Kashdan–Horowitz [E00]
New York International, round 7, 1948
[December 30]

1. d4 Nf6 2. c4 e6 3. Nf3 d5 4. g3
dxc4 5. Qa4+ Bd7 6. Qxc4 Nc6 7. Bg2
Na5 8. Qd3 c5 9. 0–0 Nc6 10. dxc5
Bxc5 11. a3 0–0 12. b4 Be7 13. Bb2 a6
14. Nbd2 Qc7 15. Rac1 Rad8 16. Nc4
Qb8 17. Qc2 Nd5 18. e4 Nc7 19. Rfd1 f6
20. e5 f5 21. Nd4 Nxd4 22. Bxd4 Nd5
23. Nb6 Bc6 24. Nxd5 Bxd5 25. Bb6
Bxg2 26. Bxd8 Be4 27. Qc7 Qxd8
28. Rxd8 Bxd8 29. Qd7 Bd5 30. Rc8
Bb6 31. Rxf8+ 1–0 (*New York International*
1948-49)

596 Kashdan–Fine [D25]
New York International, round 8, 1948
[January 1, 1949]

1. d4 d5 2. Nf3 Nf6 3. c4 dxc4 4. e3
a6 5. Bxc4 b5 6. Bb3 e6 7. a4 c6 8. 0–0
Nbd7 9. Qe2 Be7 10. e4 0–0 11. Bg5 Bb7
12. Nbd2 h6 13. Bh4 Nh5 14. Bxe7 Qxe7
15. g3 Qb4 16. Ne1 Qxd4 17. Qxh5 Qxd2
18. Rd1 Nf6 19. Qxf7+ Kxf7 20. Rxd2
Rfd8 21. Rxd8 Rxd8 22. f3 c5 23. axb5
axb5 24. Ng2 Rd2 25. Rf2 Rd4 26. Kf1
Nd7 27. Bc2 c4 28. Ke2 Ne5 29. Ke3
Rd8 30. h3 Ke7 31. Ne1 Nc6 32. f4 b4
33. e5 Na5 34. Rd2 b3 35. Bg6 c3
36. Rxd8 Kxd8 37. bxc3 Nc4+ 38. Kd4
Bd5 39. Nf3 b2 40. Bb1 Na3 0–1 (*New
York International* 1948-49)

597 Euwe–Kashdan [E35]
New York International, round 9, 1948
[January 2, 1949]

1. d4 Nf6 2. c4 e6 3. Nc3 Bb4 4. Qc2
d5 5. cxd5 exd5 6. Bg5 0–0 7. e3 h6
8. Bxf6 Qxf6 9. a3 Bxc3+ 10. Qxc3 c6
11. Nf3 Bf5 12. Be2 Nd7 13. Rc1 Qe7
14. 0–0 Nf6 15. b4 Ne4 16. Qb2 Rad8
17. Ne5 Rd6 18. a4 a6 19. b5 axb5
20. axb5 cxb5 21. Qxb5 Ra8 22. Qb2 b6
23. Ra1 Rc8 24. Rfc1 Rxc1+ 25. Rxc1 Rf6
26. Bf3 g5 27. h3 Kg7 28. g4 Bh7
29. Rc8 Nd6 30. Rc1 Nc4 31. Nxc4 dxc4
32. Bd5 Be4 33. Bxe4 Qxe4 34. Rxc4
Qf3 35. Rb4 Qd1+ 36. Kg2 Qf3+ 37. Kg1
Qxh3 38. Qe2 Rf3 39. d5 Rf6 40. Rd4
Rd6 41. Qb2 h5 42. gxh5 Kh6 43. Rh4!!

After
43. Rh4

Very clever. Besides threatening 44. Qh8 mate
White attacks the queen. Black is now forced
to go for the draw. **43. ... gxh4** ½–½ (*New
York International* 1948-49)

598 Scheltinga–Kashdan [E34]
New York vs. Amsterdam Match, 1949

1. d4 Nf6 2. c4 e6 3. Nc3 Bb4 4. Qc2
d5 5. e3 0–0 6. Nf3 c5 7. dxc5 Bxc5
8. a3 a6 9. b4 Be7 10. Bb2 dxc4 11. Bxc4
b5 12. Bb3 Bb7 13. 0–0 Nbd7 14. Rac1
Rc8 15. Qe2 Qb6 16. e4 Rfd8 17. Kh1 Nf8
18. Ne5 Qd6 19. f4 Qd2 20. Rc2 Qxe2
21. Rxe2 a5 22. f5 axb4 23. axb4 Bxb4
24. Nxf7 Kxf7 25. fxe6+ Ke8 26. e5
Nd5 27. Nxb5 Nxe6 28. Nd6+ Bxd6
29. exd6 Rxd6 30. Kg1 Ba6 31. Rxe6+
Rxe6 32. Bxd5 Bxf1 33. Bxe6 Rc2
34. Bd4 Rc1 35. Kf2 g6 36. Bd5 Bb5

37. Bf3 Bc6 38. Bxc6+ Rxc6 39. Kf3 Kf7
40. h3 Ke6 41. Ba7 Kf5 42. Bb8 Rc3+
43. Kf2 Ke4 44. Ba7 Rc7 45. Bb6 Rf7+
46. Ke2 Rb7 47. Bc5 Rb2+ 48. Kf1 Kd3
49. Ba7 Rb7 50. Bc5 Kd2 51. Kf2 Rf7+
52. Kg1 Ke2 53. Kh2 Rc7 54. Bb6 Rc4
55. Kg1 Rc6 0–1 The game was adjudicated
a win for Black.(*American Chess Bulletin*, p. 40)

599 Kashdan–Scheltinga [C65]
New York vs. Amsterdam Match, 1949

1. e4 e5 2. Nf3 Nc6 3. Bb5 Nf6 4. 0–0
Bc5 5. c3 0–0 6. d4 Bb6 7. dxe5 Nxe4
8. Bf4 d5 9. exd6 Nxd6 10. Bd3 Bg4
11. Nbd2 Qf6 12. Bg5 Qxg5 13. Nxg5
Bxd1 14. Raxd1 h6 15. Nge4 Ne5 16. Bc2
½–½ (*American Chess Bulletin* 1949, p. 13)

600 Kashdan–Rothman [E72]
Metropolitan Chess League, 1949
[April 16]

1. d4 Nf6 2. c4 g6 3. Nc3 Bg7 4. e4
0–0 5. g3 d6 6. Bg2 e5 7. Nge2 exd4
8. Nxd4 Nc6 9. Nxc6 bxc6 10. 0–0 Nd7
11. f4 Ba6 12. Qd3 Nc5 13. Qe2 Bd4+
14. Kh1 Re8 15. f5 Qd7 16. Bh6 d5
17. Qd2 dxe4 18. Rad1 Rad8 19. b4 Nd3
20. Nxe4 Bxc4 21. Qc2 Qd5 22. fxg6
hxg6 23. Ng5 Nxb4 24. Qb1 Qb5
25. Rf4 Be3 26. Rxd8 Rxd8 27. Qa1 f6
28. Rxf6 Rd1+ 29. Qxd1 Bxg5 30. Rf8+
Kh7 31. Qd7+ 1–0 A wild game! (Contributed by Dale Brandreth)

601 Vine–Kashdan [C68]
Metropolitan Chess League, 1949
[April 30]

1. e4 e5 2. Nf3 Nc6 3. Bb5 a6 4. Bxc6
dxc6 5. d4 exd4 6. Qxd4 Qxd4 7. Nxd4
Bd7 8. Be3 0–0–0 9. Nd2 g6 10. 0–0–0
Bg7 11. N4b3 b6 12. Rhe1 c5 13. f3 Ne7
14. Bf4 Nc6 15. Nc4 Be6 16. Ne3 c4
17. Na1 c3 18. b3 Rxd1+ 19. Nxd1 b5
20. a3 a5 21. b4 axb4 22. axb4 Nxb4
23. Nb3 Bxb3 If 24.cxb3 Nd3+ wins the
bishop, hence White resigns. 0–1 (Contributed
by Dale Brandreth)

602 Fink–Kashdan [C80]
North–South California Match, 1951

1. e4 e5 2. Nf3 Nc6 3. Bb5 a6 4. Ba4
Nf6 5. 0–0 Nxe4 6. Qe2 Nc5 7. Bxc6
dxc6 8. d4 Ne6 9. dxe5 Nd4 10. Nxd4
Qxd4 11. h3 Bc5 12. Nc3 Bb4 13. g4
Be6 14. Rd1 Qc4 15. Qxc4 Bxc4 16. a3
Be7 17. b3 Be6 18. Be3 h5 19. f3 hxg4
20. hxg4 Rh3 21. Kg2 Bxg4! 22. Rh1
Rxf3 23. Rh8+ Bf8 24. Bc5 0–0–0
25. Bxf8 Rxc3 26. Bxg7 Rxh8 27. Bxh8
Rxc2+ 28. Kg3 Be6 29. b4 c5 0–1 (*Cal-
ifornia Chess Reporter*, June 1951)

603 Kashdan–McDavid [C28]
Fort Worth, U.S. Open, round 1, 1951
[July 9]

1. e4 e5 2. Nc3 Nf6 3. Bc4 Nc6 4. d3
h6 5. f4 exf4 6. Bxf4 d6 7. Nf3 Be7
8. 0–0 0–0 9. Qd2 Na5 10. Bb3 Nxb3
11. axb3 Nh7 12. d4 Bg5 13. Nxg5 Nxg5
14. Rae1 Qf6 15. Nd5 Qe6? 16. Bxg5
hxg5 17. Nxc7 Qg6 18. Nxa8 Bd7 19. Nc7
Rc8 20. Nd5 Re8 21. c4 g4 22. e5 Re6
23. exd6 Kh8 24. Ne7 Qh5 25. Rxe6
Bxe6 26. d5 Bd7 27. Qa5 Qe5 28. Qd8+
Kh7 29. Qxd7 Qe3+ 30. Kh1 Qe2
31. Qf5+ g6 32. Qxf7+ Kh6 33. Qxg6
mate 1–0 (Kashdan's scoresheet)

604 Sharp–Kashdan [E38]
Fort Worth, U.S. Open, round 2, 1951
[July 10]

1. d4 Nf6 2. c4 e6 3. Nc3 Bb4 4. Nf3
0–0 5. Bg5 c5 6. Qc2 Nc6 7. e3 h6
8. Bh4 d5 9. dxc5 g5 10. Bg3 Ne4
11. Rd1 Qa5 12. Rc1 Qxa2 13. Nd2 Nxc3
14. bxc3 Qxc2 15. Rxc2 Bxc5 16. Nb3
Be7 17. c5 Bd7 18. Be2 a5 19. Bd6 a4
20. Nd4 Bxd6 21. cxd6 Nxd4 22. exd4
Bc6 23. Kd2 Rfd8 24. Ra1 Rxd6 25. Rb2
Ra5 26. Rb4 Rd8 27. Kc2 Rda8 28. Kb2
a3+ 29. Ka2 Kg7 30. Rab1 Kf6 31. Bg4
Ke7 32. Rb6 Kd6 33. Bh5 f6 34. Be2 e5
35. Bb5 Re8 36. Rxb7 Bxb5 37. R1xb5
Rxb5 38. Rxb5 exd4 39. Rb6+ Kc5
40. Rxf6 dxc3 41. Kxa3 Kc4 0–1 (*U.S.
Open* 1951)

605 Kashdan–Myers [E40]
Fort Worth, U.S. Open, round 3, 1951
[July 11]

1. d4 Nf6 2. c4 e6 3. Nc3 Bb4 4. e3
Bxc3+ 5. bxc3 d6 6. Bd3 Nc6 7. Ne2 b6
8. 0–0 Na5 9. Ng3 c5 10. e4 e5 11. f4
cxd4 12. cxd4 Qc7 13. fxe5 dxe5 14. Bg5
Bg4 15. Qc2 Nd7 16. h3 f6 17. Bd2 exd4?
18. Bf4 Qc5 19. hxg4 Rc8 20. Nf5 0–0
21. Bd6 1–0 (*U.S. Open* 1951)

606 L. Evans–Kashdan [E46]
Fort Worth, U.S. Open, round 4, 1951
[July 13]

1. d4 Nf6 2. c4 e6 3. Nc3 Bb4 4. e3
0–0 5. Nge2 d5 6. a3 Be7 7. cxd5 exd5
8. g3 c6 9. Bg2 Re8 10. 0–0 Bf5 11. f3
Bf8 12. Nf4 Na6 13. Re1 Nc7 14. e4 dxe4
15. fxe4 Bg4 16. Qd3 Ne6 17. h3 Qxd4+
18. Qxd4 Nxd4 19. hxg4 Nc2 20. g5
Bc5+ 21. Kf1 Ng4 22. Nd3 Bb6 23. Bf4
Rad8 24. Ke2 Nd4+ 25. Kd2 Nb3+
26. Ke2 Nd4+ 27. Kd2 Nb3+ 28. Ke2
½–½ (*U.S. Open* 1951)

607 Kashdan–Gonzalez [E42]
Fort Worth, U.S. Open, round 5, 1951
[July 14]

1. d4 Nf6 2. c4 e6 3. Nc3 Bb4 4. e3 c5
5. Nge2 cxd4 6. exd4 d5 7. a3 Be7 8. c5
Nc6 9. Bf4 0–0 10. g3 b6 11. b4 bxc5
12. bxc5 Ne4 13. Bg2 Nxc3 14. Nxc3
Ba6 15. Bf1 Bxf1 16. Kxf1 Qa5 17. Qd2
Bf6 18. Be3 Rfd8 19. Ra2 Rab8 20. Kg2
Rb3 21. Rc1 Rxa3 22. Rca1 Rxa2
23. Rxa2 Qb4 24. Ra4 Qb7 25. Qd3 h6
26. Nb5 Rb8 27. Nd6 Qd7 28. Qa6 e5
29. dxe5 Bxe5 30. Bf4 Bxf4 31. Rxf4
Rf8 32. Nf5 d4 33. h4 Qd5+ 34. Kh2
Re8 35. Qa1 Re4 36. Qc1 a5 37. Rf3
Kh7 38. Qd1 Ne5 39. Rf4 Rxf4 40. gxf4
Nf3+ 41. Kg3 Qxf5 42. Qxf3 Qxc5
43. Qe4+ f5 44. Qe6 h5 45. Qe8 Qd6
46. Qxh5+ Qh6 47. Qd1 But not 47. Qxf5+
as then Qg6+ would force a queen exchange
which would then allow the passed pawns to
decide the game. 47. ... Qg6+ 48. Kh2 Qg4

49. Qxd4 Qxh4+ 50. Kg2 Qg4+ 51. Kf1
Qf3 52. Kg1 Qe4 53. Qd8 a4 54. Qd6
Qf3 55. Qe5 Qh3 56. Qc7 Qg4+ 57. Kf1
Qd1+ 58. Kg2 Qd5+ 59. Kg3 a3 60. Qe7
a2 61. Qe2 Qf7 But not a1(Q) as then Qh5+
would run into a perpetual. 62. Qb2 Qg6+
63. Kh2 Qa6 64. Qa1 Qe2 65. Kg2 Qe4+
66. Kg3 Qb1 0–1 (*US Open* 1951)

608 Westbrock–Kashdan [D13]
Fort Worth, U.S. Open, round 6, 1951
[July 15]

1. d4 d5 2. c4 c6 3. cxd5 cxd5 4. Nc3
Nf6 5. Nf3 e6 6. Bf4 Be7 7. e3 a6 8. Bd3
0–0 9. h3 b5 10. a3 Bb7 11. 0–0 Nbd7
12. Ne5 Nb6 13. Qe2 Ne4 14. Bxe4 dxe4
15. Qg4 f5 16. Qe2 Rc8 17. Rfc1 Bd6
18. a4 bxa4 19. Rc2 Qe8 20. Rac1 Qe7
21. Nb1 Rxc2 22. Rxc2 Nd5 23. Nc3
Nxf4 24. exf4 a3 25. bxa3 Bxe5
26. dxe5 Qxa3 27. Qc4 Qe7 28. Na4 Rc8
29. Nc5 Bd5 30. Qc3 Qc7 31. Qg3 Qb6
32. Qa3 a5 33. Qa4 h6 Here 33. ... Rxc5??
34. Rxc5 Qe8 would be mate. 34. Qa3 Qb4
35. Qc1 a4 36. Nxa4 Rxc2 37. Qxc2 e3
38. fxe3 Qe1+ 39. Kh2 Qxe3 40. Nc5
Qxf4+ 41. Kh1 Qxe5 42. Nd7 Qd6
43. Qc8+ Kf7 44. h4 f4 45. h5 f3
46. Kg1 fxg2 0–1 (*U.S. Open* 1951)

609 Kashdan–Liepnieks [B17]
Fort Worth, U.S. Open, round 7, 1951
[July 16]

1. e4 c6 2. d4 d5 3. Nc3 dxe4 4. Nxe4
Nd7 5. Nf3 Ngf6 6. Ng3 e6 7. Bd3 Be7
8. 0–0 0–0 9. Qe2 c5 10. c3 Re8 11. Re1
Qc7 12. Ne4 h6 13. Bd2 b6 14. Ne5 Bb7
15. Nxf6+ Bxf6 16. Bb5 Bxe5 17. dxe5
a6 18. Ba4 b5 19. Bc2 c4 20. Qh5 Nc5
21. Bxh6! Qc6 22. Qg4 Qxg2+ 23. Qxg2
Bxg2 24. Be3 Be4 25. Bxe4 Nxe4 26. f3
The knight has no retreat. 1–0 (*U.S. Open* 1951)

610 Hearst–Kashdan [A28]
Fort Worth, U.S. Open, round 8, 1951
[July 17]

1. c4 e5 2. Nc3 Nf6 3. Nf3 Nc6 4. d4
exd4 5. Nxd4 Bb4 6. Bg5 h6 7. Bh4 Ne5

8. Qb3 Ba5 9. 0–0–0 Ng6 10. Bxf6 Qxf6
11. Nd5 Qxf2 12. Qa3 c6 13. Qxa5 cxd5
14. Qxd5 0–0 15. g3 Qe3+ 16. Kb1 Ne7
17. Qf3 Qxf3 18. exf3 d5 19. Bd3 dxc4
½–½ (U.S. Open 1951)

611 Kashdan–Brieger [C42]
Fort Worth, U.S. Open, round 9, 1951
[July 18]

1. e4 e5 2. Nf3 Nf6 3. Nxe5 d6 4. Nf3
Nxe4 5. d4 d5 6. Bd3 Bd6 7. 0–0 0–0
8. c4 c6 9. Nc3 Nxc3 10. bxc3 Bg4 11. h3
Bh5 12. c5 Bc7 13. Bf5 Bg6 14. Bxg6
hxg6 15. Re1 Nd7 16. Bg5 f6 17. Bd2
Re8 18. Qb1 Rxe1+ 19. Bxe1 b6 20. cxb6
axb6 21. Qxg6 Nf8 22. Qf5 g6 23. Qd3
b5 24. Bd2 Kg7 25. Qe3 g5 26. g3 Qd7
27. Re1 Bd6 28. h4 gxh4 29. Qh6+ Kg8
30. Qxh4 Nh7 31. Qh5 Nf8 32. Bh6 Qf7
33. Qg4+ Qg6 34. Qh3 Qf7 35. Nh4
Qd7 36. Nf5 Ra7 37. Qg4+ Kh7
38. Re7+ Qxe7 39. Nxe7 Rxe7 40. Bxf8
Re1+ 41. Kg2 Bxf8 42. Qd7+ Kg6
43. Qxc6 1–0 (U.S. Open 1951)

612 Kashdan–Whitaker [D36]
Fort Worth, U.S. Open, round 10, 1951
[July 19]

1. d4 d5 2. c4 e6 3. Nc3 Nf6 4. Nf3
Nbd7 5. Bg5 Be7 6. e3 0–0 7. cxd5
exd5 8. Bd3 Re8 9. 0–0 Nf8 10. Qc2 c6
11. Rfe1 Ne4 12. Bxe7 Qxe7 13. b4 Ng6
14. b5 Bd7 15. bxc6 Bxc6 16. Ne2 Rac8
17. Rac1 Bd7 18. Qb3 Bg4 19. Rxc8 Rxc8
20. Bxe4 dxe4 21. Nd2 Bxe2 22. Rxe2
Nh4 23. g3 Rc1+ 24. Nf1 Qd7! 0–1 (U.S.
Open 1951)

613 Mednis–Kashdan [C42]
Fort Worth, U.S. Open, round 11, 1951
[July 20]

1. e4 e5 2. Nf3 Nf6 3. Nxe5 d6 4. Nf3
Nxe4 5. d4 d5 6. Bd3 Bd6 7. 0–0 0–0
8. Nc3 Nxc3 9. bxc3 Bg4 10. Rb1 b6
11. h3 Bh5 12. c4 c6 13. c3 dxc4 14. Bxc4
Nd7 15. Bd3 Re8 16. Be3 Nf8 17. c4 Qc7
18. Rb3 Rad8 19. Bc2 Bh2+ 20. Kh1 Bf4
21. Qd2 Ne6 22. Bf5 Bxf3 23. Bxe6

Bxe3 24. Rxe3 Bxg2+ 25. Kxg2 Rxe6
26. Rxe6 fxe6 27. Re1 c5 28. d5 exd5
29. cxd5 Qd6 30. Rd1 b5 31. Qd3 a6
32. f3 c4 33. Qe4 c3 34. Qd4 b4 35. Qc4
a5 36. Rd4 h6 37. h4 Rd7 38. Qc8+ Kh7
39. h5 Qe7 40. Kh3 Qf7 41. Qa6 Qxf3+
42. Kh4 Qf2+ 43. Kh3 Qf5+ 44. Kg3 c2
0–1 (U.S. Open 1951)

614 Sherwin–Kashdan [D87]
Fort Worth, U.S. Open, round 12, 1951
[July 21]

1. c4 Nf6 2. Nc3 d5 3. cxd5 Nxd5
4. e4 Nxc3 5. bxc3 g6 6. d4 Bg7 7. Bc4
c5 8. Ne2 0–0 9. 0–0 Nc6 10. Be3 Qc7
11. Rc1 Rd8 12. Qd2 a6 13. f4 b5 14. Bd3
Qa5 15. dxc5 Be6 16. Rc2 Bc4 17. Nd4
Nxd4 18. cxd4 Qxd2 19. Rxd2 Bxd4
20. Kf2 Bc3 21. Bxc4 Bxd2 22. Bd5
Bxe3+ 23. Kxe3 Rac8 24. Rc1 Rc7 25. g4
e6 26. Bb3 Kf8 27. e5 Ke7 28. Bd1 Rd5
29. c6 g5 30. Bf3 gxf4+ 31. Kxf4 Rd2
32. h4 h6 33. a3 Rd3 34. Ra1 Rc3
35. Be4 Rc4 36. Ke3 Rc8 37. h5 f6
38. Rd1 Rc3+ 39. Kd4 R3xc6 40. exf6+
Kxf6 41. Rf1+ Kg5 42. Bxc6 Rxc6
43. Ke5 Kxg4 0–1 (U.S. Open 1951)

615 Kashdan–Ortega [C86]
Hollywood vs. Havana, 1951 *[September]*

1. e4 e5 2. Nf3 Nc6 3. Bb5 a6 4. Ba4
Nf6 5. 0–0 Be7 6. Qe2 b5 7. Bb3 0–0
8. c3 d5 9. d3 dxe4 10. dxe4 Bg4 11. h3
Bd7 12. Rd1 Qc8 13. Bg5 h6 14. Bh4 Re8
15. Nbd2 Nh5 16. Nxe5 Nf4 17. Bxf7+
Kh7 18. Qe3 Nxe5 19. Bxe8 Nxh3+
20. gxh3 Bxh4 21. Bxd7 Nxd7 22. e5
Be7 23. Nf3 Nf8 24. Nd4 Bc5 25. b4
Bb6 26. Qe4+ Kh8 27. Rd3 Nh7 28. Re1
Ng5 29. Qg4 Qg8 30. e6 Re8 31. e7 Qf7
32. Rde3 Nh7 33. Re6 Ng5 34. R6e3
Nh7 35. Qe6 Qh5 36. Rg3 Nf6 37. Re5
Qd1+ 38. Kg2 Ng8 39. Qf7 1–0 (*Los Angeles Times*, September 30, 1951)

616 Ortega–Kashdan [E17]
Hollywood vs. Havana, 1951 *[September]*

1. d4 Nf6 2. Nf3 e6 3. c4 b6 4. g3 Bb7

5. Bg2 Be7 6. Nc3 0–0 7. Qc2 d6 8. 0–0
Nbd7 9. b3 Re8 10. Ba3 e5 11. Rfd1 exd4
12. Rxd4 Bf8 13. Rad1 g6 14. Bb2 Bg7
15. R4d2 Nc5 16. Nd5 Nce4 17. Rd3 a5
18. Ne1 Nxd5 19. cxd5 Nc5 20. R3d2
Qe7 21. Bxg7 Kxg7 22. Bf3 Ba6 23. Ng2
Qf6 24. Rd4 Re5 25. Ne3 h5 26. a3 Bb5
27. Rf4 Qe7 28. Qc3 Kg8 29. b4 axb4
30. axb4 Ne4 31. Bxe4 Rxe4 32. Rxe4
Qxe4 33. Qxc7 Bxe2 34. Re1 Ra2
35. Qxd6 Rb2 36. Qf4 Qxf4 37. gxf4
Bb5 38. Rd1 Kf8 39. d6 Ke8 40. Nd5
Ba4 41. Re1+ Kd8 42. Nxb6 Rxb4
43. Nxa4 Rxa4 44. f5 Rg4+ 45. Kf1 gxf5
46. Re5 Rh4 47. Kg2 Rg4+ 48. Kf3 Kd7
49. Rxf5 Kxd6 50. Rxf7 Ke6 The game
was adjudicated a draw. ½–½ (*Los Angeles
Times*, September 30, 1951)

617 Graf–Kashdan [D02]
Hollywood International, round 1, 1952
[April 26]

1. d4 Nf6 2. Nf3 e6 3. Bf4 d5 4. e3 c5
5. c3 Nc6 6. Bb5 Qb6 7. Qe2 Be7 8. a4
a6 9. Bxc6+ bxc6 10. a5 Qb7 11. Ne5
Nd7 12. dxc5 Nxc5 13. b4 Ne4 14. Qg4
g6 15. 0–0 f6 16. Nxg6? Rg8 17. Qh5
hxg6 18. Qh7 Rf8 19. Qxg6+ Rf7 20. f3
Nd6 21. Qg8+ Rf8 22. Qg6+ Kd8
23. Nd2 e5 24. Bg3 Bf5 25. Qh5 Kc7
26. f4 e4 27. Nb3 Rh8 28. Qe2 Nc4
29. Nd4 Qc8 30. Rfe1 Qd7 31. Qc2 Bd6
32. Nb3 Rag8 33. Nd2 Nxd2 34. Qxd2
Kd8 35. Qd4 Ke7 36. Rad1 Be6 37. Rd2
f5 38. Red1 Kf7 39. Qb6 Ra8 40. c4
Rhb8 41. cxd5 cxd5 If 41. ... Qxb6 42.dxe6+
Qxe6 43.Rxd6 42. Qd4 Rxb4 43. Qc3 Rc8
44. Qa1 Ra4 45. Qb2 Rb8 46. Qc3 Bb4
0–1 (*Hollywood International* 1952)

618 Kashdan–Pafnutieff [C17]
Hollywood International, round 2, 1952
[April 27]

1. e4 e6 2. d4 d5 3. Nc3 Bb4 4. e5 c5
5. a3 Ba5 6. Bd2 cxd4 7. Nb5 Bxd2+
8. Qxd2 Nc6 9. f4 Nh6 10. Nd6+ Kf8
11. Nf3 f6 12. Nxd4 Nxd4 13. Qxd4 Nf7
14. Nxf7 Kxf7 15. Be2 Qb6 16. Rd1 Qxd4

17. Rxd4 Bd7 18. c4 Bc6 19. Kf2 Ke7
20. exf6+ gxf6 21. Re1 e5 22. Bf3 Kd6
23. Rd2 d4 24. fxe5+ fxe5 25. c5+ Kxc5
26. Rxe5+ Kc4 27. Be2+ Kb3 28. Bd1+
Kc4 29. Ke2 Bxg2 30. b3+ 1–0 (*Hollywood
International* 1952)

619 H. Steiner–Kashdan [E34]
Hollywood International, round 3, 1952
[April 29]

1. d4 Nf6 2. c4 e6 3. Nc3 Bb4 4. Qc2
d5 5. e3 0–0 6. a3 Be7 7. Nf3 Nbd7
8. Be2 c5 9. 0–0 cxd4 10. exd4 dxc4
11. Bxc4 a6 12. Bg5 b5 13. Ba2 Bb7
14. Qe2 Nb6 15. Rad1 Nbd5 16. Nxd5
Bxd5 17. Bb1 Bc4 18. Qc2 g6 19. Rfe1
Rc8 20. Ne5 Qd5 20. ... Bd4 would have
been better. Black is now at a disadvantage.
21. Qd2 Bb3 22. Rc1 Rfd8 23. Qf4 Kg7

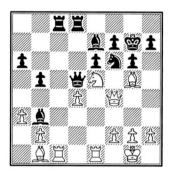

After
23. ... Kg7

24. Rc3 Rxc3 25. bxc3 Qd6 26. Re3
Bd5 27. Rh3 h5 28. Rxh5! Rd7 29. Rh8!
If 29. ... Kxh8 30. Nxf7+ wins the queen. 1–0
Notes by Steiner. (*Hollywood International* 1952)

620 Kashdan–Gligorić [E66]
Hollywood International, round 4, 1952
[April 30]

1. d4 Nf6 2. c4 g6 3. Nf3 Bg7 4. g3 c5
5. Bg2 0–0 6. 0–0 d6 7. Nc3 Nc6 8. d5
Na5 9. Nd2 a6 10. Qc2 e6 11. e4 exd5
12. cxd5 b5 13. Re1 Re8 14. Nf1 Ra7
15. f3 Rae7 16. Be3 Nc4 17. Bf2 Nxb2!
18. Qxb2 b4 19. Nd1 Nxe4 20. Qc1 Nxf2
21. Rxe7 Qxe7 22. Nxf2 Bd4 23. Kh1
Bxf2 24. Rb1 Bf5 25. Rb3 Bd4 0–1 (*Hollywood International* 1952)

621 Joyner–Kashdan [E49]

Hollywood International, round 5, 1952
[May 10]

1. d4 Nf6 2. c4 e6 3. Nc3 Bb4 4. e3
0–0 5. Bd3 c5 6. Nge2 d5 7. cxd5 exd5
8. a3 Bxc3+ 9. bxc3 This transposition of
the position is the same as Botvinnik–Capablanca, AVRO 1938, and Reshevsky–Fine,
Hamilton 1941. The usual continuation is here
9. ... b6, followed by Ba6 but White always gets
a slight plus. So perhaps Black might have done
better to play cxd4 earlier and retreat his bishop
to e2. 9. ... Re8 10. 0–0 Nc6 11. f3 Qc7
12. Ng3 Bd7 13. Ra2 Rad8 14. Re2 Bc8
15. Bb2

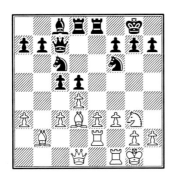

After
15. Bb2

15. ... Na5 This is a mistake even though
Black gets the White bishop for his knight.
White's center is too strong and his kingside attack soon becomes overwhelming. 16. Qe1
Nc4 17. Bxc4 dxc4 18. e4 Nd7 19. f4 f6
20. Qf2 b5 21. Re3 Nf8 22. f5 Re7
23. Nh5 Rde8 24. Qh4 Rf7 25. Rg3 Qe7
26. Rf4 Kh8 27. h3 Not immediately Rfg4
because of ...Bxf5! White's king needs a hole.
27. ... Kg8 28. Rfg4 1–0 This game was
postponed at the request of Mr. Kashdan. For
business reasons, Kashdan asked to postpone
his games against local players until the weekend
following the tournament. The game was played
on May 10. (*Hollywood International* 1952)

622 Kashdan–Martin [D19]

Hollywood International, round 6, 1952
[May 3]

1. d4 d5 2. c4 c6 3. Nc3 Nf6 4. Nf3
dxc4 5. a4 Bf5 6. e3 e6 7. Bxc4 Bb4

8. 0–0 0–0 9. Qe2 Bg4 10. Rd1 Nbd7
11. e4 Qe7 12. h3 Bxf3 13. Qxf3 e5 14. d5
Rac8 15. Bg5 h6 16. Bd2 cxd5 17. Nxd5
Nxd5 18. Bxd5 Bxd2 19. Rxd2 Nb8
20. Rad1 Nc6 21. Qb3 Nd4 22. Qxb7
Rc7 23. Qa6 Rfc8 24. Qd3 Qb4 25. f4
Qxa4 26. fxe5 Ne6 27. Kh2 Qa5 28. Rf1
Re7 29. Rdf2 Qc7 30. Qg3 Rce8 31. Rf5
Nd8 32. Ra1 Ne6 33. Ra6 Nd4 34. Rf2
Qc1 35. Bxf7+ Rxf7 36. Rxf7 Kxf7
37. Rxa7+ Re7 38. Qf2+ Ke8 39. Ra8+
1–0 (*Hollywood International* 1952)

623 Dake–Kashdan [C99]

Hollywood International, round 7, 1952
[May 4]

1. e4 e5 2. Nf3 Nc6 3. Bb5 a6 4. Ba4
Nf6 5. 0–0 Be7 6. Re1 b5 7. Bb3 d6
8. c3 Na5 9. Bc2 c5 10. d4 Qc7 11. Nbd2
0–0 12. h3 cxd4 13. cxd4 Nc6 14. d5
Nb4 15. Bb1 a5 16. Nf1 Bd7 17. Bg5
Rfc8 18. Ne3 h6 19. Bh4 g5 20. Bg3 a4
21. a3 Na6 22. Nd2 Rab8 23. Bc2 Nc5
24. Rc1 b4 25. Qf3 bxa3 26. bxa3 Qa7
27. Ndc4 Nb3 28. Bxb3 axb3 29. Rb1
Qa6 30. Nxe5 dxe5 31. Bxe5 Rb5 32. a4
Ra5 33. Nf5 Bxf5 34. Qxf5 Ne8
35. Rxb3 Rd8 36. Reb1 Qg6 37. Qxg6+
fxg6 38. Rb7 Kf8 39. Rb8 Rxa4 40. f3
Rxb8 41. Rxb8 Ra6 42. Kf2 Bc5+
43. Ke2 Ke7 44. Rb7+ Kd8 45. Rb8+
Kd7 46. Rb7+ ½–½ (*Hollywood International*
1952)

624 Kashdan–Pomar [B92]

Hollywood International, round 8, 1952
[May 6]

1. e4 c5 2. Nf3 d6 3. d4 Nf6 4. Nc3
cxd4 5. Nxd4 a6 6. Be2 e5 7. Nb3 Be6
8. 0–0 Nbd7 9. f4 Rc8 10. Be3 Be7
11. Qe1 b5 12. a3 Bc4 13. Rd1 0–0
14. Bd3 Ng4 15. Bc1 exf4 16. Bxf4 Bh4
17. g3 Bf6 18. Qe2 Qb6+ 19. Kh1 Bxc3
20. bxc3 Nge5 21. Bxc4 Rxc4 22. Rd5 f5
23. Bxe5 Rxe4 24. Qd2 Rxe5 25. Rxd6
Qb7+ 26. Qg2 Qxg2+ 27. Kxg2 Nf6
28. Nd4 Ng4 29. Rf3 Ra8 30. Rc6 g6
31. Rc7 Rae8 32. Ra7 Re1 33. Rd3 Rc1

34. h3 Ne3+ 35. Kf2 Nxc2 36. Ne6 Re1
37. Rd2 R1xe6 38. Rxc2 R8e7 39. Ra8+
Kf7 40. Rd2 Rc6 41. Rd3 Rec7 42. h4
Kf6 43. Rf8+ Kg7 44. Ra8 Kh6 45. Kg2
Kh5 46. Rf3 Rxc3 47. Rxa6 Rxf3
48. Kxf3 Rc3+ 49. Kf4 Rc4+ 50. Kf3
Ra4 51. Rb6 Rxa3+ 52. Kf4 Ra4+
53. Kf3 Rb4 54. Rb8 h6 55. Rh8 Rb1
56. Rh7 b4 57. Rh8 b3 58. Rb8 b2
59. Kg2 g5 60. Rb4 f4 0–1 (*Hollywood International* 1952)

625 Cross–Kashdan [D94]

Hollywood International, round 9, 1952
[May 11]

1. d4 Nf6 2. c4 c6 3. Nc3 d5 4. e3 g6
5. Nf3 Bg7 6. Be2 0–0 7. 0–0 Nbd7
8. b4 dxc4 9. Bxc4 Nb6 10. Bb3 Nfd5
11. Nxd5 cxd5 12. Qe2 Bf5 13. Bd2 Qd6
14. Rfc1 Rac8 15. Rc5 Be6 16. Rac1 Nc4
17. Bxc4 dxc4 18. Ng5 b6 19. Nxe6 bxc5
20. Nxf8 cxd4 21. Rxc4 Rxf8 22. exd4
Bxd4 23. g3 h5 24. Be3 e5 25. Qd2 Rd8
26. Bg5 Rd7 27. Qc2 Kh7 28. a3 Bb6
29. Rc8 Qd1+ 30. Qxd1 Rxd1+ 31. Kg2
Ra1 32. Rc3 Bd4 33. Rb3 Kg7 34. Be3
Kf6 35. Rd3 Bxe3 36. Rxe3 g5 37. Rc3
Kf5 38. Rc7 Rxa3 39. Rxf7+ Kg6
40. Rc7 g4 41. h4 gxh3+ 42. Kxh3 Ra2
43. Kg2 a6 44. Ra7 Ra4 45. Rb7 Kf5
½–½ (*Hollywood International* 1952)

626 Standers–Kashdan [C21]

Hollywood Invitational, 1953 *[February–March]*

1. e4 e5 2. d4 exd4 3. c3 dxc3 4. Nxc3
Nc6 5. Nf3 Nf6 6. Bc4 Bb4 7. e5 d5
8. 0–0 dxc4 9. Qxd8+ Nxd8 10. exf6
Bxc3 11. bxc3 gxf6 12. Nd2 Bf5 13. Nxc4
Bd3 14. Re1+ Ne6 15. Ne3 0–0–0
16. Ng4 Bc4 17. Nxf6 Rd3 18. Ne4 Rhd8
19. Ng5 Rd1 20. Be3 Rxa1 21. Rxa1 Nxg5
22. Bxg5 Rd3 23. Bf6 Bxa2 24. h4 Rd2
25. g4 a5 26. Kg2 b5 27. g5 b4 28. cxb4
axb4 29. Kg3 b3 30. f4 b2 31. Bxb2
Rxb2 32. Kg4 Be6+ 33. Kh5 Rb4 34. Re1
Bf5 35. Kh6 Kd7 36. h5 c5 37. Kg7 c4
38. Rf1 Ke6 39. Re1+ Kd6 40. Kxf7 c3

41. g6 hxg6 42. hxg6 Rxf4 43. Kf6 Bd3+
44. Kg5 Rf1 45. Re3 c2 46. Rxd3+ Ke7
47. Rc3 c1Q+ 48. Rxc1 Rxc1 49. Kh6 Kf6
0–1 (*Los Angeles Times*, February 22, 1953)

627 Kashdan–Hazard [B38]

Hollywood Invitational, 1953 *[February–March]*

1. e4 c5 2. Nf3 Nc6 3. d4 cxd4
4. Nxd4 d6 5. c4 g6 6. Nc3 Bg7 7. Be3
Nf6 8. Be2 0–0 9. 0–0 a6 10. Rc1 Bd7
11. h3 Ne8 12. Qd2 Rc8 13. Nb3 Nc7
14. Rfd1 Be6 15. Nd5 Na8 16. Bh6 f5
17. Bxg7 Kxg7 18. Nf4 Rf6 19. Qc3 Qg8
20. exf5 Bf7 21. fxg6 hxg6 22. Nd5
Bxd5 23. cxd5 Na7 24. Qe3 Rcf8
25. Qxa7 1–0 (*Los Angeles Times*, February 1, 1953)

628 Spiller–Kashdan [E49]

Hollywood Invitational, 1953 *[February–March]*

1. d4 Nf6 2. c4 e6 3. Nc3 Bb4 4. e3
0–0 5. a3 Bxc3+ 6. bxc3 c5 7. Bd3 d5
8. cxd5 exd5 9. Ne2 Nc6 10. 0–0 Re8
11. Bb2 c4 12. Bc2 Bg4 13. Qe1 Qd7
14. Ng3 Nh5 15. Qb1 Nxg3 16. hxg3 h6
17. f3 Bh5 18. g4 Bg6 19. Bxg6 fxg6
20. e4 dxe4 21. fxe4 Qxg4 22. Re1 Re7
23. Qc2 Rae8 24. e5 Rf7 25. Rad1 b5
26. a4 Ne7 27. d5 Nf5 28. e6 Rf6
29. Qe4 Qg3 30. Rf1 Qd6 31. Rf3 Rfxe6
32. dxe6 Qxd1+ 33. Rf1 Qxf1+ 0–1 (*Los Angeles Times*, February 1, 1953)

629 Almgren–Kashdan [E61]

Hollywood Invitational, round 4, 1953
[February–March]

1. d4 Nf6 2. c4 g6 3. Nc3 Bg7 4. Nf3
0–0 5. g3 d5 6. cxd5 Nxd5 7. Bg2 c5
Challenging White's center, creating difficulties for White and calling for precise treatment.
8. Nxd5 Bringing out the Black queen early to the center of the board is not altogether without hazard to her majesty. 8. ... Qxd5 9. dxc5 There are times when it is advantageous to have

the uncastled king in the thick of the fighting for the ending. But this is not one of them. The situation calls for boldness so that White may derive benefit for the threat by his bishop. For instance: 9. Be3 cxd4 10. 0–0 (threatening Nxd4) Rd8 11. Nxd4 Qh5 12. Bf3 Qc5 13. Qa4 Bd7 14. Qb3 and Black's game is OK. Another line is 12. Qh3 (instead of Qc5) 13. Qb3 Bxd4 14. Bxd4 Rxd4 15. Bxb7 and White recovers his piece. [*However, 15. ... Rb4 seems to refute this— P.P.L.*] 9. ... Qxd1+ 10. Kxd1 Na6 11. Bg5 White is puzzled as to how to proceed and quite understandably. Though 11. e4 followed by Nd2 would achieve slightly better results. 11. ... Bxb2 12. Rb1 Bf6 13. Bxf6 exf6 14. Rb5 Bd7 From now on Black dictates the terms of the struggle. Kashdan shows masterly technique of minor piece tactics. 15. Rxb7 Nxc5 16. Rc7 Ba4+ 17. Ke1 Rac8 18. Rxc8 Not 18. Rxa7? because Ne4 threatens checkmate among other things. 18. ... Rxc8 19. Nd2 Ne6 20. f4 Rc1+ 21. Kf2 Rc2

After
21. ... Rc2

And now with Black's rook on the seventh rank the White king in the center is a handicap rather than of any help. 22. Ne4 Nd4 23. Re1 Kg7 24. Ke3 Nf5+ 25. Kd3 Rxa2 26. Nc3 Ra3 27. Rb1 Ne3 With a loose knight in an open position, Kashdan is always dangerous. White would be well advised to exchange knights. As played the loss of the exchange cannot be avoided. The queening of the pawn now brings about victory. 28. Rb4 Nd1 29. Rxa4 Nb2+ 30. Kd2 Nxa4 31. Nb5 Ra2+ 32. Ke3 Nb6 33. g4 a5 34. Be4 a4 35. Bd3 Rb2 36. Kd4 Rb3 37. Kc5 a3 38. Bc2 Rxb5+ **0–1** Annotations by Herman Helms. (*American Chess Bulletin*, May-June 1953)

630 Kashdan–Blumenfeld [C83]

Hollywood Invitational, 1953 [*February-March*]

1. e4 e5 2. Nf3 Nc6 3. Bb5 a6 4. Ba4 Nf6 5. 0–0 Nxe4 6. d4 b5 7. Bb3 d5 8. dxe5 Be6 9. c3 Be7 10. Nbd2 0–0 11. Bc2 f5 12. exf6 Nxf6 13. Nb3 Bg4 14. Qd3 Bxf3 15. Qxf3 Ne5 16. Qh3 Bd6 17. Bg5 h6 18. Bh4 Qe8 19. Nd4 Qh5 20. a4 g5 21. Bg3 Qxh3 22. gxh3 bxa4 23. Rxa4 Rfb8 24. b4 Nc4 25. Nf5 Bf8 26. Rfa1 Rb6 27. Bxc7 Rc6 28. Bg3 Nd2 29. b5 Rxc3 30. Rxa6 Rxa6 31. bxa6 Nd7 32. a7 Nb6 33. Bd1 Na8 34. Bh5 Rc6 35. Rd1 Ne4 36. Rxd5 Nxg3 37. hxg3 Rc7 38. Ra5 Bc5 39. Bf3 **1–0** (*Los Angeles Times*, March 1, 1953)

631 H. Steiner–Kashdan [D19]

Hollywood Invitational, 1953 [*February-March*]

1. d4 d5 2. c4 c6 3. Nc3 Nf6 4. Nf3 dxc4 5. a4 Bf5 6. e3 e6 7. Bxc4 Bb4 8. 0–0 0–0 9. Qe2 Nbd7 10. Rd1 Ne4 11. Bd3 Ndf6 12. Qc2 Nxc3 13. bxc3 Bxd3 14. Qxd3 Be7 15. e4 c5 16. d5 exd5 17. exd5 Ne8 18. Bf4 Nd6 19. Ne5 Re8 20. Rab1 Bf8 21. Nc4 b6 22. Re1 Nxc4 23. Qxc4 Qh4 24. g3 Qf6 25. Rxe8 Rxe8 26. Qb5 Re4 27. Qd3 Qf5 28. Rd1 c4 29. Qd2 Qd7 30. d6 h6 31. h4 Re8 32. Qd5 Rc8 33. Qb5 Rc6 34. Rd4 a6 35. Qxa6 Bxd6 36. Qb5 Qc7 37. Bxd6 Rxd6 38. Qe5 Rc6 39. Qe8+ Kh7 40. Rd7 Qc8 41. Qxf7 Qg8 42. Qf5+ Kh8 43. Rf7 Rc8 44. Qg6 Rd8 45. Rb7 Rd1+ 46. Kh2 Rd2 47. Qxb6 Qd5 48. Rb8+ Kh7 49. Qb1+ Qd3 50. Kg2 Rc2 51. Qb7 Rc1 52. Kh2 Qf5 53. Qg2 Rxc3 54. Rb5 Qf3 55. Rc5 Qxg2+ 56. Kxg2 Rc1 57. Kf3 c3 58. Kg4 Ra1 59. Rxc3 Rxa4+ 60. f4 Ra5 61. h5 Rb5 62. Re3 Kg8 63. Re6 Kf7 64. Rg6 Rb4 65. Kf3 Rb3+ 66. Kg2 Rb5 67. g4 Rb2+ 68. Kg3 Rb3+ 69. Kh4 Rf3 70. f5 Kf8 ½–½ (*Los Angeles Times*, March 22, 1953)

632 Spinner–Kashdan [B71]

Hollywood Invitational, 1953 *[February–March]*

1. e4 c5 2. Nf3 d6 3. d4 cxd4 4. Nxd4 Nf6 5. Nc3 g6 6. f4 Nc6 7. Nxc6 bxc6 8. e5 dxe5 9. Qxd8+ Kxd8 10. fxe5 Nd5 11. Bd2 Bg7 12. 0–0–0 Bxe5 13. Nxd5 cxd5 14. Ba5+ Ke8 15. Rxd5 Bf4+ 16. Bd2 Bxd2+ 17. Rxd2 e5 18. Bb5+ Ke7 19. Re1 f6 20. h3 Be6 21. Bd3 Rac8 22. b3 Rhd8 23. c4 Rd4 24. Kc2 Rcd8 25. Kc3 g5 26. b4? Bxc4 27. Red1 Bxd3 28. Rxd3 Rxd3+ 29. Rxd3 Rxd3+ 30. Kxd3 f5 31. Kc4 Kd6 32. b5 f4 33. a4 e4 34. a5 e3 35. Kd3 Kc5 36. b6 axb6 37. axb6 Kxb6 38. g3 Kc5 39. h4 gxh4 0–1 (*Los Angeles Times*, February 15, 1953)

633 Kashdan–Cross [B54]

Hollywood Invitational, 1953 *[February–March]*

1. e4 c5 2. Nf3 e6 3. Nc3 d6 4. d4 cxd4 5. Nxd4 a6 6. g3 b5 7. Bg2 Bb7 8. a3 Nf6 9. 0–0 Qc7 10. Bg5 Nbd7 11. Qe2 Be7 12. Rad1 0–0 13. Bc1 Nb6 14. f4 d5 15. e5 Nfd7 16. Kh1 Bc5 17. Rd3 Rac8 18. Qh5 Rfe8 19. Nce2 Bxd4 20. Nxd4 Na4 21. g4 Nac5 22. Rh3 Nf8 23. c3 Ne4 24. f5 exf5 25. Nxf5 d4 26. Nxd4 Rxe5 27. Qh4 Qe7 28. Qxe7 Rxe7 29. Re3 Rce8 30. Nf5 Re6 31. Kg1 Nc5 32. Bxb7 Nxb7 33. Rd1 Rxe3 34. Nxe3 g6 35. Nd5 Kg7 36. Bg5 Re6 37. Kf2 Nc5 38. Be3 Ne4+ 39. Kf3 f5 40. gxf5 gxf5 41. Nb4 Kf7 42. Rd8 a5 43. Nc2 Ng6 44. Rd7+ Re7 45. Rxe7+ Kxe7 46. Nd4 Nd6 47. Nc6+ Ke6 48. Nxa5 Ne5+ 49. Ke2 Ng4 50. Bf4 Ne4 51. c4 bxc4 52. Nxc4 Ngf6 53. a4 Nd5 54. Bb8 Nc5 55. a5 Na6 56. Bd6 Nf6 57. Kd3 Ne4 58. Ba3 Nc7 59. Nd2 Ke5 60. Nxe4 fxe4+ 61. Ke2 Kd4 62. Bd6 Nd5 63. a6 Nb6 64. b4 Kc4 65. a7 Kd5 66. Bc7 Na8 67. b5 1–0 (*Los Angeles Times*, February 15, 1953)

634 Mazner–Kashdan [E34]

Hollywood Invitational, 1953 *[February–March]*

1. d4 Nf6 2. c4 e6 3. Nc3 Bb4 4. Qc2 d5 5. e3 0–0 6. Nf3 c5 7. a3 Bxc3+ 8. bxc3 Qc7 9. cxd5 exd5 10. Be2 Ne4 11. Bb2 Bf5 12. Nh4 Be6 13. 0–0 Nc6 14. Rac1 Rac8 15. Bd3 Qe7 16. Nf3 f5 17. c4 cxd4 18. cxd5 Bxd5 19. Bc4 Qf7 20. Bxd5 Qxd5 21. exd4 b5 22. Ne5 Nxe5 23. Qxc8 Nc4 24. Rxc4 bxc4 25. Qc7 Qf7 26. Qc6 Rb8 27. Bc1 h6 28. Bf4 Rb3 29. d5 Rd3 30. d6 Qd5 31. Qxd5+ Rxd5 32. f3 Nc3 33. Kf2 g5 34. Rc1 Na2 35. Rc2 gxf4 36. Rxa2 Rxd6 37. Re2 Rd4 38. g3 fxg3+ 39. hxg3 Kf7 40. Ke3 Rd3+ 41. Kf4 c3 0–1 (*Los Angeles Times*, March 8, 1953)

635 Steven–Kashdan [E25]

Hollywood Invitational, 1953 *[February–March]*

1. d4 Nf6 2. c4 e6 3. Nc3 Bb4 4. a3 Bxc3+ 5. bxc3 0–0 6. f3 d5 7. e3 c5 8. cxd5 exd5 9. Bd3 Nc6 10. Ne2 Ne7 11. Ng3 h5 12. 0–0 h4 13. Nh1 Re8 14. Ra2 Bf5 15. Nf2 Bg6 16. Bxg6 Nxg6 17. Re2 Rc8 18. e4 dxe4 19. fxe4 cxd4 20. cxd4 Rc4 21. Bb2 Nf4 22. Rc2 b5 23. Rxc4 bxc4 24. Qc2 Qd7 25. d5 Ng4 26. Kh1 Nxf2+ 27. Rxf2 Nxd5 28. Qxc4 Nb6 29. Qd4 Qxd4 30. Bxd4 Rxe4 31. Rd2 Re1+ 32. Bg1 Ra1 33. Rd3 a5 34. h3 Nc4 35. Rd8+ Kh7 36. Rd4 Nxa3 37. Rxh4+ Kg8 38. Ra4 Nc2 39. Rc4 Ra2 40. Rc8+ Kh7 41. Rc7 Kg6 42. g4 a4 43. h4 a3 44. Ra7 Rb2 45. h5+ Kh7 0–1 (*Los Angeles Times* 1953)

636 Rogosin–Kashdan [A29]

Hollywood Invitational, 1953 *[February–March]*

1. c4 e5 2. Nc3 Nf6 3. g3 d5 Here again the thrust at the center which yields the freedom craved by Black. Students of this opening will do well to mark closely the manner in which this American Master exploits the oppor-

tunities to advance his development. **4. cxd5 Nxd5 5. Bg2 Nb6 6. Nf3 Nc6 7. 0–0 Be7 8. d3 0–0 9. Bd2 f5** Serving the double purpose of a frontal attack, and a better placement of his king bishop. **10. Rc1 Kh8 11. Qc2 Bf6 12. Rfd1 Qe7 13. Be3** Conceding that White's ninth move was a loss of time. It might well be exchanged now for the knight. **13. ... Be6 14. Na4 Qf7 15. Nc5 Bd5** Naturally, not Bxa2, because of b3 in reply. **16. Ng5**

After
16. Ng5

A faulty combination, instead of which b3 might have been effective, or Ne1, the answer being Nb4. **16. ... Bxg5 17. Bxd5 Nxd5 18. Bxg5 f4** Suddenly White finds himself cut off from the lone bishop, with no help in sight. The outlook is indeed dismal. **19. gxf4 exf4 20. Kh1 h6 21. Bh4 Nd4** Ominous indeed are these two horsemen moving in for the kill; with their approach the end cannot be far away. **22. Qd2 Qh5 23. Rc4 Nxe2 24. Re4** A brave attempt, but overlooking the mate threat. 24. Rg1 is forced, but then he is minus a rook. **24. ... Qf3 mate 0–1** (*American Chess Bulletin*, May-June 1953)

637 Kashdan–Piatigorsky [B18]
Hollywood Invitational, 1953 *[February 27]*

1. e4 c6 2. d4 d5 3. Nc3 dxe4 4. Nxe4 Bf5 5. Ng3 Bg6 6. Nf3 Nd7 7. Bd3 Bxd3 8. Qxd3 Qc7 9. 0–0 e6 10. Re1 Ngf6 11. Bd2 Be7 12. c4 0–0 13. Bc3 Rfe8 14. Re2 Rad8 15. Qc2 Nf8 16. Ne5 Ng6 17. Rae1 Bd6 18. Ne4 Bxe5 19. dxe5 Nxe4 20. Rxe4 Rd7 21. h4 Qd8 22. h5 Nh4 23. Qe2 Nf5 24. g3 Kh8 25. Kg2 Rg8 26. Rh1 Rd3 27. Rf4 Rd7 28. Rxf5

exf5 **29. h6 Rd4 30. hxg7+ Rxg7 31. e6 c5 32. e7 Qe8 33. Bxd4 cxd4 34. Re1 f6 35. Qe6 d3 36. Qxf5 d2 37. Rd1 Qxe7 38. Rxd2 b6 39. b4 Kg8 40. Qc8+ 1–0** (Kashdan's scoresheet)

638 Kashdan–Altschiller [D61]
Hollywood Invitational, 1953 *[February 15]*

1. d4 d5 2. c4 e6 3. Nc3 Nf6 4. Nf3 Nbd7 5. Bg5 Be7 6. Qc2 c6 7. e3 0–0 8. Bd3 dxc4 9. Bxc4 Nd5 10. Bxe7 Qxe7 11. 0–0 Nxc3 12. Qxc3 Nb6 13. Bb3 Nd5 14. Qd2 Qb4 15. Qd3 Rd8 16. Rac1 Bd7 17. Bc2 g6 18. e4 Nf6 19. Bb3 Qf8 20. Ne5 Be8 21. Qe3 Nd7 22. Nd3 Rac8 23. f4 Qg7 24. Rfd1 Nf8 25. e5 Nd7 26. Nf2 Nb6 27. Ne4 Nd5 28. Qf2 Bd7 29. Rd3 f5 30. exf6 Nxf6 31. Nc5 Rc7 32. Bxe6+ Kf8 33. Bxd7 1–0 (Kashdan's scoresheet)

639 Kashdan–Belzer [D85]
Hollywood Invitational, 1953 *[March 22]*

1. d4 Nf6 2. c4 g6 3. Nc3 d5 4. Nf3 Bg7 5. cxd5 Nxd5 6. e4 Nxc3 7. bxc3 c5 8. Bc4 Nc6 9. Be3 0–0 10. 0–0 Bg4 11. dxc5 Bxc3 12. Rb1 Qxd1 13. Rfxd1 Rfd8 14. Rdc1 Bb4 15. Ng5 Rf8 16. h3 Bd7 17. e5 Bf5 18. Rb3 a5 19. a3 a4 20. Rxb4 Nxb4 21. axb4 a3 22. g4 a2 23. Bxa2 Rxa2 24. gxf5 gxf5 25. Rc4 h6 26. Nf3 Kh7 27. Rh4 Rg8+ 28. Kf1 Rg6 29. Nd4 e6 30. Nb5 Kg7 31. Nd6 Ra7 32. b5 1–0 (Kashdan's scoresheet)

640 Woronzoff–Kashdan [B92]
Hollywood Invitational, 1953 *[February 28]*

1. e4 c5 2. Nf3 d6 3. d4 cxd4 4. Nxd4 Nf6 5. Nc3 a6 6. Be2 e5 7. Nb3 Be6 8. 0–0 Be7 9. Be3 Nbd7 10. f4 exf4 11. Rxf4 Ne5 12. Nd5 Nxd5 13. exd5 Bd7 14. Qd2 0–0 15. Raf1 Rc8 16. Nd4 Bg5 17. R4f2 Bxe3 18. Qxe3 Qa5 19. c4 Qxa2 20. b3 Qa5 21. Bd3 Rfe8 22. Bb1 Ng4 23. Qd3 g6 24. Ra2 Qc5 25. h3 Ne3 26. Rff2 Nf5 27. Nxf5 Bxf5 28. Qd1 Bxb1 29. Qxb1 Re3 30. Kf1 Qb4 31. Rfe2

Rxb3 32. Rab2 Rxb2 33. Qxb2 Qxc4
0–1 (Kashdan's scoresheet)

641 Kashdan–König [E40]
North–South California Match, 1954

1. d4 Nf6 2. c4 e6 3. Nc3 Bb4 4. e3
Nc6 5. Bd3 e5 6. a3 Bxc3+ 7. bxc3 e4
8. Bc2 Na5 9. Qe2 0–0 10. f3 b6 11. fxe4
Nxe4 12. Nf3 f5 13. Bb2 Ba6 14. Bd3
Qe7 15. 0–0 c5 16. Rac1 Rae8 17. Rc2
Qe6 18. d5 Qh6 19. Re1 Re7 20. Bc1 Rfe8
21. g3 Qh5 22. Qf1 Bxc4 23. Bxc4 Nxc4
24. Nh4 Ned6 25. Rf2 Rf7 26. a4 Ne5
27. a5 Ref8 28. axb6 axb6 29. Nf3
Nxf3+ 30. Rxf3 Ne4 31. Kg2 Nxc3
32. Qc4 Ne4 33. Ref1 Qg6 34. Rf4 Nd6
35. Qb3 b5 36. Bb2 b4 37. Rc1 Ne4
38. Ra1 Qh5 39. Qc2 d6 40. Ra6 Re8
41. g4 Qg6 42. Qa4 Rfe7 43. h3 h5
44. Ra8 fxg4 45. hxg4 hxg4 46. Rxe8+
Qxe8 47. Qxe8+ Rxe8 48. Rxg4 Re7
49. Kf3 Nd2+ 50. Ke2 Nb3 51. Kd3 Na5
52. Rg6 Rd7 53. e4 c4+ 0–1 (*California
Chess Reporter*, June 1954)

642 H. Steiner–Kashdan [E81]
California Open, 1954 *[July]*

1. d4 Nf6 2. c4 g6 3. Nc3 Bg7 4. e4 d6
5. f3 0–0 6. Bg5 h6 7. Be3 c6 8. Qd2
Kh7 9. g4 e5 10. 0–0–0 Qe7 11. h4 Ne8
12. Nge2 Nd7 13. d5 c5 14. Ng3 a6
15. Qh2 Nc7 16. Bg5 f6 17. Be3 Rf7
18. Bd3 b5 19. b3 bxc4 20. bxc4 Ne8
21. Rdg1 Qd8 22. g5 Nf8 23. h5! fxg5
24. hxg6+ Nxg6 25. Nf5 Nh4 26. Qg3
Bxf5 27. exf5 Kg8 28. Rxh4 gxh4
29. Qg4 Kf8 30. Ne4 Nf6 31. Qxh4 Nxe4
32. Qxe4 Rb8 33. Bd2! Bf6 34. Bxh6+
Ke7 35. Bd2 Qh8 36. f4 Rg8 37. Rh1
Qg7 38. fxe5 Bxe5 39. Kc2 Qg2
40. Qh4+ Kd7 41. Qh5 Rff8 42. Qh7+
Rg7 43. Qh6 Rf6 44. Qh8 Bf4 45. Rd1
Bxd2 46. Rxd2 1–0 (*California Chess Reporter*, August 1954)

643 Zemitis–Kashdan [E72]
California Open, 1954 *[July]*

1. d4 Nf6 2. c4 g6 3. g3 Bg7 4. Bg2

0–0 5. Nc3 d6 6. e4 e5 7. Nge2 Nc6
8. 0–0 Bd7 9. h3 Ne8 10. d5 Ne7 11. f4
f5 12. fxe5 dxe5 13. exf5 Nxf5 14. g4
Nh4 15. Rxf8+ Bxf8 16. Ng3 Nxg2
17. Kxg2 Bg7 18. Nce4 h6 19. b3 Qe7
20. Be3 Nd6 21. Qd2 Kh7 22. Rf1 ½–½
(*California Chess Reporter*, August 1954)

644 Grover–Kashdan [B21]
Hollywood, Pan American, round 1, 1954
[July]

1. e4 c5 2. f4 Nc6 3. Nf3 e6 4. Be2 d5
5. d3 Nf6 6. e5 Nd7 7. Nc3 Be7 8. Bd2
0–0 9. 0–0 a6 10. Qe1 b5 11. g4 b4
12. Nd1 d4 13. g5 f6 14. exf6 gxf6
15. Qh4 Rf7 16. Rf2 f5 17. Rg2 Nf8
18. Qg3 Bb7 19. Nh4 Rg7 20. Nf2 Bd6
21. Nf3 Qc7 22. Nh3 Ng6 23. Rf2 Nce7
24. Re1 Nd5 25. Nh4 Nf8 26. Bf3 c4
27. dxc4 Qxc4 28. b3 Qc7 29. Rfe2 Rc8
30. Qg2 Ne3 31. Bxe3 dxe3 32. Bxb7
Qxb7 33. Qxb7 Rxb7 34. Ng2 Rbc7
35. Nxe3 Bc5 36. Nf2 Bxe3 37. Rxe3
Rxc2 38. R1e2 Ng6 39. Nd3 R2c3
40. Kf2 Rxd3 41. Rxd3 Nxf4 42. Rd6
Nxe2 43. Kxe2 Kf7 44. Rxa6 Rc2+
45. Kd3 Rxh2 46. Ra7+ Kg6 47. Re7
Rxa2 48. Rxe6+ Kxg5 49. Rb6 h5
50. Rxb4 h4 51. Rb8 h3 52. Rh8 Kg4
53. Rg8+ Kf3 54. Rh8 h2 55. b4 Kg2
56. Rg8+ Kf2 57. Rh8 Kg1 0–1 (*Hollywood
1954*)

645 Kashdan–Rivise [E67]
Hollywood, Pan American, round 2, 1954
[July]

1. d4 Nf6 2. c4 g6 3. Nc3 Bg7 4. Nf3
0–0 5. g3 d6 6. Bg2 Nbd7 7. 0–0 e5
8. dxe5 dxe5 9. h3 c6 10. Be3 Re8
11. Qd2 Qa5 12. Rad1 Nf8 13. Ng5 Ne6
14. Nge4 Nxe4 15. Nxe4 Qxd2 16. Bxd2
f5 17. Nd6 Rd8 18. Ba5 Rd7 19. Bb4 e4
20. Nxc8 Rxd1 21. Ne7+ Kf7 22. Rxd1 c5
23. Nxf5 gxf5 24. Ba3 b6 25. Rd5 Bf6
26. Rxf5 Nd4 27. Rh5 Re8 28. Rxh7+
Kg6 29. Rxa7 e3 30. fxe3 Rxe3 31. Bf3
Nxe2+ 32. Kf2 Bd4 33. Kg2 Ng1 34. Bg4
Rd3 35. Re7 Rd2+ 36. Kh1 Rf2 37. Re1

Nf3 38. Bxf3 Rxf3 39. Re2 Kf5 40. Kg2
Rd3 41. b3 Rd1 42. Bb2 Rg1+ 43. Kh2
Rb1 44. Ba3 Bg1+ 45. Kg2 Bd4 46. Re8
Ra1 47. Re2 Rg1+ 48. Kh2 Rb1 49. h4
Kg4 50. Re4+ Kh5 51. b4 Bg1+ 52. Kg2
cxb4 53. Bxb4 Rxb4 54. Kxg1 Rb2
55. a3 Ra2 56. Rf4 Rc2 57. Rf2 Rxc4
58. Kg2 1–0 (*Hollywood* 1954)

646 Bisguier–Kashdan [E76]

Hollywood, Pan American, round 3, 1954
[July]

1. d4 Nf6 2. c4 g6 3. Nc3 Bg7 4. e4 d6
5. f4 0–0 6. Nf3 Nfd7 7. Bd3 e5 8. fxe5
dxe5 9. d5 Nc5 10. Bc2 a5 11. Be3 Qe7
12. 0–0 Nba6 13. a3 Bd7 14. Re1 b6
15. d6 Qxd6 16. Qxd6 cxd6 17. Rad1 Be6
18. Nd5 Bxd5 19. Rxd5 Rfd8 20. Red1
Bf8 21. Nxe5 Re8 22. Ng4 Re6 23. e5
Nc7 24. Rxd6 Bxd6 25. exd6 N7a6
26. d7 Rd8 27. Bg5 Rxd7 28. Nf6+ Rxf6
29. Bxf6 Rxd1+ 30. Bxd1 Nd7 31. Bd4
Kf8 32. Kf2 Ke7 33. Ke3 Nac5 34. b4
axb4 35. axb4 Ne6 36. Ba4 Nef8
37. Ke4 Kd6 38. Bxd7 Nxd7 39. Bxb6
f5+ 40. Kf4 h6 41. Bd4 Ke6 42. h4 Nf8
43. Bg7 g5+ 44. Kf3 Ng6 45. h5 Ne5+
46. Bxe5 Kxe5 47. g3 1–0 (*Chess Review*,
September 1954)

647 Kashdan–Gordon [D73]

Hollywood, Pan American, round 4, 1954
[July]

1. d4 Nf6 2. c4 g6 3. Nc3 Bg7 4. Nf3
d5 5. g3 c6 6. Bg2 Na6 7. cxd5 cxd5
8. 0–0 0–0 9. Qb3 Qb6 10. Qxb6 axb6
11. Bg5 Be6 12. a3 h6 13. Be3 Nc7
14. Rac1 Nce8 15. Nb5 Ne4 16. Nc7 Nxc7
17. Rxc7 Nd6 18. Rxe7 Bf6 19. Rc7 Bd8
20. Rc3 Kg7 21. Rd1 Nc4 22. Bc1 Bf6
23. Ne1 Rfd8 24. Nc2 Rac8 25. Nb4 b5
26. e3 Nb6 27. Rxc8 Rxc8 28. Bd2 Be7
29. Rc1 Bxb4 30. axb4 Nc4 31. Bc3 f5
32. Ra1 Nd6 33. f3 Kf7 34. Bf1 Bd7
35. Bd3 Re8 36. Kf2 Rc8 37. h3 h5
38. Be1 Nc4 39. Bc3 Nd6 40. Ke2 g5
41. Bd2 Re8 42. Kf2 Nc4 43. Bc1 Nd6
44. b3 g4 45. Ra2 gxh3 46. Kg1 h4

47. Kh2 hxg3+ 48. Kxg3 Rg8+ 49. Kxh3
1–0 (*Hollywood*, 1954)

648 Kashdan–Ulvestad [C86]

Hollywood, Pan American, round 5, 1954
[July]

1. e4 e5 2. Nf3 Nc6 3. Bb5 a6 4. Ba4
Nf6 5. 0–0 Be7 6. Qe2 b5 7. Bb3 d6
8. a4 Bd7 9. c3 0–0 10. d4 b4 11. Bc2
bxc3 12. bxc3 Bg4 13. d5 Nb8 14. h3 Bc8
15. c4 Nfd7 16. a5 Nc5 17. Be3 Nbd7
18. Nc3 Bf6 19. Nd2 Bg5 20. Na4 Bxe3
21. Qxe3 Nxa4 22. Bxa4 Nc5 23. Bc2
Qe7 24. Rab1 Bd7 25. Nb3 Nxb3
26. Rxb3 Ba4 27. Rb2 Bxc2 28. Rxc2
Rfb8 29. Qa3 Qh4 30. Re1 Qd8 31. c5
Rb5 32. Rec1 f5 33. exf5 dxc5 34. Rxc5
Qd6 35. Qe3 Rxc5 36. Qxc5 Rd8
37. Qxd6 Rxd6 38. Rc5 Rd7 39. Kf1 Kf7
40. Ke2 Kf6 41. g4 e4 42. Ke3 Ke5
43. Rc6 Kxd5 44. Rxa6 c5 45. Re6 Kc4
46. g5 Kb5 47. Re8 c4 48. Rc8 Kb4
49. Kxe4 c3 50. f6 gxf6 51. gxf6 Kb3
52. Ke5 Ra7 53. Ke6 Ra6+ 54. Ke7 Ra7+
55. Ke8 c2 56. Rxc2 Ra8+ 57. Ke7 Ra7+
58. Ke6 Ra6+ 59. Kd7 Kxc2 60. f7 Ra7+
61. Ke6 Ra6+ 62. Ke7 Ra7+ 63. Kf6
1–0 (*Hollywood*, 1954)

649 H. Steiner–Kashdan [D56]

Hollywood, Pan American, round 6, 1954
[July]

1. d4 Nf6 2. c4 e6 3. Nc3 d5 4. Bg5
Be7 5. e3 0–0 6. Nf3 h6 7. Bh4 Ne4
8. Bxe7 Qxe7 9. Qc2 Nxc3 10. bxc3 c5
11. Be2 b6 12. 0–0 Nc6 13. e4 dxc4
14. Bxc4 Bb7 15. Rfe1 cxd4 16. cxd4
Rac8 17. Qe2 Rfd8 18. Rad1 Na5 19. Bd3
Rc3 20. Rd2 Rdc8 21. Red1 Nc4
22. Bxc4 R8xc4 23. Ne5 Rc1 24. h3 Qg5
25. Nf3 Qf4 26. d5 exd5 27. exd5 Qd6
28. Ne5 Rc5 29. Nc6 Bxc6 30. dxc6
Qxc6 31. Rd8+ Kh7 32. Qd3+ Qg6
33. Qf3 Rxd1+ 34. Rxd1 Qf5 35. Qg3
Rc2 36. a3 b5 37. Qe3 a5 38. g4 Qc5
39. Qf4 Qc4 40. Qxc4 Rxc4 41. Rd5
Rc1+ 42. Kg2 Rb1 43. a4 bxa4 44. Rxa5
Rb4 45. Ra6 g6 46. f3 Kg7 47. Kg3 h5

48. gxh5 gxh5 49. h4 Kf8 50. Ra5 Ke7 51. Rxh5 ½–½ (*Hollywood*, 1954)

650 Kashdan–Levin [C42]

Hollywood, Pan American, round 9, 1954 [*July*]

1. e4 e5 2. Nf3 Nf6 3. Nxe5 d6 4. Nf3 Nxe4 5. d4 d5 6. Bd3 Bd6 7. 0–0 0–0 8. c4 Bg4 9. cxd5 f5 10. h3 Bh5 11. Nc3 Re8 12. Re1 Nxc3 13. Rxe8+ Qxe8 14. bxc3 Bxf3 15. Qxf3 Qe1+ 16. Bf1 Nd7 17. Bb2 Qd2 18. Qe2 Qf4 19. g3 Qe4 20. Qxe4 fxe4 21. Re1 Nf6 22. c4 Bb4 23. Re3 Re8 24. Bc1 b6 25. Bg2 Kf7 26. Kf1 h6 27. Ke2 b5 28. Rb3 a5 29. cxb5 Nxd5 30. Bd2 Kf6 31. Rb2 Nc3+ 32. Ke1 Rb8 33. a3 Bxa3 34. Rb3 Nxb5 35. Bxa5 Ra8 36. Rxb5 Rxa5 If 37. Rxa5 Bb4+ regains the rook. ½–½ (*Hollywood*, 1954)

651 Gross–Kashdan [C84]

Hollywood, Pan American, round 10, 1954 [*July 19*]

1. e4 e5 2. Nf3 Nc6 3. Bb5 a6 4. Ba4 Nf6 5. 0–0 Be7 6. d4 exd4 7. Nxd4 Nxd4 8. e5 Ne6 9. exf6 Bxf6 10. Nc3 0–0 11. Ne4 Be7 12. c4 f5 13. Nc3 f4 14. Bc2 Qe8 15. Nd5 Bd8 16. Re1 Qf7 17. Qd3 g6 18. f3 d6 19. b4 c6 20. Nc3 Bb6+ 21. Kh1 Nd4 22. Ne4 Bf5 23. Bb2 c5 24. Bxd4 cxd4 25. c5 d5 26. Bb3 Bc7 27. Qxd4 Rad8 28. Nd6 Qf6 29. Bxd5+ 1–0 (*Chess Life*, January 5, 1955)

652 Kashdan–Evans [E90]

Hollywood, Pan American, round 13, 1954 [*July*]

1. d4 Nf6 2. c4 g6 3. Nc3 Bg7 4. e4 0–0 5. Nf3 d6 6. g3 c5 This line was recently analyzed by Evans in *Chess Life*. 7. Bg2 Nc6 8. d5 Na5 9. Qd3 a6 10. 0–0 Rb8 11. Rb1 b5 12. b3 b4 13. Ne2 Nxe4!? Again an Evans gamble. 14. Qxe4 Bf5 15. Qh4 Bxb1 16. Bg5 Bxa2 17. Bxe7 Qd7 18. Ng5 h6 19. Ne4 f5 After 19. ... Re8, White's attack would proceed rapidly with

20. Nf6+ Bxf6 21. Bxf6 Qf5 22. Nf4, etc. **20. Nf4** White throws everything into the attack. **20. ... g5 21. Bxg5 hxg5 22. Nxg5 Bf6 23. Nfe6 Rf7 24. Re1** A whole rook down and his house in flames on the queenside, White develops his remaining piece! **24. ... Bxb3 25. Qh6 Bxg5 26. Qxg5+ Rg7 27. Nxg7 Qxg7 28. Qh5 Qf7 29. Qg5+ Qg7 30. Qh5 Bxc4 31. Re8+ Rxe8 32. Qxe8+ Kh7 33. Qh5+ Kg8 34. Qe8+ Qf8 35. Qg6+ Kh8 36. Qh5+ Kg7 37. Qg5+ Kf7** Black must allow the opening of lines for White's remaining piece if he is to escape the checks. **38. Qxf5+ Ke7 39. Qe6+ Kd8 40. Bh3 Kc7 41. Bf5 b3 42. g4**

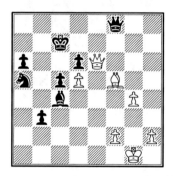

After 42. g4

White's last trump, his passed pawns, are now played out.... **42. ... Qg7 43. h4 Qa1+ 44. Kh2 Qe5+** The time pressure on Black begins to tell. Qd4 seems to win here, because the king can escape to a7 when Nb7 will stop the checks, and the White king will come into danger. **45. Qxe5 dxe5 46. h5 e4** Black is lost because the only important diagonal is in White's control. **47. h6 1–0** Black overstepped the time limit. This was the crucial game of the tournament, giving Bisguier his chance to overtake Evans. Though Black should have won with accurate defense, Kashdan is to be commended for his enterprising and brilliant play. (*The California Chess Reporter*, August 1954)

653 König–Kashdan [C86]

North–South California Match, 1955

1. e4 e5 2. Nf3 Nc6 3. Bb5 a6 4. Ba4 Nf6 5. 0–0 Be7 6. Qe2 b5 7. Bb3 d6 8. c3 Na5 9. Bc2 c5 10. d4 Qc7 11. dxc5 dxc5 12. Rd1 0–0 13. Nbd2 Rd8 14. Nf1

Be6 15. Rxd8+ Rxd8 16. Bg5 h6 17. Bh4 Nc6 18. Ne3 g6 19. a4 c4 20. axb5 axb5 21. Rd1 Kg7 22. Bg3 Rxd1+ 23. Qxd1 Bc5 24. Nd5 Qd6 25. Nxf6 Kxf6 26. Qxd6 Bxd6 27. Nd2 ½–½ (*The California Chess Reporter*, June 1955)

654 Kashdan–Taimanov [B64]
USA–USSR Match, round 1, 1955 *[July 9]*

1. e4 c5 2. Nf3 Nc6 3. d4 cxd4 4. Nxd4 Nf6 5. Nc3 d6 6. Bg5 e6 7. Qd2 Be7 8. 0-0-0 0-0 9. f4 d5 10. e5 Nd7 11. h4 Nb6 12. Be2 Bd7 13. Kb1 Rc8 14. Ncb5 a6 15. Nd6 Rc7 16. Bxe7 Qxe7 17. Qe3 Nc8 18. Nxc8 Rfxc8 19. Bd3 Nxd4 20. Qxd4 Bb5 21. c3 Bxd3+ 22. Qxd3 Rc4 23. g3 b5 24. h5 h6 25. Rhf1 b4 26. cxb4 Qxb4 27. Rc1 Rb8 28. Rc2 Rxc2 29. Qxc2 Qa3 30. Rg1 Qf3 31. Qc7 Qd3+ 32. Ka1 Rb4 33. Qc3 Qb5 34. b3 Re4 35. Re1 Rxe1+ 36. Qxe1 Qd3 37. Kb2 Qf3 38. b4 Qxh5 39. a4 Qf3 40. b5 axb5 41. axb5 d4 42. Qd2 Qf1 43. Qa5 Qe2+ 44. Kc1 d3 45. Qd2 Qe4 46. b6 Qc6+ 47. Kd1 Qxb6 48. Qxd3 Qg1+ 49. Ke2 Qg2+ 50. Ke1 g6 51. Qe3 Kh7 52. Kd1 Kg7 53. Ke1 Qh3 54. Kf2 g5 55. fxg5 Qf5+ 56. Kg2 hxg5 57. Qd4 g4 58. Qf4 Kg6 59. Kf2 Qc2+ 60. Ke3 Qb3+ 61. Kf2 Qa2+ 62. Ke3 Qa7+ 63. Ke2 Kh5 64. Qe4 Qa2+ 65. Kf1 Qa1+ 66. Kf2 Qb2+ 67. Kf1 Qc1+ 68. Ke2 Kg5 69. Qh7 Qc4+ 70. Kd2 Qd4+ 71. Kc1 Qg1+ 72. Kd2 Qf2+ 73. Kd1 Qf1+ 74. Kd2 Qf5 75. Qh8 Qf2+ 76. Kc1 Qe3+ 77. Kc2 Qe2+ 78. Kc3 Qe3+ 79. Kc4 Qe4+ 80. Kc5 Qd5+ 81. Kb6 Qd4+ 82. Kc6 Qd5+ 83. Kc7 Qc5+ 84. Kd7 Qa7+ 85. Kc6 Qa4+ 86. Kd6 Qb4+ 87. Kc6 Qe4+ 88. Kd6 Qb4+ 89. Kc6 Qe4+ ½–½ (*Chess Life*, July 20, 1955)

655 Taimanov–Kashdan [E87]
USA–USSR Match, round 2, 1955 *[July 11]*

1. c4 Nf6 2. Nc3 g6 3. e4 d6 4. d4 Bg7 5. f3 e5 6. d5 0-0 7. Be3 Ne8 8. Qd2 f5 9. 0-0-0 f4 10. Bf2 b6 11. Bd3 a5

12. Nge2 Na6 13. a3 Bd7 14. Bc2 Qe7 15. Nb5 h6 16. b4 axb4 17. axb4 Bxb5 18. cxb5 Nb8 19. Kb2 Nd7 20. Qc3 Ndf6 21. Qc6 Ra7 22. Ra1 Rxa1 23. Rxa1 Kh7 24. Ra7 Qd8 25. Nc3 Nd7 26. Bd3 g5 27. Na4 Kg6 28. Ra8 Qe7 29. Qb7 Bf6 30. Bf1 h5 31. Ra7 Rf7 32. Qc8 Rh7 33. Kb3 Kh6 34. Nb2 Rg7 35. Nc4 Rf7 36. Ra8 Rf8 37. Qb7 Rf7 38. Rc8 Rf8 39. Qc6 Bg7 40. Na5 Bf6 41. Qa8 Kg7 42. Nc6 Qf7 43. g3 g4 44. fxg4 ½–½ (From a Russian source)

656 Kashdan–Taimanov [B70]
USA–USSR Match, round 3, 1955
[July 13]

1. e4 c5 2. Nf3 Nc6 3. d4 cxd4 4. Nxd4 Nf6 5. Nc3 d6 6. g3 g6 7. Nde2 h5 8. h3 Bd7 9. Bg2 Qc8 10. Nf4 Bg7 11. Ncd5 Ne5 12. Rb1 Nxd5 13. Nxd5 Nc4 14. h4 Nb6 15. Ne3 0-0 16. 0-0 a5 17. Qd3 a4 18. c4 Be6 19. b3 axb3 20. axb3 Ra2 21. Nd5 Bxd5 22. exd5 Nd7 23. Be3 Ne5 24. Qd1 Qf5 25. Rc1 Rfa8 26. Bb6 R8a6 27. Be3 Kh7 28. b4 R6a3 29. c5 Rd3 30. Qe1 dxc5 31. bxc5 Nf3+ 32. Bxf3 Qxf3 33. c6 bxc6 34. dxc6 Be5 35. c7 Bxc7 36. Rxc7 Re2 37. Qa1 Rdxe3 38. Rc8 Re5 39. Qa8 Qxa8 40. Rxa8 Rf5 41. Kg2 e5 42. Ra3 e4 43. Kg1 Kh6 44. Rb3 g5 45. hxg5+ Kxg5 46. Rb8 Kg4 47. Kg2 e3 48. Rg8+ Rg5 49. Re8 Rxf2+ 50. Rxf2 exf2 51. Kxf2 Kh3 52. Re3 Rf5+ 53. Kg1 Ra5 54. Rf3 f5 55. Kf2 Ra2+ 56. Kf1 Kg4 57. Rf4+ Kxg3 58. Rxf5 Ra1+ 59. Ke2 h4 60. Rg5+ Kf4 61. Rh5 Kg4 62. Rh8 Kg3 63. Rg8+ Kh2 64. Kf2 Ra3 65. Rh8 ½–½ (From a Russian source)

657 Taimanov–Kashdan [E80]
USA–USSR Match, round 4, 1955
[July 15]

1. c4 Nf6 2. Nc3 g6 3. e4 d6 4. d4 Bg7 5. f3 e5 6. d5 0-0 7. Bg5 h6 8. Be3 Nh5 9. Qd2 f5 10. exf5 gxf5 11. 0-0-0 Qf6 12. Bd3 Na6 13. Nge2 Nc5 14. Bc2 f4 15. Bxc5 dxc5 16. Ne4 Qa6 17. d6! Qxc4 18. N2c3 Qd4 19. Qe2 Qe3+

20. Qxe3 fxe3 21. d7 1–0 (*Chess Review*, September 1955)

658 Kashdan–König [E16]
North–South California Match, 1956
[*May 27*]

1. d4 Nf6 2. c4 e6 3. Nf3 b6 4. g3 Bb7 5. Bg2 Bb4+ 6. Bd2 Be7 7. Nc3 d5 8. Qa4+ c6 9. cxd5 exd5 10. Ne5 0–0 11. 0–0 Nfd7 12. Nd3 Bf6 13. e4 b5 14. Qc2 Bxd4 15. exd5 Bxc3 16. Bxc3 cxd5 17. Nf4 Nb6 18. Rad1 Na6 19. Nh5 f6 20. Be4 dxe4 21. Rxd8 Raxd8 22. Nf4 Rf7 23. Rd1 Rxd1+ 24. Qxd1 Rd7 25. Qb3+ Bd5 26. Nxd5 Rxd5 27. Bd4 Nc7 28. Bxb6 axb6 29. Qc2 Ne6 30. Qxe4 Re5 31. Qc6 g5 32. h3 Kf7 33. Qxb6 h5 34. a4 bxa4 35. Qa7+ Kg6 36. Qxa4 Nc5 37. Qc2+ Kh6 38. b4 Ne4 39. f4 gxf4 40. gxf4 Re7 41. b5 Nd6 42. Qc6 Re1+ 43. Kf2 Rd1 44. b6 Rd2+ 45. Ke1 Rd3 46. b7 1–0 (*California Chess Reporter*, June 1956)

659 König–Kashdan [E87]
North–South California Match, 1957
[*June 2*]

1. d4 Nf6 2. c4 g6 3. Nc3 Bg7 4. e4 d6 5. f3 0–0 6. Be3 e5 7. d5 Ne8 8. Qd2 f5 9. 0–0–0 f4 10. Bf2 a5 11. Kb1 Na6 12. Nge2 Bd7 13. Nc1 Nc5 14. Bd3 Nxd3 15. Nxd3 b6 16. b3 Qe7 17. a3 g5 18. Qe2

Nf6 19. Kc2 Qf7 20. h3 h5 21. Ra1 Qg6 22. Rag1 g4 23. Bh4 g3 24. Bxf6 Bxf6 25. Ra1 ½–½ (*California Chess Reporter*, June 1957)

660 König–Kashdan [A20]
North–South California Match, 1960

1. c4 e5 2. g3 Nf6 3. Bg2 Bc5 4. Nc3 0–0 5. e3 Re8 6. Nge2 e4 7. 0–0 d6 8. d3 exd3 9. Qxd3 Nc6 10. Na4 Ne5 11. Qc2 Bg4 12. f3 Be6 13. f4 Nxc4 14. Nxc5 dxc5 15. f5 Bd5 16. e4 Nxe4 17. Rd1 c6 18. Nf4 Nb6 19. a4 a5 20. Ra3 Qf6 21. g4 Rad8 22. Re3 Nd6 23. Nh5 Qh4 24. Qc3 Nxf5 25. Rh3 Qxg4 0–1 (*Chess Life*, July 5, 1960)

661 Kashdan–Siff [E87]
North–South California Match, 1961
[*May 28*]

1. d4 Nf6 2. c4 g6 3. Nc3 Bg7 4. e4 d6 5. f3 0–0 6. Be3 e5 7. d5 c5 8. Bd3 Nh5 9. Qd2 f5 10. exf5 gxf5 11. Bg5 Qe8 12. Nge2 Na6 13. Nb5 Bd7 14. 0–0–0 Bxb5 15. cxb5 c4 16. Bxf5 Rxf5 17. bxa6 Nf4 18. axb7 Nd3+ 19. Kb1 Rb8 20. Nc1 e4 21. fxe4 Rf2 0–1 (*The California Chess Reporter*, June 1961) The last recorded Kashdan game. Also the last game Kashdan played in the series of the North vs. South California matches.

Simultaneous Exhibition Games (662–717)

662 Kashdan–Horneman [C02]
New York Simultaneous (Remove White's queen's rook), 1930 [*Spring*]

1. e4 e6 2. d4 d5 3. e5 c5 4. Qg4 cxd4 5. Nf3 Nh6 6. Qh3 Be7 7. Bd3 b6 8. Qg3 Nf5 9. Bxf5 exf5 10. Qxg7 Rf8 11. Nxd4 Ba6? 12. Nxf5 Nd7 13. Bg5 f6 14. e6 fxg5 (*see diagram*)
15. Qg6+! hxg6 16. Ng7 mate 1–0 (*Golden Treasury of Chess*)

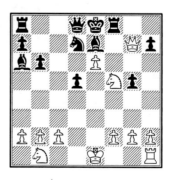

After
14. ... fxg5

663 Kashdan–McMurray [C67]

New York Simultaneous, 1930 *[December 20]*

1. e4 e5 2. Nf3 Nc6 3. Bb5 Nf6 4. 0–0
Nxe4 5. d4 Nd6 6. Bxc6 bxc6 7. dxe5
Nb7 8. Nc3 Be7 9. Qe2 0–0 10. Be3
Nc5 11. Rad1? Ba6 12. Qd2 Bxf1 13. Rxf1
d5 14. Nd4 Qd7 15. f4 f5 16. Kh1 Ne4
17. Nxe4 fxe4 18. f5 c5 19. Ne6 Qxe6
20. fxe6 Rxf1+ 21. Bg1 c6 22. g3 Raf8
23. Kg2 d4 24. Qe2 e3 25. c3 R1f2+
26. Bxf2 Rxf2+ 27. Qxf2 exf2 28. Kxf2
dxc3 29. bxc3 Kf8 0–1 In this simul conducted on December 20, 1930, Kashdan scored
20 wins, 2 losses, and one draw. (Contributed
by Larry Parr)

664 Kashdan–Thelmer [C10]

Cincinnati Simultaneous, 1931 *[February 11]*

1. e4 e6 2. d4 d5 3. Nc3 dxe4 4. Nxe4
Nf6 5. Nxf6+ Qxf6 6. Nf3 Qd8 7. Bd3
Nc6 8. 0–0 Bd7 9. Re1 Bd6 10. c3 Ne7
11. Ng5 h6 12. Ne4 Bc6 13. Qg4 Bxe4
14. Qxe4 c6 15. Qg4 Qc7 16. Qxg7 Bxh2+
17. Kh1 Rg8 18. Qf6 Nd5 19. Qh4 Bd6
20. c4 Be7 21. Qh3 Nf4 22. Qh2 Bd6
23. c5 Rxg2 24. Qxh6 Nxd3 25. cxd6
Qxd6 26. Kxg2 Nxe1+ 27. Kf1 Nc2
28. Rb1 Qxd4 29. Bg5 Kd7 30. Qh7
Qc4+ 31. Kg1 Rf8 32. Rd1+ Kc8 33. Qg7
Qg4+ 34. Kh2 Qh5+ 35. Kg3 Rh8
36. Rd2 Qh3+ 37. Kf4 Qf5+ 38. Kg3
Rh3+ 39. Kg2 Qf3+ 40. Kf1 Rh1 mate
0–1 (*Cincinnati Enquirer*, February 22, 1931)

665 Teegarden–Kashdan [B40]

Cincinnati Simultaneous, 1931 *[February 11]*

1. e4 c5 2. Nf3 e6 3. Nc3 d5 4. exd5
exd5 5. Bb5+ Nc6 6. d3 Nf6 7. 0–0 Be7
8. Ne5 Qb6 9. Bxc6+ bxc6 10. Qf3 0–0
11. h3 Be6 12. b3 a5 13. Bb2 a4 14. Ne2
Bd6 15. Ng4 Nxg4 16. hxg4 f5 17. g5 f4
18. Bc1 Qc7 19. d4 cxd4 20. Nxd4 Bd7
21. Bd2 Qd8 22. Rfe1 Qxg5 23. Ne6
Bxe6 24. Rxe6 Rf6 25. Rxf6 Qxf6
26. Re1 axb3 27. axb3 Ra1 28. Qe2 Rxe1+
29. Bxe1 h6 30. Qe8+ Bf8 31. Bb4 Qf7
32. Qc8 g6 33. Bxf8 Qxf8 34. Qxc6 Qf5
½–½ (*Cincinnati Enquirer*, February 22, 1931)

666 Kashdan–Marks [C13]

Cincinnati Simultaneous, 1931 *[February 11]*

1. e4 e6 2. d4 d5 3. Nc3 Nf6 4. Bg5
Be7 5. e5 Nfd7 6. h4 0–0 7. Bd3 Re8
8. Nh3 Nf8 9. Ne2 Nbd7 10. Qd2 c5
11. c3 f6 12. exf6 Bxf6 13. 0–0 e5
14. dxe5 Nxe5 15. Nef4 Bxg5 16. hxg5
Bxh3 17. Nxh3 Qd7 18. Be2 Rad8
19. Rad1 Nfg6 20. Rfe1 Nh4 21. Qf4
Neg6 22. Qg4 Qf7 23. Bb5 Rf8 24. Rd2
Nf5 25. Nf4 Nxf4 26. Qxf4 Nd6
27. Qxf7+ Nxf7 28. Re7 a6 29. Bd3 b5
30. g6 hxg6 31. Bxg6 Rd6 32. Bh5 g6
33. Bf3 Rfd8 34. Rc7 c4 35. Rc5 d4
36. cxd4 Rxd4 37. Rxd4 Rxd4 38. Rc6
Rd6 39. Rxd6 Nxd6 40. Kf1 Kf7 41. Ke2
Ke6 42. Bc6 Ke5 43. g3 g5 44. Kf3 b4
45. Ba4 c3 46. bxc3 bxc3 47. Bb3 Nf5
48. Ke2 Kd4 49. Bc2 Ne7 50. a3 Nd5
51. Bb3 Nf6 52. Bc2 Ne4 53. Bxe4 Kxe4
54. f4 gxf4 55. gxf4 c2 56. Kd2 c1Q+
57. Kxc1 Kxf4 58. Kd2 Kf5 ½–½ (*Cincinnati Enquirer*, February 22, 1931)

667 Kashdan–Brand [E23]

Cincinnati Simultaneous, 1931 *[February 11]*

1. d4 Nf6 2. c4 e6 3. Nc3 Bb4 4. Qb3
c5 5. dxc5 Nc6 6. Nf3 Ne4 7. Bd2 Nxc5
8. Qc2 f5 9. e3 b6 10. Be2 Qe7 11. 0–0
0–0 12. a3 Bxc3 13. Bxc3 Ne4 14. Rad1
Nxc3 15. Qxc3 a5 16. Nd4 Nxd4
17. Qxd4 Rb8 18. Bf3 Rd8 19. Qf4 Bb7
20. Bxb7 Rxb7 21. Rd2 g5 22. Qd6
Qxd6 23. Rxd6 Kf7 24. Rfd1 Ke7 25. Kf1
Rc8 26. R6d4 a4 27. Ke2 Rc5 28. h4 g4
29. f3 gxf3+ 30. gxf3 b5 31. cxb5 Rxb5
32. Rxa4 Rxb2+ 33. Rd2 Rxd2+
34. Kxd2 Rb2+ 35. Ke1 h5 36. Ra8 Rh2
37. Ra4 ½–½ (*Cincinnati Enquirer*, March 8,
1931)

668 Kashdan–A. Hermann [D00]

Allentown YMCA Simultaneous, 1931
[March 26]

1. d4 d5 2. Bf4 Bf5 3. e3 e6 4. c4
Bxb1 5. Rxb1 Bb4+ 6. Ke2 Nf6 7. c5 c6
8. Qa4 Qa5 9. Qb3 Ne4 10. a3 Qa6+

11. Qd3 Qxd3+ 12. Kxd3 Nxf2+ 13. Ke2
Nxh1 14. axb4 Na6 15. b5 Nb4 16. g3
f6 17. Bg2 Nf2 18. Kxf2 e5 19. dxe5 fxe5
20. Bg5 h6 21. Bh4 g5 22. Bxg5 hxg5
23. h3 cxb5 24. Nf3 Nd3+ 25. Ke2 e4
26. Nxg5 Nxc5 27. Rc1 b6 28. h4 Ke7
29. Bh3 a5 30. Rd1 Nd3 31. Be6 Raf8
32. Rxd3 exd3+ 33. Kxd3 Rh5 34. Bxd5
Rxg5 35. hxg5 Rf5 36. Bc6 Rxg5 37. g4
Rxg4 38. e4 Rg3+ 39. Kc2 b4 40. Bd5
Kd6 41. Bb7 b5 0–1 (*Allentown Morning Call*,
March 29, 1931)

669 Kashdan–W. Witt [D51]
Newark Simultaneous, 1931 *[March 28]*

1. d4 d5 2. Nf3 Nf6 3. c4 e6 4. Nc3
Nbd7 5. Bg5 dxc4 6. e4 Be7 7. Bxc4 b6
8. Qa4 0–0 9. 0–0 Bb7 10. Rfe1 c5 11. d5
exd5 12. exd5 Re8 13. Rad1 h6 14. Bh4
Nh5 15. Bxe7 Rxe7 16. Ne4 Ne5 17. Nxe5
Rxe5 18. Nc3 Rxe1+ 19. Rxe1 a6 20. Qd1
Nf6 21. a4 b5 22. axb5 axb5 23. Nxb5
Bxd5 24. Bxd5 Qxd5 25. Qxd5 Nxd5
26. b3 Rb8 27. Re5 Rxb5 28. Rxd5
½–½ (*Newark Evening News*, April 7, 1931)

670 Kashdan–N. Woodbridge [C49]
Newark Simultaneous, 1931 *[March 28]*

1. e4 e5 2. Nf3 Nc6 3. Nc3 Nf6 4. Bb5
Bb4 5. 0–0 0–0 6. d3 d6 7. Bg5 Bxc3
8. bxc3 Bg4 9. h3 Bd7 10. Re1 h6 11. Bc1
Re8 12. a4 a6 13. Bc4 Na5 14. Ba2 Nc6
15. Nh2 Be6 16. f4 Bxa2 17. Rxa2 exf4
18. Bxf4 Ne5 19. Nf3 Ng6 20. Bh2 Qd7
21. Nd4 Kh7 22. Nf5 d5 23. e5 Qxf5
24. exf6 Qxf6 25. Ra3 Qc6 0–1 (*Newark
Evening News*, April 7, 1931)

671 Kashdan–J. DelBourgo [C45]
Newark Simultaneous, 1931 *[March 28]*

1. e4 e5 2. Nf3 Nc6 3. d4 exd4
4. Nxd4 Nxd4 5. Qxd4 c5 6. Qe3 Be7
7. Nc3 d6 8. Bc4 Be6 9. Nd5 Nf6
10. 0–0 a6 11. a4 Nxd5 12. exd5 Bd7
13. Re1 f6 14. Bd2 Kf7 15. Qe4 g6 16. Re3
Bf5 17. Qh4 h5 18. Rae1 Re8 19. Bc3

Bxc2 20. g4 f5 21. Rxe7+ Rxe7 22. Qf6+
Ke8 23. Qh8+ Kf7 24. Rxe7+ Qxe7
25. Qxa8 Bxa4 26. Qh8 b5 27. Qg7+
Ke8 28. Qxg6+ Qf7 29. Qxf7+ Kxf7
30. Bd3 fxg4 31. Kg2 Bb3 32. Be4 b4
33. Bd2 Kf6 34. f4 Ke7 35. Kg3 a5
36. Kh4 a4 37. Kxh5 a3 38. bxa3 bxa3
39. Bc1 a2 40. Bb2 Kd7 41. Kxg4 Kc7
42. h4 Bd1+ 43. Kg5 Kb6 44. h5 1–0
(*Newark Evening News*, April 7, 1931)

672 Kashdan–H. Snowden [C21]
Newark Simultaneous, 1931 *[March 28]*

1. e4 e5 2. d4 exd4 3. Bc4 Nc6 4. Nf3
Be7 5. Nxd4 Nxd4 6. Qxd4 Bf6 7. e5
Qe7 8. f4 d6 9. 0–0 dxe5 10. fxe5 Qxe5
11. Bxf7+ Ke7 But not Kxf7, 12.Qxe5, the
bishop is pinned. 12. Qxe5+ Bxe5 13. Bb3
Bd4+ 14. Kh1 Nf6 15. c3 Bc5 16. Bf4 Bd6
17. Nd2 Bxf4 18. Rxf4 c6 19. Re1+ Kd8
20. Nf3 Bd7 21. Ng5 Re8 22. Rxe8+
Bxe8 23. Ne6+ Ke7 24. Nxg7 Bg6
25. Ne6 Nh5 26. Rf1 Rc8 27. Nd4 Ng7
28. g4 Rd8 29. Kg2 c5 30. Re1+ Kf6
31. Nf3 h6 32. h4 Ne8 33. Re6+ Kg7
34. h5 Bf7 35. Re7 Nd6 36. Bxf7 Nxf7
37. Rxb7 Kg8 38. Rxa7 Rd5 39. a4 Rd8
40. a5 Rb8 41. Rc7 Rxb2+ 42. Kg3 Ra2
43. Rxc5 Kf8 44. Nd4 Nd6 45. Kf4 Nb7
46. Rf5+ Kg7 47. Ne6+ 1–0 (*Newark Evening News*, April 28, 1931)

673 Kashdan–H. Snowden [C26]
Montclair Chess Club Simultaneous, 1931
[December 10]

1. e4 e5 2. Nc3 Nf6 3. Bc4 Bc5 4. f4
d6 5. f5 c6 6. d3 d5 7. exd5 cxd5
8. Bb5+ Nc6 9. Nf3 Qd6 10. Qe2 0–0
11. Bxc6 bxc6 12. Nh4 Re8 13. Bg5 Ba6
14. 0–0–0 e4 15. Bxf6 exd3 16. Qg4
Qxf6 17. cxd3 Rab8 18. Rhe1 Rxe1
19. Rxe1 Bf2 20. Qf4 Qh6 21. Qxh6 gxh6
22. Nf3 Bxe1 23. Nxe1 Re8 24. Kd2 Bc8
25. g4 h5 26. h3 hxg4 27. hxg4 h5
28. gxh5 Bxf5 29. Ng2 Bg4 30. Nf4 Re5
31. d4 Rf5 32. Ke3 Bxh5 33. b4 Bg4
34. a4 a6 35. b5 axb5 36. axb5 cxb5
37. Nxb5 Rg5 38. Nc7 Be6 39. Kd2 Rg4

40. Ke3 Kf8 41. Ncxe6+ fxe6 42. Nxe6+
Ke7 43. Nf4 Kd6 44. Kf3 Rg8 45. Nd3
Rd8 46. Ne5 Ra8 47. Ke3 Ra3+ 48. Kf4
Ke6 49. Nf3 Rd3 50. Kg4 Re3 51. Kf4
Re4+ 52. Kg5 Kd6 53. Kf5 Kc6 54. Kg5
Kb5 0–1 (*American Chess Bulletin*, January 1932)

674 Kashdan–Amateur [C45]
England, Simultaneous, 1932 *[February]*

1. e4 e5 2. Nf3 Nc6 3. d4 exd4
4. Nxd4 Bc5 5. Be3 Qf6 6. c3 Nge7
7. Bb5 0–0 8. 0–0 d5 9. Nxc6 bxc6
10. Bxc5 cxb5 11. Bxe7 Qxe7 12. Qxd5
Rb8 13. Nd2? Bb7? Both players missed
Rfd8. 14. Qf5 Bc8 15. Qf4 Rb6 16. Qe3
Rg6 17. f4 f5 18. Rae1 fxe4 19. Qxe4
Qc5+ 20. Qe3 Bb7! 21. Rf2

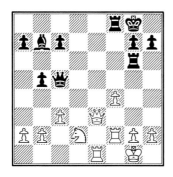

After
21. Rf2

21. Qxc5+?? leads to mate in six. 21. ... Qc6
22. Nf3 Rg4 23. h3 Rgxf4 24. Nd4 Qg6
25. Ree2 Rxf2 26. Rxf2 Re8?? 27. Qf4
c6 28. Nf5 Qf7?? 29. Nh6+ 1–0 Contributed by Aidan Woodger. Notes by Brooke.
(*Tunbridge Wells Advertiser*, February 5, 1932)

675 Abraham & Lowenthal–
Kashdan [D15]
Liverpool Simultaneous, 1932 *[February]*

1. d4 d5 2. c4 c6 3. Nc3 Nf6 4. Nf3
Nbd7 5. cxd5 cxd5 6. Bf4 e6 7. Qa4
Nh5 8. e3 Nxf4 9. exf4 Be7 10. Bd3
0–0 11. 0–0 g6 12. Rfe1 a6 13. Qd1 b5
14. Re3 Bb7 15. g4 Bf6 16. Qf1 Rc8
17. Ne5 Nb6 18. Rh3 Nc4 19. Qe2 Bg7
20. g5 Nxe5 21. dxe5 b4 22. Nd1 Qb6
23. Ne3 Qd4 24. Ng2 Rc6 25. Rd1 Qb6
26. Ne3 Rfc8 27. f5 d4 28. f6 dxe3

29. fxg7 exf2+ 30. Kf1 Rc1 31. Rg3 Qd4
32. Qd2 Rxd1+ 33. Qxd1 Qxb2 34. Bc4
Bd5 0–1 Contributed by Neil Brennen. (*Bethlehem Globe Times*, April 19, 1932)

676 Kashdan–Waxman &
Simonson & Keiser [D37]
New York Simultaneous, 1932 *[April]*

1. d4 d5 2. c4 e6 3. Nc3 Nf6 4. Nf3
Nbd7 5. Bf4 Be7 6. e3 c6 7. c5 0–0
8. Bd3 Re8 9. 0–0 Bxc5 10. dxc5 e5
11. Bg5 e4 12. Bc2 exf3 13. Qxf3 Nxc5
14. h3 Qd6 15. Rad1 Qe5 16. Bf4 Qh5
17. g4 Qh4 18. Qg2 Nfe4 19. Nxe4 Nxe4
20. f3 Nc5 21. b4 Ne6 22. Bg3 Qe7
23. b5 Qc5 24. bxc6 bxc6 25. Rfe1 Ng5
26. Rc1 Qa3 27. h4 Ne6 28. Qd2 Ba6
29. Be5 Rad8 30. Bb2 Qd6 31. Kg2 c5
32. Rcd1 d4 33. Qf2 d3 34. Ba4 d2
35. Rh1 Nf4+ 36. exf4 Re2 37. Be5
Rxf2+ 38. Kxf2 Qd3 39. Kg3 c4 40. Bc6
c3 41. Be4 Qc4 42. Rh2 Qxa2 0–1 In this
simul played at the Hotel Prince George in New
York, Kashdan scored only 6 wins, 8 draws and
13 losses, according to the *Sun*. (*New York Sun*,
April 29, 1932)

677 Kashdan–Hesse [C86]
Allentown Simultaneous, 1932 *[May 13]*

1. e4 e5 2. Nf3 Nc6 3. Bb5 a6 4. Ba4
Nf6 5. 0–0 Be7 6. Qe2 d6 7. c3 b5
8. Bb3 Bd7 9. d4 Bg4 10. Bd5 Qd7
11. dxe5 dxe5 12. Rd1 Bd6 13. Bb3 0–0
14. Bg5 Na5 15. Bc2 Qe7 16. h3 Be6
17. Nbd2 Nc4 18. Nxc4 Bxc4 19. Bd3
Be6 20. Nh4 c5 21. Nf5 Bxf5 22. exf5
Qc7 23. Bxf6 gxf6 24. Re1 c4 25. Be4
Rad8 26. Qh5 Kh8 27. Bd5 Bc5 28. Re4
Rg8 29. Bxf7? Rg5 30. Qe2 Qxf7 31. g4
Rd3 32. Kg2 Qd5 0–1 (*Bethlehem Globe
Times*, May 25, 1932)

678 Kashdan–Goerlich [D15]
Philadelphia Simultaneous, 1932 *[May 14]*

1. d4 Nf6 2. Nf3 d5 3. c4 c6 4. Nc3
Bf5 5. Qb3 Qb6 6. c5 Qxb3 7. axb3
Na6 8. Ra4 Bc2 9. Nd2 Nc7 10. e3 a6

11. Rb4 Nb5 12. Nf3 e6 13. Ne5 Be7 14. Kd2 Bg6 15. f3 Nd7 16. N×g6 h×g6 17. f4 b6 18. Ra4 0–0 19. b4 Nc7 20. Bd3 b5 21. Ra2 f5 22. Ke2 Kf7 23. Bd2 g5 24. g3 g4 25. Kf2 Rh8 26. Kg2 Rh6 27. Ne2 Rah8 28. Nc1 Nf6 29. Nb3 Ke8 30. Be1 Ne4 31. Nd2 g5 32. N×e4 d×e4 33. Bc2 g×f4 34. e×f4 Kf7 35. Bf2 Ra8 36. Bb3 Ke8 37. Raa1 Rh3 38. Rhe1 Bd8 39. Be3 Kd7 40. Bd2 Nd5 41. B×d5 e×d5 42. Red1 Kc7 43. Ra3 Kb7 44. Be3 Bf6 45. Rda1 Rah8 46. Rh1 Ka7 47. Raa1 ½–½ (*Bethlehem Globe Times*, May 25, 1932)

679 Kashdan–Ash [C28]
Philadelphia Simultaneous, 1932 *[May 14]*

1. e4 e5 2. Bc4 Nc6 3. Nc3 Nf6 4. d3 d6 5. f4 Be7 6. Nf3 Be6 7. Bb5 e×f4 8. B×f4 0–0 9. 0–0 a6 10. Ba4 b5 11. Bb3 Qd7 12. Qe2 Rae8 13. d4 B×b3 14. a×b3 Nb4 15. Qd2 d5 16. e5 Nh5 17. Be3 f5 18. Rae1 Kh8 19. Bg5 f4 20. B×e7 Q×e7 21. Re2 g5 22. Ne1 c5 23. d×c5 Q×c5+ 24. Kh1 Re6 25. Nf3 Rh6 26. Ref2? Ng3+ 27. Kg1 N×f1 28. K×f1 Qe3 29. N×d5 Q×d2 30. R×d2 N×d5 31. R×d5 g4 32. Ng5 R×h2 33. e6 Rh1+ 34. Kf2 g3+ 35. Kf3 Re1 36. Rd7 Re3+ 37. Kg4 f3 38. Nf7+ R×f7 39. e×f7 Kg7 40. K×g3 f×g2+ 41. K×g2 Re2+ 42. Kf3 R×c2 43. Ra7 R×b2 44. R×a6 R×b3+ 45. Kg4 K×f7 46. Ra7+ Ke6 47. R×h7 Kd5 48. Kf4 Kd4 49. Rd7+ Kc3 50. Ke3 Kc2+ 51. Ke2 b4 52. Rd2+ Kc3 53. Rd7 Kb2 54. Rb7 Kc1 55. Rb6 Rb2+ 56. Kd3 b3 57. Rh6 Rc2 58. Rh5 Kb1 59. Rh1+ Kb2 60. Rh5 Kb1 61. Rh1+ Rc1 62. Rh6 b2 63. Kd2 Rc2+ 64. Kd3 Rc7 65. Kd2 Ra7 0–1 (*Bethlehem Globe Times*, July 21, 1932)

680 Kashdan–Mendelsohn [E21]
Philadelphia Simultaneous, 1932 *[May 14]*

1. d4 Nf6 2. c4 e6 3. Nc3 Bb4 4. Nf3 b6 5. g3 Bb7 6. Bg2 d6 7. Qa4+ Nc6 8. Nd2 d5 9. a3 B×c3 10. b×c3 0–0 11. 0–0 Ne7 12. Qc2 Ng6 13. a4 Re8

14. a5 Qc8 15. e4 d×e4 16. N×e4 N×e4 17. B×e4 B×e4 18. Q×e4 c5 19. Be3 c×d4 20. c×d4 b×a5 21. c5 Ne7 22. R×a5 Nc6 23. Ra4 Rd8 24. Rfa1 Qd7 25. Ra6 Rac8 26. Kg2 Qd5 27. Q×d5 R×d5 28. R1a4 Kf8 29. Kf3 Ke7 30. Ke4 Rd7 31. f4 Rb7 32. Ra3 Kd7 33. R6a4 Rcb8 34. Kd3 Rb3+ 35. Kc4? The winning idea is 35. ... Na5+ 36. R×a5 Rbb4 mate! 0–1 (*Bethlehem Globe Times*, July 29, 1932)

681 Kashdan–Hutchings [C45]
Cincinnati Simultaneous, 1932 *[May 20]*

1. e4 e5 2. Nf3 Nc6 3. d4 e×d4 4. N×d4 Bc5 5. Be3 Qe7 6. Nc3 N×d4 7. B×d4 Nf6 8. B×c5 Q×c5 9. Bd3 d6 10. 0–0 Qg5 11. f4 Qh6 12. Nb5 Kd8 13. e5 Ng4 14. h3 Ne3 15. Qf3 N×f1 16. e×d6 c6 17. Nc7 Rb8 18. B×f1 Bf5 19. Qe3? Q×d6 20. Q×a7 K×c7? 21. Qa5+ b6 22. Q×f5 Qd4+ 23. Kh2 f6 24. c3 Qd2 25. Qg4! g6 26. Rd1 h5! 27. Qf3 Q×b2 28. Qe4 Rbe8 29. Q×g6 Q×a2 30. Qg7+ Kb8 31. Rd7 Qa4 32. Q×f6 Rhf8 33. Qd6+ Ka8 34. g3 h4 35. Bg2 h×g3+ 36. K×g3 Rg8+ 37. Kh2 Re2 38. Rd8+ R×d8 39. Q×d8+ Ka7 40. Qd7+ Ka6 41. Kg3 R×g2+ 42. K×g2 Qc2+ 43. Kg3 Q×c3+ 44. Kg4 b5 45. f5 b4 46. Qc8+ Kb5 47. Qb7+ Ka4 48. Qa7+ Kb5 49. Qf2 Ka4 50. Qa2+ Kb5 51. Qe6 Qd4+ 52. Kh5 Qd1+ 53. Kh6 b3 54. f6 b2 55. Qf5+ c5 56. f7 b1Q 57. f8Q Qd6+ 58. Q×d6 Q×f5 ½–½ (*Cincinnati Enquirer*, May 29, 1932)

682 Kashdan–Harris [D30]
Cincinnati Simultaneous, 1932 *[May 20]*

1. d4 d5 2. Nf3 Nf6 3. c4 e6 4. Bf4 c6 5. Nc3 Nbd7 6. e3 Qa5 7. Qc2 Ne4 8. Bd3 Ndf6 9. 0–0 N×c3 10. b×c3 d×c4 11. B×c4 Nd5 12. B×d5 c×d5 13. Ne5 Be7 14. c4 f6 15. Nd3 Bd7 16. c×d5 Q×d5 17. f3 Rc8 18. Qb2 e5 19. Bg3 e×d4 20. e×d4 Rc4 21. Bf2 0–0 22. Nf4 Qb5 23. Qe2 Re8 24. Rab1 Rb4 25. Qc2 Bd6 26. R×b4 B×b4 27. Rb1 a5 28. a3 g5 29. Nh5 Qf5 30. N×f6+ Q×f6 31. a×b4

axb4 32. Rxb4 Rc8 33. Qb2 Qf4 34. Qb3+ Kg7 35. Rc4 Qf7 36. d5 Qxd5 37. Bd4+ Kf7 38. Rb4 Qxb3 39. Rxb3 Bc6 40. Kf2 Re8 41. Be3 Kg6 42. Rc3 Re5 ½–½ (*Cincinnati Enquirer*, May 29, 1932)

683 Kashdan–G. Williams [C16]
Cincinnati Simultaneous, 1932 *[May 20]*

1. e4 e6 2. d4 d5 3. Nc3 Bb4 4. e5 Ne7 5. Bd3 Nd7 6. a3 Bxc3+ 7. bxc3 f5 8. exf6 Nxf6 9. Nf3 0–0 10. 0–0 Nf5 11. a4 Ne4 12. Bxe4 dxe4 13. Ne5 b6 14. a5 Bb7 15. a6 Bc8 16. Qe2 Qd5 17. Bb2 c5 18. c4 Nxd4 19. Qh5 Qd8 20. Rad1 Rf5 21. Qg4 Rxe5 22. c3 Qg5 23. Qxg5 Ne2+ 24. Kh1 Rxg5 25. Rd8+ Kf7 26. g3 Ke7 27. Rfd1 Nd4 28. Rh8 Bb7 29. Rxa8 Bxa8 30. cxd4 e3+ 31. Kg1 Bf3 32. Rd3 e2 33. Bc3 cxd4 34. Be1 Ra5! 35. Bb4+ Ke8 36. Rxf3 Ra1+ 37. Kg2 e1Q 38. Bxe1 Rxe1 39. Rd3 e5 40. f4 Rc1 41. fxe5 Rxc4 42. Kf3 Rc3 43. Ke4 Rc2 44. Rxd4 Rxh2 45. Rc4 Kd8 46. Rd4+ Ke7 47. Rc4 Rd2 48. Rc8 Ke6 49. Rb8 Rd7 50. Rb7 Rf7 51. Kd4 h5 52. Kc4 g5 53. Kb5 h4 54. gxh4 gxh4 55. Kc6 Re7 56. Rb8 Kf5 57. Rh8 Kg4 58. Kd6 Rg7 59. e6 h3 60. e7 Rxe7 61. Kxe7 Kg3 62. Kd6 h2 63. Kc6 Kg2 64. Rxh2+ Kxh2 65. Kb7 b5 66. Kxa7 b4 67. Kb6 b3 68. a7 b2 69. a8Q b1Q+ ½–½ (*Cincinnati Enquirer*, May 29, 1932)

684 Kashdan–Collins & Rogers [C86]
Chicago Simultaneous, 1932 *[June 11]*

1. e4 e5 2. Nf3 Nc6 3. Bb5 a6 4. Ba4 Nf6 5. 0–0 Be7 6. Qe2 d6 7. c3 Bd7 8. d4 0–0 9. d5 Nd4!? 10. cxd4 Bxa4 11. Nc3 Be8 12. dxe5 dxe5 13. Nxe5 Bd6 14. Nc4 Bc5 15. Bg5 h6 16. Bh4 b5 17. Na5 g5 18. Bg3 b4 19. Nd1 Bb5 20. Qc2 Bb6 21. Nc6 Qe8 22. Re1 Nxd5 23. Ne5 Nf4 24. Ng4 Qe6 25. Bxf4 gxf4 26. h3 f5 27. Nh2 Rad8 28. e5 a5 29. b3 Rd5 30. Nb2 Rfd8 31. Nf3 Rc5 32. Qb1 Rc3 33. Rd1 Bxf2+ 34. Kh1 Rf8 35. Na4 Rxf3 36. gxf3 Qc6 37. Kg2

Qg6+ 38. Kh1 Be2 39. Rg1 Bxf3+ 0–1 (*American Chess Bulletin*, November, 1932)

685 Kashdan–Narveson [C21]
Minneapolis Simultaneous, 1932 *[June 15]*

1. e4 e5 2. d4 exd4 3. c3 dxc3 4. Bc4 cxb2 5. Bxb2 d5 6. Bxd5 Nf6 7. Bxf7+ Kxf7 8. Qxd8 Bb4+ 9. Qd2 Bxd2+ 10. Nxd2 Nc6 11. Ne2 Re8 12. f3 Bd7 13. Nb3 b6 14. Rc1 Nb4 15. 0–0 c5 16. Rfd1 Be6 17. Rd2 Nxa2! 18. Bxf6 Nxc1 19. Nbxc1 Kxf6 20. Kf2 Red8 21. Rc2 c4 22. f4 Rd3? This is unsound, better is b5 or a5. 23. Nxd3 cxd3 24. Rc6 Rc8 25. Rxc8 Bxc8 26. Nd4 a5 27. Ke3 Ba6 28. e5+ Kf7 29. g4 Bc4 30. f5 a4 31. e6+ Ke8 32. Nc6 a3 33. Nb4 a2 34. Nxa2 Bxa2 35. Kxd3 Bd5 36. g5 Bf3 37. Ke3 Bg4 38. Ke4 b5 39. Ke5 b4 40. f6 gxf6+ 41. gxf6 Bxe6!! 0–1 (*Minnesota Chess Journal*, January-February 1972)

686 Kashdan–Sheets [D61]
Seattle Simultaneous, 1932 *[August]*

1. d4 d5 2. c4 c6 3. Nc3 Nf6 4. Nf3 e6 5. Bg5 Nbd7 6. e3 Be7 7. Qc2 0–0 8. Bd3 h6 9. Bh4 dxc4 10. Bxc4 Nb6 11. Bb3 Nfd5 12. Bg3 a5 13. a3 Re8 14. 0–0 Nxc3 15. Qxc3 Nd5 16. Qd3 b6 17. Ne5 Ba6 18. Bc4 b5 19. Ba2 c5! 20. Nc6 Qb6 21. Nxe7+ Nxe7 22. dxc5 Qxc5 23. Rac1 Qb6 24. Rfd1 Rad8 25. Qe4 Rxd1+ 26. Rxd1 Bb7 27. Qg4 Qc6 28. Be5 Ng6 29. Bc3 b4! 30. Be1 bxa3 31. bxa3 Nh4! 32. f3 Nf5 33. Qf4 Qc2 34. Rd2 Qc5 35. Rd7! g5! 36. Qc7 Bc6 37. Bd2 Qc2 38. Kf2 Qxa2 39. Qxc6 Rb8 40. g4 Ne7 41. Qd6 Re8 42. Kg3 Qa1 43. Kf2 Nd5 44. Rd8 Rxd8 45. Qxd8+ Kh7 46. Qxa5 Qh1 47. Qa7? Qxh2+ 48. Ke1 Qg1+ 49. Ke2 Nf4+! 0–1 Contributed by John Donaldson. (*Northwest Chess*, July 1980)

687 McKee & Thompson–Kashdan [D05]
Dallas Simultaneous, 1932 *[October]*

1. d4 d5 2. Nf3 Nf6 3. e3 e6 4. Bd3

c5 5. c3 Nc6 6. Nbd2 Be7 7. 0–0 0–0
8. e4 cxd4 9. e5 Nd7 10. cxd4 f5 11. exf6
Nxf6 12. Nb3 Bd6 13. Re1 Qc7 14. Qe2
Bd7 15. Bd2 Rae8 16. Rac1! Bc8 17. Ne5
Qb6 18. Be3 a5 19. Nc5 Qc7 20. f4 Qe7
21. Bb5 Bxe5 22. fxe5 Nd7 23. Nxb7
Nxd4 24. Bxd4 Bxb7 25. Rc7 Bc8
26. Bc5 Qd8 27. Bd6 Rf7 28. Rec1 Nb6
29. Bxe8 Qxe8 30. Rf1 1–0 This game was
played in a simultaneous exhibition in which
Kashdan won seven and lost this game. Earlier
on October 25, Kashdan gave an exhibition in
which he won 23, lost one, and drew one. (*Texas
Chess Magazine*, November 1932)

688 Kashdan–Rosenfeld [C21]
Dallas Simultaneous, 1932 *[October 29]*

1. e4 e5 2. d4 exd4 3. c3 Bc5 4. cxd4
Bb4+ 5. Nc3 Ne7 6. Nf3 0–0 7. Bd3 d6
8. 0–0 Bg4 9. h3 Bh5 10. Be3 Nd7 11. g4
Bg6 12. Nh4 Nc6 13. Nxg6 fxg6 14. Nd5
Ba5 15. b4 Bb6 16. Nxb6 axb6 17. b5
Ne7 18. f4 Kh8 19. f5 c6 20. Qb3 Qc7
21. Rac1 d5 22. e5 Nxe5 23. dxe5 Qxe5
24. Rf3 gxf5 25. gxf5 Nxf5 26. Rcf1 Rf6
27. Bxf5 Rxf5 28. Bxb6 Rg5+ 29. Kh1
Qe4 30. Qe3 h6 31. Qxe4 dxe4 32. Rf8+
Rxf8 33. Rxf8+ Kh7 34. bxc6 bxc6
35. Re8 Rb5 36. Bd4 Rb4 37. Be5 Rb7
38. Ra8 Re7 39. Bc3 Kg6 40. Kg2 Kf5
41. Kf2 Ke6 42. Ke3 Kd5 43. a3 g5
44. Ra6 h5 45. a4 Rf7 46. a5 c5 47. Rg6
Kc4 48. Be1 Rf3+ 49. Kxe4 Rxh3
50. Rxg5 Kb5 51. Rg2 h4 52. Rb2+ Ka6
53. Rb6+ Ka7 54. Bf2 Ra3 55. Bxc5
Rxa5 56. Kd4 h3 57. Rb1+ Ka8 58. Rh1
Ra4+ 59. Kd5 Rh4 60. Kc6 Rh6+
61. Kb5 Kb7 62. Re1 Rh7 63. Ra1 Rh8
64. Ra7+ Kb8 65. Ka6 Rh6+ 66. Bb6 h2
67. Rb7+ Kc8 68. Rc7+ Kb8 Of course if
Kd8?? then Black would lose to 69. Rh7+.
½–½ In this simul Kashdan won 14 games and
gave up this draw. (*Texas Chess Magazine*, November 1932)

689 Kashdan–Leysens [A52]
Cleveland Simultaneous, 1932 *[November]*

1. c4 Nf6 2. d4 e5 3. dxe5 Ng4 4. Nf3

Nc6 5. Bf4 Bb4+ 6. Nc3 Qe7 7. Qd5
Bxc3+ 8. bxc3 Qa3 9. Rc1 f6 10. exf6
Nxf6 11. Qd2 d6 12. e3 Bf5 13. Nd4 Ne4
14. Qc2 Nxd4 15. exd4 Ng3! 16. Bd3
Bxd3 17. Qxd3 Nxh1 18. Qe4+ Kd8
19. Kf1 Qxa2 20. Bg5+ Kc8 21. Qf5+ Kb8
22. Kg1 Qxf2+ 23. Qxf2 Nxf2 24. Kxf2
Re8 25. h4 a5 26. c5 dxc5 27. dxc5 a4
28. Ra1 Re4 29. Ra3 h6 30. Be3 Rxh4
31. g3 Rh2+ 32. Kf3 Rb2 33. Bd4 g6
34. Ke3 Kc8 35. c4 Rb3+ 36. Rxb3 axb3
37. Kd3 Ra2 38. Kc3 Rg2 0–1 (*Cleveland
Plain Dealer*, November 13, 1932)

690 Kashdan–Emary [B40]
Cleveland Simultaneous, 1932 *[November]*

1. e4 c5 2. Nf3 e6 3. d4 cxd4 4. Nxd4
e5 5. Nb5 d6 6. c4 a6 7. N5c3 Nf6
8. Bd3 Nbd7 9. 0–0 Nc5 10. Bc2 Bd7
11. Be3 b6 12. b4 Nb7 13. f3 b5 14. cxb5
axb5 15. Nd2 Bc6 16. Bd3 Qd7 17. Qe2
Be7 18. Bxb5 0–0 19. Bxc6 Qxc6
20. Rfc1 Qd7 21. Nc4 Qe6 22. Nd5 Bd8!
If 22. ... Nxd5 23. exd5 Qxd5? 24. Nb6.
23. Nxf6+ Qxf6 24. a4 Bc7 25. a5 Rfc8
26. a6 Nd8 27. b5 d5 28. exd5 Qe7
29. b6 Bb8 30. d6 Qd7 31. Qd3 Qb5
32. d7 Rc6 33. b7 Raxa6 34. Rxa6 Qxa6
35. Qd5 Qxb7 36. Rd1 Qb3 37. Bg5
Ba7+ 38. Kh1 Rxc4 39. Bxd8 Bd4
40. Re1 Qe3? This is a fatal error. Black
should have played Rc1 and then might have
secured a draw as White's pawn at d7 could not
be maintained. 41. Ba5 1–0 (*Cleveland Plain
Dealer*, November 13, 1932)

691 Kashdan–Stearns [C12]
Cleveland Simultaneous, 1932 *[November]*

1. e4 e6 2. d4 d5 3. Nc3 Nf6 4. Bg5
Bb4 5. e5 h6 6. Bd2 Bxc3 7. bxc3 Ne4
8. Qg4 Kf8 9. Bd3 Nxd2 10. Kxd2 Qg5+
11. Qxg5 hxg5 12. Nh3 f6 13. exf6 gxf6
14. f4 g4 15. Nf2 f5 16. h3 g3 17. Nd1 c5
18. Rf1 c4 19. Be2 Nd7 20. Bf3 Nf6
21. Re1 Rh4 22. Ke3 Bd7 23. a4 a5
24. Nb2 Bc6 25. Nd1 Ke7 26. Rf1 Rf8
½–½ (*Cleveland Plain Dealer*, November 13,
1932)

692 Kashdan–McLaughlin [C28]
Cleveland Simultaneous, 1932 *[November]*

1. e4 e5 2. Bc4 Nf6 3. Nc3 Nc6 4. d3
Nd4 5. f4 d6 6. f5 c6 7. Bg5 Qa5
8. Bxf6 gxf6 9. Qh5 d5 10. exd5 Nxc2+
11. Kd2 Nxa1 12. d6 Kd8 13. Qxf7 Bxd6
14. Qxf6+ Kc7 15. Qxh8 b5 16. Be6 b4
17. Ne4 b3+ 18. Nc3 Bxe6 19. Qxa8 bxa2
20. Nf3 Nb3+ 21. Ke2 Bxf5 22. Nxa2
Qxa2 23. Re1 Nd4+ 24. Nxd4 exd4
25. Kf1 Bxd3+ 26. Kg1 Bc5 27. Qe8 Qd5
28. Re5 Qc4 29. b3 Qc1+ 30. Re1 Qf4
31. Qg8 Bf8 32. h3 Kb6 33. Qe6 Bd6
34. Qg8 Qh2+ 35. Kf2 Qf4+ 36. Kg1
Qh2+ ½–½ (*Cleveland Plain Dealer*, November 13, 1932)

693 Kashdan–Lawrence [C21]
Cleveland Simultaneous, 1932 *[November]*

1. e4 e5 2. d4 exd4 3. c3 dxc3 4. Bc4
d6 5. Nxc3 Be6 6. Bxe6 fxe6 7. Nf3 Na6
8. Be3 Qd7 9. 0–0 Be7 10. Qc2 Nh6
11. Bxh6 gxh6 12. e5 0–0–0 13. a3 Rdg8
14. Kh1 Qc6 15. Qe2 Rg6 16. Rac1 Qd7
17. Nb5 Kb8 18. Rfd1 d5 19. b4 Rhg8
20. g3 c6 21. Nbd4 Nc7 22. Rc2 Rc8
23. Rb1 Ne8 24. a4 Ng7 25. a5 Nf5
26. a6 Nxd4 27. Nxd4 Bd8 28. axb7
Qxb7 29. b5 c5 30. Nc6+ Rxc6 31. bxc6
Qxb1+ 32. Kg2 Kc7 33. Qa6 Qb6
34. Qa3 Kxc6 35. Qa4+ Kc7 36. Qe8
Kc8 37. h4 h5 38. Qf7 Qc7 39. Qf8 c4
40. Qa3 Bxh4 41. Rb2 Be7 42. Qa6+
Kd8 43. Rb7 Qxe5 44. Qxa7 Qe4+
45. Kh2 Ke8 46. Rxe7+ Kf8 47. Rxh7
1–0 (*Cleveland Plain Dealer*, November 20, 1932)

694 Anderson–Kashdan [C45]
Binghamton Simultaneous, 1933 *[May 3]*

1. e4 e5 2. Nf3 Nc6 3. d4 exd4
4. Nxd4 Nxd4 5. Qxd4 Qf6 6. e5 Qe7
7. Nc3 c6 8. Be3 d5 9. 0–0–0 Be6
10. Nb5! cxb5 11. Bxb5+ Kd8 12. a3 b6
13. Bc6 Rc8 14. Bxd5 Bxd5 15. Qxd5+
Kc7 16. Qb5 Qe6 17. Rd3 Rd8 18. Rxd8
Kxd8 19. Rd1+ Kc7 20. Qa6 Bc5

21. Qxa7+ Kc6 22. Bxc5 Kxc5 23. Rd6
0–1 (*New York Post*, May 3, 1933)

695 Kashdan–Palmer [B70]
Detroit Simultaneous, 1933 *[May 6]*

1. e4 c5 2. Nf3 Nc6 3. d4 cxd4
4. Nxd4 Nf6 5. Nc3 d6 6. Be2 g6 7. h3
Bg7 8. Be3 Bd7 9. 0–0 Qc8 10. f4 h5
11. Bf3 h4 12. Qd2 Nh5 13. Nd5 Nxd4
14. Bxd4 Bxd4+ 15. Qxd4 f6 16. Rad1
Kf7 17. Nxe7 Kxe7 18. Qxd6+ Ke8
19. Bxh5 Rxh5 20. Qxf6 Qc6 21. Rd6
Qxe4 22. Rfd1 Rh7

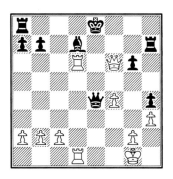

After
22. ... Rh7

If 22. ... Rd8 then 23. f5! wins. **23. Rxd7
Rxd7 24. Qh8+ Ke7 25. Qg7+ Ke8
26. Qxd7+ Kf8 27. f5! gxf5 28. Rf1 f4
29. Qd6+ Kg7 30. Qxf4 1–0** (*New York Post*, May 20, 1933)

696 Kashdan–Walton [C86]
Detroit Simultaneous, 1933 *[May 6]*

1. e4 e5 2. Nf3 Nc6 3. Bb5 a6 4. Ba4
Nf6 5. 0–0 b5 6. Bb3 Be7 7. Qe2 d6
8. c3 Bd7 9. d4 0–0 10. Rd1 Qc8
11. Nbd2 h6 12. Nf1 Re8 13. d5 Na5
14. Bc2 c6 15. dxc6 Bxc6 16. Ng3 Nb7
17. Nf5 Kf8 18. Be3 Nxe4 19. Nxe7 Kxe7
20. Bxh6 Nxc3 21. Bg5+ f6 22. bxc3
Bxf3 23. Qxf3 fxg5 24. Be4 Rb8 25. Qg3
Qe6 26. Qxg5+ Qf6 27. Qe3 Nc5
28. Bd5 Rf8 29. g3 Rb6 30. Rd2 Rfb8
31. Re1 b4 32. f4 Nd7 33. cxb4 Rxb4
34. Bc6 Rb1 35. Bxd7 Rxe1+ 36. Qxe1
Kxd7 37. fxe5 Re8 38. exf6 Rxe1+
39. Kf2 Re8 40. fxg7 Rg8 41. g4 Rxg7
42. Kg3 Rg5 43. h4 Rg8 44. g5 Re8
45. h5 Re3+ 46. Kf4 Ra3 47. Rh2 Ke6

48. h6 Ra4+ 49. Ke3 Ke5 50. h7 Ra3+ 51. Kf2 Rxa2+ 52. Kg3 1–0 (*Cleveland Plain Dealer*, May 14, 1933)

697 Kashdan–Columbia Team [A52]
Woodside Simultaneous, 1933 *[May]*

1. d4 Nf6 2. c4 e5 3. dxe5 Ng4 4. Nf3 Bc5 5. e3 Nc6 6. Nc3 Ngxe5 7. Be2 d6 8. 0–0 0–0 9. Na4 Bb6 10. Nxb6 axb6 11. Bd2 Bf5 12. Bc3 Qe7 13. Nd4 Bd7 14. Qc2 Rfe8 15. a3 Na5 16. Bxa5 Rxa5 17. Qc3 Ng4 18. h3 Nf6 19. Bf3 Ne4 20. Qc2 Ng5 21. Bg4 Bxg4 22. hxg4 Qe4 23. Qd1 Ne6 24. Re1 h5 25. f3 Qg6 26. gxh5 Rxh5 27. Nxe6 Rxe6 28. e4 Qg3 29. Qa4 Rh2 30. Qc2 Rg6 0–1 Representing the consulting Columbia Team were Bernstein, Greene, Lobel, and Hecht. Kashdan played 26 teams at Woodside. (*Brooklyn Daily Eagle* 1933, month and day unknown)

698 Kashdan–Ludlow [C28]
Cleveland Simultaneous, 1933 *[May 24]*

1. e4 e5 2. Nc3 Nf6 3. Bc4 Bc5 4. d3 Nc6 5. f4 d6 6. f5 Bd7 7. Bg5 Bb4 8. Nge2 Nd4 9. 0–0 Nxe2+ 10. Nxe2 c6 11. Kh1 Qe7 12. Ng3 0–0–0 13. c3 Ba5 14. b4 Bb6 15. a4 h6 16. Bh4 Be3 17. Nh5 Bg5 18. Bf2 Kb8 19. Nxf6 Qxf6 20. Qb3 Rhf8 21. b5 c5 22. a5 Bc8 23. Rab1 Qe7 24. Bd5 Bf6 25. Rfd1 g6 26. fxg6 fxg6 27. Rf1 Rde8 28. Qc2 Be6 29. Bxe6 Qxe6 30. Be3 Bg7 31. c4 Rxf1+ 32. Rxf1 Rf8 33. Qe2 Rxf1+ 34. Qxf1 g5 35. Kg1 Qf6 36. Qf5 Kc7 37. Kf2 b6 38. a6 Qxf5+ 39. exf5 Bf6 40. Kf3 h5 41. Ke4 Kd7 42. Kd5 Be7 43. g3 Bf6 44. h3 Be7 45. Bf2 Bf6 46. Ke4 Ke7 47. h4 gxh4 48. gxh4 Kd7 49. Kf3 Ke7 50. Kg3 Kd7 51. Be3 Ke7 52. Bg5 Kf7 53. Kf3 Be7 0–1 It is not clear that White is lost. Perhaps this was not the end of the game. (*Cleveland Plain Dealer*, June 4, 1933)

699 Kashdan–Keller [C28]
Cleveland Simultaneous, 1933 *[May 24]*

1. e4 e5 2. Nc3 Nc6 3. Bc4 Nf6 4. d3

Nd4 5. f4 d6 6. f5 h6 7. Nf3 c5 8. 0–0 Bd7 9. a4 Be7 10. Ne2 a6 11. a5 b5 12. axb6 Qxb6 13. c3 Nxf3+ 14. Rxf3 Bc6 15. Kh1 d5 16. exd5 Nxd5 17. Rg3 Bf6 18. Ng1 Bb7 19. Nf3 Qd6 20. Qe2 Kd7 21. Bd2 Rae8 22. Ne1 Nf4 23. Qf1 Bg5 24. Rg4 f6 25. Bxf4 exf4 26. Be6+ Kd8 27. Nf3 Re7 28. Nxg5 hxg5 29. Rd1 f3 30. g3 f2+ 31. Re4 Qxg3 32. Qg2 Rxh2+ 33. Qxh2 Qf3+ 0–1 Kashdan married just after the Cleveland exhibition on June 1, 1933, and just prior to the Folkestone Olympiad. (*Cleveland Plain Dealer*, June 11, 1933)

700 Barrett–Kashdan [C55]
Buffalo Simultaneous, 1933 *[May 26]*

1. e4 e5 2. Nf3 Nc6 3. Bc4 Nf6 4. Nc3 Bb4 5. d3 d6 6. Bg5 h6 7. Bh4 g5 8. Bg3 Bg4 9. Bb5 Nh5 10. h3 Nxg3 11. fxg3 Be6 12. Qd2 Qd7 13. a3 Ba5 14. d4 exd4 15. Nxd4 Bb6 16. Nd5 0–0–0 17. Nxc6 bxc6 18. Bxc6! Qxc6 19. Ne7+ Kb7 20. Nxc6 Kxc6 21. 0–0–0 Kb7 22. Qc3 Rhe8 23. Qf6 Bc4 24. Qxh6 Rxe4 25. Kb1 Re2 26. Qxg5 Rde8 27. b3 Be6 28. Qb5 Bc8 29. Qd5+ Kb8 30. Qxf7 R8e5 31. Qf1 Bf5 32. Rc1 Rf2 33. Qc4 Be6 34. Qc6 Bd5 35. Qd7 Be3 36. Rce1 Be6 37. Qd8+ Kb7 38. Rhf1 Rxg2 39. g4 Bd5 40. Rf5 Bg5 41. Rfxe5 Bxd8 42. Rxd5 Rh2 43. Rh5 c5 44. Re6 Kc6 45. g5 Ba5 46. Rhh6 Rd2 47. Kb2 c4 48. b4 Bb6 49. Kc3 Rd1 50. h4 Bc7 51. g6 Kb5 52. g7 d5 53. a4+ Kxa4 54. g8Q 1–0 Contributed by John Hilbert. (*Buffalo Evening News*, June 3, 1933)

701 Garfinkel–Kashdan [D17]
Buffalo Simultaneous, 1933 *[May 26]*

1. d4 Nf6 2. c4 c6 3. Nc3 d5 4. Nf3 dxc4 5. a4 Bf5 6. Ne5 Nbd7 7. Nxc4 Qc7 8. f3 e5 9. e4 exd4 10. Ne2 Be6 11. Bf4 Qd8 12. Nxd4 Bb4+ 13. Kf2 Bxc4 14. Bxc4 0–0 15. Qb3 Bc5 16. Rhd1 Qe7 17. Kf1 Bxd4 18. Rxd4 Ne5 19. Be2 c5 20. Rd2 Rfd8 21. Rad1 Rxd2 22. Rxd2 b6 23. Bb5 Rc8 24. Ba6 Re8 25. Qd1 h6 26. Bb5 Rf8 27. Bg3 Nh5 28. Bf2

Nf4 29. g3 Ne6 30. f4 a6 31. Bxa6 Nc6
32. Rd7 Qf6 33. Rd6 Nb4 34. Be2 Qxb2
35. Rxb6 Rd8 36. Rd6 Rxd6 37. Qxd6
Qa1+ 38. Qd1 Qb2 39. Bc4 Nd4 40. Kg2
Nbc2 41. Qd2 Qa3 42. Bxd4 Nxd4
43. Qd1 Qb2+ 44. Kh3 Qb4 45. Bd5 Qc3
46. Qh5 Ne6 47. Bxe6 fxe6 48. Qe8+
Kh7 49. Qxe6 c4 50. Qf5+ Kg8 51. e5
Qd3 52. Qe6+ Kh7 53. f5 c3 54. Qf7
c2 55. f6 Qg6 56. Qc4 gxf6 57. exf6 h5
58. Kg2 Qf5 59. f7 Kg7 60. a5 Qxf7
61. Qxc2 Qd5+ 62. Kh3 Qxa5 ½–½ Contributed by John Hilbert. (*Buffalo Evening News*,
June 10, 1933)

702 Kashdan–Watson [C66]
Toronto Simultaneous, 1933 *[May 27]*

1. e4 e5 2. Nf3 Nc6 3. d4 exd4 4. Nxd4
Nf6 5. Nc3 d6 Inviting White to transpose
into the Steinitz Variation of the Ruy Lopez.
6. Bb5 Bd7 7. 0–0 Be7 8. Re1 0–0 9. Bf4
Re8 10. Bf1 Bf8 11. Qd2 Ne5 12. Rad1
Qc8 13. Bg5 Nfg4 14. h3 Nf6 15. Bxf6
gxf6 16. Nd5 Bg7 17. Qf4 Qd8 18. Nf5
Ng6 19. Qg3 Practically pinning the knight.
19. ... Kh8 20. f4 Rg8 21. Kh2 Be6
22. Rd3 Bf8 23. Qf2 Black threatened Ne5,
winning the exchange. 23. ... c6 24. Nde3
Qc7 25. g3 Rd8 26. Ng4 Ne7 27. Nxf6
Rg6 28. Nh5 Nxf5 29. exf5 Bxf5
30. Rde3 Qb6 31. c3 Re8 32. Qd2 Rxe3
33. Rxe3 Re6 34. Rxe6 fxe6 35. Bg2 Qc7
Perhaps Kg8 and Kf7 was better. 36. Qd4+
Bg7 37. Nxg7 Qxg7 38. Qxa7 Qc7
39. Qd4+ Kg8 40. a4 c5? 41. Qf6 d5?
42. Bxd5! Qd7 Hoping for 43. Bb3 when
Qd2+ leads to a perpetual. 43. Qxf5!

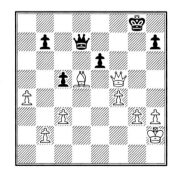

After
43. Qxf5

1–0 (*Chess World*, July-August 1933)

703 Kashdan–Pasternak [C29]
Collinsville Simultaneous, 1933 *[May 30]*

1. e4 e5 2. Nc3 Nf6 3. f4 d5 4. exd5
e4 5. Bc4 Bc5 6. d4 exd3 7. Qxd3 0–0
8. Nge2 Re8 9. Na4 Bg4 10. Qb3 Qe7
11. Nxc5 Bxe2 12. Kf2 Qxc5+ 13. Be3
Rxe3! If 14. Qxe3 then Ng4+. 0–1 (*Brooklyn
Daily Eagle*, June 8, 1933)

704 Kashdan–Regen [D52]
Philadelphia Simultaneous, 1933 *[May 31]*

1. d4 d5 2. Nf3 Nf6 3. c4 c6 4. Nc3 e6
5. Bg5 Nbd7 6. e3 Qa5 7. Qb3 Bb4
8. Rc1 e5 9. Nxe5 Nxe5 10. dxe5 Ne4
11. Bf4 Be6 12. Be2 Nc5 13. Qc2 dxc4
14. a3 Bxc3+ 15. Qxc3 Qxc3+ 16. Rxc3
Rd8 17. Bxc4? Na4 18. Rc2 Bxc4
19. Rxc4 Nxb2 0–1 (*Canadian Chessner*, 1933)

705 Kashdan–Lawrence [D66]
Woodside Simultaneous, 1933 *[December]*

1. d4 d5 2. Nf3 Nf6 3. c4 c6 4. Nc3 e6
5. Bg5 h6 6. Bh4 Nbd7 7. e3 Be7 8. Rc1
0–0 9. Bd3 dxc4 10. Bxc4 b5 11. Bd3 a6
12. e4 c5 13. e5 Nd5 14. Bg3 Bb7 15. 0–0
Rc8 16. Ne4 Nb4 17. a3 Nxd3 18. Qxd3
Bxe4 19. Qxe4 cxd4 20. Nxd4 Qb6
21. b4 Rfe8 22. Nc6 Bc5 23. Na5 Be7
24. Rc6 Rxc6 25. Nxc6 Bg5 26. h4 Be7
27. Rd1 Nb8 28. Nxe7+ Rxe7 29. Rd6
Qc7 30. Bf4 Rd7 31. Qa8 Qb7 32. Qxb7
Rxb7 33. Be3 Kf8 34. Rd8+ Ke7 35. Rg8
Nd7 36. Rxg7 Nxe5 37. Bxh6 Nc4
38. Bg5+ 1–0 (*Brooklyn Daily Eagle*, December 13, 1933)

706 Kashdan–Wallace [C45]
Washington Simultaneous, 1934 *[February 14]*

1. e4 e5 2. Nf3 Nc6 3. d4 exd4
4. Nxd4 Nxd4 5. Qxd4 Qf6 6. e5 Qb6
7. Qxb6 axb6 8. Bd3 d5 9. Bf4 Be6
10. 0–0 c6 11. Nd2 Bc5 12. Nb3 Ne7
13. Nxc5 bxc5 14. b3 c4 15. Be2 0–0
16. Be3 Rfb8 17. Bc5 Nc8 18. f4 b6
19. Be3 Ne7 20. g4 cxb3 21. axb3 c5
22. f5 Bd7 23. Bf3 Rxa1 24. Rxa1 Bc6
25. Ra7 d4 26. Rxe7 Bxf3 27. Bf4 Kf8

28. f6 gxf6 29. exf6 Rc8 30. Bh6+ Kg8
31. Re5 Bd1 32. Rg5+ Kh8 33. Rg7 Rc7
34. Rg5 Bxc2 35. Bg7+ Kg8 36. Bh6+
Bg6 37. h4 Kh8 38. Bg7+ Kg8 39. h5
Bc2 40. Bh6+ ½–½ (*Washington Post*, February 18, 1934)

707 Kashdan–Wimatt [B15]

Washington Simultaneous, 1934 *[February 14]*

1. e4 c6 2. d4 d5 3. Nc3 dxe4 4. Nxe4
Nf6 5. Ng3 e5 6. Nf3 exd4 7. Nxd4 Be7
8. Be2 0–0 9. 0–0 h6 10. Ngf5 Bc5
11. Bd3 Bxd4 12. Nxd4 Bg4 13. Qd2 Qc7
14. Nf5 Bxf5 15. Bxf5 Qe5 16. Bd3 Nbd7
17. Re1 Qh5 18. Qf4 Rfe8 19. Bd2 Nd5
20. Qg3 Nc5 21. c4 Nxd3 22. Qxd3 Nf6
23. Bc3 Rad8 24. Rxe8+ Rxe8 25. Bxf6
gxf6 26. Qd7 Qe2 27. Rf1 Re7 28. Qd4
Kg7 29. h3 Re4 30. Qxa7 Qxb2 31. c5
Qb4 32. Qb8 Re5 33. Rc1 Qb2 34. Rc4
½–½ (*Washington Post*, February 18, 1934)

708 Kashdan–LeDain [C45]

Montreal Simultaneous, 1934 *[February 17]*

1. e4 e5 2. Nf3 Nc6 3. d4 exd4 4. Nxd4
Bc5 5. Be3 Qf6 6. c3 Nge7 7. Bb5 Bb6
8. 0–0 d6 9. Na3 0–0 10. Nc4 Bd7
11. Nxb6 axb6 12. f4 Ng6 13. Qd2 Qd8
14. Bd3 Nxd4 15. cxd4 f5 16. exf5 Bxf5
17. Bxf5 Rxf5 18. g4! Rf8 19. f5 Ne7
20. Rae1 Nd5 21. Bg5 Qd7 22. a3 Ra4
23. Re4 Rc4 24. Rfe1 Qc6 25. Qf2 h6
26. Bh4 g5! 27. Bg3 Nf6 28. Re7 Nxg4
29. Qe2 Rc2 30. Qe6+ Kh8 31. d5? Qc5+
32. Kh1 Nf6 33. Rd1 Rxb2 34. Rf7 Rxf7
35. Qxf7 Qc3 36. Rf1 0–1 And Black eventually won. (*The Canadian Chessner*, 1934)

709 Kashdan–Gale [C28]

Toronto Simultaneous, 1934 *[February 21]*

1. e4 e5 2. Bc4 Nf6 3. Nc3 Nc6 4. f4
Nxe4 5. Nxe4 d5 6. Bd3 dxe4 7. Bxe4
f5 8. Bxc6+ bxc6 9. Nf3 e4 10. Ne5
Qh4+ 11. g3 Qh6 12. d3 Bc5 13. dxe4
fxe4 14. Qe2 Be6 15. Qa6 Bb6 16. Qb7
0–0 17. Qxc6 Rad8 18. f5 Bf2+ 19. Kxf2
Rd2+ 20. Bxd2 Qxd2+ 21. Kg1 Qe3+
22. Kg2 Qe2+ ½–½ Kashdan played 40

games here, winning 34, drawing 5, and losing
only one. (*Canadian Chessner*, 1934)

710 Kashdan–Nisbet [C33]

Detroit Simultaneous, 1934 *[March]*

1. e4 e5 2. f4 exf4 3. Bc4 d6 4. Nf3
Be6 5. Bxe6 fxe6 6. d4 Qf6 7. e5 Qh6
8. 0–0 Nc6 9. Qe2 0–0–0 10. Nc3 dxe5
11. dxe5 Bc5+ 12. Kh1 Nge7 13. Ne4 Be3
14. Bxe3 fxe3 15. Neg5 Nf5 16. Qe1 e2
17. Rg1 Rhf8 18. c3 Rd1 19. Qf2 Rxa1
20. Rxa1 Nxe5 21. Nxe5 Ng3+ 22. Kg1
Rxf2 0–1 (*Cleveland Plain Dealer*, April 15, 1934)

711 Kashdan–Dickman [B82]

Brooklyn Simultaneous, 1934 *[October]*

1. e4 c5 2. Nf3 e6 3. d4 cxd4 4. Nxd4
Nf6 5. Bd3 Nc6 6. Be3 a6 7. 0–0 Qc7
8. Nc3 Be7 9. Nb3 d6 10. f4 Na5 11. Qe2
Bd7 12. Rad1 Nxb3 13. axb3 Bc6 14. h3
Rd8 15. Qf2 Nd7 16. Ne2 Nc5 17. Bxc5
dxc5 18. Nc3 Bf6 19. e5 Be7 20. Be4
Rxd1 21. Rxd1 0–0 22. Qf3 Bxe4
23. Nxe4 Rd8 24. Rd3 Rd4 25. Rxd4
cxd4 26. Qd3 Qd8 27. Qc4 h6 28. Kf1
Qb6 29. Ke2 Qc6 30. Qxc6 bxc6 31. Kd3
1–0 Kashdan won 24 games, drew 5, and lost
three in this exhibition.(*Brooklyn Daily Eagle*,
October 18, 1934)

712 Kashdan–Sussman [D62]

Brooklyn Simultaneous, 1934 *[October]*

1. d4 d5 2. c4 e6 3. Nc3 Nf6 4. Nf3
Nbd7 5. Bg5 Be7 6. e3 0–0 7. Qc2 c5
8. cxd5 cxd4 9. Nxd4 Nxd5 10. Bxe7
Qxe7 11. Be2 Nxc3 12. Qxc3 Nf6 13. 0–0
e5 14. Nb5 Bd7 15. Rfd1 Bxb5 16. Bxb5
a6 17. Bf1 Rac8 18. Qb3 Ne4 19. Rac1
Rxc1 20. Rxc1 Nd2 21. Qb6 Nxf1 22. Kxf1
Rd8 23. Rc7 Rd1+ 24. Ke2 Qd8 25. Qxb7
Qd3+ 26. Kf3 Qf5+ 27. Ke2 Qd3+ ½–½
(*Brooklyn Daily Eagle*, October 18, 1934)

713 Granger & Nauheim– Kashdan [C42]

Manhattan Simultaneous, 1938 *[February 13]*

1. e4 e5 2. Nf3 Nf6 3. Bc4 Nxe4
4. Nxe5 d5 5. d3 dxc4 6. dxe4 Qxd1+

7. Kxd1 Be6 8. Nc3 f6 9. Nf3 Nc6 10. Bf4 0–0–0+ 11. Ke2 Bb4 12. Nb5 Ba5 13. c3 Rhe8 14. h3 Bf5 15. e5 fxe5 16. Be3 a6 17. Na3 b5 18. Rhd1 Bd3+ 19. Ke1 b4 20. cxb4 Bxb4+ 21. Bd2 e4 22. Ng1 e3 23. Bxb4 exf2+ 24. Kxf2 Nxb4 25. Rd2 Re4 26. Nf3 Rde8 27. Ng1 Nc6 28. Rc1 Ne5 29. b3 Rf8+ 30. Kg3 h5 31. bxc4 h4+ 32. Kh2 Bxc4 33. Nxc4 Rxc4 34. Rcd1 g5 35. Ne2 Rf7 36. Nd4 Rf6 37. a3 Kb7 38. Re2 Nc6 39. Ne6 g4 40. hxg4 Rxg4 41. Rd7 Kb6 42. Nxc7 Rfg6 43. Na8+ Ka5 44. Rd5+ Ka4 45. Nb6+ Kxa3 46. Rd3+ Kb4 47. Rb2+ 1–0 In this exhibition Kashdan won 18 games, drew 3, and lost this one game. (*American Chess Bulletin*, January-February 1938)

714 Kashdan–LaPoint [D37]

Baltimore Simultaneous, 1947 *[Fall]*

1. d4 d5 2. c4 e6 3. Nc3 Nf6 4. Nf3 Nbd7 5. e3 c5 6. cxd5 exd5 7. dxc5 Nxc5 8. Be2 Be7 9. 0–0 0–0 10. b3 Be6 11. Bb2 Rc8 12. Nd4 Nce4 13. Nxe6 fxe6 14. Nb5 Bc5 15. Rc1 Nxf2! 16. Rxf2 Bxe3 17. Rxc8 Bxf2+ 18. Kxf2 Qxc8 19. Kg1 a6 20. Nd4 e5 21. Nf3 Qc5+ 22. Kh1 Ne4 23. Qc1 Qxc1+ 24. Bxc1 Rc8 25. Be3 d4 26. Bg1 Rc1 27. Bc4+ Kf8 28. h4 d3 29. Kh2 d2 30. Be2 Hoping for d1(Q) 31. Bxd1 Rxd1 32. Nxe5 with drawing chances. **30. ... Re1 0–1** One of 38 games played in this simul in Baltimore. No further information was given. (*Chess Life*, November 20, 1947)

715 Kashdan–Rivise [C86]

Los Angeles Simultaneous, 1949 *[June]*

1. e4 e5 2. Nf3 Nc6 3. Bb5 a6 4. Ba4 Nf6 5. 0–0 Be7 6. Qe2 b5 7. Bb3 0–0 8. c3 d5 9. exd5 Nxd5 10. Nxe5 Nxe5 11. Qxe5 Bb7 12. d4 a5 13. Bc3 Ra6 14. Nd2 Rg6 15. Nf3 Bd6 16. Qf5 Rf6 17. Qg4 Nf4 18. Bxf4 Rxf4 19. Qh3 Bxf3 20. gxf3 Rh4 21. Qf5 g6! 22. Qxb5 Rh5 0–1 (*Chess Review*, July 1949)

716 Altshiller & Martin–Kashdan [C86]

Fort Worth Simultaneous, 1951 *[August]*

1. e4 e5 2. Nf3 Nc6 3. Bb5 a6 4. Ba4 Nf6 5. 0–0 Be7 6. Qe2 b5 7. Bb3 0–0 8. c3 d6 9. a4 Bd7 10. d4 b4 11. Rd1 Qb8 12. Nbd2 Na5 13. Bc2 c5 14. Bd3 Bc8 15. Nc4 Nb3 16. dxe5 dxe5 17. Rb1 Nxc1 18. Rbxc1 Nd7 19. Ne3 Re8 20. Nd5 Bd6 21. cxb4 cxb4 22. Bc4 Nf8 23. Rd3 Ne6 24. Rcd1 Bf8 25. Nh4 Nd4 26. Qh5 Be6 27. Nf5 Nxf5 28. exf5 Bxd5 29. Bxd5 Ra7 30. Rh3 h6 31. f6 Qb6 32. fxg7 Bxg7 33. Rf3 Ree7 34. Qf5 Rad7 35. Rfd3 Kf8 36. Bc6 Qxc6 37. Rxd7 Bf6 38. R7d6 1–0 While playing in the U.S. Open he played some simultaneous exhibition games as well. (Kashdan's scoresheet)

717 Kashdan–Steckel & Spiller [C12]

Fort Worth Simultaneous, 1951 *[August]*

1. d4 e6 2. e4 d5 3. Nc3 Nf6 4. Bg5 Bb4 5. e5 h6 6. Bd2 Bxc3 7. bxc3 Ne4 8. Qg4 g6 9. h4 c5 10. Bd3 Nxd2 11. Kxd2 Nc6 12. Rh3 Qe7 13. Rb1 b6 14. Rf3 Bd7 15. Rf6 c4 16. Be2 0–0–0 17. h5 g5 18. f4 Rdg8 19. fxg5 Rxg5 20. Qf3 Be8 The game is incomplete. (Kashdan's scoresheet)

United States Speed Tournament Games (718–734)

718 Kashdan–Moscowitz [D68]

Manhattan Chess Club (Speed), 1941 *[October 8]*

1. d4 Nf6 2. c4 e6 3. Nc3 d5 4. Nf3 Be7 5. Bg5 0–0 6. e3 Nbd7 7. Rc1 c6 8. Bd3 dxc4 9. Bxc4 Nd5 10. Bxe7 Qxe7 11. 0–0 Nxc3 12. Rxc3 e5 13. Qc2 e4 14. Nd2 Nf6 15. f3 Bf5 16. fxe4 Bxe4 17. Nxe4 Nxe4 18. Rb3 Rae8 19. Rf3

Kh8 20. Bd3 f5 21. a4 h6 22. h3 a6
23. Bxe4 fxe4 24. Rxf8+ Rxf8 25. Qc5?
Qf7 26. Rc3 Qf1+ 27. Kh2 Rf2 28. Kg3
Rxg2+ 29. Kh4 Qf6+ 0–1 (*American Chess
Bulletin*, September-October 1941)

719 Kashdan–Reshevsky [E40]
U.S. Lightning Championship, 1942 *[July 5]*

1. d4 Nf6 2. c4 e6 3. Nc3 Bb4 4. e3
d5 5. Nf3 c5 6. cxd5 Qxd5 7. Bd2 Bxc3
8. bxc3 0–0 9. Bd3 cxd4 10. exd4 b6
11. 0–0 Ba6 12. Bxa6 Nxa6 13. Qe2 Nb8
14. Rfe1 Nbd7 15. c4 Qd6 16. Bc3 Rfc8
17. Ne5 Nf8 18. f4 Rc7 19. Rad1 Rac8
20. Rd3 Nd5 21. Bd2 Ne7 22. Bc1 f6
23. Ba3 Qd8 24. Nf3 Rxc4 25. d5 Nxd5
26. Bxf8 Nxf4 27. Rxd8 Nxe2+ 28. Rxe2
Rxd8 29. Be7 Rd7 30. Ba3 e5 31. Kf2
Rd5 32. Bb2 b5 33. Ne1 a5 34. Nc2 Rd1
35. Ne3 Rf4+ 36. Kg3 Rd3 37. Bc1 h5
38. a3 b4 39. axb4 axb4 40. Ra2 Rc4
41. Ra8+ Kf7 42. Ra7+ Kg6 43. Ra1 Rxc1!
0–1 (*Chess Review*, June-July 1942)

720 Seidman–Kashdan [C80]
U.S. Lightning Championship, 1942 *[July 5]*

1. e4 e5 2. Nf3 Nc6 3. Bb5 a6 4. Ba4
Nf6 5. 0–0 Nxe4 6. Qe2 Nc5 7. Bxc6
dxc6 8. d4 Ne6 9. dxe5 Bc5 10. Nc3 0–0
11. Rd1 Qe7 12. Ne4 Bb6 13. Be3 Bxe3
14. Qxe3 Bd7 15. Nd4 Nxd4 16. Rxd4
Rad8 17. Rad1 Bf5 18. f4 Rxd4 19. Qxd4
b6 20. c3 c5 21. Qd5 Be6 22. Qc6 Rd8
23. Rxd8+ Qxd8 24. c4 Bxc4 25. Nc3
h6 26. h3 Qd4+ 27. Kh1 Qxf4 28. Qxc7
Qc1+ 29. Kh2 Qf4+ 30. Kh1 Qf1+
31. Kh2 Kh7 32. Qxb6 Qf4+ 33. Kh1
Qxe5 34. Qd8 Qf4 35. Qd1 Be6
36. Qd3+ Bf5 37. Qxa6 Qc1+ 38. Kh2
Qxb2 39. Qc4 Qb8+ 40. Kh1 Qc7
41. Nb5 Qe7 42. a4 Qe1+ 43. Kh2 Qe5+
44. Kh1 Be6 45. Qd3+ g6 46. Nc3 c4
47. Qf3 Kg7 48. Kg1 Bd7 49. Kh1 Qd6
50. Ne4 Qd4 51. Qc3 Qxc3 52. Nxc3 Kf6
53. Nd5+ Ke5 54. Nb6 c3 55. Nxd7+
Kd4 0–1 (*Chess Review*, June-July 1942)

721 Fine–Kashdan [D93]
U.S. Lightning Championship, 1942 *[July 5]*

1. d4 Nf6 2. c4 g6 3. Nc3 d5 4. Bf4
Bg7 5. e3 0–0 6. Qb3 c6 7. Nf3 dxc4
8. Bxc4 Nbd7 9. Be2 Nb6 10. e4 Nfd7
11. 0–0 c5 12. dxc5 Nxc5 13. Qa3 Ne6
14. Bg3 Bd7 15. Rfd1 Qc8 16. Rac1 Qc5
17. b4 Qc8 18. Nd5 Qe8 19. Ne5 Nxd5
20. exd5 Ng5 21. Qe3 h6 22. Rc7 Bc8
23. Rdc1 Nh7 24. Qc5 b6 25. Qxe7 Nf6
26. Qxe8 Rxe8 27. Bf3 Nh5 28. d6 Nxg3
29. hxg3 Bxe5 30. Bxa8 Be6 31. d7 Rf8
32. Rxa7 Bxd7 33. Rxd7 Rxa8 34. Re1
Bc3 35. Ree7 Rf8 36. a3 Bf6 37. Re3
Rc8 38. Rd6 Kg7 39. Rf3 Rc1+ 40. Kh2
Be7 41. Rxb6 1–0 (*Chess Review*, June-July
1942)

722 Kashdan–Kupchik [B85]
U.S. Lightning Championship, 1943 *[July 4]*

1. e4 c5 2. Nf3 d6 3. d4 cxd4 4. Nxd4
Nf6 5. Nc3 a6 6. Be2 e6 7. 0–0 Be7 8. f4
0–0 9. Kh1 Nbd7 10. Be3 Qc7 11. Bf3
Nb6 12. Qe2 Bd7 13. Rad1 Rac8 14. g4
Nc4 15. Bc1 b5 16. g5 Ne8 17. Qg2 b4
18. Nce2 e5 19. Nf5 Bxf5 20. exf5 Nb6
21. f6 Bd8 22. Bg4 Rb8 23. fxg7 Nxg7
24. f5 Qxc2 25. f6 Ne8 26. Bf5 Qc4
27. Qh3 Qc6+ 28. Kg1 h5 29. Qxh5 1–0
(*Chess Review*, June-July 1943)

723 Kashdan–Fine [E33]
U.S. Lightning Championship, 1943 *[July 4]*

1. d4 Nf6 2. c4 e6 3. Nc3 Bb4 4. Qc2
Nc6 5. Nf3 d6 6. g3 0–0 7. Bg2 e5
8. dxe5 dxe5 9. 0–0 Bxc3 10. Qxc3 Ne4
11. Qc2 Nd6 12. Rd1 Bf5 13. Qa4 Qe7
14. Be3 Bd7 15. Rac1 Nd4 16. Qa3 Nxe2+
17. Kh1 Nxc1 18. Rxc1 Bc6 19. Qc3 Rae8
20. b4 a6 21. Qb3 Kh8 22. a4 Nf5
23. Bc5 Nd6 24. b5 axb5 25. cxb5 Bxf3
26. Bxf3 b6 27. Bb4 e4 28. Bg2 f5
29. Rc6 f4 30. Bxd6 cxd6 31. Rxb6 e3
32. fxe3 fxe3 33. Qc3 e2 34. Qe1 Qf6
35. Rc6 Qf1+ 36. Bxf1 Rxf1+ 0–1 (*Chess
Review*, June-July 1943)

724 Reshevsky–Kashdan [D36]
U.S. Lightning Championship, 1943 *[July 4]*

1. d4 Nf6 2. c4 e6 3. Nc3 d5 4. Bg5
Nbd7 5. cxd5 exd5 6. e3 c6 7. Qc2 Be7
8. Bd3 0–0 9. Nf3 Re8 10. h3 Nf8
11. Bf4 Bd6 12. Bxd6 Qxd6 13. 0–0 g6
14. Rab1 Ne6 15. b4 Ng7 16. b5 Bf5
17. bxc6 bxc6 18. Na4 Bxd3 19. Qxd3
Ne4 20. Rfc1 f5 21. Ne5 Rac8 22. Qa6
Rc7 23. Rxc6 Rxc6 24. Qxc6 Qxc6
25. Nxc6 Ne6 26. Rb7 a6 27. Re7 Kf8
28. Rxh7 Nf6 29. Rb7 f4 30. Ne5 g5
31. Rf7+ 1–0 (*Chess Review*, June-July 1943)

725 Kashdan–Reshevsky [D93]
Metropolitan Speed Championship, 1943
[September 5]

1. d4 Nf6 2. c4 g6 3. Nc3 d5 4. Bf4
Bg7 5. e3 c6 6. Nf3 0–0 7. Qb3 dxc4
8. Bxc4 Nbd7 9. 0–0 Nb6 10. Be2 Bf5
11. Rfd1 a5 12. a4 Nfd5 13. Nxd5 cxd5
14. Rac1 Rc8 15. Rc5 Bd7 16. Rxa5 e6
17. Ra7 Bc6 18. Ne5 Bxe5 19. Bxe5 f6
20. Bg3 Nc4 21. Bxc4 dxc4 22. Qxc4
Re8 23. Qb4 e5 24. d5? Bxd5 25. e4 Be6
26. Re1 Re7 27. Rxb7 Rxb7 28. Qxb7
Qd2 29. Rf1 Rc1 30. Qb5 Bc4 31. Qe8+
Kg7 32. Qe7+ Kh6 33. h4 Rxf1+ 34. Kh2
Rxf2 35. Qf8+ Kh5 0–1 (*Chess Review*, October 1943)

726 Kashdan–Green [B40]
Metropolitan Speed Championship, 1943
[September 5]

1. e4 c5 2. Nf3 e6 3. d4 cxd4 4. Nxd4
Nf6 5. Bd3 Nc6 6. Be3 e5 7. Nb3 d5
8. exd5 Nxd5 9. Bd2 Qh4 10. 0–0 Be6
11. Nc3 Rd8 12. Qf3 Nf6 13. Rfe1 Bd6
14. Ne4 Nxe4 15. Bxe4 0–0 16. Bxc6
bxc6 17. Qxc6 e4 18. g3 Qh3 19. Qxe4
Bb4 The threat is Bd5. 20. Qe2 Bd5 21. f3
Bd6 22. Qg2 Qh5 23. g4 Qg6 24. Be3 f5
25. Rad1 Ba8 26. g5 Qh5 27. Nd4 Rde8
28. Bf2 Be5 29. Rd3 Bxd4 30. Rxd4
Bxf3 31. Qg3 Rxe1+ 32. Bxe1 Re8
33. Bc3 Ba8 34. Rd7 Qe2 35. Rxg7+ Kf8
36. Qd6+ 1–0 (*Chess Review*, October 1943)

727 Reshevsky–Kashdan [D36]
U.S. Lightning Championship, 1944 *[June 25]*

1. d4 Nf6 2. c4 e6 3. Nc3 d5 4. Bg5
Nbd7 5. cxd5 exd5 6. e3 c6 7. Bd3 Be7
8. Qc2 0–0 9. Nf3 Re8 10. Bf4 Nf8
11. h3 Bd6 12. Bxd6 Qxd6 13. 0–0 g6
14. Rab1 Nh5 15. b4 a6 16. Na4 f5
17. Qc5 Qf6 18. Nb6 Rb8 19. Nxc8
Rbxc8 20. Rfe1 Nd7 21. Qc2 Re7 22. a4
Rce8 23. b5 axb5 24. axb5 f4 25. bxc6
bxc6 26. e4 dxe4 27. Rxe4 Qd6 28. Rc1
Rxe4 29. Bxe4 c5 30. dxc5 Nxc5 31. Rd1
Qe7 32. Bxg6 hxg6 33. Qxg6+ Ng7
34. Ng5 Qe2 35. Qh7+ 1–0 (*USCF Yearbook*, 1944)

728 Denker–Kashdan [E55]
U.S. Lightning Championship, 1944 *[June 25]*

1. d4 Nf6 2. c4 e6 3. Nc3 Bb4 4. e3
0–0 5. Bd3 d5 6. Nf3 c5 7. 0–0 cxd4
8. exd4 dxc4 9. Bxc4 Nbd7 10. Qe2 Nb6
11. Bb3 a5 12. Bg5 a4 13. Bc2 a3 14. Ne4
Be7 15. Bxf6 Bxf6 16. Qd3 g6 17. Nxf6+
Qxf6 18. bxa3 Qe7 19. Qb5 Nd5 20. a4
Bd7 21. Qb2 Bxa4 22. Bxa4 Rxa4
23. Rab1 b6 24. Ne5 Rfa8 25. Ra1 Qa3
26. Qd2 Qb4 27. Rfd1 Qxd2 28. Rxd2
Rb4 29. g3 Kg7 30. Kg2 Ra3 31. h4
Rba4 32. Nf3 Nc3 33. Rb2 b5 34. Rc1
b4 35. Ne5 Rxa2 36. Rxa2 Rxa2 37. Kf3
b3!! 38. Nd3 If 38. Rxc3 b2 39. Rb3 Ra3! and
the pawn queens. 38. ... Nb5 39. Ke3 b2
40. Rb1 Na3 41. Nb4 Ra1 If 42. Rxb2 Nc4+
0–1 (*USCF Yearbook*, 1944)

729 Kevitz–Kashdan [C44]
U.S. Lightning Championship, 1944 *[June 25]*

1. e4 e5 2. Nf3 Nc6 3. c3 d5 4. Bb5
dxe4 5. Nxe5 Qd5 6. Qa4 Qxe5? This
loses a pawn. Correct is 6. ... Ne7. 7. Bxc6+
Kd8 8. Qxe4 Bd6 9. d4 Qxe4+ 10. Bxe4
Nf6 11. Bf3 Re8+ 12. Be3 Ng4 13. Bxg4
Bxg4 14. h3 Bf5 15. 0–0 c6 16. Nd2 Bd3
17. Rfe1 Kc7 18. Nf3 f6 19. Bd2 Be4
20. Re3 h6 21. Rae1 f5 22. R3e2 g5
23. Bc1 Kd7 24. Nd2 Bd5 25. Rxe8 Rxe8
26. Rxe8 Kxe8 27. c4 Bf7 28. b3 Kd7

29. h4 f4 30. hxg5 hxg5 31. Ne4 Be7 32. f3 Ke6 33. Kf2 Kf5 34. g4+ fxg3+ 35. Nxg3+ Ke6 36. Ke3 Bd6 Black should try 36. g4 and if 36. ... fxg4? 37. Bg5+ winning the bishop. 37. Ne2 Bg6 38. Kd2 Bb1 39. a3 Bg6 40. Nc3 Kf5 41. Ke2 Bh5 42. Ne4 Be7 43. Ng3+ Kg6 44. Nxh5 Kxh5 45. b4 Kh4 46. Kd3 Kg3 47. Ke4 Kf2 48. Be3+ Ke2 49. d5 cxd5+ 50. cxd5 b6 51. Bg1 a5? 52. Bxb6 axb4 53. axb4 Bxb4 54. Bd8 1–0 (*USCF Yearbook*, 1944)

730 Kashdan–Fine [D41]
U.S. Lightning Championship, 1944
[June 25]

1. d4 Nf6 2. c4 e6 3. Nf3 d5 4. Nc3 c5 5. cxd5 Nxd5 6. Nxd5 Qxd5 7. g3 Nc6 8. dxc5 Qxd1+ 9. Kxd1 Bxc5 10. e3 e5 11. Be2 Be6 12. Bd2 Rd8 13. a3 Na5 14. Ke1 Nb3 15. Rd1 f6 16. Bc3 Ke7 17. Nd2 a6 18. Ne4 Kf7 19. Nxc5 Nxc5 20. f3 Na4 21. Kf2 Nxc3 22. bxc3 Rc8 23. c4 Rc7 24. Rd6 Re8 25. Rb1 Bd7 26. e4 Ke7 27. Rdb6 Bc6 28. Ke3 Rd8 29. R6b2 g6 30. f4 Rd4 31. Bd3 Rcd7 32. Rb3 Kd6 33. Rf1 Ke7 34. Rc3 b5 35. fxe5 fxe5 36. Rfc1 bxc4 37. Bb1 Bb5 38. a4 Bxa4 39. Rxc4 Rxc4 40. Rxc4 Bb5 41. Rc5 Kf6 42. g4 g5 43. Rc8 Rd1 44. Bc2 Re1+ 45. Kf3 Rc1 46. Ke3 Ba4 47. Rc5 Bxc2 48. Kd2 Rg1 49. Kxc2 Rxg4 50. Rc6+ Kg7 51. Kd3 Rh4 52. Re6 Rxh2 53. Rxe5 h6 0–1 And Black won (*USCF Yearbook*, 1944)

731 Kashdan–Horowitz [C63]
U.S. Lightning Championship, 1944
[June 25]

1. e4 e5 2. Nf3 Nc6 3. Bb5 f5 4. d3 Nf6 5. Nc3? The correct move is 5. exf5! as played by Thomas in the Anglo-Dutch Match in 1914. 5. ... Bb4 6. 0–0 d6 7. Nd5 Bc5 8. d4 exd4 9. Nxd4 Bd7 10. Nb3 Bb6 11. Bg5 0–0 12. Nxf6+ gxf6 13. Bh6 Re8 14. exf5 Bxf5 15. Qf3 Bg6 16. Rae1 Re5 17. Bc4+ Kh8 18. Qg3 Qe7 19. Rxe5 fxe5 20. Bg5 Qg7 21. Qh4 Rf8 22. Nd2 Nd4 23. Bh6 Qf6 24. Bg5 Qg7 25. c3 Nf5

26. Qh3 c6 27. Nf3 d5 28. Bb3 e4 29. Nh4 Nxh4 30. Qxh4 Rf5 31. Be3 Qf6 32. Qg3 Kg7 33. Re1 Qe5 34. Qxe5+ Rxe5 35. a4 Bxe3 36. Rxe3 Kf6 37. Kf1 c5 38. Re1 d4 39. cxd4 cxd4 40. Rc1 Re7 41. Rc5 Rd7 42. Ke1 Rd6 43. a5 b6 44. Rb5 bxa5 45. Rxa5 Rb6 46. Ra3 Ke5 47. Kd2 Kf4 48. g3+ Kf3 49. Ke1 Kg2 50. h4 h5 51. Ke2 Rf6 52. Ke1 Rxf2 53. Bd5 Rxb2 54. Ra6 Bf5 55. Rf6 Bg4 56. Bxe4+ Kxg3 0–1 The forces are equal in the ending, but Black has a Steinitzian king. (*USCF Yearbook*, 1944)

732 Kashdan–Fine [D77]
U.S. Lightning Championship, 1945
[June 24]

1. d4 Nf6 2. Nf3 g6 3. g3 Bg7 4. Bg2 0–0 5. 0–0 d5 6. c4 e6 7. Nbd2 b6 8. Ne5 Bb7 9. Qc2 Nbd7 10. f4 c5 11. cxd5 exd5 12. e3 Rc8 13. Qa4 Nxe5 14. dxe5 Ng4 15. Nf3 f6 16. h3 Nh6 17. exf6 Rxf6 18. Bd2 Qc7 19. Bc3 Rf7 20. Bxg7 Rxg7 21. Ng5 Nf5 22. Ne6 Qd7 23. Qxd7 Rxd7 24. Kf2 Re8 25. Ng5 Nxe3 26. Rfe1 Rde7 27. Bf3 h6 0–1 (*Chess Review*, June-July 1945)

733 Moscowitz–Kashdan [D36]
U.S. Lightning Championship, 1945
[June 24]

1. d4 Nf6 2. c4 e6 3. Nc3 d5 4. Bg5 Nbd7 5. e3 c6 6. cxd5 exd5 7. Bd3 Be7 8. Qc2 0–0 9. Nge2 Re8 10. h3 Nf8 11. g4 Ne4 12. Bxe7 Qxe7 13. Bxe4 dxe4 14. Ng3 Be6 15. Ngxe4 Bd5 16. Nxd5 cxd5 17. Nc3 Rac8 18. Qb3 Qh4 19. Qxd5 Rxe3+ 20. Kf1 Re7 21. Qf3 Ne6 22. Rd1 Rd8 23. d5 Ng5 24. Qg3 Qh6 25. h4 Ne4 26. Nxe4 Rxe4 27. Kg2 Qg6 28. f3 Re2+ 29. Kh3 Rxb2 30. Qc7 Qf6 31. Rhf1 Qd6 32. Qxd6 Rxd6 33. Rc1 g6 34. Rfd1 Rxa2 35. Rc8+ Kg7 36. Rc7 Rb2 37. Re1 Rb3 38. Kg3 Rf6 39. Rf1 a5 40. g5 Rd6 41. Re1 Rxd5 42. Kg4 Rf5 43. f4 Rb4 44. Rf1 h5+ 45. gxh6+ Kxh6 46. Re7 a4 47. Re8 Kg7 48. Ra8 b5 49. Rf3 Rb1 50. Kg3 Rg1+ 51. Kf2 Rg4 0–1 (*Chess Review*, June-July 1945)

734 Tenner–Kashdan [C84]

U.S. Lightning Championship, 1945 *[June 24]*

1. e4 e5 2. Nf3 Nc6 3. Bb5 a6 4. Ba4
Nf6 5. 0–0 Be7 6. d4 exd4 7. e5 Ne4
8. Nxd4 Nxd4 9. Qxd4 Nc5 10. Nc3

0–0 11. Nd5 Nxa4 12. Qxa4 d6 13. Bf4
dxe5 14. Rad1 Bd6 15. Bg3 Be6 16. Ne3
Qe7 17. c4 c6 18. Rfe1 Rad8 19. Qc2 f5
20. c5 Bc7 21. Rxd8 Qxd8 22. Nc4 f4
23. Rd1 Qf6 24. Bxf4 Qxf4 0–1 And
Black won. (*Chess Review*, June-July 1945)

Informal, Consultation, Practice, etc. Games (735–758)*

735 Kashdan–Bentz [C33]

Correspondence Game, 1924

1. e4 e5 2. f4 exf4 3. Be2 When the game
started, the great New York 1924 International
Tournament was on. Dr. Tartakower had played
this move, the Little Bishop's Gambit, against
Bogoljubow, obtaining the better opening and
eventually winning. I had seen the game, and
thought it was an oddity worth trying. 3. ...
d5 This is the natural counter, and was played
by Bogoljubow, and later in the same tournament by Dr. Alekhine and Capablanca, with
Tartakower always on the White side. In his
notes published much later, Alekhine recommended 3. ... f5 4. exf5 (if 4. e5 d6!) Qh4+
5. Kf1 d5 6. Bh5+ Kd8 with advantage for Black.
4. exd5 Qxd5 But this is wrong. The queen
is subject to attack, and White soon gains a
strong center and better development, to com-
pensate for the sacrificed pawn. Capablanca's
continuation was 4. ... Nf6 5. c4 c6 6. d4 Bb4+
7. Kf1 leading to a remarkable position that I
shall discuss later. 5. Nf3 c6 6. Nc3 Qa5
7. 0–0 Nf6 8. d4 Bd6 9. Ne5 Threatening
the simple 10. Bxf4. If White can recover the

pawn he will obviously be far ahead in space and
development. Black's exchange is practically
forced. 9. ... Bxe5 10. dxe5 Nd5 If 10. ...
Qxe5 11. Bxf4 Qc5+ 12. Kh1. Now Black cannot
castle because of Bd6, and will have a hard time
developing. With the text, Black is ready to return the pawn for simplification, after 11. Nxd5
Qxd5 12. Qxd5 cxd5 13. Bxf4. This would be
satisfactory for White, but I preferred to go for
a direct attack. Whether this is justified or not,
is a question. I was young and ambitious, and
looking for exciting play. 11. Ne4 0–0 12. Bd3
Nd7 I was hoping for 12. ... Nb4, trying to exchange my strong bishop, when I prepared
13. Nf6+! gxf6 14. Bxh7+! Kxf7 15. Qh5+ Kg8
16. Bxf4 with a winning attack. But not 16. exf6??
Qxh5; I mention this because such moves have
been made, even in correspondence. 13. c4
Ne7 14. Bxf4 Ng6 15. Ng5 h6 16. Ne6 I
had first considered 16. Nxf7, but Black can defend by Nxf4. If then 17. Nxh6+ gxh6 18. Qg4+
Kh8 19. Rxf4 Qc5+ 20. Kh1 Nxe5, or 17. Rxf4
Rxf7 18. Bh7+ Kxh7 19. Rxf8 Nxe5, and White's
attack is gone. 16. ... Re8 Probably not realizing the strength of White's attack after the coming sacrifice. Best was still 16. ... Nxf4, with the

---

The very first game in this section is probably the earliest that we have a record of. This is also the only correspondence game on record. It was played in 1924, but it was not until 1969 that the game surfaced. In that year Kashdan became edi-tor of the Chess Correspondent. He explained in one issue why he should be the editor:

Several people have asked me, when learning that I was to be the Editor of the Chess Correspondent, *"Why a cor-respondence magazine?" I might have answered "Because it is there," or "Because no other magazine asked me." That would not be the whole truth, however.*

I played a fair amount of correspondence chess starting about a year after I first learned the game. I found it excel-lent training, and my correspondence experience speeded my chess progress.

An important point is that there is time in correspondence play to look for the best move, not merely for a good move. Each time you look deeply into the possibilities of a position, you will find new ideas. They will not always work out, of course, but when they do, the reward can be the discovery of a great combination.

To prove that I belong in CC, here is one of my early correspondence games. It was played in 1924, less than three years after I learned the moves. I was in high school at the time and a fair over-the-board-player, but far from the best in the school. My opponent, David Bentz, was the captain of the school chess team.

He then proceeded to annotate the game. It is interesting that he would point out moves that he would not make now.

continuation: 17. Nxf8 Qc5+ 18. Kh1 Nxd3 19. Nxd2 Nf2+ 20. Rxf2 (If the rook does not take, Black has a smothered mate!) Qxf2. The ending is even after 21. Qd6 Bxd7 22. Qxd7 Qxb2 23. Rf1. **17. Nxg7! Kxg7 18. Qh5 Qc5+** A necessary prelude. If at once 18. ... Rh8 19. Bxh6! Rxh6 20. Rxf7+! Kxf7 21. e6+ and Qxc5. There is that long rank again! Or if 18. ... Nxf4 19. Rxf4 Nxe5 20. Rxf7+! and once more the rook is immune. **19. Kh1 Rh8 20. Bd2 Ngxe5** I was very happy around this point, though still a piece behind. White can keep increasing the pressure, while Black's pieces are badly tied up. As an example of the possibilities, if 20. ... Ndxe5 21. Rxf7+! Kxf7 22. Bxg6+ and White wins. **21. Rae1 f6 22. Rf3 Kf8**

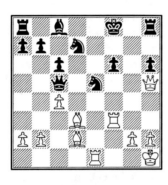

After
22. ... Kf8

This is a curious position. Black can hardly move a piece. If 22. ... Nxf3 23. Qg6+ Kf8 24. Re8 mate. If 22. ... Nxd3 23. Rg3 forces mate. Black's only chance is to get his king to the other side, and then unravel his pieces. If now, for instance, 23. Bxh6+ Ke7, Black may well escape. If White is to win, he must find something more forceful, he must open one or more lines to get to the king. There are enough White pieces in play so that sacrifices are in the wind. This is the kind of position where a combination should exist. It is just waiting to be discovered. **23. Bb4! Qxb4 24. Rxe5!** This is it. The bishop sacrifice forced the queen out of action, so that the rook can also be given up. All for the purpose of finally open the f file. Black has no choice now, as the threat is 25. Re8+, followed by Qg6 mate. **24. ... Nxe5 25. Rxf6+ Ke7** If 25. ... Kg8 or Kg7 26. Qxe5 still follows and mate is inevitable. Black's extra rook is no help at all. **26. Qxe5+ Kd8 27. Rf7 Rg8** If 27. ... Re8 28. Qc7 mate, or if 27. ... Rf8 28. Qf6+

Ke8 29. Rxf8+ Qxf8 30. Bg6+, similar to the actual game ending. Longest resistance was offered by 27. ... Bd7 28. Qxh8+ Kc7 29. Qxh8, when White has the extra rook. **28. a3** After all the fireworks, a simple quiet move ends it. It is either mate or no queen. **28. ... Qf8 29. Qf6+ Ke8 30. Rxf8+ Rxf8 31. Bg6+ 1–0** Kashdan took over as editor of the *Chess Correspondent* in 1969. To show that he was well qualified to take on this task, he gave this postal game that he had played in 1924 and just now added the notes to the game. (*Chess Correspondent*, 1969)

736 Tenner–Kashdan [D51]
Exhibition Game, New York, 1926

1. c4 Nf6 2. d4 c6 3. Nc3 d5 4. Nf3 e6 5. Bg5 Nbd7 6. e4 dxe4 7. Nxe4 Bb4+ 8. Bd2 Qa5 9. Nd6+ Ke7 10. c5 Rd8 11. Bd3 Bxd2+ 12. Nxd2 e5 13. Qe2 Kf8 14. 0–0 Qc7 15. Rae1 b6 16. f4 e4 17. N2xe4 bxc5 18. dxc5 Nxc5 19. Nxf6 gxf6 20. Qh5 Nxd3 21. Qxh7 Ne5 22. fxe5 0–1 (*The Bobby Fischer I Knew*, p. 49)

737 Kashdan & Horowitz–
H. Steiner & Frink [C42]
Consultation Game, 1926

1. e4 e5 2. Nf3 Nf6 3. Nxe5 d6 4. Nf3 Nxe4 5. d4 d5 6. Bd3 Bg4 7. 0–0 Bd6 8. c4 f5 9. cxd5 0–0 10. Nc3 Nd7 11. h3 Bh5 12. Nxe4 fxe4 13. Bxe4 Nf6 14. Bf5 Kh8 15. Bg5 h6 16. Bh4 Qe8 17. Qb3 Ne4 18. Bxe4 Qxe4 19. Rae1 Qf5 20. Ne5 Qf4 21. g4 Qxd4 22. Bg3 Bf7 1–0 (*New Yorker Staats-Zeitung*, May 9, 1926)

738 Bornholz & Samuels–
Kashdan & Horowitz [B04]
Consultation Game, 1927

1. e4 Nf6 2. e5 Nd5 3. d4 d6 4. exd6 cxd6 5. Nf3 g6 6. c4 Nb6 7. Bd2 Bg7 8. Bc3 N8d7 9. d5 Nf6 10. Bd3 0–0 11. 0–0 e5 12. dxe6 Bxe6 13. Nbd2 Rc8 14. Rc1 d5 15. Bb4 Re8 16. c5 Nbd7 17. Nd4 Ne5 18. Bb1 Bd7 19. Qb3 Nc6 20. Bc3 Nxd4 21. Bxd4 Bc6 22. Rfe1

Nd7 23. B×g7 K×g7 24. Qc3+ Qf6
25. Q×f6+ K×f6 26. b4 Re6 27. Bd3 a6
28. f4 Rce8 29. Kf2 R×e1 30. R×e1 R×e1
31. K×e1 a5! An ingenious attempt to draw
the game. 32. b5 N×c5 33. b×c6 N×d3+
34. Ke2 N×f4+ 35. Kf3 b×c6 36. K×f4
a4 37. Nf3 c5 38. g4 h6 39. h4 Ke6
40. Ke3 f5? A blunder. It is doubtful if White
could win otherwise. 41. g5 h×g5 42. h×g5
d4+ 43. Kd3 Kd5 44. Nh4 c4+ 45. Ke2
d3+ 46. Kd1 f4 47. N×g6 f3 48. Nf4+
Ke4 49. Nh3 Kf5 50. Kd2 1–0 (*American
Chess Bulletin*, January 1927, p. 15)

739 Kashdan & Horowitz & Meyer–Rubinstein [C97]
Consultation Game, 1928 *[February 16)]*

1. e4 e5 2. Nf3 Nc6 3. Bb5 a6 4. Ba4
Nf6 5. 0–0 Be7 6. Re1 b5 7. Bb3 d6 8. c3
0–0 9. h3 Na5 10. Bc2 c5 11. d4 Qc7
12. d5 Ne8 13. g4 g6 14. Bh6 Ng7
15. Nbd2 Nb7 16. Nf1 Nd8 17. Ng3 f6
18. Kh2 Nf7 19. Be3 Bd7 20. Rg1 Kh8
21. Qe2 Qb7 22. Nd2 Rg8 23. Rg2 Raf8
24. Rag1 Qc8 25. f3 Bd8 26. b3 Re8
27. c4 b4 28. h4 a5 29. h5 g5 30. a4
½–½ (*American Chess Bulletin*, March 1928, p. 54)

740 Rubinstein–Kashdan [D65]
Exhibition Game, 1928 *[May 1]*

1. c4 Nf6 2. d4 e6 3. Nc3 d5 4. Bg5
Nbd7 5. e3 c6 6. Nf3 Be7 7. Rc1 0–0
8. Qc2 a6 9. c×d5 e×d5 10. Bd3 Re8
11. 0–0 Nf8 12. Nd2 Ng6 13. Rfe1 Ng4
14. B×e7 Q×e7 15. Nf1 Bd7 16. f3 Nf6
17. Na4 Rad8 18. Nc5 Bc8 19. b4 Qc7
20. a4 Re7 21. b5 a×b5 22. a×b5 Rde8
23. b×c6 b×c6 24. Na6 B×a6 25. B×a6
Re6 26. Bd3 Ra8 27. Qc3 Rd6 28. Re2
Ne7 29. Rb1 Rdd8 30. Reb2 Ra7 31. Nd2
Rda8 32. Nb3 Nd7 33. Nc5 N×c5
34. Q×c5 g6 35. g3 Ra5 36. Qc3 Ra1
37. R×a1 R×a1+ 38. Kf2 Qa7 39. Qb4 f6
40. Qb8+ Q×b8 41. R×b8+ Kf7 42. Bb1
Ke6 43. g4 Ra6 44. Ke2 Kf7 45. h4 Ra7
46. h5 Kg7 47. Kf2 Kh6 48. Re8 g×h5
49. g×h5 f5 50. Rf8 Kg7 51. Re8 Kh6
52. Kg3 K×h5 53. Kf4 Ng6+ 54. K×f5

Rf7+ 55. Ke6 R×f3 56. Kd7 Rf6 57. Bc2
Kg4 58. Ba4 Nf8+ 59. Ke7 Re6+
60. K×f8 R×e8+ 61. K×e8 Kf3 62. Ke7
K×e3 63. Kd6 K×d4 64. B×c6 ½–½
(*Brooklyn Daily Eagle*, May 10, 1928)

741 Alekhine–Kashdan & H. Steiner [D31]
Consultation Game, 1929 *[March 24]*

1. d4 d5 2. c4 e6 3. Nc3 c6 4. Nf3
d×c4 5. a4 Bb4 6. e3 b5 7. Bd2 Qb6
8. Ne5 Nd7 9. a×b5 N×e5 10. d×e5 c×b5
11. Ne4 Be7 12. Qg4 Kf8 13. Qf4 a5
14. Be2 Bb7 15. 0–0 h5 16. Ng5 B×g5
17. Q×g5 Rh6 18. e4 h4 19. R×a5! Offering a sacrifice with telling effect! 19. ... f6
20. e×f6 N×f6 21. Q×b5 Resigns, for if
21. ... Q×b5 22. R×b5 Ba6 23. Ra5. 1–0 White
emerges at least with the exchange ahead. (*American Chess Bulletin*, November 1929)

742 Jaffe & Mishook–Kashdan & Lubowski [C77]
Consultation Game, 1931 *[January 1]*

1. e4 e5 2. Nf3 Nc6 3. Bb5 a6 4. Ba4
Nf6 5. d3 d6 6. c3 Be7 7. Nbd2 0–0
8. Nf1 b5 9. Bb3 d5 10. e×d5 N×d5
11. Qe2 Re8 12. Bd2 Bf8 13. 0–0–0 Bf5
14. Ng3 Nf4 15. B×f4 e×f4 16. Ne4 Na5
17. Bc2 c5 18. Qd2 Qc7 19. Nh4 Be6
20. Kb1 h6 21. g3 f5 22. Nf6+ g×f6
23. g×f4 Bg7 24. Rhg1 Rad8 25. Rg3
Rd7 26. Rdg1 b4 27. c×b4 c×b4 28. Ba4
Nc6 29. Qc1 Rc8 30. Qe3 Qd6 31. d4
Re8 32. d5 Q×d5 33. Bb3 Qe4+
34. Q×e4 f×e4 35. Nf5 B×b3 36. N×g7
B×a2+ 37. K×a2 Rb8 38. Nh5+ Kf8
39. Rg8+ Ke7 40. R8g7+ Kd8 41. R×d7+
K×d7 42. N×f6+ Ke6 43. N×e4 Kf5
44. Nc5 Rb5 45. Nb3 Rb6 46. Rg8 Ne7
47. Rf8+ Kg4 48. Rf7 Nd5 49. f5 ½–½
(*American Chess Bulletin*, January 1931, p. 13)

743 Sharp & Bencler & Shaw & Sack–Kashdan & Winkelman [D37]
Consultation Game, 1931 *[February 21]*

1. d4 Nf6 2. Nf3 e6 3. c4 d5 4. Nc3

Be7 5. e3 0–0 6. Bd3 dxc4 7. Bxc4 a6
8. 0–0 b5 9. Bd3 Bb7 10. Qe2 c5 11. Rd1
Qb6 12. dxc5 Bxc5 13. a3 Rc8 14. Bd2
Nbd7 15. b4 Bd6 16. Rac1 Ne5 17. Nxe5
Bxe5 18. Rc2 Rd8 19. Bc1 Rd7 20. Bb2
Rad8 21. Rcc1 Bb8 22. Nb1 e5 23. Bf5
Qc6 24. f3 Rxd1+ 25. Rxd1 Rxd1+
26. Qxd1 Qb6 27. Kf2 g6 28. Bc2 Nd5
29. Qd2 Ba7 30. Bc1 Qf6 31. Qe2 Qh4+
32. Kg1 Qh6 33. Be4 Nxe3 34. Kh1 Bxe4
35. fxe4 Qf4 36. Nc3 Qg4 37. Qf3 Qxf3
38. gxf3 f5 39. Bxe3 Bxe3 40. Nd5 Bc1
41. Nc7 Bxa3 42. Nxa6 Kf7 43. Nc7
Bxb4 44. Nxb5 Ke6 45. Nc7+ Kd6 ½–½
The game was adjourned for adjudication. It
was the feeling that the game would be drawn
despite a pawn less for White. (*Philadelphia Enquirer*, March 8, 1931)

744 Abrahams & Lowenthal– Kashdan [D15]

Liverpool, England, 1932 *[January]*

1. d4 d5 2. c4 c6 3. Nc3 Nf6 4. Nf3
Nbd7 5. cxd5 cxd5 6. Bf4 e6 7. Qa4
Nh5 8. e3 Nxf4 9. exf4 Be7 10. Bd3 0–0
11. 0–0 g6 12. Rfe1 a6 13. Qd1 b5 14. Re3
Bb7 15. g4 Bf6 16. Qf1 Rc8 17. Ne5 Nb6
18. Rh3 Nc4 19. Qe2 Bg7 20. g5 Nxe5
21. dxe5 b4 22. Nd1 Qb6 23. Ne3 Qd4
24. Ng2 Rc6 25. Rd1 Qb6 26. Ne3 Rfc8
27. f5 d4 28. f6 dxe3 29. fxg7 exf2+
30. Kf1 Rc1 31. Rg3 Qd4 32. Qd2 Rxd1+
33. Qxd1 Qxb2 34. Bc4 Hoping for 34. ...
Rxc4 when 35. Qd8+ would draw. 34. ... Bd5
0–1 (*Bethlehem Globe Times*, April 19, 1932; originally appeared in the London *Times*; contributed by Neil Brennen)

745 Kashdan–Dake [C11]

Exhibition Game, Pasadena, 1932 *[August]*

1. e4 e6 2. d4 d5 3. Nc3 Nf6 4. Bg5
dxe4 5. Nxe4 Be7 6. Bxf6 Bxf6 7. Nf3
Nd7 8. Bd3 c5 9. dxc5 Nxc5 10. Bb5+
If 10. Nxc5 then Qa5+ regains the piece. 10. ...
Ke7 11. Qxd8+ Rxd8 12. Nxc5 Rd5
13. Na6! Bxb2 14. Rb1 Rxb5 15. Nc7
Bc3+ 16. Ke2 Rxb1 17. Rxb1 Rb8 18. Na6
Ra8 19. Nc7 Rb8 ½–½ An interesting draw

by repetition. This game was played on an air-
ship during the Pasadena International tournament. (*Chess Reporter*, September 1932)

746 McKee & Thompson– Kashdan [D05]

Consultation Simul, Dallas, 1932 *[October]*

1. d4 d5 2. Nf3 Nf6 3. e3 e6 4. Bd3 c5
5. c3 Nc6 6. Nbd2 Be7 7. 0–0 0–0 8. e4
cxd4 9. e5 Nd7 10. cxd4 f5 11. exf6 Nxf6
12. Nb3 Bd6 13. Re1 Qc7 14. Qe2 Bd7
15. Bd2 Rae8 16. Rac1! Bc8 17. Ne5 Qb6
18. Be3 a5 19. Nc5 Qc7 20. f4 Qe7
21. Bb5 Bxe5 22. fxe5 Nd7 23. Nxb7
Nxd4 24. Bxd4 Bxb7 25. Rc7 Bc8
26. Bc5 Qd8 27. Bd6 Rf7 28. Rec1 Nb6
29. Bxe8 Qxe8 30. Rf1 1–0 This game was
played in a simultaneous exhibition in which
Kashdan won seven games, and this was his
only loss. Earlier on October 25 he played 25
games, winning 23, losing one and drawing
one. (*Texas Chess Magazine*, November 1932)

747 Jaffe–Kashdan [B01]

Exhibition Game, 1933 *[March]*

1. e4 d5 2. exd5 Qxd5 3. Nc3 Qa5
4. b4 Qxb4 5. Rb1 Qh4 6. Nf3 Qh5
7. Rb5 c5 8. Be2 Nf6 9. d4 e6 10. 0–0
a6 11. Rb1 b5 12. Ne5 Qh4 13. Nf3 Qh5
14. a3 Bb7 15. Nxb5! axb5 16. Ne5 Qh4
17. Bxb5+ Nbd7 18. dxc5 Rd8 19. c6
Nxe5 20. cxb7+ Nfd7 21. f4 Bc5+
22. Kh1 Ng4 23. h3 Nf2+ 24. Rxf2 Qxf2
25. Be3 Qxe3 26. Qxd7+ Rxd7 27. b8Q+
Ke7 28. Qxh8 Qxf4 29. Bxd7 Bd6
30. Qe8+ Kf6 31. Kg1 Qe3+ 32. Kh1
½–½ (*Chess Review*, April 1933)

748 Kashdan & Phillips– Alekhine & Warburg [C86]

Consultation Game, New York, 1933
[September 7]

1. e4 e5 2. Nf3 Nc6 3. Bb5 a6 4. Ba4
d6 5. c3 Bd7 6. d4 Nf6 7. Qe2 Be7
8. 0–0 0–0 9. d5 Nb8 10. Bc2 a5 11. c4
Na6 12. Nc3 Nc5 13. Be3 b6 14. h3 g6
15. Bh6 Re8 16. g4 Bf8 17. Bxf8 Rxf8

18. Nh2 Qe7 19. Qe3 h5 20. f4 hxg4
21. hxg4 exf4 22. Qxf4 Kg7 23. Rae1
Rae8 24. Kg2 Rh8 25. Re2 Rh4 26. Ref2
Reh8 27. Kg1 Be8 28. Qg5 Kf8 29. Rg2
Ncd7 30. Nb5 Ne5 31. Qxf6 Qxf6
32. Rxf6 Bxb5?

After
32. ... Bxb5

This is the turning point. If instead 32. ...
Rxh2 33. Rxh2 Rxh2 34. Kxh2 Nxg4+ 35. Kg3
and White has the advantage. After the text it
goes the other way (Kashdan). 33. cxb5 Rxh2
34. Rxh2 Rxh2 35. Rxf7+ Kxf7 36. Kxh2
Nxg4+ 37. Kg3 Ne5 38. b3 Kf6 39. Bd1
Nd3 40. Kf3 Ke5 41. Ke3 Nc5 42. Bf3
g5 43. Bh1 Nd7 44. Bg2 Nf6 45. Bf3
g4 46. Be2 Nxe4 47. Bxg4 Nf6 48. Bf3
Nxd5+ 49. Kd2 Kd4 50. a3 Nc3 51. Bc6
d5 52. Kc2 a4 53. bxa4 Kc4 0–1 The
White pawns will disappear in rapid succession.
(*Chess Review*, October 1933)

749 Horowitz & Newman–
Kashdan & Phillips [D35]

Consultation Game, New York, 1933

1. d4 Nf6 2. c4 e6 3. Nc3 d5 4. cxd5
exd5 5. Bg5 Be7 6. e3 c6 7. Bd3 Ne4
8. Bxe7 Qxe7 9. Nxe4 dxe4 10. Bc2 0–0
11. Ne2 Bg4 12. 0–0 f5 13. Qd2 Nd7
14. Nf4 g5 15. Ne6! Of course not now 15. ...
Qxe6, because of Bb3. 15. ... Rf6 16. Nxg5
h6 17. f3 Bh5 18. Nh3 exf3 19. gxf3 Kh8
20. Nf4 Rg8+ 21. Kh1 Bf7 22. Rg1 Rg5
23. h4 Rxg1+ 24. Rxg1 Nb6 25. e4 fxe4
26. Bxe4 Nd5 27. Qg2 Qf8 28. Nd3 Nf4
29. Qg3 Ne2 30. Qe5 Qd6 31. Rd1 Nxd4
32. Qxd6 Rxd6 33. Nc5 Nb5 34. Rc1
Rd2 35. Nxb7 Nd4 36. Na5 Bh5 37. Nc4
Rf2 38. Kg1 Rxb2 39. Nxb2 Ne2+

40. Kf2 Nxc1 41. Bxc6 Nxa2 ½–½ (*Brooklyn Daily Eagle*, 1933)

750 Simonson & Grossman–
Kashdan & Phillips [C86]

Consultation Game, New York, 1933
[November]

1. e4 e5 2. Nf3 Nc6 3. Bb5 a6 4. Ba4
Nf6 5. 0–0 Be7 6. Qe2 d6 7. c3 Bg4
8. h3 Bh5 9. d3 b5 10. Bb3 Na5 11. Bc2
c5 12. Be3 Nc6 13. g4 Bg6 14. Nh4 Nd7
15. Ng2 0–0 16. f4 f6 17. Bb3+ Bf7
18. Bxf7+ Rxf7 19. Na3 Nb6 20. Rad1
Bf8 21. Nc2 Na4 22. Bc1 Rd7 23. Nge3
Nb6 24. Nd5 Ne7 25. Qg2 Nbxd5
26. exd5 exf4 27. Rxf4 Ng6 28. Re4 Re7
29. Rde1 Raa7 30. d4 Rxe4 31. Rxe4
Re7 32. Ne3 cxd4 33. Rxd4 Qe8 34. Qf2
Re5 35. Kf1 Be7 36. Nf5 Bd8 37. Be3
Ne7 38. Nxd6 Qd7 39. Nf5 Nxf5
40. gxf5 Rxf5 41. Rf4 Rxd5 42. Qf3
Rd1+ 43. Kg2 Qd3 44. Rd4 Qg6+
45. Qg4 Qxg4+ 46. hxg4 Rxd4 47. cxd4
Kf7 48. Kf3 Ke6 49. Ke4 g6 50. d5+
Kd6 51. Bf4+ Kd7 52. Be3 h5 53. gxh5
gxh5 54. Bc5 Bc7 55. Bf2 Be5 1–0
(*American Chess Bulletin*, November 1933)

751 Kashdan & Phillips–
Grossman & Simonson [C86]

Consultation Game, New York, 1933
[November]

1. e4 e5 2. Nf3 Nc6 3. Bb5 a6 4. Ba4
Nf6 5. 0–0 Be7 6. Qe2 d6 7. c3 Bg4
8. h3 Bh5 9. d3 b5 10. Bb3 Na5 11. Bc2
c5 12. Be3 Nc6 13. g4 Bg6 14. Nh4 Nd7
15. Ng2 0–0 16. f4 f6 17. Bb3+ Bf7
18. Bxf7+ Rxf7 19. Na3 Nb6 20. Rad1
Bf8 21. Nc2 Na4 22. Bc1 Rd7 23. Nge3
Nb6 24. Nd5 Ne7 25. Qg2 Nbxd5
26. exd5 exf4 27. Rxf4 Ng6 28. Re4 Re7
29. Rde1 Raa7 30. d4 Rxe4 31. Rxe4
Re7 32. Ne3 cxd4 33. Rxd4 Qe8 34. Qf2
Re5 35. Kf1 Be7 36. Nf5 Bd8 37. Be3
Ne7 38. Nxd6 Qd7 39. Nf5 Nxf5
40. gxf5 Rxf5 41. Rf4 Rxd5 42. Qf3 Rd1+
43. Kg2 Qd3 44. Rd4 Qg6+ 45. Qg4
Qxg4+ 46. hxg4 Rxd4 47. cxd4 Kf7

48. Kf3 Ke6 49. Ke4 g6 50. d5+ Kd6
51. Bf4+ Kd7 52. Be3 h5 53. gxh5 gxh5
54. Bc5 Bc7 55. Bf2 Be5 0–1 (*American
Chess Bulletin*, November 1933)

752 Kashdan–Columbia Team [A52]

Consultation Game, Woodside, 1933

1. d4 Nf6 2. c4 e5 3. dxe5 Ng4 4. Nf3
Bc5 5. e3 Nc6 6. Nc3 Ngxe5 7. Be2 d6
8. 0–0 0–0 9. Na4 Bb6 10. Nxb6 axb6
11. Bd2 Bf5 12. Bc3 Qe7 13. Nd4 Bd7
14. Qc2 Rfe8 15. a3 Na5 16. Bxa5 Rxa5
17. Qc3 Ng4 18. h3 Nf6 19. Bf3 Ne4
20. Qc2 Ng5 21. Bg4 Bxg4 22. hxg4
Qe4 23. Qd1 Ne6 24. Re1 h5 25. f3 Qg6
26. gxh5 Rxh5 27. Nxe6 Rxe6 28. e4
Qg3 29. Qa4 Rh2 30. Qc2 Rg6 0–1 Representing the consulting Columbia Team were
D. Bernstein, L. Greene, H. Lobel, and S. Hecht.
Kashdan played 26 teams at Woodside. (*Brooklyn Daily Eagle*, 1933)

753 Kashdan & Phillips– Amateurs [B42]

Consultation Game, New York, 1934
[February]

1. e4 c5 2. Nf3 e6 3. d4 cxd4 4. Nxd4
Nf6 5. Bd3 a6 6. c4 d6 7. 0–0 Nbd7
8. Nc3 Qc7 9. Kh1 Be7 10. f4 0–0
11. Qe2 b6 12. Be3 Nc5 13. Bc2 Bb7
14. Bg1 d5 15. cxd5 exd5 16. e5 Nfe4
17. Nxe4 Nxe4 18. Rac1 Qd7 19. f5 Bc5
20. f6 g6 21. Nf5! gxf5 22. Qh5 Kh8
23. Rf4 Ng5 24. Bxf5 1–0 (*Chess Review*,
January-February 1934)

754 Kashdan–Turover [C42]

Exhibition Game, 1934 *[February]*

1. e4 e5 2. Nf3 Nf6 3. Nxe5 d6 4. Nf3
Nxe4 5. Qe2 Qe7 6. d3 Nf6 7. Bg5 Be6
8. Nd4 Nc6 9. Nxe6 fxe6 10. c3 h6
11. Bh4 g5 12. Bg3 0–0–0 13. Nd2 Nd5
14. 0–0–0 Nf4 15. Qf3 e5 16. Nc4 d5
17. Ne3 Qc5 18. Kb1 d4 19. cxd4 Nxd4
20. Qe4 Bd6 21. Rc1 Qb5 22. Nc4 Kb8
23. f3 Rhe8 24. h4 Re6 25. hxg5 hxg5

26. Bf2 Bf8 27. Rh7 Qe8 28. Na5 Nc6
29. Nxc6+ Rxc6 30. Rxc6 Qxc6 31. Qxc6
After 31. Qf5 White retains good winning
chances. After the text it is only a draw. 31. ...
bxc6 32. Kc2 Kb7 33. Rf7 Bd6 34. Rg7
Rh8 35. d4 exd4 36. Rxg5 c5 37. b4
cxb4 38. Bxd4 Rh1 39. Bc4 Rh2 40. Bf1
Rh1 ½–½ (*Washington Post*, April 15, 1934)

755 Reshevsky–Kashdan [D13]

Exhibition Game, New Bedford, 1934
[November]

1. d4 Nf6 2. c4 c6 3. Nc3 d5 4. Nf3 e6
5. cxd5 cxd5 6. Bg5 Nbd7 7. a3 Be7
8. e3 a6 9. Bd3 b5 10. 0–0 Bb7 11. Rc1
0–0 12. Qe2 Ne4 13. Bxe7 Qxe7 14. Ne5
Rac8 15. Nxd7 Qxd7 16. Na2 Nd6
17. Rxc8 Rxc8 18. Nc1 Nc4 19. Nb3 g5
20. Nc5 Qe7 21. f4 Rb8 22. b3 Nd6
23. a4 Bc8 24. axb5 axb5 25. Ra1 Qc7
26. Qd2 Qc6 27. Qb4 Ra8 28. Ra5 Rxa5
29. Qxa5 Kg7 30. Kf2 Bd7 31. Qd8 Be8
32. g4 Kf8 33. Qf6 Ne4+ 34. Bxe4 dxe4
35. h4

After
35. h4

Up to this point both have played with masterful exactness to command the admiration of
those present. Now White goes out to win if he
can. Instead 35. Qh8+, followed by g5+, would
have assured him at least a draw. 35. ... Qd5
36. Qh8+ Ke7 37. Qxh7 Qa8 Seizing the
open file which leads to the more or less undefended position of the White king. 38. h5
Qa2+ 39. Kg3 Qe2 40. Kh4 (*see diagram*)
If 40. hxg6 Qxe3+ 41. Kh4 Qxf4 and White
cannot play g7, on account of Qh2+, etc. 40. ...
Qxe3 41. Qg7 Qxf4 42. Qe5 Qf2+

After
40. Kh4

43. Kh3 g×h5 44. g×h5 e3 This advanced pawn decides the fate of the game. **45. Ne4 Qf3+ 46. Kh2 f6 47. Qc5+ Kf7 48. Nd6+ Kf8** Curiously enough, there is nothing to be feared from the discovered check. **49. N×e8+ K×e8 50. Qc8+ Ke7 51. Qc7+ Kf8 52. h6** There is no help. If 52. Qb8+ Kg7 53. Qg3+ Q×g3 54. K×g3 f5 55. Kf3 f4 and wins. **52. ... Qh5+ 53. Kg2 Q×h6 54. Kf3 Qh1+ 55. K×e3 Qe1+ 56. Kf3 Qd1+ 57. Kg3 Q×b3+ 0–1** (*American Chess Bulletin*, November 1934)

756 Reshevsky–Kashdan [A13]
Training Game, New York, 1948 *[January 25]*

1. Nf3 Nf6 2. c4 e6 3. g3 b6 4. Bg2 Bb7 5. 0–0 Be7 6. b3 0–0 7. Bb2 c5 8. d4 c×d4 9. Q×d4 Nc6 10. Qf4 d5 11. Rd1 Qb8 12. Ne5 Bd6 13. N×c6 B×c6 14. Qh4 Be5 15. Nc3 Ne4 16. Rac1 N×c3 17. B×c3 B×c3 18. R×c3 Qe5 19. Re3 Qb2 20. c×d5 B×d5 21. B×d5 e×d5 22. Qa4 d4 He must now lose a pawn, and should lose the game but he fights back desperately, and with little cooperation, actually earns a draw, only to throw it away! An entire tragedy in many acts. **23. Re4** Re7 was stronger. **23. ... b5 24. Q×b5 Q×a2 25. Re×d4 a6 26. Qd3 g6 27. h4 h5 28. g4 h×g4 29. h5** Overconfidence which probably should have cost him the win. The obvious recapture was best. **29. ... Rae8 30. Kf1 g3** Another bit of despair which actually succeeds. **31. h×g6** More lack of humility (an excellent quality, but little understood, for it is really a superior kind of courage). **31. ... Q×e2+ 32. Q×e2 g2+ 33. K×g2 R×e2 34. g7** Since he cannot now win legitimately, he tries tricks. A fascinating

ending follows. **34. ... K×g7 35. Rg4+ Kf6 36. Rd6+ Re6 37. R×e6+ K×e6 38. Ra4 Ra8 39. Kf3 Kd5 40. Kf4 Rb8** The best chance. Otherwise White advances either on the kingside (the king) or the queenside (the pawn). **41. Ra5+ Kd4 42. R×a6 R×b3 43. Rd6+ Kc5 44. Rd7 Kc6 45. R×f7 Kd6** This ending is a "book" draw. Though Black does not command the queening square, the White pawn is not far enough advanced. **46. Kg5 Ke6** Better was Rb8 **47. Kg6 Rb1 48. Rf3 Ke5** Excellent! He moves toward the rook and "backward" pawn; but he reverts soon to timidity, and thus loses. **49. Rf5+ Ke6 50. f4 Ke7 51. Rf7+ Ke8 52. f5 Rf1 53. Kg7 Rg1+ 54. Kf6 Rf1 55. Ra7 Rf2 56. Ra8+ Kd7 57. Rf8** The winning move— now a clear "book" win. Were Black's king on h2, it would be a draw. **57. ... Rf1 58. Kg7 Rg1+ 59. Kf7 Ra1 60. f6 Rg1 61. Re8 Rg2 62. Re1 Rg3 63. Rd1+ Kc7 64. Kf8 Rf3 65. f7 Rg3 66. Rd4 Kc6 67. Ke7 Re3+ 68. Kf6 Rf3+ 69. Ke6 1–0** I liked Kashdan's play better than Reshevsky's in this game. It showed more fight, though they both erred— Kashdan, unfortunately, the last so to do. Notes are by Helms. (*American Chess Bulletin*, January-February 1948)

757 Kashdan–Alexander Bisno
Game at odds, 1956

1. ... Rf8!

After
1. ... Rf8

If Ra8 or Rc8 2. B×c4, and R×a7 will not do because of Re8 mate. **2. B×c4 Rf1+ 3. Bg1** What now? White threatens the fatal Re8 mate and also B×d3. **3. ... Be3!!** The point of Black's plan. Obviously, if 4. R×e3 then Nf2 mate! or

Bxd3 then Rxg1 mate! **4. h3 Rxg1+ 5. Kh2 Re1!** The only move, as White will win if he succeeds in removing the bishop. Now a simple drawn endgame is enforced. **6. Bxd3 Rxe2 7. Bxe2 ½–½** The diagrammed position occurred in a game at odds of a knight between Isaac Kashdan and Alexander Bisno. White is about to regain his piece and apparently will have a decisive advantage, with a pawn plus and two strong bishops. But... (Black's first move was Rb8 to Rf8). (*Los Angeles Times*, January 29, 1956)

♦ PART THREE ♦

Appendices and Indexes

Isaac Kashdan's Overall Record

The Five Olympiads, 1928–1937

Perhaps the most significant achievement by Isaac Kashdan is his record in the five team competitions where he represented the United States from 1928 to 1937. The first team event took place in The Hague in 1928. Kashdan had the best score here of any player. The second took place in Hamburg in 1930, where Kashdan and Marshall would alternate on first board. The very next year the Olympiad was held in Prague, with Kashdan playing on board one. Then in 1933 the event was held in Folkestone, England. Kashdan did not take part when the team competition was held in Warsaw, in 1935. Then in 1937 the event was held in Stockholm. Kashdan played here on board three, behind Reshevsky and Fine. Marshall took the fourth spot. Again Kashdan had the best result of any player. Beginning with 1931 the United States won the Olympiads until 1937.

Here is Kashdan's record:

		Played	Won	Drawn	Lost	Total	Percent
1928	The Hague	15	12	2	1	13	86.7
1930	Hamburg	17	12	4	1	14	82.4
1931	Prague	17	8	8	1	12	70.6
1933	Folkestone	14	7	6	1	10	71.4
1937	Stockholm	16	13	2	1	14	87.5
Totals		79	52	22	5	63	79.5

Kashdan won four team medals, three gold, for 1931, 1933, and 1937; one silver for 1928, and five individual medals, two gold for 1928 and 1937, one silver in 1933, and two bronze in 1930 and 1931.

The United States Championships, 1936–1948

While not quite as impressive as he was in the Olympiads, Kashdan also had an excellent record in the U.S. Championships. He took part in the very first one. It was then played every two years starting in 1936 until 1948. He missed only the one in 1944. His best achievement was his tie for first with Reshevsky in 1942. He then lost in the playoff. Then in 1946 and 1948 he came in second. Here are the statistics for the U.S. Championships:

		Pos.	Played	Won	Drawn	Lost	Total	Percent
1936	1st U.S. Championship	5th	15	9	4	2	10–5	66.7
1938	2nd U.S. Championship	5th	16	8	5	3	9½–6½	59.5
1940	3rd U.S. Championship	3rd	16	7	7	2	10½–5½	65.6
1942	4th U.S. Championship	1st/2nd	15	11	3	1	12½–2½	83.3
1946	6th U.S. Championship	2nd	18	11	5	2	13½–4½	75.0
1948	7th U.S. Championship	2nd	19	12	5	2	14½–4½	76.3
Totals			99	58	29	12	70½–19½	73.2

The Tournament Record

		P	G	W	D	L	Total
1924	New York (Rice Progressive)	?	?	?	?	?	?
1924-5	Stuyesant Club Championship	?	?	?	?	?	?
1925	Albert Hallgarten (Prelims)	1st	7	5	1	1	5½–1½
1925	Albert Hallgarten (Finals)	3rd	12	5	5	2	7½–4½
1925-6	Manhattan Club Championship	1st	14	9	5	0	11½–2½
1926	New York (Rice Progressive)	1st	9	6	3	0	7½–1½
1926	Chicago International	6th	12	5	4	3	7–5
1926	New York (Rice Memorial)	3rd	6	1	3	2	2½–3½
1927	New York Junior Masters	2nd	10	4	5	1	6½–3½
1927	Manhattan Club Championship	2nd/3rd	14	10	1	3	10½–3½
1927	New York (Junior Masters)	1st	6	5	1	0	5½–0½
1927-8	Manhattan Club Championship	5th	8	1	3	4	2½–5½
1928	The Hague Olympiad	—	15	12	2	1	13–2
1928-9	Manhattan Club Championship	3rd	9	5	2	2	6–3
1929-30	Manhattan Club Championship	1st	10	8	1	1	8½–1½
1930	Hamburg Olympiad	—	16	11	4	1	13–3
1930	Berlin Quadrangular	1st	6	4	2	0	5–1
1930	Frankfurt	2nd	11	7	4	0	9–2
1930	Gyor, Hungary	1st	9	8	1	0	8½–0½
1930	Stockholm	1st	6	4	1	1	4½–1½
1931	New York International	2nd	11	6	5	0	8½–2½
1931	Prague Olympiad	—	17	8	8	1	12–5
1931	Bled, Yugoslavia	4th/7th	26	7	13	6	13½–12½
1931-2	Hastings	2nd	9	6	3	0	7½–1½
1932	London	3rd/4th	11	5	5	1	7½–3½
1932	Mexico City	1st/2nd	9	8	1	0	8½–0½
1932	Pasadena	2nd	11	5	5	1	7½–3½
1932-3	Manhattan Championship*	11th	5	2	1	2	2½–2½

*Kashdan played only 5 of the 11 games in the 1932-3 Manhattan Championship.

		P	G	W	D	L	Total
1933	Folkestone Olympiad	—	15	8	6	1	11–4
1934	Chicago (Prelims)	2nd	7	6	0	1	6–1
1934	Chicago (Finals)	5th/6th	9	2	5	2	4½–4½
1934	Syracuse International	2nd	14	7	7	0	9½–3½
1934-5	Manhattan Club Championship	1st/2nd	13	11	0	2	12–1
1935	Binghamton (N.Y. State Champ.)	1st	8	7	1	0	7½–½
1935	Milwaukee (Western) Prelims	1st	9	6	3	0	7½–1½
1935	Milwaukee (Western) Finals	3rd	10	3	7	0	6½–3½
1936	New York (U.S. Championship)	5th	15	9	2	4	10–5
1936	Philadelphia (Western) Prelims	1st	11	8	3	0	9½–1½
1936	Philadelphia (Western) Finals	4th/5th	11	5	4	2	6–5
1936	Poughkeepsie (N.Y. State Champ.)	1st	11	10	1	0	10½–.½
1936	San Juan	1st	7	6	1	0	6½–½
1936-7	Manhattan Club Championship	1st/2nd	11	9	2	0	10–1
1937	Stockholm Olympiad	—	16	13	2	1	14–2
1937-8	Manhattan Club Championship	1st	7	4	3	0	8½–1½
1938	Boston (ACF Congress) Prelims	1st	6	4	2	0	5–1
1938	Boston (ACF Congress) Finals	1st/2nd	11	8	2	1	9–2
1938	New York (U.S. Championship)	5th	16	8	3	5	9½–6½
1939	Hamilton (N.Y. State Champ.)	2nd	9	4	5	0	6½–2½
1940	Havana (Cuba)	1st	9	6	3	0	7½–1½
1940	New York (U.S. Championship)	3rd	16	7	7	2	10½–5½
1941	Hamilton (N.Y. State Champ.)	2nd/4th	10	4	6	0	7–3
1942	New York (U.S. Championship)	1st/2nd	15	11	3	1	12½–2½
1944-5	Manhattan Club Championship	3rd/4th	12	6	5	1	7½–3½
1945	Hollywood (Pan American)	5th	12	5	4	3	7–5
1946	New York (U.S. Championship)	2nd	18	11	5	2	12½–4½
1946	New York (Metropolitan Champ.)	1st	9	6	2	1	7–2
1947	Corpus Christi (U.S. Open)	1st	13	10	3	0	11½–1½
1948	Baltimore (U.S. Open)	2nd/4th	12	7	4	1	9–3
1948	Manhattan Masters	2nd	7	4	3	0	5½–1½
1948	South Fallsburg (U.S. Champ.)	2nd	19	12	5	2	14½–4½
1948-9	New York International	7th/8th	9	3	2	4	4–5
1951	Fort Worth (U.S. Open)	3rd/4th	12	8	2	2	9–3
1952	Hollywood International	7th	9	3	2	4	4–5
1953	Hollywood Invitational	1st	19	18	1	0	18½–½
1954	Hollywood (Pan American)	7th	14	8	3	3	9½–4½
1954	Santa Barbara (California Open)	3rd/6th	7	5	1	1	5½–1½
Totals			717	429	209	79	

The Match Record

			G	W	D	L	Total
1930	Jaffe (New York)	Win	3	3	0	0	3–0
1930	L. Steiner (New York)	Win	10	5	2	3	6–4
1930	Stoltz (Stockholm)	Loss	6	1	3	2	2½–3½
1937	Simonson (Manhattan Playoff)	Win	3	1	2	0	2–1
1938	Simonson (New York)	Win	4	4	0	0	4–0
1938	Horowitz (Boston Playoff)	Draw	10	2	6	2	5–5
1942	Reshevsky (U.S. Champ. Playoff)	Loss	11	2	3	6	3½–7½
1945	Kotov (USA–USSR)	Loss	2	0	0	2	0–2
1946	Kotov (USA–USSR)	Win	2	1	1	0	1½–0½
1951	Ortega (Havana–California)	Win	2	1	1	0	1½–0½
1955	Taimanov (USA–USSR)	Loss	4	0	3	1	1½–2½
Totals			57	20	21	16	

Metropolitan League Matches

A good number of games were played by Kashdan in the Metropolitan Chess League. In most of those games he played for the Manhattan Chess Club. Only in the beginning was he representing the Stuyvesant Chess Club. In the very first game, he played for the International Club. Included are also the matches he played against Philadelphia that are not part of the Metropolitan Chess League. Then after his move to California in 1951 he started playing in the matches between South and North California. He played in seven of those matches. These are not included here.

1925	Kashdan (Stuyvesant)–Schleifer (Brooklyn)	1–0
1925	Santasiere (Marshall)–Kashdan (Stuyvesant)	1–0
1926	Frink (Columbia)–Kashdan (Stuyvesant)	0–1
1926	Kashdan (Manhattan)–Sharp (Franklin)	0–1
1926	Kashdan–Pinkus (Marshall)	1–0
1927	Kashdan–Santasiere (Marshall)	0–1
1928	Kashdan–Schmid (Empire)	1–0
1928	Kashdan–Tholfsen (Marshall)	1–0
1928	Klein (Rice)–Kashdan	1–0
1929	Kashdan–L. Steiner (Hungarian)	1–0
1929	Marshall (Marshall)–Kashdan	1–0
1929	Lier (Scandinavia)–Kashdan	0–1
1929	Kashdan–Santasiere (Marshall)	1–0
1930	Mlotkowski–Kashdan	0–1
1930	Fishman (City College)–Kashdan	1–0
1930	Kashdan–Kline	1–0
1932	Kashdan–Marshall (Marshall)	1–0
1933	Siff–Kashdan	½–½

1933	Kashdan–Fine (Marshall)	½–½
1933	Kashdan–Levin	½–½
1934	Kashdan–Fine (Marshall)	½–½
1934	Goodman (Empire)–Kashdan	0–1
1935	Kashdan–Reinfeld	1–0
1935	Jaffe (Rice Progressive)–Kashdan	½–½
1936	Marshall (Marshall)–Kashdan	½–½
1937	Kashdan–Edward Lasker (Marshall)	½–½
1937	Kashdan–Shainswit	1–0
1938	Kashdan–Fine (Marshall)	0–1
1938	Kashdan–Marshhall (Marshall)	½–½
1939	Kashdan–Lessing (Rice Progressive)	½–½
1939	S. Bernstein–Kashdan	½–½
1939	Levin (Philadelphia)–Kashdan	0–1
1940	Kashdan–Marshall (Marshall)	½–½
1941	Kashdan–Reinfeld (Marshall)	½–½
1942	Pilnik–Kashdan	0–1
1942	Hanauer (Marshall)–Kashdan	0–1
1944	Edward Lasker (Marshall)–Kashdan	0–1
1946	Goodman–Kashdan	½–½
1947	Hanauer (Marshall)–Kashdan	½–½
1947	Collins–Kashdan	0–1
1947	Weinstock–Kashdan	0–1
1949	Kashdan–Rothman	1–0
1949	Vine–Kashdan	0–1
1949	Green (Manhattan)–Kashdan	0–1

Tournament Crosstables

Hallgarten 1925

Section A

	W	L
1. Kashdan	5½	1½
2.–4. Berman	4	3
2.–4. Bornholz	4	3
2.–4. Pinkus	4	3
5. Wintner	3½	3½
6. Bartha	3	4
7. Norwood	2½	4½
8. Field	1½	5½

Kashdan lost to Bornholz and drew Berman

Hallgarten 1925-6

Finals

	W	L
1. Pinkus	9½	2½
2. Steiner, H.	9	3
3. Kashdan	7½	4½
4. Samuels	7	5
5. Smirka	5½	6½
6. Berman	3	9
7. Bornholz	½	11½

Manhattan Club Championship 1925-26

	1	2	3	4	5	6	7	8	9	10	11	12	13	14	15	Score
1. Kupchik, A.	•	0	1	1	½	½	1	1	1	1	1	1	1	1	1	12
2. Kashdan, I.	1	•	1	½	½	1	½	1	½	1	1	1	1	1	½	11½
3. Horowitz, I.	0	0	•	0	½	½	½	1	1	1	1	1	½	1	1	9
4. Bornholz, R.	0	½	1	•	½	1	½	1	1	0	1	1	0	0	1	8½
5. Maróczy, G.	½	½	½	½	•	½	1	0	0	1	1	½	1	½	1	8½
6. Pinkus, A.	½	0	½	0	½	•	0	½	0	1	1	1	1	1	1	8
7. Steiner, H.	0	½	½	½	0	1	•	0	1	1	0	½	1	1	1	8
8. Tenner, O.	0	0	0	0	1	½	1	•	1	½	1	1	1	1	0	8
9. Beihoff, G.	0	½	0	0	1	1	0	0	•	0	0	1	1	1	1	6½
10. Cohen, S.	0	0	0	1	0	0	0	½	1	•	1	0	1	½	½	5½
11. Samuels, L.	0	0	0	0	0	0	1	0	1	0	•	1	1	0	1	5
12. Berman, E.	0	0	0	0	½	0	½	0	0	1	0	•	½	1	1	4½

	1	2	3	4	5	6	7	8	9	10	11	12	13	14	15	Score
13. Norwood, C.	0	0	½	1	0	0	0	0	0	0	0	0	½	•	1	1	4
14. Field, O.	0	0	0	1	½	0	0	0	0	½	1	0	0	•	½	3½
15. Halper, N.	0	½	0	0	0	0	0	1	0	½	0	0	0	½	•	2½

Rice Progressive Club Championship, New York 1926

	1	2	3	4	5	6	7	8	9	10	Score
1. Kashdan, I.	•	1	1	1	½	½	½	1	1	1	7½
2. Chajes, O.	0	•	0	1	½	1	1	1	1	1	6½
3. Kupchik, A.	0	1	•	1	½	0	1	½	1	1	6
4. Steiner, H.	0	0	0	•	1	1	1	½	1	1	5½
5. Berman, E.	½	½	½	0	•	½	1	½	0	1	4½
6. Feuer, B.	½	0	1	0	½	•	0	0	½	1	3½
7. Mishook, S.	½	0	0	0	0	1	•	1	1	0	3½
8. Simchow, A.	0	0	½	½	½	1	0	•	½	½	3½
9. Zatulove, P.	0	0	0	0	1	½	0	½	•	1	3
10. Bartha, S.	0	0	0	0	0	0	1	½	0	•	1½

Masters International, Chicago 1926
August 21–September 2

	1	2	3	4	5	6	7	8	9	10	11	12	13	Score
1. Marshall, F.	•	1	0	½	1	1	½	½	1	0	1	1	1	8½
2. Maróczy, G.	0	•	0	½	½	1	1	½	1	1	1	1	1	8
3. Torre, C.	1	1	•	0	½	½	1	0	½	1	½	1	1	8
4. Jaffe, C.	½	½	1	•	0	½	0	1	1	1	1	1	0	7½
5. Kupchik, A.	0	½	½	1	•	½	1	1	0	1	1	0	1	7½
6. Kashdan, I.	0	0	½	½	½	•	1	1	½	0	1	1	1	7
7. Factor, S.	½	0	0	1	0	0	•	1	1	½	½	1	1	6½
8. Lasker, E.	½	½	1	0	0	0	0	•	1	1	1	0	1	6
9. Fink, A.	0	0	½	0	1	½	0	0	•	1	½	½	1	5
10. Banks, N.	1	0	0	0	0	1	½	0	0	•	½	½	1	4½
11. Chajes, O.	0	0	½	0	0	0	½	0	½	½	•	1	1	4
12. Showalter, J.	0	0	0	0	1	0	0	1	½	½	0	•	0	3
13. Isaacs, L.	0	½	0	1	0	0	0	0	0	0	0	1	•	2½

Rice Memorial, New York 1926

	1	2	3	4	Score
1. Kupchik, A.	• •	1 0	½ 1	1 ½	4
2. Jaffe, C.	0 1	• •	0 ½	1 1	3½
3. Kashdan, I.	½ 1	0 0	• •	0 ½	2½
4. Chajes, O.	0 ½	0 0	1 ½	• •	2

Manhattan Club Championship 1926-27

	1	2	3	4	5	6	7	8	9	10	11	12	13	14	15	Score
1. Maróczy, G.	•	½	½	1	0	1	1	1	1	1	1	1	1	1	1	11
2. Kashdan, I.	½	•	0	1	1	1	1	0	1	0	1	1	1	1	1	10½
3. Kupchik, A.	½	1	•	1	1	½	1	0	1	1	1	1	½	0	1	10½
4. Berman, A.	0	0	0	•	1	0	1	1	1	1	1	½	1	1	1	9½
5. Horowitz, I.	1	0	0	0	•	0	1	1	1	½	1	1	½	1	1	9
6. Pinkus, A.	0	0	½	1	1	•	0	1	½	1	1	0	1	1	1	9
7. Kevitz, A.	0	0	0	0	0	1	•	1	½	1	1	0	1	1	1	7½
8. Steiner, H.	0	1	1	0	0	0	0	•	0	½	1	1	1	1	1	7½
9. Bornholz, R.	0	0	0	0	0	½	½	1	•	0	1	1	1	1	1	7
10. Tenner, O.	0	1	0	0	½	0	0	½	1	•	0	1	½	1	1	6½
11. Cohen, S.	1	0	0	0	0	0	0	0	0	1	•	1	½	1	1	5½
12. Willman, R.	0	0	0	½	0	1	1	0	0	0	0	•	1	1	1	5½
13. Bartha, F.	0	0	½	0	½	0	0	0	0	½	½	0	•	1	1	4
14. Field, O.	0	0	1	0	0	0	0	0	0	0	0	0	0	•	1	2
15. De Vries, P.	0	0	0	0	0	0	0	0	0	0	0	0	0	0	•	0

Junior Masters, New York 1927

	1	2	3	4	5	6	Score
1. Pinkus, A.	• •	½ ½	1 ½	1 1	0 ½	1 1	7
2. Kashdan, I.	½ ½	• •	½ ½	0 1	½ 1	1 1	6½
3. Santasiere, A.	0 ½	½ ½	• •	0 1	1 0	1 1	5½
4. Tholfsen, E.	0 0	1 0	1 0	• •	1 1	1 ½	5½
5. Smirka, R.	½ 1	½ 0	0 1	0 0	• •	0 1	4
6. Bornholz, R.	0 0	0 0	0 0	0 ½	1 0	• •	1½

Manhattan Club Championship 1927-28

	1	2	3	4	5	Score
1. Kupchik, A.	• •	1 ½	1 1	½ ½	1 ½	6
2. Horowitz, I.	0 ½	• •	0 1	0 1	1 1	4½
3. Pinkus, A.	0 0	1 0	• •	½ ½	½ 1	3½
4. Steiner, H.	½ ½	1 0	½ ½	• •	0 ½	3½
5. Kashdan, I.	0 ½	0 0	½ 0	1 ½	• •	2½

Manhattan Junior Masters 1927-28

	1	2	3	4	Score
1. Kashdan, I.	• •	½ 1	1 1	1 1	5½
2. Horowitz, I.	0 ½	• •	0 1	1 1	3½
3. Berman, E.	0 0	1 0	• •	1 1	3
4. Pinkus, A.	0 0	0 0	0 0	• •	0

The Hague Olympiad 1928
July 23–August 5

Round 1	Honlinger (Austria)–Kashdan	0–1	(July 23)
Round 2	Kashdan–E. Steiner (Hungary)	1–0	(July 23)
Round 3	Kashdan–Naegeli (Switzerland)	1–0	(July 24)
Round 4	[Kashdan did not play]		
Round 5	Kashdan–Blumich (Germany)	1–0	(July 25)
Round 6	[United States had the bye]		
Round 7	Kashdan–Taube (Latvia)	1–0	(July 27)
Round 8	Makarczyk (Poland)–Kashdan	1–0	(July 27)
Round 9	Kashdan–Dunkelblum (Belgium)	1–0	(July 29)
Round 10	Stoltz (Sweden)–Kashdan	0–1	(July 30)
Round 11	Pokorný (Czechoslovakia)–Kash	½–½	(July 30)
Round 12	Reca (Argentina)–Kashdan	½–½	(July 31)
Round 13	Kashdan–de Nardo (Italy)	1–0	(July 31)
Round 14	Weenink (Holland)–Kashdan	0–1	(August 1)
Round 15	Kashdan–Brody (Rumania)	1–0	(August 3)
Round 16	Norman-Hanson (Denmark)–Kashdan	0–1	(August 3)
Round 17	Kashdan–Marin (Spain)	1–0	(August 5)

Manhattan Club Championship 1928-29

	1	2	3	4	5	6	7	8	9	10	Score
1. Kevitz, A.	•	0	1	1	1	1	1	1	1	1	8
2. Kupchik, A.	1	•	½	0	1	1	1	1	0	1	6½
3. Kashdan, I.	0	½	•	1	0	1	1	1	0	1	6
4. Samuels, L.	0	1	0	•	1	0	1	½	1	1	5½
5. Willman, R.	0	0	1	0	•	½	½	1	½	1	4½
6. Fischman	0	0	0	½	½	•	½	½	1	1	4
7. Kussman, A.	0	0	½	0	½	½	•	½	½	1	3½
8. Beihoff, G.	0	0	0	1	0	½	½	•	1	0	3
9. Tenner, O.	0	1	0	0	½	0	½	0	•	1	3
10. Kline, H.	0	0	0	0	0	0	0	1	0	•	1

Manhattan Club Championship 1929-30

1. Kashdan, I.	8½	5. Arons	5½	9. Kussman, A.	3½
2. Kupchik, A.	7	6. Pinkus, A.	5½	10. Kevitz, A.	2
3. Horowitz, I.	6	7. Jackson, E.	5	11. Willman, R.	2
4. Samuels, L.	6	8. Steiner, H.	4	12. Berman, E.	0

Kashdan drew with Kupchik, lost to Samuels, and won the rest

Hamburg Olympiad 1930
(July 13–27)

Round 1	Gromer (France)–Kashdan	½–½	(July 13)
Round 2	Kashdan–Asgeirsson (Iceland)	1–0	(July 14)
Round 3	Krogius (Finland)–Kashdan	0–1	(July 15)
Round 4	Rubinstein (Poland)–Kashdan	½–½	(July 15)
Round 5	Kashdan–Macht (Lithuania)	1–0	(Default)
Round 6	Apscheneck [Apšenieks] (Latvia)–Kashdan	0–1	(July 17)
Round 7	Takács (Hungary)–Kashdan	½–½	(July 17)
Round 8	Kashdan–Balogh (Rumania)	1–0	(July 18)
Round 9	Ståhlberg (Sweden)–Kashdan	0–1	(July 19)
Round 10	Ahues (Germany)–Kashdan	0–1	(July 20)
Round 11	Kashdan–Hovind (Norway)	1–0	(July 21)
Round 12	Weenink (Holland)–Kashdan	0–1	(July 22)
Round 13	Kmoch (Austria)–Kashdan	1–0	(July 23)
Round 14	Kashdan–Desler (Denmark)	1–0	(July 24)
Round 15	Sultan Khan (England)–Kashdan	½–½	(July 25)
Round 16	Kashdan–Flohr (Czechoslovakia)	1–0	(July 26)
Round 17	Marín (Spain)–Kashdan	0–1	(July 27)

Berlin Quadrangular 1930
(August 8–14)

	1	2	3	4	Score
1. Kashdan, I.	• •	1 1	1 0	1 1	5
2. Helling, K.	0 0	• •	1 ½	1 1	3½
3. Steiner, H.	0 1	0 ½	• •	0 ½	2
4. Sämisch, F.	0 0	0 0	1 ½	• •	1½

Frankfurt 1930
(September 6–18)

	1	2	3	4	5	6	7	8	9	10	11	12	Score
1. Nimzovitch, A.	•	1	1	1	½	0	1	1	1	1	1	1	9½
2. Kashdan, I.	½	•	½	½	1	1	½	1	1	1	1	1	9
3. Ahues, C.	0	½	•	½	1	½	½	½	½	1	1	1	7
4. List, P.	0	½	½	•	½	½	1	½	1	1	1	½	7
5. Colle, E.	0	0	0	½	•	1	0	1	1	1	1	1	6½
6. Przepiórka, D.	1	0	½	½	0	•	1	½	0	½	1	1	6
7. Pirc, V.	0	½	½	0	1	0	•	½	½	½	1	1	5½
8. Sämisch, F.	0	0	½	½	0	½	½	•	½	1	1	½	5

	1	2	3	4	5	6	7	8	9	10	11	12	Score
9. Mieses, J.	0	0	½	0	0	1	½	½	•	0	1	½	4
10. Thomas, G.	0	0	0	0	0	½	½	0	1	•	0	1	3
11. Mannheimer, N.	0	0	0	0	0	0	0	0	0	1	•	1	2
12. Orbach, W.	0	0	0	½	0	0	0	½	½	0	0	•	1½

Gyor 1930
(October 2–12)

	1	2	3	4	5	6	7	8	9	10	Score
1. Kashdan, I.	•	1	1	1	1	1	½	1	1	1	8½
2. Steiner, H.	0	•	0	½	1	1	1	0	1	1	5½
3. Hoenlinger, B.	0	1	•	½	1	0	½	½	½	1	5
4. Klein, E.	0	½	½	•	½	0	1	1	½	1	5
5. Boros, S.	0	0	0	½	•	1	1	½	1	½	4½
6. Szabó, B.	0	0	1	1	0	•	½	½	½	½	4
7. Reich, L.	½	0	½	0	0	½	•	½	1	½	3½
8. Gereben, E.	0	1	½	0	½	½	½	•	½	0	3½
9. Balogh, J.	0	0	½	½	0	½	0	½	•	1	3
10. Meller, F.	0	0	0	0	½	½	½	1	0	•	2½

Stockholm 1930
(October 20–27)

	1	2	3	4	5	6	7	Score
1. Kashdan, I.	•	1	1	½	0	1	1	4½
2. Bogoljubow, E.	0	•	0	1	1	1	1	4
3. Stoltz, G.	0	1	•	½	1	1	½	4
4. Ståhlberg, A.	½	0	½	•	½	½	1	3
5. Spielmann, R.	1	0	0	½	•	½	½	2½
6. Rellstab, L.	0	0	0	½	½	•	1	2
7. Lundin, E.	0	0	½	0	½	0	•	1

New York International 1931
(April 18–May 2)

	1	2	3	4	5	6	7	8	9	10	11	12	Score
1. Capablanca, J.	•	½	1	1	1	½	1	1	1	1	1	1	10
2. Kashdan, I.	½	•	1	1	½	½	1	½	½	1	1	1	8½
3. Kevitz, A.	0	0	•	0	1	½	1	½	1	1	1	1	7
4. Horowitz, I.	0	0	1	•	½	½	0	1	1	0	1	½	5½
5. Kupchik, A.	0	½	0	½	•	½	0	1	½	½	1	1	5½

	1	2	3	4	5	6	7	8	9	10	11	12	Score
6. Steiner, H.	½	½	½	½	½	•	0	1	½	0	½	1	5½
7. Santasiere, A.	0	0	0	1	1	1	•	0	0	0	1	1	5
8. Turover, I.	0	½	½	0	0	0	1	•	1	1	½	0	4½
9. Dake, A.	0	½	0	0	½	½	1	0	•	½	0	1	4
10. Lasker, Ed	0	0	0	1	½	1	1	0	½	•	0	0	4
11. Marshall, F.	0	0	0	0	0	½	0	½	1	1	•	1	4
12. Fox, M.	0	0	0	½	0	0	0	1	0	1	0	•	2½

Prague Olympiad 1931
(July 11–July 26)

Round 1	Anderson (Denmark)–Kashdan	0–1	(July 11)
Round 2	Kashdan–Mattison (Latvia)	½–½	
Round 3	A. Steiner (Hungary)–Kashdan	0–1	
Round 4	Kashdan–Flohr (Cxechoslovakia)	1–0	
Round 5	Alekhine (France)–Kashdan	½–½	
Round 6	Kashdan–Grünfeld (Austria)	1–0	
Round 8	Kashdan–Vidmar (Yugoslavia)	1–0	
Round 9	Mikėnas (Latvia)–Kashdan	½–½	
Round 10	[United States had the bye]		
Round 11	Kashdan–Chritofferson (Norway)	1–0	
Round 12	Sultan Khan (England)–Kashdan	½–½	
Round 13	Kashdan–Roselli (Italy)	½–½	
Round 14	Weenink (Holland)–Kashdan	½–½	
Round 15	Kashdan–Bogoljubow (Germany)	½–½	
Round 16	Naegeli (Switzerland)–Kashdan	0–1	
Round 17	Kashdan–Vilardebó (Spain)	½–½	
Round 18	Erdelyi (Rumania)–Kashdan	0–1	
Round 19	Kashdan–Rubinstein (Poland)	0–1	(July 26, 1931)

Bled 1931
(August 22–September 29)

	1	2	3	4	5	6	7	8	9	10	11	12	13	14	Sc.
1. Alekhine, A.	••	1½	11	1½	½½	11	1½	1½	1½	½½	11	11	½½	11	20½
2. Bogoljubow	0½	••	½0	11	11	1½	0½	10	01	0½	00	11	½1	11	15
3. Nimzovitch	00	½1	••	11	00	0½	½½	½½	½½	½1	1½	1½	11	0½	14
4. Flohr, S.	0½	00	00	••	1½	½½	½1	10	1½	½1	11	½0	½1	½½	13½
5. Kashdan, I.	½½	00	11	0½	••	1½	½½	00	1½	½½	10	11	½½	½½	13½
6. Stoltz, G.	00	0½	1½	½½	0½	••	½1	11	½½	½1	½1	00	01	1½	13½
7. Vidmar, M.	0½	1½	½½	½0	½½	½0	••	½½	11	½0	½½	½1	½1	½½	13½
8. Tartakower	0½	01	½½	01	11	00	½½	••	½0	½½	½½	11	½½	½½	13

	1	2	3	4	5	6	7	8	9	10	11	12	13	14	Sc.
9. Kostić, B.	0½	10	½½	0½	0½	½½	00	½1	••	½½	½½	01	1½	11	12½
10. Spielmann	½½	1½	½0	½0	½½	½0	½0	½½	½½	••	0½	00	1½	11	12½
11. Maróczy, G.	00	11	0½	00	01	½0	½½	½½	½½	1½	••	½1	½½	½½	12
12. Colle, E.	00	00	0½	½1	00	11	½0	00	10	11	½0	••	0½	11	10½
13. Asztalos, L.	½½	½0	00	½0	½½	10	½0	½½	0½	0½	½½	1½	••	0½	9½
14. Pirc, V.	00	00	1½	½½	½½	0½	½½	½½	00	00	½½	00	1½	••	8½

Hastings 1931-32
(December 28–January 6)

	1	2	3	4	5	6	7	8	9	10	Score
1. Flohr, S.	•	½	½	1	1	1	1	1	1	1	8
2. Kashdan, I.	½	•	1	½	1	1	½	1	1	1	7½
3. Euwe, M.	½	0	•	½	1	0	1	½	½	1	5
4. Sultan Khan	0	½	½	•	1	0	½	0	1	1	4½
5. Jackson, Ed	0	0	0	0	•	½	½	1	1	1	4
6. Menchik, V.	0	0	1	1	½	•	0	0	1	½	4
7. Stoltz, G.	0	½	0	½	½	1	•	½	½	½	4
8. Yates, F.	0	0	½	1	0	1	½	•	1	0	4
9. Michell, R.	0	0	½	0	0	0	½	0	•	1	2
10. Thomas, G.	0	0	0	0	0	½	½	1	0	•	2

London 1932
(February 1–15)

	1	2	3	4	5	6	7	8	9	10	11	12	Score
1. Alekhine, A.	•	½	½	1	½	1	1	1	1	½	1	1	9
2. Flohr, S.	½	•	½	½	1	0	1	1	1	1	½	1	8
3. Kashdan, I.	½	½	•	½	0	½	1	1	1	1	1	½	7½
4. Sultan Khan, M.	0	½	½	•	0	1	½	1	1	1	1	1	7½
5. Maróczy, G.	½	0	1	1	•	½	½	½	½	½	½	½	6
6. Tartakower, S.	0	1	½	0	½	•	1	1	0	0	1	1	6
7. Koltanowski, G.	0	0	0	½	½	0	•	½	1	1	½	1	5
8. Menchik, V.	0	0	0	0	½	0	½	•	½	1	1	1	4½
9. Milner Barry, P.	0	0	0	0	½	1	0	½	•	½	½	½	3½
10. Thomas, G.	½	0	0	0	½	1	0	0	½	•	½	½	3½
11. Buerger, V.	0	½	0	0	½	0	½	0	½	½	•	½	3
12. Winter, W.	0	0	½	0	½	0	0	0	½	½	½	•	2½

Pasadena 1932
(August 15–29)

		1	2	3	4	5	6	7	8	9	10	11	12	Score
1.	Alekhine, A.	•	1	0	1	1	1	1	½	½	½	1	1	8½
2.	Kashdan, I.	0	•	½	1	1	½	½	1	½	½	1	1	7½
3.	Dake, A.	1	½	•	0	½	½	½	1	½	1	0	½	6
4.	Reshevsky, S.	0	0	1	•	½	0	1	½	1	0	1	1	6
5.	Steiner, H.	0	0	½	½	•	1	½	1	1	½	1	0	6
6.	Borochow, H.	0	½	½	1	0	•	0	0	1	1	1	½	5½
7.	Bernstein, J.	0	½	½	0	½	1	•	0	½	½	½	1	5
8.	Factor, S.	½	0	0	½	0	1	1	•	½	0	½	1	5
9.	Fine, R.	½	½	½	0	0	0	½	½	•	1	½	1	5
10.	Reinfeld, F.	½	½	0	1	½	0	½	1	0	•	0	1	5
11.	Araiza, J.	0	0	1	0	0	0	½	½	½	1	•	0	3½
12.	Fink, A.	0	0	½	0	1	½	0	0	0	0	1	•	3

Mexico City 1932
(October 6–18)

		1	2	3	4	5	6	7	8	9	10	Score
1.	Kashdan, I.	•	½	1	1	1	1	1	1	1	1	8½
2.	Alekhine, A.	½	•	1	1	1	1	1	1	1	1	8½
3.	Araiza, J.	0	0	•	1	0	1	1	1	1	1	6
4.	Asiain, J.	0	0	0	•	1	1	½	1	1	1	5½
5.	Vázquez, J.	0	0	1	0	•	0	1	½	1	1	4½
6.	González, E.	0	0	0	0	1	•	½	½	1	½	3½
7.	Medina, J.	0	0	0	½	0	½	•	1	½	1	3½
8.	Acevedo, Maria	0	0	0	0	½	½	0	•	0	1	2
9.	Brunner, E.	0	0	0	0	0	0	½	1	•	0	1½
10.	Soto Larrea, M.	0	0	0	0	0	½	0	0	1	•	1½

Manhattan Club Championship 1932-33

		1	2	3	4	5	6	7	8	9	10	11	12	Score
1.	Kupchik, A.	•	½	½	½	1	1	½	1	1	1	1	1	9
2.	Willman, R.	½	•	½	½	1	1	1	1	1	1	1	½	9
3.	Horowitz, I.	½	½	•	1	0	0	1	1	1	1	1	½	7½
4.	Pinkus, A.	½	½	0	•	1	1	1	0	1	1	0	½	6½
5.	MacMurray, D.	0	0	1	0	•	0	0	1	1	1	1	1	6
6.	Schwartz, E.	0	0	1	0	1	•	0	1	1	1	½	½	6
7.	Denker, A.	½	0	0	0	1	1	•	1	0	0	1	1	5½
8.	Bornholz, R.	0	0	0	1	0	0	0	•	1	0	1	1	4

	1	2	3	4	5	6	7	8	9	10	11	12	Score
9. Jackson, E, Jr.	0	0	0	0	0	0	1	0	•	1	1	1	4
10. Tenner, O.	0	0	0	0	0	0	1	1	0	•	1	1	4
11. Kashdan, I.*	0	0	0	1	0	½	0	0	0	0	•	1	2½
12. Cohen, S.	0	½	½	½	0	½	0	0	0	0	0	•	2

Kashdan played only five games, winning from Pinkus and Cohen. He drew with Schwartz, and lost to Denker and Willman.

Folkestone Olympiad 1933
(June 12–23)

Round 1	Kashdan–Asgeirsson (Iceland)	1–0	(June 12)
Round 2	Fairhurst (Scotland)–Kashdan	0–1	(June 13)
Round 3	Kashdan–Alekhine (France)	½–½	(June 14)
Round 4	Tartakower (Poland)–Kashdan	0–1	(June 15)
Round 5	Kashdan–Soultanbeieff (Belgium)	½–½	(June 15)
Round 6	Kashdan–Apscheneck [Apšenieks] (Latvia)	1–0	(June 16)
Round 7	Sultan Khan (England)–Kashdan	½–½	(June 17)
Round 8	[United States had the bye]		
Round 9	Kashdan–Grünfeld (Austria)	½–½	(June 18)
Round 10	Kashdan–Andersen (Denmark)	½–½	(June 19)
Round 11	Rosselli (Italy)–Kashdan	0–1	(June 20)
Round 12	Kashdan–Mikėnas (Lithuania)	1–0	(June 21)
Round 13	L. Steiner (Hungary)–Kashdan	0–1	(June 21)
Round 14	Ståhlberg (Sweden)–Kashdan	½–½	(June 22)
Round 15	Flohr (Czechoslovakia)–Kashdan	1–0	(June 23)

35th Western Chess Congress, Chicago 1934
(July 2–August 1)

PRELIMINARY B

	1	2	3	4	5	6	7	8	Score
1. Reshevsky, S.	1	½	1	1	1	1	1	1	6½
2. Kashdan, I.	0	•	1	1	1	1	1	1	6
3. Engholm, N.	½	0	•	1	1	1	1	1	5½
4. Woods, H.	0	0	0	•	1	1	1	1	4
5. Elo, A.	0	0	0	0	•	1	1	1	3
6. Waggoner, W.	0	0	0	0	0	•	1	1	2
7. Jackson, M.	0	0	0	0	0	0	•	1	1
8. Ilsley, B.	0	0	0	0	0	0	0	•	0

FINALS

	1	2	3	4	5	6	7	8	9	10	Score
1. Fine, R.	•	½	0	1	1	1	1	1	1	1	7½
2. Reshevsky, S.	½	•	1	½	1	½	1	1	1	1	7½

	1	2	3	4	5	6	7	8	9	10	Score
3. Dake, A.	1	0	•	½	1	½	1	1	1	½	6½
4. Denker, A.	0	½	½	•	0	1	1	½	1	1	5½
5. Eastman, C.	0	0	0	1	•	½	1	1	½	½	4½
6. Kashdan, I.	0	½	½	0	½	•	1	1	½	½	4½
7. MacMurray, D.	0	0	0	0	0	0	•	1	1	1	3
8. Araiza, J.	0	0	0	½	0	0	0	•	1	2	2½
9. Belson, J.	0	0	0	0	½	½	0	0	•	1	2
10. Engholm, N.	0	0	½	0	½	½	0	0	0	•	1½

Syracuse International 1934
(August 13–25)

	1	2	3	4	5	6	7	8	9	10	11	12	13	14	15	Score
1. Reshevsky, S.	•	½	1	½	½	1	1	1	½	1	1	1	1	1	1	12
2. Kashdan, I.	½	•	½	½	½	1	½	1	1	½	1	½	1	1	1	10½
3. Dake, A.	0	½	•	½	½	1	½	1	1	1	0	1	1	1	1	10
4. Fine, R.	½	½	½	•	½	0	1	1	1	1	0	1	1	1	1	10
5. Kupchik, A.	½	½	½	½	•	0	½	½	1	½	1	1	1	1	1	9½
6. Horowitz	0	0	0	1	1	•	½	0	½	1	1	1	½	1	1	8½
7. Steiner, H.	0	½	½	0	½	½	•	½	1	1	0	1	½	1	1	8
8. Monticelli, M.	0	0	0	0	½	1	½	•	½	1	0	½	½	1	1	6½
9. Reinfeld, F.	½	0	0	0	0	½	0	½	•	½	1	1	½	½	1	6
10. Santasiere, A.	0	½	0	0	½	0	0	0	½	•	1	1	½	1	1	6
11. Denker, A.	0	0	1	1	0	0	1	1	0	0	•	0	½	0	½	5
12. Seitz, J.	0	½	0	0	0	0	0	½	0	0	1	•	1	1	1	5
13. Araiza, J.	0	0	0	0	0	½	½	½	½	½	½	0	•	½	1	4½
14. Tholfsen, E.	0	0	0	0	0	0	0	0	½	0	1	0	½	•	1	3
15. Martin, R.	0	0	0	0	0	0	0	0	0	0	½	0	0	0	•	½

Manhattan Club Championship 1934
(October–December)

	1	2	3	4	5	6	7	8	9	10	11	12	13	14	Score
1. Kashdan, I.	•	1	1	0	1	1	0	1	1	1	1	1	1	1	11
2. Kupchik, A.	0	•	½	1	1	½	1	1	1	1	1	1	1	1	11
3. Horowitz	0	½	•	1	1	½	1	1	1	1	1	1	1	1	9½
4. MacMurray	1	0	0	•	0	1	1	1	1	1	1	0	½	1	8½
5. Schwartz	0	0	0	1	•	0	1	½	½	1	1	1	1	1	8
6. Simonson	0	½	1	0	1	•	1	1	½	0	1	1	0	1	8
7. Cohen, S.	1	0	0	0	0	0	•	0	1	0	½	1	1	1	5½
8. Denker, A.	0	0	0	0	½	0	1	•	0	½	1	1	1	0	5
9. Tenner, O.	0	0	0	0	½	½	0	1	•	1	1	0	0	1	5

	1	2	3	4	5	6	7	8	9	10	11	12	13	14	Score
10. Hassialis	0	0	1	0	0	1	1	½	0	•	0	0	1	0	4½
11. Platz, J.	0	0	0	0	0	0	½	0	0	1	•	1	1	1	4½
12. Willman, R.	0	0	0	1	0	0	0	0	1	1	0	•	½	1	4½
13. Jackson, Jr.	0	0	0	½	0	1	0	0	1	0	0	½	•	1	4
14. Richman, J.	0	0	0	0	0	0	0	1	0	1	0	0	0	•	2

Kupchik won the playoff from Kashdan 1–0.

36th Western Chess Congress, Milwaukee 1935
(July 21–August 1)

PRELIMINARY B

	1	2	3	4	5	6	7	8	9	0	Score
1. Kashdan, I.	•	½	½	1	1	1	1	1	½	1	7½
2. Belson, J.	½	•	1	1	0	½	1	1	1	1	7
3. Santasiere, A.	½	0	•	1	1	½	0	½	1	1	5½
4. Winkelman, B.	0	0	0	•	1	½	1	1	½	1	5
5. Kent, H.	0	1	0	0	•	1	0	1	0	1	4
6. Surgies, M.	0	½	½	½	0	•	1	0	½	1	4
7. Holland, K.	0	0	1	0	1	0·	•	½	1	½	4
8. Woods, H.	0	0	½	0	0	1	½	•	½	1	3½
9. Rathman, F.	½	0	0	½	1	½	0	½	•	0	3
10. Ratke, R.	0	0	0	0	0	0	½	0	1	•	1½

FINALS

	1	2	3	4	5	6	7	8	9	10	11	Score
1. Fine, R.	•	½	½	1	1	1	1	½	1	½	1	8
2. Dake, A.	½	•	½	½	½	½	1	1	1	1	1	7½
3. Kashdan, I.	½	½	•	½	½	½	½	½	1	1	1	6½
4. Chevalier, F.	0	½	½	•	½	0	½	½	1	1	1	5½
5. Factor, S.	0	½	½	½	•	1	½	1	½	½	½	5½
6. Simonson, A.	0	½	½	1	0	•	½	½	½	1	1	5½
7. Santasiere, A.	0	0	½	½	½	½	•	½	½	1	1	5
8. Morton, H.	½	0	½	½	0	½	½	•	½	0	1	4
9. Belson, J.	0	0	0	0	½	½	½	½	•	½	½	3
10. Elo, A	½	0	0	0	½	0	0	1	½	•	0	2½
11. Ruth, W	0	0	0	0	½	0	0	0	½	1	•	2

New York State Championship, Binghamton 1935
(August 19–24)

	1	2	3	4	5	6	7	8	9	Score
1. Kashdan, I.	•	1	½	1	1	1	1	1	1	7½
2. Polland, D.	0	•	1	½	1	1	1	1	1	6½
3. Lessing, N.	½	0	•	½	1	1	1	1	1	6
4. Reinfeld, F.	0	½	½	•	0	1	1	1	1	5
5. Bigelow, H.	0	0	0	1	•	1	0	1	1	4
6. Barron, T.	0	0	0	0	0	•	1	1	1	3
7. McCormick, E.	0	0	0	0	1	0	•	1	1	3
8. Goerlich, R.	0	0	0	0	0	0	0	•	1	1
9. Drummond, R.	0	0	0	0	0	0	0	0	•	0

1st U.S. Championship, New York 1936
(April 25–May 16)

	1	2	3	4	5	6	7	8	9	10	11	12	13	14	15	16	Score
1. Reshevsky, S.	•	½	½	1	1	1	½	1	0	1	1	1	0	1	1	1	11½
2. Simonson, A.	½	•	1	1	1	0	½	½	½	1	0	1	1	1	1	1	11
3. Fine, R.	½	0	•	1	1	½	½	½	½	½	1	½	1	1	1	1	10½
4. Treysman,	0	0	0	•	1	1	½	1	½	1	1	1	½	1	1	1	10½
5. Kashdan, I.	0	1	0	0	•	½	1	½	1	1	1	1	1	0	1	1	10
6. Dake, A.	0	½	½	0	½	•	1	½	½	1	0	1	½	1	1	1	9
7. Kupchik, A.	½	½	½	½	0	0	•	1	½	1	½	1	½	½	1	1	9
8. Kevitz, A.	0	½	½	0	½	½	0	•	1	0	0	1	1	½	1	1	7½
9. Horowitz, I.	1	0	½	½	0	½	½	0	•	1	1	0	½	1	0	½	7
10. Factor, S.	0	1	½	0	0	0	0	1	0	•	1	½	0	1	1	½	6½
11. Steiner, H.	0	0	0	0	0	1	½	1	0	0	•	0	1	½	1	1	6
12. Denker, A.	0	0	½	0	0	0	0	0	1	½	1	•	½	1	1	½	6
13. Bernstein, S.	1	0	0	½	0	0	½	½	0	½	1	½	•	½	0	0	5
14. Hanauer, M.	0	0	0	0	1	0	½	½	0	0	½	0	½	•	1	½	4½
15. Adams, W.	0	0	0	0	0	0	0	0	1	0	0	0	1	0	•	1	3
16. Morton, H.	0	0	0	0	0	0	0	0	½	½	0	0	1	½	0	•	3

37th Western Chess Congress, Philadelphia 1936
(August 15–30)

SECTION I

	1	2	3	4	5	6	7	8	9	10	11	12	Score
1. Kashdan, I.	•	1	½	½	1	½	1	1	1	1	1	1	9½
2. Denker, A.	0	•	½	1	1	1	1	½	1	1	1	1	9

	1	2	3	4	5	6	7	8	9	10	11	12	Score
3. Kupchik, A.	½	½	•	1	½	1	½	1	1	1	1	1	9
4. Reinfeld, F.	½	0	0	•	1	1	1	1	1	1	1	1	8½
5. Morris	0	0	½	0	•	½	½	1	1	1	1	1	6½
6. Grossman	½	0	0	0	½	•	0	1	1	1	1	1	6
7. Elo, A.	0	0	½	0	½	1	•	½	0	½	1	1	5
8. Isenberg	0	½	0	0	0	0	½	•	1	1	1	½	4½
9. Holland	0	0	0	0	0	0	1	0	•	½	½	1	3
10. Glover	0	0	0	0	0	0	½	0	½	•	½	1	2½
11. Jackson	0	0	0	0	0	0	0	0	½	½	•	1	2
12. Rivise, I.	0	0	0	0	0	0	0	½	0	0	0	•	½

FINALS

	1	2	3	4	5	6	7	8	9	10	11	12	Score
1. Horowitz, I.	•	0	1	1	½	1	1	1	½	½	½	1	8
2. Dake, A.	1	•	½	½	½	1	0	1	1	1	½	½	7½
3. Denker, A.	0	½	•	½	½	½	1	1	½	1	1	1	7½
4. Kashdan, I.	0	½	½	•	1	0	½	1	1	1	½	1	7
5. Kupchik, A.	½	½	½	0	•	½	1	½	1	½	1	1	7
6. Polland, D.	0	0	½	1	½	•	1	0	½	1	1	1	6½
7. Mugridge, D.	0	1	0	½	0	0	•	1	1	½	½	0	4½
8. Santasiere, A.	0	0	0	0	½	1	0	•	1	½	½	1	4½
9. Fox, M.	½	0	½	0	0	½	0	0	•	½	½	1	3½
10. Hanauer, M.	½	0	0	0	½	0	½	½	½	•	½	½	3½
11. Morton, H.	½	½	0	½	0	0	½	½	½	½	•	0	3½
12. Bernstein, S.	0	½	0	0	0	0	1	0	0	½	1	•	3

New York State Championship, Poughkeepsie 1936
(August 39–September 5)

	1	2	3	4	5	6	7	8	9	10	11	12	Score
1. Kashdan, I.	•	½	1	1	1	1	1	1	1	1	1	1	10½
2. Helms, H.	½	•	½	½	½	1	1	1	1	1	1	1	9
3. Shainswit	0	½	•	1	½	1	1	1	1	1	1	1	9
4. Martinson	0	½	0	•	½	1	1	1	½	1	1	1	7½
5. Soudakoff	0	½	½	½	•	½	½	1	1	½	1	1	7
6. Battell	0	0	0	0	½	•	½	½	1	1	½	1	6
7. Broughton	0	0	0	0	½	0	•	½	1	1	1	1	5
8. Barron	0	0	0	0	0	0	½	•	1	½	0	1	3
9. Carter	0	0	0	½	0	0	0	0	•	½	1	1	3
10. Evans	0	0	0	0	½	0	0	½	½	•	½	1	3
11. Wood	0	0	0	0	0	½	0	1	0	½	•	1	3
12. Slater	0	0	0	0	0	0	0	0	0	0	0	•	0

San Juan 1936
(November 12–20)

	1	2	3	4	5	6	7	8	Score
1. Kashdan, I.	•	½	1	1	1	1	1	1	6½
2. Seitz, J.	½	•	½	1	1	1	1	1	6
3. Marshall, F.	0	½	•	½	1	1	1	1	5
4. Cintrón, R.	0	0	½	•	½	½	1	1	3½
5. Benitez	0	0	0	½	•	½	1	1	3
6. Gotey	0	0	0	½	½	•	1	1	3
7. Cancio	0	0	0	0	0	0	•	1	1
8. Prieto	0	0	0	0	0	0	0	•	0

Manhattan Club Championship 1936-37

	1	2	3	4	5	6	7	8	9	10	11	12	Score
1. Kashdan, I.	•	½	1	1	½	1	1	1	1	1	1	1	10
2. Simonson, A.	½	•	1	1	1	1	½	1	1	1	1	1	10
3. Willman, R.	0	0	•	1	½	½	1	1	1	½	1	1	7½
4. Denker, A.	0	0	0	•	½	0	1	1	1	1	1	1	6½
5. Kupchik, A.	½	0	½	½	•	1	1	0	0	½	1	½	5½
6. Schwartz, E.	0	0	½	1	0	•	1	½	½	0	1	1	5½
7. Simchow, A.	0	½	0	0	0	½	•	½	1	1	1	1	5½
8. Cohen, S.	0	0	0	0	1	½	½	•	1	1	0	0	4
9. Platz, J.	0	0	0	0	1	½	0	0	•	½	1	1	4
10. MacMurray, D.	0	0	½	0	½	1	0	0	½	•	0	1	3½
11. Tenner, O.	0	0	0	0	0	0	0	1	0	1	•	1	3
12. Jackson, Jr.	0	0	0	0	½	0	0	1	0	0	0	•	1½

Kashdan won the playoff by a score of 2–1.

Stockholm Olympiad 1937

Round 1	Kashdan–Vistaneckis (Lithuania)	1–0	(July 31)
Round 2	Stoltz (Sweden)–Kashdan	0–1	(August 1)
Round 3	[Kashdan did not play]		
Round 4	Kashdan–Vukovic (Yugoslavia)	1–0	(August 2)
Round 5	Kashdan–A. Steiner (Hungary)	0–1	(August 2)
Round 6	Guimard (Argentina)–Kashdan	0–1	(August 3)
Round 7	[United States had the bye]		
Round 8	Böök (Finland)–Kashdan	0–1	(August 5)
Round 9	Baert (Belgium)–Kashdan	0–1	(August 5)
Round 10	Kashdan–Zinner (Czechoslovakia)	1–0	(August 5)
Round 11	Frydman (Poland)–Kashdan	0–1	(August 7)

Round 12	Paulsen (Denmark)–Kashdan	0–1	(August 7)
Round 13	Kashdan–Prins (Holland)	½–½	(August 9)
Round 14	Kashdan–Mezgailis (Latvia)	½–½	(August 10)
Round 15	Raud (Estonia)–Kashdan	0–1	(August 10)
Round 16	Alexander (England)–Kashdan	0–1	(August 12)
Round 17	Napolitano (Italy)–Kashdan	0–1	(August 12)
Round 18	Kashdan–Asgeirsson (Iceland)	1–0	(August 13)

Manhattan Championship 1937-38

	1	2	3	4	5	6	7	8	Score
1. Kashdan, I.	•	½	1	1	½	½	1	1	5½
2. Willman, R.	½	•	1	½	0	1	1	1	5
3. Cohen, S.	0	0	•	½	1	1	1	1	4½
4. Denker, A.	0	½	½	•	0	1	1	1	4
5. Platz, J.	½	1	0	1	•	½	0	1	4
6. Soudakoff, J.	½	0	0	0	½	•	1	½	2½
7. Newman, J.	0	0	0	0	1	0	•	½	1½
8. Tenner, O.	0	0	0	0	0	½	½	•	1

2nd U.S. Championship, New York 1938
(April 2–24)

	1	2	3	4	5	6	7	8	9	10	11	12	13	14	15	16	17	Score
1. Reshevsky, S.	•	½	1	½	1	1	1	½	½	1	1	½	½	1	1	1	1	13
2. Fine, R.	½	•	½	1	1	1	½	1	1	1	0	1	1	0	1	1	1	12½
3. Simonson, A.	0	½	•	1	½	½	½	0	1	1	½	1	1	½	1	1	1	11
4. Horowitz, I.	½	0	0	•	½	1	½	½	1	1	0	1	1	1	½	½	1	10
5. Kashdan, I.	0	0	½	½	•	0	1	1	1	1	1	1	0	½	1	1	0	9½
6. Dake, A.	0	0	½	0	1	•	1	0	½	½	1	½	½	½	1	1	1	9
7. Polland, D.	0	½	½	½	0	0	•	1	½	0	½	½	1	1	1	1	1	9
8. Kupchik, A.	½	0	1	½	0	1	0	•	½	½	½	1	1	½	½	0	1	8½
9. Bernstein, S.	½	0	0	0	0	0	½	½	½	•	1	½	½	½	1	0	1	1	7½
10. Treysman, G.	0	0	0	0	0	½	1	½	0	•	1	½	1	1	1	0	½	7
11. Santasiere, A.	0	1	½	1	0	0	½	½	½	0	•	½	0	½	½	½	1	7
12. Reinfeld, F.	½	0	0	0	0	½	½	0	½	½	½	•	1	1	0	½	1	6½
13. Cohen, S.	½	0	0	0	1	½	0	0	½	0	1	0	•	½	½	1	1	6½
14. Hanauer, M.	0	1	½	0	½	½	0	½	0	0	½	0	½	•	1	½	1	6½
15. Shainswit, G.	0	0	0	½	0	0	0	½	1	0	½	1	½	0	•	1	½	5½
16. Morton, H.	0	0	0	½	0	0	0	1	0	1	½	½	0	½	0	•	1	5
17. Suesman, W.	0	0	0	0	1	0	0	0	0	½	0	0	0	0	½	0	•	2

39th Congress of the American Chess Federation, Boston 1938
(July 11–23)

PRELIMINARY—SECTION III

		1	2	3	4	5	6	7	Score
1.	Kashdan, I.	•	1	½	½	1	1	1	5
2.	Collins, J.	0	•	1	1	1	1	½	4½
3.	Barnes, G.	½	0	•	0	1	1	1	3½
4.	Lyman, H.	½	0	1	•	0	1	1	3½
5.	Epstein	0	0	0	1	•	0	1	2
6.	Mitchell	0	0	0	0	1	•	½	1½
7.	Barron, T.	0	½	0	0	0	½	•	1

FINALS

		1	2	3	4	5	6	7	8	9	10	11	12	Score
1.	Horowitz, I.	•	½	0	1	1	1	1	½	1	1	1	1	9
2.	Kashdan, I.	½	•	1	1	0	1	1	1	1	1	1	½	9
3.	Blumin, B.	1	0	•	0	½	1	½	½	1	1	1	1	7½
4.	Polland, D.	0	0	1	•	½	1	½	½	1	1	1	1	7½
5.	Santasiere, A.	0	1	½	½	•	½	½	1	½	0	½	1	6
6.	Morton, H.	0	0	0	0	½	•	1	0	1	1	1	1	5½
7.	Shainswit, G.	0	0	½	½	½	0	•	1	½	½	1	½	5
8.	Collins, J.	½	0	½	½	0	1	0	•	0	½	0	1	4
9.	Jaffe, C.	0	0	0	0	½	0	½	1	•	1	1	0	4
10.	Moscowitz, J.	0	0	0	0	1	0	½	½	0	•	½	1	3½
11.	Rosenzweig, P.	0	0	0	0	½	0	0	1	0	½	•	1	3
12.	Dahlstrom, B.	0	½	0	0	0	0	½	0	1	0	0	•	2

The playoff was even after 10 games and the players Kashdan and Horowitz were then declared co–champions.

New York State Championship, Hamilton 1939
(August 19–26)

		1	2	3	4	5	6	7	8	9	10	Score
1.	Denker, A.	•	½	½	1	1	1	1	½	½	1	7
2.	Kashdan, I.	½	•	½	1	½	½	1	1	1	½	6½
3.	Pinkus, A.	½	½	•	½	1	½	0	1	1	½	5½
4.	Blumin, B.	0	0	½	•	0	½	1	½	1	1	4½
5.	Shainswit, G.	0	½	0	1	•	½	½	½	½	1	4½
6.	Willman, R.	0	½	½	½	½	•	½	½	0	1	4
7.	Mott-Smith, K.	0	0	1	0	½	½	•	1	0	1	4

	1	2	3	4	5	6	7	8	9	10	Score
8. Platz, J.	½	0	0	½	½	½	0	•	1	1	4
9. Chernev, I.	½	0	0	0	½	1	1	0	•	½	3½
10. Garfinkel, B.	0	½	½	0	0	0	0	0	½	•	1½

Havana 1940
(January)

	1	2	3	4	5	6	7	8	9	10	Score
1. Kashdan, I.	•	½	½	1	1	½	1	1	1	1	7½
2. Koltanowski, G.	½	•	½	½	½	1	½	1	1	1	6½
3. Planas, F.	½	½	•	½	½	1	½	½	1	1	6
4. Alemán, M.	0	½	½	•	½	1	½	½	1	1	5½
5. Blanco, R.	0	½	½	½	•	0	1	½	1	1	5
6. González, J.	½	0	0	0	1	•	1	½	1	0	4
7. Meylan, A.	0	½	½	½	0	0	•	½	½	1	3½
8. Paz	0	0	½	½	½	½	½	•	½	½	3½
9. Miss Mora	0	0	0	0	0	0	½	½	•	1	2
10. Florido	0	0	0	0	0	1	0	½	0	•	1½

3rd U.S. Championship, New York 1940
(April 27–May 19)

	1	2	3	4	5	6	7	8	9	10	11	12	13	14	15	16	17	Score
1. Reshevsky, S.	•	½	1	1	½	1	1	1	1	½	½	1	½	½	1	1	1	13
2. Fine, R.	½	•	½	½	1	0	½	1	1	½	1	1	1	1	1	1	1	12½
3. Kashdan, I.	0	½	•	½	1	1	1	½	½	½	1	0	1	½	1	1	½	10½
4. Pinkus, A.	0	½	½	•	1	½	0	½	½	½	1	½	1	½	1	1	1	10
5. Simonson, C.	½	0	0	0	•	1	½	0	1	½	½	1	1	1	1	1	1	10
6. Kupchik, A.	0	1	0	½	0	•	½	½	½	½	½	1	1	1	½	1	1	9½
7. Denker, A.	0	½	0	1	½	½	•	1	0	½	0	1	1	1	½	1	1	9½
8. Bernstein, S.	0	0	½	½	1	½	0	•	1	½	½	0	0	1	0	1	1	7½
9. Polland, D.	0	½	½	½	0	½	1	0	•	1	½	1	½	0	1	0	½	7½
10. Reinfeld, F.	½	0	½	½	½	½	½	½	0	•	½	½	½	½	½	½	1	7½
11. Shainswit, G.	½	0	0	0	½	½	1	½	½	½	•	½	½	½	½	1	½	7½
12. Adams, W.	0	0	1	½	0	0	0	1	0	½	½	•	0	1	½	1	1	7
13. Seidman, H.	½	0	0	0	0	0	0	1	½	½	½	1	•	½	½	1	1	7
14. Green, M.	½	0	½	½	0	0	0	0	1	½	½	0	½	•	½	1	½	6
15. Hanauer, M.	0	0	0	0	0	½	½	1	0	½	½	½	½	½	•	½	1	6
16. Wolliston, P.	0	0	0	0	0	0	0	0	1	½	0	0	0	0	½	•	1	3
17. Littman, G.	0	0	½	0	0	0	0	0	½	0	½	0	0	½	0	0	•	2

New York State Championship, Hamilton 1941
(August 16–23)

	1	2	3	4	5	6	7	8	9	10	11	Score
1. Fine, R.	•	½	½	½	1	1	½	1	1	1	1	8
2. Denker, A.	½	•	½	0	1	½	1	1	½	1	1	7
3. Kashdan, I.	½	½	•	½	½	1	½	1	½	1	1	7
4. Reshevsky, S.	½	1	½	•	1	½	½	½	1	1	½	7
5. Willman, R.	0	0	½	0	•	1	1	1	1	1	1	6½
6. Santasiere, A.	0	½	0	½	0	•	½	1	1	0	1	4½
7. Dr. Cruz	½	0	½	½	0	½	•	0	½	½	1	4
8. Seidman	0	0	0	½	0	0	1	•	½	1	1	4
9. Shainswit	0	½	½	0	0	0	½	½	•	1	0	3
10. Hewlett	0	0	0	0	0	1	½	0	0	•	1	2½
11. Evans	0	0	0	½	0	0	0	0	1	0	•	1½

U.S. Championship, New York 1942
(April 10–April 30)

	1	2	3	4	5	6	7	8	9	10	11	12	13	14	15	16	Score
1. Kashdan, I.	•	½	1	1	0	1	1	½	1	1	1	1	½	1	1	1	12½
2. Reshevsky, S.	½	•	1	1	1	½	1	1	1	1	½	1	1	1	½	½	12½
3. Denker, A.	0	0	•	1	½	½	1	0	1	1	½	1	1	1	1	1	10½
4. Pinkus, A.	0	0	0	•	½	1	1	1	1	1	1	0	1	1	1	1	10½
5. Steiner, H.	1	0	½	½	•	1	1	0	1	1	0	1	1	½	1	½	10
6. Horowitz, I.	0	½	½	0	0	•	1	1	½	½	1	½	½	1	1	1	9
7. Seidman, H.	0	0	0	0	0	0	•	1	0	1	1	1	1	½	½	1	7
8. Levin, J.	½	0	1	0	1	0	0	•	0	½	1	½	½	½	½	½	6½
9. Levy, L.	0	0	0	0	0	½	1	1	•	½	0	½	0	1	1	1	6½
10. Chernev, I.	0	0	0	0	0	½	0	½	½	•	½	1	0	1	1	1	6
11. Pilnick, C.	0	½	½	0	1	0	0	0	1	½	•	0	1	1	0	½	6
12. Baker, H.	0	0	0	1	0	½	0	0	½	½	0	•	½	½	½	½	5½
13. Lessing, N.	½	0	0	0	0	½	0	½	1	1	0	½	•	0	1	½	5½
14. Altman, B.	0	0	0	0	½	0	½	½	0	0	0	½	1	•	1	0	4
15. Green	0	½	0	0	0	0	½	½	0	0	1	½	0	0	•	1	4
16. Hahlbohm, H.	0	½	0	0	½	0	0	½	0	0	½	½	½	1	0	•	4

Manhattan Club Championship 1944
(October 28–December)

	Won	Lost	Drawn	Score
1. Pinkus, A.	9	1	2	10
2. Denker, A.	7	2	3	8½

		Won	Lost	Drawn	Score
3.	Kashdan, I.	6	1	5	8½
4.	Kevitz, A.	7	3	2	8
5.	Willman, R.	6	4	2	7
6.	Dr. Platz, J.	6	5	1	6½
7.	Jackson, E, Jr.	5	5	2	6
8.	Pavey, M.	5	5	2	6
9.	Rothman, A.	4	5	3	5½
10.	Kramer, G.	4	7	1	4½
11.	Byrne, R.	2	6	3	3½
12.	Shipman, W.	2	9	1	2½
13.	Byrne, D.	0	10	1	½

Pan-American, Hollywood 1945
(July 28–August 12)

		1	2	3	4	5	6	7	8	9	10	11	12	13	Score
1.	Reshevsky, S.	•	½	1	½	1	½	1	1	1	1	1	1	1	10½
2.	Fine, R.	½	•	½	½	1	½	1	1	½	½	1	1	1	9
3.	Pilnik, H.	0	½	•	½	1	½	1	½	1	½	1	1	1	8½
4.	Horowitz, I.	½	½	½	•	½	1	0	1	½	½	1	1	1	8
5.	Kashdan, I.	0	0	0	½	•	1	1	1	½	½	½	1	1	7
6.	Rossetto, H.	½	½	½	0	0	•	0	1	½	1	½	1	1	6½
7.	Adams, W.	0	0	0	1	0	1	•	½	0	0	1	1	1	5½
8.	Steiner, H.	0	0	½	0	0	0	½	•	1	1	1	1	½	5½
9.	Araiza, J.	0	½	0	½	½	½	1	0	•	½	0	½	1	5
10.	Dr. Cruz, W.	0	½	½	½	½	0	1	0	½	•	0	½	1	5
11.	Broderman, J.	0	0	0	0	½	½	0	0	1	1	•	0	½	3½
12.	Seidman, H.	0	0	0	0	0	0	0	0	½	½	1	•	1	3
13.	Camarena, J.	0	0	0	0	0	0	0	½	0	0	½	0	•	1

Metropolitan Championship 1946
(June 15–29, 1946)

1. Kashdan, I.	7–2	Kashdan lost the very first
2. Pinkus, A.	6½–2½	game to Santasire. He gave
3. Bernstein, S.	5½–3½	up a draw to Pinkus. It is
4. Santasiere, A.	5–4	not known who got the
5. Seidman, H.	5–4	other draw from Kashdan.
6. Shainswit, G.	4–5	
7. Willman, R.	3½–5½	
8. Moscowitz, J.	3½–5½	
9. Rothman, A.	2½–6½	
10. Shipman, W.	2½–6½	

U.S. Championship, New York 1946

(October 26–November 17)

		1	2	3	4	5	6	7	8	9	10	11	12	13	14	15	16	17	18	19	Score
1.	Reshevsky, S.	•	1	½	½	1	½	1	1	½	1	1	1	1	1	1	1	1	1	1	16
2.	Kashdan, I.	0	•	½	½	½	0	1	1	1	1	½	1	½	1	1	1	1	1	1	13½
3.	Santasiere, A.	½	½	•	1	½	0	1	½	½	1	½	1	½	½	1	1	1	1	1	13
4.	Levin	½	½	0	•	½	½	1	½	1	1	1	½	½	0	1	1	1	1	1	12½
5.	Denker, A.	0	½	½	½	•	0	½	1	0	1	½	1	1	1	1	½	1	1	1	12
6.	Horowitz, I.	½	1	1	½	1	•	0	1	0	½	0	1	1	1	1	0	1	½	1	12
7.	Steiner, H.	0	0	0	0	½	1	•	0	1	1	1	1	1	1	1	1	0	½	1	11
8.	Pinkus, A.	0	0	½	½	0	0	1	•	½	½	1	1	1	1	½	½	½	1	1	10½
9.	Kramer, G.	½	0	½	0	1	1	0	½	•	1	½	½	0	0	1	½	1	½	1	9½
10.	Sandrin, A.	0	0	0	0	0	½	0	½	0	•	1	1	1	1	0	0	1	1	1	8
11.	Ulvestad, O.	0	½	½	0	½	1	0	0	½	0	•	0	1	0	½	1	½	½	1	7½
12.	Rubinow, S.	0	0	0	½	0	0	0	0	½	0	1	•	1	0	1	1	1	1	0	7
13.	Adams, W.	0	½	½	½	0	0	0	0	1	0	0	0	•	0	0	1	1	1	1	6½
14.	DiCamillo	0	0	½	1	0	0	0	0	1	0	1	1	1	•	½	0	0	½	0	6½
15.	Rothman	0	0	0	0	0	0	0	½	0	1	½	0	1	½	•	0	1	1	1	6½
16.	Suesman	0	0	0	0	½	1	0	½	½	1	0	0	0	1	1	•	0	½	½	6½
17.	Drexel, G.	0	0	0	0	0	0	1	½	0	0	½	0	0	1	0	1	•	1	0	5
18.	Fink, A.	0	0	0	0	0	½	½	0	½	0	½	0	0	½	0	½	0	•	1	4
19.	Kowalski, S.	0	0	0	0	0	0	0	0	0	0	0	1	0	1	0	½	1	0	•	3½

48th U.S. Open, Corpus Christi 1947

(August 11–August 23)

Rd. 1	Gibson, J.–Kashdan	0–1
Rd. 2	Kashdan–Smith, K.	1–0
Rd. 3	Sandrin, A.–Kashdan	0–1
Rd. 4	Aleman, M.–Kashdan	1–0
Rd. 5	Kashdan–Kramer, G.	½–½
Rd. 6	Steiner, H. Kashdan	0–1
Rd. 7	Kashdan–Yanofsky, A.	1–0
Rd. 8	Ulvestad, O.–Kashdan	0–1
Rd. 9	Santasiere, A.–Kashdan	½–½
Rd. 10	Kashdan–Hartleb, G.	1–0
Rd. 11	Whitaker, N.–Kashdan	0–1
Rd. 12	Kashdan–Cuellar, M.	½–½
Rd. 13	Kashdan–Wade, R.	1–0

49th U.S. Open, Baltimore 1948

(July 5–17)

Rd. 1	Kashdan–Jenkins, T.	1–0
Rd. 2	Nash, E.–Kashdan	0–1
Rd. 3	Kashdan–Bain, O.	1–0
Rd. 4	Pilnik, C.–Kashdan	0–1
Rd. 5	Pavey, M.–Kashdan	0–1
Rd. 6	Kashdan–Kramer, G.	0–1
Rd. 7	Ulvestad, O.–Kashdan	½–½
Rd. 8	Kashdan,—Adams, W.	½–½
Rd. 9	Bisguier, A.–Kashdan	0–1
Rd. 10	Kashdan–Evans, L.	½–½
Rd. 11	Pinkus, A.–Kashdan	½–½
Rd. 12	Kashdan–McCormick, E.	1–0

Manhattan Masters 1948
(August)

	1	2	3	4	5	6	7	8	Score
1. Kramer, G.	•	½	1	1	1	½	1	1	6–1
2. Kashdan, I.	½	•	½	½	1	1	1	1	5½–1½
3. Biguier, A.	0	½	•	½	1	1	½	½	4–3
4. Pinkus, A.	0	½	½	•	0	1	1	1	4–3
5. Byrne, D.	0	0	0	1	•	1	½	1	3½–3½
6. Siff, B.	½	0	0	0	0	•	1	1	2½–4½
7. Vasconcellos	0	0	½	0	½	0	•	1	2–5
8. Williams, J.	0	0	½	0	0	0	0	•	½–6½

U.S. Championship, South Fallsburg, N.Y., 1948
(August 10–31)

	1	2	3	4	5	6	7	8	9	10	11	12	13	14	15	16	17	18	19	20	Score
1. Steiner, H.	•	½	1	0	1	1	½	1	1	½	½	½	1	1	1	½	1	1	1	1	15
2. Kashdan, I.	½	•	½	½	1	0	1	0	1	1	1	1	1	½	1	1	½	1	1	1	14½
3. Kramer, G.	0	½	•	0	0	1	½	1	½	1	1	½	1	1	½	1	½	1	1	1	13
4. Ulvestad, O.	1	½	1	•	1	1	½	0	½	½	0	½	0	1	1	½	1	1	1	1	13
5. Hesse, H.	0	0	1	0	•	1	½	0	½	0	1	1	½	½	1	1	1	1	1	1	12
6. Rubinow, S.	0	1	0	0	0	•	½	1	1	1	½	1	1	0	½	1	½	1	1	1	12
7. Shainswit, G.	½	0	½	½	½	½	•	1	½	½	½	½	½	½	½	1	1	1	1	1	12
8. Adams, W.	0	1	0	1	1	0	0	•	1	1	0	0	½	1	½	1	½	1	1	1	11½
9. Evans, L.	0	0	½	½	½	0	½	0	•	½	1	1	1	1	½	1	½	1	1	1	11½
10. Shipman, W.	½	0	0	½	1	0	½	0	½	•	½	1	½	1	½	1	1	1	1	1	11½
11. Sandrin, A.	½	0	0	1	0	½	½	1	0	½	•	½	1	0	0	1	1	1	1	1	10½
12. Santasiere, A.	½	0	½	½	0	0	½	1	0	0	½	•	1	½	1	1	½	1	1	1	10½
13. Poschel, P.	0	0	0	1	½	0	½	½	0	½	0	0	•	½	1	0	1	½	1	1	8
14. Dr. Platz, J.	0	½	0	0	½	1	½	0	0	0	½	0	0	•	1	½	½	1	0	0	7½
15. Heitner, I.	0	0	½	0	0	½	½	½	½	½	1	0	0	0	•	0	1	0	1	1	7
16. Whitaker, N.	½	0	0	½	0	0	0	0	0	0	0	0	1	½	1	•	1	½	0	1	6
17. Howard, F.	0	½	½	0	0	½	0	½	½	0	0	½	0	½	0	0	•	0	1	1	5½
18. Almgren, S.	0	0	0	0	0	0	0	0	0	0	0	0	½	0	1	½	1	•	1	0	4
19. Suraci, A.	0	0	0	0	0	0	0	0	0	0	0	0	0	1	0	1	0	0	•	1	3
20. Janes, W.	0	0	0	0	0	0	0	0	0	0	0	0	0	1	0	0	0	1	0	•	2

New York International 1948-49
(December 23–January 2)

	1	2	3	4	5	6	7	8	9	10	Score
1. Fine, Reuben	•	1	1	½	1	1	½	1	1	1	8
2. Najdorf, M.	0	•	½	1	½	1	½	1	1	1	6½
3. Euwe, M.	0	½	•	½	½	1	1	½	½	½	5
4. Pilnik, H.	½	0	½	•	½	1	½	1	½	½	4½
5. Horowitz, I.	0	½	½	½	•	½	½	0	1	1	4½
6. Kramer, G.	0	0	0	0	½	•	1	1	1	1	4½
7. Bisguier, A.	½	½	0	½	½	0	•	½	½	1	4
8. Kashdan, I.	0	0	½	0	1	0	½	•	1	1	4
9. Denker, A.	0	½	0	½	0	0	½	0	•	½	2
10. Steiner, H.	0	0	½	½	0	0	0	0	½	•	1½

52nd U.S. Open, Fort Worth 1951
(July 9–21)

Rd. 1	Kashdan–McDavid, H.	1–0	Rd. 7	Kashdan–Liepnieks	1–0
Rd. 2	Sharp, C.–Kashdan	0–1	Rd. 8	Hearst, E.–Kashdan	½–½
Rd. 3	Kashdan–Myers, H.	1–0	Rd. 9	Kashdan–Brieger, R.	1–0
Rd. 4	Evans, L.–Kashdan	½–½	Rd. 10	Kashdan–Whitaker, N.	0–1
Rd. 5	Kashdan–Gonzalez, J.	0–1	Rd. 11	Mednis, E.–Kashdan	0–1
Rd. 6	Westbrock, J.–Kashdan	0–1	Rd. 12	Sherwin, J.–Kashdan	0–1

Hollywood International Tournament 1952
(April 26–May 7)

	1	2	3	4	5	6	7	8	9	10	Score
1. Gligorić, S.	•	½	1	½	1	½	1	1	1	1	7½
2. Pomar, A.	½	•	½	½	1	1	1	1	½	1	7
3. Steiner, H.	0	½	•	½	1	½	1	½	1	1	6
4. Dake, A.	½	½	½	•	0	½	½	1	1	½	5
5. Joyner, L.	0	0	0	1	•	½	1	1	½	1	5
6. Cross, J.	½	0	½	½	½	•	½	½	½	1	4½
7. Kashdan, I.	0	0	0	½	0	½	•	1	1	1	4
8. Pafnutieff, V.	0	0	½	0	0	½	0	•	1	1	3
9. Martin, R.	0	½	0	0	½	½	0	0	•	1	2½
10. Graf, S.	0	0	0	½	0	0	0	0	0	•	½

Hollywood Invitational 1953

(February–March)

	1	2	3	4	5	6	7	8	9	10	11	12	13	14	15	16	17	18	19	20	Score
1. Kashdan, I.	•	1	½	1	1	1	1	1	1	1	1	1	1	1	1	1	1	1	1	1	18½
2. Levin, E.	0	•	½	1	1	1	1	1	½	0	1	1	1	1	1	1	1	1	1	1	16
3. Steiner, H.	½	½	•	1	0	0	1	1	1	1	1	1	1	1	1	1	1	1	1	1	15½
4. Almgren, S.	0	0	0	•	1	½	1	1	1	1	1	½	1	1	1	1	1	1	1	1	15
5. Cross, J.	0	0	1	0	•	1	0	1	1	1	½	1	1	1	1	1	1	½	1	1	14
6. Rivise, I.	0	0	1	½	0	•	0	1	½	1	0	1	1	1	1	1	1	1	1	1	13
7. Altshiller, M.	0	0	0	0	1	1	•	1	0	1	1	1	1	0	1	1	1	1	1	1	13
8. Mazner, S.	0	0	0	0	0	0	0	•	1	1	1	1	1	½	1	1	1	1	½	1	11
9. Balzer, J.	0	½	0	0	0	½	1	0	•	0	1	1	1	½	½	1	½	½	1	1	10
10. Spinner, L.	0	1	0	0	0	0	0	0	1	•	1	0	0	1	½	1	0	1	1	1	8½
11. Spiller, A.	0	0	0	0	½	1	0	0	0	0	•	½	0	1	½	1	1	1	1	½	8
12. Woronzoff, L.	0	0	0	½	0	0	0	0	0	1	½	•	1	½	½	0	1	1	1	1	8
13. Standers, L.	0	0	0	0	0	0	0	0	0	1	1	0	•	1	1	1	0	1	½	1	7½
14. Keckhut, J.	0	0	0	0	0	0	1	½	½	0	0	½	0	•	1	0	1	0	½	1	6
15. Hazard, F.	0	0	½	0	0	0	0	0	½	½	½	½	0	0	•	0	1	1	1	0	5½
16. Blumenfeld, M.	0	0	0	0	0	0	0	0	0	0	0	1	0	1	1	•	0	0	1	1	5
17. Steven, G.	0	0	0	0	0	0	0	0	½	1	0	0	1	0	0	1	•	0	½	1	5
18. Geller, S.	0	0	0	0	½	0	0	0	½	0	0	0	0	1	0	1	1	•	1	0	5
19. Piatigorsky	0	0	0	0	0	0	0	½	0	0	0	0	½	½	0	0	½	0	•	1	3
20. Rogosin, H.	0	0	0	0	0	0	0	0	0	0	½	0	0	0	1	0	0	1	0	•	2½

California Open, Santa Barbara 1954

Round 1	Kashdan	Reissman, K.	1–0
Round 2	Russell, R.	Kashdan	0–1
Round 3	Kashdan	Martin, R.	1–0
Round 4	Zemitis, V.	Kashdan	½–½
Round 5	Steiner, H.	Kashdan	1–0

Pan American, Hollywood 1954

(July 10–24)

Round 1	Grover, K.	Kashdan	0–1
Round 2	Kashdan	Rivise, I.	1–0
Round 3	Bisguier, A.	Kashdan	1–0
Round 4	Kashdan	Gordon	1–0
Round 5	Kashdan	Ulvestad, O.	1–0
Round 6	Steiner, H.	Kashdan	½–½
Round 7	Kashdan	Kaufman, A	1–0
Round 8	Pomar, A.	Kashdan	1–0

Round 9	Kashdan	Levin, E.	½–½
Round 10	Gross, H.	Kashdan	1–0
Round 11	Kashdan	Kaiser, W.	1–0
Round 12	Jacobs, R.	Kashdan	0–1
Round 13	Kashdan	Evans, L.	1–0
Round 14	Rossolimo, N.	Kashdan	½–½

Match: USA–USSR 1955
(July 9–15)

Round 1	Kashdan–Taimanov	½–½
Round 2	Taimanov–Kashdan	½–½
Round 3	Kashdan–Taimanov	½–½
Round 4	Taimanov–Kashdan	1–0

Bibliography

Tournament Books

1928   **The Hague Olympiad:** Gillam, Anthony. *The Hague Olympiad 1928*. Carlton, Nottingham: The Chess Player, 1998.

1929   **Hamburg Olympiad:** Chalupetzky, Ferenc. *Die Schacholympiade von Hamburg*. Reprint of the 1931 edition, by the *British Chess Magazine*, 1973.

       Frankfurt: Kubbel, Leonid. *Das Meisterturnier zu Frankfurt am Main*. Köln, 1930.

       Stockholm: Kalendovsky, Jan. *Stockholm 1930, le Pont, Amsterdam 1930*. Olomouc, 1995.

1930   **New York:** Aguilera, Ricordo. *New York 1931*. Madrid, 1976 (in Spanish).

1931   **Prague Olympiad:** Mrazik, Vladimir. *Šachove Olympiade v Praza*, 1932 (in Czech).

       Bled: Kmoch, Hans. *Bled 1931*. Translated from the Russian edition. Yorklyn, Delaware: Caissa Editions, 1987.

       Mueller, Hans. *Das Internationale Turnier 1931*. Vienna: Liepolt, 1932 (in German).

1931-2 **Hastings:** Gillam, Anthony. *Hastings 1931-2; Cambridge 1932*. England, 1999.

1932   **London:** Alekhine, Alexander. *London International Chess Tournament 1932*. England: Frank Hollings, 1932.

       Pasadena: Kashdan, Isaac. *Twenty Five Best Games from the International Chess Congress of 1932*. Pasadena, Calif.: Chess Reporter, 1932.

       Mexico City: Brandreth, Dale. *Mexico City International Chess Tournament 1932*. Yorklyn, Delaware: Caissa Editions, 1988.

1933   **Folkestone Olympiad:** Kashdan, Isaac. *Folkestone 1933 International Team Chess Tournament*. Woodside, New York: Chess Review, 1933.

       Gillam, Anthony. *The Folkestone Olympiad 1933*. Nottingham, England: The Chess Player, 2000.

1935   **Milwaukee:** Kashdan, Isaac. *Folkestone 1933*. Nottingham, England: The Chess Player.

       Lahde, Peter. *Milwaukee, Lodz, Sopot 1935*. Nottingham, England: The Chess Player, 2001.

1935   **Binghamton:** New York Chess Association. *The New York State Chess Championship Binghamton 1935.* New York, 1935.

1936   **New York:** Hilbert, John, and Lahde, Peter. *New York 1936: The First Modern United States Chess Championship.* Sands Point, New York: Chess Archaeology Press, 2000.

         Philadelphia: Reinfeld, Fred. *The Championship Tournament of the American Chess Federation, Philadelphia 1936.* Milwaukee: American Chess Federation, 1937.

1937   **Stockholm Olympiad:** Cozens, W. H. *The Lost Olympiad, Stockholm 1937.* British Chess Magazine Quarterly 22, 1985.

1938   **New York:** Lahde, Peter. *U.S. Championship New York 1938.* Nottingham, England, 2001.

1940   **New York:** Hilbert, John. *United States Chess Championship 1940.* Yorklyn, Delaware: Caissa Editions, 2002.

         3rd United States Chess Championship Tournament 1940. Tarrytown Press, 1941.

1942   **Reshevsky–Kashdan Match:** Fine, Reuben. *The Reshevsky–Kashdan Match.* 1943.

1945   **Hollywood:** Spence, Jack. *Pan-American Chess Congress, Hollywood, California 1945.* Omaha, 1952.

1946   **New York:** Michel, Paul. *U.S. Chess Championship, New York 1946.* Buenos Aires, Nazca 1947 (in Spanish).

1948   **Baltimore:** Spence, Jack. *49th United States Open Chess Championship.* Omaha, 1946.

1948   **South Fallsberg:** Spence, Jack. *1948 United States Chess Championship, South Fallsberg, NY.* Nebraska Chess Association, 1951.

1948-9   **New York:** Kmoch, Hans. *International Chess Tournament, New York 1948-9.* Brooklyn, NY: Albert Pinkus, 1950.

1951   **Fort Worth:** Spence, Jack. *52nd United States Open Chess Championship 1951.* Omaha, Nebraska.

1952   **Hollywood:** Ralston, Dr. H. J. *Hollywood International Tournament 1952.* California Chess Reporter, 1952.

1954   **Hollywood:** Spence, Jack. *Pan-American Chess Congress 1954.* Omaha: Nebraska.

Biographical Game Collections

Alekhine   Alekhine, Alexander. *My Best Games of Chess.* London: Bell and Sons, 1955.

Bernstein   Bernstein, Sidney. *Combat, My 50 Years at the Chess Board.* New York: Atlantis Press, 1977.

Bisguier   Bisguier, Arthur. *The Art of Bisguier.* Hazel Crest, Illinois: 3rd Millennium Press, 2003.

Bogoljubow   Spence, Jack. *The Chess Career of Bogoljubow, 1930–1952, Volume 2.* The Chess Player, 1970.

Dake   Bush, Casey. *Grandmaster From Oregon, The Life and Games of Arthur Dake.* Portland, Oregon: Chess Press, 1991.

Denker   Denker, Arnold. *If You Must Play Chess.* Philadelphia: David McKay, 1947.

Fine   Fine, Reuben. *Lessons from My Games.* New York: David McKay, 1958.

Koltanowski   Koltanowski, George. *With the Chess Masters.* San Francisco: Falcon Publishers, 1972.

Kotov   Kotov, Alexander. *Grandmaster at Work.* Translated from the Russian by Jimmy Adams. Macon, Georgia: American Chess Promotions, 1990.

Marshall   Marshall, Frank. *Marshall's Best Games of Chess,* Dover Publications, 1942.

Najdorf   Lissowski, Tomasz. *Najdorf: Life and Games.* Batsford Chess, 2005.

Reshevsky   Reshevsky, Samuel. *Reshevsky on Chess.* New York, NY: Chess Review, 1946.

Rubinstein   Donaldson, John, and Nikolay Minev. *Akiba Rubinstein: The Later Years.* Seattle: International Chess Enterprises, 1995.

Tartakower   Tartakower, S. G. *My Best Games of Chess.* 1956. Translated by Harry Golombek. Dover, 1985.

Index of Players

References are to game numbers in Part Two

Index of ECO Openings

References are to game numbers in Part Two

General Index

References are to page numbers in Part One